# *Uncle John's*
# 4-PLY BATHROOM READER

by

The Bathroom Readers' Institute

Barnes & Noble Books
New York

The following permissions are from Uncle John's 1st Bathroom Reader.

"Flipper" originally appeared in *Animal Superstars*. Copyright © 1985, by John Javna. Reprinted by permission of the author.

"Politics of Oz" originally appeared in *The Utne Reader*, July/August 1988. Copyright © 1988, by Michael Dregni. Reprinted by permission of the author.

"Doo-Wop Sounds" originally appeared in *The Doo-Wop Sing-Along Songbook*. Copyright © 1985, by John Javna. Reprinted by permission of the author.

"Caveat Eater" Copyright © 1988, by David Goines. Reprinted by permission of the author.

"7 Cool Flicks," "10 Cool Books," and "The Hipster Saint" originally appeared in *The Catalog of Cool*. Copyright © 1982, by Gene Sculatti. Reprinted by permission of the author.

"Congressional Wit," and "Party Lines" originally appeared in *Will the Gentleman Yield?* Copyright © 1988, by Bill Hogan and Mike Hill. Reprinted by permission of the publisher.

"Riddles" originally appeared in *Riddles*. Copyright © 1983, by Mark Bryant. Reprinted by permission of the publisher.



This edition published for Barnes & Noble, Inc. by St. Martin's Press.

*www.stmartins.com*

*Produced and Packaged by Javnarama*
*Design by Javnarama*

*Library of Congress Cataloging-in-Publication Data*

Bathroom Reader's Institute (New York, N.Y.)
Uncle John's Bathroom Reader.
ISBN 0-7607-3809-2
1. Wit and humor. I. Title.
PN6153.B28 1988 818'.5407

First U.S. Edition January 2003

# THANK YOU

*The Bathroom Readers' Institute sincerely thanks the people whose advice and assistance made this book possible.*

John Javna
Gordon Javna
Bob Shannon
Stuart Moore
Rachel Blau
Andrea Sohn
Gordon Van Gelder
Co-op Type
Byron Brown
Donna McCrohan
Max Allan Collins
Eric Lefcowitz
Cynthia Robins
Peter Handel
Penelope Houston
Gene Sculatti
Michael Dregni
David Goines
Dr. Lisa Berlin
Jeff Abrahams
Steve Gorlick
Leslie Boies
Jack Mingo
Franz Ross
Sam Javna
Charlie Weimer
Stephen Louis
Carla Small
Lorrie Bodger
Gideon Javna
Dayna Macy
Reddy Kilowatt
Gene Novogrodsky
Bob Migdal
Betsy Joyce
Greg Small
Adrienne Levine
Jay Nitschke
Mike Goldfinger
Doug Burnet

*Uncle John's*

# BATHROOM READER

# INTRODUCTION

There are two kinds of people in the world—people who read in the bathroom, and people who don't.

People who *do*, share a few of the subtler joys and frustrations of life—e.g., the joy of discovering a really interesting article in the latest issue of a favorite magazine as you head to the head, or the frustration of trying to find something suitable to read...at the last minute. This isn't something we talk about, but it's understood.

People who *don't* read in the bathroom haven't got a clue about why people who do, do. This book isn't for them.

*Uncle John's Bathroom Reader* is the first book especially for people who love to read in the bathroom. It was conceived in 1987, when a group of socially active citizens in Berkeley, California realized that the publishing industry had plenty of books for every room of the house (bedside readers, cookbooks, coffee-table books, etc.) *except* the bathroom—where up to 60% of Americans read. It was clearly time for bathroom readers to come out of the water closet and "Say it loud, I read in there and I'm proud!"

Consequently, they formed The Bathroom Readers' Institute to fight for the rights of bathroom readers everywhere.

Under their sensitive guidance, *The Reader* has been specially designed with the needs of bathroom readers in mind: It's full of brief but interesting articles that can be read in a few seconds, or a few minutes. It covers a variety of subjects (so a reader never has to settle for the "same old thing"). And it's arranged so a reader can just flip it open to any page; no planning, no searching. We hope you enjoy it. As we say at the Bathroom Readers' Institute: "Go With the Flow."

# CONTENTS

NOTE

Because the B.R.I. understands your reading needs, we've divided the contents by length as well as subject.

**Short**—a quick read

**Medium**—1 to 3 pages

**Long**—for those extended visits, when something a little more involved is required.

## THE NAME GAME

### Short



### Medium



## TOYLAND

### Short



### Medium



## POP-POURRI

### Short

**Medium**



**Long**



## MOUTHING OFF

**Short**

## STRANGE DEATHS

### Medium



## MYTH AMERICA

### Short



### Medium



## FOOD FOR THOUGHT

### Short



### Medium

**Long**



## WORDPLAY

**Short**



**Medium**



## AMUSEMENTS

**Short**



## SCIENCE

**Short**

## MUSIC: BEHIND THE HITS



## THE FABULOUS '60s



## CLASSIC FANTASY

## IT'S THE LAW



## IN FASHION



## THE LAST LAUGH



## PEOPLE ARE STRANGE



## HORROR



## 2-MINUTE MYSTERIES



## AMERICANA

## BANNED IN THE USA

### Short



### Medium



## BATHROOM NEWS

### Medium



## JUST FOR FUN

### Short



## ENTERTAINMENT

### Short



### Medium



### Long



## PRIVATE LIVES

### Short



### Medium



### Long



## WINNERS & LOSERS

### Medium



### Long

## HEROES & VILLAINS

### Medium



### Long



## MISCELLANEOUS

### Short



### Medium



### Long



## PLAYING AROUND

### Medium



## IT'S A CONSPIRACY

### Medium



### Long

# OUR ANTHEM

*Ever have people banging on the bathroom door, telling you to "hurry up and get out of there"? Then you'll be glad to know your response has already been immortalized in a classic soul tune. From* Behind the Hits, *by Bob Shannon.*

In the '60s, Memphis' Stax Records had the most talented lineup of studio musicians and singers in the south. There was Otis Redding, Rufus Thomas, Booker T. and the M.G.'s, Carla Thomas, Eddie Floyd, and Sam and Dave.

Sam Moore and Dave Prater joined the Stax family in 1965. They were assigned to the writing/production team of Dave Porter and Isaac Hayes, and the partnership clicked big, producing a string of near-perfect Soul masterpieces. First to hit the charts was "You Don't Know Like I Know"; and their first big hit was "Soul Man." In between was a song that almost made the pop Top 20—a record that would have been a much bigger hit if it hadn't been for radio censorship.

White Top 40 stations were just getting used to playing black Soul records in 1966 when "Hold On, I'm Comin'" was released. Because of its suggestive title, many radio stations refused to air it at all. And those that did often made the situation worse as deejays drooled over the sexual implications of the song. In reality, the lyrics were simply about one lover giving the other support "when times are bad." "Coming" just meant "coming to the rescue." Sam and Dave's macho, boastful delivery and sly laughs throughout the song didn't help their case, although they helped to make it a great record. Stax changed the title to "Hold On, I'm A-Comin'" to placate the FCC, but the damage was already done.

If only the radio jocks had known the true story of its conception! You see, Hayes and Porter were in the studio, writing some songs. Porter left for a minute, and when he didn't come back, an impatient Hayes went looking for him. His room-to-room search finally ended up at—you guessed it—the men's room door. Porter was taking his time in there, and Hayes yelled at him to hurry up. Porter's irritated reply: "Hey man, hold on. I'm comin'." And a song was born.

**The most valuable bathtub in the world is valued at $5 million. It is solid gold.**

# BATHROOM LORE

*It seems appropriate to begin this volume with a little background on the room you're probably sitting in right now.*

## THE FIRST BATHROOM

The idea of a separate room for the disposal of "bodily waste" goes back at least 10,000 years (8,000 B.C.). On Orkney, an island off the coast of Scotland, the inhabitants combined stone huts with a drainage system that carried the waste directly into a nearby stream.

## THE FIRST SOPHISTICATED PLUMBING

- Bathtubs dating back to 2000 B.C. have been found on the island of Crete (where there's also evidence of the first flush toilet). Considering they were built almost 4,000 years ago, the similarity to modern baths is startling.
- Around 1500 B.C., elite Egyptians had hot and cold running water; it came into their homes through a system of copper tubing or pipes.

## THE FIRST SOCIAL BATHING

The ancient Romans took their bathing seriously, building public facilities wherever they settled—including London. The more elaborate of these included massage salons, food and wine, gardens, exercise rooms, and in at least one case, a public library. Co-ed bathing was not uncommon, nor frowned upon.

## BACK TO FILTH

- As Christianity became increasingly powerful, techniques of plumbing and waste disposal—and cleanliness in general—were forgotten; only in monasteries was this knowledge preserved.
- For hundreds of years people in Europe basically stopped washing their bodies, in large part because nudity—even for reasons of health or hygiene—was regarded as sinful by the Church.

• In some cases a reverence for dirt arose in its place. St. Francis of Assisi, for example, believed "dirtiness was an insignia of holiness."
• Upper-class citizens tried to cover up the inevitable body odors with clothes and perfume, but the rest of the population suffered with the rank smells of filth.

## CHAMBER POTS AND STREET ETIQUETTE

• Until the early 1800s, Europeans relieved themselves in chamber pots, outhouses, streets, alleys, and anywhere else they happened to feel like it.
• It was so common to relieve oneself in public that people were concerned about how to behave if they noticed acquaintances "urinating or defecating" on the street. Proper etiquette: Act like you don't see them.
• Chamber pots were used at night, or when it was too cold to go outside. Their contents were supposed to be picked up once a day by a "waste man," who carted the community's leavings to a public cesspool.
• But frequently, the chamber pot was surreptitiously dumped at night, which made it dangerous to go strolling in the evening.

## DISEASE AND CHANGE

The lack of bathing took an enormous toll on the European population of the Middle Ages, as epidemics caused by unsanitary living conditions became matter-of-fact. But in the 1830s, a London outbreak of Cholera—a disease the English believed could only be contracted by inferior races—finally convinced the English government to put its power behind public sanitation. Over the next 50 years, the British constructed major new public facilities that set the pace for the rest of the world.

## THE MODERN FLUSH TOILET

The modern flush toilet was invented by an Englishman named Alexander Cumming in 1775. Cumming's toilet emptied directly into a pipe which then carried the undesirable matter to a cesspool. Other toilets had done this, too; but Cumming's major improvement was the addition of a "stink trap" that kept water in the pipe, and thus blocked odor.

**About 10 billion cigarettes are produced annually throughout the world.**

## THOMAS CRAPPER

It is widely believed that an Englishman named Thomas Crapper invented the toilet. Not true. That was a hoax.

## HEAD FOR THE JOHN

• In the mid-1500s in England, a chamber pot was referred to as a *Jake*. A hundred years later, it became a *John*, or *Cousin John*. In the mid-1800s, it was also dubbed a *Joe*.
• That still may not be the source of the term *John* for the bathroom—it may date to the 1920s, when Men's and Ladies' rooms became common in public places. They were also referred to as *Johns* and *Janes*—presumably after John and Jane Doe.
• The term *potty* comes from the pint-sized chamber pot built for kids.

## BATHROOMS

• The bathroom we know—with a combination toilet and bath—didn't exist until the 1850s. And then only for the rich.
• Until then, the term bathroom—which came into use in the 1820s or 1830s—meant, literally, a room with a bathtub in it.

## A FEW AMERICAN FIRSTS

• First American hotel with indoor modern bathrooms: The Tremont House in Boston, 1880s.
• First toilet in the White House: 1825, installed for John Quincy Adams (leading to a new slang term for toilet—a *quincy*).
• First city with modern waterworks: Philadelphia, 1820.
• First city with a modern sewage system: Boston, 1823.

## THE FIRST TOILET PAPER

• Toilet paper was introduced in America in 1857, as a package of loose sheets. But it was too much like the paper Americans already used—the Sears catalog. It flopped.
• In 1879, an Englishman named Walter Alcock created the first perforated rolls of toilet paper. He couldn't sell them.
• In 1880, things got rolling. Philadelphia's Scott Brothers saw the potential for a product that would constantly have to be replaced and introduced Waldorf Tissue (later ScotTissue), which was discreetly sold in plain brown wrappers. The timing was right—there were enough bathrooms to make them a success.

# PRIME-TIME PROVERBS

*TV's comments about everyday life in America. From* Prime Time Proverbs, *a forthcoming book by Jack Mingo.*

**ON FOOD:**
"Why am I bothering to eat this chocolate? I might as well apply it directly to my thighs."

**—Rhoda Morgenstern,**
***Mary Tyler Moore Show***

**Gracie:** "The reason I put the salt in the pepper shaker and the pepper in the salt shaker is that people are always getting them mixed up. Now when they get mixed up, they'll be right.."

***—Burns and Allen***

"Six years, and you haven't learned *anything*—it's *white wine* with Hershey Bars."

**—Harvey Barnes,**
***Making the Grade***

**ON THE BATTLE OF THE SEXES:**
"Early to bed, early to rise, and your girl goes out with other guys."

**—Bob Collins,**
***Love That Bob***

"Carmine and I have an understanding. I'm allowed to date other men, and he's allowed to date ugly women."

**—Shirley Feeney,**
***Laverne and Shirley***

**ON MARRIED LIFE:**
**Edith:** "Do you like bein' alone with me?"
**Archie:** "Certainly I like being alone with you. What's on television?"

***—All in the Family***

**ON MONEY:**
"There are two things [I won't do for money]. I won't kill for it and I won't marry for it. Other than that, I'm open to about anything."

**—Jim Rockford,**
***The Rockford Files***

**CURRENT EVENTS:**
"What's this I hear about making Puerto Rico a steak? The next thing they'll be wanting is a salad, and then a baked potato."

**—Emily Litella**
**(Gilda Radner)**
***Saturday Night Live***

**Only 1/4 of the American population lives in rural areas.**

# THE FABULOUS '60S

*Odds and ends about America's favorite decade, from 60s!, by John and Gordon Javna.*

**CUT 'EM SOME SLACKS.** It wasn't considered "lady-like" to wear pants in the '60s. In 1968, for example, *Women's Wear Daily* polled several employers about it. Some of the comments: Macy's, New York: "We don't allow it"; First National Bank of Boston: "We would allow our women employees to wear pants if they continue to act like women"; Citizens and Southern National Bank, Atlanta: "We would not want to be among the first...."

**OFF WITH HER PANTS.** In 1969 Judy Carne, a star of "Laugh-In," visited the posh "21" Club wearing a "tunic-topped pants suit." When the management refused to let her in because of its policy against women in pants, she took off her pants, checked them in the checkroom, and sailed off into the dining room wearing only her tunic—barely long enough to be called a micro-mini-skirt. The club changed its policy on pants the next day.

**WHICH DOPE?** Spiro Agnew's daughter was suspended from school while they investigated her for smoking dope.

**FAST FOOD:** A few '60s fast-food flops you never ate at: Johnny Carson's "Here's Johnny's!" restaurants; Mahalia Jackson's Glori-Fried Chicken; Mickey Mantle's Southern Cooking; Tony Bennett Spaghetti House; Alice's Restaurants.

**TV OR NOT TV?** In 1967, a lady went on "Let's Make a Deal" dressed as a little girl holding a baby bottle. Monty Hall took away her baby bottle and said, "All right, for two hundred dollars, show me another nipple."

**WHY WE DON'T OWN THE MOON:** The U.S. waived any claim to the moon by signing the Treaty on Exploration and Use of Outer Space in 1967. This established the lunar surface as the property of all mankind.

**One slice to go: America's first pizzeria opened in New York City in 1895.**

# FAMOUS FOR 15 MINUTES

*Andy Warhol was prophetic when he said, "In the future, everyone will be famous for 15 minutes." Here are a few examples of what we have to look forward to.*

**THE STAR:** Annabella Battistella, a.k.a Fanne Foxe, "The Argentine Firecracker," voluptuous Latin "exotic dancer."

**THE HEADLINE:** "Stripper sinks political career."

**WHAT HAPPENED:** Late one night in October 1972, a suspicious Washington, D.C. cop pulled over an erratically moving vehicle. The inebriated driver turned out to be Congressman Wilbur Mills of Arkansas, a 36-year veteran of the House and chairman of its powerful Ways and Means Committee. In the car with him were his next-door neighbor, 38-year-old Annabella Battistella (a stripper known on stage as Fanne Foxe), and some friends—all headed home after a night of carousing. At some point during the confrontation—no one is sure exactly why—Annabella suddenly ran screaming from the car and jumped or slipped into the Tidal Basin, a shallow section of the Potomac river. The event became front page news, and it was revealed that the staid Mills—happily married for 40 years—had been having an affair with Fanne.

Shock waves rippled through Washington, but Fanne cashed in immediately, booking a tour of East Coast strip joints as "the Washington Tidal Basin Girl" ("You've read about her, now see her in person!"). She claimed to be making $3,000 a week, and that a "big toy company" was planning a Fanne doll. She even got the Harvard Republican Club's "Newcomer of the Year" award.

**THE AFTERMATH:** Mills' career was jeopardized, but it seemed as though he'd pull through—until two months later, when he suddenly appeared onstage in a seedy Boston strip joint, and gave Fanne a kiss. That was it. "I'm a sick man," he told colleagues when they challenged his authority. Mills was hospitalized, and Fanne continued to take it off, but faded into obscurity.

**THE STAR:** Scott Halprin, a San Francisco teenager.

**THE HEADLINE:** "Rock Star for a Night: Kid From Audience Steps Forward."

**WHAT HAPPENED:** In 1973 the Who were in San Francisco playing the first show of what was to be a major U.S. tour. As the opening bars of "Won't Get Fooled Again" burst from the massive sound system at the Cow Palace, the group's unpredictable drummer, Keith Moon, suddenly slumped over, totally out of it, unable to hit another cymbal. Moon was escorted offstage and returned shortly after, seemingly revived. But a few minutes later, he collapsed again, this time completely unable to continue.

In a bizarre fantasy-come-true, the Who's leader, Pete Townsend, went to the edge of the stage and asked for volunteers. A 19-year-old named Scott Halprin bounded forward...and soon he found himself playing "Magic Bus" and "My Generation." "It happened really quick," said Halprin later. "I didn't have time to think about it and get nervous. I really admired their stamina...I only played three numbers and I was dead."

**THE AFTERMATH:** Keith Moon recovered (at least for a few more years). Halprin didn't become a star, but he was the subject of a small piece in *Rolling Stone*. "That drummer," said lead singer Roger Daltry, "was really good."

**THE STAR**: Peg Entwistle, aspiring actress.

**THE HEADLINE:** "Starlet Plunges to Death in Desperate Dive."

**WHAT HAPPENED:** Young Peg Entwistle had been a success on the Broadway stage, and she arrived in Hollywood expecting to build a career in motion pictures. Unfortunately, it didn't work out. So in September of 1932, she decided to end it all. She did it in the grand Cecil B. DeMille style: she climbed to the top of the 50-foot-high H in the "Hollywood" sign above the city, and leaped to her death. It made national news, although it was a little too late to do her career any good.

**AFTERMATH:** Hollywood, "the city of broken dreams," had a new fad. Disappointed would-be movie stars continued to take their own lives by jumping off the sign.

**The biggest recorded bubble ever blown with bubble gum was 22 inches in diameter.**

**THE STAR:** Sacheen Littlefeather, a Native American political activist, and an Oscar stand-in for Marlon Brando.

**THE HEADLINE:** "Brando Refuses Oscar, Sends Surrogate in Protest Over Indian Rights."

**WHAT HAPPENED:** In 1972, Marlon Brando was nominated for a Best Actor Oscar for his role in *The Godfather*. Brando was becoming increasingly politicized and at the time, the plight of the American Indians was his primary interest. So he arranged to have a young activist named Sacheen Littlefeather accept the award (if he won) in his place, handing her a three-page speech to read. When the time came, dressed in full Indian regalia, Ms. Littlefeather shocked the audience and TV network—and Roger Moore, the man trying to present it—by refusing the award for Brando and reading a short speech (the Academy refused to allow the long one) which decried the treatment of the Indian in Hollywood films.

**AFTERMATH:** Littlefeather had regularly played bit parts in films herself, but after the incident found herself blacklisted for several years. She was also harassed by both the FBI and unknown individuals. She is still an activist, but feels bitter about the experience.

**THE STAR:** Eddie Gaedel, a 3' 7" midget.

**THE HEADLINE:** "Small Man in Big Leagues: A Veeck Stunt."

**WHAT HAPPENED:** It was a Sunday doubleheader with the Detroit Tigers on August 19, 1951, and the St. Louis Browns were celebrating the 50th anniversary of the American League. Between games, Brown owner Bill Veeck wheeled a huge cake out onto the field, and out popped Eddie Gaedel, wearing a Browns uniform with the number 1/8 on it. During the first inning of the next game, Gaedel popped out of the dugout and informed the umpire he was pinch hitting. Challenged, Veeck produced a valid contract. Pitching is difficult as it is, but a 3'7" person has a strike zone of about 18 inches. Gaedel walked on four straight pitches. He then left for a pinch-runner.

**AFTERMATH:** Gaedel made a quick 100 bucks for his appearance, and American League president Will Harridge issued a solemn declaration barring midgets from baseball, and warning Veeck not to try any similar stunts.

**Life span: The oldest known goldfish lived to 41 years of age. Its name was Fred.**

# WORDPLAY

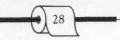

*Here are the origins of a few common phrases.*

FALL GUY
*Meaning*: Someone who takes the blame.
*Background*: The first people to "fall" were Adam and Eve, who fell from grace and were booted out of Eden. In England, this gave rise to the term "take a fall," meaning "to be arrested," often in conjunction with taking the rap for someone else. Someone who took a fall was known as a "fall guy."

BETWEEN A ROCK AND A HARD PLACE
*Meaning*: In trouble, stuck with two undesirable choices.
*Background*: This is an updated version of an expression dating back to the Ancient Greeks, "between Scylla and Charybdis." The former was a large rock that endangered seamen in the Straits of Messina, the latter was a potentially fatal whirlpool on the opposite side. Sailors tried to avoid sailing between them. It is speculated that Charybdis is known as "a hard place" partly because it's so hard to pronounce.

KEEP YOUR SHIRT ON
*Meaning*: Stay calm.
*Background*: Probably from the age-old response to a challenge to fight. You rip your shirt off to fight, and you keep it on if you're avoiding one.

SWAN SONG
*Meaning*: A final, best performance.
*Background*: Though in actuality swans don't make many sounds, in legends the bird was believed to give a final, wonderful song just before it died.

STOOL PIGEON
*Meaning*: An informer, a traitor.
*Background*: To catch passenger pigeons (now extinct), hunters would nail a pigeon to a stool. Its alarmed cries would attract other birds, and the hunters would shoot them by the thousand. The poor creature that played the traitor was a "stool pigeon."

**Weighty stuff: The heaviest dog on record was a St. Bernard that weighed 310 pounds.**

# THE TWILIGHT ZONE

*Picture, if you will, a 5-foot, 5-inch ex-boxer who produced, created, and often wrote what may be the best television program in history.*
*From* Cult TV, *by John Javna.*

You're traveling through another dimension, a dimension not only of sight and sound, but of mind; a journey into a wondrous land whose boundaries are that of the imagination. That's the signpost up ahead! Your next stop...the Twilight Zone!"

**HOW IT STARTED**

In the mid-'50s, Rod Serling was an award-winning writer for the celebrated TV anthology series, "Playhouse 90." However, he became frustrated with the inane changes sponsors insisted on making to his scripts. One sponsor (an auto maker) demanded that the Chrysler building be painted out of a scene. Another (a tobacco company) deleted the word "lucky" from a script because Lucky Strikes weren't their brand. And when an insurance company refused to allow a central character to commit suicide, Serling quit. People were shocked that the outspoken playwright left a cushy job at one of TV's most prestigious programs to write and produce his own "fantasy" show. But Serling knew exactly what he was doing. By operating under the cover of fantasy, Serling could get his message across without getting it censored.

In 1957, he reworked a script that had aired years before on a local Cincinnati station, and presented it to CBS as the "Twilight Zone" pilot. CBS wasn't interested, but Desilu Productions aired it as an episode of "Desilu Playhouse." It generated more viewer response than any other show that season, and CBS decided to take another look. They requested a second script from Serling ("The Happy Place"), which was deemed too depressing. So he wrote a third, this time keeping the concept simple and straightforward. In February, 1959, "Where Is Everybody" was accepted by CBS as a pilot; in March, Gener-

**According to *Guinness*, an Arkansas boy grew a 260-lb. watermelon in 1985.**

al Foods bought it; and on October 2, 1959, living rooms across America entered "The Twilight Zone."

**INSIDE FACTS**

**The Amazing Serling:** In real life, Rod Serling was a nervous wreck in front of the camera. It was his idea to introduce and close the episodes himself, but he remained an uneasy, sweating mess right through the last show. "Only my laundress really knows how frightened I am," he said of his appearances.

He was incredibly productive. He worked 18-hour days, and could turn out a completed "Twilight Zone" script in around 35 hours—much of it dictated into a tape recorder while he sat by the swimming pool of his L.A. home. In the first season, he wrote a phenomenal 80% of the scripts; by the fifth season, he was still producing about 50% of them.

Sadly, Serling died during open heart surgery in 1975. He was 50 years old.

**Calling All Writers.** One of Serling's biggest complaints about network procedure was that new talent was constantly being smothered by the system. So he invited amateur writers to send in their manuscripts if they thought they were good enough. It was an interesting lesson—he received 14,000 scripts in five days. Of the 500 that Serling and his staff got around to reading, only two of those were of "professional quality." Did he use those two? He couldn't—they "didn't fit the show."

**Name Game.** Fans think that Rod Serling invented the term "Twilight Zone." So did Serling. He'd never heard anyone use it before, so he assumed he'd created it. He was in for a surprise: after the show debuted, he was informed that Air Force pilots used the phrase to describe "a moment when a plane is coming down on approach and it cannot see the horizon."

**Belated Thanks.** Although it was considered a "prestige" show, "The Twilight Zone" never had good enough ratings to excite advertisers. Sometimes, in fact, sponsors didn't even understand what the show was about. In the first season, one of the sponsors called up CBS every Monday to demand an explanation of Friday's show. "And then," said Serling, "he demanded an explanation of the explanation."

**According to one survey, 2/3 of the men in America believe in love at first sight.**

# THE WRONG IDEA

*Some words try their best to mislead you.*

**French Fries** actually came from Belgium, not France.

**Fairy tales** are seldom about fairies.

**One horsepower** represents the amount of power it takes to move 550 pounds one foot in one second. Actually, it would take one-and-a-half horses to pull off this feat.

Your **funny bone** is a nerve, not a bone.

**Fabric softeners** grease and lubricate the fibers of material to make it feel soft—they do not actually soften them.

**Great Danes** hail from Germany, not Denmark.

**Brazil nuts** are seeds, not nuts (but they do come from Brazil).

**Shooting stars** are meteors, not exploding stars.

**Hardwood** comes from deciduous trees. **Softwood** comes from evergreen trees. But the terms "hard' and "soft" have nothing to do with how tough or weak the wood really is. Balsa wood, for example—which you can practically cut with fingernails—is technically a hardwood.

Your **backbone** is actually thirty-three different bones.

**Rice Paper** has absolutely no rice in it.

**Moth-holes** in sweaters are created by larvae before they become grown-up moths.

**Mountain Goats** do live in the hills, but they aren't goats—they're small antelopes.

**Coconuts** are really giant seeds, not nuts.

**10-gallon hats** are for oversize heads, but they only hold about a gallon of liquid.

**Electric eels** are capable of producing a whopping 650 volts—but they aren't eels.

# BRAINTEASERS

*We've included a few simple logic problems in the book. For obvious reasons, they don't require heavy math or pencil and paper.* *Answers are on p. 234.*

My Uncle Gordon is quite absent-minded. One day I ran into him on the street. He was mumbling to himself, and seemed quite perplexed.

"What's the matter, Uncle Gordon?" I asked.

"Hmm? Oh, it's you, nephew. I was just trying to figure out what day today is."

"Well that's easy enough," I replied, a little relieved that it wasn't anything serious. "Today is—"

Uncle Gordon cut me off.

"Now, I now that the day before the day after tomorrow will be Saturday. And the day after the day before yesterday was Thursday. But what is today?"

Can you help him?

Uncle Gordon and I were sitting on a park bench together. I was reading a book, and Gordon was reading the newspaper.

"Well, well," he musedch. "Here's a little poem I don't understand". And he recited it:

*"A box without hinges, key or lid.*
*Yet golden treasure inside is hid."*

"It's a riddle," I explained.

"But what's the answer?" he demanded.

Do you know?

Uncle Gordon was puzzled by a math problem: "If one car starts from New York at 11 A.M. and travels 55 m.p.h, and another car starts from Boston at 1.P.M. and travels 60 m.p.h., which car will be nearer New York when they meet?"

"But Uncle Gordon, " I chided him, "That's easy."

You know the answer, of course.

**The first beer can was used by Kreuger Beer, and introduced in 1935.**

# A FOOD IS BORN

*These foods are common, so you've probably never even wondered where they came from. Here are the answers anyway.*

**BAGELS.** According to *The Bagels' Bagel Book:* "In 1683 in Vienna, Austria, a local Jewish baker wanted to thank the King of Poland for protecting his countrymen from Turkish invaders. He made a special hard roll in the shape of a riding stirrup—'Beugel' in Austrian—commemorating the king's favorite pastime, and giving the bagel its distinctive shape."

**MAYONNAISE.** Originally brought to France by Duke Richelieu, who tasted it while visiting Mahon, a city on the island of Minorca. It was eventually dubbed Mahonaisse by French chefs, and considered a delicacy in Europe. In America, it became known as mayonnaise, but for over a century was still regarded as suitable for only the most elegant meals. Finally, in 1912, Richard Hellman, a German immigrant, began packing it and selling it in jars from his New York deli. This transformed mayonnaise from a carefully-prepared treat for the select few, to a mass-merchandised condiment.

**GATORADE.** According to *60s!*, by John and Gordon Javna: "In 1965, Dr. Robert Cade was studying the effects of heat exhaustion on football players at the University of Florida (whose team name is the Gators). He analyzed the body liquids lost in sweating and within three minutes came up with the formula for Gatorade. Two years later, Cade sold the formula to Stokely-Van Camp. Soon, annual sales were well over $50 million and Gatorade could be found on the training tables of over three hundred college sports teams, a thousand high school squads, and all but two pro football teams."

**7-UP.** According to *Parade* magazine: "In October 1929, just before the stock market crash, St. Louis businessman Charles L. Grigg began marketing a beverage called Bib-Label Lithiated Lemon-Lime Soda. His slogan: 'Takes the "Ouch" out of grouch.' The drink was a huge success during the Depression, perhaps because it contained lithium, a powerful drug now prescribed for manic-depressives....The drink's unwieldy name was later changed to 7-UP. The '7' stood for its 7-ounce bottle, the 'UP' for 'bottoms up,' or for the bubbles rising from its heavy carbonation, which was later reduced. The lithium was listed on the label until the mid-'40s."

**CHEWING GUM.** American Indians chewed resin from freshly cut spruce bark, and colonial settlers occasionally chewed "a limp paraffin," but it wasn't until the late 1860s that chewing gum become a commercial success. A Staten Island inventor named Thomas Adams noticed that his visiting neighbor from Mexico—the deposed dictator Santa Ana—"seemed to enjoy chewing...lumps of gum from the sapodilla plant, now known as chicle"....Adams decided chicle was better than paraffin, and went to market with "Adams New York Gum—Snapping and Stretching." Later, he tried adding flavors and found that licorice tasted best. Still later, he invented a "gum-making machine" that made mass production possible.

**POPSICLES.** Eleven-year-old Frank Epperson accidentally left a mixture of powdered soda mix and water on his back porch one winter night in 1905. The next morning, Frank found the stuff frozen, with the stirring stick standing straight up in the jar. He pulled it out, and had the first "Epperson icicle"—or "Epsicle." He later renamed it "Popsicle," since he'd made it with soda pop. It was patented in 1923, eighteen years later.

**THE ICE CREAM CONE.** It happened at the 1904 World's Fair in Saint Louis (where the hot dog and the hamburger were also popularized). An ice cream vendor who was selling cups of the frozen dessert had so many customers in the hot weather that he ran out of cups. In desperation, he looked around to see if another nearby vendor might have some spare containers, but all he could find was a waffle concession. He quickly bought some waffles and began selling them wrapped around a scoop of ice cream. The substitute became even more popular than the original, and it spread around the country.

**Patty Hearst's prison T-shirt: "Being kidnapped is always having to say you're sorry."**

# 7 COOL FLICKS

*7 unsung cool films recommended by Gene Sculatti, author of* The Catalog of Cool.

**CAGED MEN** (1973). Wrestling great Abdullah the Butcher and his (real life) midget manager make screen debuts, playing desperate lifers trying to grow pot in a jail greenhouse. Hammerlocks and hopheads.

**CHE!** (1969). Unwatchable, even within its genre (bogus "revolutionary" films of the late sixties), but singularly brilliant for its perverse casting: Jack Palance as Fidel Castro. Arriba!

**DECOY FOR TERROR** (1970). Beatnik artist murders his models ("They always *move*!") by freezing them. Cool climax: a power outage causes one, frozen posed with a bow and arrow, to release the arrow, killing artist who's just finished his masterpiece. Neil Sedaka sings "Do the Waterbug" (Do the Cow/If you want to right now...").

**HIT LADY** (1964). Women's lib comes knocking in sharp threads: Yvette Mimeux as a bikini-clad mob assassin. Groovy.

**KITTEN WITH A WHIP** (1964). Ann-Margaret, as a delinquent-on-the-run, holes up with Senator John Forsythe and threatens to cry rape if he chucks her.

**R.P.M.** (1970). The only thing that could beat Ann-Margaret playing a campus radical is Anthony Quinn as a left-leaning, motorcycle-riding professor named Taco. R.P.M. offers both.

**THUNDER ROAD** (1958). Flickdom's granddaddy of cool, bad Bob Mitchum in a barbiturate-soaked performance....When some creep tries running moonshiner Mitch off the road, Mr. Heavylids cooly removes the old cig from his lip and flicks it across his car, out the window, and into the creep's car. It lands on his lap and he drives screaming to his death over an embankment. Mitchum never changes his expression.

**In 1987, a 1,400-year-old lump of still-edible cheese was unearthed in Ireland.**

# TOY ORIGINS

*You've loved them. You've played with them.*
*You've probably lost parts to them.*
*Now, here's where they came from.*

**SCRABBLE.** Created in 1931 by an out-of-work architect named Alfred Botts. He hoped he could support his family by inventing a successful word game, but before the game was refined, he had his job back. That was just as well; when he finally showed his hand-made "Criss-Cross" to toy companies, they insisted it had no potential—it was too intellectual.

In 1948, Botts and a friend went into business manufacturing the game—now called Scrabble—in an old schoolhouse. It was an unsophisticated cottage industry that enabled the friend to barely eke out a living. But in the summer of 1952, for no apparent reason, Scrabble suddenly became a fad. In two years, the partners went from selling less than ten thousand games a year to selling more than four million. To meet the growing demand, the rights were sold to Selchow-Righter, and thirty years later, Scrabble ranks as the second-best selling game in history.

**LINCOLN LOGS.** In 1916, Frank Lloyd Wright went to Tokyo to supervise construction of the Imperial Palace Hotel, a magnificent building, assembled with an inner frame of wood so it would withstand earthquakes better. Wright brought his son John with him, and as John watched workers move the huge timbers required for the structure, he came up with an idea for a wooden construction toy. When he returned to America, John created Lincoln Logs.

**SILLY PUTTY.** In 1945, an engineer at a General Electric laboratory in New Haven, Connecticut, was assigned the task of trying to create synthetic rubber. One day he combined boric acid with silicone oil. The result: a bizarre substance with a variety of fascinating properties (it bounced, stretched, and could be broken with a hammer), but no practical use. It became a New Haven conversation piece.

**#1 Dead entertainer: In 1988, Elvis earned an estimated $15 million.**

Several years later, a marketing man named Peter Hodgson saw a group of adults playing with the stuff at a cocktail party. Hodgson was putting together a mail order catalog for a toy store at the time, and decided to include this "nutty putty" in it. The response was amazing. Even without a photo, the "putty" outsold everything in the catalog except crayons. Hodgson knew he had a winner—so he bought $147-worth of putty from G.E., and packaged it in little plastic eggs. In the first five years, over 32 million containers of the stuff were sold worldwide.

**RUBIK'S CUBE.** Devised by Hungarian mathematician Erno Rubik in 1974 as an aid for teaching math concepts to his students. Rubik realized the puzzle's possibilities as a toy, and ended up selling two million of the cubes in Hungary alone—a total of one cube for every five Hungarians. In 1980, the Ideal Toy Corporation bought the rights, and the puzzle became a world-wide craze. Rubik reportedly became "the first self-made millionaire in a Communist country."

**SLINKY.** Richard James, a marine engineer, was trying to invent a spring that could be used to offset the effects of a boat's movement on sensitive navigational instruments. One day he knocked a sample spring off a high shelf—but instead of simply falling, it uncoiled like a snake and "crawled" down to the floor. James realized he had a toy product, gave it a name, and formed the James Toy Company to manufacture it.

**TINKER TOYS.** Charles Pajeau, an Evanston, Illinois stone-worker, conceived of Tinker Toys in 1913 after observing some kids playing with "pencils, sticks, and empty spools of thread." He designed it in a garage in back of his house, and brought the finished toy—packed in its famous cannister—to the 1914 American Toy Fair. But the public wouldn't buy it. So Pajeau had to prove his marketing genius again; at Christmastime, he dressed some midgets in elf costumes and had them play with Tinker Toys in the windows of New York's Grand Central Station and Chicago's Marshall Field's department store. The publicity this stunt attracted made all the difference—a year later, over a million sets had been sold.

**The first stereo record went on the market in 1958.**

# WILL ROGERS SAID...

*A tiny piece of the rich legacy left by America's national humorist during the '20s and '30s.*

"You can't say civilization don't advance, for in every war they kill you a new way."

"Half our life is spent trying to find something to do with the time we have rushed through life trying to save."

"Being a hero is about the shortest-lived profession on earth."

"I don't make jokes—I just watch the government and report the facts."

"Everybody is ignorant, only on different subjects."

"Everything is funny as long as it's happening to somebody else."

"The American people are generous and will forgive almost any weakness with the exception of stupidity."

"I guess the truth can hurt you worse in an election than about anything that could happen to you."

"American people like to have you repent; then they are generous."

"Income Tax has made more liars out of the American people than golf."

"Nobody wants to be called common people, especially common people."

"Lord, the money we do spend on Government and it's not one bit better than the government we got for one third the money twenty years ago."

"It must be nice to belong to some legislative body and just pick money out of the air."

"Half the people in the U.S. are living on interest paid by people who will never get the last mortgage paid."

"No man is great if he thinks he is."

"A remark generally hurts in proportion to its truth."

**The first scheduled TV broadcast, in 1931, featured George Gershwin and Kate Smith.**

# MYTH AMERICA

*You've believed these stories since you were a kid. Most Americans have, because they were taught to us as sacred truths. Well, sorry. Here's another look.*

## SAVAGES

**The Myth:** "Scalping" was a brutal tactic invented by the Indians to terrorize the settlers.

**The Truth:** Scalping was actually an old European tradition dating back hundreds of years. Dutch and English colonists were paid a "scalp bounty" by their leaders as a means of keeping the Indians scared and out of the way. Finally the Indians caught on and adopted the practice themselves. The settlers apparently forgot its origins and another falsehood about Indian cruelty was born.

## MOTHER OF THE FLAG

**The Myth:** Betsy Ross, a Philadelphia seamstress, designed and sewed the first American flag at the behest of the Founding Fathers.

**Background:** This story first surfaced in 1870 when Betsy Ross's grandson told a meeting of the Pennsylvania Historical Society that his grandmother had been asked to make a flag for the new nation. The tale must have touched a nerve, because it quickly spread and soon was regarded as the truth.

**The Truth:** While Betsy Ross did in fact sew flags for the Pennsylvania Navy, there is no proof to back up her grandson's tale. Ironically, no one is sure who designed the flag. The best guess is that the flag's design is derived from a military banner carried during the American Revolution.

## MIDNIGHT RAMBLER

**The Myth:** Paul Revere made a solitary, dramatic midnight ride to warn patriots in Lexington and Concord that the British were coming.

**Background:** Revere's effort was first glorified in Henry Wadsworth Longfellow's poem, "The Midnight Ride of Paul

**The #1 nonfiction book of 1959: Pat Boone's *Twixt Twelve and Twenty* (advice to teens).**

Revere." Longfellow may have written the ode out of guilt—his grandfather had tried to court-martial Revere during the Revolutionary War. The charge: "Unsoldierly behavior tending toward cowardice." (Revere was not convicted.)

**The Truth:** Paul Revere was actually one of two men who attempted the famous ride...and it was the other one, William Dawes, who made it to Concord. Revere didn't make it—he was stopped by British troops. As for Revere's patriotic motives: According to Patricia Lee Holt, in *George Washington Had No Middle Name*, "Paul Revere billed the Massachusetts State House 10 pounds 4 shillings to cover his expenses for his ride."

## INDIAN MADE

**The Myth:** Pochahontas and Captain John Smith were in love. When her father tried to chop Smith's head off, Pochahontas put her own neck on the line and begged her father to spare her beloved.

**Background:** John Smith told people this had occurred.

**The Truth:** Smith probably made it up. He did know Pochahontas in Jamestown, but they weren't an item. All that's known about her is that "she apparently entertained the colonists by performing cartwheels in the nude."

## AMERICUS THE BEAUTIFUL

**The Myth:** Amerigo Vespucci, a Florentine navigator, made four trips to the New World from 1497 to 1502. The newly discovered land was named America in his honor.

**Background:** Vespucci wrote an account of his four voyages. An Italian mapmaker was so impressed by it that he put "Americus's" name on the first known map of the New World.

**The Truth:** America is named after a probable fraud. Scholars doubt Vespucci really made those trips at all.

## THANKSGIVING

**The Myth**: The Pilgrims ate a Thanksgiving feast of turkey and pumpkin pie after their first year in the New World, and we've been doing it ever since.

**The Truth:** Thanksgiving didn't become a national holiday until Abraham Lincoln declared it in 1863, and the Pilgrims ate neither the bird we call turkey, nor pumpkin pie.

**About 1/6 of the male population in America weighs over 200 lbs.**

# MOVIE OF DOOM

*Getting a job in a movie can be hazardous to your health—in unexpected ways.*

**THE VICTIMS:** More than 90 of the 220 people working on the film *The Conqueror*, including director Dick Powell, stars John Wayne, Agnes Moorhead, and Susan Hayward, and dozens of secondary players and crew members.

## THE CIRCUMSTANCES

On May 19, 1953, the U.S. government tested a powerful A-bomb at Yucca Flats, Nevada. In St. George, Utah, 100 miles to the west, people were fascinated by the event. As *Macleans* magazine described it: "Some of the people went up on the hillside outside town to watch the blast, because nobody told them not to. A few hours later, grey ash began to sift over the Black Hill west of the city; it drifted across the lawns, clung to laundry on the lines, burned the skin of people in the streets....The town's citizens were merely instructed to wash the ash off their automobiles. They were urged not to worry."

A year later, the cast and crew of the film *The Conqueror*, a schlock version of the life of Genghis Khan (John Wayne was Genghis), arrived in St. George to film on location at a nearby desert. They—and the fulltime residents of St. George—were unaware that radiation levels were extraordinarily high in the area...and that, in fact, the entire perimeter may have been contaminated by fallout.

**The result:** Wayne and almost 100 others—about 45% of the people associated with the filming—died of cancer over the next 30 years. Residents of St. George also had an unusually high incidence of cancer.

## UNANSWERED QUESTIONS

- Was the cancer caused by the cumulative, long-lasting effects of low-level radiation?
- Was the area contaminated?

**The first city in history to boast a million inhabitants was London, in 1811.**

• Did the government know about it, and intentionally conceal the information?

**POSSIBLE CONCLUSIONS**

• Government officials were as naive as the citizens of St. George, believing that it was adequate (as they told one St. George resident) to take a shower and change one's clothes when exposed to low-level radiation.

• The low-level radiation didn't cause the cancer that killed so many of the cast and crew of *The Conqueror*. Certainly, not all of them blamed atomic testing for it. (Wayne, a fervent anti-communist, never did. On the other hand, actress Jeanne Gerson, asserting she was the last of the film's stars still living, sued the government when she, too, contracted cancer at age 76.) Still, while no definite link has been (or can be) proven, the situation is highly suspicious; about 45% of the crew contracted cancer, a rate which far exceeds any reasonable statistical probability.

• The government knew it was endangering the lives of American citizens—it had essentially doomed the people working on the movie—but felt it was worth the sacrifice of a few lives to further their knowledge of nuclear power. Considerable evidence which points to this conclusion is coming to light. "Documents made public in 1979," says *Macleans*, "show a long-term pattern to confuse and mislead the public about the dangers of fallout."

For example: An official memo written in 1953—the year of the Yucca Flats test—insisted that "people have got to learn to live with the facts of life, and part of the facts of life is fallout." Another said, "We must not let anything interfere with these tests—nothing." And a subsequent study in 1963 which indicated serious health risks to people exposed to high levels of radiation was suppressed by the Atomic Energy Commission because, one official wrote, "The public would know they have not been told the truth."

So it may, in fact, be true that the U.S. government was responsible for the death of Duke Wayne. And the 1954 B-film, which he reluctantly took on, turned out to be a bomb in more ways than one.

**The first heart transplant took place on December 3, 1967.**

# THE JAVA JIVE

*This might well be the B.R.I. membership's favorite drink. But did you know...*

• Americans drink about 400 million cups of coffee per day—or 146 billion cups every year.

• Coffee has absolutely no nutritional value.

• Legend has it that coffee was discovered over 1,000 years ago, when an Abyssinian goatherder noticed his goats prancing on their hind legs after sampling the fruit of a wild coffee tree. He tried the raw berries himself and began dancing wildly.

• Four out of five adults in the US drink coffee. They put away an average of two cups a day, which adds up to about a third of the world's supply.

• The coffee tree is really an evergreen shrub. It grows to about 25 feet high.

• Per capita, Finns drink the most coffee in the world.

• Hot Water Politics:
Tea was the most popular drink in the Colonies until 1773, when King George III levied a tax on it. After the Boston Tea Party, coffee became the drink of preference, and much of the Revolution was planned in the patriots' favorite new type of meeting place—the coffee house.

• Over 10,000 different studies have analyzed the medical effects of caffeine—and there still are no conclusive results.

• Caffeine is tasteless.

• An average cup of coffee contains 100 milligrams of caffeine; a cup of espresso has 200.

• Signs of caffeine overdose:
1) Cold Sweat
2) The Shakes
3) Heart Palpitations, plus a feeling of Impending Doom

• The symptoms of caffeine withdrawal:
1) Headaches
2) Nervousness
3) Irritability

• Researchers believe that heavy coffee drinkers use the drug to treat themselves for the most common psychiatric condition: depression.

**2/3 of the books published in America are paperbacks.**

# PRESIDENTIAL AFFAIRS

*Until details of John Kennedy's private life began to surface, Americans believed their presidents were above "playing around." Now we know better. Some samples:*

## THOMAS JEFFERSON

The egalitarian aristocrat of Virginia who theoretically opposed slavery, yet owned dozens of slaves, was quite fond of one in particular—the light-skinned Sally Hemings. Jefferson fathered five children with Hemings, four of whom survived. The children apparently passed into the white community with little trouble, and Jefferson's will directed that after his death they be "freed." They were. One son, Madison Heming, resembled Jefferson closely, and reportedly wrote about his life at Monticello in 1873.

## WARREN HARDING

One of America's most inept chief executives, he was so indiscreet with his affairs that some historians speculate that his wife retaliated by poisoning him while he was in office.

Harding carried on long liaisons with at least two different women. One, a Mrs. Phillips, was the wife of a department store owner in Marion, Ohio. She tried to cash in on her relationship with Harding when he was nominated for president by the Republicans, and was probably sent to Japan with a huge chunk of cash in exchange for maintaining her silence.

Harding's romantic poetry to her was discovered after her death. An excerpt: "I love you more than all the world. Possession wholly imploring. Mid passion I am oftimes whirled, oftimes admire—adoring. Oh God! If fate would only give Us privilege to love and live!"

Another of Harding's lovers, Nan Britton, wrote a book in 1927 in which she claimed to have given birth to his daughter in 1919. Her story is less documented than Mrs. Phillips's, but is regarded by historians as probably true.

## DWIGHT D. EISENHOWER

This paragon of middle-American virtue gave in to temptation during World War II. While his wife, Mamie, followed his career from the states, another woman—Kay Summersby—kept him company. Eisenhower was the head of the Allied forces in Europe; Kay was his driver for over three years. In her 1977 book, *Past Forgetting: My Love Affair with Dwight D. Eisenhower*, Summersby (a former British model) details what actually happened between the two during the war. Apparently, she and Eisenhower tried on several occasions to consummate their affection for each other—but Ike was unable to really "rise" to the moment. An unhappy marriage had apparently stripped the 5-star General of his libido and work was the substitute he used in its place.

## LYNDON BAINES JOHNSON

LBJ had no such problem; as his former press secretary, George Reedy, commented in a Johnson biography: "[LBJ] had the instincts of a Turkish sultan in Istanbul." One tale: In 1950 one of his many sexual partners became pregnant. According to the woman, Madeline Brown, Johnson quietly took care of her—both before and after the birth of a son named Steven. For twenty-one years the two carried on, with Johnson setting her up in an apartment for discreet get-togethers.

## JOHN KENNEDY

The stories about JFK's sexual exploits are too numerous to recount. He chased women like a man possessed, but his family name and connections helped keep that part of his personal life out of the news until years after his death. Movie stars, White House workers, "staff" members and gangsters' girlfriends were all the subject of Kennedy's penetrating lifestyle. Some reports now acknowledge that often two women were included in the fun.

## FRANKLIN ROOSEVELT

The love of FDR's life apparently wasn't Eleanor, but a woman named Lucy Mercer, Eleanor's one-time social secretary. Their affair was discovered by Mrs. Roosevelt, who confronted FDR with the information. He promised to end the relationship, but it is reported that Mercer was with him when he died in 1945—almost 30 years after the relationship had begun.

**Elvis collected statuettes of Joan of Arc and Venus de Milo.**

# BRAIN TEASERS

*These simple logic problems have appeared in American game books in various forms for almost a century. We confess that they're not as hard as they first seem to be—we've stayed away from heavy math problems and—for obvious reasons—anything you'd need a pencil to solve.*

A man needs something specific for his house, so he goes to a hardware store to purchase it. When he asks the clerk the price, the clerk answers that "the price of one is fifty cents, the price of thirty is one dollar, and the price of one hundred forty-four is one dollar and fifty cents." What is the man buying?

Two boys were playing on a tool shed roof when the roof collapsed with a crash. The boys fell uninjured to the floor below, but when they picked themselves up, the face of one boy was covered with dirt and the other boy's was still clean. Instantly, the boy with the clean face ran off to wash his face, while the one with the dirty face remained placidly behind. Why did the boy with the clean face act as he did?

A tree has one blossom on it at the beginning of June. The blossoms double in area every 24 hours. It takes the entire month for the tree to be covered completely with blossoms. On what date will the tree be half-covered?

You have one match. You enter a room that contains a wood-burning stove, a kerosene lamp and a fireplace. Which should you light first?

# DEFINITIONS

*While you're sitting there, you might like to improve your vocabulary a bit. Here are some obscure words and definitions to study.*

**Peccadillo:** A slight or trifling sin; a fault
**Sesamoid:** Having the shape of a sesame seed
**Anserine:** Gooselike, as in goose bumps on skin
**Wanion:** Disaster or bad luck
**Joad:** A migratory worker
**Pettifogger:** An inferior lawyer
**Feverwort:** A weedy herb
**Squamous:** Covered with scales
**Cachinnate:** To laugh noisily
**Erubescence:** Process of turning red, blushing
**Histoplasmosis:** A respiratory illness caused by inhaling festered bat dung
**Paraselene:** A mock moon appearing on a lunar halo
**Yerk:** To tie with a jerk
**Bilbo:** A finely tempered Spanish sword
**Verisimilitude:** Appearance of truth
**Salubrious:** Wholesome
**Fecund:** Fruitful
**Epistemology:** A school of philosophy that includes the study of the nature of human knowledge
**Yowie:** A small ewe
**Parsimony:** Stinginess
**Holm:** An island in a river
**Coriaceous:** Tough, leathery texture
**Mullion:** A vertical dividing piece between window lights or panels
**Sippet:** A triangular piece of toasted or french bread used to garnish a dish of hash
**Infrangible:** Not breakable
**Sudorific:** Causing perspiration
**Cerulean:** Sky blue
**Pomology:** The study of fruit
**Rusticate:** To send into the country
**Agnomen:** An added name due to some special achievement
**Saponification:** Process of making soap
**Motet:** A sacred musical composition for several voices
**Lycanthropy**: The power of turning a human being into a wolf by magic or witchcraft. Wolfman science.

**The most common bird in the world is the starling.**

# GILLIGAN'S ISLAND

*Few TV shows have been both as reviled and beloved as "Gilligan's Island"—sometimes by the same people. Two unanswered questions remain about this program: 1) Where did they get all those clothes? 2) How did they last for three years without sex?*

## HOW IT STARTED

In 1963, veteran TV writer Sherwood Schwartz ("The Red Skelton Show", "I Married Joan") was ready to break away from writing other people's shows and create his own sitcom. A literate man with degrees in zoology and psychology, Schwartz had an idea for a meaningful show: He'd take representative members of American society, strand them on an island (this was inspired by Defoe's *Robinson Crusoe*), and their interaction would be a microcosm of life in the U.S.

How this idea turned into "Gilligan's Island" is anyone's guess. In the end, Sherwood's castaways were more caricatures than characters. He called them *clichés*: "The wealthy, the Hollywood glamour girl, the country girl, the professor, the misfit, and the resourceful bull of a man." He added, "Anybody who is watching can identify with someone." Yes, but would they want to?

Schwartz brought his concept to CBS and United Artists; both agreed to finance a pilot. But after the pilot was filmed, CBS started playing with the premise. Network president Jim Aubrey felt it should be a story about a charter boat that went out on a new adventure every week. "How would the audience know what those guys were doing on the island?" he wanted to know. It looked like Schwartz's original idea was sunk. Then he had a brainstorm—explain the premise in a theme song! He wrote his own tune and performed it at a meeting of CBS brass (probably a first). And on the basis of that song, CBS ok'd the castaways. Now do we thank them or what?

## INSIDE FACTS

Even "Gilligan's Island" wasn't sanitized enough for the censors!

Never mind that there wasn't a hint of sex in three years on a deserted island. CBS censors still objected to Tina Louise's low-cut dresses and Dawn Wells' exposed navel.

•Believe it or not, some viewers took the show seriously. The U.S. Coast Guard received several telegrams from concerned citizens asking why they didn't rescue the *Minnow*'s crew.

•Schwartz picked the name "Gilligan" from out of the Los Angeles phone book.

•Schwartz originally wanted Jerry Van Dyke to play Gilligan. He turned it down in favor of the lead in a different TV series—"My Mother the Car." Another actor wanted to play the Skipper, but was rejected: Carroll "Archie Bunker" O'Connor.

## EVERYONE'S A CRITIC

The public loved Gilligan, but most critics hated it. A sample:

•*L.A. Times:* "'Gilligan's Island' is a show that should never have reached the airwaves, this season or any other."

•*S.F. Chronicle:* "It is difficult to believe that this show was written, directed, and produced by adults. It marks a new low in the networks' estimation of public intelligence."

## THE PILOT FILM

•It was shot in Hawaii, just a few miles from the spot where *South Pacific* was filmed.

•One of the major problems faced by the production crew during the pilot's filming: frogs. Inexplicably, they piled up by the hundreds outside the doors of the on-site cottages.

•Filming of the pilot was completed on November 22, 1963—the day J.F.K. was assassinated.

## ABOUT THE ISLAND

•It was man-made, located in the middle of an artificial lake at CBS's Studio Center in Hollywood, and surrounded by painted landscapes, artificial palm trees, and wind machines.

•At one point, the concrete lake-bottom leaked. So it had to be completely drained, repaired, and filled again.

•It cost $75,000 to build.

**Killer Ant: The black bulldog ant of Australia and Tasmania can kill a person.**

# CRYONICS

*At one time or another, everyone has toyed with the idea of eternal life—or at least, of being able to put things on hold and come back, when cures for today's terminal diseases have been found. Enter the technology of cryonics, the attempt to preserve human life by storing bodies at subfreezing temperatures.*

## WHAT IT IS

Theoretically, cryonics is a way of putting nature on ice, of creating suspended animation in human beings by freezing them—a notion that can be traced back to 1964, when physics professor Robert Ettinger wrote and published a book called *The Prospect of Immortality*.

At death, the body is cooled to near freezing and the blood is removed and replaced with a synthetic solution. Then the body is placed in a stainless steel tank filled with liquid nitrogen. The reason: when living tissue is cooled at a controlled rate to the temperature of liquid nitrogen, all molecular and biological activity stops. Theoretically, with its biological clock stopped, the tissue stays viable via suspended animation.

The body is kept in the tank at subfreezing temperatures, until the anticipated day when technology makes "re-animation" possible.

When will that be? According to a committed cryonicist: "The technology of freezing is still very primitive, and will require advances in thawing and resuscitation that may not be available for two centuries, if ever."

## IS IT STRICTLY FOR LUNATICS?

At first a lot of scientists thought it was a money-making scam (and many still do), a false hope for people who are unable to accept the inevitability of their own deaths. But recently theory has given way to practice as biologists at the University of California have been able to revive ice-cold hamsters and dogs.

Freezing, said one of the UC scientists, "is nature's way of saying 'time out.' It's a way of putting life on hold. For in-

**According to *Billboard*, the #1 song of the '60s was "Theme from a Summer Place."**

stance, some frogs go through the winter with 1/3-to-1/2 of their body's water turned into ice. They can go without breathing, eating or even without a heartbeat. In the spring, they thaw out and go on with their lives."

Throughout the years, the basic doctrine of cryonics has not varied: the dead are considered temporarily incurable.

**WHAT IT IS NOT**

Cryonics shouldn't be confused with cryobiology, a recognized branch of medical research that studies the effects of very low temperatures on living tissue. Cryobiology has enabled scientists and physicians to freeze blood, corneas, bone marrow, sperm and even human embryos for use at a future time. However, organs such as the pancreas, the kidney and the human heart (to be used in transplant surgery) have proven to be unusable if frozen (which makes the whole premise behind cryonics highly suspect).

**FREEZER FACTS**

• The American Cryonics Society says that its membership numbers 100 people who have committed themselves for freezing after death.

• In three cryonics centers in California and Michigan, the earthly remains of 15 people are on ice. There used to be 45, but 30 of the tanks leaked.

• Freezing doesn't come cheap. The price tag for return in the 21st century varies between $100,000 and $125,000.

• For a reduced price of $30,000 one may have his head frozen instead of his entire body. The head may or may not be grafted onto a healthy body at some future date; the guiding idea is that cloning will make other body parts easy to replicate in the future when the technology is available.

• Cryonicists do have a sense of humor. Their slogan is: "Freeze, Wait, Reanimate." The standard joke is "Many are cold, but few are frozen."

• "There's a poem we like to quote," says one cryonicist:

"I really think that I could freeze,
My mother-in-law with the greatest of ease.

**In Kentucky, 50% of the people who get married for the first time are teenagers.**

The only thing that gives me pause,
Is what will happen when she thaws."

• **Whoops:** When Saul Kent's mother, Dora, died after years of suffering from arthritis and a degenerative brain disease, he hired Alcor Life Extension Foundation, a cryonics facility in Fullerton, California, to freeze her head until it could be revived and attached to a new body. There was one hitch, however: Dora Kent may not have been dead before her head was removed. Besides, the old woman may not have wanted to be turned into a human ice cube; she never signed the consent forms.

**RECENT DEVELOPMENTS:** Research physiologists at the University of California at Berkeley froze a three-year-old beagle named Miles and revived him.

• Miles was anaesthetized and placed on a bed of ice until his temperature fell from his normal 100.5 degrees (F) to 68 degrees.

• Next, the pooch, drained of his own blood (which was replaced with a clear, synthetic blood that wouldn't clot in the cold) was frozen.

• Legally "dead" for the hour his body spent at below 50 degrees, Miles was thawed, given back his blood and returned to perfect doggie health.

**FOR NOW:** While the Miles experiments may lead scientists to give ailing humans "the big chill" until cures for their diseases have been found, experiments with freezing a patient's own blood may alleviate a lot of problems right now. Surgery requires a lot of donated blood (which may or may not be contaminated); with freezing and the use of synthetic blood, a patient's own blood can be recycled.

## WHAT ABOUT UNCLE WALT?

The most enticing rumor associated with cryonics is that Walt Disney had his body frozen and is planning to return some day. Is it true? In the book *Disney's World*, an associate reveals: "My information is that he *is* frozen down....[And] if he does come back, there's going to be hell to pay. He wouldn't approve of much that's gone on at the [Disney] Studios...."

**Thomas Wedgwood took the world's first photograph in 1802.**

# FLIPPER

*The most famous aquatic animal superstar is the dolphin who starred in her own TV series. Here's the inside scoop on Flipper, from* Animal Superstars, *by John Javna.*

**ORIGIN:**
"Lassie in a wet suit," as one TV critic jokingly described "Flipper," was exactly what underwater stunt man Ricou Browning had in mind when he created Flipper in the early '60s.

"I was watching 'Lassie' on television with my kids one night," he says, "and I thought, 'Wouldn't it be great to do an animal show similar to "Lassie" with a kid and a dolphin?'" He envisioned the story as a book, but the idea was turned down by every publisher Browning sent it to.

So he tried movie producers instead. At the time, very little was known about dolphins, and no one knew if they could be trained to become film performers. But when Browning sent his ideas to producer Ivan Tors, Tors couldn't resist the challenge. "Let's make a movie of...that story of yours," he told Browning. The result: two films, a TV series, and the #1 aquatic superstar of all time.

**ABOUT THE STAR**
Species: Dolphin

- Length: seven feet
- Weight: 300 lb.
- Number of teeth: 84
- Speed: Up to 40 miles per hour
- Favorite foods: Mullets and butterfish
- Sex: Female
- Name: Mitzi was the star of two Flipper films. Suzy starred in the TV series—until she became too rough with the actors. Then Cathy replaced her.

**INSIDE FACTS**

- **Secrets of success:** Unlike previous dolphin trainers who worked on dry land, everyone connected with "Flipper" interacted with the animals in the water. This cut training time from six months per trick to three weeks.

•Flipper's most memorable trick—carrying a boy on her back—was really a "fetch." Browning threw his nine-year-old son in the water and ordered Flipper to retrieve him. She put her fin under his arm, and off they went.

## TRICKS AND TRAINING

•**The Trainer:** Although Ivan Tors worked with the dolphins sometimes, Ricou Browning was their trainer. Browning had been a diver on "Sea Hunt," and (are you ready for this?) played the creature in *The Creature from the Black Lagoon*.

•The stars of "Flipper" could learn new tricks in one shot, as long as their human trainers were "smart enough" to communicate what they wanted.

•Each dolphin could learn the 35 basic maneuvers that the role of Flipper required in only six months.

•Essential tricks included "fetching" (Mitzi could fetch up to five things at once), towing a boat with a rope, shaking hands with her flipper, hitting the water with her tail, and letting a person hold her flipper while she swam.

## STAR GOSSIP

Ivan Tors had a very special relationship with Suzy, the dolphin who played Flipper on TV—she'd saved his life.

•When Suzy was first being trained, Tors swam out into a lagoon to meet her. But she swam away, refusing to let him near her. Tors chased her until he was exhausted. Then he surfaced to get his breath—and was overwhelmed by a huge wave. As he desperately called for help, he suddenly felt Suzy's dorsal fin underneath him. He grabbed it, and she towed him to safety, winning his gratitude—and a starring role on the show.

## SCREEN CREDITS

•1963: *Flipper* (film). Co-stars: Chuck Connors, Luke Halpin.

•1964: *Flipper's New Adventures* (film). Co-stars: Brian Kelly, Luke Halpin.

•1964-67: "Flipper" (TV series). 88 episodes. Co-stars: Brian Kelly, Luke Halpin, Tommy Norden, Pete the Pelican, Spray the Retriever.

**Elvis owned 18 TVs, including one installed on the ceiling over his bed.**

# PRIME-TIME PROVERBS

*TV comments about everyday life in America. From* Prime Time Proverbs, *by Jack Mingo.*

**ON MARRIAGE:**
"Son, stay clear of weddings because one of them is liable to be your own."
**—Pappy Maverick,** ***Maverick***

"Just because I've been married for twenty-five years is no reason to stop being sexy."
**—Ralph Kramden,** ***The Honeymooners***

**Groucho:** "Are you married, Georgette?"
**Contestant:** "Yes, I've been married to the same man for thirty-one years."
**Groucho:** "Well if he's been married for thirty-one years, he's not the same man."
***—You Bet Your Life***

**ON TELEVISION:**
"Well, Beaver, this may be hard for you to believe, but life isn't exactly like television."
**—Ward Cleaver,** ***Leave It to Beaver***

"It's just plain foolishness, squattin' all day in front of that little black box, starin' bleary-eyed at people who ain't more than two inches high. It's a passin' fancy, I tell you, like buggy whips and high button shoes."
**—Grandpa Amos McCoy** ***The Real McCoys***

**Maggie:** "It's four o'clock in the morning and you're watching a test pattern."
**Dave:** "I know, but I want to see how it ends."
***—My Mother the Car***

**ON RACE & RELIGION:**
"Jesus was a Jew, yes, but only on his mother's side."
**—Archie Bunker,** ***All In the Family***

"Have you always been a Negro, or are you just trying to be fashionable?"
**—Dr. Morton Chesley,** ***Julia***

"You keep talking about minorities. Well mister, you're a psycho, and they're a minority, too."
**—Sgt. Joe Friday,** ***Dragnet***

**A dragonfly, the fastest flying insect, can move up to 35 m.p.h.**

# WHAT A DOLL!

*Barbie is the product that toymakers dream of. She never goes out of style...and each succeeding generation loves to play with her. What a doll!*

Children have been playing with dolls for thousands of years, but the most popular doll in the history of the world has only been in existence since 1959. It's Barbie, of course. Since Mattel's buxom fashionplate was first introduced, more than 400 million Barbie dolls have been sold. And the number is growing every day.

Some toys are just toys. But Barbie is a way of life.

From the outset, she encouraged little girls to be good consumers. "Barbie was important not for herself, but for all that could be added to her," explains Thomas Hine in *Populuxe*. "She had party dresses, and gowns for the prom, and a wedding ensemble....She had a boyfriend, Ken, a little sister, and a Corvette. There was always something new to buy for her—a more stylish outfit, a new kind of fashion, a different fantasy."

But Barbie carried other social messages besides the joys of consumerism. The joy of sex, for example. With her large breasts and hourglass figure, Barbie resembled a teenage Jayne Mansfield; she was clearly a traditional sex object. Yet you knew you'd never see Barbie stuck in anyone's kitchen, barefoot and pregnant. It's no coincidence that Barbie debuted at about the same time as The Pill. As much as any child's toy could in 1960, she represented an ideal of sexual freedom.

And how about Barbie's obsession with looks and possessions? Sure, they propagated a shallow set of values to the little girls who adored her. But they also implied independence. Prior to Barbie, every popular doll in America was a baby doll. Barbie signified a change. Girls didn't have to play "mommy" anymore. They had a new kind of role model—a career girl who could be a model, a nurse, a nightclub singer...even an astronaut. Sure, Barbie had expensive taste, but she didn't de-

**Only 2/3 of all American kids think we can avoid a nuclear war.**

pend on her boyfriend for anything. In fact, Barbie was the boss in that relationship. It was *Barbie*'s Corvette, remember—Ken just went along for the ride.

## BARBIE'S ROOTS

The real Barbie (yes, there was one) was the daughter of Ruth and Eliot Handler, who founded Mattel after World War II. The idea for the teenage fashion doll came to Ruth when she noticed that Barbie preferred playing with shapely paper dolls to playing with baby dolls. The Handlers gambled that other modern girls would feel the same way. The Handlers had a son, too, named Ken.

Barbie was introduced at the New York Toy Fair in February, 1959. The first Barbie dolls cost $3—today, in mint condition, they're worth over $1,000. And the figure keeps rising.

Barbie's creators based her appearance on the prevailing standards of beauty in 1959—Brigitte Bardot, with her perky pony tail and knock-out figure, and Grace Kelly's patrician blondness.

She was originally called a three-dimensional fashion drawing. Said Ruth Handler, "Barbie was originally created to project every little girl's dream of the future," and part of that future meant being grown up. Grown up to a little girl, was having breasts. It was no accident that a lingerie line was one of the first sets of Barbie clothes available.

Collectors seem certain that the design for Barbie was lifted from a German doll named "Lilli"—which was, in turn, based on a cartoon character created for the daily newspaper *Bild-Zeitung*. Ironically, the German Lilli was not a wholesome teenager, but a winsome, sexually loose gold-digger. Maybe that explains her body.

## ALL DRESSED UP...

Barbie was sold as a teenage fashion model, but her wardrobe was definitely haute couture, or as close to Parisian fashion as one could come with a doll. Whenever new costumes were planned for the doll, Mattel designer Charlotte Johnson and her staff traveled to Europe to see the collections of Dior, Jacques Fath, Balenciaga, Givenchy, Mme. Gres, Balmain and Schiaparelli. Then they adapted what they saw.

Barbie has always been on the top of pop fashion trends. In

**The longest-lived insects are queen termites, which live for up to 100 years.**

the late'50s and early '60s, her wardrobe included white gloves and pillbox hats. By the '70s, she was the prototypical exercise nut in leotards and tights—so she'd look great in her hot pants outfits and fringed suede vests. By 1980, she was a disco singer wearing glitter togs and toting a microphone.

**...AND NO PLACE TO GO**

Overall, the most popular Barbie outfits are wedding gowns. But although she has all the necessary gear for a fancy wedding (and has for about 30 years), Barbie has never actually taken the plunge. She and Ken haven't even set a date.

•Mattel is the world's largest manufacturer of "women's" clothing. They produce 20 million Barbie outfits a year.

**BARBIE FACTS**

•In 1987, Mattel sold $450 million worth of Barbie merchandise—that's almost $1 billion on the retail level.

•Barbie's last name is Roberts.

•Barbie is a college graduate. She attended a generic educational institution called State College.

•The Barbie Fan Club has over 600,000 members worldwide.

•Not that you care, but...what would happen if you laid all the Barbie dolls that have been sold since 1959 in a line, head-to-toe? According to Mattel press releases, "that's enough dolls to circle the earth more than three-and-a-half times."

•Some Barbie features over the years: Fashion Queen Barbie had wigs in 1963; in 1966, Barbie's hair and clothes changed color "when swabbed with a special solution"; there was "a motorized stage in 1971, which, when activated, made Live Action Barbie dance"; 1980's Western Barbie winked. And the beat goes on.

**BARBIE FLOPS**

•Two Barbie flops: "Colored Francy," and "Kissing Barbie." "Kissing Barbie"'s lips moved, but Mattel didn't make a "Kissing Ken," so there was nobody for Barbie to pucker up with.

•In 1986, Mattel tried to introduce a Barbie clothing line for real girls from 7 to 14 years old. Their slogan: "We Girls Can Do Anything." Mattel marketed the clothes in stores like J.C. Penney and K-Mart; but it didn't work.

**Ostriches measure up to nine feet from head to feet. They weigh as much as 350 pounds.**

# CUSTOMS

*Where did they come from? A few random examples.*

## TIPPING

Some think it began in the 17th century, when restaurants had boxes labelled T.I.P.—To Insure Promptness—on the wall beside their entrances. Patrons who wanted their food in a hurry deposited a few coins in the box before they sat down.

## AN APPLE FOR THE TEACHER

Now an outmoded custom, it stems from the days when public school teachers were paid with whatever the community they served could afford. Often they were given food or goods in lieu of cash.

## THE TOOTH FAIRY

In Germany, where the idea apparently originated, the tooth was not placed under a pillow. Instead, it was put in a rat hole because it was thought that the new tooth growing in would take on the "dental quality" of the animal who found it.

## STRIPED BARBER POLES

Barbers were once a lot more versatile than they are today. They not only cut hair, they performed surgery as well. When the barbers finished, the towels used to soak up excess blood were hung outside to dry on a pole. As the wind dried them they wrapped around the pole, making a design, so to speak, of red and white stripes.

## ADVICE TO SINGLES

From the 1700s: "If you want to get married, stand on your head and chew a piece of gristle out of a beef neck and swallow it, and you will get anyone you want."

**The zipper was invented in 1893, for use in shoes.**

# MARILYN SAID...

*Marilyn Monroe was known for saying exactly what was on her mind. A fascinating collection of quotes is in* Marilyn Monroe: A Never-Ending Dream, *by Guus Luijters.*

"I think femininity and beauty are ageless and can't be faked, and that true glamour—I know the manufacturers aren't going to like this—isn't a factory product. Not real glamour, in any case, which is based on femininity. Sexuality is only attractive when it's natural and spontaneous."

"Bobby Kennedy promised to marry me. What do you think of that?"

"A career is a wonderful thing, but you can't snuggle up to it on a cold night."

[*After JFK had surreptitiously slipped his hand under her dress*] "I bet he doesn't put his hand up Jacqueline's dress. I bet no one does. Is she ever stiff!"

"I've noticed that men generally leave married women alone and treat them with respect. It's too bad for married women. Men are always ready to respect someone who bores them. And if most married women, even the pretty ones, look so dull, it's because they're getting too much respect."

"My ass is way too big. They tell me men like it like that. Crazy, huh?"

"Blonde hair and breasts, that's how I got started. I couldn't act. All I had was my blonde hair and a body men liked. The reason I got ahead is that I was lucky and met the right men."

"People are always looking at me as if I were a kind of mirror instead of a person. They don't see me, they see their own hidden thoughts and then they whitewash themselves by claiming that I embody those secret thoughts."

**Kotex was first manufactured as bandages, during World War I.**

# VALENTINE'S DAY

*Beginning in kindergarten, we exchange cards with classmates and friends on Valentine's Day. Later, it's flowers and presents for loved ones. Here's why we do it.*

**VALENTINE'S DAY**
This "lovers' holiday" is an anomaly. It was actually an effort by the Catholic Church to *keep* teenagers from becoming lovers.

Before Christ was born, it was a Roman tradition for teenage girls and boys to gather every February in the name of the god Lupercus, and randomly select a "mate" for a year. They were permitted to do anything they liked together (and what else would teenagers do?).

When Christians gained power in the Roman Empire, they wanted to bring this practice to an end. So they selected a substitute for Lupercus (to be the focus of a parallel holiday)—St. Valentine, a bishop who had reputedly been tortured and executed by Emperor Claudius II in 270 A.D, for performing marriages after Claudius had outlawed them in the Empire. This symbol of more "wholesome" love, was reluctantly accepted by the Romans. But just to be sure no one gave in to temptation, the Catholic Church made it a mortal sin to worship Lupercus. Eventually, Valentine's Day became a recognized holiday throughout Western Europe.

## VALENTINE CARDS

If teens couldn't get together in February, what could they do? They could send each other respectful notes of affection. And they did, although it seems like a poor substitute. At any rate, sending lover's greetings became a part of the Valentine's day ritual, and when Christian influence grew, the practice of sending notes on February 14 spread with it.

The first greeting cards didn't appear until the 18th century. Printed cards were common in Germany by the 1780s; they were called *Freundschaftkarten*, or "friendship cards." The first American cards were manufactured in the 1870s, at an amazing cost of up to thirty-five dollars apiece.

**If an orangutan belches at you, watch out. He's warning you to stay out of his territory.**

# ENQUIRING MINDS...

*The* National Enquirer, *"America's most popular newspaper," deals in gossip coupled with oddity. Celebrity "confessions" share space with miracle cures, religious wonders (Jesus's face in a taco), advice on relationships, psychic predictions, UFO/alien kidnap tales, weight loss schemes, interesting trivia and occasionally, a legit news scoop.*

VITAL STATS

**Circulation:** Over 4.5 million weekly

**Weekly readership:** 15-20 million

**Founder:** Generoso Pope, Jr., who died on September 25, 1988.

**Earnings:** Unknown, because the *Enquirer* is privately held.

**Headquarters:** Lantana, Florida (Pope moved the paper from New Jersey to Florida because he liked the weather.)

**Staff:** Largely British, Scottish and Australian—writers and editors steeped in the tradition of England's Fleet Street tabloid operations, where they essentially make the news up if it's not exciting enough.

**Salaries:** Staff is paid on a scale that far surpasses more traditional journalists. In 1981, it was revealed that beginning reporters made over $40,000 and editors could make as much as $80,000; presumably that salary base has risen drastically. However, story editors are paid according to how many of their staff's articles appear in print, so the competition for space in the *Enquirer* is stiff and the burn-out factor is very high. Reporters who last longer than 18 months are a rare breed.

**Philosophy:** To Pope's way of thinking, the *Enquirer* was not out to win prizes—it is mass entertainment, pure and simple.

In the *Enquirer*'s inner sanctum, the highest compliment Pope could pay an editor was that he had a "Hey Martha!" story—one "so astonishing and compelling" that the reader would stop mid-sentence and turn to his wife or someone nearby and say "Hey Martha, get a load of this!" The rest of the editors had to settle for "Gee-whiz" stories.

## SCOOPS AND STORIES

*Some memorable efforts by the* Enquirer:

**THE SCOOP:** A photo of Elvis Presley in his coffin.
**HOW THEY DID IT:** When Elvis died on August 16, 1977, the *Enquirer* flew staff members to Memphis and set up headquarters in a boarding house. The reporters were instructed to find a "blockbuster" scoop, something to eclipse the emerging stories about the King's drug habit. One staffer came up with the idea of a photograph of Presley in his coffin, and that was it. The night before the funeral, reporters bought a number of cameras and handed them out to "mourners" along with a liberal sprinkling of cold, hard cash.

The day after the funeral, the command center was littered with snaps of the King lying in state. The next issue of the *Enquirer* went on sale with Elvis' corpse on the cover. It quickly became the newspaper's all-time biggest (at that time) seller.

**THE SCOOP:** A Photo of Bing Crosby in *his* coffin.
**HOW THEY DID IT:** This time a reporter dressed as a priest conned his way into the private ceremony held for Bing. As he left the service with his snapshot, the priest/reporter admonished ABC reporter Geraldo Rivera not to bother the Crosby family at such a sensitive moment.

**THE SCOOP:** Photographs of Democratic presidential candidate Gary Hart in Bimini with Miami model Donna Rice. The photos (snapped by Rice's friend Lynn Armandt) showed Rice sitting on Hart's lap and Hart, surrounded by Rice, Armandt and a male friend, standing on the stage of a Bimini bar holding a pair of maracas.

The story details the long, romantic weekend the two spent aboard the yacht, *Monkey Business*, and quotes Rice as saying to several unnamed friends that Hart had said he loved her, and that he would divorce his long-suffering wife, Lee, *after* he was elected president.

Quotes like this one: "When Gary has a few beers, he becomes a wild and crazy guy, nothing like the straight serious man you see on TV" sank Hart's campaign for good.
**HOW THEY DID IT:** More than 12 editors and researchers

were involved in tracking down people who had either seen Hart and friends in Bimini or knew Donna Rice and her friend Lynn. Most of the story was drawn from what the loose-lipped Rice later told friends about the weekend. The tab for the photos came to a reputed $25,000.

**THE SCOOP:** The last hours of John Belushi as told by Cathy Evelyn Smith....and a confession by Smith that it was she who gave Belushi his final "speedball," the injection of cocaine and heroin that killed him.
**HOW THEY DID IT:** *Enquirer* reporters actually uncovered more information on Belushi's death than the Los Angeles Police Department. Then they tracked Smith down and paid her $15,000 to talk to them. The tell-all interview led police to reopen the case and further investigate her role in the incident. Eight months later, a Los Angeles grand jury indicted Smith for murder along with 13 counts of administering a dangerous drug. The evidence against Smith included the *Enquirer*'s interview tapes.

**THE SCOOP:** Carol Burnett was seen acting "boisterous and disorderly" in a Washington, D.C. restaurant.
**HOW THEY DID IT:** By stretching the facts. At least, that's what Burnett said as she sued them for big bucks... and won. In a rare retraction, the *Enquirer* admitted the error of its ways, but not without a parting shot.

The Quote: "As far as we're concerned," said an editor, "the Carol Burnett decision essentially means that Carol Burnett is now the only woman in America officially adjudicated as 'not the life of the party.'"

**THE SCOOP:** The Three Mile Island disaster was sabotage.
**HOW THEY DID IT:** According to an ex-reporter, they took a statement by a local cop that an elderly couple at a nearby motel looked a little suspicious to him...combined it with a similar statement that the radio and can opener the old couple had could conceivably be called a "dangerous weapon" and "sophisticated communications equipment," and pieced the rest of the totally misleading story together from there.

**The first transcontinental phone call: 1915, from New York to San Francisco.**

# ANCIENT RIDDLES

*These old riddles—and hundreds more—have been reproduced in the book* Riddles—Ancient and Modern, *by Mark Bryant, published by Peter Bedrick Books. They're more "what am I?" than traditional riddles. Some of them are pretty hard, but they're all very clever. And all are authentically old.*

**1.** "The beginning of eternity,
The end of time and space,
The beginning of every end,
And the end of every place."
**Hint:** *It's in front of you right now.*

**2.** "I never was, am always to be,
None ever saw me, nor ever will,
And yet I am the confidence of all
Who live and breathe on this terrestrial ball."
**Hint:** *It never comes.*

**3.** "Runs over fields and woods all day,
Under the bed at night sits not alone,
With long tongue hanging out,
A-waiting for a bone."
**Hint:** *It's something very close to you.*

**4.** "At night they come without being fetched, and by day they are lost without being stolen."
**Hint:** *They belong to the night.*

**5.** "Fatherless and motherless,
Born without a skin,
Spoke when it came into the world,
And never spoke again."
**Hint:** *If you had no nose, you'd never know this one.*

**6.** "What gets wet when drying?"
*No hint.*

**7.** "There was a green house.
Inside the green house there was a white house.
Inside the white house there was a red house.
Inside the red house there were lots of black babies.
**Hint:** *A fruit.*

**The biggest known pumpkin in history weighed almost 700 pounds.**

# BYPASS SURGERY

*For a change of pace, here's some medical history. Written by Dr. Lisa Berlin.*

Today open heart surgery is performed using a cardiopulmonary bypass pump, a mechanical device that pumps blood and performs gas exchange. It allows surgeons to enter the heart directly without risking damage to other organs through lack of blood and oxygen.

Before mechanical bypass systems were perfected, one of the pioneers in this area, Dr. Walton Lillehei, used the heart and lungs of another living person to perform these vital functions. The patients usually were young children with life-threatening congenital heart defects, and the donors were usually parents. Child and parent lay side by side on separate tables in the operating room, and tubes connected the circulatory systems of each. The tubing went from the superior and inferior vena cavae of the child, major veins draining oxygen-poor blood into the heart, to a large vein in the parent. The blood then went to the parent's heart and lungs, picked up oxygen and released carbon dioxide, and then traveled back to the infant's aorta, or major artery, through a second tube placed in the parent's aorta.

Although this technique allowed for the correction of otherwise inoperable heart defects at a relatively small risk to the child, there were some complications involving the donors. It was eventually replaced by the purely mechanical systems in use today.

## TOTALLY UNRELATED NEWS REPORT

*A few years ago, someone sent us this article.*

Ironton, Ohio. "Church members burned records albums and cassettes, after hearing evangelist Jim Brown of Psalms 150 in South Point say the "Mr. Ed" television theme conveys a satanic message to unwary listeners.

"'A horse is a horse'—when played backwards—contains the message 'the source is Satan' and 'Someone sung this song for Satan,' Brown said."

**The theme song to "Mr. Ed" was written by the composers who wrote "Que Sera, Sera."**

# THE POPE

*It was a tragedy that the Pope passed away. But there was nothing anyone could have done about it...or was there?*

**THE VICTIM:** Pope John Paul I, leader of the Roman Catholic Church for a scant thirty-three days.

**THE CIRCUMSTANCES:** On September 29, 1978, the deceased Pope was discovered in his own bed; he had apparently died during the night. The cause, according to his doctors, was a heart attack. This didn't come as a surprise, however. Vatican offcials explained that the Pope had been ailing for some time. Fourteen hours later, the Pontiff was embalmed...without an autopsy.

**UNANSWERED QUESTIONS:** An entire book—*In God's Name: An Investigation Into the Murder of Pope John Paul I*—has been written about them by author David Yallop. A few of the more interesting ones:

- Why would the Vatican doctors claim to know the cause of death without performing an autopsy? Why didn't they do an autopsy? And what was the hurry to get the body embalmed?
- Why did the Vatican claim they anticipated a heart attack when all available evidence indicates the opposite? Three months before his death, for example, the Pope had an EKG which indicated a healthy heart; and his blood pressure was low.
- Why was he reported to have been reading a Medieval religious text when he died, when he had actually been reading some "personal papers"? What were the papers? And why did the Vatican say the Rev. John Magee discovered the corpse when it was really a nun named Sister Vincenza? What did the Sister see?

**POSSIBLE CONCLUSIONS:**

- It's just another conspiracy theory with no basis in reality.
- The Pope was murdered by conservative elements within the

**Einstein couldn't speak fluently when he was nine. His parents thought he might be retarded.**

Church because he planned a liberalization of some important rules, particularly regarding birth control.

•He was murdered by forces connected to the Vatican Bank scandals. As it was later revealed, the Vatican Bank was mixed up in a number of shady transactions involving some equally shady characters at that time—including Michael Sindona, a banker whose Mafia connections were exposed after the Franklin National Bank (which he owned) failed.

Sindona was later convicted of hiring hit men to kill an official of the Italian government who was investigating him. Why wouldn't he repeat the approach if the Pope had decided to expose him? Sindona, by the way, died of poisoning in jail.

There were several other questionable characters dealing with the Vatican Bank. Any of them or their associates might have assassinated the Pope if they felt sufficiently threatened. But as one author points out, we'll probably never know what really happened.

## DEATH BY WATER BED

*Reported by* The Realist *in the '60s.*

"Malcolm Coors, a University of Arizona grad student in economics, became the first fatality of the waterbed fad. He had been watching a late-night talk show on his tiny Sony television, which had frayed electrical connecting wires. The set fell into a puddle—the result of his cat clawing at the waterbed—and he was electrocuted. The electrically charged water seeped up and surrounded his body before he could reach safety. Coors would have been 23 years old two days later."

## KILLER TALK SHOW

*The Realist* also reported the rather bizarre circumstances of the death of publisher and health-food advocate J. I. Rodale. Rodale, who created the popular *Prevention* magazine, made an appearance on "The Dick Cavett Show" in the late '60s, confidently discussing his physical well-being. "He said that doctors had given him 6 months to live 30 years ago, but because of the food he ate, he would live to be a hundred." A little later in the show he appeared to have fallen asleep, and Cavett and guest Pete Hamill chuckled about it...until they realized he was dead. The taped show did not air.

# CONFUCIUS SAY...

*Yes, there really was a Confucius. He was a Chinese sage and philosopher who lived from 551 to 479 B.C. Here are a few of the things he actually said.*

"They who know *the truth* are not equal to those who love it, and they who love it are not equal to those who delight in it."

"The superior man has neither anxiety nor fear."

"Without knowing the force of words it is impossible to know men."

"We don't know yet about life, how can we know about death?"

"Being true to oneself is the law of God. To try to be true to oneself is the law of man."

"To be fond of learning is to be near to knowledge."

"Silence is a true friend who never betrays."

"The superior man thinks always of virtue; the common man thinks of comfort."

"He does not preach what he practices till he has practiced what he preaches."

"He who learns but does not think, is lost! He who thinks but does not learn is in great danger!"

"It is only the wisest and the very stupidest who cannot change."

"To see what is right and not to do it is want of courage."

"Our greatest glory is not in never falling but in rising every time we fall."

"True goodness springs from a man's own heart. All men are born good."

"The superior man is firm in the right way, and not merely firm."

"Sincerity and truth are the basis of every virtue."

"The strength of a nation is derived from the integrity of its homes."

**Big Bucks: In 1988, Michael Jackson earned an estimated $60 million.**

# FAMOUS OVERDUBS

*Sometimes a few words can make a big difference in a film. Here are three examples of voices being added to movies without the public knowing about it.*

**GIANT**
James Dean's last film was an adaptation of Edna Ferber's *Giant*. "The last big speech Jimmy, as Jett Rink, made [was] when he addressed all of the Texas crowd who had spurned him. It was a drunken soliloquy, and Dean, in his attempt at accurate excellence, had slurred some meaningful words so badly, they had to be re-recorded." Unfortunately, by this time Dean had had his fatal accident. So his friend Nick Adams stepped in and did the overdub. "Nick, a noted mimic, could imitate anybody from Cary Grant...to Robert Wagner. He was able to redo parts of Jimmy's last speech so perfectly, it was years before anyone knew all those words had not come directly from Dean's own lips."

**DR. STRANGELOVE**
At the end of Stanley Kubrick's masterpiece of black humor, a B-52 with a doomsday bomb is headed for Russia. "Inside the B-52 Kong [played by Slim Pickens] and his men are opening their survival kits while over the intercom the major itemizes the incongruous contents." Slim Pickens, with his heavy Southern accent, comments: "Shoot, a fellah could have a pretty good weekend in Vegas with all that." Actually, the original line was "a fellah could have a pretty good weekend in Dallas with all that." But Wills went in and overdubbed the name of the city after JFK was assassinated.

**THE EXORCIST**
One of the most potent scenes in *The Exorcist* is "the voice of-the devil emanating from the on-screen mouth of fourteen-year-old Linda Blair." How did she do it? She didn't. The voice turned out to belong to actress Mercedes McCambridge, who commented: "If people had heard her saying some of those obscenities, they would have fallen over laughing."

# CAMPAIGN SMEARS

*Campaign smears are ugly, but they're a part of American politics, and have been since the first elections. A few notable examples:*

**THE 1828 PRESIDENTIAL CAMPAIGN**

During his second try for the presidency, Andrew Jackson was subjected to vicious slander by incumbent John Quincy Adams.

Jackson was termed "a blood-thirsty wild man, the son of a black and a prostitute and a murderer who had put to death soldiers who offended him." And he was accused of being an adulterer. This hit home. Unfortunately, Jackson's wife Rachel had married him unaware that she was still legally married to someone else; her previous marriage hadn't been officially dissolved. It was merely a technicality, but Adams's supporters relentlessly pursued it, dragging Rachel's name through the mud throughout the country.

By the time the matter was straightened out, Jackson had won the election....But he went to the White House alone. Rachel Jackson died of a heart attack; Jackson and his supporters attributed it to the brutal attacks during the campaign.

**THE 1884 PRESIDENTIAL CAMPAIGN**

In 1884 the governor of New York, Grover Cleveland, was closing in on the Democratic nomination for president when a Buffalo newspaper accused him of fathering an illegitimate boy ten years earlier.

Had he? Cleveland, a bachelor at the time, had indeed dated the woman. And he had contributed to the support of a child. But Cleveland was never proven to be the child's father; in fact, the woman admitted it could have been any one of a number of men. Nonetheless, when the presidential campaign began, the child was a part of it. Cleveland had to live with the chant: "Ma, Ma, Where's my Pa? Gone to the White House, ha! ha! ha!"

Interestingly, Cleveland's opponent, James G. Blaine, had his own problems—political scandals in his home state of Maine, and anti-Catholic prejudice—and wasn't able to capitalize on Cleveland's vulnerable position. Cleveland won.

## THE 1864 PRESIDENTIAL CAMPAIGN

Anticipating the next election, Abraham Lincoln's enemies tried to undermine his presidency. A whispering campaign in Washington suggested that Lincoln's wife, Mary Todd, was secretly aiding the Confederates. It was a spurious charge, but it gained enough credibility to force the president to appear before a secret congressional committee investigating the matter. His prestige was slightly tarnished, but Lincoln was still re-elected.

## THE FLORIDA SENATORIAL CAMPAIGN OF 1950

This is a textbook case of a politician using rhetoric to pander to the fears of less-educated people. Congressman George Smathers was challenging incumbent Senator Claude Pepper in Florida's Democratic senatorial primary in 1950. Smathers, the underdog, circulated printed material in the rural towns of central and northern Florida accusing Pepper of the following "indecencies":

- That his brother was a "practicing Homosapien."
- That he had a sister in New York who was a "thespian."
- And that Pepper himself had "matriculated" with young women.

To top it off, Smathers jumped on the early McCarthy bandwagon and saddled Claude with the nickname "Red" Pepper. Smathers won.

## THE PRESIDENTIAL CAMPAIGN OF 1988

It keeps coming back. Sounding every bit like Joseph McCarthy, George Bush accused his opponent, Michael Dukakis, of being "a card-carrying member" of the American Civil Liberties Union—an organization devoted to upholding the Constitution and, ironically, one defending Oliver North at the time. The motive: people who knew nothing about the ACLU would respond to the phrase "card-carrying," identifying it with "commie." It worked.

**As a person ages, the first sense to go is the sense of smell.**

# REAGANISMS

*Some of Ronald Reagan's choicest comments.*

"I'm not medical. I'm not a lawyer and I'm not medical, either."

"I'm no linguist, but I have been told that in the Russian language there isn't even a word for freedom."

"The taxpayer—that's someone who works for the federal government but doesn't have to take a civil service examination."

"Imagine if people in our nation could see the Bolshoi Ballet again, while Soviet children could see American plays and hear groups like the Beach Boys. And how about Soviet children watching 'Sesame Street'?"

"I'm concentrating on dog heaven."

"Boy, after seeing *Rambo* last night, I know what to do the next time this happens."

[On South Africa] "They have eliminated the segregation that we had in our own country, the type of thing where hotels and restaurants and places of entertainment and so forth were segregated—that has all been eliminated."

"Nuclear war would be the greatest tragedy, I think, ever experienced by mankind in the history of mankind."

"I'm not a lawyer, and I don't intend to get into too many legal areas where I might be caught short."

"If you've seen one redwood, you've seen them all."

"Why should we subsidize intellectual curiosity?"

"Government exists to protect us from each other. Where Government has gone beyond its limits is in deciding to protect us from ourselves."

"The best minds are not in government. If any were, business would hire them away."

**The "first electronic computer" was built in 1889 for the U.S. Census Bureau.**

# SUPERSTITIONS

*Many of us secretly believe far fetched legends— that broken mirrors and black cats really do bring bad luck, for example. It's amusing to discover the sources of our silliness.*

**LADDERS:** The belief that walking under a ladder propped up against a building will bring bad luck comes from the early Christians. They held that the leaning ladder formed a triangle, and that this symbol of the Holy Trinity shouldn't be violated by walking through it. Those who did were considered in league with the devil.

**FRIDAY THE THIRTEENTH:** Friday, in general, is considered an unlucky day. An old poem goes: "Now Friday came. Your old wives say / Of all the week's the unluckiest day."

Adam and Eve were supposed to have been kicked out of the Garden of Eden on a Friday; Noah's great flood started on a Friday; and Christ was crucified on a Friday. Couple this with the fact that 12 witches plus the Devil—totalling 13—are necessary for a Satanic meeting, and the resulting combination (of Friday plus 13) is a deadly one.

**SNEEZES:** The European/American tradition of saying "God bless you" when someone sneezes originated during the sixth century. It was already customary to congratulate someone when they sneezed (the prevalent idea being that a sneeze expelled evil from the body), but when a plague whose symptoms included violent sneezes began spreading around southern Europe, the Pope stepped in. He declared that since a sneeze could be a sign of imminent death, people should bless the sneezer. The phrase caught on and became commonplace.

**BREAKING A MIRROR:** At one time in the ancient world, mirrors were used to tell fortunes. If a mirror was broken during the reading, it meant the person was doomed. Later, this was amended; a person's image was interpreted as a symbol of health, and a cracked image in a mirror meant imminent illness. But ultimately, the superstition of seven years bad luck is common today because it was used to scare European servants in the 1400s and 1500s into using extra care when polishing their masters' expensive mirrors. No servant (or anyone, for that matter) wanted to court a lifetime of bad luck. The belief spread, and became ingrained in European culture.

**SALT:** The origin of this nearly worldwide superstition is hard to trace, but it logically stems from salt's historic importance as a spice and medicine. If you were the kind of person who could spill something as precious as salt, you were clearly headed for trouble. Some historians attribute the rituals surrounding salt to Judas spilling the stuff at the table during the Last Supper, but that's spurious. The antidote—throwing a few grains over your left shoulder—is a little puzzling. The best explanation: in some cultures, people believed that nasty spirits inhabited the left side, and tossing some salt over the shoulder hit them right in the eyes—thus preventing their evil deeds.

**ST. CHRISTOPHER MEDALS:** Supposedly the patron saint of travellers. But many authorities don't believe there ever was a Saint Christopher.

**BLACK CATS:** In ancient Egypt, cats were regarded as spiritual creatures, and among the most exalted Goddesses was Bast, a black female cat. But in European culture, the black cat became an animal to avoid. Apparently in the Middle Ages, when ignorant peasants were convinced that witches and evil demons were living among them, cats were singled out as suspicious creatures (perhaps because of their silent, fluid movements, or the way they stare, or even their occasionally unworldly wailing). The fact that some of the women who cared for the cats were old and grizzled—i.e., witch material—probably added to the legend. Ultimately, people came to believe that a black cat was the nighttime embodiment of a witch.

**LADYBUGS:** "Ladybird, ladybird, fly away home...." It's considered bad luck to kill one of these orange, spotted insects because it represents the Virgin Mary.

**In 1986, the program "Wheel of Fortune" earned over $100 million.**

# FAMILIAR NAMES

*Some people achieve immortality because their names become commonly associated with an item or activity. You know the names—now here are the people.*

**R. J. Lechmere Guppy.** A clergyman living in Trinidad. He sent several species of tropical fish to the British Museum, including a tiny specimen which now bears his name.

**Dr. J. I. Guillotin.** A French physician. Moved by mercy, he endorsed what he thought was a more humane method of execution than hanging. Ironically, the guillotine—which he did not invent—"is now synonymous with needless and brutal slaughter."

**Jules Leotard.** A renowned French acrobat of the nineteenth century. Designed and introduced the tight-fitting oufit "that does not hide your best features."

**Tom Collins.** A nineteenth century English Bartender at Limmer's Old House in London.

**Amelia Jenks Bloomer.** An outspoken late-nineteenth century feminist. Did not invent bloomers, but advocated their use by women (instead of corsets and cumbersome hoop skirts).

**Nicholas Chauvin.** Fanatically loyal soldier in Napoleon's army. Inspired the word *chauvinism.*

**Cesar Ritz.** A Swiss hotelier. Founded a chain of fancy hotels, which he named after himself.

**John Duns Scotus.** A respected scholar and theologian of the thirteenth century. Two hundred years after his death in 1308, his followers were known as "Scotists, Dunsmen, and Dunses," and were reviled for their resistance to the new ideas of the Renaissance. More enlightened thinkers chided the Dunses for their ignorance. Eventually *Dunses* became *dunces.*

**Pirates thought that wearing an earring in a pierced ear improved their eyesight.**

**Jean Nicot.** French ambassador to Portugal in the 1550s. First brought tobacco to France. When nicotine was found in tobacco leaves in 1818, it was named after him.

**Henry Shrapnel.** English inventor. Created the shell that helped beat Napoleon in 1815.

**Helen Porter Mitchell.** A celebrated opera singer whose professional name was Melba (taken from her hometown of Melbourne, Australia). When she was dieting, she ate thin, crisp slices of bread now called Melba Toast. When she wasn't, she ate a dessert called Peach Melba.

**Sylvester Graham.** A food faddist of the early 1800s. Advocated vegetarianism and high fiber; he was called "the poet of bran meal and pumpkins" by Ralph Waldo Emerson. His followers were called *Grahamites*, and food he recommended included *Graham crackers* and *Graham flour*.

**Etienne de Silhouette.** Louis XIV's unpopular controller-general in 1759. He made shadow portraits, "recommending them for their cheapness," and they were named after him.

**Haile Selassie.** The emperor of Ethiopia, known as "The Lion of Judah." His real name was "Ras Tafari"—which explains the origin of the term *Rastafarian*.

**Charles Wenburg.** A nineteenth century shipping mogul. He discovered a new recipe for lobster and passed it on to Lorenzo Delmonico, who named it after him—*Lobster Wenburg*. Shortly after, Wenburg was ejected from Delmonico's Restaurant for fighting. His punishment: the first three letters of the dish were transposed; *Lobster Wenburg* became *Lobster Newburg*.

**Charles Cunningham Boycott.** A tyrannical land agent for an absentee owner. The Englishman was overseer of the Earl of Erne's estate in Ireland. When, after two consecutive bad potato harvests, farmers demanded lower rents, Boycott tried to evict them. The result: the farmers banded together and harrassed Boycott until he fled Ireland.

**Around 200 people die while watching football games every year.**

# MYTH AMERICA

*Very little of what we are taught about the "taming of the West" is true, and the legend of George Armstrong Custer is a perfect example.*

**A BRAVE INDIAN FIGHTER?**

**The Myth:** General George Armstrong Custer was one of the U. S. Army's great soldiers during the western expansion. His valiant battle at the Little Bighorn—fighting a horde of renegade Indians that outnumbered his small cavalry unit 1,000 to 1 (Custer's Last Stand)—was an example of the fearlessness that made the white man's victory over the red man inevitable.

At one time so many people believed it that Custer was the hero of several films, and the main character in a prime-time TV series. ("The Legend of Custer" ran for a few months in 1967 on ABC.) Custer was also the subject of a million-selling record, "Please Mr. Custer," in 1958.

**The Truth:**

- Custer was a lieutenant colonel, not a general. (He had briefly been a major general during the Civil War, but was immediately demoted to captain when the war ended.)
- Custer was far from an exemplary soldier. He finished last in his class at West Point in 1861. And in 1867, he left his command to visit his wife; when he was caught, he was court-martialed and kicked out of the service for a year. He was allowed to return only because the Army needed help fighting Indians.
- Custer's Last Stand wasn't heroism, it was stupidity. Custer's division was supposed to be a small part of a major attack, led by General Alfred Terry—who was planning to meet Custer in two days with his troops. Custer was instructed to wait for Terry. Instead, he led his 266 men into battle, where they were all slaughtered. Historians speculate that the foolishly ambitious Custer believed a victory would earn him a presidential nomination, or that he had unwarranted contempt for the Indians' fighting ability.

# WHAT AM I?

*In the late twenties, America's intellectual elite devised a word game called "What Am I?" The idea was to offer literate clues to the identity of a common object or phenomenon without giving the answer away. These four examples are from the 1920s book about the game.* *Answers are on page 234.*

1. I wear the face of a leader of men. My financial worth is small and my appearance not impressive, yet my presence is a passport to any country and society. I have the entrée alike to the boudoir and the armed camp; I penetrate to royal palaces and to the far corners of the earth. In my youth I am bright and fresh-looking; later, my face is marred and disfigured and I am cast aside as nothing; but when I am very old I am eagerly sought, and a safe refuge is provided for me, where I am exhibited to admiring visitors. What am I?

2. Everything that is presented to me I return at once. Although helpless I can wound; although speechless I can encourage. People are afraid of my fabled revenge so I am seldom hurt. Children adore me. A widely known character once went through me and discovered an amazing country. What am I?

3. Changeless through uncounted centuries, I am still the symbol of inconstancy. I am dead and cold in death, yet I exercise irresistible power, renewed every day, over that which is thousands of miles distant from me. I cause strange sensations in dogs and lovers and once inspired athletic ambitions in the domestic cow. I am a symbol of mania and of a formidably rising nation. Though I have a well-rounded character nobody has ever seen more than one side of me. What am I?

4. I am positively the worst ever. I am absolutely the best on record. I am always surpassing myself. My past is negligible, my future a matter of universal concern and infinite conjecture. Most people profess a prophetic vision of me, but birds and animals know more about me than they do. Everybody complains of me, but nobody ever does anything to correct or improve me. What am I?

**A Swiss scientist named A. E. Fick invented contact lenses in 1887.**

# NIXON SEZ

*It's probably been a while since you've thought about Tricky Dick. Just in case you're beginning to wonder why you didn't trust him in the first place, here's a refresher.*

"I'll speak for the man, or against him, whichever will do him most good."

"We cannot judge it before it is concluded, and we cannot judge it even after it has been concluded."

"I rate myself a deeply committed pacifist."

"You won't have Nixon to kick around any more, gentlemen. This is my last Press Conference."

"Let us begin by committing ourselves to the truth, to see it like it is and to tell it like it is, to find the truth, to speak the truth and live with the truth. That's what we'll do."

"You can say that this Administration will have the first complete, far-reaching attack on the problem of hunger in history. Use all the rhetoric, so long as it doesn't cost money."

"I never made the [football] team...I was not heavy enough to play the line, not fast enough to play halfback and not smart enough to be a quarterback."

"When the President does it, that means it is not illegal."

"I like the job I have now, but, if I had my life to live over again, I'd like to have ended up as a sports writer."

"I would have made a good pope."

"I hear that whenever anyone in the White House tells a lie, Nixon gets a royalty."

"I'm not a lovable man."

"Call it paranoia, but paranoia for peace isn't that bad."

"Once you get into this great stream of history, you can't get out."

**The first stewardesses were on United Airlines, in 1930. They had to be registered nurses.**

# M*A*S*H

*"M*A*S*H" was the first comedy on television to deal directly with the ugly facts of war, as well as the funny ones. The American public responded by making it one of the most popular programs in the history of the medium.*

**HOW IT STARTED:** When Richard Hornberger [pen name: Richard Hooker] completed the memoirs of his days with the 8055th MASH unit in Korea, he hardly expected he'd have a best-seller on his hands. And for the next eight years, his expectations were borne out—by rejection slips. He couldn't even get it published.

Finally in 1968, after securing a partner to polish up the manuscript, *M*A*S*H* was published by William Morrow and Co. Initially the book was a flop. But it caught the eye of Ingo Preminger (Otto's brother), who bought the movie rights and commissioned a screenplay (adapted by Ring Lardner, Jr.). Directed by Robert Altman, and starring Eliot Gould and Donald Sutherland, *M*A*S*H* was a phenomenal success—which caused *M*A*S*H* (the book) to become a surprise best-seller. 20th Century Fox elected to further capitalize on the movie by creating a low-budget television pilot using sets and props from the film.

When CBS decided to give the series a shot (or at least finance a pilot), nothing had been written yet. So producer Gene Reynolds called his friend Larry Gelbart in England and asked for a script. Gelbart whipped one out in two days.

*M*A*S*H* (the TV show) premiered in September, 1972 to low ratings and poor reviews. But CBS didn't lose faith. It allowed the show to struggle through its first season and, in an unusual act of foresight, kept it going into the next season—when it became a hit.

## INSIDE FACTS:

**Just the facts.** More than half of the *M*A*S*H* storylines were the product of painstaking research. Larry Gelbart worked with photocopies of '50s issues of *Time* magazine and kept a master list of Korean names, a map of Korea, and an Army handbook on his desk.

**Ladies' man.** Alan Alda's support of the feminist movement is a tribute to Sister Elizabeth Kenney, whose cure for infantile paralysis (discovered during World War I) wasn't recognized by the male-dominated medical profession for nearly 20 years. The application of her theories cured Alda's childhood case of polio.

**The real thing.** The model for the *M*A*S*H* 4077th was the 8055th. In real life, the 8055th had a staff of 10 doctors and 12 nurses, and treated roughly 200 patients at a time.

**The last show.** The final 2 1/2 hour episode, *Goodbye, Farewell, and Amen*, was broadcast on February 28, 1983. Commercial time for the episode sold briskly at $450,000 per 30 second spot ($50,000 more than for the Super Bowl telecast), and over 125 million viewers were on hand (35 million more than watched *Roots*).

**Funnier than fiction.** Many of the episodes were based on stories purchased from Korean War MASH unit veterans.

**Right Flank.** Richard Hornberger (author of *M*A*S*H*) is actually a conservative Republican who fashioned Hawkeye after himself (real hometown: Crabapple Cove, Maine)—and didn't like the way Alda portrayed him at all. In fact, he was offended by the anti-war message of the show.

**Korea or Vietnam?** Make no mistake—the apparent anti-Vietnam bent of the early *M*A*S*H* wasn't coincidental. It was specifically written that way. Reynolds and Gelbart managed to air a weekly vilification of U.S. involvement in Southeast Asia by pre-dating it 20 years. Neat trick.

**The set.** *M*A*S*H* outdoor scenes were shot at the 20th Century Fox Ranch (now Malibu Canyon State Park). But most of the footage was shot at Fox Studios, where the *M*A*S*H* compound measured only 45' x 90', and came complete with a Korean landscape backdrop and a **rubber** floor!

**Bill Cosby made an estimated $50 million in 1988.**

# THE POLITICS OF OZ

*This fascinating story of how The Wizard of Oz might really be a political allegory comes from the* Utne Reader, *"The Best of the Alternative Press." Written by Michael Dregni.*

Who would believe that the battle between the gold and the silver standard in turn-of-the-century U.S. politics would make a good plot for a children's fantasy book?

And who would believe that a story as delightful as *The Wizard of Oz* could also have meaning for adults?

*In These Times* (Feb. 18, 1987) exposes *Oz* as a parable of populism, the 1890s Midwestern political movement led by William Jennings Bryan. The populists challenged Eastern banks and railroads, which they charged with oppressing farmers and industrial workers. Bryan felt that farmers were being crucified on a cross of gold; a switch to silver-backed currency would make money plentiful for all.

*Oz* author L. Frank Baum was a populist—and also a bit of a fantasizer. As editor of a South Dakota newspaper, he advised poor farmers to feed wood shavings to starving livestock, after fitting the beasts with special green glasses so they would think they were eating grass.

After Bryan's 1896 bid for the presidency failed, Baum was so moved to write the first of his long-running Oz series.

The allegory begins with the title: Oz is short for ounce, the measure for gold. Dorothy, hailing from the populist stronghold of Kansas, represents the common person. The Tin Woodsman is the industrial worker who is rusted solid, referring to the factories shut down in the 1893 depression. The Scarecrow is the farmer who lacks the brains to realize his own political interests. And the Cowardly Lion is Bryan himself, with a loud orator's roar but little else.

After vanquishing the Wicked Witch of the East (the Eastern banker) Dorothy frees the Munchkins (the little people). With the witch's silver slippers (the silver standard), Dorothy starts down the Yellow Brick Road (the gold standard) to the Emerald City (Washington). There the group meets the Wizard (the president), who, like all good politicians, appears as whatever people wish to see. When the Wizard is defrocked, the Scarecrow denounces him as a humbug, which is the core of Baum's message, writes Michael A. Genovese in the Minneapolis *Star Tribune* (March 22, 1988).

Dorothy saves the day by dousing the Wicked Witch of the West with water, evoking the drought that was plaguing Midwestern farms at the time. The Wizard flies away in a hot-air balloon, the Scarecrow is left in charge of Oz, the Tin Woodsman rules the East, and the Cowardly Lion returns to the forest—Bryan had lost the election.

In the 1939 movie starring Judy Garland, the populist parable lost out to Hollywood escapism, and Dorothy's silver slippers were inexplicably changed to ruby. However, Baum might have applauded the use of black and white film depicting the grim reality of Kansas farm fortunes and color stock for the fantasy world of Oz. And the song "Somewhere Over the Rainbow" suited well the populist dream.

## TOTALLY UNRELATED GOSSIP

According to Ed Lucaire in *Celebrity Trivia*:

•Clark Gable had no teeth; he wore dentures—which bothered the actresses he worked with. "His false teeth were just too much," complained Grace Kelly. And Vivian Leigh swore she would quit doing love scenes with him in *Gone With the Wind* "unless he washed out his mouth."

•Hugh Hefner was still a virgin on his 22nd birthday.

•Charles Bronson got his first part in a movie, *You're In the Navy Now* (1951), because "he could belch on cue."

•Adolf Hitler owned about 9,000 acres of land in Colorado. Hitler's favorite film was *King Kong*. His favorite song was Walt Disney's "Who's Afraid of the Big, Bad Wolf?"

•Jerry Lewis never wears the same pair of socks twice.

**In Los Angeles, there are fewer people than there are automobiles.**

# QUOTES FROM JFK

*Some better-known remarks made by our 35th president.*

"There is no city in the United States in which I get a warmer welcome and less votes than Columbus, Ohio."

[*To his brother in 1960, before the election*] "Do you realize the responsibility I carry? I'm the only person standing between Nixon and the White House."

"When we got into office, the thing that surprised me most was to find that things were just as bad as we'd been saying they were."

[*At a press conference prior to the 1960 election*] "I have just received the following telegram from my generous Daddy. It says, 'Dear Jack: Don't buy a single more vote than is necessary. I'll be damned if I'm going to pay for a landslide.'"

"When power corrupts, poetry cleanses."

*Question*: "The Republican National Committee recently adopted a resolution saying you were pretty much of a failure. How do you feel about that?"
*Pres. Kennedy*: "I assume it passed unanimously."

"When written in Chinese, the word "crisis" is composed of two characters: one represents danger, the other represents opportunity."

"In a free society, art is not a weapon."

"Failure has no friends."

"Conformity is the jailer of freedom and the enemy of growth."

"Let us never negotiate out of fear. But let us never fear to negotiate."

"We must use time as a tool not as a couch."

"The war against hunger is truly mankind's war of liberation."

"The blessings of liberty have too often stood for privilege, materialism and a life of ease."

# THE LOUIE, LOUIE STORY

*"Louie, Louie" is arguably the most recorded rock 'n' roll song of all time. The following history is from* Behind the Hits, *by Bob Shannon and John Javna. The authors credit the "extensive liner notes" written by Doc Pelzell for Rhino Records' "Louie, Louie" album—an album consisting completely of different versions of the song.*

Besides groupies and recording contracts, what do Frank Zappa, Julie London, Iggy Pop, Barry White, Tom Petty and the Heartbreakers, Blondie, the Beach Boys, David McCallum, Toots and the Maytals, and the Kinks have in common? You guessed it. They—and thousands of other artists—have all performed versions of "the most easily recognizable rock 'n' roll song of all time"—"Louie, Louie." This three-chord wonder has been singled out by many critics as *the* definitive rock 'n' roll song. Yet it wasn't until seven or eight years *after* it was originally recorded that most American teens heard it for the first time.

In 1955, Richard Berry, a young black musician, was playing in Los Angeles with a Mexican group called Ricky Rivera and the Rhythm Rockers. One of the band's songs, "El Loco Cha Cha Cha," had a contagious rhythm figure in it that Berry just couldn't get out of his mind. And while he was waiting backstage to perform at the Harmony Club Ballroom one night, the words "Louie, Louie" popped into his head and superimposed themselves around the persistent riff; "the rest just fell into place." His main lyrical influence: a composition called "One for My Baby," which was sung from the viewpoint of a customer who was speaking to a bartender named Joe. In it, the singer said: "One for my baby/One for the road/Set 'em up Joe." In Berry's composition, the bartender became Louie, and the customer was telling Louie how he intended to sail to Jamaica to find his true love. The speech patterns and the use of Jamaica in the song were inspired by Berry's exposure to Latin music, and by Chuck (no relation) Berry's "Havana Moon," a similarly styled song that was popular at the time.

When Berry wrote "Louie, Louie," he was under contract to

Modern Records. But because of a dispute over the royalties for the sixty-plus songs he had written for the label, he saved the tune until his contract expired and he could record it for Flip Records. Flip released it in 1956 and it became a respectable R&B hit, selling (according to Berry) around 130,000 copies. A year later, however, sales had tapered off, and Berry needed some money for his upcoming wedding. So he sold the record sales publishing rights to "Louie Louie," retaining only the radio and television performance rights. He philosophically chalks this sale up to "experience." After all, who could have predicted the bizarre set of circumstances that would, a few years later, turn this song into a monster hit?

About five years later in Seattle, Washington, an obscure singer by the name of Rockin' Robin Roberts discovered Berry's recording of "Louie Louie" while browsing through the bargain bin of a local record store. "Louie" soon became Roberts' signature song and he took it with him through a succession of local bands. Finally, he joined one of the area's more popular groups, the Wailers (no relation to Bob Marley's contingent), and they decided to cut the song for their own Etiquette Records label. It was a regional hit in the Northwest, but when Liberty Records released it nationally, it flopped.

Kids in most of America still didn't know the song, but in Portland, Oregon, "Louie, Louie" was hot. One night, a Portland Top 40 band called the Kingsmen were playing a local dance with friendly rivals Paul Revere and the Raiders. During one of their breaks, they happened to notice that a lot of their audience had gathered around a juke box, and were dancing enthusiastically to the Wailers' record. Since this reaction was exactly what the Kingsmen were looking for in their own performances, they decided to include the song in their act; each member agreed to learn the song by their next rehearsal. But the only one to follow through on the pact was lead singer Jack Ely. Consequently, he had to teach it to the rest of the group; when he remembered it incorrectly, no one knew it. He taught the band a 1-2-3, 1-2, 1-2-3, 1-2 version, rather than the Wailers' 1-2-3-4, 1-2-, 1-2-3-4, 1-2 rendition. The result: he made the tune faster. It's interesting to speculate: would the song have been as successful if Ely hadn't accidentally altered it?

Anyway, the group got the response they were looking for. They were asked to play it as much as eight or nine times a night. One Friday in May, 1963, the band decided, just for kicks, to do a marathon version of the song to see who could last longer, the dancers or the band. Even bass player Bob Norby, who didn't sing, warbled a few verses just to keep the song going for approximately forty-five minutes. Despite the band's boredom, audience response was so positive that arrangements were made that night to record "Louie, Louie" the next day.

Actually, the Kingsmen had been wanting to get into the studio for some time. Their reason: a summer job. "That's really what 'Louie, Louie' was intended for," members of the band admit now, "an audition tape for a job on a steamship line for the summer. To Australia. We never got there, though. We had this hit record instead and had to go play the White House. And Wyoming. And Iowa." After pooling their money to come up with the $50 they needed for the two-hour session, the group went to the only recording studio in Portland and made their demo. Facilities were, at best, primitive. Mikes were placed next to amps that had been muffled with coats and blankets. Jack Ely's lead vocal was yelled up to a mike that was suspended near the studio's fifteen-foot ceiling—which explains the garbled lyrics that ultimately helped make the Kingsmen's record so successful. Strange twist: the very next day, Paul Revere and the Raiders, with Mark Lindsay on Sax, went into the same studio to record *their* version of "Louie, Louie."

Both the Kingsmen and Paul Revere's versions got local airplay, and Revere's actually did much better at the outset.

**THE KINGSMEN**: "Radio stations in those days used to promote their own shows—dances, record hops, local supermarket openings...and the Kingsmen were the house band for a station called KISN—y'know, we'd go out and do all the shows with all the jocks. And so, as soon as we recorded 'Louie, Louie,' of course, they put it on the air...Paul Revere's version got instant play all up and down the West Coast as soon as it was released; ours was only played in the Portland area, basically. But after a few months, toward the end of '63, a copy of two of our records got back to Boston. A disc jockey named Early

**In 1984, a New Jersey man opened a summer camp for Cabbage Patch dolls.**

Bird on an FM R&B station started playing it, thinking that we were an East Coast Rhythm and blues group or something. There was no precedent for this type of sound east of the Rockies. Eventually, Arnie 'Woo-Woo' Ginsberg on WBZ started blasting it all over the Northeast. Then it spread out all over the East Coast, into New York City. And then it became a national hit."

Going back a few months: after "Louie, Louie" began getting airplay in Boston, it was picked up for pressing and distribution by Wand Records. It fared well; by September, the record had reached #94 on the *Billboard* charts, and was climbing rapidly. But the final shot-in-the-arm that boosted the record to the top of the charts for four months caught even the Kingsmen off-guard; someone, somewhere, decided that the words were dirty. Without warning, rumors spread that Ely's slurred vocals were laced with obscenities, and soon every teenager in America was trying to figure out what Ely was "really" saying. They even did it at the band's live performances.

**THE KINGSMEN**: "It was kind of disheartening at first. Before we knew that there was this 'dirty lyrics' controversy, we thought that something was wrong with the band because we'd be playing all night long and when we'd hit our closer, which was 'Louie, Louie'—at the time our only hit—everyone would stop watching us. No one would pay attention any longer; they'd all pull these pieces of paper out of their pockets and start reading along...and singing. And they're going, 'Y'know, which version is right?' It was weird, having all these people come up to you like that." J. Edgar Hoover certainly wasn't going to stand for obscenity on the airwaves (neither was the state of Indiana, which banned "Louie"). The FBI and FCC launched a "Louie, Louie" investigation, playing the record at every speed from 16 to 78 rpm. They called in both Jack Ely and Richard Berry to testify about the lyrics. And in the end: the FCC concluded that, "We found the record to be unintelligible at any speed we played it." They hadn't found what they were looking for, but the FCC's efforts weren't entirely fruitless—they helped create a rock 'n' roll classic. With all that "negative" publicity, the record took off. It sold over eight million copies. "Well, you know," a member of the Kingsmen laughs today, "when the FBI and Lyndon Baines Johnson say, 'You can't do this,' that really does wonders for record sales."

# MOST COMMON WORDS

*How's your vocabulary? Not particularly good, according to one etymologist.*

One of the most entertaining books to peruse in the bathroom is Stuart Flexner's *I Hear America Talking*, an examination of America's speech. According to Flexner, there are an estimated 600,000 words in our English language—but the average American only understands around 2%-3% of them...and actually uses only *half* that amount. "Of these," Flexner says, "just 10 basic words account for over 25% of all speech and 50 simple words for almost 60%, with between 1,500 and 2,000 words accounting for 99% of everything we say." The most commonly used word is *I*, followed by *you*, *the*, and *a*. Of our written language, Flexner says: "[It] is only a little more varied than our spoken one, 70 words making up 50% of it....We are more likely to qualify our words and to use *but*, *or*, *if*, *so*, *which*, and *who*. In general, too...we use shorter sentences, fewer auxiliary verbs, and more active verbs."

## The 50 Most Common Words

| | | | |
|---|---|---|---|
| I | A | About | Do |
| You | An | Now | Are |
| He | On | Just | Want |
| She | To | Not | Can |
| It | Of | That | Would |
| We | In | This | Go |
| They | For | Is | Think |
| Me | With | Get | Say |
| Him | Out | Was | Be |
| Her | From | Will | See |
| Them | Over | Have | Know |
| What | And | Don't | Tell |
| The | | | Thing |

The first sound recording ever made was "Mary Had a Little Lamb," in 1877 by Tom Edison.

# HULA HOOPS

*The Hula Hoop was a pioneer, the first major fad created and fueled by the new power in America—TV ads.*

The Hula Hoop originated in Australia, where it was simply a bamboo exercise ring used in gym classes. In 1957, an Australian company began selling the ring in retail stores—which attracted the attention of a small California toy manufacturer named Wham-O.

Wham-O's owners made a few wooden rings for their kids ("They just wouldn't put the hoop down"), took them to cocktail parties ("Folks had to have a couple of drinks in them to take a whack at it")...and then decided they had a hot item on their hands. They began producing a plastic version, naming it a Hula Hoop after the motion it resembled—the Hawaiian hula dance.

Wham-O introduced it to the American public in January 1958, and it quickly became the biggest toy craze in history (up to that time). During the year over 20 million—$30 million worth—were sold. The Hula Hoop was the quintessential fad item, though; by November 1958 the Wall Street Journal was already announcing: "Hoops Have Had It." A brief comeback occurred in 1965, when Wham-O introduced the "Shoop-Shoop" Hula Hoop, with a ball-bearing in it to make noise, but it just wasn't the same.

**HOOP FACTS:**

- According to the *British Medical Journal*, the Hula Hoop was responsible for an increase in back, neck, and abdominal injuries.
- Indonesia banned Hula Hoops because they "might stimulate passion." Japan forbade them on public streets.
- The official news agency in China called Hula Hoops "A nauseating craze." In the Soviet Union the hoop was seen as a "symbol of the emptiness of American Culture."
- Hula Hoop Endurance records: longest whirl—four hours (over 18,000 turns), by a 10 year old Boston boy; most hoops twirled simultaneously—14, by an 11-year-old in Michigan.

**You're more likely to catch people's colds from shaking hands with them than their sneezes.**

# THE HUNTING ACCIDENT

*To people who noticed it in the obituaries on November 10, 1977, it seemed like just another unfortunate accident. But it may have been something more....*

**THE VICTIM:** William C. Sullivan, former third-in-command in the FBI under J. Edgar Hoover, "the only liberal Democrat ever to break into the top ranks of the Bureau." For a decade, he ran the FBI's Domestic Intelligence division (including the investigation following JFK's assassination). In 1971 he was summarily fired by Hoover. Sullivan subsequently emerged as an active—and effective—critic of the Bureau.

**THE CIRCUMSTANCES:**
On November 9, 1977, shortly after daybreak, Sullivan went to meet two hunting companions near his Sugar Hill, New Hampshire home. He never made it. On the way, he was shot to death by the eighteen-year-old son of a state policeman. The young man claimed that (despite the fact that his rifle was equipped with a telescopic sight) he had mistaken Sullivan for a deer.

Two months later, the killer received his sentence in court: a $500 fine and a ten-year suspension of his hunting license.

**UNANSWERED QUESTIONS:**
Was it an accident, or the elimination of an adversary who knew too much? Consider these coincidences:

- As the FBI's illegal activities came to light in the mid-'70s, Bureau men were being brought to trial. At the time of his death, Sullivan was scheduled to be the chief witness against ex-agent John Kearny, who had been indicted for illegal wiretapping.
- At the time of the accident, Sullivan was writing a tell-all book about his years in the FBI. The book was ultimately com-

pleted by his co-author and was published by W. W. Norton and Company. But it had no author to champion it to the media, and no one to do a sequel—the author was dead.

• In 1976, Congress voted to open its own investigation of the JFK and Martin Luther King assassinations. "Sullivan would have been questioned by the Assassinations Committe in 1978," says Anthony Summers in his book about the death of JFK (*Conspiracy*). He goes on: "Sullivan had been head of the FBI's Division Five, which handled much of the King and Kennedy investigations....In 1975, Sullivan responded in opaque fashion to a question from a Congressional committee about Oswald. Asked whether he had seen anything in the files to indicate a relationship between Oswald and the CIA, Sullivan replied, 'No, I think there may be something on that, but you asked me if I had seen anything. I don't recall ever having seen anything like that, but I think there is something on that point....It rings a bell in my head.' Sullivan's fatal accident occurred before the Assassinations Committee could ask him to be more specific about the source of that bell in his mind."

**POSSIBLE CONCLUSIONS:**

• *It was a hunting accident.* Sullivan's co-author on *The Bureau*, Bill Brown, says he flew to New Hampshire and checked it out—and was satisfied that the incident really was an accident.

• *It was an assassination.* We asked several hunting enthusiasts about the probability of the shooting being an accident, based on their experience. The conclusion: they're skeptical that an experienced hunter with a telescopic sight could confuse a man with a deer. Among other things, the hunter would have to look carefully to verify that the "deer" was old enough—and the right sex—to shoot legally. If it wasn't a hunting accident? Two possibilities: either people associated with the FBI who would be damaged by Sullivan's testimony/revelations decided to eliminate him; or someone associated with the Kennedy assassination wanted him silenced.

What's your guess?

**You're more likely to get stung by a bee on a windy day than in any other weather.**

# CAR NAMES

*They're a part of your life; you know them as well as you know your own name. But do you know where they come from?*

## SOME REAL PEOPLE

**Chevrolet.** Louis Chevrolet, a race car driver and designer who co-founded the company which later merged with GM.

**Oldsmobile.** Ransom Eli Olds, an auto pioneer who started the Olds Motor Vehicle company in 1897.

**Rolls-Royce.** A combination of Sir Henry Royce's and Charles Rolls's names. Royce founded the company in 1903, Rolls promoted the car.

**Mercedes-Benz.** The *Benz* is Karl Benz, believed by many to be the inventor of the automobile in 1879. *Mercedes* comes from a young girl named Mercedes Jellinek, whose father was a German diplomat and an investor in the company.

**Dodge.** John and Horace Dodge. Set up the Dodge Brothers Machine Shop in Detroit in 1901, and were immediately hired to make transmissions for Ransom Olds. In 1914, they started their own car company, building low-cost autos to compete with Ford.

**Buick.** David Dunbar Buick, a Scotsman. Gave up his failing Buick Motor Car Company to William Durant, who in 1908 turned it into the nation's most successful—and used it as the cornerstone of the General Motors empire. Buick died broke; he was "so poor he could afford neither a telephone nor a Buick."

**Chrysler.** Walter Chrysler. A huge man, all of his Chrysler cars were designed extra-large, so they'd be comfortable for him to sit in.

## SOME INSTANT WORDS

**Caravan.** A car combined with a van—a Car-a-van!

**Nissan Sentra.** According to one of the men who named it: "It's the company's mainstream, or central, car, and they wanted consumers to understand that it was quite safe, even though it was small. The word *Sentra* sounds likes *central*, as well as *sentry*, which evokes images of safety."

**Corvair.** A combination of the sporty Corvette and the family-oriented Bel Air.

**Volvo.** Means *I roll* in Latin.

**Camaro.** According to GM in 1967, it meant pal in French, a fitting title because "the real mission of our automobile is to be a close companion to its owner." But a French auto executive corrected them: "It doesn't mean anything in English, and it doesn't mean anything in French, either."

**Toronado.** Literally means, in Spanish, *floating bull.* But that has nothing to do with the car; GM just thought it sounded classy and exciting.

## SOME SECOND CHOICES

**Mustang.** Original name: Torino.

Ford expected to appeal exclusively to young sports car lovers with this vehicle. The name *Torino* was chosen because it sounded like an Italian sports car; the projected ad campaign called it "the new import...from Detroit." But last-minute market research showed that the car could appeal to all buyers, and a new name had to be chosen. Colt, Maverick, and Bronco (all used for later cars) were considered. But Mustang seemed best, bringing to mind cowboys, adventure, and the Wild West. As one Ford man put it, "It had the excitement of the wide-open spaces, and it was as American as all hell."

**Pontiac Firebird.** Original name: the Banshee.

The press releases were out, the initial announcement had been made, and then someone at Pontiac discovered that in Irish folklore, a Banshee is "a supernatural being whose wailing foretells death." That, of course, would have been a public relations disaster; it would have been like calling a car "the Grim Reaper." Who would dare buy it? The firebird, a creature of Native American legends, was chosen instead.

**Elephant trivia: elephant trunks hold up to 1 1/2 gallons of liquid.**

# BIRTH OF THE BIKINI

*Conservatives have long pointed to the bikini as an example of our moral decline; yet history shows that the bikini is related to the A-bomb and war, not simply sex.*

The atomic bomb is responsible for many terrible things and at least one attractive thing—the bikini.

In July 1946, the American government announced that it would be exploding an atomic bomb. It was just a test, but this was the first *announced* atomic bomb blast, and people's imaginations ran wild. Rumors spread that it was going to be a "super bomb" that could easily get out of control, start a massive chain reaction, and blow up the world.

**Party Time.**

These rumors were especially prevalent in Paris, which had recently suffered through the trauma of German occupation in World War II. Parisians simply couldn't take any more pressure....So instead of protesting the impending explosion, they celebrated. Hostesses used the bomb threat as an excuse to hold "end-of-the-world" parties; young men used it as an excuse to convince reluctant girl friends to give in (if the world was going to end, why not break *all* the rules?). And when it was revealed that the test would take place in the then-unheard-of Bikini Atoll, the parties became "Bikini" parties.

**A Publicity Stunt**

Meanwhile, a fashion show was being planned for the Piscine Molitor in Paris on July 5, 1946 (note: *piscine* is French for swimming pool). Its promoters wanted to attract attention, and since people seemed to be throwing modesty to the wind, the promoters came up with the idea of a "Bikini" costume—one that would go as far as anyone dared go with a bathing suit. So in the middle of the fashion show, Paris model Micheline Bernardini suddenly stepped out before the audience wearing a scanty two-piece bathing suit—the world's first "bikini." Of course the scandalous suit got international publicity...and a new style was born.

**Nothing new under the sun:** Archaeologists have now found evidence that bikinis were worn in Sicily as early as 2000, B.C.

# STAR TREK

*This is the show that started the cult TV boom. It has now spawned an industry that includes movies, toys, videos, etc. Here are some facts about it, from* Cult TV, *by John Javna.*

**HOW STAR TREK BEGAN:** Gene Roddenberry, the head writer for a popular western called *Have Gun, Will Travel*, was also a science fiction buff. He saw a lot of similarities between space exploration and the experiences of the American pioneers—so he conceived of a TV space fantasy that would be similar to a western series, complete with continuing characters (which hadn't ever been done). He based his idea on a popular show named *Wagon Train*. He called his idea a "wagon train to the stars." A star trek.

In 1964, while producing an MGM series *The Lieutenant*, Roddenberry created a workable format for his space show. MGM turned it down, but Desilu bought it and sold the idea to NBC. The network financed the pilot called "The Cage." This was filmed in November and December. It cost $630,000—an outrageous amount for the time—and featured only two members of the final cast—Majel Barret and Leonard Nimoy. The captain's name wasn't Kirk—it was Pike. he was played by Jeffrey Hunter.

The pilot was submitted to NBC in February, 1965. They rejected it. But the project wasn't canned; NBC still saw promise in the series and authorized an unprecedented second pilot—including an almost entirely new cast. The new film was entitled "Where No Man Has Gone Before." It featured Shatner as Kirk, Nimoy as Science Officer Spock, Doohan as Scotty, and Takei as Physicist Sulu. For the record, the doctor's name was Mark Piper. He was played by Paul Fix.

The second pilot was submitted in January, 1966. A month later NBC accepted it for their coming fall schedule.

## INSIDE FACTS

**Easier than landing.** The Enterprise's "transporter" was developed as a cost-cutting measure. It provided an inexpensive means to transport characters from the ship to the next set (landings are expensive). The "glittering" effect (as the transporter dissolved and relocated the passengers' atoms) was provided by aluminum dust.

**The Starship Enterprise.** Three models of the Enterprise were used in filming: a 4-inch miniature, a 3-foot model, and a 14-foot plastic model that now hangs in the Smithsonian.

**Those Ears.** Spock's pointed ears were originally included as a throw-in when Roddenberry contracted with a special-effects house to produce three monster heads.

- The first pair were "gruesome," according to Nimoy. "They were rough and porous, like alligator skin." But two days before shooting, they were finally modified to everyone's satisfaction.
- Nimoy objected to wearing the ears, but Roddenberry offered a compromise—wear them for a while, and if they didn't work out, Spock could have "plastic surgery" and have them altered. Nimoy agreed.
- A typical pair of ears lasted from three to five days.

**On the air.** Believe it or not, the highest *Star Trek* ever ranked in a year's prime time rating was #52.

**Logical thinking.** One of Leonard Nimoy's contributions was the Vulcan nerve pinch. In one scene, he was supposed to sneak up behind a character and whack him on the head with a gun. But he objected that Vulcans wouldn't be so crude. As a substitute, he made up the legendary maneuver on the spot.

**The Source.** Incipient Trekkies who want a first-hand look at the inspiration for many of *Star Trek's* distinctive features should view the 1956 film *Forbidden Planet*, which starred Walter Pidgeon, Anne Francis, and Leslie Neilsen. Some of the "similarities" are amazing.

**Fat City.** Alert fans can tell in what part of the season an episode was filmed just by observing William Shatner's stomach. Always in top shape before shooting began, Shatner appeared trim and fit in early-season episodes. But as the season wore on, time to exercise became harder to find, and his waistline expanded.

**In Germany more people have the last name of Schultz than any other name.**

# COMMON PHRASES

*What do these familiar phrases really mean? Etymologists have researched them and come up with these explanations.*

**SMELL A RAT**

*Meaning:* To sense that something is wrong.

*Background:* In earlier times, it was fairly common for people to have rats infesting their houses. And if a rat died in a place where it wasn't visible—inside a wall, for example—the person who lived in the house didn't know about it until he could literally smell the decaying rodent. That's how he could tell something was amiss.

**HAM ACTOR (HAM)**

*Meaning:* Someone who enjoys putting on a show, or who plays rather obviously to an audience (though not necessarily on stage).

*Background:* An American phrase originating in the 1880s. Minstrel shows, mass entertainment of the time, often featured less-than-talented performers who overacted. They frequently appeared in "blackface," and used ham fat to remove their make-up. Thus they were referred to as "ham fat men," later shortened to "ham."

**WHIPPING BOY**

*Meaning:* A scapegoat, or someone who is habitually picked on.

*Background:* Hundreds of years ago, it was normal practice for a European prince to be raised with a commoner of the same age. Since princes couldn't be disciplined like ordinary kids, the commoner would be beaten whenever the prince did something wrong. The commoner was called the prince's *whipping boy*.

**RAINING CATS AND DOGS**

*Meaning:* Torrential rain

*Background:* In the days before garbage collection, people tossed their trash in the gutter—including deceased house pets—and it just lay there. When it rained really hard, the garbage, including the bodies of dead cats and dogs, went floating down the street. So there had to be a hell of a lot of water for it to rain cats and dogs.

## HIT THE PANIC BUTTON

*Meaning*: "Speaking or acting in unnecessary haste."
*Background*: Coined during World War II, by men in the Air Force. According to Lt. Col. James Jackson, in *American Speech* magazine: "The actual source seems...to have been the bell system used in [B-17 and B-24] bombers for emergency procedures such as bailout and ditching. In case of fighter or flak damage so extensive that the bomber had to be abandoned, the pilot rang a 'prepare to abandon' ring, and then a ring meaning 'jump.' The bell system was used since the intercom was apt to be out if there was extensive damage. The implications of the phrase seem to have come from those few times when pilots hit the panic button too soon and rang for emergency procedures over minor damage, causing their crews to bail out unnecessarily."

## HACK WRITER

*Meaning*: Writer who churns out words for money.
*Background*: In Victorian England, a hackney, or "hack," was a carriage for hire. (The term is still used in reference to taxi drivers, who need their "hack's licenses" to work.) It became a description of anyone who plies their trade strictly for cash.

## PIE IN THE SKY

*Meaning*: An illusion, a dream, a fantasy. An unrealistic goal.
*Background*: Joe Hill, a famous labor organizer of the early 20th century, wrote a tune called "The Preacher and the Slave," in which he accused the clergy of promising a better life in Heaven while people starved on Earth. A few of the lines: "Work and pray, live on hay, you'll get pie in the sky when you die (That's a lie!)."

## HARD AND FAST

*Meaning*: "Unalterable."
*Background*: "Refers to a vessel that is stuck on the bottom, which is hard, where it is held fast."

**The animal with the largest eyes on earth: the giant squid, with eyes as big as pie plates.**

# ROCK CHARACTERS

*Many pop songs are about real people, although most of the public never knows exactly who. Here are a few examples, from* Behind the Hits, *by Bob Shannon and John Javna.*

**DONNA**, Ritchie Valens. 1959/Top 5. Donna Ludwig was Ritchie's high school girlfriend. Valens quit high school to go on tour when his record was released. It hit #2 in December, 1958, and Ritchie was killed a few months later in the February, 1959, plane crash with Buddy Holly and Big Bopper Richardson.

**LET IT BE**, the Beatles. 1969/#1. Who is "Mother Mary"? Paul McCartney: "My mother's name was Mary, so that was probably what that was about."

**CATHY'S CLOWN**, the Everly Brothers. 1960/#1. Cathy was Don Everly's high school girlfriend in Knoxville, Tennessee.

**KILLING ME SOFTLY WITH HIS SONG**, Roberta Flack. 1973/#1. The singer referred to in the song is Don McLean, composer of "American Pie." Songwriter Lori Lieberman saw him perform in Los Angeles, and was so knocked out that she wrote a ten-minute song about it. Roberta Flack rewrote the tune and had a hit with it.

**DIANA**, Paul Anka. 1957/#1. Diana Ayoub was an older girl with whom 15-year-old Paul Anka was infatuated. "She was a girl I saw at church and saw now and then at functions," he says. "She was a little out of my league. She was twenty and I was fifteen—and she really didn't want anything to do with me, which made it even worse." Worse still, Diana was babysitting for Anka's younger brother and sister, so it was hard to avoid her. Anka wrote a poem about her and set it to music. It became a #1 hit and a million-seller, and launched his show business career.

**OH! CAROL**, Neil Sedaka. 1959/Top 10. Carol was Carole Klein, whom singer Neil Sedaka described as "a scrawny girl,

**Elvis Presley was thrown out of the Grand Ole Opry in 1954.**

with dirty blonde hair, a long nose, and funny buck teeth." She was a fan of Sedaka's Brooklyn high school group, the Tokens, and used to hang around with Sedaka. After "Oh! Carol" hit, the real Carole put out an answer record called "Oh Neil," which flopped. Later she married Gerry Goffin and after changing her name to Carole King, she wrote classic pop songs like "Up on the Roof."

**ROSANNA**, Toto, 1982/#2. It's about actress Rosanna Arquette.

**SEXY SADIE**, the Beatles. 1968/"The White Album." Not a single, but worth mentioning. Sadie was the Maharishi Mahesh Yogi, father of "Transcendental Meditation" ("TM"), whom the Beatles followed to India in 1967. John Lennon dubbed him "sexy" after he found out the Maharishi had tried to make it with Mia Farrow, a disciple who was staying at the Maharishi's retreat at the same time the Beatles were.

**WINDY**, the Association. 1967/#1. Although the Association sang about a *girl* named Windy, the song was actually written about a man. The composer was Ruthann Friedman and Windy, her boyfriend, was an original hippie, living in San Francisco's Haight-Ashbury district. In that context the lyrics make a lot more sense. Example: he's "tripping" down the streets of the city. The song was originally written in waltz (3/4) time.

**HEY JUDE**, the Beatles. 1968/#1. Jude is Julian Lennon. In 1968, John Lennon had fallen in love with Yoko Ono and wanted to divorce his wife, Cynthia. It was messy at first—Cynthia retreated to Italy with her mother and son, Julian. But finally she returned to England to discuss terms of the divorce. "The only way I could get in touch with John was through Peter Brown at Apple," she says, "and when I finally did meet him, Yoko was there. He insisted she should stay." Julian was feeling the effects of the battle, and Paul McCartney, who was good friends with the boy, went to see him. As McCartney drove he began improvising a consoling melody. The words that went with it were "Hey Jules..." McCartney: "Then I thought a better name was Jude. A bit more country and western for me." Ironically, John Lennon thought that McCartney had written the song for *him*.

**Americans spend $8 billion a year on pornography.**

# ST. LENNY SAYS...

*No one explained the innate contradictions of society better than Lenny Bruce.*

"All my humor is based on destruction and despair. If the whole world were tranquil, without disease and violence, I'd be standing in the breadline—right back of J. Edgar Hoover."

"Every day people are straying away from the church and going back to God. Really."

[About drugs] "I'll die young ...but it's like kissing God."

"[The Crucifixion] was just one of those parties that got out of hand."

"People should be taught what is, not what should be."

"There's nothing sadder than an old hipster."

"If the bedroom is dirty to you, then you are a true atheist, because...if anyone in this audience believes that God made his body, and your body is dirty, the fault lies with the manufacturer."

[*The dedication to his autobiography*] "I dedicate this book to all the followers of Christ and his teachings; in particular to a true Christian—Jimmy Hoffa—because he hired ex-convicts as, I assume, Christ would have."

"We're all the same people....And it discourages me that we try so desperately to be unique."

[*On his legal problems*] "What I need is a lawyer with enough juice to get Ray Charles a driver's license."

"I'm not original. The only way I could truly say I was original is if I created the English language. I did, man, but they don't believe me."

"Marijuana will be legal some day, because the many law students who now smoke pot will some day become Congressmen and legalize it in order to protect themselves."

**According to one poll, nearly 3/4 of all American women wear a bra that is the wrong size.**

# CONGRESSIONAL WIT

*Even congressmen can be funny—albeit sometimes unintentionally. Bill Hogan and Mike Hill scoured the Congressional Record and came up with Congress's most amusing moments for their book,* Will the Gentleman Yield?, *published by* **Ten Speed** *Press.*

## SHEA A LITTLE LONGER

Mr. *Domenici.* Will the Senator yield for a question without losing his right to the floor?

Mr. *D'Amato.* Certainly.

Mr. *Domenici.* If the Senator is going to stay here and talk until Saturday night, would he give me his ticket to the Mets game? He can stay here and I will go.

***—Sens. Pete V. Domenici (R-N. Mex.) and Alfonse M. D'Amato (R-N.Y.)***
***October 16, 1986***

## POTATO, GRENADA

Mr. Speaker, some 40 years ago, George Gershwin popularized a little ditty that went like this:

"You like po-ta-to and I like po-tah-to,
You like to-ma-to, and I like to-mah-to,
Po-ta-to, po-tah-to, To-ma-to, to-mah-to!
Let's call the whole thing off!"

At about the same time that Mr. Gershwin was writing his tune, Mr. Reagan was starring in the kind of movies that recent incidents in Grenada cannot help but remind one of. Think about it for a moment—a small Caribbean island, a band of bearded local militia, a lot of beautiful and confused residents, and throw in a few angry tourists for comic relief. Unfortunately, this is not a grade B movie, it is not even a very good script—two American marines have already lost their lives.

But if that is the way Mr. Reagan persists in looking at these issues maybe he will listen to a little advice from Mr. Gershwin. If Gershwin were alive today, perhaps he would consider this rewrite:

You like po-ta-to, I like po-tah-to,
You say Gre-na-da, I say Gre-nah-da,
Po-ta-to, po-tah-to, Gre-na-da, Gre-nah-da,
Let's call the whole thing off.

*—Rep. James M. Shannon (D-Mass.)*
*October 26, 1983*

**TEED OFF AT THE POST OFFICE? REMEMBER LARRY**

Mr. Speaker, a recent item in the *Washington Star* told of one Larry Ryan who scored a hole-in-one while playing in the Pittsfield, Mass., Post Office Golf Tournament. But his was a dubious achievement. He drove from the third tee and the ball went 180 yards away—into the cup on the first green.

Some would find this an apt analogy to the operations of the Postal Service. So, whenever you receive mail intended for another—a not uncommon occurrence—it is a safe guess that our Postal Service is using the Larry Ryan method of delivery.

*—Rep. Charles H. Wilson (D-Calif.)*
*June 10, 1975*

**OH GOD**

I recall something that involved my good Baptist friend, Bill D. Moyers....

President Johnson called on Bill one day to open a Cabinet meeting with prayer. Bill was sitting at the end of the Cabinet table, and when he had finished the prayer, the President said, "Bill, we couldn't hear you up here."

Bill said, "I wasn't talking to you, Mr. President."

*—Rep. Brooks Hays (D-Ark.)*
*May 19, 1977*

**CONE HEAD**

Mr. Speaker, I have introduced a resolution declaring July Ice Cream Month and July 15 as Ice Cream Day....Ice cream is good for you.

If you feel dejected or frustrated, eat ice cream; if the legislative processes frustrate you, eat ice cream; if you are happy and want to celebrate, eat ice cream. Not only will you help an industry and American workers but it is good, it is just plain good.

*—Rep. E de la Garza (D-Tex.)*
*June 7, 1984*

GOLDEN OLDIE

I am reminded of the time when Emanuel Celler was in the House, and I served with him. Emanuel Celler was the oldest Member of that body at that time. He was...speaking in support of a measure I had introduced, and he forgot certain facts about which I reminded him.

He said, "Oh yes, yes. How clearly I recall that now. You know, there are three signs of aging. The first is that you tend to forget things rather easily—and for the life of me, I don't know what the other two things are."

[Laughter.]

*—Sen. Spark M. Matsunaga (D-Hawaii)*
*March 12, 1980*

STARK DIFFERENCES

Mr. Speaker, the *Washington Post* reports that the Army has granted a $139,000 contract to the University of Maryland to conduct a study of how to prepare healthy food that tastes good. I submit that the Army asking a college food service about healthy, tasty food is rather like Phyllis Diller asking Joan Rivers about beauty aids....

*—Rep. Fortney H. (Pete) Stark (D-Calif.)*
*October 10, 1986*

UPS AND DOWNS

Mr. Speaker, after careful and scholarly study I have concluded that the principal cause of congressional inefficiency is the elevator system in the Longworth Building.

*—Rep. Andrew Jacobs, Jr. (D-Ind.)*
*June 15, 1976*

The first all-talking movie was called *The Lights of New York.*

# BUTCH AND SUNDANCE

Butch Cassidy and the Sundance Kid, *starring Paul Newman and Robert Redford, is the highest-grossing cowboy film of all-time. For those of you who assume that the pair's wild on-screen exploits were pure fantasy, here's a surprise.*

Of all the outlaws, desperadoes and personalities of the West, perhaps none have captured the fancy of Americans more than Butch Cassidy and the Sundance Kid. They were master bank and train robbers, outlaws who seldom used their guns, and among the very few who lived to spend and enjoy the enormous wealth they captured in the waning days of the Wild West.

Cassidy, whose real name was Robert Leroy Parker, was born in 1866 to Mormon parents in Utah. Harry Longabaugh, the Sundance Kid, probably hailed from New Jersey or Pennsylvania sometime in the late 1860s. Both Cassidy and Sundance were products of the times, when small ranchers and businessmen were often overwhelmed by the well-financed "robber barons" of the era. Some historians believe their robbery exploits were a reaction to the emerging monopoly capitalism mentality, while others feel it was simply a case of "bad company."

At any rate, Cassidy, Sundance, and their gang—known both as the Hole in the Wall Gang and the Wild Bunch—were masters of the big heist. They perfected the technique of the three-man robbery—one man to hold the horse, one to hold the gun, and of course, one to grab the cash. The gang was particularly famous for their stylish technique. When the boys took a train, they blew up the baggage cars with dynamite...but *never* hurt the passengers or crew. And the robberies were always well planned out from start to finish—which accounts for their long and lucrative careers.

In 1900, with the Wild Bunch's numbers diminishing (due to the steady pursuit of the famous Pinkerton Detective Agency), Cassidy, Sundance and a third man robbed a bank in a remote part of Nevada and netted over $32,000 in cash. They split up to meet again in Texas, where a wild spending spree ensued.

In 1901, the two discussed plans to go to South America, then pulled a final train robbery, demolishing a baggage car and making off with thousands in bank notes. After a brief visit to New York City, the pair and Sundance's lover went to Argentina and bought a ranch. There they apparently led a quiet life. But in 1906, probably because they were running out of money, they robbed a bank in a nearby town.

After a trip back to the United States by Sundance and his ailing mistress, the pair met up again, sometime around 1909 in Bolivia. A violent shoot out with the Bolivian cavalry (probably during a robbery) ensued, and it was from that point on that their legend began to really take shape. Accounts of what happened during and after the shootout vary: Some say both men died; some think Cassidy survived; but most are now convinced that both outlaws actually escaped, with Sundance rejoining his long-time lover and living quietly in Wyoming until 1956. As for Cassidy, he probably changed his name and died in a nursing home in Washington state in 1937.

Whatever the real story, it's clear that Butch Cassidy and the Sundance Kid were among the cleverest and shrewdest outlaws ever to emerge from the Old West.

## FACTS ABOUT THE WEST

- Billy the Kid was from Brooklyn, New York.
- The most common causes of death for old-time cowboys: pneumonia and riding accidents.
- Most cowboys didn't like carrying guns—they got in the way when they were riding, and scared their horses or cattle.

# TOP TEN BABY NAMES

*What's in a name? Sugar and spice? Or the herd instinct?*
*Here's what parents have been naming*
*their kids for the last fifty years.*

**Most popular baby names in 1925:**

| *For Girls:* | *For Boys:* |
|---|---|
| 1. Mary | Robert |
| 2. Barbara | John |
| 3. Dorothy | William |
| 4. Betty | James |
| 5. Ruth | Charles |
| 6. Margaret | Richard |
| 7. Helen | George |
| 8. Elizabeth | Donald |
| 9. Jean | Joseph |
| 10. Ann | Edward |

**Most popular baby names in 1948:**

| *For Girls:* | *For Boys:* |
|---|---|
| 1. Linda | Robert |
| 2. Mary | John |
| 3. Barbara | James |
| 4. Patricia | Michael |
| 5. Susan | William |
| 6. Kathleen | Richard |
| 7. Carol | Joseph |
| 8. Nancy | Thomas |
| 9. Margaret | Stephen |
| 10. Diane | David |

**Most popular baby names in 1974:**

| *For Girls:* | *For Boys:* |
|---|---|
| 1. Jennifer | Michael |
| 2. Michelle | John |
| 3. Christine | Robert |
| 4. Lisa | David |
| 5. Maria | Christopher |
| 6. Melissa | Anthony |
| 7. Nicole | Joseph |
| 8. Elizabeth | Jason |
| 9. Jessica | James |
| 10. Erica | Jose |

**Most popular baby names in 1987:**

| *For Girls:* | *For Boys:* |
|---|---|
| 1. Jessica | Michael |
| 2. Jennifer | Christopher |
| 3. Ashley | Matthew |
| 4. Amanda | Daniel |
| 5. Christine | Joseph |
| 6. Sara(h) | David |
| 7. Nicole | Andrew |
| 8. Stephanie | Steven |
| 9. Melissa | Brian |
| 10. Danielle | Robert |

# MONOPOLY

*Monopoly is the best selling game in history. It has been published in twenty-eight countries and nineteen different languages and is more popular in the eighties than ever.*

If there was ever a way to introduce the concept of capitalism to children, this game is it.

**Background**: In 1904, "The Landlord's Game," a board game which included the purchasing of property, utilities and a "public park" space, was patented. Apparently Charles Darrow, the father of Monopoly, "borrowed" much of this game.

**The Origin**. Following the stock market crash of 1929, Darrow—an engineer by trade—found himself unemployed and short of cash like the rest of the country. To kill time (and keep his spirits up), he began devising a game involving "plenty of money for the player to invest or speculate with." Because he was interested in real estate he made that the primary focus; and because he personally didn't believe in credit or borrowing money, he made the whole thing a cash proposition.

Darrow had visited Atlantic City shortly before the stock market crashed, so he transferred his fond memories of the town to the board—thus the Boardwalk, railroad lines and property of the New Jersey resort are represented there.

The original version of the game was crudely painted on a piece of linoleum. But that didn't stop family and friends from getting hooked on it—and demanding their own sets. "I hadn't anything better to do, so I began to make the games," Darrow explained. "I charged people $4.00 a copy." Although Darrow did no advertising, he soon began to receive orders from all over the country. He was shocked but excited. Looking for more distribution, he took the game to Parker Brothers...and was turned down cold. Says one writer: "George and Charles Parker thought Monopoly took much too long to play, the rules were hopelessly complicated, and there were at least fifty-two

**The most common street name in America is "Park Street."**

other weak points they believed ruled the game out as far as they were concerned."

Darrow was upset by the decision, but decided to distribute the games on his own. He took them to two major retailers—Wanamaker's Department Store in Philadelphia, and FAO Schwartz, New York's most prestigious toy store—and convinced them to stock Monopoly. When both quickly sold out their entire stock, the Parker brothers reconsidered. They purchased the rights to make the game...and watched, astounded, as Monopoly sold so fast that it kept the toy company—which was on the edge of insolvency—from going under.

Parker Brothers sold every Monopoly set they could manufacture for Christmas, 1934, and the demand didn't die down after the holidays. They were soon literally inundated with requests for more; orders were so plentiful they had to be stacked in laundry baskets and stored in hallways. The company had never even heard of a product being so much in demand.

By mid-February of the following year, Parker Brothers was selling more than twenty thousand sets of Monopoly per week. Darrow, as one would imagine, was financially set for life. And the reluctant toy company had its hands on the most lucrative game in the history of the toy industry.

## GUINNESS ON MONOPOLY

- Largest Monopoly game in history: Took place on full-size sidewalks and streets in Huntington, Pennsylvania, on a board that was bigger than a square city block. Sponsored by students at Juniata College, who cast huge foam dice from a third-story fire escape and kept players informed of their moves by using walkie-talkie-equipped bicycle messengers. April, 1967.
- Longest Monopoly game underwater: 1,008 hours, by the Lodi, California, Diving School. That's forty-two days, one hundred forty players.
- Longest Monopoly game in a moving elevator: sixteen days.
- Longest Monopoly game ever: 1,416 hours. Players: McCluer North Games Club, Florissant, Missouri.
- Longest Monopoly game in a bathtub: 99 hours.
- Longest anti-gravitational Monopoly game: 36 hours.

**In 1985, "The Cosby Show" was the highest-ranking TV program in South Africa.**

# 10 COOL BOOKS

*From Gene Sculatti, here's a list of ten obscure but hip books which may be suitable for future bathroom reading.*

**BEEN DOWN SO LONG IT LOOKS LIKE UP TO ME** —*Richard Fariña*
The fact that he may inadvertently have invented Tom Robbins should not be held against this late great. This ...is *the* missed link between the beatbooks of Kerouac, Brossard, etc. and the great hippie novels that were never written. Maybe the flower kids took one look at *Been Down So Long* and gave up.

**CONFESSIONS OF A HOAXER** —*Alan Abel*
OK, there've been odder political candidates than Yetta Brosten, more ludicrous rock stars than Count Von Blitzstein, social protests every bit as ill-founded as the campaign to clothe nude animals. But they didn't all have a single mastermind behind them. Alan Abel got away with the above and more (including staging the debut of the world's first topless string quartet). *Confessions* makes it look easy, as well as eminently worthwhile.

**A CONFEDERACY OF DUNCES**
—*John Kennedy Toole*
The coolest American hero of recent years wore earflaps, caroused with b-girls in a Bourbon Street dive called the Night of Joy, and contended with a mad world and a mother who feared he'd become "a communiss." They don't make 'em like this anymore. A Pulitzer Prize winner.

**FLASH AND FILIGREE**
—*Terry Southern*
The brilliant comic writer's first novel, containing the boss TV game show "What's My Disease," a seduction scene comprised solely of grappling maneuvers, and "Ononono-pleaseno's." Surpassed only by his short story "Blood of a Wig" (in *Red Dirt Marijuana and Other Tastes*).

**GORMENGHAST TRILOGY** —*Mervyn Peake*
One critic described *Titus Groan*, *Gormenghast*, and *Titus Alone* as "Charles Dickens on opium." Psycho-

More Americans visit Tijuana than any other foreign city.

logically rich, koo-koo characters live in a huge crumbling castle located somewhere in Peake's brain. The first two novels are great, the third isn't. A companion novella *Boy in Darkness*, is even more unreal.

**MINE ENEMY GROWS OLDER** —*Alexander King*
By 1958, the man Lenny Bruce christened "the junkie Mark Twain" had seen it all and done most of it twice. Long before he became a high-watt fixture on Jack Paar's TV show, Alex the Great had painted covers for Mencken's *Smart Set* magazine, scrawled Chinese murals on the walls of kosher deli's and been photo editor of *Life*....He'd also been a morphine addict, submitted to bagel therapy at an asylum as batty as Kesey's cuckoo's nest, and played chess with A-bomb "spy" Alger Hiss. Bonus: King explains why, between 1917 and 1948 he only wore pink neckties.

**OZZIE** —*Ozzie Nelson*
Dedicated to Harriet. It takes 309 pages, but Daddy-O spills it all in this 1977 autobio: what he did for a living all those years on *Ozzie and Harriet*, his days on the road, that time at Rutgers when a young student presented him with a lit marijuana cigarette. (Oz put it in his pocket. It burned.)

**THE SECRET LIFE OF SALVADOR DALI**
A Forties autobiography from the twentieth century's most profound comedian. Mind-boggling anecdotes, opinions, and self-analysis spill out over the page, filtered through Dali's aristo-punk attitude. (He once shellacked his hair.) Always outrageous, *never* dull.

**THE WANDERERS** —*Richard Price*
The coolest, craziest juvenile delinquent trip ever put down. Noo Yawk at its most fearsome, funniest. Irish Ducky Boys roam their gang turf like midget dinosaurs, Chinese Wongs take no shit, and everybody listens to Dion.

**WRITE IF YOU GET WORK: THE BEST OF BOB & RAY**
Worth hunting for if you remember their insane commercials, *Mad* articles, or the deadpan dada of their radio comedy. Reprints classic bits—"Spelling Bee," "Lightbulb Collector," and more.

# THE REAL ARTICLE

*A random sampling of first-person articles, dialogue, correspondence. You are there.*

## SOUR GRAPES

*In 1957, Frank Sinatra—a teen idol in the '40s—wrote this piece about rock 'n' roll in a magazine called* Western World:

"My only deep sorrow is the unrelenting insistence of recording and motion picture companies upon purveying the most brutal, ugly, degenerate, vicious form of expression it has been my displeasure to hear and naturally I'm referring to the bulk of rock 'n' roll.

"It fosters almost totally negative and destructive reactions in young people," he said. "It smells phony and false. It is sung, played, and written for the most part by cretinous goons and by means of its almost imbecilic reiterations and sly, lewd—in plain fact—dirty lyrics, it manages to be the martial music of every sideburned delinquent on the face of the earth."

## FORGETTABLE FIRST FILM

*On September 15, 1937,* Variety *reviewed a film called* Love Is On the Air*—which happened to be Ronald Reagan's first movie appearance. Ironically, Reagan starred as a citizen who exposed a corrupt link between businessmen and politicians.*

"In the lead, Ronald Reagan, whom Warners is trying to build up into a juvenile lead, is a spot-newscaster on a radio station. If he exceeds in authority and importance that role played in radio actually, the public probably won't notice. But they are bound to notice that the plot is the one about the newspaperman who, against the advice and even threats from higher-ups, does his community the good turn of dragging into the open the connections between racketeering gangsters and the businessmen and political job-holders who protect the lawless and share the booty....

"Reagan, before the camera all the way, gives rather an in-and-out performance. He's best when in fast physical action...."

## FARTS IN SPACE

*An official NASA transcript of a conversation between astronauts John Young and Charles Duke during the moon launch on April 21, 1972.*

*Young*: "I got the farts again. I got 'em again, Charlie. I don't know what the hell gives 'em to me."

*Duke*: [unintelligible]

*Young*: "Certainly not—I think it's acid in the stomach. I really do."

*Duke*: "Probably is."

*Young*: "I mean, I haven't eaten this much citrus fruit in twenty years. And I'll tell you one thing—in another twelve...days, I ain't never eating any more. And if they offer to serve me potassium with my breakfast, I'm going to throw up. I like an occasional orange, I really do. But I'll be damned if I'm going to be buried in oranges."

## ABE LINCOLN'S BEARD

*A copy of the letter—written to Abraham Lincoln while he campaigned for president in 1860—which inspired Lincoln to grow a beard.*

Westfield, Chautauqua Co., N.Y.
October 15, 1860

Dear Sir,
I am a little girl 11 years old, but want you should be President of the United States very much so I hope you won't think me very bold to write to such a great man as you are.

Have you any little girls about as large as I am if so give them my love and tell her to write me if you cannot answer this letter. I have got four brothers and part of them will vote for you any way and if you will let your whiskers grow. I will try to get the rest of them to vote for you. You would look a great deal better, for your face is so thin. All the ladies like whiskers and they would tease their husbands to vote for you and then you would be President.

Grace Bedell

Over 450 million copies of author Barbara Cartland's books have been sold—a record.

## REAGAN'S RESOLUTION

*In November, 1955, Ronald Reagan wrote an article for* The Hollywood Reporter *about his work in TV, films, and politics. Among his comments:*

"I have for the past months been doubling, combining television and motion picture chores. This manifold job has taught me one thing for sure: never again will I allow myself to get into a position where I must make a choice between a seat in Congress and a comfortable position in the arms of my leading lady.

"Actors are citizens and should exert those rights by speaking their minds, but the actor's first duty is to his profession. Hence, you can rest assured that I will never again run for mayor or anything but head man in my own household...."

## HANK WILLIAMS' LAST WORDS

*Hank Williams died on December 31, 1952, sitting in the back of his Cadillac. When his body was discovered, a piece of paper was found clutched in his right hand. On it were Hank Williams's last words. They were:*

"We met, we lived and dear we loved, then comes that fatal day, the love that felt so dear fades far away. Tonight love hath one alone and lonesome, all that I could sing, I you you [sic] still and always will, but that's the poison we have to pay."

## MODEL CITIZEN

*Twiggy was a hero to millions of girls in the '60s.* Esquire *magazine quoted this encounter with a reporter who actually asked her a real question.*

**Reporter:** "Twiggy, do you know what happened at Hiroshima?"
**Twiggy:** "Where's that?"
**Reporter:** "In Japan."
**Twiggy:** "I've never heard of it. What happened there?"
**Reporter:** "A hundred thousand people died on the spot."
**Twiggy:** "Oh, God! When did you say it happened? Where? Hiroshima? But that's ghastly! A hundred thousand dead? It's frightful. Men are mad."

A beehive hairdo that stood 6 feet, 6 inches is the tallest recorded hairdo in the world.

# MARK TWAIN SAYS...

*No one in the history of American literature combined sardonic wit, warmth, and intelligence as Mark Twain did in his novels.*

"Adam and Eve had many advantages, but the principal one was that they escaped teething."

"Reader, suppose you were an idiot. And suppose you were a member of Congress. But I repeat myself."

"Get your facts first, and then you can distort them as much as you please."

"It is better to keep your mouth shut and appear stupid than to open it and remove all doubt."

"It is by the goodness of God that we have in our country three unspeakably precious things: freedom of speech, freedom of conscience, and the prudence never to practice either."

"Truth is the most valuable thing we have. Let us economize it."

"A man pretty much always refuses another man's first offer, no matter what it is."

"Be good, and you will be lonesome."

"There are three kinds of lies—lies, damned lies and statistics."

"Noise proves nothing. Often a hen who has merely laid an egg cackles as if she has laid an asteroid."

"The principle difference between a cat and a lie is that a cat only has nine lives."

"Man is the only animal that blushes. Or needs to."

"I believe that our Heavenly Father invented man because he was disappointed in the monkey."

"War talk by men who have been in a war is always interesting, whereas moon talk by a poet who has not been in the moon is likely to be dull."

# PLACES' NAMES

*The fascinating history of place-naming in America is captured in the classic* Names on the Land. *Author George R. Stewart demonstrates several of the main sources for common U.S. names.*

**RIVERS.** "On August 4, 1830, the inhabitants of an...undistinguished western village filed [to become a town]. They had previously been known as Fort Dearborn, but Dearborn (the man for whom it was named)...had merely been Secretary of War under Jefferson, and was no hero....So, in accordance with the fashion of the time, the town-founders took the name of the river, and wrote Chicago upon their [application]. It was a good example of a name adopted without knowledge of its meaning, for if the founders had known it to be Onion river, or allegedly Skunk or Smelling River, they would very likely have kept Dearborn."

**HEROES**. "At San Jacinto, on April 21, 1836, General Sam Houston waved his old campaign hat as a signal, and the Texans charged, shouting 'Remember the Alamo!' Within a few months a town was laid out near the battlefield; its promoters combined patriotism with advertisement, and called it Houston."

**THE ANCIENT WORLD.** "[John Charles] Fremont made his best stroke in California. The Spaniards had neglected to supply a name to the passage connecting San Francisco Bay with the ocean. Although Fremont had never been to Constantinople, he fancied a resemblance between that ancient harbor and the western strait;...He wrote accordingly: 'I give the name *Chrysoplaye*, or *Golden Gate*; for the same reasons that the harbor of Byzantium was called *Chrysoceras*, or *Golden Horn*.'"

**LANDOWNERS.** "One of the five boroughs of New York City...is always *The Bronx*, never just a naked *Bronx*....This dates from the 17th century, a time when a man named Jonas Bronck farmed...land north of Manhattan Island. When people back then said they were going to the Broncks, they really meant it."

**In 1976, a Los Angeles secretary formally married her fifty-pound pet rock.**

# GLOBAL VILLAGE

*B.R.I. member Eric Lefcowitz contributed this batch of world statistics. Unfortunately, stats are generally buried in books that are too large and cumbersome for bathroom reading.*

With the advent of computers and lasers, and both digital and satellite technology, Marshall McLuhan's late Sixties version of a "global village" is more relevant than ever. The media's ability to transmit information is just a small part of the development of global consciousness, however. The depletion of the earth's oxygen through the destruction of rain forests, the ozone layer and the "greenhouse effect" have become world issues. As we found out with Chernobyl, one country does not have a nuclear accident—they all do.

So maybe Uncle Walt was right: it's a small world, after all....Actually, if you want to be precise, it's not so small—the land area of the world is 135,841,000 kilometers, or 52,500,000 square miles.

**Here are some other world statistics.**

There are approximately

- 1.2 billion households
- 5 billion people
- 1.8 billion people working
- 1.5 billion children under 15
- 32 million teachers
- 4 million doctors
- 8,240 daily newspapers
- 72 million movie seats
- 527 million television sets
- 453 million telephones
- 300 million passenger cars
- 250,000 movie theaters

**Here are some world averages:**

- Approximate life expectancy at birth: 62 years
- Life expectancy, female: 59 years; male: 53 years
- Literacy rate: 70%
- Daily Calorie Supply per Capita: 2,607
- Size of a Household: 4.1
- Gross Global Product (GGP): $2,633

However, drastic differences come to light when you subject global averages to quantitative analysis. For example, in terms of male life expectancy, the country of Iceland ranks the highest with 73 years. On the low end of the scale are the African nations of Togo (31.50), Chad (29) and Gabon (25). Neither America nor England are in the top 10.

For female life expectancy, Iceland again ranks number one at 79.20 years. Upper Volta, however, brings up the rear with 31.10.

**Other global highs and lows:**

- Hottest place—Aroune, Mali. Highest recorded temperature: 130 degrees Fahrenheit (54.4 Centigrade).
- Coldest place—Eismitte, Greenland. Lowest recorded temperature: -85 degrees Fahrenheit (-64.8 Centigrade).
- Wettest place—Cherrapunji, India. Highest recorded rainfall (in 1983): 425 inches of rain.

**The Media**

**TV:** According to a 1980 poll, Canada has the most hours of TV broadcasting in the world—over 6 million per year. The U.S. is in second place with 5 1/2 million, followed by Japan and Brazil. England is tenth. If you lived in Cyprus , Norway, Pakistan, or about a dozen other countries, you could watch less than 3,000 hours...if you watched TV *every single minute* there was something on the air. Compare that with the viewing habits of (and influences on) the average American, who routinely watches me than 8 hours of television per day.

**Movies:** People in the U.S.S.R. watch more movies than anyone in the world—about a third of all movie attendance. Among the countries that average the most films seen per capita: Iceland, the Falkland Islands, Singapore, Hong Kong, and Grenada. The least: Uganda, Tanzania, and other African nations.

You have about 10 gallons of water inside you, making up about 60% of your weight.

# FIVE BEATLE SONGS

*It's fun to learn the origin of any Beatles song; here is a random selection of five tunes to read about, from* Behind the Hits, *by Bob Shannon and John Javna.*

**PLEASE PLEASE ME**, 1964
**LENNON** (in an interview with *Playboy*): "It was my attempt at writing a Roy Orbison song, would you believe it? I wrote it in the bedroom in my house at Menlove Avenue, which was my auntie's place...I heard Roy Orbison doing 'Only the Lonely' or something. And...I was intrigued by the words of 'Please lend your little ears to my pleas'—a Bing Crosby song. I was always intrigued by the double use of the word *please*. So it was a combination of Bing Crosby and Roy Orbison." The Beatles, by the way, were once the opening act for headliner Roy Orbison on a British tour.

**MICHELLE**, 1966
**McCARTNEY** (to Paul Gambaccini): "I just fancied writing some French words....I had a friend whose wife taught French...and I just asked her, you know, what we could figure out that was French. We got words that go together well. It was mainly because I always used to think the song sounded like a French thing...I can't speak French, really, so we sorted out some actual words."

**ELEANOR RIGBY**, 1966
**McCARTNEY** (in *Paul McCartney in His Own Words*): "I think it was 'Miss Daisy Hawkins' originally, picking up the rice in a church after a wedding....At first I thought it was a young Miss Daisy Hawkins...but then I saw I'd said she was picking up the rice in a church, so she had to be a cleaner, she'd missed the wedding and she was suddenly lonely. In fact, she had missed it all—she was the spinster type.

"[But] I didn't really like 'Daisy Hawkins'—I wanted a name that was more real. The thought just came, 'Eleanor Rigby picks up the rice and lives in a dream,' so there she was. The

One company manufactures an edible set of Monopoly, made of chocolate and butterscotch.

next thing was Father Mackenzie. It was going to be Father McCartney, but then I thought that was a bit of a hang-up for my dad, being in this lonely song. So we looked through the phone book. That's the beauty of working at random—it does come up perfectly, much better than if you try to think it with your intellect. Anyway, there was Father Mackenzie, just as I had imagined him, lonely, darning his socks."

**NOWHERE MAN**, 1966
**LENNON**: "I was just sitting, trying to think of a song, and I thought of myself sitting there, doing nothing and getting nowhere. Once I'd thought of that, it was easy. It all came out. No, I remember now, I'd actually stopped trying to think of something. Nothing would come. I was cheesed off and went for a lie-down, having given up. Then I thought of myself as a 'Nowhere Man,' sitting in his nowhere land."

**DO YOU WANT TO KNOW A SECRET**, 1964
**LENNON** (in *Playboy* again): "My mother...was a comedienne....She used to get up in pubs and things like that. She had a good voice....She used to do this little tune when I was just a one- or two-year-old. The tune was from a Disney movie—[singing] 'Want to know a secret? Promise not to tell. You are standing by a wishing well.'

"I wrote [the song] and gave it to George to sing. I thought it would be a good vehicle for him because it only had three notes and he wasn't the best singer in the world."

**MISCELLANEOUS BEATLES STATS**

- In less than a decade, they sold over 125 million singles and 85 million LPs.
- They had the most #1 records during the '60s—17—compared to the second-place Supremes, who had 12.
- They had the most Top 10 hits in the '60s—29.
- In one year—1964—they had 31 songs that hit the charts.
- On April 4, 1964, they had all of the top 5 songs on the Billboard charts: 1) "Can't Buy Me Love"; 2)"Twist and Shout"; 3)"She Loves You"; 4) "I Wanna Hold Your Hand"; 5) "Please Please Me."

# THE FABULOUS '60s

*If you were there, you remember the "topless" controversy of the mid-'60s. If you weren't, this might give you an idea of what it was like.*

**THE INSIDE STORY: The Origin of the Topless Bathing Suit**

The topless suit began simply as a prediction. One day in 1963, in an interview, fashion designer Rudi Gernreich commented that "in five years every American woman will be wearing a bathing suit that is bare above the waist." After saying that, he realized that if *he* didn't make that topless suit immediately, someone else would. But should he?

Before he could decide, Hess Brothers department store in Allentown, Pennsylvania, ordered some. Then other stores across the United States did, too. Gernreich put the suit into production.

One of the things that focused national attention on the topless suit was that 1964 was an election year, and the Republican party seized on it as a symbol of the "decadence" in America.

This produced millions of dollars worth of publicity for Gernreich, who said in amazement: "I never dreamed it would go beyond the fashion business into sociology."

By the way, the topless suit was never popular to wear—only three thousand were sold.

**'60s MADNESS**

**Topless Bathing**

**June 1964**—New York City Commissioner of Parks Newbold Morris said women wearing topless bathing suits on N.Y.C. beaches would be issued summonses by police for indecent exposure. L.A. police issued the same warning.

**July 1964**—The Vatican newspaper *L'Osservatore Roma* headlined an article on topless bathing suits "The Ultimate Shame," and said it "negates moral sense."

**June 1964**—In an article entitled "Back to Barbarism," the Soviet newspaper *Izvestia* called the topless suits a sign of America's moral decay. "So the decay of the moneybags society continues," it said.

**July 1964**—The topless suit was modeled in the *San Francisco Chronicle*—by a four-year-old-girl.

**THE REVEREND ED WATT**

In Dallas, the Reverend Ed Watt and a group of protesters from the Carroll Avenue Baptist Mission picketed a department store that was displaying a topless bathing suit in its window. Their placards read: "We Protest these Suits in the Name of Christ." Watt said that church action was long overdue—topless shorts would be next.

The picketing continued until the department store removed the one topless suit it had from its display.

Were the protesters successful? Not exactly. They attracted so much attention to the suit that someone went into the store and bought it.

**MORE '60S MADNESS:**

**Bottled Eggs**

September 3, 1962: "Fresh eggs sold by the bottle are being test-marketed in National Tea Co. stores. The secret (which the developer, Chicago's David Cleaver Produce Co., won't reveal) is in the 'simple but patentable method' of getting the shell-less eggs into the bottle without breaking the yolks. The eggs readily pour out of the bottle one at a time, yolks cushioned by the whites. National Tea claims that refrigerated bottled eggs keep longer than eggs in the shell (six to eight weeks vs. four to six) because the capped bottle offers an airtight seal while the shell is porous. The bottles come in one-pound (about ten eggs) and two-pound (twenty eggs) sizes. Cost: About eight cents more per dozen than eggs in the carton."

**Puppy Love.**

*1962*: A fallout shelter for pets was put on the market, "to give pets an equal chance for survival."

1966: Upjohn introduced an oral contraceptive for dogs, for "Planned Puppyhood."

**Elvis Presley had more records on the *Billboard* charts—107—than any other artist.**

# DOO-WOP SOUNDS

*You've heard classic street-corner rock 'n' roll tunes before—"Why Do Fools Fall in Love," "Come Go With Me," etc. And you've probably noticed the crazy syllables the groups sing in the background. Ever wonder what they'd look like spelled out? Here are 20 great doo-wop syllables from* The Doo-Wop Sing-Along Song Book.

1. **Hooodly-Papa-Kow, Papa-Kow, Papa-Kow (YEAH), Hooodly-Papa-Kow, Papa Kow, Papa Kow.** A gem from Frankie Lymon and the Teenagers.

2. **Pa-pa-pa-pa-pa-pa-pa-Oom-A-Mow-Mow, Papa-Oom Mow Mow.** One of the most famous rock syllable combos, from a group called the Rivingtons and a semi-doo-wop tune called—big surprise—"Papa Oom Mow Mow."

3. **Oop-Shoop, Shang-A-Lack-A-Cheek-A-Bock.** One of the all-time greats, a background section from the Earls' "Remember Then" (1961).

4. **Diddle-iddle-iddle-iddle-it (YEAH), Diddle-iddle-iddle-iddle-it.** Notable for its persistence, in a classic doo-wop tune by Herb Cox and the Cleftones, "Little Girl of Mine" (1956).

5. **Neh-neh-neh-neh, neh neh-neh-neh neh-neh-neh, Neh-neh-neh-neh-neh, neh-neh-neh-neh (repeat the whole thing two more times), Werp-A-Tul-Werp, Neh-Neh-Neh-Neh, Neh-Neh-Neh-Neh.** A perfect example of why you have to hear doo-wop to appreciate it. The opening of "The Closer You Are," by the Magnificent Four.

6. **I Su-mokem Boo-eye-ay, I sumokem boo.** Doo-wop's classic drug reference. From "Ling Ting Tong," by the Five Keys.

**7. (Bom-bom) Cheer-Up, (Bom-bom) Cheer-up, (Bom-Bom) Cheer-Up, (Bom-bom) Cheer-Up.** A favorite adaptation of a real word into a doo-wop. From the Pentagons' "To Be Loved."

**8. Rama Lama-Lama-Lama-Lama Ding Dong, Rama Lama-Lama-Lama-Lama-Lama Ding.** That's the Edsels playing homage to George Jones, Jr.'s girlfriend, "Rama Lama Ding Dong."

**9. Rang Tang Ding Dong, Rankety Sing.** Weird syllable combination from "Ring Tang Ding Dong (I am the Japanese Sandman)," by the Cellos.

**10. Ka-Ding-Dong, Ding-Dong, Ka-Ding-Dong, Ding-Dong, Ding.** The sound of the singer's heart in the G-Clefs' thriller, "Ka-Ding-Dong."

**11. Yip, Yip, Yip, Yip Boom, Sha-Na-Na-Na, Sha-Na-Na-Na-Na.** It's from "Get A Job" by the Silhouettes and it's not only a great doo-wop, it's the symbol of the '70s doo-wop revival. The quasi-greaser band from Columbia University got its name from this background.

**12. Sho-Dot'n' Shoby-Doh, Sho-Dot'n' Shoby-Doh.** From Fred Parris and the Five Satins' classic "In the Still of the Night." Strangely, although it's sold millions of records, the highest this song ever reached on the *Billboard* charts was #25.

**13. Dom-Dooby-Dom Woh-oh, Dooby Dooby, Dom Dooby Dom, Woh-oh, Dooby Dooby, Dom Dooby Dom Woh-Oh, tonight I fell in love.** Sort of a white bread doo-wop, but kind of catchy. From the Tokens' "Tonight I Fell In Love."

**14. Tuh-tuh-tuh-tuh-tuh-tuh-tuh-aaa-ooo-ooo-ooo-ooo-ooo.** A super doo-wop. This is the end of a line in "Unchained Melody," by Vito and the Salutations. The one that starts "Oh my love, my darling, I hunger for your...." Originally, the next word was "touch." In doo-wop it became this 13-syllable creature.

**15. A-Wop-bop-A-Loo-bop-A-Bop--Bam-Boom.** For sentimental reasons. From Little Richard's "Tutti Frutti."

**The first sperm banks opened in 1964; they were located in Tokyo and Iowa City.**

**16. Iminni-ma-ma-ma-Iminni-ma-ma-ma-gin-A-tion. Imin-i-ni-ma-ima-ima-ma-gin-aaaa-tion.** The doo-wop spelling for the word "imagination," as interpreted by the Quotations.

**17. Shoh-Be-Doo-Wop-Wah-Da.** The controversial last line in "What's Your Name," by Don and Juan. No one seems to agree on what they're saying. Here's my version.

**18. Wah-Wah-OOO, Chop Chop Chop.** An original from "Tell Me Why," by the Rob Roys.

**19. Wop-wop-Doodly-wop-Wop-wop. Wop-wop, Doodly-wop-Wop-Wop.** The El Doradoes lead into the instrumental break in "At My Front Door."

**20.** And of course: **Bomp-ba-ba-bomp, Ba-bom-ba-bom-bomp, Ba-ba-bomp-ba-ba-bomp, A-dang-a-dang-dang. A-ding-a-dong-ding, Bluuuue Moooon.**

From the Marcels' adaptation of the Rogers and Hart classic, "Blue Moon." Originally, this song was written for a '30s film—Jean Harlow was supposed to sing it! She never did.

The Marcels, from Pittsburgh, Pa., however, made it the #1 song in America in 1961.

SAD NEWS. *Variety*, March 6, 1968

"Frankie Lymon, 26, a click disk artist as a moppet blues singer back in 1956-58, died of an apparent overdose of narcotics in the New York apartment of a friend. A GI, Lymon had come to New York to start a disk comeback with Roulette Records.

"Lymon was among the original youngsters to ride in on the rock 'n' roll cycle early in the 1950s. His big hits included "Why Do Fools Fall In Love," "Goody, Goody," and "I'm Not a Juvenile Delinquent," recorded with a combo called the Teenagers. He clicked both in rhythm and blues and pop grooves for a few years.

"As the youngster grew up and lost his precocity, he also lost impact and faded into obscurity. He was arrested a few times on assorted charges, including narcotics raps. In the last year, he claimed to have rid himself of the dope habit and had written stories about how he had kicked the habit.

"His wife survives him."

**California has had the most Miss Americas since the pageant began in 1921.**

# JUNK FOOD CONTROVERSY

*As junk food has become an integral part of American life, it has also become the focal point in issues unrelated to eating.*

## FRITOS CORN CHIPS

***Background***: Invented 1932, by Elmer Doolin. Doolin, a Texan, bought the recipe—and the whole concept of the corn chip—from a cook at a Mexican border cafe. (He paid $100 for it.) Then he began turning out the chips by hand in his mother's kitchen, ten pounds per hour. When demand increased, Doolin invented a machine that would make the chips automatically. As the company grew, it moved into larger quarters in Dallas, Texas. In 1945, the Frito Company merged with H. W. Lay and Co., Atlanta-based maker of Lay's potato chips, and achieved national distribution.

***The Controversy:*** In the '60s, Frito-Lay was accused of anti-Mexican racism (an ironic assertion, considering the origin of the product). The reason: it introduced the Frito Bandito, a mustachioed cartoon character who showed up on TV in 1967, ready to steal your Fritos Corn Chips.

In his prime, the Bandito devised some pretty sneaky ways of fleecing gringos. One commercial showed the Apollo astronauts landing on the moon. Who do you think they found there waiting for them? The Frito Bandito, standing next to a parking meter with his burro. "I ham the moon parking lot attendant," he announced. "Now if you will kindly deposit one bag of cronchy Fritos corn cheeps for the first hour..."

But after Frito-Lay decided to use him in all its commercials, the Mexican-American Anti-Defamation Committee protested publicly that the Bandito was spreading the "racist message that Mexicans are sneaky thieves." Frito vehemently denied any hidden meaning or racist intent. But several California TV stations quickly banned the commercials and the Anti-Defamation Committec announced its intention of asking the FCC for equal time.

Although he was an effective TV salesman, the Frito Bandito was ultimately withdrawn from Frito commercials.

## HOSTESS TWINKIES

***Background***: Invented in 1931 by James Dewar, manager of Continental Bakeries' Chicago factory. He envisioned the product as a way of using the company's thousands of shortcake pans (which were otherwise employed only during the strawberry season) full-time...and as a way of having a low-priced snack to sell during the Depression. The cakes were originally called Little Shortcake Fingers, but during a business trip Dewar and a friend noticed a shoe factory sign that read "Home of Twinkle Toe Shoes." Dewar had been looking for a new name for his product; his friend suggested he call it "Twinkle Fingers," which was shortened to Twinkies. The five-cent snack soon became one of Continental's best-selling items.

***The Controversy***: In 1979, a San Francisco employee named Dan White went on a rampage and killed two important politicians—Mayor George Moscone and Supervisor Harvey Milk—in City Hall. His case seemed indefensible...but in the ensuing trial White's attorney, Douglas Schmidt, did come up with a palatable defense. He blamed his client's behavior on junk food—specifically Twinkies. Psychiatrist Martin Blinder testified that White had eaten too many Twinkies, and that their high sugar content had resulted in "diminished mental capacity." It sounded preposterous, but to the shock of the grieving city, the jury bought this explanation and convicted White of voluntary manslaughter instead of murder. In San Francisco, people still refer to it as the "Twinkie defense."

## PRINGLE'S POTATO CHIPS

***Background***: The potato chip was invented in 1853 by a chef named George Crum in Saratoga Springs, New York. Apparently, a customer at the restaurant where Crum worked kept sending back French Fries, complaining that they were too thick. Finally, the exasperated Crum cut the potatoes paper-thin...and the customer loved them. "Saratoga Chips" became the specialty of the house, and ultimately a national snack.

For many years, large food companies avoided manufacturing

potato chips, despite their popularity. The reason: potato chips were hard to transport long distances without heavy breakage. And they got stale too quickly.

Then in 1969, General Mills and Proctor & Gamble each introduced "newfangled" kinds of potato chips. General Mills called theirs "Chipos." P & G called theirs "Pringle's Potato Chips."

This new product wasn't a sliced potato (as the traditional chip is), but a wafer made from "reconstituted potato granules." Each chip was made from scratch, so each could be formed in exactly the same shape and size—which meant the chips could now be designed to be stackable, and thus they could be packaged in break-proof cannisters, complete with preservatives. A food conglomerate's dream.

***The Controversy:*** Would this mean the end of the potato chip as we knew it? Potato chip manufacturers were afraid it would—so in 1970, the Potato Chip Institute (the trade organization for potato chip makers around the U.S.) went on the offensive and sued General Mills for calling their Chipos "new fashioned potato chips." Chipos, the chipmakers asserted, were not "authentic" chips, and General Mills had no right to equate them with America's classic snack. "We don't like synthetics riding on the potato chip's reputation," said Francis X. Rice, the president of the organization.

By the time the suit gathered steam, however, it was clear that the new chips would never be as popular as the old ones. So the suit was quietly dropped.

Frito-Lay, the nation's largest potato chip manufacturer, straddled the issue. They joined as a party in the Potato Chip Institute's suit, but also came out with their own new-style chip—Munchos...just in case.

## UNRELATED COMMENT

"Being in politics is like being a football coach. You have to be smart enough to understand the game, and dumb enough to think it's important."

***—Ex-Senator Eugene McCarthy***

# ELVIS' TOOTHBRUSH

*A bizarre—but true—tale of fan weirdness, from the book* How to Meet the Stars, *by Missy Laws. Published by Ross Books, Berkeley, CA.*

**THE SCENARIO:** *A rabid Elvis fan called "Sir Mordrid" and two women were visiting Las Vegas. A celebrity they met in a casino invited them "to meet my good friend Elvis."*

"The four of them went to the Hilton Hotel, where Elvis was performing two shows nightly. They entered the backstage area and confronted a mob. Sir Mordrid could feel the pounding of his heart as he grew nearer to the superstar's private dressing room.

"Because he had an enormous collection of Elvis memorabilia and had attended a vast quantity of his concerts, Sir Mordrid considered himself to be the number one fan of the legendary performer.

"Upon seeing Elvis, Sir Mordrid began to feel dizzy and got sweaty palms. In order to hide his nervous behavior, he headed for a table of food in the corner. Nonstop, he crammed lobster, finger sandwiches and strawberries into his mouth. Between bites, he could see across the room where [the celebrity] was introducing the two girls to Elvis.

"'Where's Sir Mordrid?' [the celebrity] questioned. But upon noticing him hunched over the snack table, he continued, 'Sir Mordrid, come on over. I want to introduce you to Elvis.'

"Panic struck Sir Mordrid as he almost choked on an entire sandwich. Hesitantly he walked over to his idol.

"Sir Mordrid meekly said, 'Hi,' but then, without giving Elvis a chance to speak, he chattered on, attempting to cover his anxiety. The only thing he could think of to say was a joke that he had learned the previous day. Elvis quietly listened, certain that there must be some significance to the joke if this guy insisted on telling it at what seemed to be such an inappropriate time.

[Sir Mordrid told the joke and, staring at Elvis, asked him if he knew what the punchline was.]

"Smiling, the singer answered, 'What?'

"Suddenly, Sir Mordrid was so absorbed in his own feelings of anxiety that he couldn't remember the punchline. He panicked. He could feel the lobster, finger sandwiches and strawberries threatening to come up.

"He broke away from the singer and muttered, 'Excuse me.' He sprinted towards a gentleman standing near the doorway. He pleaded, 'Do you know where the rest room is? I feel really sick!'

"The man pointed to Elvis' private bathroom and said, 'I think it's in there.' Although it was obvious that this was designated as an exclusive chamber for only Elvis, Sir Mordrid ignored this minor detail as he hurled himself inside, slamming and locking the door.

"While Sir Mordrid expelled every bit of food from his stomach, there was a knock. A voice firmly called, 'I'm sorry, but you're not allowed in there.'

"Sir Mordrid ignored this remark. After several minutes of screaming and banging on the door, the man stopped trying to get Sir Mordrid out of the rest room.

"Sir Mordrid stood in silence and noticed a disgusting taste in his mouth. Glancing at the sink, he saw a clear, oblong box engraved with the initials 'E.P.' Inside was a toothbrush. A tube of toothpaste rested behind it.

"After checking to make sure the door was indeed locked, he brushed his teeth with his idol's personal toothbrush. Afterward, he dried it off and replaced it exactly as he had found it. He returned to the party, but kept his distance from Elvis for the rest of the evening."

## ELVIS FACTS

• For one stretch of two years, the singer reportedly ate nothing but meat loaf, mashed potatoes, and tomatoes.

• His idol was General Douglas MacArthur.

• He memorized every line of dialogue from the George C. Scott film, *Patton*.

**Dream on: Every year, the average human being has about 1,500 dreams.**

# ON THE BALLOT

*There's no easier way to get your name into print than to run for office...unless you try to get a laugh at the same time. Some notable politicians' names:*

**SISTER BOOM-BOOM.** A transvestite who dresses as a nun, he/she ran for mayor of San Francsico in 1982...and received 23,121 votes.

**JELLO BIAFRA.** Lead singer of the Dead Kennedys, a San Francisco-based rock band. Ran for mayor of San Francisco in 1982.

**NONE OF THE ABOVE.** Never actually made it to the ballot, but his heart was in the right place. Luther Knox changed his name (legally) to *None of the Above* in order to give Louisianans a choice "to say no" to mainstream candidates in their 1979 gubernatorial election.

**BANANAS THE CLOWN.** Another almost-made-it...onto the ballot, that is. When Lester Johnson decided to run for a seat on the city council in Salt Lake City, he submitted this name. He was rejected, although he accurately protested that "it wouldn't be unprecedented for a clown to be in city government."

**LOUIS ABALOFIA.** It's not a weird name, and we're not even sure it's the right spelling, but Louis deserves some mention here. Running for president, he passed out leaflets bearing his official campaign photo—a picture of himself stark naked. His campaign slogan, emblazoned at the top: "I have nothing to hide."

**TARQUIN FINTIMLINBINWHIMBINLIN BUS STOP-F'TANG-F'TANG-OLE-BISCUIT BARREL.** In 1981, a new political party—the Raving Looney Society of Cambridge—nominated this candidate (a real person otherwise known as John Lewis) for a seat in the British Parliament. The media referred to him as "Mr. Tarquin Biscuit-Barrel," and more than two hundred people actually voted for him.

**In 1980, the Yellow Pages accidentally listed a Texas funeral home under frozen foods.**

# CAVEAT EATER

*By David Goines*

*The ten fundamental rules for selecting an eating place in an unfamiliar environment are simple to remember and easy to follow.*

**1.** Never eat in anything that moves, i.e., trains, airplanes, and revolving restaurants. As a corollary, never eat any food that can be purchased and consumed without leaving your car.

**2.** Never eat on the top of anything, i.e., any restaurant situated at the top of any building or structure, such as "The Top of the Mark."

**3.** Never eat in anyplace with a theme: waitresses dressed as pirates, menus die-cut in the shape of a cowboy hat, cute incomprehensible names for ordinary beverages and dishes. As a corollary, shun foods allegedly prepared by animals, elves, or pixies: Granny Goose potato chips, etc.

**4.** Never eat anyplace that serves an infinite amount of food at a fixed price.

**5.** Never eat anyplace that has a name formatted "The (adjective) (noun)," i.e., "The Hungry Hunter," "The Velvet Turtle," etc.

**6.** Eat the local product. Beef in Kansas City and Chicago, Jewish delicatessens in New York. Seafood in New Orleans. Bread, wine, and salad in San Francisco. If there is no local product, as in Salt Lake City, don't eat. Or pack a lunch.

**7.** Never eat in an ethnic restaurant in which no people of that ethnicity are eating.

**8.** Never eat anyplace called "Mom's," or incorporating the concept of motherhood into the restaurant or food product. Doubly to be avoided is the concept of grandmotherhood.

**9.** Never drink anything with more than two ingredients: Ice is an ingredient.

**10.** The quality of a restaurant is in inverse proportion to the size of its pepper grinders.

**According to *Billboard* magazine, the "Top Artist" of the '70s was Elton John.**

# JUST THE FACTS

*"Dragnet" is the most popular cop show in TV history. It spanned two generations (running from 1951 to 1959, then returning in 1967 for three seasons). Its monotoned hero, Sgt. Joe Friday, became so familiar that thirty-five years after the show debuted, Dan Ayckroyd's film parody of Friday and his exploits was one of the biggest movie hits of 1987.*

"Dragnet" played an important role in television history. It was the first realistic crime show ever to air, and the first TV show to treat law enforcement as a day-to-day job—portraying the police as normal working stiffs. Other shows like "Gangbusters" glamorized police work—but Sgt. Joe Friday wasn't colorful, didn't wear a snappy costume, wasn't even particularly interesting. He was a guy with a job to do, and he plodded through it day after day ("12:14 PM. We approached the suspect's house. It looked deserted. We rang the doorbell."). "Dragnet"'s enormous popularity inspired other police shows to take the same approach. "We couldn't have shows like 'Hill Street Blues' if it hadn't been for 'Dragnet,'" comments one TV critic.

**HOW IT STARTED:** In 1948, after struggling to break into the movies, a radio performer named Jack Webb finally landed a small part in a police thriller called *He Walked By Night*. One day during the filming, Webb was hanging around with his friend, Sgt. Marty Wynn of the L.A.P.D. (the movie's technical adviser). Wynn made a suggestion: "Jack," he said, "I can arrange for you to have access to all the cases in the L.A. police files, and maybe you could do something with them."

Wynn went on to explain that he wanted to hear a radio drama that portrayed police work honestly. No "Gangbusters" stuff. Webb insisted that "Gangbusters" was what people wanted and declined the offer.

But the more he thought about Wynn's idea, the better he liked it. About ten months after the conversation, Webb began writing an outline for this "realistic" show. He did research by accompanying Wynn and his partner in their patrol car.

In Elizabethan England, spoons were so rare that people brought their own.

When Webb had a format, characters, and a title, he made a radio audition record of the show and brought it to NBC...which signed him as a summer replacement at $150 a week, starring and directing. *Dragnet* premiered on June 3, 1949; within two years, it was the top show on radio. The jump to TV was inevitable, but Webb held out until NBC gave him $38,000 to film a pilot (instead of doing it live). The pilot aired on December 16, 1951, and the series began its official run about four weeks later. It immediately became the #2 show on television (behind "I Love Lucy"), and remained popular for 11 years.

## INSIDE FACTS

**Smoky places.** The early '50s shows were sponsored by Chesterfield cigarettes, and Webb and others in the cast often took time to elaborately light up and smoke, to plug the sponsor's product. The '60s shows are much less smoky.

**Police Disguise.** Each episode of *Dragnet* was based on an actual case. It was selected from the files provided to Webb by a special detail of three L.A.P.D. officers. After Webb picked the case, he adapted it to a script, altering enough details to make it unrecognizable—even to the criminal—but retaining the basic facts.

**It's only TV, lady.** Sgt. Friday was so real to the public that people often went to L.A.P.D. headquarters to meet him. At first the department was at a loss about how to deal with them. But later, they came up with a standard answer: "Sorry, it's Joe's day off."

**Sgt. Everyman.** Webb on the name: "Some (people) have said I was thinking of Robinson Crusoe and his man Friday. Or that I thought of it on Friday. I really didn't know where it came from, except that I wanted a name that had no connotations at all. He could be Jewish, or Greek, or English, or anything. He could be all men to all people in their living room."

**Friday's return.** "Dragnet" was going to return as a 1967 TV movie-of-the-week. But the film came off so well that it was used as a pilot for a new series instead. Retitled "Dragnet '67," it became a virtual parody of itself, with anti-drug preaching, and embarrassing Hollywood hippies. It was "camp" humor to much of its audience.

**There is enough phosphorus inside you to make about 250 matchheads.**

# RUMORS

*Why do people believe wild, unsubstantiated stories? According to some psychologists, "rumors make things simpler than they really are." And while people won't believe just anything, it's surprising what stories have flourished in the past. Many of these tales are still in circulation today....*

**RUMOR:** McDonald's adds earthworms to its hamburger meat.
**HOW IT SPREAD:** Apparently the stories began in Atlanta in 1979 and were originally aimed at a competitor, Wendy's. "But," as a psychologist commented, "industrial rumors tend to gravitate to the industry leader." Another possibility: an article in *Reader's Digest* about worm farms mentioned that such farms tend to attract animals that like to eat worms, making the farm "a veritable McDonald's" for such animals.
**WHAT HAPPENED:** To fight it, McDonald's held a press conference in Atlanta and produced a letter from the U.S. Secretary of Agriculture stating that the burgers were, and always had been, 100% beef.

**THE RUMOR:** Sweaters at K-Mart are infested with hatching baby snakes.
**HOW IT SPREAD:** The story—that a shopper was trying on sweaters, felt something prick her skin, and discovered she'd been bitten by a rare poisonous snake from Taiwan—was probably started by a competitor.
**WHAT HAPPENED:** K-Mart has chosen to ignore it.

**THE RUMOR:** Mikey, the cute kid in the Life cereal commercials, died by exploding after ingesting a combination of "Pop Rocks" candy and soda pop.
**HOW IT SPREAD:** Unknown.
**WHAT HAPPENED:** This rumor was so prevalant that Life Cereal redesigned their box to include a photo of several kids

and Mikey, now grown up. The object was to identify Mikey, and of course, reassure us that he hadn't exploded after all.

**THE RUMOR:** A teenage girl was squeezed to death while sitting in the bathtub in cold water trying to shrink her new Levis.
**HOW IT SPREAD:** Unknown.
**WHAT HAPPENED:** No action taken, but a great story.

**THE RUMOR:** A woman attempted to dry her poodle in a microwave oven and the dog exploded.
**HOW IT SPREAD:** A classic example of how a rumor reflects fears, this one stemming from concerns about new technology.
**WHAT HAPPENED:** The public's awareness of microwave ovens was increased, and as people realized the story was just a rumor, they relaxed and accepted the product as safe.

**THE RUMOR:** Bubble Yum gum, made by Life Savers, had spider eggs in it.
**HOW IT SPREAD:** Apparently this story began in New York City, where kids began telling each other not to buy Bubble Yum because it contained the aforementioned additive.
**WHAT HAPPENED:** Life Savers at first paid little attention to the story, but a senior vice president wanted to find out how the story began, so he ordered a phone survey and asked consumers and their parents if they'd heard the rumors. He next checked with retailers to see what they knew....In fact, many were upset and wanted the company to reassure them. In the end, Life Savers published a full-page newspaper ad which said, "Somebody is telling your kids very bad lies about a very good gum." It worked, and the story died. Bubble Yum maintained its position as the #1 selling bubble gum.

**THE RUMOR:** Another Soviet nuclear accident—similar to the 1986 disaster at Chernobyl—occurred.
**HOW IT SPREAD:** Apparently it originated in either Stockholm or Moscow and reached world financial markets.
**WHAT HAPPENED:** The dollar surged in value, but only temporarily. The following day, February 4, 1988, the *Wall*

**The largest airline in the world is Aeroflot, the official Soviet airline.**

*Street Journal* reported that the "accident" was just a rumor. Nonetheless, its effect on world economic markets was undeniable. When the truth became known, the dollar then eased back to its relative value against other currencies.

**THE RUMOR:** A leper worked in the factory where Spud cigarettes—the first king size menthol filter brand—were manufactured in the 1940s.
**HOW IT STARTED:** Unknown.
**WHAT HAPPENED:** Within six months, the brand vanished from stores.

**THE RUMOR:** Procter & Gamble's company trademark is a satanic symbol signifying a pact with the devil.
**HOW IT STARTED:** Surfaced in 1980. Refers to the profile of a man-in-the-moon and 13 stars in the trademark, which was created in 1850.
**WHAT HAPPENED:** In June of 1982, P & G received 15,000 telephone inquiries. The company responded by filing lawsuits against individuals linked to the story and recruiting religious leaders, including Rev. Jerry Falwell, to refute the rumor and publicly declare the company "pure."

**THE RUMOR:** Xerox copy machine toner gives you cancer.
**HOW IT STARTED:** 1978, a research team found that extracts of a copier toner caused mutations in bacteria cells and another team reported mutations in mouse cells. The story was picked up by a newspaper which inflated the results from mutagenic to cancer-causing. Though the toner was not Xerox's, the company's name became associated with the findings. An Australian newspaper featured the headline, "Tens of Thousands at Risk."
**WHAT HAPPENED:** Thousands of customers called Xerox. Every query was answered by company representatives. Health records of 60,000 Xerox employees were reviewed for cancer. A Xerox Vice president presented facts in defense of his company to the Environmental Protection Agency, which resulted in an EPA news release assuring copier users not to be concerned.

# ELVIS: WAR ON DRUGS

*The secret life of "The King" included a secret visit to the FBI and a desire to meet "the greatest living American," J. Edgar Hoover. Totally bizarre.*

After Elvis Presley's death in 1977 we learned about his tragic drug problems. Coroners found a veritable pharmacy in the King of Rock 'n' Roll's bloodstream.

The revelations of Elvis' drug abuse were shocking to his loyal fans but not to insiders. Presley's bodyguard, Red West, described him as a "walking pharmaceutical shop who took pills to get up, pills to go to sleep, and pills to go out on the job."

The supreme irony of his drug habit is that Presley, himself, was a dedicated antidrug crusader. According to Penny Stallings book, "Rock 'n' Roll Confidential": "At one time he'd even turned his home into an arsenal, with the idea of meting out backwoods justice to local drug pushers whose names he'd obtained from the Memphis narcs. He sometimes had to be physically restrained from carrying out his plan."

The most bizarre twist in this story is Presley's visit to Washington D.C. in late 1970. During his visit, Presley (who was already addicted to barbiturates and amphetamines) received a special agent's badge of the Bureau of Narcotics and Dangerous Drugs from then-President Richard Nixon.

After his meeting with Nixon, Presley requested a personal audience with the man he considered "the greatest living American": J. Edgar Hoover. Thanks to the Freedom of Information Act, the files of this event are now available.

From the available data it seems that the FBI—always conscious of its image—was quite concerned with Elvis' visit. In an official memorandum dated 12-30-70, the question of whether Presley should meet the Director was discussed. "During the height of his popularity," the memo stated, "during the latter part of the 1950s and early 1960s, his gyrations while performing were the subject of considerable criticism by the public and comment in the press."

**An African ostrich egg weighs about 30 lbs. A 200-lb. man can stand on it without breaking it.**

The memo concluded: "Presley's sincerity and good intentions notwithstanding, he is certainly not the type of individual whom the Director would wish to meet. It is noted at the present time he is wearing his hair down to his shoulders and indulges in wearing all sorts of exotic dress."

Although a meeting with Hoover was ruled out (Presley's entourage was told he was out of town), the FBI did arrange for a special tour of their facilities on December 31, 1970.

The following is an account of his tour from FBI files:

"Presley...and six individuals who provide security for Presley visited FBI Headquarters and were afforded a very special tour of our facilities in accordance with plans approved by the Director.

"Regrets were expressed to Presley and his party in connection with their request to meet the Director. Presley indicated that he has long been an admirer of Mr. Hoover, and has read material prepared by the Director including 'Masters of Deceit,' 'A Study of Communism' as well as 'J. Edgar Hoover on Communism.' Presley noted that in his opinion no one has ever done as much for his country as has Mr. Hoover, and that he, Presley, considers the Director 'the greatest living American.' He spoke most favorably of the Bureau.

"Despite his rather bizarre personal appearance, Presley seemed a serious minded individual who expressed concern over some of the problems confronting our country, particularly those involving young people. In this regard, in private comments made following his tour, he indicated that he, Presley, is the 'living proof that America is the land of opportunity' since he rose from truck driver to prominent entertainer almost overnight. He said that he spends as much time as his schedule permits informally talking to young people and discussing what they consider to be their problems with them. Presley said that his long hair and unusual apparel were merely tools of his trade and provided him access to and rapport with many people particularly on college campuses who considered themselves 'anti-establishment.' Presley said that while he has a limited education, he has been able to command a certain amount of respect and attention from this segment of the population and in an informal way point out the errors of their ways. He advised that he does not consider himself competent to address large groups but much rather prefers small gatherings in community centers and the like, where he makes himself accessible for talks and discussions regarding the evils of narcotics and other problems of concern to teenagers and other young people.

"Following their tour, Presley privately advised that he has volunteered his services to the President in connection with the narcotics problem and that Mr. Nixon had responded by furnishing him with an Agent's badge of the Bureau of Narcotics and Dangerous Drugs. Presley was carrying this badge in his pocket and displayed it.

"Presley advised that he wished the Director to be aware that he, Presley, from time to time is approached by individuals and groups in and outside the entertainment business whose motives and goals he is convinced are not in the best interests of this country and who seek to have him lend his name to their questionable activities. In this regard, he volunteered to make such information available to the Bureau on a confidential basis whenever it came to his attention. He further indicated that he wanted the Director to know that should the Bureau ever have any need of his services in any way that he would be delighted to be of assistance.

"Presley indicated that he is of the opinion that the Beatles laid the groundwork for many of the problems we are having with young people by their filthy unkempt appearances and suggestive music while entertaining in this country during the early and middle 1960s. He advised that the Smothers Brothers, Jane Fonda, and other persons in the entertainment industry of their ilk have a lot to answer for in the hereafter for the way they have poisoned young minds by disparaging the United States in their public statements and unsavory activities...

"He noted that he can be contacted any time through his Memphis address and that because of problems he has had with people tampering with his mail, such correspondence should be addressed to him under the pseudonym, Colonel Jon Burrows."

The file concludes: "Presley did give the impression of being a sincere, young man who is conscious of the many problems confronting this country. In view of his unique position in the entertainment business, his favorable comments concerning the

**A leopon is a cross between a leopard and a lion. Such creatures really exist.**

Director and the Bureau, and his offer to be of assistance as well as the fact that he has been recognized by the Junior Chamber of Commerce and the President, it is felt that a letter from the Director would be in order."

## LITTLE-KNOWN FACTS ABOUT J. EDGAR HOOVER

•Hoover wanted to be president, and believed he could unseat FDR in 1936.

•He had FBI agents conduct a top-secret, unofficial poll in the South and Southwest, where he thought he had the strongest support. "He's a great man," the agents were told to say. "Many people think we'd be better off if Hoover were president." Hoover was shocked to discover that many law enforcement chiefs didn't even want him to continue as director of the FBI.

•Hoover gave up chasing the presidency, and focused his sights on attorney general instead. He planned to use that position as a stepping-stone to become a justice of the Supreme Court. To achieve this goal, he surreptitiously backed and assisted Thomas Dewey in his presidential race against Harry Truman in 1948. Dewey lost.

•He assisted Richard Nixon in his race against JFK in 1960, supplying sensitive data to Nixon for the debates. Nixon lost.

•Hoover once told a top lieutenant that he'd never married "because God had made a woman like Eleanor Roosevelt."

•Whether that's true or not, he rarely fraternized with women, and he and his top aide, Clyde Tolson, went everywhere together.

•In his 48 years with the FBI, Hoover never made an arrest or conducted an investigation.

•Hoover never once left America while he was in charge of the FBI.

•According to a top aide, Hoover didn't even know how to use a gun.

# GROUCHO SEZ...

*A few choice words from the master.*

"I must say I find television very educational. The minute somebody turns it on I go into the library and read a good book."

"Please accept my resignation. I don't want to belong to any club that will accept me as a member."

"I didn't like the play, but then I saw it under adverse conditions—the curtain was up."

"Dig trenches? With our men being killed off like flies? There isn't time to dig trenches. We'll have to buy them ready made."

"Do you suppose I could buy back my introduction to you?"

"I've worked myself up from nothing to a state of extreme poverty."

*Mrs. Teasdale*: "He's had a change of heart."
*Firefly [Groucho]*: "A lot of good that'll do him. He's still got the same face."

"Military intelligence is a contradiction in terms."

"Any man who says he can see through a woman is missing a lot."

"A man is as young as the woman he feels."

"She got her good looks from her father—he's a plastic surgeon."

"There's one way to find out if a man is honest—ask him. If he says 'Yes,' you know he is a crook."

[Feeling patient's pulse] "Either he's dead, or my watch has stopped."

"Age is not a particularly interesting subject. Anyone can get old. All you have to do is live long enough."

"Send two dozen roses to Room 424 and put 'Emily, I love you' on the back of the bill."

# WORD PLAY

*What do these familiar phrases really mean? Etymologists have researched them and come up with these explanations.*

**Fly Off the Handle**
*Meaning:* To get irrationally angry.
*Background:* Refers to axe heads, which, in the days before mass merchandising, were sometimes fastened poorly to their handles. If one flew off while being used, it was a dangerous situation...with unpredictable results.

**Get a Bad Break**
*Meaning*: To be unlucky.
*Background*: Refers to the game of pool, which begins with a player hitting the cue ball into the rest of the balls and "breaking" them apart (separating them). If the player gets a good break, he pockets several balls. If it's a bad break, he gets nothing. Other terms: "Gets all the breaks," "them's the breaks," etc.

**Peeping Tom**
*Meaning*: Someone who looks in the windows of people's homes.
*Background*: From the legend of Lady Godiva, who rode naked through the streets of Coventry in order to get her husband, Lord Leofric, to reduce taxes. She requested that the citizens stay inside and close their shutters while she rode. Everyone did "except the town tailor, Tom, who peeped through the shutters."

**High on the Hog**
*Meaning*; Luxurious, prosperous.
*Background*: The tastiest parts of a hog are its upper parts. If you're living high on the hog, you've got the best it has to offer.

**Pull the Wool Over Someone's Eyes**
*Meaning:* Fool someone
*Background:* "Goes back to the days when all gentlemen wore powdered wigs like the ones still worn by the judges in British courts. The word wool was then a popular, joking term for hair....The expression 'Pull the wool over his eyes' came from

the practice of tilting a man's wig over his eyes, so that he'd be unable to see what was going on."

**Hooker**
*Meaning*: A prostitute.
*Background*: Although occasionally used before the Civil War, its widespread popularity can probably be traced to General Joseph Hooker, a Union soldier who was well-known for the liquor and whores in his camp. He was ultimately demoted, and Washington prostitutes were jokingly referred to as "Hooker's Division."

**To Talk Turkey**
*Meaning*: To speak frankly
*Background*: Derived from a popular, if demeaning, joke in Colonial America:
"A white man and an Indian went out hunting together, agreeing to divide whatever they bagged equally. At the end of the day, they had two crows and two turkeys. 'You can have whichever you like,' the white man told his companion—'Either I'll take the turkeys and you take the crows, or you take the crows and I'll take the turkeys.' The Indian demurred, saying, 'You talk all turkey for you, but you not talk turkey to me.'"

**Rack Your Brain**
*Meaning*: Think hard
Background: Refers to a Medieval instrument of torture, the rack, on which people were stretched until—in the worst cases—their limbs were pulled off. When you rack your brain, you subject yourself to a sort of mental torture, stretching it as far as it will go.

**Let the Cat Out of the Bag**
*Meaning:* Reveal the truth
*Background*: Refers to con game practiced at country fairs in old England. "A trickster would try to palm off on an unwary bumpkin a cat in a burlap bag, claiming it was a suckling pig." If the victim figured out the trick and insisted on seeing the merchandise, the cat had to be let out of the bag.

**The earliest known board game was used around 3,000 B.C. It is an ancestor of backgammon.**

# TOY ORIGINS, PART II

*More stories about America's favorite playthings.*

**TWISTER.** The first game in the history of the American toy industry "to turn the human body into a vital component of play," enjoyed instant popularity when Milton Bradley introduced it in 1966. Why? TV and sex.

When it first came out, Bradley's PR firm brought Twister to the Tonight Show and showed it to Johnny Carson's writers. They thought it was hilarious, and promised to get it on the show right away.

They were true to their word. Carson's guest that night was Eva Gabor, and when millions of viewers saw the two glamorous celebrities climbing all over each other as they played the game on national television, the public understood exactly what Twister was really about—SEX. The next day, toy stores were flooded with demands for the game.

That year, over 3 million games were sold—more than ten times the amount that Milton Bradley anticipated. It became the most popular new game of the '60s, and is still selling over twenty years later.

**BINGO.** In 1929, a tired, depressed toy salesman named Edwin Lowe set out on a night-time drive from Atlanta, Georgia to Jacksonville, Florida. On the way he noticed the bright lights of a carnival; he decided to stop to investigate. Lowe found only one concession open—a tent full of people seated at tables, each with a hand-stamped, numbered card and a pile of beans. As the emcee called out numbers, players put beans on the corresponding squares on their cards. If they got five beans in a row, they won a Kewpie doll. The concessionaire called his game Beano. Lowe was so impressed that he tried it at his own home, where one young winner became so excited that she stammered out "B-b-b-ingo!" instead of "Beano." So that's what Lowe called it.

**Streaking record: 1,200 college students streaked at the same time in Boulder, Colo., 1974.**

# HOLY PUNCTUATION!

*What's the difference between good and evil? Maybe just a little grammar. The following are excerpts from real church bulletins, collected by B.R.I.'s Les Boies.*

"This afternoon there will be a meeting in the south and north ends of the church. Children will be baptized at both ends."

"Tuesday, at 4 PM, there will be an ice cream social. All ladies giving milk, come early."

"Wednesday, the Ladies Liturgy Society will meet. Mrs. Johnson will sing, 'Put Me In My Little Bed,' accompanied by the Pastor."

"Thursday, at 5 PM, there will be a meeting of the Little Mothers Club. All those wishing to become little mothers, please meet the pastor in his study."

"This being Easter Sunday, we will ask Mrs. Johnson to come forward and lay an egg on the altar."

"The service will close with 'Little Drops of Water.' One of the ladies will start quietly and the rest of the congregation will join in."

"On Sunday, a special collection will be taken to defray the expense of the new carpet. All those wishing to do something on the new carpet, come forward and get a piece of paper."

"The ladies of the church have cast off clothing of every kind and they may be seen in the basement on Friday afternoon."

"A bean supper will be held Saturday evening in the church basement. Music will follow."

"The rosebud on the altar this morning is to announce the birth of David Alan Belser, the sin of Rev. and Mrs. Julius Belser."

"Altar flowers are given to the glory of God in memory of her mother."

**Life span: An average elephant lives for about 55 years.**

# MYTH AMERICA

*All it takes to create a widely accepted myth is a popular "historical" movie or television show... or a damn good liar, like Davy Crockett*

**The Myth:** Davy Crockett was an American hero, a clean-cut frontier superman who:

- "Killed him a b'ar when he was only three"
- Was the greatest Indian fighter of his day
- Could shoot a rifle better than any man alive
- Was a respected Congressman who considered running for president
- Was the last man to die at the Alamo

**Background:** Much of this "information" was taken from Crockett's autobiography and a series of Crockett *Almanacs* which were published between 1835 and 1856.

But it was Walt Disney who made the legend stick. In December, 1954 he unveiled a TV mini-series about Crockett with an episode called "Davy Crockett, Indian fighter." The folk hero became an instant national fad, surprising even Uncle Walt. In a matter of months, merchants sold millions of dollars worth of official Davy Crockett coonskin caps, bubble-gum cards, toy guns, fringed jackets, etc. Fourteen-million copies of Crockett's life story were sold. The Davy Crockett theme song hit the national top 20 four times in one year, with four different versions. Sample verse: "Fought single-handed through the Injun War, Till the Creeks was whipped and peace was in store, And while he was handlin' this risky chore, Made hisself a legend forevermore."

**The Truth: Crockett was:**

- A drunk who deserted his wife and children
- A "scout" who avoided going into battle against the Indians by hiring a substitute
- A congressman with one of the worst absentee records in history.

**In 1980, a secretary at Deere & Co. was fired "for making a Xerox copy of her bottom."**

The only thing that seems to be consistent with the legend is that Crockett did die at the Alamo. But that, says author Paul Sann in *Fads, Follies, and Delusions*, was "more bungling and stupidity than heroism."

During the Crockett craze, several journalists researched the new American hero. Some sample comments:

"He was never king of anything, except maybe the Tennessee Tall Tales and Bourbon Samplers' Association. When he claimed that he had shot 105 bear in nine months, his fellow tipplers refused to believe a word of it, on the grounds that Davy couldn't count that high."

**—John Fisher, *Harper's* magazine.**

"He was out on the frontier only because it was an easier place to live than in a home with a growing brood. Davy had a flock of children and he left them and never bothered with any of them again. He set the cause of married life back about 200 years." **—Harry Golden, syndicated columnist**

"Davy grew up to be a very brave young man, who would bear any hardship to escape a routine day's work."

**—Murray Kempton, *New York Post***

Ironically Fess Parker, who played the lead in the Disney version of Crockett's life—and became a star as a result—was also a bit of a fraud. Says Leonard Mosley in *Disney's World*, "Parker hated Wild West roles. As in the case of most minor Hollywood actors, hunger had sometimes forced him to play in Western films, and he found he was allergic to horses and loathed the clothing cowboys wore. His...lip curled in derision and distaste when he saw the drawings of Davy Crockett's outfit.....But eventually hunger won out, and Parker signed up for the film. They had to teach him how to ride a horse, first, and do it without having him come down with a case of hives. His leather breeches were specially sprayed before he wore them, and when he was out of camera range he shied away from them as if they were a bunch of poison ivy, swearing they would give him "crotch rot." Parker later played TV's Daniel Boone for 6 years.

**Grace Slick named her child "god" with a small "g" because "we've got to be humble."**

# DEAD MAN'S CURVE

*This is one of rock's classic disaster songs. But it's the only one that was actually fulfilled by the man who wrote it.*

Dead Man's Curve" was a top ten hit for Jan and Dean in 1964. But it became even more famous when Jan—who co-wrote the song with Los Angeles disc jockey Roger Christian—actually had an accident that paralleled the crash in the song. An eerie prediction? A simple coincidence? A cursed song? No one will ever know.

But we do know the story behind the song:

**ROGER CHRISTIAN**: "Dead Man's Curve is in Los Angeles, right near UCLA, on Sunset Boulevard. It's a downhill, winding turn that's bowed to the outside, so centrifugal force, comin' down the hill, will throw you into the opposite lane if you don't watch it. And that's just what happened. I was a deejay at KRLA in Los Angeles, and I was reading the news one night. I read that Mel Blanc had been seriously injured and he was on the verge of death, from an accident where he was struck at Dead Man's curve.

"Blanc was like my idol because he was a voiceover man and could do all kinds of voices [note: Blanc was the voice of Bugs Bunny, Porky Pig, etc.]. I watched the news copy every hour to see how he was doing; they didn't think he was gonna live—but he did. He was in the hospital for six months.

"I thought someone ought to write a song about Dead Man's Curve. I said, 'Well, we ought to make it into a race,' because Jan and I were really into racing. Every Saturday night we'd meet and go to Sunset and Vine...and we'd race. I had a Jaguar XKE, and Jan had a Stingray—the same cars that are in the song."

The weirdest part of the story is that Roger didn't intend for "Dead Man's Curve" to be a "disaster" song at all—he wanted the race to end in a tie.

But Jan *insisted* that the song end with a disastrous crash. And in real life, shortly after, Jan was paralyzed in a serious car accident...on Dead Man's Curve.

# I LOVE LUCY

*I Love Lucy ran from 1951 to 1957. It was the #1 show in America for 4 of those 6 years.*

**HOW IT STARTED:** In 1948, Lucille Ball became a radio star in the CBS series, *My Favorite Husband.* It co-starred Richard Denning as her spouse, a Midwestern bank president.

Two years later, CBS decided to move the show to TV, with Denning continuing as her "husband." But to their surprise, Lucy refused. She insisted that the only way she'd do a TV series was if her real-life husband—Desi Arnaz—was her co-star. CBS balked. "Who," they asked, "would believe that a redheaded movie star and a Cuban bandleader were married?" But Lucy was determined; she thought it was the only way to save her marriage.

To prove to CBS that the public would accept them together, Lucy and Desi put together a vaudeville act and went on the road, performing live. They were billed as *Desi Arnaz and Band with Lucille Ball.* They got rave reviews in New York and Chicago—and interest from NBC.

CBS didn't want to let Lucy get away, so they capitulated and half-heartedly authorized a pilot. At first they couldn't find a sponsor for it, and had practically given up on the project when Phillip Morris cigarettes finally agreed to back it.

But there was still a problem. The sponsors wanted the show done live in New York, (where the biggest audience was), and the Arnazes refused to leave Hollywood. They came up with a unique (for the time) compromise: each program was filmed in front of a live audience in California, then edited and transported to the East Coast for a "live" broadcast. This made it the first TV series ever filmed, and gave us *I Love Lucy* reruns.

**INSIDE FACTS:**

**Sorry about that, chief.** On January 20, 1953, two important events were televised: Lucy's birth to Little Ricky in the "Lucy Goes to the Hospital" episode of *I Love Lucy*, and Dwight D.

Eisenhower's inauguration. Lucy outdrew Ike by 15 million viewers—44 million to 29 million.

**Good timing.** When *I Love Lucy* premiered, Lucy was 40, Desi was 35, Vivian Vance was 39 and William Frawley was 64.

**Out of sight.** After the success of *I Love Lucy*, Desi changed hats again, this time from actor to producer. One of his productions, *The Untouchables*, put mobster Al Capone in such a bad light that a contract was reportedly put out on his life. After selling his share of Desilu to Lucy for $2,552,975 in 1962 (she sold it for $17 million just five years later), he retired to a ranch east of Los Angeles to raise thoroughbred horses. He died in 1986.

**Name Game.** Coming up with a name for the program was a struggle. Sponsors wanted to call it The Lucille Ball Show, but Lucy wanted Desi's name on it, too. They finally agreed that *I Love Lucy* was acceptable, since the "I" referred to Desi, and it came first in the title. Clever solution to a potentially volatile problem.

**Paley's folly.** Bill Paley, president of CBS, thought there was absolutely no hope for a series about a dingbat redhead and her Cuban bandleader husband. So he cheerfully handed over all future rights for *I Love Lucy* to Desilu Productions.

**Star Wars.** While all appeared calm to viewers at home, squabbles on the set were common. Lucy and Desi's tiffs were the stuff of legends, while William Frawley and Vivian Vance really couldn't stand each other. Vance couldn't see why anyone would believe she was married to "that old man"; Frawley often referred to Vance as "that sack of doorknobs."

**Red-dy Or Not:** During the McCarthy "red scares" in the early '50s, Lucille Ball was accused of being a communist by columnist Walter Winchell, who discovered that she had once joined a leftist organization in the '30s. Believe it or not, this revelation actually threatened her career. Desi went to her defense: "The only thing red about Lucy," he responded, "is her hair. And that's not even real." Lucy is not a true redhead.

**It's the Law: In Washington, D.C. no building can be taller than the Capitol.**

# THE 20-YEAR PRESIDENTIAL CURSE

*From 1840 to 1980, every president elected in a year that ended in zero died while in office. Only Ronald Reagan managed to escape the presidential curse—and he barely survived an assassination attempt.*

**THE VICTIMS:** Seven presidents of the United States: William Henry Harrison (the ninth president), Abraham Lincoln (the sixteenth president), James Garfield (the twentieth president), William McKinley (the twenty-fifth president), Warren G. Harding (the twenty-ninth president), Franklin D. Roosevelt (the thirty-second president), and John F. Kennedy (the thirty-fifth president).

**THE CIRCUMSTANCES:**

- Harrison was elected in 1840. He died of pneumonia on April 4, 1841, one month after taking office.
- Lincoln was elected in 1860. He was assassinated during his second term, in 1865.
- Garfield was elected in 1880. He was shot by a deranged man as he boarded a train in July, 1881. He died two months later.
- McKinley was elected to his second term in 1900. He was assassinated in 1901 by an anarchist who "wanted to kill a ruler."
- Harding was elected in 1920. He supposedly died of pneumonia in 1923, but it is suspected that he was poisoned.
- FDR was elected to his third term in 1940. He died of a cerebral hemorrhage, shortly after being elected to his 4th term.
- JFK was elected in 1960. He was assassinated in Dallas in 1963.

**UNANSWERED QUESTIONS:** How is it possible that for the last 120 years, *all* of the presidents elected during a year ending in zero died while in office?

**POSSIBLE CONCLUSIONS:**
No rational ones. A curse? A cosmic sick joke?

**In 1977, a 13-year-old boy discovered a tooth growing on his left foot.**

# NAME THAT FOOD

*We take these household names for granted, but they had to start somewhere. Here's where.*

**Aunt Jemima:** Charles Rutt invented America's first pancake mix, but it bombed without a catchy name. One night in 1889, he saw a blackface vaudeville show featuring a tune called *Aunt Jemima*—which was sung by an actor in drag. Somehow, that inspired the image of Southern hospitality Rutt was looking for...and it worked. Instant success.

**Spam Luncheon Meat:** Combines the SP from spice and the AM from ham.

**Baby Ruth candy bar:** Most people think this was inspired by baseball's Babe Ruth. Not true. Originally called Kandy Kake, it was renamed in the 1920s to honor a contemporary celebrity—ex-President Grover Cleveland's daughter, Ruth, the first child born in the White House, and known to the public as "Baby Ruth" despite the fact she was in her late twenties. Within a few years, it was the best-selling candy in America. Footnote: N.Y. Yankee Babe Ruth once tried marketing his own brand of candy, *Babe Ruth's Home Run Candy*; the Curtiss Candy Co. took him to court and enjoined him from using his own name.

**Tootsie Roll:** Leo Hirschfield, an Austrian immigrant, originally hand-rolled the candies for his daughter, Tootsie.

**Crackerjacks:** This unnamed combination of peanuts, popcorn and sugar had been around since the 1870s, but was bulk-shipped in wooden crates; when it arrived in stores, it would be stuck together in massive lumps. In 1890, the company finally licked the problem with a new sugar-coating process. A salesman tasted it and exclaimed "That's cracker jack!" The

**In Switzerland, it is against the law to slam your car door.**

phrase was slang at the time for something great or excellent.

**Chef Boy-ar-dee Spaghetti & Meatballs:** Boy-ar-dee is a phonetic spelling of the inventor's name—Hector Boiardi. An Italian immigrant and restauranteur, Boiardi devised the recipe in a small room above his Cleveland restaurant in 1929. His picture still appears on the label.

**Oreo Cookies:** Oreo means *hill* in Greek. The original version of the cookie was mound-shaped, not flat.

**Fig Newtons:** In 1895, a new machine was installed at a Massachusetts cookie company called the Kennedy Biscuit Works. Among the machine's capabilities: it could wrap cookie dough around jam. The first jam the company tried it with just happened to be "made from figs." And since their policy was to name their products after neighboring towns, Newton, Mass. was honored in the title. Hence *Fig Newtons*.

**Wonder Bread:** Introduced after W.W.I.; it was the successor to *Mary Maid*, a popular brand of bread manufactured by the Taggart Baking Company of Indianapolis, Indiana. They wanted to maintain the appeal of their previous product, and the name *Wonder* filled the bill—it was easy to remember, and implied "goodness." Footnote: the balloons on the wrapper were inspired by the International Balloon Race, held at the Indianapolis Speedway. A Taggart vice president saw the sky filled with multi-colored balloons and decided to incorporate them into a package design.

**Coca Cola:** Named for two of its original ingredients—coca leaves (yes, the ones that give us cocaine), and Kola nuts.

**Budweiser Beer:** In the 1870s, German-born Adolphus Busch and his partner produced a light-colored beer, inspired by a beer they'd seen brewed in Budweis, Czechoslovakia.

**The geographical center of the North American continent: Rugby, North Dakota.**

# OFF TO SEE THE WIZARD

*The original* Wizard of Oz *is one of the most popular children's series ever. L. Frank Baum wrote the first one in 1901, perhaps as a political allegory (see "The Politics of Oz," elsewhere in this book). It was so popular that he wound up writing several more. In modern America, the book's long-term popularity is guaranteed by the lasting appeal of the 1939 film starring Judy Garland. These excerpts are from the original manuscript of* The Wizard of Oz.

**ON THE ROAD THROUGH THE FOREST**

"Tell me something about yourself and the country you came from," said the Scarecrow, when Dorothy had finished her dinner. So she told him all about Kansas, and how gray everything was there, and how the cyclone had carried her to this queer Land of Oz.

The Scarecrow listened carefully, and said, "I cannot understand why you should wish to leave this beautiful country and go back to the dry, gray place you call Kansas."

"That is because you have no brains," answered the girl. "No matter how dreary and gray our homes are, we people of flesh and blood would rather live there than in any other country, be it ever so beautiful. There is no place like home."

The Scarecrow sighed.

"Of course I cannot understand it," he said. "If your heads are stuffed with straw, like mine, you would probably all live in the beautiful places, and then Kansas would have no people at all. It is fortunate for Kansas that you have brains."...

**THE SCARECROW**

"It was a lonely life to lead, for I had nothing to think of, having been made only the day before. Many crows and other birds flew into the cornfield, but as soon as they saw me they flew away again, thinking I was a Munchkin; and this pleased me and made me feel that I was quite an important person. By and by an old crow flew near me, and after looking at me carefully he perched upon my shoulder and said:

"'I wonder if that farmer thought to fool me in this clumsy manner. Any crow of sense could see that you are only stuffed with straw.' Then he hopped down at my feet and ate all the corn he wanted. The other birds, seeing he was not harmed by me, came to eat the corn too, so in a short time there was a great flock of them about me.

"I felt sad at this, for it showed I was not such a good Scarecrow after all; but the old crow comforted me, saying, 'If you only had brains in your head you would be as good a man as any of them, and a better man than some of them. Brains are the only things worth having in this world, no matter whether one is a crow or a man.'

"After the crows had gone I thought this over, and decided I would try hard to get some brains. By good luck, you came along and pulled me off the stake, and from what you say I am sure the Great Oz will give me brains as soon as we get to the Emerald City."

"I hope so," said Dorothy earnestly, "since you seem anxious to have them."

"Oh, yes. I am anxious," returned the Scarecrow. "It is such an uncomfortable feeling to know one is a fool."...

**THE TIN WOODMAN**

"My head is quite empty," answered the Woodman. "But once I had brains, and a heart also. So, having tried them both, I should much rather have a heart."

"And why is that?" asked the Scarecrow.

"I will tell you my story, and then you will know."

So, while they were walking through the forest, the Tin Woodman told the following story:

"I was born the son of a woodman who chopped down trees in the forest and sold the wood for a living. When I grew up I too became a woodchopper, and after my father died I took care of my old mother as long as she lived. Then I made up my mind that instead of living alone I would marry, so that I might not become lonely.

"There was one of the Munchkin girls who was so beautiful that I soon grew to love her with all my heart. She, on her part, promised to marry me as soon as I could earn enough money

**In the early '80s, a toad was discovered that meows instead of croaking.**

to build a better house for her. So I set to work harder than ever. But the girl lived with an old woman who did not want her to marry anyone, for she was so lazy she wished the girl to remain with her and do the cooking and the housework. So the old woman went to the Wicked Witch of the East, and promised her two sheep and a cow if she would prevent the marriage. Thereupon the Wicked Witch enchanted my ax, and when I was chopping away at my best one day, for I was anxious to get the new house and my wife as soon as possible, the ax slipped all at once and cut off my left leg.

"This at first seemed a great misfortune, for I knew a one-legged man could not do very well as a wood-chopper. So I went to a tinsmith and had him make me a new leg out of tin. The leg worked very well, once I was used to it. But my action angered the Wicked Witch of the East, for she had promised the old woman I should not marry the pretty Munchkin girl. When I began chopping again, my ax slipped and cut off my right leg. Again I went to the tinner, and again he made me a leg out of tin. After this the enchanted ax cut off my arms, one after the other; but, nothing daunted me, I had them replaced with tin ones. The Wicked Witch then made the ax slip and cut off my head, and at first I thought that was the end of me. But the tinner happened to come along, and he made me a new head out of tin.

"I thought I had beaten the Wicked Witch then, and I worked harder than ever; but I little knew how cruel my enemy could be. She thought of a new way to kill my love for the beautiful Munchkin maiden, and made my ax slip again, so that it cut right through my body, splitting me into two halves. Once more the tinner came to my help and made me a body of tin, fastening my tin arms and legs and head to it, by means of joints, so that I could move around as well as ever. But alas! I had now no heart, so that I lost all my love for the Munchkin girl, and did not care whether I married her or not. I suppose she is still living with the old woman, waiting for me to come after her.

"My body shone so brightly in the sun that I felt very proud of it and it did not matter now if my ax slipped, for it could not cut me. There was only one danger—that my joints would rust. But I kept an oil-can in my cottage and took care to oil

**The first known brothel opened its doors in 550 B.C. in Athens, Greece.**

myself whenever I needed it. However, there came a day when I forgot to do this, and, being caught in a rainstorm, before I thought of the danger my joints had rusted, and I was left to stand in the woods until you came to help me. It was a terrible thing to undergo, but during the year I stood there I had time to think that the greatest loss I had ever known was the loss of my heart. While I was in love I was the happiest man on earth; but no one can love who has not a heart...."

## THE COWARDLY LION

"You are nothing but a big coward."

"I know it," said the Lion, hanging his head in shame. "I've always known it. But how can I help it?"

"What makes you a coward?" asked Dorothy, looking at the great beast in wonder, for he was as big as a small horse.

"It's a mystery," replied the Lion. "I suppose I was born that way. All the other animals in the forest naturally expect me to be brave, for the Lion is everywhere thought to be the King of Beasts. I learned that if I roared very loudly every living thing was frightened and got out of my way. Whenever I've met a man I've been awfully scared. But I just roared at him, and he has always run away as fast as he could go. If the elephants and the tigers and the bears had ever tried to fight me, I should have run myself—I'm such a coward; but just as soon as they hear me roar they all try to get away from me, and of course I let them go."

"But that isn't right. The King of Beasts shouldn't be a coward," said the Scarecrow.

"I know it," returned the Lion, wiping a tear from his eye with the tip of his paw. "It is my great sorrow, and makes my life very unhappy. But whenever there is danger, my heart begins to beat fast."

"Perhaps you have heart disease," said the Tin Woodman.

"It may be," said the Lion.

"If you have," continued the Tin Woodman, "you ought to be glad, for it proves you have a heart. For my part, I have no heart, so I cannot have heart disease."

"Perhaps," said the Lion thoughtfully, "if I had no heart I should not be a coward."

"Have you brains?" asked the Scarecrow.

"I supposed so. I've never looked to see," replied the Lion.

"I am going to the Great Oz to ask him to give me some," remarked the Scarecrow, "for my head is stuffed with straw."...

"Do you think Oz could give me courage?" asked the Cowardly Lion.

"Just as easily as he could give me brains," said the Scarecrow.

"Or give me a heart," said the Tin Woodman.

"Or send me back to Kansas," said Dorothy.

"Then, if you don't mind, I'll go with you," said the Lion, "for my life is simply unbearable without a bit of courage."

"You will be very welcome," answered Dorothy, "for you will help to keep away the other wild beasts. It seems to me they must be more cowardly than you are if they allow you to scare them so easily."

"They really are," said the Lion, "but that doesn't make me any braver, and as long as I know myself to be a coward I shall be unhappy."

**RANDOM GOSSIP:**

•Author Margaret Mitchell's only casting suggestion for the film *Gone With the Wind*: She thought Groucho Marx should play Rhett Butler.

•Bob Newhart became a successful comedian without performing at clubs—while he was an accountant in the Illinois State Unemployment Office, he just recorded some wacky phone conversations he made to a friend...and sold them to a record company.

•Peter O'Toole is obsessed with green sox. He always wears them, even while sleeping. In fact, he once almost lost a movie role because he wouldn't take them off. In the end, he agreed to carry them in his pocket instead.

•Comedian Albert Brooks's real name is Albert Einstein.

•Ludwig von Beethoven never took a bath during the time he was writing his Ninth Symphony.

•Attila the Hun was probably a dwarf.

•Charlton Heston, a noted conservative, was once an artists' model who posed in the nude.

**About 1 million Americans say they drink Coca Cola for breakfast.**

# CELEBRITY MANIA

*This gets the Ed Wood, Jr. Award for Weirdness. Missy Laws, a professional celebrity-chaser, has written a book entitled* How to Meet the Stars *(Ross Books, Berkeley, CA). The volume offers a glimpse into the mind of a Fan, and boy is it strange. In case you're scheming to meet the celeb of your dreams, here's a sample of Missy's advice to you. Used courtesy of Ross Books.*

**PRETEND YOU'RE AN OLD FRIEND.** To portray an old friend, you must inform your star that you have met him previously. All you need to know is a place he has visited and the approximate time he was there.

Your opening line would be, "Hi. I don't know if you remember, but I met you before at (name of place he has been before)."

You may wonder how you can say this if it isn't true. The well-known meet so many strangers that it is simply impossible to remember them all. Therefore, if you insist that the two of you have previously met, your celebrity has little reason to doubt you. Even if he questions your accuracy, it's likely he'll be polite and not dispute your claim.

Perhaps you are certain that your star frequented a particular restaurant in the month of June. You could claim to have met him there. Maybe you know he cut an album at a specific recording studio. You could say that you originally introduced yourself to him there.

However, do not blindly invent a place and circumstance, or your luminary may unravel the lie and label you a fool.

Why is it a good idea to pretend to be an "old friend" by saying that the two of you met before? Partly because it's a good icebreaker. You leave the lines of communication open. In an obscure way, it gives you both something in common.

Also, if your celebrity thinks he has previously met you, he may feel more comfortable in your presence. If the two of you really had come in contact and he doesn't remember, then it's obvious you didn't cause trouble. Your star wouldn't forget if he had a reason to dislike you.

## PRETEND TO BE RICH

There are a couple of things to remember when portraying an important person. First, if you dress and act as if you're wealthy, not only will you be more believable in the role, but you may also make your celebrity less leery of you.

Famous people are often suspicious of strangers, and rightly so, for often outsiders have insincere reasons for wanting to know the renowned. Money, for example, may be their objective. Dressing as if you're rich may help alleviate your celebrity's worries.

People are generally more comfortable with those on the same monetary level as they are, and most stars fall into the category of upper-level income citizens. They may more readily accept you as their equal if you outfit yourself to look like you're from the same social class. This could ease you into either a personal or business relationship more rapidly.

It's easy to fake wealth. You could find a classy, expensive-looking outfit at a thrift shop or garage sale. Inexpensive baubles could dangle from your ears and drape around your neck. If someone has the nerve to ask you, "Are those jewels real?" you could skirt the issue by responding, "They were a gift." Perhaps they were a gift to yourself from yourself!

I used to borrow prestigious antique automobiles from my friends or relatives when I really wanted to impress a luminary. If a star was extremely important to me, I'd appear in a different car each time I visited him. On Monday night I might have a Mercedes. On Tuesday I might have a Corvette, and on Wednesday I might have a Ferrari. Some celebrities probably thought I was wealthier than they were!

**Mary Tyler Moore:** "I know a funny Carol Burnett story. Once a fan followed her into the bathroom. The fan poked her head under the stall and shoved a pen and a piece of paper at Carol [for an autograph]."

# PERRY MASON

*Lawyer shows have always been popular on TV, but without a doubt, this is the most popular of them all. It inspired an entire generation to become attorneys. From* Cult TV.

**HOW IT STARTED:** In the early '20s, a lawyer named Erle Stanley Gardner decided to give up his practice and become a full-time mystery writer. He wrote like a madman. He wrote so much that his fingers started bleeding. But it didn't pay off—no one wanted to buy his stories, not even the lowly pulp magazines he was trying to write for.

Eventually, his style improved, and he began selling literally hundreds of short mystery stories to magazines every year. Then, in 1933, he wrote two novels. One featured a lawyer named Ed Stark. The other was about a detective named Samuel Keene (who doubled as an astrologer). No one bought them, but the head of the William Morrow Publishing Co. suggested that Gardner combine his two heroes into one, creating a lawyer/detective. Gardner obliged. He created *Perry Mason*, whose first adventure, *The Case of the Velvet Claw*, was published in 1934.

By 1955 there were 70 Perry Mason novels, and Perry had become a popular movie and radio character.

But Gardner never liked what movie studios did with his hero. So when he got an offer to sell the TV rights for $1 million, he turned it down. Instead, he and his former agent, Cornwell Jackson, formed Paisano Productions to do their own *Mason* TV show. Jackson's wife, Gail, became executive producer. It aired for the first time on September 21, 1957, and lasted on CBS until the end of the 1965-1966 season.

**INSIDE FACTS:**

**Deja vu.** Gardner was so prolific that he couldn't remember what he'd written previously. Sometimes he'd be halfway through a new Perry Mason story before he or his staff realized he'd already used the plot before.

**Court is adjourned.** In Perry's last case, "The Case of the Final

Fade-Out," the judge was played by his creator, Erle Stanley Gardner. And the killer was...Dick Clark.

**Win some, lose some.** Surprise! Perry did NOT win every case. He lost at least three of them. But there were extenuating circumstances, of course. And the second was a trick:

1. In "The Case of the Terrified Typist," the killer was an imposter, pretending to be Perry's real client; the guilty verdict was thrown out.
2. "The Case of the Witless Witness" opened with Perry losing a civil suit to a judge he later defended for murder in the same episode. Doesn't really count, does it?
3. And in "The Case of the Deadly Verdict," his client was falsely convicted when she withheld key evidence. They got the *real* killer in the end.

**Barbara Hale, 1963:** "I occasionally attended meetings of legal secretaries, and the first thing they want to know is 'How do you arrange to go out with the boss every night?' The next is 'Why don't we ever see your typewriter?' "

**He can dream, can't he?** Erle Stanley Gardner liked Raymond Burr's performance but was particularly fond of Bill Talman as Hamilton Burger. "He actually looks like he expects to win a case," Gardner said, admiringly.

**By the book.** The *Perry Mason* radio show was more a romance than a detective series. It began with the emphasis on mysteries, but Gardner found that his courtroom dramas didn't adapt well to radio. As a soap opera, however, it was enormously successful. When it moved to television it remained a soap. The name was changed from *Perry Mason* to *Edge of Night*.

**Book 'em, Perry.** Gardner did not write the teleplays, but almost all of the 70+ Perry Mason novels were adapted for the series.

**He's Back**: Raymond Burr was so popular as Perry Mason that when he came back as the character in 1985, in a made-for-TV movie called *The Return of Perry Mason*, the show was higher-rated than any TV film of the season.

# THE MAGIC DRAGON

*"Puff the Magic Dragon" is probably one of the best-known folk songs in the world. But is it really about drugs? Here's the answer, from* Behind the Hits, *by Bob Shannon.*

Lenny Lipton's first year of college wasn't easy. Not because he was homesick—he was glad to finally be out of Brooklyn—but for some reason, he was having a hard time getting used to being on his own. There were so many things to think about: girls; money; a career. Growing up obviously wasn't going to be easy. Lenny secretly began to miss his childhood.

The fall of 1958 and winter of 1959 passed. So did Lenny, who managed to survive at Cornell in spite of his emotional turmoil. And then one evening in the spring of 1959, a few days after his nineteenth birthday, Lenny made one of the most important decisions of his life. He decided to go to the library.

He was supposed to have dinner that night with a friend who lived off-campus, but it was still early. So Lenny wandered over to the library in the Cornell Student Union. He scanned the shelves until he found a volume of poems by Ogden Nash, then pulled it from the shelves and retired to a chair with it. Lenny was struck by a simple rhyme about the "Really-o Truly-o Dragon." In fact, he was inspired by it. "If Ogden Nash can write that kind of stuff, so can I," he thought.

Lenny returned the book and left the library and headed for his friend's house. As he walked down the hill that led from Cornell into the town of Ithaca, he thought of Ogden Nash's dragon. And then he thought of his own dragon. As he approached his friend's house, Lenny incorporated his dragon into a little poem about a subject that was never far from his mind in those days—the end of childhood.

When Lenny got to 343 State Street, he knocked on the door. No answer. Apparently neither his friend nor his friend's roommate, Peter Yarrow, was home. But Lenny wanted to get this poem onto paper, so he went inside anyway. He headed straight for a typewriter—which happened be Yarrow's. Lenny

**On the average, a working man spends 8 minutes a day cooking. A working woman spends 50.**

sat down and began typing as fast as he could. In three minutes, he typed out his poem—and then he got up and left. He didn't bother taking "Puff the Magic Dragon" with him. He didn't care, he'd gotten it out of his system. He just left it sitting in the typewriter.

Folk music was popular at Cornell in the late '50s, and Peter Yarrow was a big man in the folk scene. Although he was still an undergraduate, he taught a class on folk music, performed, and often organized concerts. As Lipton tells it, Yarrow returned home that night, found the poem sitting in his typewriter, and wrote a melody for it. Eventually Yarrow became part of Peter, Paul, and Mary, and they included the song about "Puff" in their act.

Years went by. And Lipton forgot all about this three-minute poem. Until a friend from Cornell happened to mention that he'd seen Peter Yarrow perform "Puff" with his new group. Yarrow had told him that Lenny had written it. Was it true?

Suddenly, Lenny's little poem came back to him.

In the world of rock 'n' roll, one inevitably runs into stories about unscrupulous operators who've stolen songs from their rightful owners. So it's nice to be able to write about a case in which an honest man went out of his way to find a writer. That's what happened here. When it began to look as if "Puff" was really going to be worth something, Peter Yarrow tracked Lenny Lipton down to let him know about it. And he's always listed Lipton as co-writer—even when Lenny didn't remember having invented the world's most popular dragon.

For years, people have speculated about the meaning of "Puff." But Lenny is quite clear about what was on his mind when he wrote it: "Loss of innocence, and having to face an adult world," he says. "It's surely not about drugs. I can tell you that at Cornell in 1959, *no one* smoked grass." None of the "suggestive" names were thought out—they just popped into his head as he was walking along that night. "I find the fact that people interpret it as a drug song annoying," he says. "It would be insidious to propagandize about drugs in a song for little kids. I think it's a very sentimental tune."

It's had remarkable success for a poem that took three minutes to compose. It reached Number Two on the national charts in 1963, and in the '70s became the basis of a continuing series of children's cartoons.

**In 1984, the National Coca Company of Peru introduced toothpaste with cocaine in it.**

# A-BOMB VS. YOUR CAR

*This article first appeared in a 1957 car magazine which is now defunct. It revealed the "shocking truth" about a car's chance of surviving a nuclear blast. B.R. Institute member Steve Gorlick has been saving it for years, hoping for a chance to share it. "It's real* Atomic Cafe *stuff," he says. "In retrospect, it's preposterous....But people ate it up in 1957. We were so naive back then."*

The story of "Your Car vs. The Bomb" began on the barren Nevada desert in the chill gray hours before dawn of March 17, 1953. At exactly 5:20 AM on that St. Patrick's Day, the rugged landscape suddenly became brighter than the sunniest day in June. The earth rocked and rolled and a king-sized shock wave swept across the sand as the awesome mushroom cloud of a nuclear explosion began its ascent into the stratosphere.

A split-second earlier, the desert near the site of the blast had appeared like a small parking lot with 51 automobiles—some old and some new—standing at various distances from the tall steel tower which supported the nuclear device. Some were within one-half mile of the structure—much too close to escape obliteration from a hydrogen bomb, but near enough to the atomic weapon to provide a good test of a car's sturdiness.

As the terrific roar reverberated through the Nevada mountain, these same cars stood almost as they had a few moments earlier, but there was a difference—a difference which can mean much to millions of American car owners.

A few cars had rolled over, some were on fire, broken glass was scattered throughout the area and almost all vehicles appeared to have been struck by a giant fist. Tops were dished in and sides and fenders were crumpled.

## Experts Inspect Cars

When experts from the Federal Civil Defense Administration and the Society of Automotive Engineers inspected the cars, they found that:

**Fabulous Flop: Former Yippie Jerry Rubin declared in 1980 that "My goal is at the age of**

**1.** Cars which would run before the blast *would* run after the blast, if they had not burned.

**2.** All cars had survived the blast with *no appreciable structural damage* to frames, front and rear suspensions, and motor mounts.

**3.** Safety plate glass in cars near ground zero of the weapon was blown out in large pieces which were badly cracked, *but did not shatter*. In most cases, *all cars escaped damage to windows*. There were a number of instances where safety glass gave under the blast impact but did not blow entirely out of the frame.

In a few cars, only a relatively small hole was blown in the center of the caved-in glass!...Curved windshields and rear windows generally resisted the blast better than small or similar sized flat glass surfaces.

**4.** The percentage of cars lost to fire was very low. Where fire occurred it apparently began with smoldering seat covers, head liners and door panels. There was some scorching of paint, tire sidewalls and other exposed surfaces. There was no evidence that gasoline tanks or fuel systems had contributed to the initial fire hazard. There were no fuel tank explosions, even where the car was burned out.

**5.** There was no significant difference between makes or models of cars, with exception of wooden-bodied station wagons. These suffered more. No convertibles were tested.

**6.** The only tire failures were due to fire.

**7.** In cases where car windows were closed, the greatest damage was done to dished roofs and side panels.

## What About Occupants?

All right—so much for the cars themselves. But what would have happened if you had been in one of these crates?

To answer this question, Civil Defense engineers placed

**35 to act like I'm 15." Within a few years, he was running a "networking" service and**

mannequins in many of the cars, all seated as if in driving position. Some of these mannequins showed a great deal of heat flash damage within three-quarters of a mile from the tower. Human skin at this distance would have been badly burned. In many instances the dished tops were pressed down hard on the mannequins' heads, indicating severe or fatal injury if it had been your head.

Thus it was found that while automobiles offered some protection from the bomb—if they were out of the area of complete destruction and if the occupants had had time to duck down below window level—basements and other permanent type shelters would be your best bet for protection from the bomb. However, a brick house standing a few hundred feet further away from the blast than were some of the cars was completely demolished.

## One of the most important findings in the test was this:

Cars which could be operated before the blast still would run after the blast.

## What does this mean to the average motorist?

The Federal Civil Defense Administration is vitally concerned with this question. Its experts point out that the nation has no guarantee that a potential enemy will not launch an attack against our cities and industries. Nor will we ever have assurance that natural disaster—flood, fire, tornado, hurricane, blizzard and earthquake—will spare us before, during and after attack, if the latter should come. Those who might escape the bombs still could face the threat of natural disaster at any time.

## New Cars Would Be Out

If this country ever is hit with nuclear weapons, you can be certain that our automobile plants will be knocked out—if the enemy can do it—stopping production completely. If the plants escape the raids their output most certainly will be diverted to military demands. In any event, *you just won't be able to get a*

**talking about how wonderful it was to make money.**

*new car for no one knows how long.* Many cars would be destroyed in such raids and a lot of family jalopies would be damaged. It's the damaged cars which may mean the difference between survival for you and your family, and further disaster.

**The surest way to escape any kind of trouble is:**
Just don't be there when it happens.

The family car can play an important part in helping you obey this axiom because it provides three essential elements vital to escape from danger.

• **First,** if we are to put distance between ourselves and the source of danger, we must have dependable, speedy transportation from the trouble spot. The family car is a must on this.

• **Second,** no matter where we are the family must have shelter. Despite its relatively small size (but they're growing bigger every year), the American automobile is a sort of house on wheels. It provides a haven from sun, wind, rain, and snow. It can shelter you from insects and even wild animals. It can also shield, to some degree, against the deadly radioactive fallout from a nuclear bomb—the stuff Adlai Stevenson kicked about in the last presidential election campaign.

• **Third,** the family car provides storage for food, clothing and other items vital during an emergency. The roomy luggage compartment of your car can easily accommodate several days' supply of food, clothing and other gear.

However, the car will serve this purpose only if you equip it properly and keep it in good condition. Good luck.

**Close shave: In the course of a decade, a man is likely to shave off a pound of whiskers.**

# GANDHI SPEAKS

*The fact that Mahatma Gandhi was a man of compassion and peace makes him unique among the powerful politicians of the 20th century.*

"Freedom is not worth having if it does not connote freedom to err."

[*Responding to an interviewer who asked what Gandhi thought of Western civilization*] "I think it would be a good idea."

"If non-violence is the law of our being, the future is with women."

"All fear is a sign of want of faith. Cultivate the quiet courage of dying without killing. For man lives freely only by his readiness to die."

"Non-violence is not a garment to be put on and off at will. Its seat is in the heart and it must be an inseparable part of our very being."

"I have known many meat-eaters to be far more non-violent than vegetarians."

"A non-violent revolution is not a program of seizure of power. It is a programme of transformation and relationships, ending in a peaceful transfer of power."

"The slave clings to his chains and he must have them struck from him."

"No sacrifice is worth the name unless it is a joy. Sacrifice and a long face go ill together."

"Honesty is incompatible with amassing a large fortune."

"There is enough for the needy but not for the greedy."

"To a man with an empty stomach food is God."

"Prayer is not an old woman's idle amusement. Properly understood and applied it is the most potent instrument of action."

"There is more to life than increasing its speed."

# WEIRD INSPIRATIONS

*You can find the inspiration for that great rock song you're trying to write in the oddest place. These are from* Behind the Hits, *by John Javna and Bob Shannon.*

**ALL SHOOK UP, Elvis Presley.** 1957/#1

This story will probably come as a pleasant surprise to Pepsi Cola. They don't know that their product inspired one of the all-time great Elvis tunes.

**1957:** Otis Blackwell was sitting in his office at Shalimar Music, desperately trying to come up with a follow-up to his composition, "Don't Be Cruel." It wasn't going to be easy to match; recorded by Elvis, "Don't Be Cruel" had been #1 on the charts for *eleven* weeks, making it the top song of 1956. Now Presley wanted another song and Otis wanted to give him one. But nothing came. Then Al Stanton, one of the partners at Shalimar, happened to wander in.

**Blackwell**: "He walked in with a bottle of Pepsi, shaking it as they did at the time. Al said, 'Otis, I've got an idea. Why don't you write a song called "All Shook Up?"' A couple of days later I brought the song in and said, 'Look man, I did something with it!'" So did Presley. It hit #1 and stayed there for nine weeks, enough to make an Otis Blackwell song the most popular record of the year *again*! All from a fizzing bottle of Pepsi.

**MONY, MONY — Tommy James and the Shondells.** 1968/#3

People who work for the Mutual of New York Insurance Company—also known as M.O.N.Y—probably can't imagine that the staid, conservative company has something to do with rock 'n' roll. They think it's just a coincidence that the name of their company is also the title of this song....But it isn't.

M.O.N.Y.'s central office in New York City is a 40-story building located at 1740 Broadway. On top is a huge old sign that flashes the company's name in neon at night. This sign inspired Tommy James' 1968 hit.

**James:** "The night we wrote the song, we were absolutely devastated because we couldn't come up with a 'Bony Moronie,' a 'Sloopy' kind of title, and we knew that's what it had to be. It had to be a girl's name that nobody had ever heard of before.

"We were going through the dictionary, but nothing was happening. We were just totally frustrated. I walked out onto my terrace—I lived in Manhattan at the time—and I was just sort of scanning around, looking for just any part of a name, anything. I was just kind of staring out into space, and all of a sudden, I looked up and I saw [what I was looking for]...I said [to my manager], 'Ritchie, c'mere.' He came over and I said, 'Look.'...And all of a sudden, here's this 'M.O.N.Y.' with a dollar sign in the middle of the 'O.' The song was kind of etched in stone in New York, I guess. We both just fell down laughing."

**Other Weird Ones:**

•Paul Simon was inspired to write **"Mother and Child Reunion"** by a chicken-and-egg dish in a Chinese restaurant.

•**"Heartbreak Hotel,"** Elvis's first #1 hit, was inspired by a highly publicized suicide note that was printed on the front page of the Miami Herald. It began with the line, "I walk a lonely street...."

•The Teddy Bears' 1958 #1 song, **"To Know Him Is to Love Him,"** was inspired by the epitaph on group-member Phil Spector's father's tombstone.

•Melanie's million-seller, **"Brand New Key,"** came to her after she'd broken a strict vegetarian diet by eating a McDonald's hamburger.

•**"Be-Bop-A-Lula"** was inspired by a Little Lulu comic book.

•Ray Davies of the Kinks got the idea for the chord changes in **"You Really Got Me"** from a performer he saw on TV who "played" half-filled glasses of water with spoons.

•**"Running on Empty"** came to Jackson Browne because, in a tough period of his life, he kept forgetting to fill up his car with gas.

# ANDY GRIFFITH SHOW

*Although lots of city slickers don't care for the corn-ball world of Mayberry, U.S.A., this show is one of America's cult classics. Here's some info, from* Cult TV, *by John Javna.*

**HOW IT STARTED:** While he was still riding high in the movies in the '50s, Andy Griffith avoided TV. But when his films started receiving less kind reviews and the quality of the scripts he was offered fell off, he figured it was time to make the jump to the small screen.

In 1960 he let his agents at William Morris know that he was looking for a TV series. They, in turn, contacted Sheldon Leonard, executive producer of *The Danny Thomas Show*, and asked him to devise a show specifically for their client.

Griffith's forte seemed to be playing "hillbillies" (as in *No Time For Sergeants*, where he played fresh-off-the-farm Will Stockdale). So Leonard came up with a rural sitcom featuring Andy as the sheriff, mayor, justice of the peace, and newspaper editor of a small North Carolina town. Andy didn't like the idea—but he liked Sheldon Leonard—so he agreed to give it a try. They decided to air the pilot as an episode of *The Danny Thomas Show*, to showcase it for potential sponsors.

Griffith took ten days off from *Destry*, a Broadway play in which he was starring, went to Hollywood, and shot the pilot (which featured Ronny Howard and Frances Bavier). Called *Danny Meets Andy Griffith*, it aired on February 15, 1960 as the final *Danny Thomas Show* episode of the 1959-60 season.

It was so well received that the sponsor for the *Thomas* show, General Foods, signed up for the *Griffith* show immediately. They were on the air six months later.

**INSIDE FACTS:**

Mayberry is loosely based on Andy Griffith's North Carolina hometown, Mount Airy. "Andy never left Mount Airy," a resident told *TV Guide* in 1966. "He plain took it to Hollywood with him."

**In 1984, a Canadian farmer began renting ad space on his cows.**

**Fatherly advice.** Ronny Howard was only six when he was cast as Opie, so his father, actor Rance Howard, chaperoned him. The first time Ronny had a tantrum about cooperating with the director, his father came up and spanked him right on the set. He rarely complained after that, and developed a reputation with the cast as a great kid.

**Going straight.** Many of the comic attributes which were originally planned for Andy were shifted to Barney Fife; Andy then became Mayberry's straight man, and Barney its clown.

**About Barney.** Don Knotts described his interpretation of Barney Fife this way: "I thought of Barney as a childlike man who was funny mainly because he was never able to hide anything in his face. If he was sad, he really looked sad. If he was angry, he acted angry. Children do that—pout, get overjoyed, or whatever. Barney never hid anything. He wasn't able to. In my mind that was really the key to Barney's character."

**Communications breakdown.** Don Knotts left the show in 1965 because he understood that Andy Griffith didn't want to do the show for more than five years. Knotts had already negotiated a movie contract with Universal Pictures when Andy changed his mind, and couldn't stay on as a regular. He did return, though, to make five more appearances as Barney in the last three seasons.

**The real Mayberry.** *The Griffith Show* was shot in three locations. The interior scenes were shot at Desilu Studios (the jail, Andy's house, etc.). The exterior scenes of Mayberry were shot at a lot in Culver City (where the main street was constructed). And the bucolic shots (the opening scene, etc.) were shot at Franklin Canyon, a Los Angeles reservoir.

**Now you see 'em...**

- Jack Nicholson appeared in two episodes.
- Howard McNear (Floyd the Barber) was out of the series for over a year (including the whole 1963-64 season) after he had a stroke. He returned in 1964 and stayed until 1967.
- George Lindsay auditioned for the part of Gomer Pyle and was rejected. Later, he was offered Goober's role.

**Phone Crazy: The Pentagon made almost $85 million worth of phone calls in 1986.**

# INVENTIONS IN THE NEWS

*We thought it would be interesting to take a look at the 1st newspaper reports on various inventions that changed our lives. These are excerpts from the actual articles.*

*The Flashlight...*

**LIGHT FROM AN ELECTRIC CURRENT**

**October 22, 1877**

"Electricity in a hand-lamp is the most recent fruit of inventive enterprise. Messrs. Voison and Drouier, of Paris, have just patented a new scheme for obtaining light from an electric current. The apparatus consists of a single cell enclosed in a light mahogany case....The whole operation is performed so quickly that it may be said to be almost simultaneous with the pressing of the finger on the plunger.

"The principle of the invention is, of course, well known, but the mode of applying it is altogether novel. The apparatus is very simple, and it is noiseless in its working."

*Music over the wire...*

**MUSIC BY TELEGRAPH**

**July 23, 1876**

"The *Boston Traveller* prints the following statement: A few nights ago Prof. Bell was in communication with a telegraph operator in New York, and commenced experimenting with one of his inventions pertaining to the transmission of musical sounds. He made use of his phonetic organ and played the tune of 'America,' and asked the operator in New York what he heard. 'I hear the tune of "America,"' replied New York; 'give us another.' Prof. Bell then played 'Auld Lang Syne.' 'What do you hear now?' 'I hear the tune of "Auld Lang Syne," with the full chords, distinctly,' replied New York. Thus the astounding discovery has been made that a man can play upon musical instruments in New York, New Orleans, or London, or Paris, and be heard distinctly in Boston! If this can be done, why cannot distinguished performers execute the most artistic and beautiful music in Paris and an audience assemble in Music Hall, Boston, to listen? Prof. Bell's other improvement, viz., the transmission of the human voice, has become so far perfected that persons have conversed over one thousand miles of wire with perfect ease, although as yet the vocal sounds are not loud enough to be heard by more than one or two persons. But if the human voice can now be sent over the wire, and so distinctively that when two or three known parties are telegraphing the voices of each can be recognized, we may soon have distinguished men delivering speeches in Washington, New York, or London and audiences assembled in Music Hall or Faneuil Hall to listen."

*Television...*

**BELIN SHOWS TELE-VISION**

**December 2, 1922**

"Tele-vision or 'long-distance sight' by wireless, had a preliminary experimental demonstration at the Sorbonne today by Edward Belin, inventor of the transmission of photo-graphs by wire. Flashes of light were directed on a selenium element, which, through another instrument, produced sound waves. These waves were then taken up by a wireless apparatus that reproduced the flashes of light on a mirror.

"This was offered as proof that the general principle of projecting a stationary scene had been solved."

*Radio...*

**TOPICS OF THE TIMES**

**May 26, 1897**

"English electricians, particularly those connected with the army and navy, are much interested in the Marconi system of telegraphy without wires. Some remarkable work has already been done with this machine, and improvements being made are expected to add many miles to the two or three over which it is already effective.

The system, it is thought, will be of especial use to the commanders of fleets at sea by enabling them to communicate with their other vessels without the use of visible signals."

*Movie projector...*

**REALITIES OF ANIMAL MOTION**

**November 18, 1882**

"Prof. Eadweard Muybridge, whose success in instantly photographing the motion of the horse in running has overturned all previous ideas on the subject, lectured last evening in the Turf Club

About 96% of all American children can recognize Ronald McDonald.

Theatre under the auspices of the Turf Club....

"Prof. Muybridge's subject was 'The Romance and Reality of Animal Motion,' and he illustrated his lecture upon a large screen by means of a *zoopraxiscope*, which an eminent English writer describes as 'a magic lantern run mad.' With this instrument the Professor produced upon the canvas, first stationary figures of the horse in the different positions assumed in the walk, the pace, the rack, the canter, and the gallop, and afterward displayed the figure of the animal, first at a walk across the canvas, then pacing, cantering, galloping, and even jumping the hurdle... the spectator could almost believe that he saw miniature horses with their riders racing across the screen."

*Pocket Calculator...*

**POCKET COMPUTER CAN HANDLE TASKS OF UNIT 150 TIMES ITS SIZE**

**October 20, 1961**

"Texas Instruments, Inc., has developed a vest pocket computer.

The gadget isn't much bigger than a pack of cigarets and weighs only 10 ounces, but it will do the same tasks as a conventional transistorized computer 150 times its size and 48 times heavier, the company claims.

Texas Instruments built the compact computer for the Air Force, to show it could be done. But it is offering components for sale that could be used to build almost any electronic equipment now using vacuum tubes or transistors.

P.E. Haggerty, president, says the little parts will be competitively priced for 'high reliability, small-run military requirements in 1963.' But their initial offering price runs something like 50 times the equivalent weight in good diamonds. In lots of 1,000 the components will sell for $50 to $65; since it takes 587 components to make a computer, the parts would be priced at $29,350 or more.

Initial use of equipment made from the networks is expected to be in the missile and space field....Future price reductions and development will lead to industrial uses in a few years and perhaps eventual consumer uses, the company feels. At the moment the company can suggest no immediately practical industrial or consumer uses, but officials are in no way perturbed."

# THE HIPSTER SAINT

*Contributed by Gene Sculatti, one of America's hippest cultural observers, and author of* The Catalog of Cool. *Gene believes that the late great Lord Buckley is one of the hippest cats ever to make the scene in America.*

Maybe we shouldn't be talking about Lord Buckley at all.

It's just that, having been a secret so long, could he stand the public acclaim? Besides, words were his axe, and when it comes to that instrument, nobody blew it better.

Richard "Lord" Buckley (1906-60) was the embodiment of life lived coolly. If the coolest one can be is fashioning an accurate expression of what's inside, then Buckley was easily, to borrow a phrase from him, one of "the wildest, grooviest, hippest, swingin'-est, double-frantic, maddest, most exquisite" cats that ever breathed.

It also helps if what's inside is good to start with. Like maybe a huge heart. Tons of compassion. A mind that spontaneously generates material to entertain itself even when there are no audiences around. Or a conviction that language itself is the headiest brew and that staying drunk is divine.

Lord Buckley had all this inside. You'll know that when you hear his records. They're all that survive a life and a "career" that was by all accounts unpredictable and gloriously insane.

Much of the material on albums like *Way Out Humor* and *A Most Immaculately Hip Aristocrat* takes the form of parables. The best known may be his life of Christ "The Nazz" ("The sweetest far-out cat that ever stomped on this Sweet Green Sphere!"). There are also routines on Gandhi ("The Hip Gahn"), Jonah and the whale, Poe's "Raven," and Marc Antony's oration at Caesar's funeral.

The two that made a believer of me are Buckley's profile of the Spanish explorer Alvar Nuñez de Vaca and—best of all—his interpretation of the life of Einstein called "The Hip Einie."

On the multicandle brainpower of this most eminent "sphere-gasser" and his continual job loot predicaments: "Now here was a cat who carried so much *wiggage*—he was gig-less! He *could* not find a wheel to turn! He sounded all the hubcaps within' reach but nathan shakin'. He could *not* connect." Buckley rolls on, in an extrapolation of black jazz-rap, to clue us in on Einstein's subsequent relocation to Switzerland: "Now, not digging the lick, you see, of these double-square kicks the cats were puttin' down, he saved his beans and finally he swung with a Swiss passport, *swooped* the scene and lit in the land of the Coool, to prove and groove with the Alpine-heads!"

Ultimately, the Hip Einie connects with a gig, a pad, a wife and kids. Writing down his scientific theories, he soon becomes "the king of all Spaceheads," flips the physics-chemistry community on its ear, ascends to top dog status at the U of Zurich, and wows the world. Buckley shouts, whispers, wails like an evangelist wired to a generator, stomps through the tale (there is no way to repeat or paraphrase his explication of Einstein's theory—you have to be there) and finally winds down.

Buckley's personal (and sometimes highly public) life was a true trip itself. Born of Indian extraction in California's Mother Lode gold country in '06, he gravitated to Frisco, then to the Texas oil fields. He spent the Thirties doing standup in Capone-style Chicago speakeasies, made it to New York and married "Lady" Buckley. By the mid-Fifties he was reigning hepcat to a circle of admirers that included Sinatra, Robert Mitchum and Stuart Whitman. Ed Sullivan put him on TV; Jonathan Winters, Redd Foxx, and every other comedian dug him. Ultimately, he suffered the Bruce-type fuzz busts—in New York City in '60, where he died in November.

Which is great and dramatic, and somebody should (and somebody else will) make a movie of it someday. But what really counts is first-person Buckley, his work. Here's a sample:

"Now you see in Hip Talk, they call William Shakespeare 'Willie the Shake!' You know why they call him 'Willie the Shake?' Because HE SHOOK EVERYBODY!! They gave this Cat five cents' worth of ink and a nickel's worth of paper and he sat down and wrote up such a breeze, WHAMMMMM!! Everybody got off! Period! He was a hard, tight, tough Cat. Pen in hand, he was a Mother Superior."

The average American consumes almost ten pounds of "chemical additives" annually.

# FABULOUS FOOD FLOPS

*Americans will eat almost anything. We consume billions of Twinkies, drink oceans of Kool-Aid, devour millions of pounds of processed cheese spread. But even we have our limits—some food products are so outrageous that no one will touch them. Like these.*

**CORN FLAKES WITH FREEZE-DRIED FRUIT.** In the '60s, the lure of space-age food technology was too seductive for cereal giants Kellogg and Post to resist.

The year was 1964. Freeze-drying had been "perfected" by NASA, so Post decided to add freeze-dried strawberries to its cornflakes. Just add milk, they told wide-eyed consumers, and these dried-out berries miraculously turned back into real fruit.

"Corn Flakes with Strawberries" took off like a rocket; supermarkets couldn't keep the product on their shelves. Exulting, Post built a multi-million dollar plant to produce the cereal and added two new fruity varieties to their line: "Corn Flakes with Blueberies," and "Corn Flakes with Peaches."

Meanwhile, Kellogg's was test-marketing its own version of high-tech fruit 'n' cereal: "Corn Flakes with Instant Bananas." The Battle Creek cereal giant bought the rights to the song, "Yes We Have No Bananas," and hired Jimmy Durante to croak new lyrics at a piano: "Yes, we now have bananas...." But the prognosis wasn't good. One Kellogg's salesman described the product as "cardboard discs in a box."

It turned out that freeze-dried fruit got soft on the outside, but stayed crunchy on the inside. What's worse: by the time the fruit was soft enough to eat, the cereal was soggy. Millions of families bought "Corn Flakes with Strawberries" once, but never came back for a second helping—leaving both cereal giants stuck with a bountiful harvest of unwanted pseudo-fruit.

**OTHER FREEZE-DRIED FLOPS:** Freeze-dried mushrooms in a box, from Armour foods; freeze-dried cottage cheese ("with cultured sour cream dressing"), from Holland Dairies.

## WEIRD BEER

Here are two beer ideas that America refused to swallow:

- In 1965, Dr. Robert Cade came up with the formula for Gatorade. Two years later, he sold it to Stokely-Van Camp. What did he do with the profits? He developed "Hop 'n' Gator," a mixture of beer and Gatorade. The Pittsburgh Brewing Company actually produced it in 1969...but it was canned right away.
- Not to be outdone, the Lone Star Brewing Company retaliated with flavored beer in 1970. It was available in three exciting tastes: cola, grapefruit, and lemon-lime. But of course, it wasn't available too long. Cola-flavored beer?

## McDONALD'S MISTAKE

In the '50s, Catholics still weren't permitted to eat meat on Friday's—a problem for McDonald's. Since the fast food giant only had hamburgers on its menu, sales slumped every week in Catholic areas. McDonald's needed a creative alternative...and Ray Kroc, Chairman of the Board, had one. Putting his marketing genius to work, he came up with the "Hula Burger."

Picture a toasted bun, covered with a piece of melted American cheese, mustard, ketchup, a pickle...and a slice of grilled pineapple. Sound appetizing?

The "Hula Burger" had no meat, so it was perfect for Fridays. But it had another problem—Kroc couldn't get anyone to buy it. Customers all said, "I love the Hula, but where's the burger?" McDonald's' vegetarian experiment was abandoned after a few months. It wasn't until 1962 that the religious crisis was solved with the "Filet-O-Fish" sandwich.

## A QUICK ONE

In the mid-'60s, Hires developed a brand new product and rushed it out to supermarkets...where it went sour. The product: root beer-flavored milk.

## GIMME A LIGHT

Believe it or not, "light beer"—a huge success today—was a dud in 1967. Two light beers were introduced that year.

The first was Gablinger's—also known as "the Edsel of

Beers." Brewed on the East Coast by Reingold, it was named after the Swiss chemist who'd formulated it—Hersch Gablinger. Reingold put his picture on the cans, trying to make him a celebrity, but it was no use. The "no carbohydrate" beer was so watery it wouldn't even hold a head. And the slogan, "It doesn't fill you up," didn't mean anything to beer-drinkers in 1967.

If that wasn't enough, the federal government seized a shipment of Gablinger's because of "misleading" statements on the label, and a Reingold competitor filed a lawsuit, charging that the product was falsely promoted. Reingold made all the necessary changes, but by that time Gablinger's was a lost cause.

The other "light" beer was called...Lite Beer. That's right—the same one that over-the-hill athletes have promoted on television for the last decade. In 1967, it was marketed by a Cincinnati brewery named Meister Brau. They called it "low calorie beer," and their ads featured "Miss Lite," a 21-year-old California blonde in a leotard. But Lite was ahead of its time, and people who were into low-cal foods weren't into drinking beer. Lite lasted for about a year, then disappeared.

**IT AIN'T OVER TIL IT'S OVER:** In the late '70s, the Miller Brewing Company purchased Meister Brau and its various assets—including the trade name *Lite*. Styles had changed in a decade, and the time was right for "diet beer." So in 1979, Miller launched its "new" beer with a memorable ad campaign featuring aging macho men fighting over whether Lite was more attractive because it tasted good or because it didn't make them feel full. The result: the beer that flopped in '67 was the second-leading beer in America (behind Bud) twenty years later.

**BEER NOTES**

- Legally, a beer doesn't actually have to be lower in calories to call itself "light" beer. All that's required is for the beer to be light in color.
- In 1986, Anheuser-Busch sold more beer than any brewery in history—72,300,000 barrels.
- Smoke and drink? Tastes good, but doubles your health risk.

# ONE-LINERS

*Occasionally a random phrase in a conversation inspires a hit record. Here are some examples.*

**MY BOYFRIEND'S BACK,** the Angels. 1963/#1
Abraham Lincoln High School in Brooklyn was fertile ground for musicians and singers. Neil Sedaka and the Tokens went there. So did songwriter/producer Bob Feldman. Bob graduated in 1958 and moved across the East River to Manhattan, where he became a staff writer for April-Blackwood Music.

Five years later he heard that the Sweet Shoppe across the street from Lincoln High, his favorite hangout in the '50s, was being torn down. So he went back for a last look. "While I was there," Feldman recalls, "an altercation started between a young girl and a hoody-looking young man with a leather jacket and a great D.A. [duck's-ass hairstyle]. She was pointing a finger at him and screaming, "My boyfriend's back and you're gonna be in trouble. You've been spreading lies about me all over school and when he gets ahold of you, you're gonna be sorry you were ever born.'"

That night Bob told his writing partners, Jerry Goldstein and Richard Gotterher, about the incident and they sat down and wrote a song about it. The Angels recorded the tune a few weeks later, and it became a million-seller—one of the biggest hits of 1963.

**OH PRETTY WOMAN, Roy Orbison.** 1964/#1
Roy Orbison's wife, Claudette, was already a famous rock 'n' roll name by the '60s. Orbison wrote the flip side of the Everly Brothers' 1958 classic, "All I Have to Do Is Dream," as a tribute to her. But the tune she inspired in 1964 meant even more to Roy's career; he sang it himself.

It started with a shopping trip. Roy and Billy Dees, a songwriter Orbison collaborated with, were sitting in the Orbisons' house when Claudette announced she was going into town to

In 1647, New York became the first city in America with a paved street.

buy some groceries. "Do you need any money?" Roy asked. Dee said, "A pretty woman never needs any money." Then he turned to Roy and said, "Hey, how about that for a song title?" Orbison liked the idea of a "pretty woman," but not the part about the money. After Mrs. Orbison left, Roy and Billy began turning the phrase into a song. And when she returned, carrying her bags of food, she was greeted by the debut performance of Roy's second #1 tune.

In 1982, Van Halen remade the song.

## OTHER ONE-LINERS

•Otis Redding and drummer Al Jackson were discussing the problems of going on tour, and Redding started complaining too much. Jackson said, "What are you griping about? You're on the road all the time. All you can look for is a little respect when you come home." Redding took the line and wrote **"Respect"** from it.

•**"He Ain't Heavy, He's My Brother"** was inspired by Father Flanagan's Boy's Town poster. The poster had a picture of a priest on one side, and a two kids facing him, one sitting on the other's shoulders. The caption read, "He ain't heavy Father, he's my brother."

•Marvin Gaye's biographer visited Gaye in Belgium, where the singer was living in 1982 after a bitter divorce. The biographer noticed sado-masochistic magazines in Gaye's apartment, and suggested that Gaye needed some "sexual healing." It inspired the tune **"Sexual Healing,"** Gaye's first top 10 hit in five years, and a Grammy-winner.

•"The Jack Benny Show" occasionally featured a used car salesman who swore that every car had been owned by "a little old lady from Pasadena." Jan Berry, of Jan and Dean, was studying geriatrics at the time; he based a million-selling song on the phrase—**"The Little Old Lady From Pasadena."**

•Lamont Dozier was having a fight with his girlfriend. He shouted at her, **"Stop in the name of love!"**

The first pay phone was installed in a Hartford, Connecticut bank in 1889. The price: 5¢.

# EINSTEIN SAYS...

*A few words of wisdom from the white-maned genius.*

[Explaining the concept of relativity] "When you are courting a nice girl an hour seems like a second. When you sit on a red-hot cinder a second seems like an hour. That's relativity."

"The most beautiful thing we can experience is the mysterious. It is the source of all true art and science."

"Imagination is more important than knowledge."

"The hardest thing in the world to understand is the income tax."

"God is subtle, but he is not malicious."

"An empty stomach is not a good political adviser."

"Nothing is more destructive of respect for the government and the law of the land than passing laws which cannot be enforced."

"We should take care not to make the intellect our god; it has, of course, powerful muscles, but no personality."

"I don't believe in mathematics."

"The release of atom power has changed everything except our way of thinking, and thus we are being driven unarmed towards a catastrophe."

[When asked how he felt about seeing his ideas used in the atomic bomb] "If only I had known, I should have become a watchmaker."

"Art is the expression of the profoundest thoughts in the simplest way."

"Everything should be made as simple as possible, but not simpler."

"Science without religion is lame, religion without science is blind."

"Whoever is careless with the truth in small matters cannot be trusted with important matters."

Thomas Edison demonstrated the first practical electric lightbulb on December 20, 1879.

# THE FBI: WATCHING TV

*According to a former ranking agent, the FBI spends an extraordinary amount of time and money on p.r. ...and not nearly enough on solving crimes. A case in point:*

In 1986, it was revealed that between 1959 and 1963 the FBI employed agents to watch, report on, and try to influence the content of the TV series "The Untouchables." The reason: Director J. Edgar Hoover was incensed that it portrayed Treasury Agent Eliot Ness as the major crime-buster of his era, ignoring the FBI completely.

"Hoover fumed when episodes showed Ness solving a crime that fell under the FBI's regular jurisdiction," wrote William Barret in *Rolling Stone*. "'We must find some way to prevent FBI cases from being used,' [he] wrote. His staff launched an immediate investigation into published reports—apparently false—that ex-FBI agents were writing scripts for the show."

Actually, J. Edgar Hoover's monitoring of "The Untouchables" barely scratched the surface of the FBI's elaborate surveillance of Hollywood scripts during his tenure as director (48 years). Hoover's obsession with Hollywood's depiction of the Bureau in films and on television led to some strange investigations. FBI files on Rock Hudson, Groucho Marx and Walt Disney reveal the paranoid scope of the Bureau's efforts to reshape its image for public consumption.

As an unelected government official at the whim of periodic presidential reappointments, Hoover—who served as director from 1924 until his death in 1972—had every reason to protect the G-Man's glorified position in popular culture. FBI-sanctioned projects, such as "The FBI" TV series (1965-73) starring Efrem Zimbalist, Jr., helped solidify the Bureau's pre-Watergate public standing and thus Hoover's stranglehold as director.

Hoover himself admitted in a posthumously published article written for *TV Guide* (May 20, 1972) that the Bureau had final approval rights over the scripts, sponsors and actors portraying FBI agents in "The FBI" TV series. The Director also collected a neat $500 per episode. "We know," Hoover wrote in *TV Guide* "that a less than first-rate program could cheapen the FBI's name and have an adverse effect on its image.... Perhaps we are inclined towards Puritanism in an increasingly permissive world."

Only after Hoover's death and the post-Nixon flurry of bureaucratic reform—such as the re-amended Freedom of Information Act of 1974 which subjected FBI documents to declassification—did the truth behind the FBI's Hollywood surveillance become known.

During his almost 50-year reign as Bureau chief, Hoover had been rumored to have amassed a Personal and Confidential file on every major player in both political and entertainment circles, including intimate (but often unsubstantiated) details of drinking, drugging and sexual peccadillos. Unfortunately, the contents of Hoover's P&C files will never be known, thanks to his private secretary Helen Gandy, who shredded every file upon Hoover's death, except one: the pedigree of his terriers, G-Boy and Cindy. (That file, incidentally, had been saved for Clyde Tolson, Hoover's right hand man—some say literally—and brief successor at the Bureau.)

Fortunately, various bits of Hooverana in the form of Official and Confidential files managed to survive the purge. These documents—available for public scrutiny (and cheap thrills) at the FBI's Freedom of Information Act Reading Room in Washington—have revealed the methods by which Hoover managed to meddle into any film production or television series that included a portrayal of an FBI agent.

The following are some examples:

## WALT DISNEY

Not even Uncle Walt could escape the Bureau's dragnet. The movie in question was *Moon Pilot,* a harmless Disney pre-*I Dream of Jeannie* comedy about an astronaut who meets an alien before a space mission.

After learning that *Moon Pilot*'s script portrayed FBI agents as ineffectual bumblers, Hoover ordered the chief of the Bureau's Los Angeles division to contact Disney for a meeting, where he was asked to change the film's reference from FBI agents to Federal security agents. Despite Disney's protestations that the change was "unrealistic," dialogue changes were tailored to meet Hoover's specifications.

The real snafu started when Hoover was sent a newspaper review of *Moon Pilot* which referred to the bureau's portrayal "as a mass of dolts." On the margin of the review (which is included in Disney's FBI file), Hoover scrawled "I am amazed Disney would do this. He probably has been infiltrated."

Apparently, the squabble carried over to another Disney production, *That Darn Cat* (1964), which was also closely monitored by the Los Angeles division for references to the FBI. The matter was dropped—according to an FBI memorandum in Disney's file—after "an established source at the Disney studios" confirmed that the script depicted "the FBI in a most complimentary manner."

## ROCK HUDSON

In 1982, Rock Hudson's FBI file was rush-released in the midst of the media circus surrounding his AIDS-related death. The most quoted part of the released documents was as follows: "Rock Hudson has not been the subject of an FBI investigation. During 1965, however, a confidential informant reported that several years ago while he was in New York he had an 'affair' with movie star Rock Hudson. The informant stated that from personal knowledge he knew that Rock Hudson was a homosexual. The belief was expressed that by 'personal knowledge' the informant meant he had personally indulged in homosexual acts with Hudson or had witnessed or received the information of individuals who had done so."

This document had been sent to Mildred Stegall, White House staff-member during LBJ's presidency.

Since Hoover himself had been rumored to be gay (never proven but he was a bachelor all his life), he had particular interest in major figures who were gay. For example, Tennessee Williams' FBI files include this: "Subsequently, in connection with the investigation for the Department in 1961 (expurged) the Bureau ascertained that Thomas Lanier Williams has the reputation of being a homosexual. (Expurged.) Further, the Office of Naval Intelligence, in a separate inquiry, secured statements from individuals who admitted participating in homosexual acts with Williams."

**Only 10% of the athletes who sign pro baseball contracts ever make it into the major leagues.**

Hoover, then, was particularly alarmed to find out that Rock Hudson might be playing an FBI agent in a movie. According to *Daily Variety* (9/5/67), Hudson had been signed to play "an FBI agent who becomes involved with a jewel thief." This revelation sent shockwaves through the Bureau. An investigation into the movie called *The Quiet Couple* (eventually released as *A Fine Pair*) proved that *Daily Variety's* information was erroneous—Hudson's role was that of an ex-police officer. Still, the Bureau made several follow-up reports (and wasted untold thousands of taxpayers' dollars) to make sure Hudson did not play an FBI agent.

## GROUCHO MARX

Obviously, any Jewish celebrity with the name Marx was going to be under Hoover's intense scrutiny. Although Marx's FBI files include inconclusive investigations into his possible Communist affiliations, it is the references to his TV series, "You Bet Your Life," that show the Bureau's sensitivity to every mention of the FBI.

*Included in Marx's files are the following entries:*

"(Expurged) called on 2/29/60 to advise that he had been listening to the captioned program on last Thursday, 2/25/60, on NBC, Channel 4, and that one of the contestants was an individual described by (expurged) as a 'stumble bum' who admitted being a former pugilist and bootlegger. (Expurged) said that when this contestant, whose name he did not recall, stated he had been a bootlegger, Marx asked, 'You mean you were a bootlegger for the FBI?' in an apparent effort to be funny. (Expurged) said the contestant made some non-committal answer and there was little laughter from the audience. (Expurged) stated that he felt that Marx's question was in poor taste and simply wanted to call it to the Bureau's attention."

"We received a letter from (Expurged) Los Angeles 48, California, suggesting that the director see Romaine Rielding talk Russian to Groucho Marx on the Groucho Marx television show Thursday evening, January 29, 1959.

"The show was monitored and there was nothing on it concerning the Bureau or matters of any interest to us."

# WORD PLAY

*Common phrases and their origins*

**To Peter Out**
Possibly comes from France, where peter means "fart." According to one expert: "'Peter out' would then be equivalent to 'fizzle out,' since...the original 'fizzle' was a noiseless fart."

**A Wild Goose Chase**
A game played in Elizabethan England—a crazy version of follow-the-leader, on horseback. People believed wild geese acted this way.

**Red Tape**
The stuff used by bureaucrats in the 19th century to tie together packets of official documents.

**Different Drummer**
Coined by Henry David Thoreau. In his own words: "If a man does not keep pace with his companions, perhaps it is because he marches to a different drummer."

**To Quit Cold Turkey**
"Typically, a person [who quits drugs or drinking] undergoes bouts of sweating and chills, with goosebumps. ....Anyone who has seen a plucked turkey prepared for the oven...will at once understand the image."

**The Jig Is Up**
"First heard during Shakespeare's time. Jig was then a slang word for *trick*, so the phrase simply meant, 'Your trick or deceit has been found out.'"

**Toodle-oo**
Derived from the French phrase, *Tout a l'heure*, which means "See you later."

**Jerk**
In Victorian times, masturbation was considered the road to insanity. People who showed the "results" of self-abuse—stupidity, dimwittedness, etc.—were referred to as *Jerk-offs*. Later, just calling someone a *jerk* was sufficent to get the point across.

**Someone's Gone to Pot**
Like food that's cooked and eaten....It's gone to (the) pot. It's done, finished, over.

# FRANKS & DOGS

*Some food is so much a part of our lives that we never stop to ask where it comes from. Here are some answers you can chew on.*

**THE SAUSAGE: ANCIENT HISTORY**

• The Babylonians were the first to come up with the concept over 3,500 years ago by stuffing spiced meat into animal intestines.

• Other civilizations adopted and modified the sausage. The Greeks called it "orya." In the 9th Century B.C., the Greek poet Homer praised the sausage in his epic the *Odyssey*.

• The Romans, whose army marched on its stomach, loved the sausage. It is mentioned in the oldest known Roman cookbook, dated 228 A.D. They called it "salsus"—which ultimately became *sausage*.

**THE WEINER.** Over the next 1000 years, the popularity of sausages spread throughout Europe. By the Middle Ages, they began to take on regional characteristics; their shape and size varied from country to country, and local creations were named for the towns in which they originated. Austria gave birth to the "Vienna sausage" or *wienerwurst*, from which the term "weiner" is derived.

**THE FRANKFURTER.** The modern hot dog—the frankfurter—is descended from a spiced, smoked, slightly curved, thin sausage developed in Frankfurt, Germany.

• According to German lore, the shape of this "Frankfurter" was a tribute to a popular pet dachshund that belonged to a local butcher. The result: by the 1850s, it was commonly called a "dachshund sausage." It was customarily eaten with sauerkraut and mustard. But no bun.

• In the 1890s, a German immigrant named Charles Feltman began selling "dachshund sausages" on the street in Coney Island, NY. He became so successful that he was able to open a "frankfurter" restaurant—the first in the United States.

**THE BUN.** In 1904, at the St. Louis "Louisiana Purchase Exposition," another Frankfurt native sold "dachshund" sausages.

The effect was far-reaching: besides popularizing the food nationwide, this entrepreneur improved the package by introducing the bun. Here's how: Gloves were customarily supplied for customers to wear while eating their frankfurters. But at the fair, too many people walked away still wearing them; the vendor soon ran out of spare gloves. In desperation, he convinced a nearby baker to make frank-shaped rolls as a substitute for gloves. The rolls actually worked better; a new tradition was born.

**THE HOT DOG.** The name *Hot Dog* was coined in 1906. A syndicated cartoonist named Tad Dorgan was enjoying a baseball game at New York's Polo Grounds. Inspired by the vendors' call of "Get your red hot dachshund dogs!" he went back to his office and began sketching a cartoon based on the notion of a real dachshund in a bun, covered with mustard. When he couldn't come up with the correct spelling of dachshund, he supposedly just settled for "hot dog." The name stuck. Ironically, although Dorgan is clearly given credit for the name, the original cartoon has never been found.

## THE HAMBURGER

• The hamburger originated with the warring Mongolian and Turkish tribes known as Tatars who shredded low-quality beef before cooking to make it taste better.

• The dish was introduced to Germany sometime before the 14th century where it was spiced and prepared cooked or raw. From the town of Hamburg the dish became known as "Hamburg steak."

• In the 1880's, German immigrants brought the Hamburg specialty to America where it became known as "hamburger steak." It was also known as "Salisbury Steak," named after the English Dr. J.H. Salisbury, who recommended to his patients that they eat beef three times a day.

• The "hamburg" began its ascent to unparalleled popularity when it was served as a sandwich at the 1904 St. Louis World's Fair. Unfortunately, no one knows exactly how its association with ketchup started, or who thought of serving it on a bun.

• Today, the hamburger is *the* most popular entrée in American restaurants.

**The average American eats between 15 and 20 pounds of apples annually.**

# PARTY LINES

*People often ask if there's really any difference between the two major political parties. To answer the question, Rep. Andrew Jacobs of Indiana rose in the House of Representatives and offered this delineation. It was recorded in* Will the Gentleman Yield?, *by Bill Hogan and Mike Hill, and is reprinted with permission of Ten Speed Press.*

**TO BE READ ALOUD BY A DEMOCRAT TO A REPUBLICAN, OR A REPUBLICAN TO A DEMOCRAT:**

Democrats seldom make good polo players.

The people you see coming out of white wooden churches are Republicans.

Democrats buy most of the books that have been banned somewhere. Republicans form censorship committees and read them as a group.

Republicans are likely to have fewer but larger debts that cause them no concern.

Democrats owe a lot of small bills. They don't worry either.

Republicans consume three-fourths of all the rutabaga produced in this country. The remainder is thrown out.

Republicans usually wear hats and almost always clean their paintbrushes.

Democrats give their worn-out clothes to those less fortunate. Republicans wear theirs.

Republicans post all the signs saying *No Trespassing* and *These Deer are Private Property* and so on. Democrats bring picnic baskets and start their bonfires with signs.

Republicans employ exterminators. Democrats step on bugs.

Republicans have governesses for their children. Democrats have grandmothers.

Democrats name their children after currently popular sports figures, politicians and entertainers. Republican children are named after their parents or grandparents according to where the most money is.

Large cities such as New York are filled with Republicans—up until 5 p.m. At this point there is a phenomenon much like an automatic washer starting the spin cycle. People begin pouring out of every exit of the city. These are Republicans going home.

Democrats keep trying to cut down on smoking, but are not successful. Neither are Republicans.

Republicans tend to keep their shades drawn, though there isn't any reason why they should. Democrats ought to, but don't.

Republicans fish from the stern of a chartered boat. Democrats sit on the dock and let the fish come to them.

Republicans study the financial pages of the newspaper. Democrats put them in the bottom of the bird cage.

Most of the stuff you see alongside the road has been thrown out of car windows by Democrats.

On Saturday, Republicans head for the hunting lodge or the yacht club. Democrats wash the car and get a haircut.

Republicans raise dahlias, Dalmatians and eyebrows. Democrats raise Airedales, kids and taxes.

Democrats eat the fish they catch. Republicans hang them on the wall.

Democrats watch TV crime and Western shows that make them clench their fists and become red in the face. Republicans get the same effect from presidential press conferences.

Christmas cards that Democrats send are filled with reindeer and chimneys and long messages. Republicans select cards containing a spray of holly, or a single candle.

Democrats are continually saying, "This Christmas we're going to be sensible." Republicans consider this highly unlikely.

Republicans smoke cigars on weekdays.

Republicans have guest rooms. Democrats have spare rooms filled with old baby furniture.

Republican boys date Democratic girls. They plan to marry Republican girls, but feel they're entitled to a little fun first.

Democrats make up plans and then do something else. Republicans follow the plans their grandfathers made.

Democrats purchase all the tools—the power saws and mowers. A Republican probably wouldn't know how to use a screwdriver.

Democrats suffer from chapped hands and headaches. Republicans have tennis elbow and gout.

Republicans sleep in twin beds—some even in separate rooms. That is why there are more Democrats.

# SOUNDS OF SILENCE

*The unusual history of the record that made Simon and Garfunkel famous, from the book* Behind the Hits, *by Bob Shannon and John Javna.*

As late as March 1965, Simon and Garfunkel were still just another unknown folk duo who played at Greenwich Village coffee houses. Their act consisted of a few folk standards, a few Dylan tunes, and a few originals.

Then they got a break; Paul Simon managed to interest Columbia producer Tom Wilson in his material. The result: Simon and Garfunkel's first album, a record called "Wednesday Morning, 3 AM." It featured Simon on acoustic guitar, and included "Sounds of Silence," which Paul had written the previous year.

It bombed, and Simon and Garfunkel broke up. Paul moved to England; Artie went back to college.

That could have been the end of the story. But unknown to the singers, a Boston radio station began playing "Sounds of Silence" regularly...and Columbia suddenly became interested. They'd had Top 40 success with the folk-rock music of the Byrds, so they decided it was worth trying to turn S&G into a folk-rock act, too.

The secret: All Columbia had to do was add electric instruments to the S&G tracks already on tape. That task fell to Tom Wilson. Without telling Simon and Garfunkel about it, he gathered a bunch of studio musicians at the Columbia recording studios in New York City and had them add their own music to S&G's. Vinnie Bell was the guitarist in that session.

**Vinnie Bell**: "We had no idea what we were going to work on that day—we were just doing a session. So we got there and there were no artists...and we had no music; they just played a ...record of these two guys singing....Well, everybody got out their own paper and we started jotting down music. We each made up our own parts because there was no arranger on it. And then we played along to this existing track."

So, thanks to a handful of anonymous New York sidemen, the acoustic version of "Sounds" became electrified. Then Columbia issued it as the new single from their latest "folk-rock discovery," Simon and Garfunkel. Top 40 stations, unaware that the duo no longer existed, immediately played it and soon it was shooting up the charts.

A few weeks later, Paul Simon got a call in England telling him that his record was the #1 song in America. You can imagine his shock—he didn't even know it existed! Of course, Simon flew back to the States, S&G reunited, and America had two new poet-heroes. Simon, however, apparently had no idea who'd played the electric instruments on his record—which proved embarrassing when he and Garfunkel appeared on NBC's prime time rock 'n' roll TV show, "Hullaballoo." Here's what happened:

**Vinnie Bell**: "I was working [in the house band] on 'Hullaballoo,' and of course we'd get all the big groups on the show. It was a lot of fun for me, because I would see all my friends. I recorded with all those people. The Stones used to come on—I worked with them. Dionne Warwick was a regular guest....All those people, y'know. Well, now Simon and Garfunkel have a big hit, 'Sounds of Silence,' so they came on the show. And during the rehearsal, Paul Simon talked to the musical conductor, Peter Matz. He said, 'I'd like to show the guitar player how to play this [part].' But Peter Matz knew I did the record; he said, 'I think he knows.' But Paul Simon insisted. He said, 'No, I did a special thing on the record that I want him to do with the sound.' And Peter Matz looked at me, and he said, 'All right, go ahead.' So Simon walked through the orchestra and when he got to me, he said, 'Hi, I'm Paul Simon.' I said, 'Hi, I'm Vinnie Bell.' He said, 'I'd like to show you, if you don't mind, how I did this thing on the record. We have a record out, I don't know if you know it, it's a big hit, "Sounds of Silence."' So I said to him, 'Yes, I know the record. To tell you the truth, I know just what to play.' He said, 'No, here, just watch my fingers,' and showed me with his guitar. 'Paul,' I said, '*I did the record*.' And of course there was silence. And he said, 'Well...okay....Are you sure you did the record?' I said, 'Yeah, it's *this*, right?' And I played [the part for him]. He said, 'Yeah, that's it.' I just told him, "Don't worry.'"

**The most money ever paid for a cow in an auction was $1.3 million.**

# PETER PAN

*This is one of the most engaging works of fantasy you'll find anywhere. After seeing Walt Disney's sugary version, you'll be surprised how ironic and sophisticated the original is.*

## BACKGROUND

Peter Pan *was written by Sir James Matthew Barrie, one of England's most celebrated writers. It was first presented as a play in London in 1904, and was so well received that in 1906 Barrie wrote a sequel called* Peter Pan in Kensington Gardens. *In 1911, Barrie finally published* Peter Pan and Wendy, *the famous prose adaptation of the original play. The following is excerpted from that work.*

Mrs. Darling first heard of Peter when she was tidying up her children's minds. It is the nightly custom of every good mother after her children are asleep to rummage in their minds and put things straight for the next morning, repacking into their proper places the many articles that have wandered during the day. If you could keep awake (but of course you can't) you would see your own mother doing this, and you would find it very interesting to watch her. It is quite like tidying up drawers. You would see her on her knees, I expect, lingering humorously over some of your contents, wondering where on earth you had picked this thing up, making discoveries sweet and not so sweet, pressing this to her cheek as if it were as nice as a kitten, and hurriedly stowing that out of sight. When you wake in the morning, the naughtiness and evil passions with which you went to bed have been folded up small and placed at the bottom of your mind; and on the top, beautifully aired, are spread out your prettier thoughts, ready for you to put on.

I don't know whether you have ever seen a map of a person's mind. Doctors sometimes draw maps of other parts of you, and your own map can become intensely interesting, but catch them

**Guzzlers: Americans drink an average of 90 million cans of beer every day.**

trying to draw a map of a child's mind, which is not only confused, but keeps going round all the time. There are zigzag lines on it, just like your temperature on a card, and these are probably roads in the island; for the Neverland is always more or less an island, with astonishing splashes of colour here and there, and coral reefs and rakish-looking craft in the offing, and savages and lonely lairs, and gnomes who are mostly tailors, and caves through which a river runs, and princes with six elder brothers, and a hut fast going to decay, and one very small old lady with a hooked nose. It would be an easy map if that were all; but there is also first day at school, religion, fathers, the round pond, needlework, murders, hangings, verbs that take the dative, chocolate pudding day, getting into braces, say ninety-nine, threepence for pulling out your tooth yourself, and so on; and either these are part of the island or they are another map showing through, and it is all rather confusing, especially as nothing will stand still.

Of course the Neverlands vary a good deal. John's, for instance, had a lagoon with flamingoes flying over it at which John was shooting, while Michael, who is very small, had a flamingo with lagoons flying over it. John lived in a boat turned upside down on the sands, Michael in a wigwam, Wendy in a house of leaves deftly sewn together. John had no friends, Michael had friends at night, Wendy had a pet wolf forsaken by its parents; but on the whole the Neverlands have a family resemblance, and if they stood in a row you could say of them that they have each other's nose, and so forth. On these magic shores children at play are forever beaching their coracles. We too have been there; we can still hear the sound of the surf, though we shall land no more.

Of all delectable lands the Neverland is snuggest and most compact; not large and sprawly, you know, with tedious distances between one adventure, but nicely crammed. When you play at it by day with the chairs and tablecloth, it is not in the least alarming, but in the two minutes before you go to sleep it becomes very nearly real. That is why there are night-lights.

Occasionally in her travels through her children's minds Mrs.

**Life Span: Rattlesnakes live for about nineteen years.**

Darling found things she could not understand, and of these quite the most perplexing was the word Peter. She knew of no Peter, and yet he was here and there in John and Michael's minds, while Wendy's began to be scrawled all over with him. The name stood out in bolder letters than any of the other words, and as Mrs. Darling gazed she felt that it had an oddly cocky appearance.

'Yes, he is rather cocky,' Wendy admitted with regret. Her mother had been questioning her.

'But who is he, my pet?'

'He is Peter Pan, you know, mother.'

At first Mrs. Darling did not know, but after thinking back into her childhood she just remembered a Peter Pan who was said to live with the fairies. There were odd stories about him; as that when children died he went part of the way with them, so that they should not be frightened. She had believed in him at the time, but now that she was married and full of sense she quite doubted whether there was any such person.

'Besides,' she said to Wendy, 'he would be grown up by this time.'

'Oh no, he isn't grown up,' Wendy assured her confidently, 'and he is just my size.' She meant that he was her size in both mind and body; she didn't know how she knew it, she just knew it.

Mrs. Darling consulted Mr. Darling, but he smiled pooh-pooh. 'Mark my words,' he said, 'it is some nonsense Nana has been putting into their heads; just the sort of idea a dog would have. Leave it alone, and it will blow over.'

But it would not blow over; soon the troublesome boy gave Mrs. Darling quite a shock.

Children have the strangest adventures without being troubled by them. For instance, they may remember to mention, a week after the event happened, that when they were in the wood they met their dead father and had a game with him. It was in this casual way that Wendy one morning made a disquieting revelation. Some leaves of a tree had been found on the nursery floor, which certainly were not there when the children went to bed, and Mrs. Darling was puzzling over them when Wendy said with a tolerant smile:

'I do believe it is that Peter again!'

'Whatever do you mean, Wendy?'

'It is so naughty of him not to wipe,' Wendy said, sighing. She was a tidy child.

She explained in quite a matter-of-fact way that she thought Peter sometimes came to the nursery in the night and sat on the foot of her bed and played his pipes to her. Unfortunately she never woke, so she didn't know how she knew, she just knew.

'What nonsense you talk, precious. No one can get into the house without knocking.'

'I think he comes in by the window,' she said.

'My love, it is three floors up.'

'Were not the leaves at the foot of the window, mother?'

It was quite true; the leaves had been found very near the window.

Mrs. Darling did not know what to think, for it all seemed so natural to Wendy that you could not dismiss it by saying she had been dreaming.

'My child,' the mother cried, 'why did you not tell me of this before?'

'I forgot,' said Wendy lightly. She was in a hurry to get her breakfast.

Oh, surely she must have been dreaming.

But, on the other hand, there were the leaves. Mrs. Darling examined them carefully; they were skeleton leaves, but she was sure they did not come from any tree that grew in England. She crawled about the floor, peering at it with a candle for marks of a strange foot. She rattled the poker up the chimney and tapped the walls. She let down a tape from the window to the pavement, and it was a sheer drop of thirty feet, without so much as a spout to climb up by.

Certainly Wendy had been dreaming.

**Tall tale: The average person is about a quarter of an inch taller at night.**

But Wendy had not been dreaming, as the very next night showed, the night on which the extraordinary adventures of these children may be said to have begun.

On the night we speak of all the children were once more in bed. It happened to be Nana's evening off, and Mrs. Darling had bathed them and sung to them till one by one they had let go her hand and slid away into the land of sleep.

All were looking so safe and cozy that she smiled at her fears now and sat down tranquilly by the fire to sew. It was something for Michael, who on his birthday was getting into shirts. The fire was warm, however, and the nursery dimly lit by three night-lights, and presently the sewing lay on Mrs. Darling's lap. Then her head nodded, oh, so gracefully. She was asleep. Look at the four of them, Wendy and Michael over there, John here, and Mrs. Darling by the fire. There should have been a fourth night-light.

While she slept she had a dream. She dreamt that the Neverland had come too near and that a strange boy had broken through from it. He did not alarm her, for she thought she had seen him before in the faces of many women who have no children. Perhaps he is to be found in the faces of some mothers also. But in her dream he had rent the film that obscures the Neverland, and she saw Wendy and John and Michael peeping through the gap.

The dream by itself would have been a trifle, but while she was dreaming the window of the nursery blew open, and a boy did drop on the floor. He was accompanied by a strange light, no bigger than your fist, which darted about the room like a living thing; and I think it must have been this light that awakened Mrs. Darling.

She started up with a cry, and saw the boy, and somehow she knew at once that he was Peter Pan. If you or I or Wendy had been there we should have seen that he was very like Mrs. Darling's kiss. He was a lovely boy, clad in skeleton leaves and the juices that ooze out of the trees; but the most entrancing thing about him was that he had all his first teeth. When he saw she was a grown-up, he gnashed the little pearls at her.

**Doctors in ancient China were paid when patients were healthy, not sick.**

# ALLENISMS

*Some of Woody Allen's coolest comments.*

"Thought: Why does man kill? He kills for food. And not only food: frequently there must be a beverage."

"Showing up is 80 percent of life."

"I'm not afraid to die. I just don't want to be there when it happens."

"If only God would give me some clear sign! Like making a large deposit in my name at a Swiss bank."

"I'm a practicing heterosexual...but bisexuality immediately doubles your chances for a date on Saturday night."

"My brain: it's my second favorite organ."

"I don't want to achieve immortality through my work...I want to achieve it through not dying."

Q. "Have you ever taken a serious political stand on anything?"

A. "Yes, for twenty-four hours I refused to eat grapes."

"Eternal nothingness is OK if you're dressed for it."

"Not only is there no God, but try getting a plumber on weekends."

"Is sex dirty? Only if it's done right."

"Money is better than poverty, if only for financial reasons."

"I want to tell you a terrific story about oral contraception. I asked this girl to sleep with me and she said 'no.'"

"My one regret in life is that I'm not someone else."

"I asked the girl if she could bring a sister for me. She did. Sister Maria Teresa. It was a very slow evening. We discussed the New Testament. We agreed that He was very well adjusted for an only child."

# CARY GRANT, ACID-HEAD

*We think of Timothy Leary, Jimi Hendrix , etc. as the quintessential LSD freaks. But Cary Grant—of all people—was into acid before those guys ever heard of it.*

Before Timothy Leary and the counterculture discovered LSD—before it was even illegal—the unflappable, ultimately dignified Cary Grant was tripping out every Saturday.

It was 1957. Grant's wife, Betsy Drake, had been going to the Psychiatric Institute of Beverly Hills to undergo an unusual form of chemical therapy. The Institute's directors believed that the little-known drug LSD "acted as a psychic energizer, emptying the subconscious mind and intensifying emotions a hundred times." Drake had been taking it regularly, and it had done wonders for her. So when she realized that Grant was on the verge of a nervous breakdown, she convinced him to try it, too.

Working with Dr. Mortimer Hartman, whom the actor referred to as "My wise Mahatma," Cary began the sessions under strict medical supervision. First he was given a dose of LSD in the therapist's offices; he spent several hours in treatment. Then he was given a depressant to calm him down. Finally, he was driven home to rest and recover for a day. Grant found the effects of the drug astounding. "The first thing that happens to you," he told friends, "is you don't want to look at who you are. Then the light breaks through; to use the cliché, you are enlightened." Hallucinating under the drug gave the otherwise staid Briton a new freedom. Once, he admitted, "I imagined myself as a giant penis launching off from Earth like a spaceship."

Grant continued this treatment for two years; he took hundreds of acid trips. Previously he had been reluctant to talk about his personal life. (An instructive anecdote: a reporter once cabled this question to him: "How old Cary Grant?"

**If a room contains 100 American women, 4 will probably not be wearing panties.**

Grant's evasive reply: "Old Cary Grant fine.") Now at age 55, thrilled by the new outlook on life that the drug gave him, he spoke to friends, the media, college students—anyone who would listen—about the benefits of LSD therapy.

"I have been born again," he declared. I have been through a psychiatric experience which has completely changed me. It was horrendous. I had to face things about myself which I never admitted, which I didn't know were there. Now I know I hurt every woman I ever loved. I was an utter fake, a self-opinionated bore, a know-all who knew very little."

**A Sampling of Grant's "Acid Revelations"**

- "Respect women because they are wiser than men...(they) have an innate wisdom we men try to despoil from the time we're sixteen years old."
- "The only way to remain happy is to know nothing or everything. Unfortunately, it is impossible to know nothing for very long."
- "A man owes it to me—if I have to look at him—to keep his hair combed and his teeth cleaned."
- "Deplore your mistakes. Regret them as much as you like. But don't really expect to learn by them."
- "Don't expect to be rewarded if you...tell the truth. Hypocrisy no longer has any power to shock us. We encounter it every day. But we encounter the truth so seldom that it shocks and embarrasses us, and we run from it."

Unfortunately, Grant's acid-inspired statement that "My next marriage will be complete" wasn't accurate—although he did have the child he said he was now ready to "beget." When he and actress Dyan Cannon (who swore she had only taken acid once before their marriage—and never during) decided to divorce, it turned ugly. She accused him of being an "apostle of LSD," "an unfit father," and said he insisted that she trip out. "He told me the new me would be created through LSD," she declared in court.

In later years, Grant refused to discuss the remarkable drug. "My intention in taking LSD," he finally told a reporter, "was to make myself happy. A man would have to be a fool to take something that *didn't* make him happy."

# PRESIDENTIAL QUIZ

*Odds and Ends about American presidents.*

1) In which state were the most presidents born?

2) The first president not born a British subject was:
a) Martin Van Buren
b) William Henry Harrison
c) Andrew Knox Polk

3) The only president who was never elected to any national office was...

4) Which president was into boxing and jujitsu?
a) Abe Lincoln
b) Teddy Roosevelt
c) John Kennedy

5) The first woman appointed to the cabinet was Frances Perkins. Who appointed her?

6) Who was the first president to weigh over 300 lbs.?

7) The first president to have documented nervous breakdowns (he had five before he became president) was...

8) The only president known to have ancestors who were American Indians was...

9) Which of these presidents was a bowling enthusiast?
a) Herbert Hoover
b) Harry Truman
c) Richard Nixon

10) What is the significance of the film, *Hellcats of the Navy* ?

11) Who was the first U.S. president to appear on national public TV?

12) Who was the first president to be inaugurated in Washington, D.C.?
a) George Washington
b) Thomas Jefferson
c) Andrew Jackson

13) The first bachelor president is considered likely to have been homosexual (his V.P., nicknamed "Miss Nancy," was thought to be his lover). Who was he?

14) More presidents were officially residents of this state when they were elected than any other. Which state?

15) How many presidents have there been?

# CAR BOMB: THE EDSEL

*In the lore of American business, the name Edsel is synonomous with total failure. Yet hardly anyone knows anything about the Edsel. The story is almost too stupid to believe, but here it is. Judge for yourself.*

The story of the Edsel sounds like a *Mad* magazine parody of the auto industry of the '50s: The people at Ford were so intent on using the latest novelty gadgets, super-sophisticated marketing techniques, and "personality surveys" to sell their new vehicle that they forgot to give their customers a car, too. Everything, from beginning to end, was done wrong ....And to top it off, Ford had the bad luck to unveil its upscale bomb during an economic slump that was responsible for the worst overall car sales in a decade. Things couldn't have gotten much worse.

"How much planning went into the Edsel? In a sense, it must be the most thoroughly planned product ever introduced."
**—*Fortune* magazine, September, 1957.**

**THE PLAN:** Ford, the #2 car manufacturer in the '50s, was losing too much business to GM in the "trade-up" field. Upwardly mobile consumers who started with an ordinary Ford or Chevrolet eventually wanted something a little more prestigious. Surveys showed that they "traded up" to either an Oldsmobile or a Buick—rarely a Mercury, which was all Ford had to offer in the upper range. So in the early '50s, Ford executives decided to create a whole new line of cars to attract "the young executive or the professional family on its way up." It was to be "the first new line of cars...started from scratch by a major manufacturer" since the Mercury was introduced in 1938. Ford committed $250 million to the project.

**THE EXECUTION:** Ford concentrated on three key elements: Design, Dealers, and "Personality."

**DESIGN:** Roy Brown, from the Lincoln division, was assigned the task of styling the Edsel. "His first move," reported one magazine, "was to take his stylists out to a busy intersection to look at cars. To no one's surprise, they decided all American cars looked pretty much alike."

"I wanted a car with strong identity, " Brown explained before the Edsel's unveiling, "one that could be recognized instantly from the front, the side, or rear." An example: Struck by the fact that front grilles on American cars were all "massive and horizontal," Brown decided a vertical grille would set the Edsel apart visually. His 1957 analysis of the result: "It is crisp and fresh-looking. That grille could become a classic." [It did, of course, but not exactly the way Brown foresaw it; the famous "toilet-seat" grille remains a classic example of tasteless excess in car design.]

**The interior** was next. Neil Blume was assigned the task of "loading it with exciting things for Edsel dealers to talk about." He came up with 23 selling points, most of which were simply cosmetic. Some examples: "A drum-like speedometer that glows a menacing red when the car exceeds a preset speed;" "a thermometer that registers the temperature both inside and outside the car;" "a single-dial heating and ventilating control;" and "gearshift buttons sensibly located in the steering wheel hub."

**DEALERS:** Ford wanted exclusive dealers for the Edsel—not salesmen who also handled Fords, Mercurys, or any other brand. The reason: they figured the car stood a better chance of succeeding if the Edsel was all a dealer had to offer. So beginning in 1955, they began trying to woo dealers away from their competition, offering the the chance of a lifetime to become the first Edsel dealers. The amazing thing is that it worked. Almost 200 GM dealers jumped to the Edsel; 150 Chrysler-Plymouth dealers took the bait; another 200 dealers from smaller manufacturers went for it. Each had to plunk down over $100,000 (1957 money), and in some cases, they hadn't even seen the car—they took it on faith that Ford was behind the project 100%...and how could Ford miss? It was like buying a ticket on the *Titanic*.

**PERSONALITY:** The Edsel may have been the first auto to rely on sophisticated marketing profiles to target its potential customers. Ford wanted to know what the car's "personality" should be, so they hired a marketing expert named David Wallace to tell them. Begining in 1955, Wallace worked with the Bureau of Applied Social Research at Columbia University, doing market studies and polling consumers to find out how they *felt* about various makes of automobiles. It was he who determined that the Edsel should be positioned as "the smart car for young families."

But it was a crazy survey. They approached their new car strictly as a status symbol, asking questions about what *impressed* people, without asking what people would *buy*. "The trouble here," commented one critic, "[is] that they didn't ask questions that elicited meaningful replies. Ford asked no questions at all about car prices, cost of upkeep, cost of operation, cars too long for garages, etc. In fact, the consumer research program...completely ignored automobiles as functioning machines of transportation."

In addition, Ford frequently ignored the research and reverted to its standard decision-making techniques..."If you ask how a policy was determined, like the choice of green as the Edsel's color" said one writer at the time, "you may still be told 'Well, So-and-so liked it, and he has the power. That's the way it is.'" The marketing men weren't particularly pleased with the choice of the name Edsel, either. [Edsel Ford was Henry Ford II's father—it's obvious who picked that one.] "Just look at the associations," complained one. "Edsel, diesel, pretzel—Good Lord! It's a wonderful name for a plow or a tractor, but a car? They can make it elegant, but it will take them two or three years and $50 million to do it." [An aside: Wallace corresponded with poet Marianne Moore about names for the new car. The ones she suggested included: Mongoose Cigique, Pastelogram, Pluma Piluma and Utopian Turtletop.]

In the end, Wallace shrugged it off. "All we can do is advise them how to merchandise the car," he said. "We can't tell them how to create it."

**THE UNVEILING**: "On September 4, 1957, after a year of intensive and elaborate build-up (in which no detail of the car was revealed) and better than a month before any of the 1958 models were out, the public was finally invited to see the dream made real." People couldn't resist the invitation; for the first week, Edsel showrooms were packed. But within a month,

**According to Gallup, the woman most admired by Americans in 1986 was Mother Teresa.**

it was clear that customers had just come to look. No one was buying the car. Ford announced that "They're simply waiting to see what the other makes will offer; they'll be back," but Ford was dreaming. October's sales were worse than September's, and November's were so bad that dealers started going bankrupt. The main Edsel dealer in New York City quit, declaring that "The Ford Motor Company has laid an egg."

Ford used every trick it knew to lure people into the showrooms—it raised the Edsel ad budget to a record $20 million, offered the car to state highway officials at huge discounts to give the car some road respectability, offered rebates to dealers...But nothing worked.

In retrospect, perhaps the most amazing thing about this new product is the fact that Ford concentrated so much effort on the "sell" that the car itself was overlooked. Not only did it offer nothing new—it was even inadequately supplied with the basics. The brakes, for example, were the same as Ford used on its smaller cars, although the Edsel was considerably heavier than the rest of the Ford line.

**TEST REPORTS:** Here are a few of the comments *Consumer Reports* made when it test-drove the celebrated new auto:

- "The public expected the new name to be on a new-from-the-ground-up car. CU's answer: the Edsel has no...advantages over other brands. The car is almost entirely conventional in construction, utilizing components from the 1957 Ford...and Mercury."
- "Edsels offer nothing new in passenger accommodations—unless 'contour seats' feel different to you....The interior dimensions are, for the most part, those of the 1957 Ford Fairlane, one of the least roomy of last year's cars."
- "The amount of shake present...on rough roads—which wasn't long in making itself heard as squeaks and rattles—went well beyond any acceptable limit."
- "As a matter of simple fact, combined with the car's tendency to shake like jelly, Edsel's handling represents retrogression rather than progress in design and behavior."
- "The 'luxury-loaded' Edsel—as one magazine cover described it—will certainly please anyone who confuses gadgetry with true luxury."

**A sneeze zooms out of your mouth at over 600 m.p.h.**

•"The center of the steering wheel is not, in CU's opinion, a good pushbutton location....To look at the Edsel buttons pulls the driver's eyes clear down off the road."

• "The Edsel instrument panel is a mismanaged dilly."

And so it went. Fundamentally, the magazine had nothing good to say about Ford's new product—except that it had great acceleration.

## EVEN MORE REASONS IT FLOPPED:

• It was an effort to get into the mid-sized car market....But in 1956 and 1957, the mid-sized car was in trouble. Anyone in the auto industry knew that. What Ford should have done was to bring out a low-priced, innovative economy model, a car to compete with the German Volkswagen. Instead, Ford produced an instant white elephant.

•Rotten timing. In September 1957, the stock market was in a downturn. In fact, the Edsel and the economic recession hit the market at exactly the same time.

•Ford introduced its new car with its 1958 prices at exactly the same time that the 1957 models were being discounted to clear them out. Consequently, the attention the company had sought for its new baby focused instead on its price. Consumers, dealers and bankers alike, balked at higher car prices in general—but because Edsel was the first car to announce them, the brunt of the public's displeasure landed right at Edsel's doorstep.

•The over-designed status symbol appeared a month before Russia successfully launched its Sputnik. In the wake of the U.S.S.R.'s feat, embarrassed Americans shunned opulent new cars as symbols of a misguided national priority. The emphasis in American culture temporarily shifted to academics and practicality.

## THE AFTERMATH

The Edsel lasted for two years. Shortly after it bombed, the *Wall Street Journal* ran this little squib: "Ford Motor has called on the Institute of Motivational Research to find out why Americans buy foreign economy cars."

**P.S.:** Edsel Ford, the car's unfortunate namesake, was a progressive minded, artistic thinker whose death preceded that of his father. Neither he nor Henry Ford ever saw the Edsel.

# THE FABULOUS '60S

*More odds and ends about America's favorite decade, from 60s!, by John and Gordon Javna*

**FLASH-IN-THE-PANTIES.** In the summer of 1960, Macy's installed a men's underwear vending machine. It was national news; throngs of people swarmed into the store to get a look at the contraption—so many, in fact, that Macy's had to move it from the ground level to the fifth floor to avoid store traffic jams. But it died there; the bare facts were that nobody wanted to buy boxer shorts from a machine.

**AUTO MANIPULATION.** Ford's Thunderbird was so popular in the early '60s that when John F. Kennedy requested 25 of them for his inaugural parade, Ford had none to supply; they were all sold out, and none of the waiting buyers would relinquish his claim to a new T-Bird (not even for the President). After some desperate juggling, Ford finally decided to make a few of its customers wait until after the inauguration.

**UNFRIENDLY SKIES.** In 1967 in Ankara, Turkey, farmers marched to the American and Soviet embassies and demanded compensation for flood damages to their crops. The floods, they charged, were caused by Russian and American spaceships, which had torn "holes in the sky." The Russian ambassador suggested that if they really thought there was a hole in the sky, they ought to be trying to figure out how to fix it, not complaining to him about it.

**POLITICAL IMAGE.** After JFK's election in 1960, Robert J. Donovan's book *PT 109*—an account of the heroic rescue Kennedy pulled off during World War II—became a bestseller. A movie version wasn't far behind; but who would star? JFK, it turns out, wanted Warren Beatty to play him. But the director considered Beatty too unstable, and hired Cliff Robertson for the part instead. Kennedy sent his press secretary, Pierre Salinger, to protest the choice. The director's reply to the president: "Don't tell *me* how to make an exploitation movie."

# BRAINTEASERS

*Still more logic puzzles. Remember—no heavy math or pencils needed.*

"You know," said my Uncle Gordon, "an eccentric friend of mine decided that one of his two sons should take over his horse-breeding business. Being a sporting man, he arranged a horse race between the two sons. But being eccentric, he decided that the son who owned the *slowest* horse would win the business. Naturally each son was worried that the other would cheat by holding his horse back and not letting it run freely. So they decided to ask me for advice. I don't mean to be immodest," he said, grinning, "but I solved their problem with two words."

What did Uncle Gordon say?

"You know," said my Uncle Gordon, "people on Wall Street say that 1987 dollars are worth more than 1985 dollars."

"Uncle Gordon, you old faker," I said, "everybody knows that."

Why is it true?

"I know a man," said Uncle Gordon, "who lives on the 25th floor of an apartment building. Every morning he rides the elevator down to the street level, gets out and goes to work. But when he comes home at night, he only rides the elevator to the 8th floor and then walks up the stairs the rest of the way. Know why?"

"I haven't the foggiest idea," I answered.

Do you?

"Once in Asia," said Uncle Gordon, "I was captured by bandits. They told me: 'Make a statement—if you speak the truth, we'll hang you...if you say something false, we'll shoot you.' I thought it over for a minute, and then uttered a phrase that confused the robbers so completely that they let me go."

What did he say?

# HOLIDAYS

*We celebrate them every year without having the slightest idea where they really came from... Here are a few enlightening tidbits.*

## EASTER

Although we know it as the Christian celebration of the Resurrection of Christ, the name "Easter" derives from Eostre, the dawn goddess of Anglo-Saxon myth—who was traditionally honored with an annual festival at the beginning of spring. This celebration happened to coincide with Christian holy days, and so was co-opted by that religion. In America, Easter was largely ignored until immediately after the Civil War. The war-torn country needed a holiday which stressed rebirth, so observance of Easter became important.

## EASTER RABBIT

Take your pick: The rabbit is either a traditional symbol of fertility that represents spring, or the rabbit was the earthly symbol of the goddess Eostre.

## EASTER EGG

The egg represents birth and resurrection. It was apparently an ancient pre-Christian tradition to give people decorated eggs as gifts in the spring.

## APRIL FOOL'S DAY

Until 1564, it was a tradition to begin the New Year with a week of celebration, ending with a big party. But the calendar was different then, and the New Year began on March 25—which meant that the annual party was held on April 1. In 1564, a new calendar was instituted, making January 1 the New Year. People who forgot—or didn't realize—what had happened, and still showed up to celebrate on April 1, were called "April fools."

## MOTHER'S DAY

Created in response to the prolific letter-writing campaign of a Miss Anna Jarvis, a West Virginia school teacher who wanted to honor her own deceased mother. How could anyone say no? In 1914, six years after Jarvis began her campaign, President Woodrow Wilson signed a bill proclaiming the second Sunday in May as America's official Mother's Day. Jarvis was named the head of the official Mother's Day committee, and greeting card, flower, and candy sellers—thrilled at the opportunity to sell more of their goods—supported the effort with advertising. (In 1986 it was reported that over 150 million cards and 8 million bouquets of flowers were sent on Mother's Day.)

By the mid-'30s, however, Anna Jarvis was so disgusted with the commercialization of the holiday that she disavowed it. This didn't faze American businesses one bit. They set up their own organization to support Mother's Day, and with the backing of the American public, the holiday continues to flourish.

## CHRISTMAS

No one knows exactly when Christ was born, but according to accounts in the Bible, it might well not be December 25—the activities of the shepherds described in conjunction with the event are associated with spring, not winter. Nor did Christians celebrate Christ's birth when the religion was new. It wasn't until around the third century A.D. that December 25 was sanctioned as a holy day by the Church. The reason: It seems likely that Christian fathers were trying to compete with another growing religion, Mithraism—the worship of a sun god—whose big day was December 25.

## THE CHRISTMAS TREE

Might have begun in pre-Christian Europe, where the Nordic people believed that fruit trees and evergreens were embodiments of powerful spirits, although there are several other equally plausible legends. German families in the 16th century began bringing evergreens into their homes during the holiday season. They were known as *Christbaume* or "Christ trees," and were decorated with fruit, candles, and cookies.

The *Christbaum* was taken to England by Queen Victoria's German husband, Prince Albert. The first American Christmas trees were brought by German immigrants in the 1820s, but it wasn't until the beginning of the 20th century that Christmas trees became a mainstream custom in the States.

**Only about 5% of American men say they are satisfied with the way they look.**

## HANGING CHRISTMAS STOCKINGS

The custom of hanging stockings on the mantel to receive small gifts originated with St. Nicholas, the Turkish version of our own Santa Claus. Long ago, St. Nick was supposed to have provided dowries for the three daughters of a poor nobleman. He threw bags of money through their windows (in one version, down the chimney), where the gifts happened to fall into a stocking that was hung out to dry by the fire.

## SANTA CLAUS

The first Santa was the bishop of Myra of Asia Minor, St. Nicholas—who today remains a principal saint of the Eastern Orthodox church. In the 4th Century, he distributed presents to good children on his feast day, December 6.

During the Protestant Reformation, St. Nicholas was replaced in many countries by the Christmas Man, known in England as Father Christmas and in France as Pere Noel. But in the Netherlands, where St. Nicholas was the patron saint of sailors, he remained popular. There he was known as Sint Nikolaas or Sinterclaas, and Dutch children expected him to leave goodies in their wooden clogs on his feast day. Both this tradition and the name were Americanized. Sinterclaas became Santa Claus.

Amazingly, most of the things American kids believe about Santa originated with the 1822 poem, "The Night Before Christmas," by Dr. Clement C. Moore; the image of the tubby, jolly man in the red suit can be attributed to some 1860s illustrations by celebrated political cartoonist, Thomas Nast.

## WASHINGTON'S BIRTHDAY

Surprisingly, the Father of Our Country's birthday was first celebrated as a national holiday in 1780, during his lifetime. But it was his real birthday, February 11, they celebrated.

## GROUNDHOG DAY

Originally, this was a European planting superstition—if hedgehogs saw their shadows when they emerged from hibernation, planting was put off a few weeks. American settlers adapted the day to the groundhog.

# MONKEE TALES

*In 1987, the Monkees returned, spurred by exposure on MTV and books like* A Monkees Tale, *by Eric Lefcowitz.*

HISTORY

On September 8, 1965, director Bob Rafelson and producer Bert Schneider (together as Raybert Productions) placed an ad in *Variety* magazine that read:

"Madness!! Auditions
Folk & Rock Musicians-Singers
For Acting Roles in New TV Series
Running Parts for 4 Insane Boys, Age 17-21
Want Spirited Ben Frank's Types
Have Courage To Work
Must Come Down For Interview"

The idea was to create an American TV version of the Beatles—a pre-fab four.

In all, 437 applicants showed up at Raybert's offices trying to become the four finalists for a "musical situation comedy" called "The Monkees." Among those rejected were Harry Nilsson, Paul Williams, Danny Hutton (Three Dog Night), Rodney Bingenheimer, Steven Stills and, according to legend, Charlie Manson. Eventually Rafelson and Schneider narrowed it down to four: Davy Jones, Micky Dolenz, Michael Nesmith and Peter Tork. NBC bought the pilot, RCA agreed to distribute the records and almost overnight, the Monkees were a pop phenomenon.

With corporate power and a crack creative team behind them (director Paul Mazursky co-wrote the pilot), the Monkees first single, "Last Train To Clarksville," sold 250,000 copies before the series even debuted—despite the fact that the group did little more than sing on cue. Later it hit number one—as did the group's first album...and the group's second single...and the group's second album...etc.

The show debuted in the 1966-67 season, and never rated

highly. One problem: Many NBC affiliates refused to carry a show that had long-haired "hippie" types as the heroes. But it was a respected program. Most people aren't aware that in addition to having hit records (including the #1 song of 1967, "I'm a Believer"), the Monkees won two Emmy awards for best sitcom.

At the end of the second season NBC cancelled the series, so the group concentrated its efforts on a movie called *Head* (now a cult classic) instead. It was released with little fanfare in 1968.

The group's last project with all four members was a bizarre TV special entitled "33 1/3 Revolutions Per Monkee," which featured Jerry Lee Lewis, Fats Domino and Little Richard as guests. NBC ran the show against the Oscars, dooming it to obscurity. The Monkees themselves soon disappeared, splitting in 1970.

**MONKEE FACTS**

• In 1965, Peter Tork was playing with Stephen Stills in the Buffalo Fish—an early incarnation of the Buffalo Springfield. It was Stills, in fact, who tipped off Tork—then washing dishes for $50 a week—that TV producers were still casting for the Monkees (Stills auditioned, but lost out due to bad teeth and a receding hairline). Tork was the last hired and the first to quit the group in 1968.

• Micky Dolenz wasn't a drummer. He agreed to play drums only after the other Monkees refused.

• Davy Jones' big break came with the stage musical "Oliver!" where he played the role of the Artful Dodger. When the musical moved from London to New York, Jones became an instant teen star, winning a Tony nomination for his role. Ironically, Jones—along with the rest of the cast of "Oliver!"—appeared on the Ed Sullivan Show which included the Beatles' first American TV appearance.

• In terms of fan mail, Jones was always the most popular Monkee.

•Michael Nesmith's mother, Bette Nesmith, was a commercial artist who invented Liquid Paper (i.e., typewriter correction fluid). Michael inherited millions of dollars from her.

**Where does the name condom come from? Dr. Charles Condom (1630-1685).**

• Jack Nicholson co-wrote *Head*. Nicholson also made a cameo appearance in the movie.

• Frank Zappa made a rare guest appearance on "The Monkees" TV series and in *Head*.

• Due to Davy Jones' popularity, another English singer named Jones was forced to change his real name to...David Bowie.

• Monkeeing Around: Davy Jones was due to be drafted for duty in Vietnam when suddenly (by coincidence?) someone broke into the local Army recruitment branch and stole the file cabinet with Jones' file.

• Jimi Hendrix was the Monkees' opening act on their 1967 summer tour of the States. Micky Dolenz had seen Hendrix perform in a New York club and later signed Hendrix following his historic show at Monterey Pop (where both Dolenz and Tork were stage announcers). Monkees fans, however, were unprepared for the overt sexuality and strange guitar work of the Jimi Hendrix Experience—they kept cheering, "We Want the Monkees." Finally, after the group's show at Forest Hills, New York, Hendrix and the Monkees amicably split company. The official excuse for Hendrix leaving the tour was the Daughters of The American Revolution had banned him for being too sexually suggestive.

• Bob Rafelson and Bert Schneider later went on to form BBS Productions, which produced films such as *Easy Rider*, *The Last Picture Show* and *Hearts and Minds*.

• In 1980, Michael Nesmith received the first video Grammy award for his one-hour video special, "Elephant Parts." Nesmith has produced such movies as *Tapeheads* and *Repo Man*.

• In 1986, Micky Dolenz, Peter Tork and Davy Jones reunited for a massively-successful 20th Anniversary Monkees Tour. Although Nesmith declined to tour, he did show up for the encore at the group's 9/6/86 appearance at Hollywood's Greek Theatre. Thanks to MTV exposure of the original series, the Monkees experienced a surge in popularity, culminating in the hit single, "That Was Then, This Is Now." In an unprecedented showing on the *Billboard* charts, the Monkees had seven albums in the Hot 200, six of which were reissues of original albums.

# BRAINTEASERS

*A few more simple logic problems to entertain you. Remember: no heavy math or pencils needed.*

"This is a true story," my uncle Gordon said. "When I was living in Vermont, the minister of a local church fell asleep during the services. He dreamed he was a French nobleman during the French Revolution, had been sentenced to die, and was waiting for the blade of the guillotine to fall. Right then, his wife noticed he was asleep and poked him on the back of the neck with a pencil to wake him up. It was a terrible thing—the shock was so great that he had a heart attack and fell over, dead."

"Come on, Uncle Gordon," I replied. "That can't possibly be true."

How could I be so sure that my uncle was kidding me?

One day, Uncle Gordon and I were walking down a busy street, and we noticed four workmen digging. "Hm-m-m," my uncle mused. "If it takes four men four days to dig four holes, how long would it take one man to dig half a hole?"

What's the answer?

Every summer my Uncle Gordon goes to his house in the country. One summer, he asked me to forward his mail to him. I assured him I would. A month went by, and one night he angrily called to ask where his mail was—he hadn't received any yet.

"I'm sorry Uncle Gordon," I replied, "but you forgot to give me your mailbox key."

He apologized profusely, and promised to mail me the key right away. Another month went by, and when he returned, he was fuming.

"I never got a bit of mail!" he screamed. "How could you be so irresponsible?!!"

"Sorry, unk, but it wasn't my fault," I replied.

What did I mean?

**The first known contraceptive was crocodile dung, used by Egyptians in 2000 B.C.**

# THE LASER

*Tired of reading about music and TV? Try this.*

In a scant 30 years, the laser (short for Light Amplification by Stimulated Emission of Radiation) has become as indispensable to the fields of communication, medicine, industry, manufacturing and the military, as the wheel. The concentrated beam of a laser can bore a hole through a diamond or mend a detached retina. It can slice through a sheet of metal like a hot knife through aged Brie or it can read the price code on a can of creamed corn at your local supermarket check-out counter.

## DEVELOPMENT

Lasers were developed in the late '50s and early '60s, growing out of earlier research studies of microwave amplifying devices called masers. Because of this parallel development, early lasers were called *optical masers* because they amplified light in the same manner that masers amplified microwaves. The first laser was produced by Theodore H. Maiman at Hughes Research Laboratory using a ruby crystal as the amplifying medium.

## HOW THEY WORK

Simply put, lasers collect and harness light to produce an intense beam of radiation in a single, pure color.

To know something about how lasers work is to have a crash course in the basic nature of the atom. Every atom stores energy. The amount of energy in the atom depends on the motion of the electrons that circle the nucleus of the atom. When the atom absorbs energy, its own energy level increases and the atom becomes "excited."

To return to its normal unexcited state, the atom must release its extra energy in the form of light. This release is called "spontaneous emission." When the atom returns to its lower energy state, it emits a "photon," the basic unit of all radiation.

**1984 headline in the *National Examiner*: "Nixon Was Grooming Elvis for President."**

An ordinary light source, such as the common electric bulb, emits photons of light independently in a random manner. That light is called "incoherent." Wavelengths of light issuing from a laser, on the other hand, are organized or "coherent," and work in conjunction with one another, producing an amplified stream of photons which all have the same wavelength and move in the same direction.

Because of its highly directional beam (unlike radio waves, laser beams spread only slightly as they travel), lasers can transmit information with little interference. And because they operate on a higher frequency than conventional electronic transmitters, lasers can carry more information than radio waves, allowing them to transmit both telephone and television programs at the same time.

## THREE DIFFERENT KINDS

The three major types of lasers, based on their light-amplifying medium are solid lasers, gas lasers and liquid lasers:

**Solid Lasers:** The light-amplifying substance may be a crystal, glass or a semiconductor. For instance, crystal lasers have a fluorescent crystal, such as a ruby. Ruby lasers produce intensely powerful bursts of light that can drill through solid steel. A garnet crystal laser which emits a continuous beam of light may be used as a drill or a range finder. Glass lasers are used by scientists in experiments with plasmas. And semiconductor lasers, which convert electricity into coherent light, are useful in the communications industry.

**Gas lasers:** The light-amplifying source, a mixture of gases, is contained in a glass or quartz tube. Unlike ruby or glass lasers, gas lasers can produce a continuous beam of light which has a narrow frequency range than the light from a solid laser. Gas lasers are used in communications and in measuring.

**Liquid lasers:** Chemical dyes dissolved in methanol and contained in a glass tube are the light-amplifying sources for liquid lasers. The only kind of laser that can have its light frequency adjusted, liquid lasers are used by scientists to study the properties of atomic and molecular systems.

**The air that leaves your body when you exhale floats out at a rate of about 15 m.p.h.**

## THE LASER IN YOUR LIFE

In the '60s, people who understood lasers looked forward to the day when they would be a part our everyday lives. In 1963, for example, *Life* magazine reported of a laser test: "This dazzling demonstration only hints at the vast power and versatility of laser beams. Although lasers today are still laboratory tools, scientists foresee a variety of future uses."

Then, in the '70s, the laser came into its own—not only as those eerie green special effects projected during elaborate rock shows, but as technical medical marvels—"bloodless scalpels" used to treat certain types of cancers, to stop bleeding stomach ulcers and, more recently, to perform complicated microsurgeries.

Today, the dreams of scientists two decades ago have largely come true. The impact of laser technology encompasses everything from child care (pricking holes in baby-bottle nipples) and home entertainment (creating audio equipment systems that can reproduce sound with studio or live-performance accuracy) to cost-effective communications (lowering the cost of transoceanic telephone calls through the use of optical fibers) and "national defense" (creating space-based "Star Wars" weaponry).

## TOTALLY UNRELATED INFORMATION

**Weird Lawsuits:** In 1985, a Budweiser radio commercial featured a recreation of the Bill Mazeroski home run that won the 1960 World Series for the Pittsburgh Pirates. It went: "Ditmar delivers...Mazeroski swings...It's going back, back...." The thing is, Ralph Terry was the pitcher who threw that ball for the Yankees, not Art Ditmar—and Ditmar was angry to hear his name mentioned. So he sued Anheuser-Busch for half-a-million dollars, charging "his reputation had been tarnished."

# PRIME-TIME PROVERBS

*More comments about everyday life in America. From* Prime Time Proverbs, *a forthcoming book by Jack Mingo.*

**ON TELEVISION:**
"Television has done much for psychiatry by spreading information about it...as well as contributing to the need for it."

**—Alfred Hitchcock,**
***Alfred Hitchcock Presents***

**George:** "Gracie, what do you think of television?"
**Gracie:** "I think it's wonderful—I hardly ever watch radio anymore."

***—Burns and Allen***

**ON GROWING UP:**
"You don't need any brains to grow up. It just happens to ya."

**—Gilbert Bates,**
***Leave It to Beaver***

"I used to do a year in 365 days. Now they go by much faster."

**—Dr. Graham,**
***Ben Casey***

**ON MONEY:**
**The Riddler:** "This is my dream come true!...Nothing stands between me and the Lost Treasure of the Incas!...And it's worth millions...MILLIONS!!!
**Batman:** "Just remember, Riddler, you can't buy friends with money."

***—Batman***

"There's only one thing more important than money— and that's more money."

**—"Pappy" Maverick,**
***Maverick***

**ON PHYSICS:**
"A dog can't get struck by lightning. You know why? Cause he's too close to the ground. See, lightning strikes tall things. Now, if they were giraffes out there in that field, now then we'd be in trouble. But you sure don't have to worry about dogs."

**—Barney Fife,**
***The Andy Griffith Show***

**ON EATING RIGHT:**
**John Burns:** "I try to eat only natural things."
**Louie DePalma:** "How'd you like a sack of dirt?"

***—Taxi***

Your fingernails grow up to four times faster than your toenails.

# ALICE TAKES A TRIP

*The final selection in our* Bathroom Reader*—and the longest—is from* Through the Looking Glass, *by Lewis Carroll. This is a particular favorite, because it is one of the few works of fiction you can pick up and begin anywhere (a bathroom reading requisite). In this passage, Alice meets Humpty Dumpty. Due to space limitations, we've cut out some of the poetry. But if you enjoy what's here, you can pick up an unabridged copy for your bathroom.*

*Alice finds herself in a grocery store, talking to a sheep.*

"I should like to buy an egg, please," she said timidly. "How do you sell them?"

"Fivepence...for one—twopence for two," the Sheep replied.

"Then two are cheaper than one?" Alice said in a surprised tone, taking out her purse.

"Only you *must* eat them both, if you buy two," said the Sheep.

"Then I'll have *one* please," said Alice, as she put the money down on the counter. For she thought to herself, "They mightn't be at all nice, you know."

The Sheep took the money and put it away in a box: then she said, "I never put things into people's hands—that would never do—you must get it for yourself." And so saying, she went off to the other end of the shop, and set the egg upright on the shelf.

"I wonder why it wouldn't do?" thought Alice, as she groped her way among the tables and chairs, for the shop was very dark towards the end. "The egg seems to get further away the more I walk towards it. Let me see, is this a chair? Why, it's got branches, I declare! How very odd to find trees growing here! And actually here's a little brook! Well, this is the very queerest shop I ever saw!"

So she went on, wondering more and more at every step, as everything turned into a tree the moment she came to it, and she quite expected the egg to do the same.

However, the egg only got larger and larger, and more and more human; when she had come within a few yards of it, she saw that it had eyes and a nose and mouth; and, when she had come close to it, she saw clearly that it was HUMPTY DUMPTY himself. "It can't be anybody else!" she said to herself. "I'm as certain of it, as if his name were written all over his face!"

It might have been written a hundred times, easily, on that enormous face. Humpty Dumpty was sitting, with his legs crossed like a Turk, on the top of a high wall—such a narrow one that Alice quite wondered how he could keep his balance—and, as his eyes were steadily fixed in the opposite direction, and he didn't take the least notice of her, she thought he must be a stuffed figure after all.

"And how exactly like an egg he is!" she said aloud, standing with her hands ready to catch him, for she was every moment expecting him to fall.

"It's *very* provoking," Humpty Dumpty said after a long silence, looking away from Alice as she spoke, "to be called an egg—*very!*"

"I said you *looked* like an egg, Sir," Alice gently explained. "And some eggs are very pretty, you know," she added, hoping to turn her remark into a sort of compliment.

"Some people," said Humpty Dumpty, looking away from her as usual, "have no more sense than a baby!"

Alice didn't know what to say to this: it wasn't at all like conversation, she thought, as he never said anything to *her*; in fact, his last remark was evidently addressed to a tree—so she stood and softly repeated to herself:

*"Humpty Dumpty sat on a wall:*
*Humpty Dumpty had a great fall.*
*All the King's horses and all the King's men*
*Couldn't put Humpty Dumpty in his place again."*

"That last line is much too long for the poetry," she added, almost out loud, forgetting that Humpty Dumpty would hear her.

"Don't stand chattering to yourself like that," Humpty Dumpty said, looking at her for the first time, "but tell me your name and your business."

"My *name* is Alice, but—"

A hard rain falls at the rate of about 20 m.p.h.

"It's a stupid name enough!" Humpty Dumpty interrupted impatiently. 'What does it mean?'

"*Must* a name mean something?" Alice asked doubtfully.

"Of course it must," Humpty Dumpty said with a short laugh: "*my* name means the shape I am—and a good handsome shape it is, too. With a name like yours, you might be any shape, almost."

"Why do you sit out here all alone?" said Alice, not wishing to begin an argument.

"Why, because there's nobody with me!" cried Humpty Dumpty. "Did you think I didn't know the answer to *that*? Ask another!"

"Don't you think you'd be safer down on the ground?" Alice went on, not with any idea of making another riddle, but simply in her good-natured anxiety for the queer creature. "That wall is so *very* narrow!"

"What tremendously easy riddles you ask!" Humpty Dumpty growled out. "Of course I don't think so! Why, if ever I *did* fall off—which there's no chance of—but *if* I did—"

Here he pursed his lips, and looked so solemn and grand that Alice could hardly help laughing. "*If* I *did* fall," he went on, "*the King has promised me*—ah, you may turn pale, if you like! You didn't think I was going to say that, did you? *The King has promised me—with his very own mouth*—to—to—"

"To send all his horses and all his men," Alice interrupted, rather unwisely.

"Now I declare that's too bad!" Humpty Dumpty cried, breaking into a sudden passion. "You've been listening at doors—and behind trees—and down chimneys—or you couldn't have known it!"

"I haven't indeed!" Alice said very gently. "It's in a book."

"Ah, well! They may write such things in a *book*," Humpty Dumpty said in a calmer tone. "That's what you call a History of England, that is. Now, take a good look at me! I'm one that has spoken to a King, *I* am: mayhap you'll never see such another: and, to show you I'm not proud, you may shake hands with me!" And he grinned almost from ear to ear, as he leant forwards (and as nearly as possible fell off the wall in doing so) and offered Alice his hand. She watched him a little anxiously as she took it. "If he smiled much more the ends of his mouth might meet behind," she thought: "And then I don't know *what* would happen to his head! I'm afraid it would come off!"

"Yes, all his horses and all his men," Humpty Dumpty went on. "They'd pick me up again in a minute, *they* would! However, this conversation is going a little too fast; let's go back to the last remark but one."

"I'm afraid I can't quite remember it," Alice said, very politely.

"In that case we start afresh," said Humpty Dumpty, "and it's my turn to choose a subject—" ("He talks about it just as if it was a game!" thought Alice.) "So here's a question for you. How old did you say you were?"

Alice made a short calculation, and said "Seven years and six months."

"Wrong!" Humpty Dumpty exclaimed triumphantly. "You never said a word like it!"

"I thought you meant 'How old *are* you?'" Alice explained.

"If I'd meant that, I'd have said it," said Humpty Dumpty.

Alice didn't want to begin another argument, so she said nothing.

"Seven years and six months!" Humpty Dumpty repeated thoughtfully. "An uncomfortable sort of age. Now if you'd asked my advice, I'd have said 'Leave off at seven'—but it's too late now."

"I never ask advice about growing," Alice said indignantly.

"Too proud?" the other enquired.

Alice felt even more indignant at this suggestion. "I mean," she said, "that one can't help growing older."

"*One* can't, perhaps," said Humpty Dumpty; "but *two* can. With proper assistance, you might have left off at seven."

"What a beautiful belt you've got on!" Alice suddenly remarked. (They had quite enough of the subject of age, she thought: and, if they really were to take turns in choosing subjects, it was her turn now.) "At least," she corrected herself on second thoughts, "a beautiful cravat, I should have said—no, a belt, I mean—I beg your pardon!" she added in dismay, for Humpty Dumpty looked thoroughly offended, and she began to wish she hadn't chosen that subject. "If only I knew," she thought to herself, "which was neck and which was waist!"

**Estimate: By the year 2,000, there will be more than 100,000 people over the age of 100.**

Evidently Humpty Dumpty was very angry, though he said nothing for a minute or two. When he *did* speak again, it was in a deep growl.

"It is a—most—provoking—thing," he said at last, "when a person doesn't know a cravat from a belt!"

"I know it's very ignorant of me," Alice said, in so humble a tone that Humpty Dumpty relented.

"It's a cravat, child, and a beautiful one, as you say. It's a present from the White King and Queen. There now!"

"Is it really?" said Alice, quite pleased to find that she *had* chosen a good subject after all.

"They gave it me," Humpty Dumpty continued thoughtfully as he crossed one knee over the other and clasped his hands round it, "they gave it me—for an un-birthday present."

"I beg your pardon," Alice said with a puzzled air.

"I'm not offended," said Humpty Dumpty.

"I mean, what *is* an un-birthday present?"

"A present given when it isn't your birthday, of course."

Alice considered a little. "I like birthday presents best," she said at last.

"You don't know what you're talking about!" cried Humpty Dumpty. "How many days are there in a year?"

"Three hundred and sixty-five," said Alice.

"And how many birthdays have you?"

"One."

"And if you take one from three hundred and sixty-five what remains?"

"Three hundred and sixty-four, of course."

Humpty Dumpty looked doubtful. "I'd rather see that one on paper," he said.

Alice couldn't help smiling as she took out her memorandum book, and worked the sum for him:

$$\begin{array}{r} 365 \\ \underline{-1} \\ 364 \end{array}$$

Humpty Dumpty took the book and looked at it carefully. "That seems to be done right—" he began.

"You're holding it upside down!" Alice interrupted.

**Ivan the Terrible built the Kremlin—then gouged the architect's eyes out to**

"To be sure I was!" Humpty Dumpty said gaily as she turned it round for him. "I thought it looked a little queer. As I was saying, that *seems* to be done right—though I haven't time to look it over thoroughly just now—and that shows that there are three hundred and sixty-four days when you might get un-birth-birthday presents—"

"Certainly," said Alice.

"And only one for birthday presents, you know. There's glory for you!"

"I don't know what you mean by 'glory,'" Alice said.

Humpty Dumpty smiled contemptuously. "Of course you don't—till I tell you. I meant 'there's a nice knock-down argument for you!'"

"But 'glory' doesn't mean 'a nice knock-down argument,'" Alice objected.

"When *I* use a word," Humpty Dumpty said, in rather a scornful tone, "It means just what I choose it to mean—neither more nor less."

"The question is," said Alice, "whether you *can* make words mean so many different thing."

"The question is," said Humpty Dumpty, "which is to be master—that's all."

Alice was too much puzzled to say anything; so after a minute Humpty Dumpty began again. "They've a temper, some of them—particularly verbs: they're the proudest—adjectives you can do anything with, but not verbs—however, *I* can manage the whole lot of them! Impenetrability! That's what *I* say!

"Would you tell me please," said Alice, "what that means?" "Now you talk like a reasonable child," said Humpty Dumpty, looking very much pleased. "I meant by 'impenetrability' that we've had enough of that subject, and it would be just as well if you'd mention what you mean to do next, as I suppose you don't mean to stop here all the rest of your life."

"That's a great deal to make one word mean," Alice said in a thoughtful tone.

"When I make a word do a lot of work like that," said Humpty Dumpty, "I always pay it extra."

"Oh!" said Alice. She was too much puzzled to make any other remark.

"Ah, you should see 'em come round me of a Saturday night," Humpty Dumpty went on, wagging his head gravely from side

**prevent him from ever designing another structure like it.**

to side, "for to get their wages, you know."

(Alice didn't venture to ask what he paid them with; so you see I can't tell *you*.)

[*Humpty Dumpty explains Jabberwocky to Alice, and then recites his own poem...*]

"I sent a message to the fish:
I told them this is what I wish.

The little fishes of the sea,
They sent an answer back to me.

The little fishes' answer was,
'We cannot do it, Sir, because—'"

"I'm afraid I don't quite understand," said Alice.

"It gets easier further on," Humpty Dumpty replied.

"I sent to them again to say,
'It will be better to obey.'

The fishes answered, with a grin,
'Why, what a temper you are in!'

I told them once, I told them twice:
They would not listen to advice.

I took a kettle large and new,
Fit for the deed I had to do.

My heart went hop, my heart went thump:
I filled the kettle at the pump.

Then someone came to me and said,
'The little fishes are in bed.'

I said to him, I said it plain,
'Then you must wake them up again.'

I said it very loud and clear,
I went and shouted in his ear."

Humpty Dumpty raised his voice almost to a scream as he repeated this verse, and Alice thought with a shudder, "I wouldn't have been the messenger for anything!"

"But he was very stiff and proud:
He said, 'you needn't shout so loud!'

And he was very proud and stiff:
He said, 'I'd go and wake them, if—'

I took a corkscrew from the shelf:
I went to wake them up myself!

And when I found the door was locked,
I pulled and pushed and kicked and knocked

And when I found the door was shut,
I tried to turn the handle, but—"

There was a long pause.

"Is that all?" Alice timidly asked.

"That's all," said Humpty Dumpty. "Good-bye."

This was rather sudden, Alice thought: but, after such a very strong hint that she ought to be going, she felt that it would hardly be civil to stay. So she got up and held out her hand. "Good-bye, till we meet again!" she said as cheerfully as she could.

"I shouldn't know you again if we did meet," Humpty Dumpty replied in a discontented tone, giving her one of his fingers to shake: "you're so exactly like other people."

"The face is what one goes by, generally," Alice remarked in a thoughtful tone.

"That's just what I complain of," said Humpty Dumpty. "Your face is the same as everybody has—the two eyes, so—" (marking their places in the air with his thumb) "nose in the middle, mouth under. It's always the same. Now if you have the two eyes on the same side of the nose, for instance—or the mouth at the top—that would be *some* help."

"It wouldn't look nice," Alice objected, but Humpty Dumpty only shut his eyes, and said, "Wait till you've tried."

Alice waited a minute to see if he would speak again, but, as he never opened his eyes or took any further notice of her, she said, "Good-bye!" once more, and, getting no answer to this, she quietly walked away: But she couldn't help saying to herself as she went, "Of all the unsatisfactory...people I ever met—" She never finished the sentence, for at this moment a heavy crash shook the forest from end to end.

# SOLUTION PAGE

**PAGE 32, BRAINTEASERS:**
1. Friday; 2. An egg; the riddle is by J. R. R. Tolkien; 3. Neither—when they meet, they're the same distance from N.Y.

**PAGE 46, BRAINTEASERS:**
1. House numbers; 2. He saw the other boy's face and assumed his was just as dirty; 3. June 29, the next-to-last day of the month; 4. The match

**PAGE 65, ANCIENT RIDDLES:**
1. The Letter "E"; 2. Tomorrow; 3. A shoe; 4. The stars; 5. A fart; 6. A towel; 7. A watermelon

**PAGE 79, WHAT AM I?**
1. A postage stamp; 2. A mirror; 3. The moon; 4. The weather

**PAGE 207, PRESIDENTIAL QUIZ:**
1. Virginia; 2. a, Martin Van Buren; 3. Gerald Ford, who was appointed to the vice presidency before he became president; 4. b, Teddy Roosevelt; 5. Franklin D. Roosevelt; 6. William Howard Taft; 7. Warren G. Harding; 8. Calvin Coolidge; 9. c, Richard Nixon; 10. It is the first Hollywood film in which a future president (Ronald Reagan) and first lady (Nancy Davis) co-starred; 11. Dwight Eisenhower; 12. b, Thomas Jefferson; 13. James Buchanan; 14. New York; 15. 41 as of January, 1989.

**PAGE 214, BRAINTEASERS:**
1. "Trade horses"; 2. $1987 is worth more than $1985; 3. He's a midget, and the highest button he can reach is the one for 8th floor; "I will die by shooting." If they shot him, that would be true, so he would have to die by hanging—but that would make his statement false. Unable to reconcile the two, they gave up.

**PAGE 221, BRAINTEASERS:**
1. If the minister died without ever waking up, it would be impossible to know what he'd been dreaming; 2. You can't dig half a hole; 3. He mailed me the key, but I couldn't get into the mailbox to get it.

*Uncle John's*

# SECOND BATHROOM READER

"The Birds" and "You Animal!" originally appeared in *Animal Superstars*. Copyright © 1985, by John Javna. Reprinted by permission of the author.

"A Bizarre Genius" Copyright © 1989, by Jim Morton, and "What's the Beef" Copyright © 1989, by Mike Wilkins, originally appeared in *Popvoid* magazine. Reprinted by permission of the authors.

"See Europe in the U.S." Copyright © 1989, by Mike Wilkins. Reprinted by permission of the author.

"Sweet Nuthin's" Copyright © 1989, by Jim Morton. Reprinted by permission of the author.

"The Nut Behind Grape Nuts" Copyright © 1977, by Bull Publishing Co. Originally appeared in *The New Nuts Among the Berries*, by Ronald M. Deutsch. Reprinted by permission of the publisher.

"Which Stooge Are You?" Copyright © 1989, by The Church of the Sub-Genius, appeared in the *Northwest EXTRA*. Reprinted by permission of the publisher.

Excerpts from *Everybody's Business* (in "The Great Rockefeller," "The Condensed Man," and parts of "Uncle Walt's Secrets") by Milton Moskowitz, Michael Katz, and Robert Levering. Copyright © 1980, by Harper & Row Publishers, Inc. Reprinted by permission of the publisher.

"Cooking with Power Tools" Copyright © 1983 by Jack Mingo. Originally appeared in *The Official Couch Potato Handbook*. Reprinted by permission of the author.

"But They'd Never Been There," "Mack the Knife," "Only In America," "Maniac," "96 Tears," "We've Only Just Begun," "Layla," and "Who Was That Man?" originally appeared in *Behind the Hits*, Copyright © 1985, by Bob Shannon and John Javna. Reprinted by permission of the authors.

"Get Smart," "Hello, I'm Mr. Ed," "Leave It to Beaver," "The Three Stooges," "The Addams Family," "Lost In Space," and "Batman on TV," originally appeared in *Cult TV*. Copyright © 1985, by John Javna and Gordon Javna. Reprinted by permission of the authors.

"The Fabulous '60s," "Tales of '60s TV," "Fabulous Flops," "The Mini-Skirt Saga," Mustang: Car of the '60s," and "How Pantyhose Hatched" originally appeared in *60s!*. Copyright © 1983, by John Javna and Gordon Javna. Reprinted by permission of the authors.

Excerpts from *Extraordinary Origins of Everyday Things* (in "The Origin of Dracula," "One Good Yawn Deserves Another," "Nothing to Sneeze At," "The Frisbee Story," "Gimme Some Skin," and "The Story of Uncle Sam") by Charles Panati. Copyright © 1987 by Charles Panati. Reprinted by permission of Harper & Row, Publishers.

# THANK YOU

*The Bathroom Readers' Institute sincerely thanks the people whose advice and assistance made this book possible.*

Michael Brunsfeld
Richard Kizu-Blair
John Javna
Gordon Javna
Bob Shannon
Stuart Moore
Rachel Blau
Andrea Sohn
Gordon Van Gelder
Fifth Street Computers
Eric Lefcowitz
Mike Wilkins
Jim Morton
Gene Brissie
Ivan Stang
Northwest EXTRA
Carol Schreiber
Penelope Houston
Fritz von Springmeyer
Gene Sculatti
Pat Mitchell

Steve Gorelick
Leslie Boies
Jack Mingo
Franz Ross
Sam Javna
Charlie Weimer
Stephen Louis
Carla Small
Lorrie Bodger
Gideon Javna
Reddy Kilowatt
Gene Novogrodsky
Bob Migdal
Betsy Joyce
Greg Small
Adrienne Levine
Jay Nitschke
Mike Goldfinger

And all the Bathroom Readers

# INTRODUCTION

When the Bathroom Readers' Institute put together our first *Uncle John's Bathroom Reader* last year, we urged America's secret readers to come out of the water closet, to "sit down and be counted." And they did, pouring into bookstores around America by the tens of thousands.

Clearly, we've flushed out a new "silent majority"—which is great, because as you might imagine, we really love our work.

- First, it's a challenge to come up with interesting ideas for pieces in the book.
- Second, it's a pleasure to write for an audience we know is going to read every page at least once...and sometimes two or three times.
- And finally, *The Bathroom Reader* gives us a chance to do some throughly enjoyable research; rest assured that everything included here has been tested under actual Bathroom Readers' conditions.

What has the B.R.I. learned about bathroom reading?

- The ideal piece of lavatory lit is a unique blend of light reading and weighty subject matter.
- The topics should be heavy enough to provide food for thought, but avoid clogging the reader's mind wth details.
- The bits of information should be easy to absorb.
- Ideas should flow smoothly from one article to the next.
- A person's mind is more fluid when he or she is in the john, so the best bathroom reading is informative as well as entertaining.

We could go on and on (as we often do), but if you're a bathroom reader, you can already read the writing on the wall.

Go ahead and take the plunge into *Uncle John's Second Bathroom Reader*. And remember: "Go With the Flow."

# UNCLE JOHN'S MAILBAG

*Our first* Uncle John's Bathroom Reader *brought in lots of mail with interesting comments...and suggestions for this second volume. Here's a random sample*

**Dear Fellow Bathroom Connoisseurs:**
I thoroughly enjoyed your first book....For many years I would search my house for something interesting to read before I would enter my asylum. I have even been known to do my homework while I was in the bathroom. In fact, when I was younger I once watched a whole quarter of the Super Bowl while in the bathroom. It's relaxing and quiet in there, and no one bothers you—except for the few who don't understand, and ask you every few minutes if you've fallen in.

—*Adam B., Richmond Heights, Missouri*

**Dear Uncle John,**
I am from a long line of Bathroom Readers. At first I thought it was an Italian thing to do crosswords and read for long periods of time in the head, because my father is Italian and my grandfather was straight off the boat....Now I know better.

—*Vinnie B.*

**Uncle John,**
It was a strain writing, but now that we've started, it's a relief. I'm sure the feeling will pass, so being brief, we'd like to "sit down and be counted"—It's the only way to get a-head in life. We've enjoyed the book—it has really bowled us over! We were unable to flush out any discrepancies....Well, that about wipes it up.

—*Mike and Dan M., Colora, Maryland*

**Dear Sirs:**
What about the possibility of inserting a picture of a wayside comfort station such as were common in the Roman Empire days? In case you are not familiar with this convenience, let me say that it would normally consist of a group of holes, perhaps 25 in number, in an open location in the main part of an ancient city or town. All

seats were side by side without any pretence or privacy. I can imagine that such a citizen convenience was a hub of gossip and activity for both men and women.

*—R. Wilfed B., Totonto, Canada*

**Dear B.R.I.**

We really enjoyed Volume I of your book and have a great idea for a few pages in Volume II: Elvis Presley sightings!! They've been rampant this year, most notably in Kalamazoo, Michigan, where the King reportedly frequents all-night grocery stores and Burger Kings.

*—Ron and Lisa B., Des Moines, Iowa*

**Uncle John—**

We always kept the Sears Catalog in our outhouse and used the paper. We had already bought what we wanted out of it, of course. Talk about rough—that stuff was worse than corn cobs!

*—Dan R., Athens, Georgia*

**Dear B.R.I.—**

All right, I confess! I read your book cover-to-cover on an airplane—not in the bathroom!

*—Julie S., Merritt Island, Florida*

**Gentlemen:**

I enjoyed the footnotes immensely. Maybe some of them can be questions next time, such as:

• Why are hot dog buns packed 8 to a package while the hot dogs themselves always come 10 to a package? To even things out, you have to buy 5 packs of buns, and 4 packs of weiners.

• Why are toilet papers and tissues scented? You shouldn't be able to smell tissues if your nose is stuffed up, and you shouldn't be putting toilet paper up to your nose....Should you?

*—Andy D., Gainesville, Fla.*

**Dear Uncle John:**

I laughed so hard while reading your book that I dropped it in the toilet. Don't worry—I bought another one.

*—Bill D., Tenafly, N.J.*

# THOMAS CRAPPER: MYTH OR HERO?

*If our mail was any gauge, the most controversial tidbit in the first* Bathroom Reader *was our comment that the widely accepted notion that Thomas Crapper invented the toilet is a hoax. Readers sent all kinds of evidence "proving" that Crapper was real. But was he? Let's take a closer look.*

## FLUSHED WITH PRIDE

The name Thomas Crapper appears to have been unknown among bathroom historians until 1969, when English writer Wallace Reyburn published a 99-page book entitled *Flushed With Pride—The Story of Thomas Crapper.*

This biography (which Reyburn's publisher calls "The Little Classic of the Smallest Room") begins this way:

"Never has the saying 'a prophet is without honor in his own land' been more true than in the case of Thomas Crapper. Here was a man whose foresight, ingenuity, and perseverence brought to perfection one of the great boons to mankind. But is his name revered in the same way as, for example, that of the Earl of Sandwich?"

Of course not. Not, anyway, until Reyburn's book was published.

## CRAPPER, THE MAN

According to Reyburn:

- Tom Crapper was born in 1837, and died in 1910.
- He is responsible for many toilet innovations—including, as bathroom-ologist Pat Mitchell puts it, "the toilets that flush in a rush seen in public restrooms today, and the...trap in plumbing that keeps sewer gas from rising into our homes."
- But the most important of Crapper's alleged accomplishments was "Crapper's Valveless Water Waste Preventer," an apparatus that made flushing more efficient. *Cleaning Management* magazine calls it "the forerunner of our present-day flush system."
- For this contribution, Crapper was supposedly appointed the Royal Plumber by King Edward VII.

• Crapper's name was stenciled on all the cisterns—and later, toilets—his company manufactured: "T. Crapper & Co., Chelsea, London." American soldiers stationed in England during World War I began calling a toilet a "crapper."

## FACT OR FICTION?

Beats us. But here are a few possibilities to consider:

• The premier bathroom history, an impressive tome called *Clean and Decent,* makes absolutely no mention of Thomas Crapper.

• Reyburn followed up *Flushed With Pride* with another social "history," entitled *Bust Up: The Uplifting Tale of Otto Titzling and the Development of the Bra.*

• Charles Panati, in *Extraordinary Origins of Everyday Things,* notes that "the acculmulation of toilet-humor puns, double-entendres, and astonishing coincidences eventually reveals...Reyburn's hoax." He offers some examples: "He moved to London and eventually settled on Fleet Street, where he perfected the 'Crapper W.C. Cistern after many dry runs.'...The installation of a flushing toilet at the Royal Palace was 'a high-water mark in Crapper's career.'... He was particularly close with his niece, 'Emma Crapper,' and had a friend named 'B.S.' "

• On the other hand, Pat Mitchell sent us this information: "It seems that in recent years, a certain Ken Grabowski, researcher at the Field Museum of Natural History in Chicago, has unselfishly, unswervingly, and unrelentingly sought to uncover the truth. His findings? Indeed, there was a Thomas Crapper (1836-1910). And Crapper founded a London plumbing fixture company in 1861. His efforts did produce many improvements in the fixtures he manufactured. His company's products (with his name upon them) were distributed all over Europe. Military barracks included. These were still there during World War I."

## CONCLUSION

The Bathroom Readers Institute is stuck; we can't relieve the tension or wipe away the rumors. The legend of Crapper seems to have survived all the stink people have made about his life. Or, as Pat Mitchell puts it, "I'm not certain the legend can be killed, but if it could, does B.R.I. want to be the executioner?"

**It's not polite to stare, but a butterfly probably can't help it—it has 12,000 eyes.**

# COMMON PHRASES

*In the first* Bathroom Reader *we supplied the origins of familiar phrases. Here are some more.*

**STEAL SOMEONE'S THUNDER**

***Meaning:*** To pre-empt; to draw attention away from someone else's achievements in favor of your own.

***Background:*** English dramatist John Dennis invented a gadget for imitating the sound of thunder and introduced it in a play in the early 1700s. The play flopped. Soon after, Dennis noted that another play in the same theater was using his sound-effects device. He angrily exclaimed, "That is my thunder, by God; the villains will play my thunder, but not my play." The story got around London, and the phrase grew out of it.

**PAY THROUGH THE NOSE**

***Meaning:*** To pay a high price; to pay dearly.

***Background:*** Comes from ninth-century Ireland. When the Danes conquered the Irish, they imposed an exorbitant Nose Tax on the island's inhabitants. "They took a census (by counting noses) and levied oppressive sums on their victims, forcing them to pay by threatening to have their noses actually slit." Paying the tax was "paying through the nose."

**HAPPY AS A CLAM**

***Meaning;*** Blissfully happy; perfectly content.

***Background:*** The original phrase was, "Happy as a clam at high tide." Why at high tide? Because people can't dig clams out then. They're "safe and happy" until low tide, when their breeding grounds are exposed. The saying was shortened through use.

**TO LAY AN EGG**

***Meaning:*** To fail.

***Background:*** From the British sport of cricket. When you fail to score, you get a zero—which looks like an egg. The term is also taken from baseball, where a zero is a "goose egg."

**There are more cars in Southern California than there are cows in India.**

# SWEET NUTHIN'S

*Interesting facts about American candies from B.R.I. member Jim Morton.*

**THREE MUSKETEERS.** Most people today have no idea where the name for the Three Musketeers bar came from. Advertising in the fifties and sixties suggested the candy bar was so named because it was big enough for three people to share. The truth is, Three Musketeers bars were originally made of three separate nougat sections: vanilla, chocolate and strawberry. Eventually, the strawberry and vanilla nougat sections were eliminated, leaving only chocolate nougat in each Three Musketeers bar.

**BLACK CROWS.** The Mason Candy Company decided to introduce a new candy treat in 1890. The candy, a licorice-flavored gumdrop, was to be called Black Rose. But the printer misunderstood the instructions and printed the wrappers with the name "Black Crows." The printer refused to reprint the job, claiming it was Mason's mistake. Rather than pay to reprint the wrappers, the folks at Mason decided to change the name of the product. Today, one-hundred years later, Black Crows are still available by that name.

**M&Ms.** In 1930, Frank Mars, a candy-maker in Chicago, told his son Forrest to get out of the country and not come back. Forrest went to England with a few thousand dollars and the recipe for Milky Ways. He quickly set up shop and began selling his own versions of his father's candy bars. While in England, Forrest discovered "Smarties," a candy-coated chocolate treat that was popular with the Brits. He bought the rights to market "Smarties" in America, where he went into partnership with a business associate named Bruce Murrie. The candies were called M&Ms; short for Mars and Murrie.

**HERSHEY'S.** Milton Hershey, the inventor of the Hershey Bar, was an unusual man. As a child he was brought up in a strict Mennonite family. Unlike most entrepreneurs, he never sought the usual material wealth that accompanies success. In 1909 he took a large sum of the money he had earned making candy bars, and opened the

Milton Hershey School for orphaned boys. Nine years later he donated the candy company to a trust for the school. Today, the Milton Hershey School and School Trust still own 56% of the Hershey Company.

**SPARKLERS.** Wintergreen LifeSavers, when chewed in the dark, give off sparks. This is due to a chemical process known as triboluminescence.

**SUGAR DADDY.** Robert O. Welch, the inventor of the Sugar Daddy, is also the founder of the John Birch Society.

**MEXICAN HATS.** Heide's Mexican Hats candies were originally called "Wetem and Wearems." Kids were supposed to lick the candies and stick them to their foreheads. What possible reason for kids wanting to use the candies in this fashion is unknown.

**CRACKER JACKS.** The dog on the Cracker Jack package is named Bingo, after the folk song that generations of kids were forced to learn in grade school.

**OH HENRY.** Every day at about the same time, a young man named Henry would stop in at the Williamson Candy Company in Chicago, and flirt with the girls making the candy. Soon the girls were asking Henry to do things for them. Whenever he came into the store they would start, "Oh Henry, will you do this! Oh Henry, will you do that!" When Williamson introduced a new candy bar in 1920, one of the salesmen suggested that they call the bar "Oh Henry" in honor of the likeable young fellow.

**CHARLESTON CHEW.** Sometimes the names of candy bars come from fads that are popular when they are introduced. The Charleston Chew was introduced during the roaring twenties when the Charleston dance craze was in full swing.

**CLARK BAR.** Often candy manufacturers spend hours agonizing over what to call their confections. But David L. Clark wasn't one to waste time on such efforts. When he introduced his candy bar in 1917 he simply named it after himself.

**Estimates show that it may take a plastic container 50,000 years to decompose.**

# THE LAST LAUGH: EPITAPHS

*Who collects unusual epitaphs? Lots of people, we're discovering. Here are some authentic ones, supplied by B.R.I. members.*

*Seen in Falkirk, Scotland:*
**Solomon Pease**
Here under this sod, and under
these trees
Is buried the body of Solomon
Pease
But here in his hole lies only
the pod,
His soul is shelled out, and
gone up to God.

*Seen in Hatfield, Massachusetts:*
**Arabella Young, 1771**
Here lies as silent clay,
Miss Arabella Young.
Who on the 21st of May,
Began to hold her tongue.

*Seen in Bradford, Vermont:*
**Mary S. Hoyt, 1836**
She lived—what more can
then be said?
She died—and all we know
she's dead.

*Seen in Skaneatles, New York:*
**Sally Briggs**
Underneath this pile of stones,
Lies all that's left of Sally
Jones.
Her name was Briggs, it was
not Jones,
But Jones was used to rhyme
with stones.

*Seen in Topsfield, Massachusetts:*
**Mary Lefavour, 1797**
Reader pass on and ne'er waste
your time
On bad biography and bitter
rhyme.
For what I am this cum'brous
clay insures
And what I was, is no affair of
yours.

*Seen in Lincoln, Maine:*
**Sacred to the memory of
Jared Bates,**
Who died Aug. the 6th, 1800.
His widow, aged 24, lives at
7 Elm Street,
Has every qualification for a
good wife,
And longs to be comforted.

*Seen in Kent, England:*
Grim death took me without
any warning.
I was well at night, and dead
in the morning.

*Seen in Tombstone, Arizona:*
**Lester Moore**
Here lies
Lester Moore
Four slugs from a 44.
No Les
No more.

**With the amount of fuel held in a jumbo jet, you could drive around the world in a car 4 times.**

# ELEMENTARY, MY DEAR STEVE

*The famous sleuth, Leslie Boies, and her faithful companion, Steve, have a few simple mysteries for you to solve. Answers on p. 454*

The celebrated detective, Leslie Boies, was home working on a case one day when Steve came wandering in.

"I just saw the strangest thing," he mused. "A man walked into Effie's Bar down on Carlotta Street and ordered a glass of water. Suddenly the bartender pulled out a gun and pointed it at him."

"What happened then, Steve?" Leslie looked up, interested.

"That's the strange part—the man said " 'Thank you,' and left"

"Well, I expect he would," Leslie chuckled. "The bartender did him a favor."

**What had happened in the bar?**

**2.** Steve was reading the newspaper, and Leslie was combing her hair.

"Here's a story about a guy named Moore," Steve told her, "whose life was saved by a *dream*. Apparently, he owns some sort of factory and commutes into the city every morning at 7:00 A.M.. Then he takes the 5:30 P.M. train home every night.

"One morning last week, he met the night watchman as he arrived at work. The night watchman told him that he'd had a dream the previous night that the 5:30 train would crash that day...and he warned Moore not to take his regular train. Would you believe it—Moore actually waited and took a later train. And afterwards, he heard that the 5:30 P.M. train *did* crash! Now, Moore is trying to figure out how to reward the night watchman. What do you think he should do, Les?"

Leslie looked up and thought for a second.

"Well, Moore should give the him a bonus...and then he should fire the guy."

Steve was startled. "Huh? Why do you say that, Les?"

"Why Steve, I'm surprised at you. It's elementary."

**What was Leslie thinking?**

**Turtles don't have any teeth.**

# AD TRICKS

*Former adman Terry Galanoy once wrote a book called* Down the Tube, *in which he revealed many secrets of making TV ads, including these:*

**BEER ADS**

"For years, static pictures of a glass of beer have been made with a light-grade motor oil in the bottom of the glass and a foamy head of whipped-up detergent on top."

**SHAMPOO ADS**

The models "washing" their hair in shampoo commercials are often really using something else on their heads. According to Galanoy, they either use laundry detergent, because "it whips up creamy and frothy and rich-looking," or "beaten egg whites, which are carefully laid on the hair not by beauticians, but by home economists, who ice up the lady's head as if they were icing up a cake."

**FOOD ADS**

"There are a lot of everyday camera tricks for making food look better. Soap chips are sprinkled on cereal because they look more like sugar than sugar does. Lard is scooped out to make ice cream shapes in a sundae dish because ice cream melts under hot lights and lard doesn't. Small stones replace boiled rice because boiled rice goes out a sticky mess."

**HAIR COLOR ADS**

"You...can't be sure at whom you are looking. For example, one commercial for Clairol hair coloring used one girl for the front of the hair and another for the back. The back of the first girl's hair wasn't attractive enough, but they wanted her face, so they hired a back-of-the-head backup for her."

**TESTIMONIALS**

Those hidden camera commercials?..."Sometimes they have to shoot 100 women and enough film to make three features in order to get one 'spontaneous' endorsement."

**Until 1796, the state of Tennessee was known as Franklin.**

# PRIME TIME PROVERBS

*TV's comments about everyday life in America, collected by Jack Mingo and John Javna for their book,* Prime Time Proverbs*—an excellent supplement for your bathroom library.*

**ON REVENGE**

**Sam:** "Let me give you some advice, Carla. I suggest you turn the other cheek."
**Carla:** "Mooning her isn't enough—I want to hurt her!"

—*Cheers*

**ON RELIGION**

"Let's leave religion to the televangelists. After all, they're the professionals."

—**Cheviot,**
***Max Headroom***

"Edith, Sunday's supposed to be the day of rest. How can I rest when I'm going to church?"

—**Archie Bunker**
***All in the Family***

"I thought I was on my way to Nirvana. All I ended up with was recurrent flashbacks of the original Mouseketeers."

—**Reverend Jim Ignatowski,**
***Taxi***

**ON OPPORTUNITY**

"How do you like my luck? Every time opportunity knocks, I ain't got enough money to open the door."

—**Sgt. Ernie Bilko,**
***The Phil Silvers Show***

**ON SINGLE MOTHERS**

**Blanche:** "It says here in this Spock book that it's important to have male role models during your formative years."
**Rose:** " Well, what does Spock know about raising babies? On Vulcan they're all in pods."

—***The Golden Girls***

**ON LIFE**

**Coach Ernie Pantusso:** "How's life, Norm?"
**Norm Peterson:** "It's a dog-eat-dog world, and I'm wearing Milkbone underwear."

—*Cheers*

**Wednesday Addams:** "Look, a black widow spider village."
**Gomez Addams:** "Amazing, just like a tiny human world."
**Wednesday:** "Yes, all they do is fight."
**Morticia Addams:** "Well, that's life."

*The Addams Family*

# RUMORS

*Here's the second installment of a feature we included in* BR #1. *Rumors are a special kind of gossip—outrageous stories that, one expert explains, "reveal the desires, fears, and obsessions of a society." They're also a lot of fun. Did you hear the one about...*

**RUMOR:** Proctor & Gamble is secretly owned by the Moonies (Reverend Sun Myung Moon's Unification Church).

**HOW IT STARTED:** Apparently, it was originally fueled by widespread paranoia about Moon's flower-selling legions. (They're everywhere!) The secret tipoff was supposed to be P&G's logo—the man in the moon. It was "a signal" to other Moonies.

**WHAT HAPPENED:** Proctor & Gamble executives first got wind of the rumor in 1979 and ignored it...until they got over 1,000 phone inquiries about the matter in a single month. Alarmed, they sent a letter to newspaper editors around the country pointing out that neither the Unification Church nor Rev. Moon owned even one share of stock in the company. Despite this, P&G continued to get 300 inquiries about it every month for several years.

**THE RUMOR:** A few years ago, three white Midwestern women, visiting New York City for the first time, were on an elevator in their hotel. A large black man with a big dog got on and hissed, "Sit, Lady." The terrified women immediately slid to the floor—whereupon the man informed them he was actually talking to his dog, Lady. The embarrassed women got up and contritely began asking about restaurants. They got the gentleman's recommendation for a good one, went, and enjoyed it. And when it came time to pay the bill, they were informed it had already been taken care of...by Reggie Jackson, the man they'd "met" in the elevator.

**HOW IT STARTED**: Unknown, but the story was reported as fact all over the country, including stories in newspapers in New York, L.A., Detroit, and Salt Lake City.

**WHAT HAPPENED:** A New York reporter finally called Jackson and asked him to confirm it. Jackson's reply: "I've heard that story a million times and it's not true. I would never own a dog in New York. It would be cruel."

**THE RUMOR:** Green M&Ms are an aphrodisiac.
**HOW IT STARTED:** Unknown.
**WHAT HAPPENED:** M&M Mars, the company that makes the candy, gets frequent requests for custom-packed bags of green M&Ms. They always refuse.

**THE RUMOR:** While President Richard Nixon was visiting China, he tried to steal a priceless Chinese teacup by slipping it into his briefcase. The Chinese spotted him. But instead of confronting Nixon directly, they entertained him with a magician who—while performing—surreptitiously retrieved the cup and substituted a worthless replica. Nixon didn't realize it 'til he got back to the U.S.
**HOW IT STARTED:** The official Chinese news agency released the story.
**WHAT HAPPENED:** The American government ignored it. Experts explained that the Chinese used it as propaganda to reinforce their self-image: "It symbolized," said one expert, "the victory of the resourceful Chinese over the crafty foreigner, and the ability of the Chinese to know how to act without having anyone lose face."

**THE RUMOR:** McDonald's owner Ray Kroc contributed a big chunk of his company's profits to the Church of Satan, a devil-worshiping cult in San Francisco.
**HOW IT STARTED:** Unknown, but a McDonald's manager first heard it in a Georgia fundamentalist church in 1979.
**WHAT HAPPENED:** Not wanting to give it credibility, McDonald's ignored it until it spread so far that an Ohio minister claimed Kroc had actually admitted it was true on "The Phil Donahue Show," and a few religious groups began calling for a boycott of the food chain. The company's public relations director quickly obtained a transcript of the program to prove Kroc had said nothing of the kind, then made appearances before several fundamentalist groups to explain the situation. It worked—they retracted boycott calls and dropped the matter.

**THE RUMOR:** When Army brass was planning its 1983 invasion of Grenada, they decided they needed someone who could speak Spanish, to communicate with the Grenadian citizens. So they convinced a Spanish-speaking supply sergeant named Ontiveros to land with the first paratroopers. He jumped, came under fire, and spent the entire invasion morning shouting 'Qué pasa?' at uncomprehending Grenadians. Finally, Sergeant Ontiveros realized that the Army had screwed up—Grenadians speak English, not Spanish.

**HOW IT STARTED:** It was a popular rumor in the Army, "reflecting," as one source put it, " the feelings of enlisted soldiers toward the officers who had planned the invasion."

**WHAT HAPPENED:** A reporter checked the names listed on the invasion force, and found there was no one named Ontiveros in it. An Army press officer added: "I don't doubt the story for a minute.... Except that it's not true."

**THE RUMOR:** Dr. Pepper's secret ingredient is prune juice.

**HOW IT STARTED:** Unknown, but it's been whispered for about 40 years. The company speculates that the combination of Dr. Pepper's unidentifiable "fruity taste" and their penchant for secrecy about the soft drink's formula stimulates kids' imaginations.

**WHAT HAPPENED:** The company prepared a pamphlet which they send out to people who ask about the ingredients. It says: "There are 23 flavors and other ingredients (none of which are prunes) that produce the inimitable taste of Dr. Pepper."

**THE RUMOR:** Mama Cass of the group, "the Mamas and Papas," died by choking on a ham sandwich.

**HOW IT STARTED:** When the 220-lb. Mama died suddenly in 1974, her doctor issued a quick statement speculating that "she probably choked on a sandwich."

**WHAT HAPPENED:** The bizarre report was picked up by newspapers, including *The New York Times* and *Rolling Stone* magazine, and presented as fact. Actually, when the coroner's report was issued a week later; it gave the cause of death as a heart attack "brought on by obesity." Too late—the rumor was already circulating.

**THE RUMOR:** Ex-president Jimmy Carter saw a UFO.

**HOW IT STARTED:** Carter is responsible. He told someone: "I don't laugh at people any more when they say they've seen UFOs, because I've seen one myself." He then described it in detail.

**WHAT HAPPENED:** The Air Force issued a statement explaining that Carter had mistaken the planet Venus for an alien spacecraft.

**Census report: U.S. men live longest in the Pacific states (Ore., Cal., Hawaii, Alaska, Wash.).**

# TALES OF '60s TV

*Weird things happened on TV during the '60s. Here are a few examples.*

## THE SAGA OF ARNOLD ZENKER

On March 29, 1967, television actors went on strike. And Walter Cronkite—the most popular newscaster in America—decided to walk out with them. CBS was forced to fill his anchor spot with one of their executives—but who could take Cronkite's place? They auditioned seven men for the spot, and all of them seemed too tense.

Finally, in desperation, they picked their 28-year-old manager of programming, Arnold Zenker—without an audition—because he had looked calm on a local newscast that morning. And for no apparent reason, he was an overnight smash. He received 3,000 fan letters. In fact, he was so popular that when Cronkite returned a few weeks later, he opened his first show with, "Good evening. This is Walter Cronkite, sitting in for Arnold Zenker."

"Bring back Zenker" buttons could be seen in TV studios for a while, but the novelty gradually wore off. Zenker, however, was still in shock. "There's nothing like breaking in on the 'Cronkite Show,' " he said in a classic understatement.

## LONG GREEN

On January 13, 1965, the irreverent TV host Soupy Sales was suspended from his New York children's program. Why? Because he told young viewers to reach in their fathers' billfolds and send him "those little green pieces of paper." The station manager announced he was afraid the joke might be "misinterpreted" by viewers.

## THE WEDDING

One of the most-watched televison events of the decade (and certainly one of the most talked-about) was the marriage of Tiny Tim to Miss Vicky Budinger on "The Tonight Show."

Tiny Tim, the ukelele player who'd been catapulted to fame on "Laugh-In," had mentioned that he was getting married, within earshot of a "Tonight Show" publicist. The PR man suggested to

**Census results: American women live longest in the South (Ken., Tenn., Miss., Ala.).**

Johnny Carson that he offer to let Tim get married right on the program. Tim's response: "Oh, could we?"

NBC went all out. For the man who sang "Tiptoe Through the Tulips," they ordered ten thousand tulips directly from Holland and filled the stage with them. Miss Vicky wore a $2,500 Victorian gown, Tim a black silk frock coat with a top hat. They passed up Carson's champagne toast in favor of a milk-and-honey drink that Tim concocted, and when they were pronounced man and wife, they kissed. "The fifth kiss we ever had," said Tiny.

Then they flew off to their honeymoon and at least three days of celibacy. ("S-E-X is the least important part of marriage," explained Mr. Tim.)

### THE NEW NIXON

In 1968 the Republican candidate for president, Richard Nixon, went on "Laugh-In" and said, "Sock It to Me." Believe it or not, this little event might have helped him squeak by Hubert Humphrey in the presidential election. Why? Nixon's image for two decades had been that of a humorless, colorless character. His appearance on a "hip" show lent credibility to his claim that he was a "new" Nixon. Ironically, Hubert Humphrey was also asked to appear, but declined. Rowan and Martin planned to have him say "Sock it to him, not me" right after Nixon went on. When Humphrey realized his mistake, he asked to appear also. But it was too late.

### TOURIST BONANZA

"Bonanza" was the #1 TV show in America in 1964 and 1965. It seemed so real to people that they refused to believe the Ponderosa Ranch was an imaginary place. To accommodate them, a special tour was set up near Lake Tahoe, where outdoor scenes for "Bonanza" were filmed. Guides brought tourists to an anonymous old shack in the Lake Tahoe area and told them it was the "real" Ponderosa.

### UH-H-H-H

Walter Cronkite was known for his ability to keep talking on the air, no matter what was going on. But one time—and only one time—he was left speechless.

What did it? The moon landing. "I just went blank," Cronkite explained afterward.

**The only place you can see the sun rise on the Pacific and set on the Atlantic is Panama.**

# PHOBIAS

*Are you struck with terror at the thought of wool? If someone mentions spiders, do you go limp? Maybe you've got a phobia. See if any of these rings a bell:*

**Aulophobia:** Fear of flutes
**Neophobia:** Fear of anything new
**Bogyphobia:** Fear of demons and goblins
**Triskaidekaphobia:** Fear of the number 13
**Gamophobia:** Fear of marriage
**Scopophobia:** fear of being stared at
**Aurophobia:** Fear of gold
**Chrematophobia:** Fear of money
**Astraphobia:** Fear of thunder and lightning
**Blennophobia:** Fear of slime
**Phasmophobia:** Fear of ghosts
**Arachnephobia:** Fear of spiders
**Hedonophobia:** Fear of pleasure
**Chaetophobia:** Fear of hair
**Catoptrophobia:** Fear of mirrors
**Ombrophobia:** Fear of rain
**Isopterpophobia:** Fear of termites
**Laliophobia:** Fear of talking
**Pogonophobia:** Fear of beards
**Theophobia:** Fear of God
**Ecclesiophobia:** Fear of churches
**Taurophobia:** Fear of bulls
**Teratophobia:** Fear of monsters
**Tapinophobia:** Fear of small things
**Homichlophobia:** Fear of fog
**Geumophobia:** Fear of flavors
**Hadephobia:** Fear of hell
**Gymnophobia:** Fear of nudity
**Levophobia:** Fear of things on the left side of the body
**Ichthyophobia:** Fear of fish
**Mechanophobia:** Fear of machines
**Pteronophobia:** Fear of feathers
**Politicophobia:** Fear of politicians
**Siderodromophobia:** Fear of trains (or traveling on them)
**Symmetrophobia:** Fear of things that are symmetrical
**Xenophobia:** Fear of foreigners and unfamiliar things
**Zoophobia:** Fear of animals
**Anthrophobia:** Fear of people
**Ophidiophobia:** Fear of snakes
**Graphophobia:** Fear of writing in public
**Linonophobia:** Fear of string
**Pantophobia:** Fear of everything

**Hear, hear: You'll find a snake's ears in its jaws.**

# FAMILIAR NAMES

*Some people achieve immortality because their names become commonly associated with an item or activity. You already know the names—now here are the people.*

**Joel Roberts Poinsett.** A lifelong American diplomat, secretary of war under Martin Van Buren. While ambassador to Mexico, he brought the first *poinsettia* back to the United States.

**Patrick Hooligan.** A notorious hoodlum who lived in London in the mid-1800s. His name became a generic term for "trouble-maker."

**Leopold von Sacher-Masoch.** An Austrian novelist. His books reflected his sexual disorder, a craving which was later dubbed *masochism*.

**Frederick S. Duesenburg.** An automobile manufacturer. His 1930 Duesenburg SJ was the most exquisite vehicle of its time, so impressive that its nickname—the Duesey—became a slang term for something really terrific. When someone says, "That's a real doozey," they're talking about Frederick.

**Charles Mason / Jeremiah Dixon.** English surveyors. In the 1760s, they were called in to settle a boundary dispute between two prominent Colonial families—the Penns of Pennsylvania, and the Calverts of Maryland. A hundred years later, the line they laid out became the North/South border.

**Arnold Reuben.** A New York deli owner in the '40s and '50s. He put corned beef, sauerkraut, and Russian dressing on a piece of rye bread and named the whole thing after himself—the Reuben sandwich.

**Alexander Graham Bell.** Inventor of the telephone (1876). The standard measurement of "sound intensity," the *decibel*, was named in his honor.

**Sir Benjamin Hall.** The "chief commissioner of works" for the British government in the 1850s, when the tower clock on the Houses of Parliament got its largest bell. Newspapers of the time dubbed it "Big Ben," after Hall.

**Pierre Magnol.** A French professor of botany in the 1600s. Gave us the flower name *magnolia.*

**Alessandro Volta.** A celebrated Italian physicist. His experiments with electricity in the late 1700s led to the invention of the dry-cell battery. The *volt* was named for him.

**Belinda Blurb.** A model portrayed on a book jacket by American illustrator Gelett Burgess. She inspired the common term for a publisher's comments on a book cover.

**Samuel A. Maverick.** Texas cattle baron in the mid-1800s. Had so many unbranded stray calves that they became known as *mavericks.* Eventually, the term came to include independent-minded people as well.

**Franz Anton Mesmer.** An Austrian physician. Popularized outrageous medical theories on animal magnetism in Paris in 1780s. He *mesmerized* the public.

**Guy Fawkes.** English political agitator who tried to blow up Parliament in 1605, but was caught and executed. The British began celebrating November 5 as Guy Fawkes Day, burning effigies of "the old Guy." Since the effigies were dressed in old clothes, the term *guy* came to mean *bum.* In America during Colonial times, its meaning was broadened to mean any male.

**William Russell Frisbie.** American pie maker. Founded the Frisbie Pie Company in Bridgeport, Connecticut, in 1871. In the early 1900s, students from Yale—located up the road in New Haven, Connecticut—found they could flip the Frisbie pie tins like flying saucers.

**Madame de Pompadour.** Mistress of King Louis XV of France in the mid-1700s. Popularized the hairstyle that reappeared, in modified form, on the heads of Elvis and James Dean.

**Why do flamingoes hold their heads upside down? It's the only way they can eat.**

# CELLULOID HEROES

*Popular films often inspire musicians to write their best songs. Here are a few examples.*

**THAT'LL BE THE DAY,** by Buddy Holly and Jerry Allison (The Crickets).
**INSPIRATION:** *The Searchers.*
John Wayne's favorite—and maybe his best—cowboy film, *The Searchers*, was released in 1956.

Wayne's character in the movie was a defiant, macho loner, an anti-hero who fit right in with the James Dean/Marlon Brando image of the mid-'50s. Whenever anyone said something he disagreed with, he'd sneer, "That'll be the day." The phrase caught on among teenagers, and two high school musicians from Lubbock, Texas, Buddy Holly and Jerry Allison, used it in a song.

They recorded it with their band, the Crickets, in 1957, and it became the first hit in a series of records that made Holly a rock legend.

**THE MIGHTY QUINN,** by Bob Dylan.
**INSPIRATION:** *The Savage Innocents.*
Who—or what—inspired Bob Dylan to write "The Mighty Quinn (Quinn the Eskimo)"? He's not saying, but chances are it was a little-known 1960 film called *The Savage Innocents.*

What does the movie have to do with Quinn the Eskimo? Well, it starred Anthony Quinn. And he played an Eskimo.

**NIGHT MOVES,** by Bob Seger.
**INSPIRATION:** *American Graffiti.*
"The song was inspired by *American Graffiti*," Seger says. "I came out of the theater in 1972 thinking, 'Hey, I've got a story to tell, too! Nobody has ever told about how it was to grow up in my neck of the woods.' "

So Seger wrote "Night Moves" about the early '60s, when he and his teenage friends around Ann Arbor, Michigan would drive into farmers' fields to party. "Everybody had their headlights on, so there was light to dance," Seger recalls. "They'd play 45s, and we'd be blasting them out: Ronettes, Crystals...." Seger's personal

**A queen bee can lay as many as 3,000 eggs in a day.**

"American Graffiti" sold over a million copies and became the favorite tune of his career. "I don't know if I'll ever write one as good as that again," he says.

**BIG GIRLS DON'T CRY,** by Bob Crewe and Bob Gaudio (The Four Seasons).
**INSPIRATION:** A "B" movie on TV.
This was one of the biggest hits of 1962. According to Bob Crewe, the man who co-wrote it:

"I was up late one night in my apartment, watching a dreadful movie—I think it was with John Payne and some blonde bombshell. I had been drinking...and I was drifting in and out of sleep. I woke up at one point and Payne was smacking the blonde across the face and knocked her on her bottom. He said something like, 'Well, whadda ya think of that, baby?' She gets up, straightens her dress, pushes her hair back, stares at him and says, 'Big girls don't cry,' and storms out the door. I ran and jotted down the line. The next day we turned it into a song."

**BEAT IT,** by Michael Jackson.
**INSPIRATION:** *West Side Story*.
There's a distinct similarity between the "Beat It" video and the filmed musical *West Side Story* —which tends to indicate that Michael Jackson was inspired by the award-winning 1961 film. Indeed, he's known to have studied it. "The theme of my song," he said, "is about two gangs coming together to rumble, to fight." Just like the Sharks and the Jets.

But the best evidence is this: The first two words in *West Side Story* —spoken when a member of the Sharks accidentally wanders into Jet territory—are "Beat it!"

**SCHOOL'S OUT,** by Alice Cooper.
**INSPIRATION:** A Bowery Boys movie.
From 1937 to 1958, Leo Gorcey, Huntz Hall, and the rest of the Bowery Boys gang appeared in dozens of low-budget films. Alice Cooper was inspired by one of them. "I heard the phrase 'School's out' in a Bowery Boys' movie." he says. "It was used the same way that someone would say 'Get smart, Satch.' "
Cooper then used it in the song that became his first Top 10 hit.

**America's first nudist organization was founded in 1929, by 3 men.**

# W.C. FIELDS SEZ

*The original movie curmudgeon had a lot to say.*

"Never give a sucker an even break."

"Women are like elephants to me I like to look at 'em, but I wouldn't want to own one."

"Anyone who hates children and dogs can't be all bad."

"Reminds me of my safari in Africa. Somebody forgot the corkscrew and for several days we had to live on nothing but food and water."

"Never try to impress a woman because if you do, you'll have to keep up that standard the rest of your life."

"Show me a great actor and I'll show you a lousy husband; show me a great actress, and you've seen the devil."

"I've been asked if I ever get the DTs. I don't know. It's hard to tell where Hollywood ends and the DTs begin."

"I am free of all prejudices. I hate everyone equally."

"I never vote *for* anyone. I always vote against."

"Start every day off with a smile, and get it over with."

"A thing worth having is a thing worth cheating for."

"'Twas a woman who drove me to drink....And I never had the courtesy to thank her for it."

"I always keep a supply of liquor handy in case I see a snake—which I also keep handy."

"All my available funds are completely tied up in ready cash."

"I have never struck a woman. Never! Not even my poor old mother."

"I like children. If they're properly cooked."

"If at first you don't succeed, try again. Then quit. No use being a damn fool about it."

**A whopping 60% of all new cars sold in the '80s were recalled for some defect.**

# UNCLE JOHN'S LETTER OF THE YEAR

*Of all the mail we received—and there was plenty—one stood out as our "Letter of the Year." Here it is.*

**BACKGROUND:** In our previous volume, we included a comment from Mary Tyler Moore about how far fans will go to get autographs. She said:

"I know a funny Carol Burnett story. Once a fan followed her into the bathroom. The fan poked her head under the stall and shoved a pen and a piece of paper at Carol for an autograph."

Okay, got it? Now here's our Letter of the Year.

June 4, 1989

**Dear Uncle John,**

I am a third grade teacher...I teach a literature selection during the year...and this year I selected *The Wizard of Oz*, one of my personal favorites. My son suggested that I read the excerpts and comments about this story in *Uncle John's Bathroom Reader*. I did, and was fascinated by the political implications of this child's tale.

However, this is not why I write. I am astounded to tell you that as I thumbed through your pages, I found an article on page 152—"Celebrity Mania"—that was about ME! I am referring to a quote of Mary Tyler Moore's regarding Carol Burnett.

Here is the real scoop. *I* was the fan referred to in the story. However, it does my heart good to know that not only the common people, but also the rich and famous like to embellish a good story now and then.

Many years ago, sometime in the early sixties, my husband and I had gone to Las Vegas. We tried to get tickets to see Carol Burnett's show. I think it must have been one of her very first forays away from the world of television and Garry Moore. [*Uncle John's note: She got her start on daytime TV, in "The Garry Moore Show".*]

We were told that she was sold out. The disappointment of my life! (So far—I was young then.) Trudging away from the desk, I happened to see Carol going into the ladies' room. On impulse, I followed her in. Now my recollections are just a little different from Miss Burnett's. Ever the lady, I waited outside the stall, just as I would to use the facilities. I had no intention of "peeking under the stall." When Carol came out, I zipped inside, shut the door and sat down. Oh!, be still my heart—the seat was still warm. (Isn't this gross? Remember, I was very young.) That would have been enough for me. To live to tell the tale. Yet, when I came out to wash my hands, SHE was still there by the sink. Gathering up my courage I said to her . . .

"Oh MissBurnett,I'msosorrythatIcan'tgetticketsto seeyour-show whileweare-here.It'sabigdisappointment.CanIhaveyourautograph? Yourshowisallsoldout!!!!"

Whereupon she grabbed her head as only Carol Burnett can do and said in that great voice, "I had no idea that so many people would want to see me!" She added, "Why don't you and your husband come in to watch the dress rehearsal" . . . or whatever it was they were doing. "Just tell them at the door that I said it's O.K."

Well, I got my autograph—went to find my husband—walking on air! He said, "Sure, sure, sure. Who did you *really* get to sign that envelope?" He wouldn't go with me because he thought I was making it up, and I was too frightened to go alone. I never did get to see Carol Burnett do a show, but I still have the autograph. I'll never part with it.

Addendum: Just a couple of weeks ago I was installing a new toilet seat in my bathroom and I thought of Carol. (I'm sure she would be *thrilled* to know that I think of her every time I sit there!) Anyway, I was thinking that I should probably box up the old one and send it to her. Maybe she would like to sit on one of mine for a change.

Anyway, she has given me years of pleasure, not only in watching her, but in the telling and re-telling of my story. I know fans can be a pain...but I'd do it all over again.

Sincerely,

Cynthia L.

**It takes 1/2 gallon of water to cook a pot of macaroni...and a gallon to wash the pot.**

# THE PATENTED CAR

*This is a bit of lost history. We take it for granted that anyone who wants to can build a car. Few people realize that that right actually had to be won in court at the beginning of this century, by Henry Ford.*

## CASHING IN

In the late 1870s George Selden, a lawyer/inventor specializing in patents, heard about the development of the automobile in Europe. He realized that it was a product of the future, and "set his mind to working out the precise legal definition and wording of a patent that would give him the sole right to license and charge royalties on future automobile development in America." Some twenty years later, with the auto industry beginning to show signs of life, he set up a partnership with a few wealthy Wall Street sharks and began asserting his "rights" with automakers. To his surprise, even the five biggest car manufacturers agreed to pay him royalties rather than go to court.

## THE CARMAKERS' CARTEL

By 1903, this royalty-paying alliance of carmakers had officially become the Association of Licensed Automobile Manufacturers (ALAM). Henry Ford, then a fledgling automaker, applied for membership...and was refused. His reaction: "Let them try to put me out of business!" He took out ads telling his dealers that "the Selden patent does not cover any practicable machine," and dared Selden's group to take him to court. They did.

## BATTLING IN COURT

Ford and the ALAM battled it out for six years. Then in 1909, a Federal judge determined that Selden's patent was valid; Selden and his allies legally owned *all rights* to the car. Immediately, carmakers that had held off on joining the ALAM —including the newly formed General Motors—fell in line to pay royalties.

The ALAM magnanimously offered to settle cheaply with Ford, but Henry fought on. "There will be no let up in this legal fight," he announced angrily. Finally, on January 9, 1911, a Federal Court of Appeals ruled in Ford's favor. Selden and his cronies were forced to give up; the ALAM was never heard from again.

**Dirty snow melts quicker than clean snow.**

# YOU'RE PUTTING ME ON!

*The history of some modern wearables.*

## WHAT A HEEL

In the 1600s, Louis XIV of France added a few inches to the heels of his boots because he was so short. To his annoyance, he started a fad in the Royal Court—soon everyone was wearing elevated heels. So he made his even higher. And so did everyone else. This went on until it got ridiculous. Eventually, men's heels got smaller—but women's stayed high. In the 1800s, American women copied the styles of Paris, and high heels—called "French heels" at first—became a part of American fashion.

## TIES THAT BIND

The necktie fashion originated with a band of Croatian soldiers who showed up in France in the mid-1600s. Part of their uniforms were fancy scarves made of linen or muslin; and this looked so impressive to the French that they began wearing fancy linen scarves themselves. They called the scarves *cravats*. Meanwhile, King Charles II of England picked up on the fashion—and when cravats became part of *his* daily wear, the rest of England followed. Over the next century, the cravat evolved into the modern tie.

## SNEAKING AROUND

The modern sneaker was introduced in 1917, when the National India Rubber Company came up with *Peds*. Or at least, that's what they wanted to call their new shoe. It turned out that the name *Peds* was already registered; so they quickly changed the name to *Keds* (with a *K* for "kids"). The original sneakers had black soles and brown tops, because those were the popular colors for traditional men's footwear.

## TUX & ROLLS

Pierre Lorillard IV, scion of the tobacco company, lived in Tuxedo Park, N.Y. In 1886, he decided he was sick of the formalwear of the day, and had his tailor make suits without tails. In a daring move for Victorian high society gent, he planned to wear one of these scandalous suits to the annual Autumn Ball. But he chickened out at the last minute. Instead, his son and his son's friends wore the suits. No scandal here; since the Lorillards were rich, everyone copied them. The outrageous suit became a fashion. It was even named for its birthplace. And a century later, the tuxedo industry is grossing a half a billion dollars annually.

## WRANGLING AROUND

The Blue Bell Overall company was the largest manufacturer of denim bib overalls in the world, but after World War II, they wanted to expand—and decided to add blue jeans to their line of clothing. The name they picked for their new product was Wrangler. At first, since Levi-Strauss had the better stores all sewn up, Blue Bell sold its Wranglers only to discount chains, like J. C. Penney's. But eventually they hired Hollywood stars to plug the jeans, and they became as fashionable as Levi's.

## STRAIGHT-LACED

The shoelace was invented in England in 1790. Until then, shoes were always fastened with buckles.

## MADE IN THE SHADES

According to Gene Sculatti, in *The Catalog of Cool*: "The first sunglasses were made in 1885 in Philadelphia. Seeking an alternative to costly amber and micalens glasses, a glazier simply put small circles of window glass out in the sun, exposing them to several summers' rays." Sunglasses were popular, but weren't faddish until the '20s, when a bankrupt French comb manufacturer began turning out an assortment of bizarre sunglass frames, trying to find something people would buy. They were shaped like "peacocks, butterflies, pistols, wings, masks, etc. These were gobbled up by the international pre-jet set of the '30s, and soon became true 'trinkets of the bourgeoisie.' " Since then, luminaries like Jackie O., Elton John, Marcello Mastroianni, Audrey Hepburn, and even Barry Goldwater have kept them stylish.

## NEHRU WOULD BE PROUD

The Nehru jacket was popularized—briefly—by Johnny Carson, who wore it on TV in the '60s.

Just one part oil per million parts of water will make drinking water taste and smell funny.

# MONSTER MOVIES

*The inside dope on a few of the all-time great horror flicks.*

**FRANKENSTEIN (1931).** The role that made Boris Karloff a star was originally offered to both Bela Lugosi and John Carradine; both turned it down. One of the factors: the monster costume weighed 62 pounds and the makeup took four hours to apply every day.

• Karloff had to wear 22-pound size 24 boots. He also donned two pairs of pants with steel struts shoved in them, and a double-thickness quilted suit.

• His facial makeup was one-sixteenth of an inch thick, and the bolts on the sides of his neck left long-term scars.

• The famous scene in which the monster carries Dr. Frankenstein was memorable for Karloff, too—he strained his back, and ultimately had to have an operation to fix it.

• Bette Davis wanted the part of Mrs. Frankenstein, but was turned down because she was "too aggressive."

**DRACULA (1931).** Bela Lugosi became the first great monster of the talkie era with his role in this film. He had been playing Count Dracula on Broadway since 1927, so he already knew the part. Unfortunately, he was only paid $500 for his classic film performance.

• Among the film's lighting tricks: "Twin pencil-spotlights" were shined in Lugosi's eyes to give Count Dracula his legendary hypnotic stare.

• The Castle Dracula and Carfax Abbey sets were so expensive to build that Universal Pictures kept and reused them. You can spot them in numerous Universal films of the '30s.

• The enormous spider web on Dracula's staircase was actually a string of rubber cement. And the mountains shown in the first scenes were really the Rockies—not the Alps or Carpathians.

**THE MUMMY (1932)** Boris Karloff's second big monster flick was inspired by the discovery of King Tut's tomb in 1922...and the widespread belief—because several men on the Tut expedition had died mysteriously—that there was a real-life curse connected to it.

• Karloff was wrapped every day in linen and gauze, and was covered with mud.

**Survey results: 98% of American drivers think they drive better than anyone else.**

• He had become so famous as Frankenstein's monster the previous year that he was billed simply as "Karloff." Only Greta Garbo could match that.

**THE WOLF MAN (1941).** Lon Chaney, Jr. starred; it was his favorite role. Based on a popular 1935 English film, *Werewolf of London*, it was a surprise hit. Universal released it two days after Pearl Harbor, and expected low box office receipts. But instead of being distracted *by* the news, Americans wanted to be distracted *from* it.
• Chaney's werewolf makeup took five hours to apply every day.
• The same makeup man who created the Mummy and Frankenstein's monster for Boris Karloff created Chaney's werewolf.
• The werewolf costume was actually made of yak hair.

**THE THING (1951).** Director Howard Hawks's flick about an alien discovered near an Arctic research station is notable for two reasons: First, it kicked off the whole "it came from outer space" genre in the '50s; and second, the actor playing the monster was James Arness—"Gunsmoke" 's Matt Dillon. Arness, who's 6 feet-5 inches tall, wore four-inch lifts. He was onscreen about 3 minutes.

**THEM! (1954).** Another B-film breakthough—the first of the "giant mutated insects" genre. In this one, huge killer ants were found in the desert. But again, it was one of the actors who made the film memorable—Fess Parker. In 1954 Walt Disney, planning a feature about Davy Crockett, couldn't find the right man to play the lead...until he saw *Them!* He immediately hired Parker, who became one of America's hottest actors as the King of the Wild Frontier—and later, as Dan'l Boone. Also featured in the film: Arness, who was a year away from TV stardom, and Leonard Nimoy.

**THE CREATURE FROM THE BLACK LAGOON (1954).** The star of this 3-D epic, the scaly creature who's become the symbol of all '50s cheapo monsters, was actually modeled after the Oscar statue given at the Academy Awards.
•Two different actors appeared inside the latex costume. On land, it was a big fellow named Ben Chapman. In water, it was champion swimmer Ricou Browning, whose main claim to fame was that a decade later, he created and trained TV's most famous aquatic hero—Flipper.

**Michael Landon played the title role of *I Was a Teenage Werewolf* in 1957.**

# MYTH AMERICA

*You've probably believed these stories since you were a kid. Most Americans have, because they were taught to us as sacred truths. Well, here's another look at them.*

## HILL OF BEANS

**The Myth:** The Battle of Bunker Hill—where the Americans first faced the Redcoats—was the colonists' initial triumph in the Revolutionary War.

**The Truth:** Not only did the British wallop the Americans in the encounter, the whole thing wasn't even fought on Bunker Hill. The American troops *had* actually been ordered to defend Bunker Hill, but there was an enormous foul-up and somehow, they wound up trying to protect nearby Breed's Hill, which was more vulnerable to attack. They paid for it—when the fighting was over, the Americans had been chased away by the British troops. Casualties were heavy for both sides; about 450 Americans were killed, and a staggering 1,000 (out of 2,100 soldiers) Redcoats bit the dust.

## PILGRIMS' PROGRESS

**The Myth:** The Pilgrims were headed for Massachusetts.

**The Truth:** They were headed for "Hudson's River." Because of poor navigation and unexpected winds, the first land they sighted was Cape Cod. They tried to sail south, but "dangerous shoales and roaring breakers" prevented it. So they reluctantly turned back. By this time, the crew of the *Mayflower* (no, the ship wasn't manned by Pilgrims) was sick of them and hustled them off the boat as fast as they could.

**The Myth:** The Pilgrims landed at Plymouth Rock.

**Background:** This tale originated in 1741, more than 100 years after the Pilgrims arrived. It has been attributed to a then-95-year-old man named Thomas Fraunce, who claimed his father had told him the story when he was a boy. However, his father hadn't landed with the pilgrims—he reached America 3 years after they did.

**The Truth:** The Pilgrims first landed in Provincetown, Massachusetts.

## AND SO FOURTH...

**The Myth:** American independence was declared on July 4th.

**Background:** Because the Declaration of Independence is dated July 4th, people associate that date with American independence. In fact, independence was declared first...and was confirmed with the document a few days later.

**The Truth:** The Continental Congress declared independence on July 2nd. One of the Founding Fathers, John Adams, is quoted as having written his wife on July 3rd: "The 2nd day of July, 1776, will be the most memorable...in the history of America. I am apt to believe it will be celebrated by succeeding generations, as the great anniversary Festival."

• **Note:** Actually, the first Independence Day celebration—by the Continental Congress—was on July 8th, 1776.

## A SIGN OF THE TIMES

**The Myth:** In a hushed hall in Philadelphia on July 4, 1776, each signer of the Declaration of Independence proudly and publicly took his turn affixing his signature to the document.

**Background:** This tale was apparently concocted by Thomas Jefferson and Benjamin Franklin, who wrote about it in letters after the event.

**The Truth:** Only 2 people—John Hancock and Charles Thomson—signed the Declaration of Independence on July 4th. It wasn't until about a month later, on August 2, that the majority of the delegates signed it. And it wasn't until 5 years later, in 1781, that the last signature was finally added.

• How public was the signing? The Continental Congress would only admit that Hancock's and Thomson's names were on the document. Everyone else signed in secrecy. It wasn't until the following January that the signers' names were made public.

## YANKEE DOODLE

**The Myth:** "Yankee Doodle" was originally a patriotic song.

**The Truth:** It was composed in England as an anti-American tune. The phrase "stuck a feather in his cap and called it macaroni" referred to a foppish English group called the Macaroni Club, whose members wore ludicrous "continental" fashions they mistakenly believed to be elegant. The British laughed at "Yankee Doodle dandies," bumpkins who didn't know how silly they really were.

**Texas is the most expensive place in the U.S. to get a divorce. Idaho is the cheapest.**

# BUSHSPEAK

*President Bush has a unique way of presenting his ideas. Newspapers have dubbed it "Bushspeak."*

"America's freedom is the example to which the world expires."

*To a gathering of Hispanic high school students:*
"You don't have to go to college to achieve success. We need the people who do the hard, physical work."

*On his years with Ronald Reagan:*
"For seven and a half years I have worked alongside him, and I am proud to be his partner. We have had triumphs, we have made mistakes, we have had sex..."

*On a tour of a Nazi death camp:*
"Boy, they were big on crematoriums, weren't they?"

"If this country...ever loses its interest in fishing, we got real trouble."

*Political analysis while on the campaign trail:*
"It's no exaggeration to say the undecideds could go one way or another."

*To the head of the Jordanian Army:*
"Tell me, General, how dead is the Dead Sea?"

"I can announce that our dog is pregnant. This happened yesterday. A beautiful experience. We expect to have puppies in the White House."

"This isn't a signal. It's a direct statement. If it's a signal, fine."

*On his gun control position:*
"And you know, you look at the amount of people committing crimes with a gun—I looked up the gun registration, which I oppose. I went down —I told you or you heard me say this: But I had the guy doing up a file today."

"When I ran for office in Texas, they said, 'This guy's from New England.' I said, 'Wait a minute. I couldn't help that, I wanted to be near my mother at the time.' "

"He would have been in deep doo-doo."

# ADVICE TO SINGLES

*Before self-help books like* How to Pick Up Girls *and* How to Marry the Man of Your Choice *were available, people relied on aphrodisiacs and rituals to score with the opposite sex. These honest-to-goodness recipes were collected by love-starved historians.*

**FOR THE MARRIAGE-MINDED:**
"If you want to get married, stand on your head and chew a piece of gristle out of a beef neck and swallow it, and you will get anyone you want."

***—American folklore***

❤

"If you can walk around the block with your mouth full of water, you will be married within a year."

***—American folklore***

❤

" To win your beloved's affection: Take a piece of clothing into which you have freely perspired, and burn and powder it with some of your hair. Mix with your spit and blood and introduce it into the food and drink which your loved one will consume."

***—English folklore***

❤

**APHRODISIACS:**
"Take three pubic hairs and three from the left armpit. Burn them on a hot shovel. Pulverize and insert into a piece of bread. Dip bread in soup and feed to a lover."

***—Albertus Magnus,***
***Medieval philosopher***

❤

"Shed your clothes completely, and at the stroke of midnight beneath a cloudless moon, walk three times around a house. For each step you take, throw a handful of salt behind you. If no one has seen you by the time you have finished, the person you love will be mad for you."

***— Dutch folklore***

❤

**Annual event: The U.S. uses more steel making bottle caps than car bodies.**

# BASEBALL NAMES

*If you're a baseball fan, you know these names by heart. But you probably don't know where they came from. Here are the stories behind some famous names.*

**Los Angeles Dodgers.** Formed in Brooklyn, New York, in 1890. Brooklyn had hundreds of trolleys zig-zagging through its streets, and pedestrians were constantly scurrying out of their way. That's why their baseball team was called the Brooklyn Trolley Dodgers (later shortened to Dodgers). The team moved to L.A. in 1958.

**Houston Astros.** Formed in 1961, they were originally called the Colt .45s, after the famous gun. But by 1965, when their new stadium opened, Houston had become famous as the home of NASA's Mission Control. Both the stadium (Astrodome) and the team were named in honor of America's astronauts.

**Pittsburgh Pirates.** In 1876, they were known as the Alleghenies (after the neighboring Allegheny River). But in the 1890s, they earned a new nickname—the Pirates—when they stole a few players from a rival Philadelphia baseball club.

**San Francisco Giants.** The New York Gothams baseball club were fighting for a National League championship in 1886. After one particularly stunning victory, their manager proudly addressed them as "My big fellows, my giants." The name stuck. The New York Giants moved to San Francisco in 1958.

**Cleveland Indians.** From 1869 to 1912, the Cleveland baseball team had five different names—including the Forest Citys, the Naps, and the Spiders. Then in 1913 a popular player named Luis Francis Sockalexis died. He had been the first American Indian ever to play pro baseball and the team was renamed in his honor.

**Chicago Cubs.** Apparently they had no official nickname at the turn of the century (although they were informally called the Colts and the Orphans). Then, in 1902, a sportswriter dubbed them "the

**You can feed 24 people with one ostrich egg.**

Cubs" because it was short enough to fit into a newspaper headline. The name caught on, and 5 years later the team officially adopted it.

**Cincinnati Reds.** Formed in 1869, the team was originally called the Red Stockings. Later, they were known as the Reds—until the early '50s, when McCarthyism was rampant. No one wanted to be called a "Red" then—it sounded too much like "Commie." So the team actually made an official name change, to Redlegs. When the patriotic panic died down, they quietly switched back to Reds.

**Detroit Tigers.** Legend says that the Detroit Creams (the cream of the baseball crop) became the Tigers in 1896, when their manager decided their black and brown striped socks reminded him of tiger stripes.

**Montreal Expos.** The Canadian city was awarded a baseball franchise in 1968, partly because its 1967 World's Fair—called Expo '67—had been successful. The team was named in honor of the event.

**New York Yankees.** They were first called the Highlanders or Hilltoppers, because their ballfield was located at the highest point in the city. Again, sportswriters got fed up trying to fit the names into headlines. So in 1909, a newsman arbitrarily called them Yankees—patriotic slang for "Americans." After World War I, when jingoistic fervor was rampant ("The Yanks are coming"), the team officially became the Yankees.

**Baltimore Orioles.** Were named for the Maryland state bird in the early 1900s.

**Kansas City Royals, San Diego Padres, Seattle Mariners, Texas Rangers, Toronto Blue Jays.** All 5 are expansion teams. All 5 got their names in public "name-our-new-team" contests. The Padres, although formed in 1969, got their name in 1935. The original contest was held to name a *minor league* team. Thirty-four years later, San Diego was awarded a major league franchise, and the new ballclub adopted the old name.

**The most-watched film in history is *The Wizard of Oz*. Over a billion people have seen it.**

# WHICH STOOGE ARE YOU?

***The B.R.I. is pleased to present this penetrating social analysis by Ivan Stang, the brains behind the Church of the Sub-Genius.***

There are three kinds of people in this world. I know, you've heard that before. Everybody has their "three types of people," or their four types, or five types....

But there are three, and the models for these types come neither from psychology nor ancient religion. They come from Columbia Studios, and they are archetypally embodied in The Three Stooges.

The Stooges unwittingly—of course—left us a rich legacy of deft interpretations of the most primal human behavior patterns. Their short films, seen as a whole, form a tapestry in which the interactions of people as individuals, corporations, and nations are distilled to a microcosm, a pure essence of existential folly.

There are but a small percentage of Moes in any given population: perhaps five percent. There are even fewer Curlys. The vast bulk of humanity are Larrys. (Though represented by male characters, the three types also apply to women.)

## THE MOE PERSONALITY

Moe is the active personality, and if not always dominant, always striving to be. Moe is the one who spurs the others into action. He devises plans to better their lot, but when his plans fail the other two suffer the consequences. But is Moe any less the fool because they follow his plans?

He is a natural manipulator, only partially because the others are waiting to be manipulated. He would want to manipulate them anyway, even if they weren't so willing.

## THE LARRY PERSONALITY

Larry is a born follower, a blank slate that only reacts (and slowly at that) to external stimuli. He never initiates action. He is Moe's absolute tool, the truest "stooge." When Moe's abuse finally does make him angry, he lashes out not at Moe, but at Curly. No matter how he suffers under Moe's yoke, he never really rebels. He argues, but gives up easily.

Were it not for the presence of his friends, Larry probably would live in peace—a dull, flat, mechanical peace. Though clumsy, he is still the most employable of the three—for the other two are incapable of following orders, although for different reasons.

## THE CURLY PERSONALITY

Curly is the only likeable one, a truly rare human model. He is the holy man, the Divine Fool. He is as creative and active as Moe—but it is a spontaneous and joyous kind of creativity, no good for the kind of plotting and scheming required by a Moe-dominated society. He is a free spirit, but correspondingly unable to function well in a world of Moes and Larrys. He, like Larry, is perpetually abused, but he intuitively understands what is happening to him and reacts far more angrily—if equally ineffectually. He is everyone's favorite Stooge because he is the funniest; through his innate nobility and natural humility he constantly bests Moe, but it is in an unconscious way, and it is only apparent to the outside observer. Curly himself is hardly aware of his talents; his weakness is that he does not know his own strength, and cannot trust his own luck.

In real life, Curlys are usually branded by the Moes and Larrys around them as retarded, schizophrenic, maladjusted, or just plain stupid...whereas in reality, it is only Curly who understands the truth. Remaining cheerful through adversity, he wins battles not by fighting, but by "accidentally" unleashing "accidents" in which his enemies injure themselves.

## STOOGE CO-EXISTENCE

Alien to feelings of avarice or ambition, Curly is the opposite of Moe. Yet the two are drawn together by some inexplicable balancing force of nature. The Larrys, though, are ever the in-betweeners, slug-like nonentities caught in the crossfire of cosmic dualities—yet remaining there by some herding instinct that makes being a casualty of the Moe-Curly battle preferable to life alone with other Larrys.

Only the existence of the blameless, bovine Larrys makes that of Moe or Curly possible. They are able to maintain their level of glandular brutality and senseless destruction only at the expense of the unquestioning, loyal worker drone whose income partially supports their excesses. Were he not there to diffuse Moe's anger by becoming another recipient of his blows, Curly would have been killed long ago, and Moe would have committed suicide out of

**Americans owned 2.1 million computers in 1981. In 1989 we own 37.8 million of them.**

loneliness.

The horror of it all is that the three types need each other to survive. Of all nature's cycles of parasitic symbiosis, the one involving the three human types is the most nightmarish. It rages around us all the time in real life, spreading death and madness, yet when we see it on the screen we call it "comedy."

## NYUK NYUK NYUK: THE STOOGES IN ACTION

*A doctor doubts the Stooges' qualifications as surgeons.*
**Doctor:** "Why, you don't even know how to deliver an anesthetic."
*The Stooges pull out wooden mallets.*
**Moe:** "Give him some anethesia."
*Larry and Curly clobber him on the head with their mallets.*

*The Stooges are about to operate on a patient, planning out their strategy by playing tic-tac-toe on the sheet covering him.*
**Moe:** "Give him another anesthetic, boys. I think it's wearing off.
**Patient** (sitting up): "No it isn't."
**Larry** (roughly pushing him down): "Lay down. Are you trying to make a fool out of us doctors?"
Wham!

**Moe:** "Whaddya up to now?"
**Curly** (bowling): "I just got a poifect score!"
**Moe:** "No ya haven't. Ya need another strike."
Wham!

*Curly is holding an unwrapped cigar up to his ear.*
**Moe:** "What're ya doin'?"
**Curly:** "Listenin' to the band. Nyuk, nyuk, nyuk."
**Moe:** "Would you like to hear some birdies?"
**Curly:** "I'd love it!"
**Moe:** "Take off yer hat!"
Wham!

**Secretary:** "Mattie Herring is here to see you."
**Moe:** "Mattie Herring? Sounds fishy. Send her in."
**Secretary:** "Now?"
**Moe:** "No, marinate her first."
**Curly:** "And don't forget the onions. Nuyuk, nyuk, nyuk."

**The speed of a hard rain is about 20 mph.**

# DEFINITIONS

*In the first* Bathroom Reader *we included some uncommon words, and their meanings, to help build anemic vocabularies. Here's another batch.*

**Franch:** To eat greedily
**Rhotacism:** Excessive use of the letter "R"
**Manumission:** The official act of freeing a slave
**Netop:** A friend
**Gash-gabbit:** Having a protruding chin
**Girn:** To bare your teeth in anger or in sadness
**Wamfle:** To walk around with flapping clothes
**Charientism:** An elegantly veiled insult
**Juglandaceous:** Pertaining to walnuts
**Kakistocracy:** Government of a state by its worst citizens
**Ergophile:** A person who loves to work
**Lingible:** Meant to be licked
**Cicisbeo:** A married woman's well-known lover
**Moll-buzzer:** A thief whose specialty is robbing women
**Yerd:** To beat with a stick
**Mubblefubble:** Mental depression
**Nash-gob:** An arrogant gossip
**Zuber:** The European breed of buffalo
**Nazzard:** A lowly or weak person
**Alliaphage:** A garlic eater
**Nuddle:** To push something with your nose
**Glossolalia:** Gibberish; babble
**Ribazuba:** Ivory from a walrus
**Eristic:** Argumentative
**Roddikin:** A cow or deer's fourth stomach
**Mabble:** To wrap your head
**Scobberlotcher:** An idle person
**Irrefragable:** Undeniable
**Shench:** To pour a drink for someone
**Palilalia:** Helplessly repeating a phrase faster and faster.
**Shongable:** A shoemaking tax
**Slibbersauce:** A disgusting substance
**Walm:** To bubble up
**Cherubimical:** Inebriated
**Dendrofilous:** Loving trees enough to live in them
**Kinetosis:** Travel sickness
**Oligophrenia:** Extreme mental retardation
**Ranarium:** A frog farm

**American grow tomatoes at home more often than any other fruit or vegetable.**

# ONLY IN AMERICA

*It started out as a social protest song, and wound up a boring patriotic anthem. Here is a fascinating true story of how politics can influence popular music.*

## BACKGROUND

The story of "Only in America," recorded by Jay and the Americans in 1963 for United Artists Records, reveals a lot about the racial consciousness of the music business—and about how political censorship takes place behind the scenes in the U.S.

## THE SONG:

The year was 1963. American blacks were demonstrating for civil rights. One black leader, Medgar Evers, was shot and killed in Jackson, Mississippi and another, Martin Luther King, led a massive March on Washington, delivering his immortal "I have a dream" speech.

On the radio, a young white group called Jay and the Americans was following up its 1962 hit, "She Cried," with a seemingly patriotic pop tune, "Only in America." Lead singer Jay Black sang about the very American dream from which blacks were saying they were excluded. In "the land of opportunity," he sang, a poor boy could be parking cars one day and be a movie star the next, grow up to be President, or win the ultimate rock 'n' roll prize, a "classy girl."

But the irony of "Only in America" was that it was originally written for an all-black vocal quartet called the Drifters—one of the most popular groups in America—who had consistently scored with million-sellers like "Under the Boardwalk" and "On Broadway." And the original lyrics had a far different slant.

## BEHIND THE SCENES

According to co-writer Barry Mann, the song was intended to deliver a strong message about black life in the United States. An original verse was: "Only in America / Land of opportunity / Can they save a seat in the back of the bus just for me./ Only in America / Where they preach the Golden Rule / Will they start to march when my kids want to go to school."

Arguing that the pop charts weren't ready for such strident social commentary, Atlantic Records asked for new lyrics.

"They said it would never get played," Mann recalls, "so we changed it to fit a WASP." But with the Drifters singing the revamped version, the song took on a different sort of irony. According to producer Mike Stoller, "They were afraid of it. They thought they'd get too much flak. It would be too controversial. We felt it would make a strong ironic statement—that it would be more effective—four black guys singing about what was obviously not taking place."

Stuck with an unreleasable song, the producers took their instrumental track over to the other label they worked with, United Artists, where Jay and the Americans recorded. The group loved the song, UA bought the music tracks from Atlantic, and a whitewashed "Only in America" wound up in the Top 25 in 1963.

Mike Stoller was disappointed. Because of the changes in the song and who sang it, people wouldn't have a clue about its original theme. "It was straight ahead. It didn't have any irony in it at all, as done by Jay and the Americans. The point behind the message in the lyrics was lost, as far as we were concerned. It had to have been done with a black group. With a white group, it was just a kind of patriotic song."

## UNRELATED TRIVIA

**According to *Celebrity Trivia,* by Edward Lucaire:**

• "After his high school graduation, Johnny Carson hitchhiked to California, acquired a naval cadet's uniform, and managed to do three noteworthy things: He danced with Marlene Dietrich at the Stage Door Canteen; he was sawed in half by Orson Welles in a magic act (he volunteered from the audience); and he was arrested by the Military Police for impersonating a serviceman."

• Before she became an actress, Margaret Hamilton—who scared the daylights out of millions of children as the Wicked Witch of the West in the film version of *The Wizard of Oz*—taught nursery school and kindergarten.

• Once, while visiting Monte Carlo, Charlie Chaplin entered a "Charlie Chaplin look-alike contest." He not only didn't win…he came in *third.*

• Gary Cooper's real name was Frank. His agent renamed him "Gary" because her hometown was Gary, Indiana.

# THE FRISBEE STORY

*Playing with a Frisbee is one of America's most popular outdoor activities. The story behind the product, from Charles Panati:*

**THE ORIGINAL FRISBIE**

"In the 1870s, New England confectioner William Russell Frisbie opened a bakery that carried a line of homemade pies in circular tin pans embossed with the family surname. Bridgeport historians do not know if children in Frisbie's day tossed empty tins for amusement, but sailing the pans did become a popular diversion among students at Yale University in the mid-1940s. The school's New Haven campus was not far from the Bridgeport pie factory, which served stores throughout the region...."

**THE INVENTOR**

"The son of the inventor of the sealed-beam automobile headlight, [Walter Frederick] Morrison was intrigued with the possibility of alien visits from outer space, a topic that in the '50s captured the minds of Hollywood film makers and the American public. Hoping to capitalize on America's UFO mania, Morrison devised a lightweight metal toy disk (which he'd later construct of plastic) that in shape and airborne movements mimicked the flying saucers on movie screens across the country. He teamed up with the Wham-O Company of San Gabriel, California, and on January 13, 1957, the first toy 'Flyin' Saucers' debuted in selected West Coast stores."

**THE FRISBEE IS BORN**

"Within a year, UFOs in plastic were already something of a hazard on California beaches. But the items remained largely a Southern California phenomenon.To increase sales, Wham-O's president, Richard Knerr, undertook a promotional tour of Eastern college campuses, distributing free plastic UFOs. To his astonishment, he discovered students at two Ivy League schools, Yale and Harvard, playing a lawn game that involved tossing metal pie tins. They called the disks 'Frisbies' and the relaxation 'Frisbie-ing.' The name appealed to Knerr, and unaware of the existence of the Frisbie Pie Company, he trademarked the word "Frisbee" in 1959. And from the original pie tin in the sky, a national craze was launched."

# DUMB PREDICTIONS

*Elsewhere in* The Bathroom Reader, *we've included amazingly accurate predictions. These are amazingly dumb ones.*

The abolishment of pain in surgery is a chimera. It is absurd to go on seeking it today. Knife and pain are two words in surgery that must forever be associated in the consciousness of the patient. To this compulsory combination we shall have to adjust ourselves."

**—Dr. Alfred Velpeau, 1839**
***Anesthesia was introduced 7 years later***

"While theoretically and technically television may be feasible, commercially and financially I consider it an impossibility, a development of which we need waste little time dreaming."

**—Lee De Forest,**
**"Father of the Radio," 1926**

"At present, few scientists foresee any serious or practical use for atomic energy. They regard the atom-splitting experiments as useful steps in the attempt to describe the atom more accurately, not as the key to the unlocking of any new power."

**—*Fortune* magazine, 1938**

"What can be more palpably absurd than the prospect held out of locomotives traveling twice as fast as stagecoaches?"

**—*The Quarterly Review*, 1825**

"The ordinary 'horseless carriage' is at present a luxury for the wealthy; and although its price will probably fall in the future, it will never, of course, come into as common use as the bicycle."

**—*The Literary Digest*, 1889**

"The energy necessary to propel a ship would be many times greater than that required to drive a train of cars at the same speed; hence as a means of rapid transit, flying could not begin to compete with the railroad."

**—*Popular Science* magazine, 1897**

# YOU ANIMAL!

*They're as famous as most human stars, but what do we really know about them? Some gossip about America's favorite animals:*

**LASSIE**

The most successful animal actor ever, starred in 7 feature films and a TV series that ran for 19 years—2nd on the all-time list behind "Gunsmoke." But there wasn't just 1 Lassie—there were 6 of them. And they were all female impersonators. Lassie was supposed to be a she-dog; in real life, "she" was always a he.

Lassie was created by writer Eric Knight in a 1938 *Saturday Evening Post* short story. But although the dog went on to make more money than any animal actor in history, Knight got no royalties—he'd already sold the rights to MGM in 1941 for a paltry $8,000.

**SMOKEY THE BEAR**

Smokey is the only celebrity in America with his own ZIP code—20252. He's also the only bear in the world with his own secretarial staff; the U.S. government employs 3 full-time secretaries to answer his mail. Smokey was named after "Smokey Joe" Martin, Assistant Fire Chief in New York City between 1919 and 1930.

**CHEETAH**

Tarzan's favorite chimp seemed angelic in the Tarzan movies, but was dangerous to work with. During one scene in 1932's *Tarzan the Ape Man*, a little of Jane's (Maureen O'Sullivan's) hair got in Cheetah's eyes, blinding the chimp. Cheetah went crazy on the set and bit O'Sullivan. Another time, Cheetah was supposed to kiss O'Sullivan during a scene. As their faces met, the chimp sneezed all over her.

One of the reasons Cheetah looked so convincing as a "thinking" animal was that many of the tricks the chimp already knew were written into the Tarzan scripts. For example, Cheetah was adept at crawling on his stomach. So in *Tarzan and His Mate* (1934), a scene was included in which the chimp escaped from an attacking rhinoceros by crawling through the tall grass.

**RIN TIN TIN**

Rinty was film's first bona fide animal superstar. He made his film debut in 1922, and his box office success over the next few years literally saved Warner Brothers' Studio from bankruptcy. During the '20s, when he made some 22 movies and was voted the #1 movie star in America (no kidding), Rinty was insured for $250,000. In the early '30s, he lived in a Hollywood mansion across the street from Jean Harlow. His sons and grandsons were among the dogs used in later films, and in the 1954-59 TV series.

**ELSIE THE COW**

The Borden milk symbol started as a cartoon in Borden's ads in 1938. But at the 1939 New York World's Fair, visitors to the Borden exhibit kept asking, "Where's Elsie?" Borden needed an answer, so they picked the most attractive cow in their milking exhibit—a 975 lb. Jersey named "You'll Do, Lobelia"—and renamed her Elsie. They built her a special display—a "bovine boudoir"—that was so successful she got a screen contract, playing Buttercup in the 1940 version of *Little Men*. Elsie became a national celebrity: She went on tour and raised $10 million in U.S. War Bonds; she gave birth to a calf in the window of Macy's department store (behind a modest curtain, of course); she was even awarded a "Doctorate of Bovinity" at Ohio State in 1948.

**MORRIS THE CAT**

America's best-known catfood salesman was originally named "Lucky" by his owner—because he was discovered at an animal shelter in Hinsdale, Illinois about 20 minutes before he was going to be "put to sleep." As Morris, he was the the first animal star ever featured on "Lifestyles of the Rich and Famous."

**TOTO**

Almost didn't make it into MGM's 1939 film *The Wizard of Oz*; the MGM prop department was using W. W. Denslow's original illustrations as a casting guide, but they couldn't identify the breed of dog in the pictures. Sketches were sent all over the world, but no one responded—until Hollywood trainer Carl Spitz happened to see the illustrations. He knew right away that they were looking for his Cairn Terrier, Terry. When Spitz took Terry to the studio, someone grabbed him and shouted "That's the dog we want!"

# COOKING WITH POWER TOOLS

*Here's a handy cooking idea from Jack Mingo, author of the* Official Couch Potato Handbook.

Many of you have power tools sitting around your homes that you never use. Almost all of them, with a little imagination, can be adapted for food preparation. For example: Take a household power drill, poke the bit through the plastic lid of a 15 oz. styrofoam cup, and voilà! You've got a blender that's ideal for highspeed whipping. A jigsaw is great for slicing and dicing. A good belt sander will peel potatoes in a jiffy. And a butane torch is perfect for Pop Tarts flambé.

**Caution:** Power tool cooking should be attempted only if tools are properly shielded and grounded. Wear safety lenses. Some power tools will interfere with TV reception, so confine preparation to commercials. Power tool cookery is NOT recommended while bathing.

*Here are three of our favorite power tool recipes:*

### THE CHEESE CHOC-DOG

#### Ingredients

- 1 Package hot dogs
- 1 Loaf generic white bread
- 1 Can aerosol cheese product
- Electric Drill with 1/4" bit
- 1 Squeeze-bottle of Hershey's Chocolate syrup
- Safety Lenses

#### Instructions

1. Put on safety lenses.
2. Hold unopened package of hot dogs with ends pointing toward you.
3. Using slow speed, carefully drill each hot dog lengthwise.
4. Open package and remove hot dogs. Each should now have a hole down the center.
5. Fill cavities with aerosol cheese product.
6. Place hot dog on slice of white bread. Pinch bread into a trough around the hot dog and squirt liberally with chocolate syrup. Pop

in toaster oven for 10-12 minutes, or until cheese is runny.

## TUBE-STEAK PATÉ

This is the award-winning recipe in the 1982 Chef Aldo International Couch Potato Bake Off. I highly recommend it for its near-European sensibility.

### Ingredients

- 1 Oscar Mayer all-meat hot dog
- 1 Tsp. sweet pickle relish
- 2 Green olives, pimentos left in
- 8 Saltine crackers
- Mayonnaise
- Pepper
- Power tool blender (or real blender)

### Instructions

1. Rev blender up to full speed and drop in hot dog.
2. Add relish and olives. Let blend at high speed for 90 seconds.
3. Spread the saltine crackers generously with mayonnaise.
4. Spread paté on crackers; add pepper to taste. Makes 8 servings.

## EXTRA SHARP CARROT CAKE

This extra-easy version of the old favorite is almost indistinguishable from traditional recipes (the cola and spices even turn the Bisquick a rich, golden brown color). You can double the recipe and use a regular size aluminum pie tin.

### Ingredients

- 2-3 Skinny carrots
- 1/2 Handful brown sugar
- 1 Can generic cola
- 1 Pot pie tin
- 1 Handful Bisquick
- 1/2 Handful pumpkin pie spices
- Electric pencil sharpener

### Instructions

1. Shred carrots in clean pencil sharpener.
2. Line bottom of pot pie tin with carrot shavings.
3. Add Bisquick, sugar, and spices.
4. Knead slowly with hands, adding a small amount of the cola. Continue to knead and add cola until batter is the consistency of fresh Play-Doh.
5. Adjust sugar and spices to taste.
6. Bake in toaster oven at 400° for 15-22 minutes.
7. Remove from oven. When cool, carrot cake can be frosted with canned or aerosol frosting. A real health treat.

# INVENTION IN THE NEWS:

*While many B.R.I. members enjoy reading current newspapers on the seat of learning, the B.R.I.'s staff historian is particularly fond of old ones. "It's like reliving history," he says. For some time now, he's been searching through old issues of* The New York Times, *looking for an account of the Wright Brothers' flight in 1903. He hasn't found it, and here's why: Only one newspaper, the* Norfolk Virginia Pilot, *published an account of the first airplane flight. Luckily, B.R.I. member Gene Brissie had a copy. Here's part of it.*

## FLYING MACHINE SOARS 3 MILES IN TEETH OF HIGH WIND OVER SAND HILLS AND WAVES AT KITTY HAWK ON CAROLINA COAST

### No Balloon Attached to Hold It!!

December 17, 1903

The problem of aerial navigation without the use of a balloon has been solved at last!

Over the sand hills of the North Carolina coast yesterday, near Kittyhawk, two Ohio men proved that they could soar through the air in a flying machine of their own construction, with the power to steer and speed it at will.

This, too, in the face of a wind blowing at the registered velocity of twenty-one miles an hour!

Like a monster bird, the invention hovered above the breakers and circled over the rolling sand hills at the command of its navigator and, after soaring for three miles, it gracefully descended to earth again, and rested lightly upon the spot selected by the man in the car as a suitable landing place.

While the United States government has been spending thousands of dollars in an effort to make practicable the ideas of Professor Langley, of the Smithsonian Institute, Wilbur and Orville Wright, two brothers, natives of Dayton, Ohio, have, quietly, even secretly, perfected their invention and put it to a successful test.

They are not yet ready that the world should know the methods they have adopted in conquering the air, but the *Virginian Pilot* is able to state authentically the nature of their invention, its principles and its chief dimensions. . . . [Ed. note: the flight began with the plane rolling down a track.]

Wilbur Wright, the chief inventor of the machine, sat in the operator's car, and when all was ready his brother unfastened the catch which held the invention at the top of the slope. The big box began to move slowly at first, acquiring velocity as it went, and when halfway down the hundred feet the engine was started. . . . When the end of the incline was reached the machine shot out into space without a perceptible fall.

Keeping its altitude, the machine slowly began to go higher and higher until it finally soared sixty feet above the ground.

Maintaining this height, the forward speed of the huge affair increased until a velocity of eight miles was attained.

All this time the machine headed into a twenty-one-mile wind.

The little crowd of fisherfolk and coast guards, who have been watching the construction of the machine with unconcealed curiosity since September, were amazed.

They endeavored to race over the sand and keep up with the thing in the air, but it soon distanced them and continued its flight alone.

Steadily it pursued its way, first tacking to port, then to starboard, and then driving straight ahead.

"It is a success," declared Orville Wright to the crowd on the beach after the first mile had been covered.

But the inventor waited. Not until he had accomplished three miles, putting the machine through all sorts of maneuvers en route, was he satisfied.

Then he selected a suitable place to land and, gracefully circling, drew his invention slowly to the earth, where it settled, like some big bird, in the chosen spot.

"Eureka!" he cried.

The success of the Wright brothers in their invention is the result of three years of hard work.

The spot selected for the building and perfecting of the machine is one of the most desolate upon the Atlantic seaboard; no better place could scarcely have been selected to maintain secrecy.

It is said the Wright brothers intend constructing a much larger machine, but before this they will go back to their homes for the holidays.

**The real James Bond was an ornithologist, not a spy.**

# COMMON PHRASES

*What do these familiar phrases really mean? Etymologists have researched them and come up with these explanations.*

**FEATHER IN YOUR CAP**
*Meaning*: An achievement.
*Background*: Dates back to 1346, when, according to scholars, "the English Black Prince was awarded the crest of John, King of Bohemia—3 ostrich feathers—after distinguishing himself at the Battle of Crecy." It started a tradition; thereafter, any knight who fought well was allowed to wear a feather in his helmet.

**PRIVATE EYE**
*Meaning*: A private detective.
*Background*: The Pinkerton Detective Agency, founded in 1850, used the motto "We Never Sleep," and accompanied it with a picture of an open eye. It was commonly referred to as "The Eye," and Pinkerton agents, hired by private concerns, were called "Private Eyes."

**LOCK, STOCK, AND BARREL**
*Meaning*; The whole thing.
*Background*: Guns. The lock (firing mechanism), stock (wooden mount), and barrel constituted the main parts of an old rifle.

**DOG DAYS**
*Meaning*: The hottest days of summer.
*Background*: The Ancient Romans believed that there was a period during the summer when "the brightest star in the heavens, the dog star 'Sirius,' added its heat to the sun's, making these days a veritable inferno."

**GREAT SCOTT!**
*Meaning*: An exclamation of surprise or amazement.
*Background*: One of America's most admired soldiers during the 19th century was General Winfield Scott, hero of the Mexican War in 1847. He inspired the phrase in the mid-1800s.

# FAMOUS CHEATERS

*You've heard the old adage, "Cheaters never win." But when they do win, we never find out about them. We only know about the ones who get caught. Like these folks:*

**THE CULPRIT:** Rosie Ruiz, a 26-year-old New Yorker.

**SCENARIO:** Ms. Ruiz appeared to be the fastest woman runner in the 26-mile Boston Marathon in 1980, stumbling across the finish line with an impressive time of 2 hours, 31 minutes, and 56 seconds. The only thing was, no one remembered seeing her run the course. And she couldn't recall anything about the route she was supposed to have taken. Very suspicious. Then a friend revealed that Ruiz's impressive showing in the New York Marathon a few months earlier was a fraud. Rosie, claimed the friend, had skipped most of the race and taken the subway to the finish line. Was Boston a fraud, too? Ruiz denied it.

**VERDICT:** After an embarrassing public controversy, race officials determined that Rosie had only run the last two miles of the marathon, and stripped her of her title.

**AFTERMATH:** In 1984, Ruiz was arrested in Miami for trying to sell two kilos of cocaine to a cop. Police said she was a member of an all-woman cocaine ring.

**THE CULPRIT:** Dave Bresnahan, a catcher for the Williamsport (Pennsylvania) Bills.

**SCENARIO:** It was September, 1987, a minor league baseball game—Williamsport vs. Reading.

Reading was at bat, with two outs and a man on third. After a pitch, the catcher (Bresnahan) leaped to his feet and threw to the third baseman, apparently trying to catch the runner off base. He missed by a mile—the "ball" sailed into the outfield and the runner headed home...only to find the catcher waiting there with the ball in his hand, ready to tag him out. How did Bresnahan get the ball so fast? Answer: he never actually threw the ball—instead, he threw a potato he'd hidden in his uniform.

**VERDICT:** Unfortunately, the authorities didn't appreciate this prank. Not only was the runner called safe and Bresnahan ejected from the game, but the following day the parent Cleveland Indians released Bresnahan from the team.
**AFTERMATH:** Bresnahan moved to Arizona and got a job selling real estate. But his stunt became so famous that a year later, the Williamsport Bills invited him back to recreate it...and to honor him by retiring his number!

**THE CULPRIT:** Janet Cooke, a reporter for the *Washington Post.*

**SCENARIO:** Cooke arrived at the Post with impressive credentials—she said she'd graduated from Vassar with honors and had gotten a master's degree at the University of Toledo. She was assigned to do local stories, and in 1980 told her editor that she'd heard of an 8-year-old who was addicted to heroin. "Find that kid," the editor reportedly told her, "and it's a front-page story." Cooke came back with a detailed account of how a ghetto woman had allowed her lover to inject—and addict—her young son. The tale was titled "Jimmy's World," and it caused an immediate furor in Washington. Cooke refused to reveal her sources, so the mayor put the full resources of the police behind an effort to find the child. The board of education was bombarded with questions and complaints. But the newspaper stood by Cooke. In fact, they nominated her for a Pulitzer Prize, journalism's most prestigious award. And she won. But as reporters gathered biographical information for their story about her, they discovered she had lied about her background. And the Post's executives discovered, to their horror, that Cooke had fabricated the entire story of "Jimmy's World."
**VERDICT:** Cooke, in tears, offered her resignation. The *Post* accepted it. The Pulitzer went to Teresa Carpenter of the *Village Voice*, instead.
**AFTERMATH:** The *Post* published a front-page story criticizing itself. On the legal front, several members of the Washington Board of Education sued Cooke and the *Post* to recover the money the city has spent trying to find "Jimmy," and for damages for being falsely accused of concealing "Jimmy" 's identity.

**All gondolas in Venice must be painted black, unless they belong to high public officials.**

# FABULOUS FLOPS

*Next time you read about some amazing overnight success, remember these equally fabulous stinkers.*

**THE GTO SHOE**

In the '60s, Thom McAn Shoes cashed in on every fad. They marketed Beatle Boots, Monkee Boots, Chubby Checker Twister boots, and even Ravi Shankar "Bombay Buckles." But they lost their magic touch when they tried to ride the hot car fad of the mid-'60s with GTO shoes, "the world's first high-performance shoe." Promoted in conjunction with Pontiac's celebrated GTO, the footwear came equipped with "pointed toes, beveled accelerator heels, and double-beam eyelets."

The Pontiac GTO was a huge success, but most of Thom McAn's GTO shoes wound up being donated to charity.

**INSTANT FISH.**

In the early '60s, one of the owners of the Wham-O Mfg. Co.—makers of Hula Hoops and Frisbees—was on vacation in Africa. One evening, he camped beside a dry lake bed; during the night it rained, and the lake filled up. The next day he noticed there were fish in the lake. "How could that be?" he thought. "Fish don't grow overnight."

When he got back to California, he asked a biologist friend what had happened, and was told that there was indeed a fish in that part of the world whose eggs lay dormant until they were exposed to water. Then the eggs hatched and the fish emerged.

It sounded like an incredible idea for a product—"Instant Fish." At his urging, Wham-O hurriedly built huge fish tanks in their factory and imported thousands of fish so they could start collecting their eggs.

Meanwhile, the annual New York Toy Fair, where toy store owners from all over the U.S. buy merchandise, was taking place....And "Instant Fish" was the smash of the show. In one week, Wham-O took orders for $10 million worth of fish (an incredible amount in the mid-'60s). Even when the company refused to take any more orders, people sneaked to Wham-O's hotel rooms

**What does the word "Karate" mean? Empty hand.**

and slipped orders under the door. "Instant Fish" was a gold mine.

Except that nobody told the fish. They just couldn't lay eggs fast enough to supply all the excited toy store owners. Desperate, Wham-O owners tried everything they could think of: They tried covering the windows to darken the inside of their plant; they tried warmer room temperatures...and they tried cooler ones; they even tried piping romantic music into the tanks. But nothing worked. Wham-O finally had to admit that "Instant Fish" had laid its own enormous egg. And after shipping only a few of the fish, they canceled all the orders.

### "TURN ON"

In 1968 and 1969, "Laugh-In" was TV's #1 show. Hoping to buy themselves a copycat hit, ABC hired "Laugh-In" executive producer George Schlatter to create an identical series. And by mid-1969, he'd put together "Turn-On," which ABC promoted as "the second coming of 'Laugh-In'," a "visual, comedic, sensory assault." "Turn-On" premiered on Feb. 5, 1969. It was so bad that the next day, phone calls poured in from ABC affiliates all over the U.S., saying that they refused ever to carry the show again. Embarrassed, the network cancelled it immediately, making it the shortest-lived primetime series in TV history.

### THE ANIMAL OF THE MONTH CLUB

In the '50s and '60s, mail order "thing-of-the-month" clubs were big business—worth close to a billion dollars a year. Americans were buying a Fruit-of-the Month, a Candy-of-the-Month, a House-of-the-Month (architectural plans), a Cheese-of-the-Month, Flowers-of-the-Month, and so on. How far could the fad go? Creative Playthings took it to the limit when it introduced an "Animal of the Month Club" in the late '60s. Every month, the company promised, an exotic "pet," such as an Argentine toad snail, a musk turtle, a newt, a Mongolian gerbil, or others, would arrive in the mail at subscribers' houses.

But shipping exotic pets turned out to be a crazy—and cruel—idea. In 1968, for example, Creative Playthings had orders for 4,000 Argentine toads and couldn't find enough of them in the Argentine swamps to supply the demand. But that wasn't the worst of their problems. Ever try bulk-mailing animals? The creatures-of-the-month often arrived squashed, or dehydrated. Mercifully, Creative Playthings took its losses and gave up.

# UNCLE WALT'S SECRETS

*Everyone knows about Walt Disney—or do they? Check it out for yourself.*

## STRANGE LOVE AFFAIR

Walt once confessed, "I love Mickey Mouse more than any woman I've ever known."

## HIS PASSION FOR TRAIN WRECKS

Like Gomez Addams, Walt relaxed with model trains—but Walt's were big enough to ride on: The Disney "ride 'em" scale model railroad was half a mile long; it circled his estate, and even wound through a tunnel under his wife's flower beds.

The Disneys spent a great deal of time riding the little train. If you were a really good friend, Uncle Walt made you an official "vice president" of his railroad.

But Disney was more like Gomez than met the eye. According to *Everybody's Business*: "Disney especially enjoyed planning wrecks because he had so much fun repairing the damage. Once, after buying two new engines, he told George Murphy (then an actor and one of the road's 'vice-presidents'; later a U.S. senator): 'Boy, we're sure going to have some wrecks now!' "

## PEN-ULTIMATE SECRETS

• Most people believe that Walt was a cartooning genius. But according to author Richard Schickel in *The Disney Version*, he couldn't draw Donald Duck or any of his other famous characters! According to *Everybody's Business*:

•"Disney was known to ask his animators to show him how to turn out a quick sketch of Mickey Mouse to accompany autographs."

• "Walt grew up on a small farm in Missouri, where he picked up a feeling for what middle America wanted in their movies. He also picked up a bit of anti-Semitism, which he showed in a rather nasty caricature of a Jewish peddler in his first big cartoon success, *The Three Little Pigs*."

• "Disney's real signature bore no resemblance to the famous logo that appeared on all his products. Ironically, a number of people have thrown away authentically signed books and records under the impression that the autographs were fake."

# THE BIRTH OF A FLAKE

*You probably think that corn flakes have always been with us. Not so. The cereal flake was accidentally born less than a century ago. Here's the tale.*

**BACKGROUND**

It all started with a devoutly religious woman named Sister Ellen Harmon White, a Seventh Day Adventist who in 1844 decided it was time for her to ascend to heaven in a laundry basket. Along with others in her congregation, she stood for hours on a Maine hilltop, waiting to be carried away...but nothing happened. Sister Ellen wasn't disappointed, however. She took it as a sign that God still had important things for her to do in this world—and she set out to accomplish them.

In 1863, she and her husband traveled to Otsego, Michigan, where she had a vision: The Lord told her that people could only achieve "purity of mind and spirit" by eating properly—water, fruits, and vegetables, with a little bit of bread made from Graham flour. Another vision told her to open a sanitarium in nearby Battle Creek, where people could heal themselves with this diet.

**THE BATTLE CREEK SANITARIUM**

1866, the Western Health Reform Institute at Battle Creek was opened. It had no doctor on its staff for ten years. But in 1876, a 25-year-old Adventist who had just graduated from Bellevue Medical College—Dr. John Harvey Kellogg—was hired to run it. Kellogg's first official act was to hire his younger brother, William Keith (W. K.) as chief clerk.

Kellogg set out to turn the institution into an influential one. He changed the name to Battle Creek Sanitarium, and screened potential patients so that no one who was seriously ill was ever admitted. What he wanted were "tired businessmen, sufferers from dyspepsia...and neurotics." So people were invariably cured, and the San (as it was called) began attracting the wealthy and famous from all over the country. John D. Rockefeller, Henry Ford, Harvey Firestone, and others were among the guests. At the same time, Kellogg wrote voluminously, making his somewhat looney medical views influential with common Americans who would never make it to Battle Creek.

## KELLOGG GETS FLAKEY

The diet in this now world-famous institution was strictly vegetarian. But to make the food more palatable to non-vegetarians, the Kelloggs and their staff set up a special kitchen in which they experimented with new dishes. Among their creations: hamburger substitutes, a coffee substitute called Caramel Coffee, and cereal flakes.

The flakes were an accident. Kellogg originally required his patients to begin each meal by chewing a piece of hard zwieback bread. But when a patient broke a tooth on it, he started experimenting with substitutes. One experiment entailed running boiled wheat dough through rollers, turning it into thin sheets before it was toasted and ground into flour.

On one occasion in 1895, Kellogg left some pans full of dough sitting while he was called away on an emergency. When he returned (it's not clear exactly how much later), he ran the dough through the rollers—but instead of thin sheets, he got a bunch of flakes. He toasted them and served them to his patients... who loved them. The flake was born.

## NOT A CORNY JOKE

Kellogg and his staff came up with two flake variations—rice and corn. The corn was a flop (too tough and tasteless) until someone got the idea to use only the heart of the corn, and to flavor it with malt. Then it instantly became the most requested variety.

Realizing that he was sitting on a commercial bonanza, Dr. Kellogg set up the Sanitarium Health Food Company with his brother (keeping it separate from the San and the Adventist Church) and began selling his flakes. In the first year, he sold over 100,000 pounds of them. Business kept growing, and Kellogg kept getting wealthier.

## "CEREAL SODOM"

But then things suddenly got out of hand. Dozens of cereal entrepreneurs moved in on Kellogg's territory and cut his profits. Subtly capitalizing on the reputation of the San, 42 Battle Creek-based cereal companies sprang up, each making ludicrous health claims for its products...and each making a fortune. Sister Ellen Hanson White was furious; she felt Dr. Kellogg had desecrated the Divine vision that inspired the San, and Battle Creek had now become a "cereal Sodom." On the other side, Will Kellogg was pressuring his brother to cash in like all the other cereal companies—which Dr. Kellogg adamantly opposed. His practices were already attracting some unfavorable attention from the medical profession, and he didn't want to focus any more attention on himself.

## DR. KELLOGG LOSES CONTROL

Here's what happened: Dr. Kellogg, a tight man with a dollar, had been giving out stock in his cereal company to employees in lieu of pay raises. But it backfired, because his brother Will quietly bought the stock up until, in 1906, he had control of the entire enterprise—which he renamed the Kellogg Toasted Corn Flakes Company. He immediately placed an advertisement in the *Ladies' Home Journal*, which brought in a flood of orders. Sales leapt from 33 cases a day to 2,900 cases a day. But Dr. Kellogg wasn't happy about it. He called William a traitor...and the two never spoke to each other again.

Meanwhile, the Kellogg's Corn Flake Company prospered. As *Everybody's Business* puts it: "By 1909 the company was selling more than 1 million cases a year. Two years later, the advertising budget had reached $1 million, part of which was used to erect the world's largest electric sign on the Mecca Building at Times Square in New York, with K in *Kellogg* 66 feet tall."

## THE KELLOGGS' FATE

Both of the Kellogg brothers were expelled from the Seventh Day Adventist church. The San, even without religious affiliation, flourished under Dr. Kellogg's direction until 1933. Then the Depression deprived it of many wealthy clients, and its source of revenue. Deeply in debt, it was forced to close in 1938. John Harvey Kellogg lived until 1942 when, at the age of 91, he succumbed to pneumonia.

William (W. K.) Kellogg, whose signature is on every box of Kellogg's cereal, lived to be 92 years of age. He died in 1951. His legacy: a $5 billion dried breakfast cereal business.

## BY THE WAY...

Remember these cereals? Rice Krinkles; King Vitaman; Frosty-Os; Crispy Critters; Apple Jacks; Puffa Puffa Rice; Wheat Honeys....

# THE ADDAMS FAMILY

*"They're creepy and they're kooky, mysterious and spooky...."*
*You know the rest. But here are a few things you* didn't
*know about TV's weirdest sitcom family.*

## HOW IT STARTED

Charles Addams' ghoulish cartoon characters first appeared in *The New Yorker* magazine and developed a cult following strong enough to warrant several volumes of cartoons. It was one of these collections that inspired the TV show. Early in 1963, TV executive David Levy noticed an Addams book in a N.Y. store window. "Eureka!" he thought. "There's an idea for a great TV show." Unaware that Addams had already rejected other TV offers, Levy called *The New Yorker* and made an appointment to meet him. They met at the Plaza Hotel.

"Addams was tall and young-looking for his age, with a twinkle in his eye," recalls Levy. "He spoke laconically, with a very dry wit. I remembered a famous quote of his: Emerging from a big screening of Liz Taylor's Cleopatra with actress Joan Fontaine on his arm, he was asked if he enjoyed the movie. He said 'Yes.' What part? 'I liked the asp.'

"I had all this in mind when I met him, but for two hours over drinks we talked of *nothing* but novelist John O'Hara!"

It was a strange way to discuss a TV series.

Addams and O'Hara, it turned out, had been drinking buddies since Prohibition. And Levy had worked with O'Hara on TV adaptations of his short stories. The O Hara connection made all the difference. After two hours, Addams suggested that they meet the next day to finalize an agreement...and "The Addams Family" TV series was born.

## INSIDE FACTS

### Go, Gomez

After John Astin's first sitcom, "I'm Dickens, He's Fenster," was cancelled, he auditioned for "The Addams Family," and was turned down...for the part of *Lurch*. He didn't even try out for Gomez. But the producer spied John leaving the room, grabbed him, and offered him the lead role on the spot. The only condition: Astin had to grow a mustache. He grabbed the role.

**Hair Today...**

It took Carolyn Jones two hours every day to put on Morticia's makeup. The final touch: she wore a wig made of—what else?—human hair.

• Believe it or not, Jones was only the producer's *3rd* choice to play Morticia! ABC insisted that they needed a "name" actress, and Jones was the only well-known performer in the running (she had been nominated for an Oscar in 1956)—so she got the part.

**Itt's Alive!**

Cousin Itt's (you remember, the ball of fur with a hat on) voice was supplied by "Addams" producer Nat Perrin, who recited gibberish into a tape recorder and played it back at a higher speed.

**Name Game**

Addams, who'd never given his characters first names, had to come up with some for the TV show. (It was one of the few contributions he actually made to the sitcom; other than that, he did nothing except give his approval.) Within a week he'd decided on all of them—except for Mr. Addams, who almost wound up being called "Repelli" (for repellent) instead of Gomez.

**True Fans**

• When Ringo Starr met John Astin in 1965, he greeted Astin by grabbing his hand and kissing his way up his arm. And Astin hadn't said a word of French!

• In the early '80s, punk-rocker Siouxsie Sioux, of Siouxsie and the Banshees, wrote in a "portrait-of-the-artist" column, "My role model, inspiration, and heroine is Morticia Addams."

• Lurch got fan mail from teenage girls who thought he was cuter than the Beatles.

**Home Sweet Home**

The unique interior of the Addams house was inspired by the real-life Manhattan apartment of Charles Addams, which contained suits of armor, an antique cross-bow collection, and other odds-and-ends (with the emphasis on "odds").

# ROAD KILL

*One of the stranger studies in human behavior we've ever heard of was a recent experiment to find out how people react to animals on the highway. Here's what they found out.*

## THE TEST

David Shepherd, a biology professor at Southeastern Louisiana University, put rubber reptiles "on or near roads" and watched how 22,000 motorists reacted to them. His conclusion: "There are apparently very few animals hit accidentally on the highway."

## WHAT THEY DID

To find out how drivers would respond to reptiles on the road, Shepherd and his crew put fake snakes and turtles in places where drivers would hit them if they kept driving straight; they also put the rubber reptiles where drivers had to go way out of their way to hit them. Shepherd's comment: "We found that while eighty-seven percent of drivers tried to avoid the animals, six percent went out of their way to hit them—with snakes getting squashed twice as often as turtles."

## WEIRD REACTIONS

Apparently, there's something about a reptile on the road that makes some drivers bloodthirsty. A few examples Shepherd witnessed:

- "A truck driver crossed the center line, went into the opposite lane of traffic, and drove onto the shoulder of the road to run over a 'turtle.' "
- A normal housewife who saw what she thought was a snake in the road swerved to kill it, "then turned around to run over it five more times."
- "A policeman crushed a 'snake' with his tires, then stopped and pulled his gun. I quickly jumped from some bushes and explained it was a fake."

**His conclusion:** "Some people just have a mean streak toward animals."

**The patent for the ball-point pen was awarded to John J. Loud of Weymouth, Mass. in 1888.**

# MANIAC

*Believe it or not, the gruesome horror flick,* The Texas Chainsaw Massacre, *inspired one of the best-selling dance tunes of the '80s.*

## GOOFING AROUND

One night, musician/songwriter Michael Sembello and his writing partner rented a copy of *The Texas Chainsaw Massacre*, a particularly gruesome horror film. After watching it on Sembello's VCR, they decided—just for kicks, because they were sick of love songs—to write a tune about a mass-murderer. They did a rough version of the song, put it on cassette, then went back to working on other projects.

## RUSHIN' ROULETTE

A few weeks later, record producer Phil Ramone asked Sembello to supply some music for an upcoming Paramount film—a dance movie called *Flashdance*. Michael came up with 2 or 3 songs he thought might work; then he asked his wife to copy them onto a tape and send them off to Paramount. She went into the studio and picked up a cassette, did the copying, and rushed it into the mail.

The next day his wife took a call from someone at Paramount. The guys at the studio had listened to all the songs, and there was one they were crazy about—they'd tested it with a specific dance scene, and it worked perfectly. They definitely wanted to use it in the film. "Which song?" she asked. The reply: "I don't know. It's the song at the very end of the tape that keeps repeating something about a maniac." Sembello's wife was horrified—it was the song about the mass murderer! She'd sent the tape without realizing it was at the very end of the cassette. "No, no, that's not supposed to be on the cassette!" she pleaded. But Paramount was adamant—they loved it and wanted it.

## NEW CHARACTER

When Michael found out, he was so shocked that he didn't even believe his wife. But Ramone confirmed it, adding that Paramount wanted the lyrics changed to fit the dance scene. In this new version, the maniac was dance-crazy, not bloodthirsty.

"Maniac"—the song no one was ever supposed to hear—became Sembello's first hit—a million-seller, #1 song, and Oscar nominee.

# WARHOLISMS

*Andy Warhol understood modern America. Some comments:*

"Try the Andy Warhol New York City Diet: When I order in a restaurant, I order everything I don't want, so I have a lot to play around with while everyone else eats."

"An artist is a person who produces things that people don't need to have but that he—for some reason—thinks it would be a good idea to give them."

"It's not what you are that counts, it's what they *think* you are."

"Employees make the best dates. You don't have to pick them up and they're always tax deductible."

"Sex is the biggest nothing of all time."

"Being born is like being kidnapped. And then sold into slavery."

"It's the movies that have really been running things in America ever since they were invented. They show you what to do, how to do it, when to do it, how to feel about it, and how to *look* when you feel about it."

"The most exciting attractions are between opposites that never meet."

"The nicer I am, the more people think I'm lying.'"

"I always run into strong women who are looking for weak men to dominate them."

"I never think that people die. They just go to department stores."

"After being alive, the next hardest work is having sex."

"Dying's the most embarrassing thing that can ever happen to you."

"I am a deeply superficial person."

"The more information you get, the less fantasy you have."

"Muscles are great. Everybody should have at least one that they can show off."

# THE CONDENSED MAN

*One of the most famous names in American food is Borden's. This tale of Gail Borden, an inventor and classic American eccentric, comes from* Everybody's Business.

## SMALL IS BEAUTIFUL

"Gail Borden was obsessed by the idea that food could be preserved by condensing, but his early experiments were unsuccessful....A condensed meat 'biscuit' he invented for Texans headed for California during the 1850s Gold Rush proved to be nutritious, but tasted awful....Undeterred, Borden continued his experiments with dehydrating and concentrating foods. 'I mean to put a potato into a pillbox, a pumpkin into a tablespoon, the biggest sort of watermelon into a saucer,' he declared."

## THE PERFECT HOST

"He once subjected friends to a dinner party consisting entirely of the products of his experiments: condensed and concentrated soups, main course, fruits, and extracts. While Borden ate heartily and discoursed enthusiastically on the fine flavors of his concoctions, his guests toyed unhappily with their food. All firmly refused second helpings.

"Afterward, the unfortunate diners were lured onto another of Borden's inventions, the 'land schooner,' a contraption that used wind power to move on land. Its sails raised, the schooner moved down the beach, gaining speed at an alarming rate. Borden's passengers yelled for him to stop—at which point it was discovered that the braking mechanism was ineffective. As panic broke out, Borden swung the rudder the wrong way, and the schooner splashed into the waves, capsizing and dumping all hands into the sea. Unhurt, the group scrambled ashore. 'Where's Gail?' inquired one of Borden's dripping guests....'Drowned, I...hope!' "

## CONDENSED FOR ETERNITY

"Neither drowned nor discouraged, Borden went on...to found what...became a giant corporation, built on his 1863 discovery of a process for making condensed milk. As he rode the train to work in New York City each day, he passed a cemetery where he had built his own tombstone—in the shape of a can of condensed milk."

# THE FABULOUS '60s

*Odds and ends about America's favorite decade, from the fabulous book 60s!, by John and Gordon Javna.*

## SOUP'S ON

Not everyone appreciated Pop Art. When Andy Warhol's first Campbell's Soup Can paintings went on display in an L.A. art gallery in 1961—for $100 apiece—another gallery down the street contemptuously stacked soup cans in its windows with the sign: "The real thing, 29¢."

## WARHOL AGAIN

For a show at a gallery in Toronto in 1965, Warhol moved 80 of his Pop Art sculptures of Brillo boxes, cornflakes boxes, and the like across the Canadian border—only to discover that they were classified as "merchandise" instead of "art" by the Canadian government. That meant that the gallery owner had to pay an import duty, which he refused to do. He told newsmen that Canada had embarrassed itself and was now the "laughingstock of the art world." Government spokesmen countered that the boxes looked too much like their commercial counterparts, and "the only thing the artist adds is his signature."

"But," said Warhol, "I don't sign them."

## MR. SPACEMAN

On April 12, 1961, one of man's impossible dreams was realized when Yuri Gagarin, a 27-year-old Russian test pilot, orbited the earth. He thus became the first man in history to actually see our planet. His 108-minute flight for the Soviet Union made him a worldwide hero. After the experience, he returned to testing new aircraft. Tragically, he was killed in a plane crash in 1968 and did not live to see man walk on the moon.

## GIMME A BURGER, BABY

McDonald's menu in 1964:

- Hamburgers 15¢
- French fries 12¢
- Shakes 20¢.

## FIVE REACTIONS TO THE MOON LANDING

In 1969, the whole world watched as Neil Armstrong and crew walked on the moon. Some unusual reactions.

**1. In Ghana:** Nagai Kassa VII, a tribal chief, listened to the Apollo 11 saga on his shortwave radio through the Voice of America. Reportedly, he was worried that the astronauts would fall off the moon, and was amazed that they were able to fit on it at all. "The moon is so small as I see it that I didn't think there would be enough room," he said.

**2. In India:** Astrologers wondered if the moon was "too tainted for use in soothsaying, now that a man has walked on it."

**3. In Alaska:** Unimpressed by the scientific aspects of the lunar escapade, an Eskimo interpreted the moon landing for a reporter as a way to predict the weather. He said it was a sure sign of a "hard winter next year."

**4. Somewhere in the Arab World:** Al Fatah, the terrorist organization, objected that Arab newspapers were giving more attention to the moon landing than to "terrorist missions against Israel."

**5. In New York City:** The lunar landing was celebrated with a "moon bash" in Central Park. The Department of Parks invited the millions of New Yorkers to enjoy huge screens with live TV coverage, searchlights, a film collage, synthetic Northern Lights, dancing to "moon music," inflatable sculpture, and a blue-cheese picnic.

## MISS AVERAGE AMERICA

Our all-time favorite beauty contest is the National College Queen Pageant, a little-known pageant that awarded some lucky college girl a title and prizes for excelling in the most mundane activities imaginable. "We are idealizing the well-rounded average," explained the show's promoter in 1962. Some of the events in which contestants had to compete:

- Blouse-ironing
- Cooking hamburgers
- "Doodling designs with colored inks on electric blankets"
- Carrying coffee cups and pots across a room to the judges' table and pouring (to evaluate "skill and poise as a hostess")
- Sandal decoration
- A fierce debate on "right and wrong hairstyles."

# TV's RULES TO LIVE BY

*More words of wisdom from* Prime Time Proverbs.

"Remember—the Eagle may soar but the weasel never gets sucked up into a jet engine."

**—Rick Simon,**
***Simon and Simon***

"The first thing to do when you're being stalked by an angry mob with raspberries, is to release a tiger."

**—John Cleese,**
***Monty Python's Flying Circus***

"Always enter a strange hotel room with extreme caution, especially one with a samurai warrior in it."

**—Thomas Magnum,**
***Magnum P.I.***

"If you can't fight 'em, and they won't let you join 'em, best get out of the county."

**—Pappy Maverick,**
***Maverick***

"Just keep laughin'."

**—Bozo the Clown,**
***Bozo's Circus***

"The older you get, the better you get—unless you're a banana."

**— Rose,**
***The Golden Girls***

"Like my old skleenball coach used to say, 'Find out what you don't do well, then don't do it.' "

**— Alf,**
***ALF***

"As we say in the sewer, if you're not prepared to go all the way, don't put your boots on in the first place."

**—Ed Norton,**
***The Honeymooners***

"An ounce of prevention is worth a pound of bandages and adhesive tape."

**—Groucho Marx,**
***You Bet Your Life***

"It's been the lesson of my life that nothing that sounds that good ever really happens."

**—Alex Reiger,**
***Taxi***

"Never wear polyester underwear if you're going to be hit by lightning."

**—Roz,**
***Night Court***

"A watched cauldron never bubbles."

**Morticia Addams,**
***The Addams Family***

**Donald Duck comics were banned from libraries in Finland because he doesn't wear pants.**

# GIMME SOME SKIN

*When you meet someone socially, what do you do? Shake hands? Tip your hat? Here's the background story on some traditional greetings.*

## THE HANDSHAKE

From *Extraordinary Origins of Everyday Things*:

"In its oldest recorded use, a handshake signified the conferring of power from a god to an earthly ruler....

"In Babylonia, around 1800 B.C., it was required that the king grasp the hands of a statue of Marduk, the civilization's chief deity. The act, which took place annually during the New Year's festival, served to transfer authority to the potentate for an additional year. So persuasive was the ceremony that when the Assyrians defeated and occupied Babylonia, subsequent Assyrian kings felt compelled to adopt the ritual, lest they offend a major heavenly being....

"Folklore offers an earlier, more speculative origin of the handshake: An ancient villager who chanced to meet a man he didn't recognize reacted automatically by reaching for his dagger. The stranger did likewise, and the two spent time cautiously circling each other. If both became satisfied that the situation called for a parley instead of a fight to the death, daggers were reinserted into their sheaths, and right hands—the weapon hands—were extended as a token of goodwill. This is also offered as the reason why women, who throughout history were never the bearers of weapons, never developed the custom of the handshake."

## TIPPING YOUR HAT, BOWING, CURTSYING, ETC.

From *Extraordinary Origins of Everyday Things*:

"The gentlemanly practice of tipping one's hat goes back in principle to ancient Assyrian times, when captives were required to strip naked to demonstrate subjugation to their conquerors. The Greeks required new servants to strip from the waist up. Removing an article of clothing became a standard act of respect. Romans approached a holy shrine only after taking their sandals off. And a person of low rank removed his shoes before entering a superior's home—a custom the Japanese have brought, somewhat modified,

**Each $1,000 raise in a wife's salary increases the chances for divorce or separation by 1%.**

into modern times. In England, women took off their gloves when presented to royalty. In fact, two other gestures, one male, one female, are remnants of acts of subjugation or respect: the bow and the curtsy; the latter was at one time a full genuflection.

"By the Middle Ages in Europe, the symbol of serfdom to a feudal lord was restricted to baring the head. The implicit message was the same as in earlier days: 'I am your obedient servant.' So persuasive was the gesture that the Christian Church adopted it, requiring that men remove their hats on entering a church.

"Eventually, it became standard etiquette for a man to show respect for an equal by merely tipping his hat."

## GIVING A MILITARY SALUTE.

The formal military salute seems to have started in medieval England, when soldiers were commonly clad in armor. Two possible explanations for its origin:

• At jousting tournaments, knights paraded past the queen with hands held over their eyes, a symbolic gesture suggesting they were protecting themselves from her "blinding beauty."

• When two knights in armor met on the road, they raised their visors to show respect...and to demonstrate that they had no violent intentions. This position—one hand held at the forehead—became a formal military greeting. It outlasted the practice of wearing armor.

## BUSINESS CARDS

Today, business cards are a means of establishing credibility as a professional. But until the early part of this century, they were "calling cards," and they were used exclusively for social purposes. They were "upper class"; presenting a calling card when you met or visited someone indicated that you didn't have to work for a living. And there was an elaborate etiquette surrounding their use (e.g., should a single woman leave a calling card for a gentleman?). But as the middle classes got into the act, the calling card became another means of making a business contact. Today, that's all it is.

## GOOD-BYE

Good-bye is probably a shortened version of the old term, "God be with you."

**The average American generates a ton of garbage every year.**

# FAMOUS FOR 15 MINUTES

*We included this feature—based on Andy Warhol's comment that "in the future, everyone will be famous for 15 minutes"—in the first Bathroom Reader. Here it is again, with new stars.*

**THE STAR:** Robert Opel, a 33-year-old unemployed actor.

**THE HEADLINE:** "Streaker Steals Oscar Show."

**WHAT HAPPENED:** Near the end of the 1974 Academy Awards ceremony, host David Niven was introducing the woman who would present the Best Picture award—Elizabeth Taylor. "She is," he was saying fondly, "a very important contributor to world entertainment, and someone quite likely—"

Suddenly his speech was interrupted by screams and laughter as a naked man streaked across the stage in back of him. Niven stuttered for a second, then recovered and commented, "Ladies and gentlemen, that was bound to happen. Just think, the only laugh that man will probably ever get is for stripping and showing off his shortcomings." Then he gave the floor to Taylor, who quipped, "That's a pretty tough act to follow."

Meanwhile, the streaker had been caught backstage and was produced by security, fully clothed, for the press. "I have no official connection with the Academy," Robert Opel told reporters. But observers speculated that Oscar show producer Jack Haley, Jr. had created the whole incident as a publicity stunt. He denied it, declaring: "I would have used a pretty girl instead."

**THE AFTERMATH:** Opel made an appearance on "The Mike Douglas Show," debuted as a stand-up comedian in Hollywood, and was hired to streak at other Hollywood affairs (e.g., one honoring Rudolf Nureyev). Then he disappeared from public view. Five years later, he made the news again when was brutally murdered at a sex paraphernalia shop he owned in San Francisco.

**THE STAR:** Jimmy Nicol, a little-known English drummer.

**THE HEADLINE:** "Ringo Heads to Hospital as Beatles Tour with New Drummer."

**WHAT HAPPENED:** In June, 1964 the Fab Four were getting

publicity shots taken at a photographer's, when drummer Ringo Starr suddenly collapsed. He was rushed to a hospital, and was diagnosed as having tonsillitis. This was a huge problem—the Beatles were about to leave for a world tour. Their solution: They hired a local session drummer named Jimmy Nicol to play with them while Ringo recovered. Overnight, the bewildered Nicol became a member of the world's most popular band.

Nicol played with the Beatles for two weeks—in Holland, Hong Kong, and Australia. Ringo finally felt well enough to join the band Down Under, and after one last performance—with Ringo watching—Jimmy reluctantly returned to England.

**THE AFTERMATH:** Inspired, Nicol started his own band, called the Shubdubs. Unfortunately, they went nowhere.

**THE STAR:** Jackie Mitchell, 17-year-old lefthanded pitcher for the Chattanooga Lookouts, a minor league baseball team.

**THE HEADLINE:** "Female Hurler Fans Ruth and Gehrig."

**WHAT HAPPENED:** It was April 2, 1931. The mighty New York Yankees were "working their way north at the end of spring training," playing minor league teams along the way. Today, they were in Chattanooga, Tennessee. When the first two Yankee batters got hits, the manager decided to make a pitching change. He brought in his latest acquisition, a local player who had never pitched in a pro game before—Jackie Mitchell. She was, in fact, the first woman *ever* to play in a pro game. And the first batter she had to face was Babe Ruth. A tough situation; but she was tough. Jackie struck the Babe out in 5 pitches...and then proceeded to strike out "Larrupin' Lou" Gehrig in 3.

It was an impressive debut for a rookie, but it was a little suspect—Joe Engel, owner of the Lookouts, was known for publicity stunts, and this game had been planned for April 1 (the April Fools' Day game was rained out). Still, Jackie insisted to her dying day that it was on the level, and you can't argue with record books.

**AFTERMATH:** *The New York Times* praised Jackie in an editorial, hailing her feat as a blow for women's rights.

Mitchell never made it as a pro—she played ball around Chattanooga for 6 years, then quit to marry and to take over the family business (optometry). She died in 1987.

**THE STAR:** Harold Russell, a disabled World War II veteran.
**THE HEADLINE:** "Non-actor Wins Oscar for First Film Role."
**WHAT HAPPENED:** In 1946, director William Wyler made a film called *The Best Years of Our Lives*, depicting the personal struggles of several returning World War II vets. It was a hot topic, and the movie attracted a first-class cast: Frederic March, Myrna Loy, Virginia Mayo, Dana Andrews...and Harold Russell.

Russell had lost both his hands in an explosion at a Georgia training camp during the war. The Army asked him to appear in a short film about disabled veterans, and Wyler spotted him in it.

The director essentially cast Russell as himself—a severely disabled man trying to readjust to everyday life. Wyler wouldn't let him take acting lessons; and his performance was so powerful that it carried the film. *The Best Years of Our Lives* captured 7 Oscars—including best picture, best actor (Frederic March), best director, best screenplay, and best supporting actor—Russell.
**AFTERMATH:** Russell didn't appear in another film for 34 years. He can be seen in the 1980 feature, *Inside Moves*.

**THE STAR:** Valerie Solanas, founder of SCUM—the Society for Cutting Up Men.
**THE HEADLINE:** "Warhol Felled By SCUM."
**WHAT HAPPENED:** Valerie Solanas had hung around Andy Warhol's studio in the '60s. She'd even appeared in his movie, *I, a Man*. So the artist whom friends called "the ultimate voyeur" was shocked when Valerie pulled out a gun one day in June, 1968 and shot him. Solanas, it turned out, was irked that Warhol hadn't bothered commenting on the script of a play she'd left with him.

Andy was seriously wounded; doctors only gave him a 50-50 chance to survive. Meanwhile Valerie turned herself in, telling the patrolman to whom she surrendered, "He had too much control over my life." She was immediately sent for psychiatric observation, while she and her organization were splashed across the tabloid front pages.
**AFTERMATH:** Warhol lived, Solanas was imprisoned, and the whole incident stands as an ironic reminder that no one—not even the man who first articulated the idea—is immune when someone's 15 minutes arrive.

# NEAR MISSES

*A surprising amount of movie parts that turn lesser lights into stars are cast simply because bigger stars have turned the roles down. Take these, for example:*

**CASABLANCA (1942).** The lead role was originally offered not to Humphrey Bogart, but to movie tough guy George Raft—who turned it down because he didn't like the script. Earlier, Raft also turned down the part of Sam Spade in *The Maltese Falcon* (1941) because he didn't trust the young director (John Huston), and the lead in *High Sierra* (1941) because he thought it was bad luck to die onscreen. Bogart took both of those roles, too, and built a career on them.

**DRACULA (1931).** The choice for the film was Universal's master of horror, Lon Chaney, Sr. But Chaney died in August, 1930, a few months before filming began. Second choice: Bela Lugosi, who'd played the vampire on Broadway. Lugosi was rushed to Hollywood, became a surprise star, and was typecast as a movie ghoul for the rest of his career.

**THE WIZARD OF OZ (1939).** This was supposed to star "Americas's Sweetheart," Shirley Temple. MGM was willing to trade the services of its two biggest stars—Clark Gable and Jean Harlow—to 20th Century Fox to get the little actress. But Darryl Zanuck, Fox's chief, refused—so the part of Dorothy went to little-known Judy Garland. Ironically, Miss Temple was cast in a similar movie the following year, called *The Blue Bird.* It bombed and ruined her film career.

**More Shuffling:**

- W. C. Fields was supposed to be the Wizard, but he was dropped when he held out for more money. His replacement was Frank Morgan.
- Ray Bolger was supposed to be the Tin Woodsman, and Buddy Ebsen was supposed to be the Scarecrow. But they traded parts. Then Ebsen's lungs got infected when he inhaled the metallic dust sprayed on his costume, and he spent the next six weeks in an iron lung. He was replaced by Jack Haley.

**MIDNIGHT COWBOY (1969):** Dustin Hoffman's intended co-star was Michael Sarazin. But Sarazin turned it down...and Jon Voight became an overnight star.

**GONE WITH THE WIND (1939):** The original Scarlett and Rhett were Bette Davis and Errol Flynn. That was Jack Warner's idea, anyway, when Warner Brothers still planned to finance the film. But Davis absolutely refused to have anything to do with Flynn, so Warner pulled out. When MGM got involved, producer David O. Selznick asked them for Gary Cooper to play Rhett—but he was refused. Finally he wound up with Clark Gable, who took the part simply because he wanted some quick money to finance an impending divorce.

• Despite the hoopla about finding *the* actress to play Scarlett at the last minute, Selznick apparently knew who he wanted quite early. When he saw Vivien Leigh in the British film *A Yank at Oxford*, his mind was made up. The rest was just p.r.

**FRANKENSTEIN (1931):** After the success of *Dracula*, Bela Lugosi was in line for all the good monster parts—including this one. But he turned *Frankenstein* down when he found out the monster wouldn't have any dialogue. Instead, an English actor named William Henry Pratt (Boris Karloff) got the role and became an international star.

**ON THE WATERFRONT (1954):** Marlon Brando won an Academy Award for his performance, but the producers originally wanted Montgomery Clift to star instead.

**SOMEBODY UP THERE LIKES ME (1956):** Young, little-known actor Paul Newman lost several choice parts to James Dean—including the role of Cal in *Giant*, and the lead in this biography of boxer Rocky Graziano. Then suddenly, before shooting on *Somebody Up There* started, Dean was dead. Newman was picked to step in, and the movie was his springboard to stardom.

**TARZAN THE APE MAN (1932):** Swimming star Johnny Weissmuller made a living with Tarzan pictures for decades, but only because Clark Gable turned the first one down.

**You use up as many calories sitting in a sauna for 15 minutes as you do jogging for a mile.**

# THEIR REAL NAMES

*We know them as Doris Day, Woody Allen, etc. But that's not what their parents called them. Here are some celebs' real names.*

**Muddy Waters:** McKinley Morganfield
**Liberace:** Wladziu Valentino Liberace
**Wolfman Jack:** Bob Smith
**Stan Laurel:** Arthur Stanley Jefferson
**Dean Martin:** Dino Crocetti
**Twiggy:** Leslie Hornby
**Peter Lorre:** Laszlo Lowenstein
**Jerry Lewis:** Joseph Levitch
**Lauren Bacall:** Betty Perski
**James Stewart:** Stewart Granger
**Yves Montand:** Ivo Livi
**Shelley Winters:** Shirley Schrift
**Van Morrison:** George Ivan
**W. C. Fields:** W. C. Dunkenfield
**Roy Rogers:** Leonard Slye
**Charles Bronson:** Charles Buchinsky
**Irving Berlin:** Israel Baline
**Stevie Wonder:** Steveland Judkins Morris
**Doris Day:** Doris Kappelhoff
**Boris Karloff:** William Henry Pratt
**Natalie Wood:** Natasha Gurdin
**Tammy Wynette:** Wynette Pugh
**Kirk Douglas:** Issur Danielovitch
**Rock Hudson:** Roy Fitzgerald
**Sophia Loren:** Sophia Scicolone
**Tony Curtis:** Bernie Schwartz
**John Wayne:** Marion Michael Morrison
**David Bowie:** David Jones
**Greta Garbo:** Greta Gustafsson
**Woody Allen:** Allen Konigsberg
**Fred Astaire:** Fred Austerlitz
**Lucille Ball:** Dianne Belmont
**Anne Bancroft:** Anne Italiano
**Jack Benny:** Joseph Kubelsky
**Yul Brynner:** Taidje Kahn, Jr.
**George Burns:** Nat Birnbaum
**Michael Caine:** Maurice Mickelwhite
**Joan Crawford:** Lucille Le Sueur
**Rodney Dangerfield:** John Cohen
**John Denver:** Henry John Deutschendorf, Jr.
**Werner Erhard:** Jack Rosenberg
**Douglas Fairbanks:** Julius Ullman
**Redd Foxx:** John Sanford
**Mel Brooks:** Mel Kaminsky

**How big is a standard grave? 7' 8" long x 3' 2" wide x 6' deep.**

# MYTH AMERICA

*Here are a few more patriotic stories we all learned when we were young...and which are all 100% baloney.*

**The Myth:** Nathan Hale, an American soldier during the Revolutionary War, was captured by the British and sentenced to hang. When the Redcoats asked if he had any last words, he replied defiantly: "I regret that I have but one life to lose for my country."
**The Truth:** He never said that—or anything close to it. According to the diary of a British soldier who was there, Captain Frederick MacKenzie, Hale's last words were brave, but not very inspiring. They were: "It is the duty of every good officer to obey the orders given him by his commander-in-chief."

**The Myth**: Abraham Lincoln hurriedly composed his most famous speech—the Gettysburg Address—on the back of an envelope while riding on a train from Washington, D.C. to the site of the speech in Gettysburg.
**Background:** The story apparently originated with Lincoln's son, Robert, who first created it in a letter he wrote after his father was assassinated.
**The Truth:** Lincoln actually started writing the speech two weeks before the event, and wrote at least five drafts before even leaving Washington for Gettysburg. He wasn't particularly keen on speaking spontaneously—in fact, he even refused to say anything to the crowd that met him at the Gettysburg train station because he was afraid he might say something foolish.

**The Myth:** The Liberty Bell got its name when it was rung on July 4, 1776 to commemorate declaring independence.
**Background:** This tale was invented by writer George Lippard in his 1847 book, *Legends of the American Revolution.*
**The Truth:** The Liberty Bell was installed in Philadelphia in 1753—23 years before the colonists rebelled—and it has nothing whatsoever to do with the Revolution. Its nickname, "Liberty Bell," was coined by abolitionists in 1839. They were referring to the end of slavery in America, not freedom from England.

# MUSTANG: CAR OF THE '60s

*The original Ford Mustang, a sporty car for "everyman," introduced in 1964, is now a symbol of the entire decade. Its early history is fascinating.*

The Mustang was the most successful car ever introduced by the American auto industry. But in terms of the '60s, it was more than a car. Its popularity was an expression of the simple truth of the decade—that everyone wanted to look, feel, and act young.

## ORIGIN OF THE CAR

• The Mustang was the pet project of Ford General Manager Lee Iacocca, who kept notes on new car ideas in a little black book. Because Ford kept getting letters from car buffs who wanted a car like the 1955 T-Bird, Iacocca felt there was a market for a new "personal sports car" waiting to be developed. Research also showed that the population was getting younger, and that young people bought more cars per capita than any other segment of the population.

• Based on these findings—and Iacocca's instinct—Ford decided to create a car that was sporty yet low-priced, so young people and middle-income groups could afford it. But it also had to be capable of taking enough options to make it a luxury car.

• The new project was dubbed "T-5." Ford engineers and designers worked under maximum security in a windowless room, known as "The Tomb"; even the wastepaper was burned under supervision.

• Over a three-year period they came up with many two-seat prototypes—XT-Bird, Allegro, Aventura, and Mustang I (loved by car enthusiasts, but considered too sporty by Iacocca)—but all were scrapped in favor of a four-seat model with a large trunk. It was completed in spring 1963.

• The Mustang was designed to be versatile. The buyer had options: two different engines, whitewalls, power disc brakes, racing hubcaps, sports console, and so on. As Dr. Seymour Marshak, Ford's market research manager, said admiringly, "This flexibility makes this car the greatest thing since the Erector Set."

•Since Ford figured the T-5's market was the young sports car

**The most popular color for cars is white. 10% of all cars sold in the U.S. are white.**

buyer, the name "Torino" was chosen because it sounded like an Italian sports car. The projected ad campaign called it "the new import . . . from Detroit."

• But last-minute market research showed that this car could appeal to all buyers, and a new name had to be chosen. Colt, Bronco, and Maverick (all used for later cars) were considered. But "Mustang" seemed best for T-5, bringing to mind cowboys, adventure, and the Wild West. As one Ford man put it, "It had the excitement of the wide-open spaces, and it was American as all hell."

• The Mustang was introduced on April 17, 1964. On that day, over 4 million people visited the 6,500 Ford dealers across the country to get a look at it...and they bought 22,542 of them.

• In the first three months of production, a record 100,000 Mustangs were sold. It was an instant status symbol, with people vying for the limited supply as though it was a contraband item.

## MUSTANG FEVER

*The introduction of the Mustang on April 17, 1964 was a big event. Here are 5 of the bizarre things that happened that day.*

**1.** A Mustang was the pace car for a stock car race in Huntsville, Alabama. When it drove onto the track, thousands of people scaled the retaining wall to get a better look at it. The race was delayed for over an hour.

**2.** A cement truck crashed through the plate-glass window of a Seattle Ford dealer when the driver lost control of his vehicle. The reason: He was staring at the new Mustangs on display there. They looked "like some of them expensive Italian racers," he explained.

**3.** A Chicago Ford dealer was forced to lock the doors of his showroom models because too many people were trying to get into them at the same time.

**4.** A Texas dealer put a new Mustang on a lift to show a prospective customer the underside of the vehicle. By the time his demonstration was over, the showroom was filled with people, and he had to leave the Mustang up in the air for the rest of the day.

**5.** A New Jersey Ford dealer had only one Mustang and 15 eager buyers, so he auctioned it off. The winner of the auction insisted on sleeping in the car to be sure the dealer didn't sell it to someone else before his check cleared.

# STRANGE LAWSUITS

*These days, it seems like people will sue each other over practically anything. Here are a few real-life examples of unusual legal battles.*

**THE PLAINTIFF:** An unidentified 40-year-old woman from Poughkeepsie, New York.

**THE DEFENDANT:** Her plastic surgeon.

**THE LAWSUIT:** The woman had an operation to tighten her stomach in 1979. When it was over, she discovered that her belly-button was now 2-1/2 inches off center. She claimed "the operation had left a large deformed hole in her stomach and had disrupted her business and her life." She sued the doctor for malpractice.

**VERDICT:** She was awarded $854,000 by the New York State Supreme Court, and ultimately settled with the doctor for $200,000. A year later, she had her bellybutton surgically corrected.

**THE PLAINTIFF:** An unidentified woman from San Francisco.

**THE DEFENDANT:** Her priest.

**THE LAWSUIT:** The woman embezzled around $30,000 from the Catholic Church, and was overcome by guilt. "I couldn't take the pressure anymore," she said. "I needed to talk with someone, and the only person I could talk with was my priest." So she went into the confessional and admitted what she'd done. She expected absolution and forgiveness; instead, the priest turned her in to the police. She spent 7 months in jail, and when she got out, she sued the priest for $5 million for "violation of confidentiality."

**VERDICT:** Settled out of court.

**THE PLAINTIFFS:** Bruce and Susan S., from Manitoba, Canada.

**THE DEFENDANT:** Winnipeg International Airport.

**THE LAWSUIT:** One day in 1988, the couple and their baby daughter, Anna, showed up at the Winnipeg Airport to catch a flight. At the gate, the airport security guard X-rayed their carry-on luggage—and then picked up Anna and sent her through the X-ray

**According to *Playboy* magazine, 99% of cat and dog owners talk to their pets.**

machine, too. The couple immediately took their daughter to a hospital to see if the X-rays had harmed her. She was okay, but they still sued the airport—"for the time lost while waiting for test results as well as the fare of the missed flight."
**VERDICT:** Settled out of court.

**THE PLAINTIFF:** Robert K., "a 36-year-old Philadelphia real estate manager."
**THE DEFENDANT:** The Transcendental Meditation Society and the guru Maharishi Mahesh Yogi.
**THE LAWSUIT:** Mr. K. worked with TM groups for 11 years, but he finally sued them because "he was never able to achieve the 'perfect state of life' they promised, and he suffered psychological disorders as a result. One broken agreement: he had been told he would be taught to 'fly' through self-levitation, but he learned only to 'hop with the legs folded in the lotus position.' "
**VERDICT:** "A U.S. district court jury in Washington, D.C. awarded him nearly $138,000 in damages."

**THE PLAINTIFF:** A 19-year-old man from New York City.
**THE DEFENDANT:** The City Transit Authority.
**THE LAWSUIT:** The 19-year-old decided to commit suicide by throwing himself off a subway platform into the path of an oncoming train. The train didn't stop in time to avoid hitting him, but it didn't kill him, either—he lost a leg, an arm, and part of the other arm. So he sued the Transit Authority, claiming "the motorman was negligent in not stopping the train quickly enough."
**THE VERDICT:** They settled out of court for $650,000—despite the fact that while they were negotiating the settlement, the man threw himself off a subway platform—and failed to kill himself—a second time.

**AND LET'S NOT FORGET...**
Two 1974 cases involving CBS-TV. The first one, a claim by studio technician Hamilton Morgan that "The Beverly Hillbillies" was originally his idea, was settled out of court (reportedly with a big cash settlement to Morgan). The second charged that CBS's Paladin character in "Have Gun, Will Travel" was pirated from a retired rodeo performer. The case went to court, and CBS lost.

**The book most often read by high school English classes: Shakespeare's *Romeo and Juliet*.**

# "COME UP AND SEE ME..."

*Comments from film actress Mae West.*

"Marriage is a great institution, but I'm not ready for an institution yet."

"It's hard to be funny when you have to be clean."

"She's the kind of girl who climbed the ladder of success, wrong by wrong."

"Between two evils, I always pick the one I haven't tried before."

"I generally avoid temptation—unless I can't resist it."

"It's not the men in my life that counts—it's the life in my men."

"He who hesitates is last."

"When women go wrong, men go right after them."

"Too much of a good thing can be wonderful."

"I used to be Snow White...but I drifted."

"I only like two kinds of men—domestic and foreign."

"Is that a gun in your pocket, or are you glad to see me?"

"Give a man a free hand and he'll run it all over you."

"I've been in more laps than a napkin."

"A man in the house is worth two in the street."

"He's the kind of man a woman would have to marry to get rid of."

"Brains are an asset...if you hide them."

"I don't look down on men, but I certainly don't look up to them either. I never found a man I could love—or trust—the way I loved myself."

"When I'm good, I'm very good. But when I'm bad, I'm better."

"I always say, keep a diary and one day it will keep you."

"I've always had a weakness for foreign affairs."

# WE'VE ONLY JUST BEGUN

*Ads are so pervasive in society that we often don't even know one when we hear it. Like this one.*

Some people think "We've Only Just Begun" is a great love song. Actually, it's a bank commercial.

**BACKGROUND:** In 1968, officials of the Crocker Bank in California approached a San Francisco ad agency about trying to attract young people to their institution. There was a strong anti-establishment feeling among college graduates at the time, and the bank felt it had to make an extra effort to reach them.

The ad executive in charge of the project came up with a basic approach. "The one thing that all young people have in common," he explained later, "is that they're starting out on new things—beginning careers, setting up a household for the first time, and so on. So the ad campaign was developed around that theme." The slogan: "We've only just begun."

**THE BUCK STARTS HERE:** The ad exec got an inspiration—he decided to pay a songwriter to create a *real* song called "We've Only Just Begun," instead of just a coming up with a jingle. That way, if the song made the charts, there would be extra benefits to his client whenever it was played on the radio. So he commissioned tunesmith Paul Williams to write a song with the phrase "We've Only Just Begun" in it.

As part of the deal, the bank used it on their commercials—but Williams was also free to do whatever he wanted with it.

What did he do with it? He sold it to the Carpenters, who recorded a saccharine version that sold millions of records, and became a wedding and elevator standard.

Meanwhile, the bank made its money back by licensing commercial right for the song to other banks around the country.

**THE ULTIMATE IRONY:** The bank realized it didn't *want* young people's business. Young adults flocked to the Crocker Bank to borrow money, but they didn't have any collateral. They turned out to be bad risks, and the ad campaign was stopped.

# NOTHING TO SNEEZE AT

*Why do we say "God Bless You" when we sneeze? Charles Panati checked it out, and came up with the answer in his* Extraordinary Origins of Everyday Things.

Gesundheit,' say Germans; 'Felicita,' say Italians; Arabs clasp hands and reverently bow. Every culture believes in a benediction following a sneeze. The custom goes back to a time when a sneeze was regarded as a sign of great personal danger."

## SNEEZING SUPERSTITIONS

"For centuries, man believed that life's essence, the soul, resided in the head and that a sneeze could accidentally expel the vital force. This suspicion was reinforced by the deathbed sneezing of the sick. Every effort was made to hold back a sneeze, and an inadvertent or unsuppressed sneeze was greeted with immediate good luck chants."

## THE GREEK SNEEZE

"Enlightenment arrived in the fourth century B.C. with the teachings of Aristotle and Hippocrates, the 'father of medicine.' Both Greek scholars explained sneezing as the head's reaction to a foreign or offensive substance that crept into the nostrils. They observed that sneezing, when associated with existing illness, often foretold death. For these ill-boding sneezes, they recommended such benedictions as 'Long may you live!' 'May you enjoy good health!' and 'Jupiter preserve you!' "

## THE ROMAN SNEEZE

"About a hundred years later, Roman physicians extrapolated the lore and superstition surrounding a sneeze.

"The Romans preached the view that sneezing, by an otherwise healthy individual, was the body's attempt to expel the sinister spirits of later illnesses. Thus, to withhold a sneeze was to incubate disease, to invite debility and death. Consequently, a vogue of sneezing swept the Roman Empire and engendered a host of new post-sneeze benedictions: 'Congratulations' to a person having robustly executed a sneeze; and to a person quavering on the verge of an exhalation, the encouraging 'Good luck to you.' "

## THE CHRISTIAN SNEEZE

"The Christian expression 'God bless you' has a still different origin. It began by papal fiat in the sixth century, during the reign of Pope Gregory the Great. A virulent pestilence raged throughout Italy, one foreboding symptom being severe, chronic sneezing. So deadly was the plague that people died shortly after manifesting its symptoms; thus, sneezing became synonymous with imminent death.

"Pope Gregory beseeched the healthy to pray for the sick. He also ordered that such well-intended though leisurely phrases as 'May you enjoy good health' be replaced with his own more urgent and pointed invocation, 'God bless you!' And if no well-wisher was around to invoke the blessing, the sneezer was advised to exclaim aloud, 'God help me!'

"Pope Gregory's post-sneeze supplications spread throughout Europe, hand in hand with the plague, and the seriousness with which a sneeze was regarded was captured in a new expression, which survives to this day: 'Not to be sneezed at.' "

## WORLD-CLASS SNEEZING

- According to the *Guinness Book of World Records*, "The most chronic sneezing fit ever recorded is that of Donna Griffiths." On January 13, 1981, the 12-year-old from Pershore, England began sneezing and kept sneezing every day for 978 days. The previous record was 194 days.
- In the first year, she sneezed an estimated one million times.
- Her first "sneeze-free day" in almost three years was September 16, 1983.

The *Guinness Book* has somehow also come up with an account of the most powerful sneeze ever recorded:
"The highest speed at which expelled particles have been measured to travel," it says, is "103.6 miles per hour."

## MISC. LAST THING ON THE PAGE

The phrase "Bring home the bacon" comes from the 1700s, when the term *bacon* was criminal slang for "booty" or "loot." If you brought home the *bacon*, you fulfilled your mission and returned with "the goods," which is how we use it today.

# SO LONG, ROUTE 66

*You may not know it, but America's most famous highway is slowly disappearing, a victim of progress.*

Although many American highways have been celebrated, few can match the romance and lore of Route 66—the 2,200-mile-long highway that was once the primary route between Chicago and Los Angeles. Route 66 has been immortalized in song ("Get Your Kicks on Route 66") and on the screen (the hit 1960s TV series).

Although it has now been bypassed by superhighways, it's still cherished by an enthusiastic cult of motorists who venture off the new interstates in search of a piece of America's history—which they seem to find on the old Route 66 backroads that still exist.

**ROUTE 66 FACTS**

• Route 66 began as a series of cattle and wagon train trails. By the early 1900s, the route was known as the "National Old Trails Highway."

• It was first designated Route 66 in 1926, while it was still mostly dirt and gravel. At the time, East-West routes were given even numbers, North-South got odd numbers. Route 66's Midwest path landed it between Route 2 (the northernmost route running from Maine to Idaho) and Route 96 (on the southern Texas border).

• In 1937, paving was completed. The finished highway went through eight states (Illinois, Missouri, Mississippi, Oklahoma, Texas, New Mexico, Arizona, and California) and three time zones.

• Route 66 was the road of choice for "Dust Bowl" Okies fleeing to California during the Depression of the early 1930's. John Steinbeck included Route 66 in his classic *The Grapes Of Wrath*, calling it "the mother road" on which the Joad family travelled West.

• Route 66 nicknames: The Will Rogers Highway, the Postal Highway, and the Ozark Trail.

• The TV show "Route 66" was actually filmed in Oregon and Florida. The series ran from October 7, 1960 until September 18, 1964. It starred Martin Milner and George Maharis as Tod Stiles and Buz Murdock. They drove a '62 Corvette.

Only about 1/4 of all Americans say they eay "a lot" of red meat.

• **The beginning of the end:** President Eisenhower ordered the construction of 42,500 miles of interstate highways in 1956. New superhighways like Interstate 40—which runs parallel to Route 66 from Oklahoma City to L.A.—eventually replaced the country backroads. As a result, small businesses which once thrived by the highway began to disappear in favor of fast-food franchises and hotel chains. Three interstates—40, 44, and 55—eventually replaced Route 66, whose last original stretch of highway (Williams, AZ) closed in the mid-1980s.

## THE SONG

• In 1946, Bobby Troupe was driving from his home in Pennsylvania to try and make it as a songwriter in Los Angeles. At one point in the trip, his wife, Cynthia, suggested that he try and write a song about Highway 40. Troupe didn't think much of the suggestion. "Then later, out of Chicago, when we realized that we'd be following the same highway all the way to California," Troup recalls. "She whispered, kind of hesitantly because of the put-down on the first suggestion, 'Get your kicks on Route 66.' " By the time Troupe and his wife hit L.A. the song was nearly complete. Nat King Cole was the first to record it—everyone from Nelson Riddle and the Rolling Stones to Depeche Mode have done their version of "Route 66."

## ROUTE 66 LANDMARKS

• Route 66 officially began on Jackson Boulevard and Michigan Avenue in Chicago. It ended at Ocean Avenue and Santa Monica Boulevard in Santa Monica, California, where a plaque can still be found dedicated to the Will Rogers Highway. It reads: "This Main Street of America Highway 66 was the first road he travelled in a career that led him straight to the hearts of his countrymen."

• The state of Arizona has preserved 105 miles of Route 66 as a historic state highway—it contains the longest drivable stretch of the road that still exits, running from Seligman to Topock, Arizona.

• Clark Gable and Carole Lombard spent their first honeymoon night on Rte. 66, in the Beale Hotel in Kingman, Arizona in 1939.

• Route 66 crosses the Texas panhandle and goes through Amarillo, home of the Cadillac Ranch (immortalized by Bruce Springsteen).

• Major cities you can still see on Route 66: Chicago, St. Louis, Oklahoma City, Amarillo, Albuquerque, and L.A.

**The leaders in per capita consumption of chocolate: #1, Switzerland; #2, Norway. #3, Britain.**

# HELLO, I'M MR. ED

*A horse is a horse, of course, of course. Unless he's on TV. Then anything can happen. Mr. Ed is probably TV's first legitimate animal folk hero.*

**HOW IT STARTED.**
Arthur Lubin couldn't understand it. His films about *Francis the Talking Mule* had made a small fortune, but he still couldn't interest the TV networks in a similar concept he'd created for the small screen. He envisioned a show about a talking horse named Mr. Ed. (The idea was inspired by a series of magazine stories about a horse that not only talked, but frequently got drunk.) But no one—not even his projected star, comedian Alan Young—would consider the series when Lubin proposed it in 1954.

Lubin kept trying, and three years later, in 1957, he finally found a backer who agreed to bankroll a pilot film—comedian George Burns, who along with his pal, Jack Benny, thought the concept of a talking horse was hilarious.

Now that Lubin had some money, he approached Young again with a concrete offer. But again Young turned him down. "It's not the kind of thing I want to do," said Alan, who'd had his own CBS variety show in the early '50s (but was now working in England). Lubin went ahead and made a pilot anyway, using a different actor; in fact, all the stars in the original pilot were different from the TV show—even Mr. Ed. But he still couldn't sell the show.

Lubin was nothing if not persistent. He offered the part to Young *again* a few years later. And this time Young decided it was his only chance to get back into American TV. So he accepted. Lubin wanted to call it "The Alan Young Show," but Young refused that. "Why should I take the rap if it bombs?" he asked. So it became "Mr. Ed."

When the networks didn't pick up the show, the Studebaker Company (a now-defunct auto maker) purchased it and put it into syndication in 1960. To everyone except Lubin's (and Burns's) surprise, it was an instant hit. A year later, CBS bought it, making it the first syndicated show ever to be picked up by a network. It aired until 1965 on Sunday nights.

## INSIDE FACTS

### Les Is More

• Mr. Ed, an 1100-lb. golden palomino, wouldn't respond to any of his co-stars. He only took orders from his trainer, Les Hilton—which meant that Hilton had to be on the set all the time, barking out commands or giving them with hand signals.

• Hilton was often hidden in the scene or lying on the floor just out of camera range. If you're watching Mr. Ed and you want to know where Hilton is, just watch Ed's eyes. Ed is always looking at him (even if it seems that he's involved in the action).

### Vital Stats

Ed's real name was Bamboo Harvester. He was born in 1954, and supposedly died in 1979 at the age of 25. His daily diet was 20 lbs. of hay, washed down with a gallon of sweet tea.

### Take Five

Like any star, Ed could be moody and difficult to work with. When he was tired of working, he'd just walk off the set. And when he was hungry, shooting stopped while he strolled over to his bale of hay and ate. When he was bored, he'd cross his hind legs and yawn.

### Historic Preservation

The classic Mr. Ed theme was first recorded in Italy—by an opera singer! It was so bad that Arthur Lubin started looking for a new song to use. But Jay Livingstone, Oscar-winning ("Que Sera, Sera") co-writer of the tune, recorded his own version which Lubin liked enough to use on the show. Livingstone sings it on the air.

### Stunt Horse

There was no stand-in while Ed performed his stunts. He could really open the barn door (left or right side) and answer the telephone. He couldn't really talk, though. His lips were moved by a nylon bit.

### The Voice

The voice of Mr. Ed was kept a secret. It was actually Allen "Rocky" Lane, a former cowboy star. For obvious reasons, Lane billed himself as "an actor who prefers to remain anonymous."

**In 1900 only 41% of all Americans lived to be 65. In 1989, 79% do.**

# FREUDIAN SLIPS

*From the mind of Sigmund Freud...*

"America is a mistake, a giant mistake!"

"When a man is freed of religion, he has a better chance to live a normal and wholesome life."

"Anatomy is destiny."

"What progress we are making. In the Middle Ages they would have burnt me; nowadays they are content with burning my books."

"Thought is action in rehearsal."

"The great question...which I have not been able to answer, despite my thirty years in research into the feminine soul, is 'What do women want?' "

"Sometimes a cigar is just a cigar."

"The more the fruits of knowledge become accessible to men, the more widespread is the decline of religious belief."

"Neurosis seems to be a human privilege."

"The goal of all life is death."

"The first human being who hurled an insult instead of a stone was the founder of civilization."

"When one of my family complains that he or she has bitten his tongue, bruised her finger, and so on, instead of the expected sympathy, I put the question, 'Why did you do that?' "

"We hate the criminal, and deal with him severely, because we view in his deed, as in a distorting mirror, our own criminal instincts."

"When making a decision of minor importance, I have always found it advantageous to consider all the pros and cons. In vital matters, however, such as the choice of a mate or profession, decisions should come from the unconscious, from somewhere within ourselves. In the important decisions of our personal lives we should be governed by the deep inner needs of our nature."

**41% of all Americans say they want their child to be President of the United States.**

# PRESIDENTIAL CURIOSITIES

*Nowadays, former presidents—even disgraced ones—are treated with respect and deference. So it's enlightening to find out that the presidential office wasn't always a royal one.*

**FACT:** The government of the United States completely ignored the death of one former president because he was considered a traitor.

**THE PRESIDENT:** John Tyler (10th president, 1841-45).

**BACKGROUND:** A Virginia aristocrat, Tyler was William Henry Harrison's running mate in 1840. When Harrison died in 1841, he became president. But 20 years later, the 71-year-old joined the Confederacy. He died in 1861 while serving as a Virginia representative in the Confederate Congress, and was buried with full honors by the rebels. In Washington, however, his death was never publicly acknowledged.

**FACT:** One president had to borrow money to get to his own inauguration.

**THE PRESIDENT:** George Washington (1st president, 1789-97).

**BACKGROUND:** Washington wasn't poor—he was among America's largest landowners. But when it came time to travel to New York City for his inauguration in 1789, he didn't have any money. So "The Father of Our Country" had to borrow about $600 to get there. One consolation: his presidential salary was $25,000.

**FACT:** One ex-president was so destitute in his final years that circus impresario P. T. ("There's a sucker born every minute") Barnum actually offered him $100,000 to take a nationwide tour with his personal memorabilia.

**THE PRESIDENT:** Ulysses S. Grant (18th president, 1869-77).

**BACKGROUND:** In the early 1880s, Grant invested his life savings—about $100,000—in a banking firm in which one of his sons was a partner. The head of the company turned out to be a swindler, and the firm went broke in 1884. Grant was not only penniless, but had terminal cancer when Barnum wrote that year and suggested a quick money-making tour. Grant refused. Instead, in an effort to leave his wife something after his death, he wrote his memoirs. Mark Twain published them posthumously, and they earned over $500,000 for the Grant estate.

**FACT:** Another ex-president was so broke that friends created a lottery in his name and began selling raffle tickets in Washington.

**PRESIDENT:** Thomas Jefferson (3rd president, 1801-1809).

**BACKGROUND:** Brilliant in other fields, Jefferson apparently had no head for business. When he came close to bankruptcy in his final years, friends and political allies put together the "Thomas Jefferson Lottery" to benefit the ex-president. Fortunately, Jefferson was spared this embarrassment when enough money was raised privately to keep him financially afloat.

**FACT:** One president never voted in a presidential election until *he* was the one running for office.

**THE PRESIDENT:** Zachary Taylor (12th president, 1849-50).

**BACKGROUND:** "Old Rough and Ready," a national military hero in the Mexican War, was completely apolitical until he was bitten by the presidential bug. When an aide first suggested that he run for the office, he reputedly answered "Stop your nonsense and drink your whiskey!"

When he actually was nominated by the Whigs, he didn't find out about it until weeks after the convention. The Whig party's letter informing him of the news arrived collect, and Taylor refused to pay the postage due—so he never read it. The nominators had to send another letter—prepaid—to tell him. When Taylor voted in the national elections of 1848, it was the first time he'd ever voted for a president—and he probably wouldn't have bothered then either, if he hadn't been on the ballot.

**FACT:** One president was a licensed bartender.

**THE PRESIDENT:** Abraham Lincoln (16th president, 1861-65).

**BACKGROUND:** In 1833, Honest Abe was co-owner of a saloon in Springfield, Illinois, called *Berry and Lincoln*. He needed his license to sell booze.

# MONEY TALK

*What do you really know about your money?*

**THE GREENBACK DOLLAR**
The Federal government didn't start printing paper money until 1861.

• When the Civil War broke out, people began hoarding coins—and soon there was virtually no U.S. money in circulation. So Congress was forced to authorize the Treasury Department to create paper currency.
• These bills were nicknamed "Greenbacks" after the color ink used on one side. Lincoln, then president, was pictured on them.
• Congress stipulated that paper money had to be signed either by the Treasurer of the United States or people designated by him. Today the signature is printed on the bills, but in 1862 money had to be signed by hand. So 6 people—2 men and 4 women—worked in the attic of the Treasury building every day, signing, sorting, and sealing our first $1 and $2 bills.

**THE BUCKS START HERE**
Today, paper money worth over $12 billion is printed every year—an average of more than $10 million a day.
• About 2/3 of the paper money printed is $1 bills.
• A $1 bill lasts for about 1-1/2 years in circulation.
• The average bill is exchanged 400 times in its lifetime.
• It costs the government about 2.5¢ to print a $1 bill. It costs the same amount to print a $100 bill.
• Modern U.S. currency is printed on special paper, a blend of rag bond, cotton, and linen, supplied by a single manufacturer, Crane and Company of Massachusetts.
• U.S. paper money is printed three separate times—once each for front and back, and then it's reprinted with an overlay of green ink.
• The current U.S. dollar is 1/3 smaller than it was in 1929.

**VITAL STATS**
**Size of a bill:** 2.61 inches x 6.14 inches.
**Thickness:** .0043 inches. (233 of them make a stack an inch high.)
**Weight:** 490 bills equals a pound. A million $1 bills weigh approximately a ton.

**Laid end-to-end around the equator, it would take 257,588,120 dollar bills to circle the earth.**

## THE BIG BUCKS

• There are officially 12 different denominations of U.S. paper money, ranging from $1 to $100,000.
• The highest denomination printed in the last 45 years is a $100. In fact, everything over $100 has been officially "retired" from circulation for 30 years.
• The $100,000 bill has never been available to the public. It's only for transactions between the Treasury Department and the Federal Reserve.
• The $2 bill was resurrected in 1976—the only piece of new engraved currency in 60 years. It was a flop; the mint recently got rid of the last remaining bills in storage by burning them.
• Who's on what? $50—Ulysses S. Grant ; $100—Ben Franklin; $500—William McKinley; $1,000—Grover Cleveland; $5,000—James Madison; $10,000—Salmon P. Chase; $100,000—Woodrow Wilson.

## COIN OF THE REALM

• The first U.S. coin to bear the words, "United States of America," was a penny piece made in 1727. It was also inscribed with the plain-spoken motto: "Mind your own business."
• All American coins struck since 1792, when the first United States mint was established in Philadelphia, have been stamped with the word, "Liberty."
• The average coin circulates for a minimum of 15-20 years.
• Originally, the dime, quarter, and half dollar were 90% silver, 10% copper. But in the early '60s, the price of silver began to climb, and government officials worried that people would melt coins down for the precious metals.
• The result: Congress passed the 1965 Coinage Act, eliminating all silver from the three coins. Instead, the composition was changed to "clad" metal—a combination of three strips of metal. The faces are made of 75% copper and 25% nickel; the core is pure copper, which you can see on the side.
• In 1965, anticipating the disappearance of old quarters due to the value of the silver, the government issued almost 2 billion new ones (compared to an average annual production of 225 million). That's why you find so many 1965 quarters in circulation.
• Nickels are now made of 75% copper, 25% nickel.
• Pennies are now bronze. They contain 95% copper, 5% zinc.

**Although they had many million-sellers, Creedence Clearwater Revival never had a #1 song.**

# AROUND THE HOUSE

*The origins of a few common items.*

**BAND-AIDS (1921).**
In 1921 Earle Dickson, an employee of Johnson & Johnson, married a woman who kept injuring herself in the kitchen.
• As he carefully bandaged her cuts and burns with gauze and adhesive tape numerous times, he became frustrated; the clumsy bandages kept falling off. So he decided to create something "that would stay in place, be easily applied, and still retain its sterility." He stuck some gauze in the center of a piece of adhesive tape, and covered the whole thing with crinoline to keep it sterile. It worked.
• He made up a bunch for his wife, and took a few in to show his co-workers. The company's owner, James Johnson, heard about it and asked for a demonstration—which convinced him to begin manufacturing the product
• By the '80s, over 100 billion Band-Aids had been sold. Dickson, who became an exec at J & J, was amply rewarded for his efforts.

**IVORY SOAP (1879).**
Harley Procter and his cousin, chemist James Gamble, came up with a special new soap in 1878. It was smooth and fragrant, and produced a consistent lather...but it wasn't Ivory—it was called White Soap—and it didn't float.
• One day in 1879, the man operating P & G's soap-mixing machine forgot to turn it off when he went to lunch. On returning, he discovered that so much air had been whipped into the soap that it actually floated.
• For some reason, the batch wasn't discarded—it was made into bars and shipped out with the other White Soap. Soon, to their surprise, P&G was getting letters demanding more of "that soap that floats." So they started putting extra air in every bar
• Now that they had a unique product, they nedded a unique name. And they found it in the Bible. Procter was reading the 45th Psalm—which says: "All thy garments smell of myrrh, and aloes, and cassia, out of the ivory palaces..." —when it hit him that *Ivory* was just word he was looking for.
• In October, 1879 the first bar of Ivory Soap was sold.

**That's huge: In the 4th century, the Romans had a stadium that held 380,000 spectators.**

**VELCRO (1957).**
A young Swiss inventor named George De Mestral went for a hike one day in 1948. When he returned, he was annoyed to find burrs stuck to his clothes. But his annoyance turned to fascination. Why, he wondered, wouldn't it be possible to create synthetic burrs that could be used as fasteners?
• Most people scoffed at the idea; but a French weaver took him seriously. Using a small loom, the weaver hand-wove two cotton strips that stuck together when they touched. The secret: one strip had hooks, the other had loops.
• But De Mestral had to figure out how to mass-produce it...and he needed tougher material than cotton, which quickly wore out.
• Years passed; De Mestral experimented constantly. Finally he found a suitable material—nylon, which, it turned out, became very hard when treated with infrared light.
• Now he knew how to make the *loops* by machine—but he still couldn't figure out how to mass-produce the *hooks*.
• Finally a solution hit him. He bought a pair of barber's clippers and took them to a weaver. With the clippers, he demonstrated his idea—a loom that snipped loops as it wove them, creating little nylon hooks. He worked on the project for a year—and when it was finally completed, Velcro ("Vel" for velvet, "cro" for crochet) was born. The product had taken a decade to perfect.

**THE ELECTRIC TOASTER (1919).**
The first electric toasters, which appeared around 1900, were primitively constructed heating coils that were terrible fire hazards.
• However, they were a luxury—it was the first time in history that people didn't need to fire up a stove just to make a piece of toast.
• There was a built-in problem, though—the bread had to be constantly watched or it would burn to a crisp.
• In 1919, Charles Strite, a Minnesota factory worker, got sick of the burnt toast in the company cafeteria. So in his spare time, he designed and patented the first pop-up toaster. Then he went into business manufacturing them. It took years to work out the bugs, but by 1926, Strite's "Toastmasters" were relatively foolproof.
• A few years later, a New York businessman purchased Strite's company, and invested heavily in advertising—which proved to be the key ingredient in making the toaster a common household. appliance. Every home "had to have one"...and now they do.

**That's a lotta nerve: You have 45 miles of nerves in your body.**

# ACCORDING TO JEFFERSON

*Wisdom from Thomas Jefferson, one of our Founding Fathers.*

"A little rebellion now and then is a good thing."

"The man who reads nothing at all is better educated than the man who reads nothing but newspapers."

"The tree of liberty must be refreshed for time to time with the blood of patriots and tyrants. It is its natural manure."

"I tremble for my country when I reflect that God is just."

"Never buy what you do not want, because it is cheap; it will be dear to you."

"Question with boldness even the very existence of a God; because, if there be one, he must more approve of the homage of reason than that of a blindfolded fear."

"Never spend money before you have it."

"The art of life is the avoiding of pain."

"The Earth belongs...to the living. The dead have neither rights nor powers over it."

"The tax which will be paid for education is not more than the thousandth part of what will be paid to kings, priests, and nobles who will rise up among us if we leave the people to ignorance."

"Resistance to tyrants is obedience to God."

"To the press alone, chequered as it is with abuses, the world is indebted for all the triumphs which have been gained by reason and humanity over error and oppresion."

"Do not bite at the bait of pleasure till you know there is no hook beneath it."

"The legitimate powers of government extend to such acts as are injurious to others. But it does me no injury for my neighbor to say there are twenty gods, or no God. It neither picks my pocket nor breaks my leg."

**If you're average, you've got a vocabulary of about 10,000 words.**

# LIMERICKS

*Limericks have been around since the 1700s. The authors of these silly ditties (except for the one by Edward Lear) are unknown.*

There was a young fellow named Clyde,
Who once at a funeral was spied.
When asked who was dead,
He smilingly said,
"I don't know—I just came for the ride."

There was a young man of Calcutta
Who had a most terrible stutta,
He said: "Pass the h. . .ham,
And the j . . .j . . .j . . .jam,
And the b....b...b...b...b... b...butta."

There was a young man from Darjeeling,
Who got on a bus bound for Ealing;
It said at the door:
"Don't spit on the floor,"
So he carefully spat on the ceiling.

There was an old fellow named Cager
Who, as the result of a wager,
Offered to fart
The whole oboe part
Of Mozart's *Quartet in F Major*.

There was a young fellow of Lyme
Who lived with three wives at one time.
When asked: "Why the third?"
He replied: "One's absurd,
And bigamy, sir, is a crime."

There was a brave fellow named Gere,
Who hadn't an atom of fear.
He indulged a desire
To touch a live wire,
And any last line will do here.

An epicure, dining in Crewe,
Once found a large mouse in his stew.
Said the waiter: "Don't shout,
Or wave it about,
Or the rest will be wanting one, too."

A mouse in her room woke Miss Dowd,
Who was frightened and screamed very loud.
Then a happy thought hit her—
To scare off the critter,
She sat up in bed and meowed.

***—Edward Lear***

**What color was Christopher Columbus's hair? Blonde.**

# INSIDE MOTHER GOOSE

*We've sung and recited these rhymes since we were kids. Little did we know that they weren't just nonsense. Here's the inside scoop about what they really meant.*

***Humpty Dumpty** sat on a wall, Humpty Dumpty had a great fall. All the King's horses and all the king's men, couldn't put Humpty together again.*

**Background:** According to Katherine Thomas in *The Real Personages of Mother Goose*, this rhyme is 500 years old and refers to King Richard III of England. In 1483 his reign ended when he fell from his mount during battle; he was slain as he stood shouting "My kingdom for a horse!"

• Richard's fall made him Humpty Dumpty. Originally the last line was "Could not set Humpty up again"—which can be interpreted as either putting him back on his horse, or back on the throne.

***Old King Cole** was a merry old soul, a merry old soul was he. He called for his pipe and he called for his bowl, and he called for his fiddlers three."*

**Background:** There was actually a King Cole in Britain during the third century. No one knows much about him, but historians agree that he's the subject of the poem. Of interest: There's a Roman amphitheater in Colchester, England which has been known as "King Cole's Kitchen" for centuries.

***Little Jack Horner** sat in a corner, eating his Christmas pie. He stuck in his thumb and he pulled out a plum, and said "What a good boy am I."*

**Background:** In the mid-1500s, when King Henry VIII was confiscating lands belonging to the Catholic church, the Abbot of Glastonbury—the richest abbey in the British kingdom—tried to bribe the monarch by sending him a special Christmas pie. Inside the pie, the abbot had enclosed the deeds to 12 manor houses.

The courier who delivered the pie to the king was the abbot's aide, Thomas Horner.(The name "Jack" was contemporary slang for any male, particularly a "knave"). On his way, Horner stopped, stuck in his hand, and pulled out one of the deeds from the pie—a plum called Mells Manor. Shortly after, Horner moved into Mells, and his family still lives there today (although they deny the story).

Ironically, the abbot was later put on trial for his life—and Horner was one of the judges who condemned him to death.

***Jack be nimble****, Jack be quick, Jack jump over the candlestick.*

**Background:** for centuries, jumping over a candlestick was a method of fortune-telling in England. According to *The Oxford Dictionary of Nursery Rhymes*: "A candlestick with a lighted candle was placed on the floor and if, when jumping over it, the light was nmot extinguished, good luck was supposed to follow during the coming year."

***Ring around the rosy,*** *a pocket full of posies.*
*Ashes, ashes, we all fall down*

**Background:** According to James Leasor in *The Plague and the Fire*, this "had its origin in the [London Plague of 1664]. Rosy refers to the rosy rash of plague....The posies were herbs and spices carried to ward off the disease; sneezing was a common symptom of those close to death. In the *Annotated Mother Goose*, the authors note that the third line is often given as a sneezing noise ("At-choo, at-choo"), and that " 'We all fall down' was, in a way, exactly what happened."

## WHO WAS MOTHER GOOSE?

No one's quite sure. There are at least two possibilities, according to *The Annotated Mother Goose*:

- Charles Perrault, a French writer, "published a collection of fairy tales called *Tales of My Mother Goose* in 1697. The book contains eight stories: 'Little Red Riding Hood,' 'Bluebeard,' 'Puss In Boots,' " etc.
- But many scholars maintain that Mother Goose was actually one Elizabeth Foster Goose, of Boston, Mass. In 1692, when she was 27, Elizabeth married a widower named Isaac Goose and immediately inherited a family of 10 children. One of her step-daughters married a printer several years later and the printer enjoyed listening to "Mother Goose" recite old rhymes to the younger children. In 1719, he published a collection called *Songs for the Nursery, or Mother Goose's Melodies*.

**In 1980, there was only one country in the world with no telephones—Bhutan.**

# BUT THEY'D NEVER BEEN THERE

*Songs about places can be so convincing that it's hard to believe the people who wrote them haven't been there themselves. But that's often the case. Three prime examples:*

**TAKE ME HOME, COUNTRY ROADS; JOHN DENVER**

John Denver sounds so sincere singing this song that it's hard to believe he wasn't born and raised in West Virginia. But he wasn't. Denver didn't even write it; two musicians named Bill Danoff and Taffy Nivert did.

And they didn't grow up in West Virginia either. In fact, they'd never even been there when the song was composed.

It was actually written while they were on their way to a Nivert family reunion in *Maryland*. As they drove through the countryside, along the winding, tree-lined roads, Bill passed the time by writing a little tune about their rural surroundings. Gradually, it became "Take Me Home, Country Roads."

How did West Virginia get into the song? A friend of Bill's kept sending him picture postcards from the Mountain State with notes like, "West Virginia's almost heaven." Bill was so impressed by the postcards that he incorporated them into the lyrics of the song.

John Denver discovered the tune in 1970, while he was performing at a Washington, D.C. folk club. Bill and Taffy were also performing there, and one evening they played Denver their half-finished "Country Roads." The three of them stayed up all night finishing it. Denver put it on his next RCA album; it made him a star, and made Bill and Taffy some hefty royalties. Presumably, they've been to West Virginia by now.

**WOODSTOCK; CROSBY, STILLS, NASH, AND YOUNG**

The most famous tribute to the most famous musical event in rock history was written by Joni Mitchell. Millions of young Americans have listened to the hit versions by Crosby, Stills, Nash, and Young and by Matthews' Southern Comfort (as well as an album cut featuring Joni herself) and imagined enviously what it was like to be at Woodstock.

But what they don't know is that Joni *wasn't at the festival.* She was watching it on TV, like most of America.

She'd been traveling with Crosby, Stills and Nash (who played one of their first gigs ever at the mammoth rock concert), and they were all staying in New York City before heading up to the festival. But Mitchell's managers, David Geffen and Elliot Roberts, decided she wouldn't be able to make her scheduled appearance on "The Dick Cavett Show" if she went to Woodstock—so they cancelled her appearance there; Joni was left behind in New York.

Mitchell says: "The deprivation of not being able to go provided me with an intense angle on Woodstock. I was one of the fans."

But in the song, she sounds like one of the eyewitnesses.

**PROUD MARY;**
**CREEDENCE CLEARWATER REVIVAL**

This million-selling single about an old Mississippi paddlewheeler established Creedence Clearwater Revival as America's chief exponent of "swamp rock."

They were quickly recognized as the most promising artists to emerge from New Orleans since Fats Domino.

There was only one catch: Creedence Clearwater Revival wasn't from New Orleans. They were from El Cerrito, California. And they had never even been to New Orleans. In fact, the farthest east that songwriter John Fogarty had ever gotten was to Montana. And the closest thing to a bayou that he'd ever seen was the swampland around Winters, California.

Actually, Proud Mary wasn't originally going to be a Mississippi riverboat at all. Fogarty initially envisioned her as a "washer woman." But the first few chords he played with reminded him of a paddle-wheel going around. That brought him to thoughts of the Mississippi River, and Mary became a boat.

How did Fogarty manage to pull it off so well? The best explanation he could come up with for his "authentic" sound was that he'd listened to a lot of New Orleans music (like Fats Domino) when he was young.

**IRRELEVANT NOTE:** Not even one of the 13 actors who played Charlie Chan in movies, radio, Broadway, or TV were Chinese or of Chinese ancestry.

**The most extras ever used in a movie was 300,000, for the film *Gandhi* in 1981.**

# PRIME-TIME PROVERBS

*TV's comments about everyday life in America*
*From* Prime Time Proverbs, *by Jack Mingo and John Javna.*

## ON AGING

**Dorothy:** "Age is just a state of mind."
**Blanche:** "Tell that to my thighs."

**—*The Golden Girls***

**Fred Sanford:** "I still want to sow some wild oats!"
**Lamont Sanford:** "At your age, you don't have no wild oats—you got shredded wheat!"

**—*Sanford and Son***

## ON RELATIONSHIPS

"You can make a man eat shredded cardboard. . . . If you know the right tricks."

**—Jeannie's sister,**
***I Dream of Jeannie***

**Sam Malone:** "You've made my life a living hell."
**Diane Chambers:** "I didn't want you to think I was easy."

**—*Cheers***

## ON HUMAN NATURE

"I'm only human, Meathead… and to be human is to be violent."

**—Archie Bunker,**
***All in the Family***

"Everyone's a character—some of us just haven't met the right writer yet."

**—Dash Goff,**
***Designing Women***

"I think man is the most interesting insect, don't you?"

**—Marvin Martian,**
***The Bugs Bunny Show***

## ON ANATOMY

**Cosmetic Clerk:** "You know what the fastest way to a man's heart is?"
**Roseanne:** "Yeah. Through his chest!"

**—*Roseanne***

## ON MARRIAGE

"Just because we're married to men doesn't mean we've got anything in common with them."

**—Ethel Mertz,**
***I Love Lucy***

"Why can't they invent something for us to marry instead of women?"

**—Fred Flintstone,**
***The Flintstones***

**All wet: The average 150-lb. man should consume 2.9 quarts of water (in any form) each day.**

# MARK TWAIN & POLITICS

*In 1912, Mark Twain declared he was running for the presidency. Here's what he told the press:*

**On His Reasons for Running:** "A patriotic American must do something around election time, and...I see nothing else to do but become a candidate for President. Even the best among us will do the most repulsive things when smitten with a Presidential madness."

**On His Position:** "I am in favor of anything and everything anybody is in favor of."

**On His Character:** "The rumor that I buried a dead aunt under my grapevine was correct. The vine needed fertilizing; my aunt had to be buried, and I dedicated her to this high purpose. Does that unfit me for the Presidency? The Constitution of this country does not say so. No other citizen was ever considered unworthy of this office because he enriched his grapevine with his dead relatives. Why should I be selected as the first victim of an absurd prejudice?"

**On Corruption:** "We have humble God-fearing Christian men among us who will stoop to do things for a million dollars that they ought not to be willing to do for less than two million."

**On the Arms Race:** "The idea is that these formidable new war-inventions will make war impossible by and by—but I doubt it."

**On Women's Rights:** "Their wonderful campaign lasted a great many years, and is the most wonderful in history, for it achieved a revolution—the only one achieved in history for the emancipation of half a nation that cost not a drop of blood."

**On Civil Rights:** "It is a worthy thing to fight for one's freedom; it is another sight finer to fight for another man's."

**On Liberty:** "I believe we ought to retain all our liberties. We can't afford to throw them away. They didn't come to us in a night. The trouble with us in America is that we haven't learned to speak the truth. We have thrown away the most valuable asset we have—the individual right to oppose both flag and country when by one's self we believe them to be in the wrong."

# GET SMART

*The most popular satire in the history of TV was this spy takeoff starring Don Adams and Barbara Feldon.*

**HOW IT STARTED.**

The spy craze began quietly in 1963 with the release of the first James Bond film, *Dr. No.* By the end of 1964, there were 2 more Bond epics and a hit TV spinoff ("The Man from UNCLE"). Spies were everywhere, and Dan Melnick, a packager at Talent Associates, decided to parody them on TV. He picked comedy writers Mel Brooks (still years away from his first film) and Buck Henry to create the satire. "No one had ever done a show about an idiot before," Brooks said in 1965. "I decided to be the first."

The appropriate name for a sitcom idiot, they figured, was Smart. And since every secret agent needed a number, they gave theirs 86—the code bartenders use to cut off service to a drunk ("86 that guy"). Smart also needed a beautiful companion, so they created a slightly daffy Mata Hari named "99" (instead of "69") to costar.

"We had no special comedian in mind for Smart," Henry said at the time. "We wrote dialogue suitable for any standup comedian. But we had our eyes on a definite Mata Hari—Barbara Feldon."

ABC loved the idea and commissioned a pilot script. But when they read what Brooks and Henry had written, they backed out of the deal. The story had the evil KAOS threatening to blow up the Statue of Liberty, which ABC called "dirty and un-American." Instead, the show was sold to NBC.

"Get Smart" became the highest-rated new show of the 1965–66 season, and the episode ABC rejected was nominated for an Emmy.

**SIC 'EM**

Barbara Feldon was the first of many models who became famous by starring in TV ads. Her big break: A commercial for a men's hair product called Top Brass. She stretched out on a rug and purred, "Sic 'em, tiger." That got her so much attention that she was offered TV guest roles as an actress. A spot as an industrial spy on a show called "East Side, West Side" earned her the role of 99.

## WOULD YOU BELIEVE...

Don Adams and comedian Bill "Jose Jimenez" Dana were old friends. So when Dana got his own sitcom in 1963 ("The Bill Dana Show"), he included Adams in the cast, playing a dumb house detective named Byron Glick—essentially the same role he played as Maxwell Smart. Dana's show was cancelled in 1965, leaving Adams free to take the starring role in "Get Smart" the same year.

## THE VOICE

In the '50s, Adams' stand-up comedy routine included impersonations of famous personalities, including actor William Powell. For Max's voice, he just did his Powell imitation in a higher pitch.

## THE OLD ONE-LINER TRICK

Max was famous for one-liners like "Sorry about that, Chief," and "Would you believe..." They became fads, with kids adopting them as hip slang. But it wasn't an accident. From the outset, Don Adams anticipated it and insisted the show's writers build them into the stories. Most of them were already part of Adams' comedy routine. He brought "Would you believe..." from "The Bill Dana Show" and borrowed "Sorry about that" from Ernie Kovacs' protege, Joe Mikalos. As the old lines got stale, writers began adding new ones, like "The old _____ trick."

## THE BURGER KING

Here's a whopper. Which cast member had the most successful post-"Get Smart" acting career? King Moody, who played the semi-regular villain, Starker. He became Ronald McDonald on McDonald's TV commercials.

## TRUE CONFESSIONS

Don Adams on the quality of the show: "At first, I wanted every show to be a classic. [But] I then came to the realization that when you do a show every week, you can't be a classic. If you can do 3 out of 5 which are good, you should be happy with that."

## NAME GAME

According to Buck Henry, Agent 99's real name was never revealed. In one episode, she was introduced as "Susan Hilton." But in the end, she explained to Max that it was just a cover name.

**Room to breathe: In 1610, the population of the American colonies was 350 people.**

# MORE EPITAPHS

*More unusual epitaphs and tombstone rhymes from our wandering B.R.I. tombstone-ologists.*

*Seen in Enosburg, Vermont:*
**In memory of Anna**
Here lies the body of our Anna,
Done to death by a banana.
It wasn't the fruit that laid her low,
But the skin of the thing that made her go.

*Seen in Burlington, Mass.:*
**Anthony Drake**
Sacred to the memory of Anthonly Drake,
Who died for peace and quietness sake.
His wife was constantly scoldin' and scoffin',
So he sought for repose in a $12 coffin.

*Seen in Winslow, Maine:*
**Beza Wood, 1792-1837**
Here lies one Wood enclosed in wood,
One within the other.
The outer wood is very good.
We cannot praise the other.

*Seen in Boot Hill Cemetery, Dodge City, Kansas:*
He played five Aces.
Now he's playing the harp.

*Seen in the English countryside:*
**Mary Ford, 1790**
Here lieth Mary—the wife of John Ford.
We hope her soul is gone to the Lord.
But if for Hell she has changed this life,
She would rather be there than be John Ford's wife.

*Seen in Canaan, N.H.:*
**Sarah Shute, 1803-1840**
Here lies, cut down like unripe fruit,
The wife of Deacon Amos Shute.
She died of drinking too much coffee,
Anno Domini eighteen forty.

*Seen in Burlington, N.J:*
**Mary Ann Lowder, 1798**
Here lies the body of Mary Ann Lowder,
Who burst while drinking a Seidlitz powder.
Called from this world to her Heavenly Rest
She should have waited till it effervesced.

**If a Turkish person is wearing violet, he or she might be in mourning.**

# THE ORIGIN OF LEVI'S

*Blue jeans are as American as apple pie and bathroom reading. In fact, you might have a pair around your ankles right now.*

## CANVASING THE CUSTOMERS

In 1850—during the California gold rush—a 17-year-old named Levi Strauss moved from New York City to San Francisco to sell dry goods to the miners. • He tried to sell canvas to them for their tents, but found little interest in it. So he made pants out of the material instead.

• The miners loved them. Although the pants weren't particularly comfortable, they were the first pants durable enough to withstand the miners' rugged living conditions.

• People nicknamed the pants Levi's, after their creator.

## A RIVETING EXPERIENCE

Some years later, Levi Strauss began using denim in his pants. It was still tough, but it was softer and more comfortable than canvas.

• He also found that when the denim pants were dyed blue, they wouldn't show soil and stains as much. Miners appreciated this, and Levi's became even more popular.

• Meanwhile, miners found that after heavy use, the pockets often ripped the pants at the seams.

• A Nevada tailor named Jacob Davis solved that problem for his customers by securing each pocket seam with a rivet. It worked so well, in fact, that Davis wrote to Levi Strauss offering to sell him the idea. Strauss took him up on it; copper rivets first appeared on Levis in 1873. They became a hallmark of the company's product.

## LEVI'S' MIDDLE-AGE SPREAD

Levi's were working people's pants for their first 75 years. Then, in the '30s, an advertisement for jeans ran in *Vogue* magazine. The reaction was so great that jeans became the rage. Jitterbugging teenagers started wearing them with the cuffs rolled up, and they've been fashionable ever since.

• Meanwhile, the Levi Strauss Company branched out into manufacturing other items as well as blue jeans...and by 1970 it had become the largest clothing manufacturer in the world.

# MYTH AMERICA

*Here's a myth in reverse—a tale most people believe is fictional, but is actually true.*

**THE MYTH:** Uncle Sam is a fictional character, created by cartoonists as a symbol of America's government and our "national character."

**BACKGROUND**: Ironically, while Americans routinely believe historical tales which are completely false, we're skeptical of some that are actually true. This is a case in point. For years, it was assumed there was no real Uncle Sam. Then, in 1961, a historian stumbled on proof that "Uncle Sam" had actually existed.

**THE TRUTH**: There's a detailed account of the Uncle Sam story in Charles Panati's book *Extraordinary Origins of Everyday Things*: Here are some excerpts:.

## BACKGROUND

• "Uncle Sam was Samuel Wilson. He was born in Arlington, Massachusetts, on September 13, 1766....At age 14, [he] joined the army and fought in the American Revolution."

• "With independence from Britain won, Sam moved in 1789 to Troy, New York, and opened a meat-packing company. Because of his jovial manner and fair business practices, he was affectionately known to townsfolk as Uncle Sam."

## OUR "UNCLE SAM" IS BORN

• "During the War of 1812, government troops were quartered near Troy. Sam Wilson's fair-dealing reputation won him a military contract to provide beef and pork to soldiers. To indicate that certain crates of meat produced at his warehouse were destined for military use, Sam stamped them with a large 'U.S.'—for 'United States,' though the abbreviation was not yet in the vernacular."

• "On October 1, 1812, government inspectors made a routine tour of the plant. They asked a meat packer what the ubiquitously stamped 'U.S.' stood for. The worker, himself uncertain, joked that the letters must represent the initials of his employer, Uncle Sam."

• "The error was perpetuated. Soon soldiers began referring to all military rations as bounty from Uncle Sam. Before long, they were calling all government-issued supplies property of Uncle Sam. They even saw themselves as Uncle Sam's men."

## UNCLES SAM'S WARDROBE

"The...familiar and colorful image of Uncle Sam we know today arose piecemeal, almost one item at a time, each the contribution of an illustrator."

• "The first Uncle Sam illustrations appeared in New England newspapers in 1820."

• "Solid red pants were introduced during...Jackson's presidency."

• "The...beard first appeared during Abraham Lincoln's term, inspired by the President's own beard, which set a trend at the time."

• "By the late nineteenth century, Uncle Sam was such a popular national figure that cartoonists decided he should appear more patriotically attired. They adorned his red pants with white stripes and his top hat with both stars and stripes. His costume became an embodiment of the country's flag."

• "It was Thomas Nast, the famous...cartoonist of the Civil War and Reconstruction period, who made Uncle Sam tall, thin, and hollowcheeked. Coincidentally, Nast's Uncle Sam strongly resembles drawings of the real-life Sam Wilson. But Nast's model was actually Abraham Lincoln."

•"The most famous portrayal of Uncle Sam—the one most frequently reproduced and widely recognized—was painted in this century by American artist James Montgomery Flagg. The stern-faced, stiff-armed, finger-pointing figure appeared on World War I posters captioned: 'I Want You for U.S. Army.'...Flagg's Uncle Sam, though, is not an Abe Lincoln likeness, but a self-portrait."

## A MYTH UNCOVERED

• "During these years ...the character of Uncle Sam was still only a myth. The identity of his prototype first came to light in early 1961. A historian, Thomas Gerson, discovered a May 12, 1830, issue of the *New York Gazette* newspaper in the archives of the New York Historical Society. In it, a detailed firsthand account explained how Pheodorus Bailey, postmaster of New York City, had witnessed the Uncle Sam legend take root in Troy, New York."

• Sam was officially acknowledged during JFK's administration, "by an act of the 87th Congress, which states that 'the Congress salutes 'Uncle Sam' Wilson of Troy, New York, as the progenitor of America's National symbol.' "

# THE BIRTH OF G.I. JOE

*G.I. Joe, the first successful doll for boys, seems to be going as strong today as he was the year he was introduced.*

**HIS BIRTH.** By 1963 Mattel's Barbie doll was so popular that Don Levine, creative director of the Hasbro Toy Co., suggested manufacturing a boys' version. "But instead of fashion," he explained, "we'll make it a soldier, and we'll sell extra uniforms and weapons."

• But would boys buy dolls? Hedging its bets, Hasbro decided never to call it a "doll"—only an "action soldier." And they decided to give it a scarred face to make it seem more masculine.

**HIS NAME.** Hasbro planned to make different sets of uniforms for each branch of the service (Army, Navy, Air Force, Marines) and give each a different name—Salty the Sailor, Rocky the Marine, etc. But the marketing department insisted on one name. One night, Levine happened to see the 1945 film *The Story of G.I. Joe* on television, and realized that "G.I. Joe" was perfect.

**HIS BODY.** Unlike Barbie, the boy's doll had to be fully movable. But Hasbro wasn't sure if it could be done. One day Levine was walking past an art-supply store when he noticed a display of small wooden, jointed models that artists use to draw different body positions. He bought a dozen, and they copied the construction.

**HIS LIFE.**

**1964:** Joe is introduced to the toy industry; toy store owners avoid him, sure that American parents won't buy their sons dolls. But Hasbro sticks with it, and in the first year over $30 million worth of G.I. Joe and accessories are sold—including 2 million dolls.

**1968:** With the increasing unpopularity of the war in Vietnam, parents begin to reject war toys. Joe's sales plummet to less than a third of their previous level. He's almost wiped out, but Hasbro saves the day by changing him from a soldier to an adventurer.

**1978:** *Star Wars* action figures are hot, and no one wants a G.I. Joe anymore. He's dead meat. Hasbro drops him from their line.

**1982:** Joe returns. Raised from the dead with his "G.I. Joe Team," he storms the toy market and becomes the #1 seller again. From 1982-88, he racks up over $600 million in sales. Go Joe!

# POLITICAL DOUBLE-TALK

*Every year, the Committee on Public Doublespeak of the National Council of Teachers of English "honors" public figures (or organizations) who "use language that is grossly deceptive, evasive, confusing, and self-contradictory." Here are some examples, taken from their annual news releases.*

**In 1980:**
• President Jimmy Carter declared that the failed effort to rescue American hostages in Iran was an "incomplete success."

**In 1981:**
• The Department of Agriculture decided that ketchup was a vegetable and could "be counted as one of the two vegetables required as part of the school lunch program."

**In 1982:**
• The Environmental Protection Agency prohibited its employees from using the term "acid rain." Instead, they were told to use the term "poorly buffered precipitation."
• Lewis Thurston, chief of staff for New Jersey's governor, Thomas Kean, insisted that "staff members do not have chauffeurs." Rather, they have "aides who drive."
• When it was pointed out that a commercial sponsored by the Republican National Committee misrepresented the facts, a Republican official declared: "Since when is a commercial supposed to be accurate?"

**In 1984:**
• When American troops in Lebanon were evacuated to ships offshore, Secretary of Defense Caspar Weinberger claimed this did not constitute a withdrawal. "We are not leaving Lebanon," he said. "The Marines are merely being deployed two or three miles to the west."
• Investigating an accident, the National Transportation Safety Board called an airplane crash "controlled flight into terrain."
• The Pentagon called peace "permanent pre-hostility."
• The CIA called mercenary soldiers hired to fight in Nicaragua "unilaterally controlled Latino assets."

**In 1986:**

•NASA referred to the *Challenger* astronauts' bodies as "recovered components," and their coffins as "crew transfer containers."

• Disregarding Due Process of Law, Attorney General Edwin Meese suggested that if a person is arrested, he's almost certainly guilty. "If a person is innocent of a crime," he explained, "he is not a suspect." Then he insisted to a reporter that "I...consider myself in the forefront of the civil rights movement in the country today."

• The Defense Department defined a hammer as a "manually powered fastener-driving impact device," a flashlight as an "Emergency Exit Light," and a tent as a "frame-supported tension structure."

• When a missile flew out of control and crashed, the Defense Dept. said it had merely "impacted with the ground prematurely."

**In 1987**

• Oliver North said he wasn't lying about his actions in Iran-Contra—he was "cleaning up the historical record," and creating "a different version from the facts." In discussing a false chronology of events which he helped to construct, North said he "was provided with additional input that was radically different from the truth," adding: "I assisted in furthering that version."

• The U.S. Army called killing "servicing the target."

• The U.S. Navy called a limited armed conflict "violent peace."

• South Africa's Deputy Minister for Information set the record straight, commenting that "We do not have censorship. What we have is a limitation of what newspapers can report."

**In 1988:**

• Senator Orrin Hatch of Utah explained that "Capital punishment is our society's recognition of the sanctity of human life."

• The Chrysler Corporation, on laying off 5,000 workers, said it had simply "initiated a career alternative enhancement program."

• In a report, the U.S. Department of Agriculture called cows, pigs, and chickens "grain-consuming animal units."

• General Motors announced, as it closed an entire plant, that it was making a "volume-related production schedule adjustment."

• The Massachusetts Department of Public Works called road signs "ground-mounted confirmatory route markers."

**Dieter's secret: If you eat 11 pounds of potatoes, you only gain one pound of weight.**

# BATHROOM ECOLOGY

*We all know and love the bathroom—but we still have a lot to learn about it. Believe it or not, the way we use it can affect the world around us in significant ways. Here's some valuable information from the great new book,* 50 Simple Things You Can Do to Save the Earth, *by the Earthworks Group.*

**THE TOILET**

• Each time your toilet is flushed, it uses 5 to 7 gallons of water—in fact, 40% of the pure water you use in your house is flushed down the toilet.

**Bathroom Ecology:** You can save 1-2 gallons with each flush if you put something in the tank that reduces the amount of water the tank will hold. This is called a "displacement device."

• Don't use a brick. Small pieces can break off and damage your plumbing system.

• Small juice bottles, dishwashing soap bottles, or laundry soap bottles work well. Soak off the label, fill the bottle with water, put on the cap, and put it in the tank.

• Be careful that the bottle doesn't interfere with the flushing mechanism.

• You may need to experiment with bottle sizes—different toilets need different amounts of water to flush effectively. Option: put a few stones in the bottom of the bottle to weight it down.

*Savings:* 1-2 gallons per flush.

**Results:** If the average toilet is flushed about 8 times a day, that means a savings of 8-16 gallons every day, 56-112 gallons a week, 2900-5800 gallons a year. If only 10,000 people were to put a bottle in the tank, that would equal a savings of 29 to 58 million gallons a year! And if 100,000 people did it...well, use your own imagination.

**THE SINK**

• A running faucet puts 3-5 gallons of water down the drain every minute.

• You use 10-15 gallons of water if you leave the tap running while you brush your teeth.

• If you shave with the water on, you use 10-20 gallons each time.

**Bathroom Ecology:** If you just wet and rinse your brush when you brush your teeth, you use only 1/2 gallon of water. *Savings*: Up to 9 gallons each time you brush.

• If you fill the basin when you shave, you use only 1 gallon of water. *Savings*: Up to 14 gallons each time you shave.

• Install a Low-Flow Faucet Aerator. It's a simple device that screws onto the end of your faucet and cuts the flow *in half*. But don't worry—since it mixes air in with the water, the water comes out just as fast as before.

• Low-flow faucet aerators sell for less than $4 at hardware and plumbing stores everywhere.

## THE SHOWER & BATH

• Showers account for a whopping 32% of home water use.

• A standard shower head has a flow rate of 5 to 10 gallons of water per minute. So a 5-minute shower uses around 25 gallons.

**Bathroom Ecology:** First of all, take showers instead of baths. Depending on the size of the tub, a bath will generally use around 50 gallons of water...or more—which is about double the water use of a shower.

• Try installing a "low-flow shower head." It can reduce your overall water use by 50% or more.

• With a low-flow shower head, a family of four accustomed to 5-minute showers will save nearly 22,000 gallons of water per year.

• For a family of four, the $ savings from a low-flow shower head can amount to $100 a year in water saved, plus $150 a year in energy costs-—for all that hot water you don't have to heat.

• So the cost of a low-flow shower head—generally, less than $15 at any plumbing supply or hardware store—can be recouped in a month.

## AEROSOL CANS

• At one time, aerosol cans routinely used gases called CFCs as propellants. But it was discovered that CFCs were harmful to the Earth's ozone layer, and CFCs were banned. End of problem? No. Their replacements—gases like butane and propane—are also harmful to the environment. They mix with sunlight to create smog...which contributes to the acid rain problem.

**Bathroom Ecology:** Use non-aerosols whenever possible.

# MODERN MYTHOLOGY

*These characters are as famous in our culture as Pegasus or Hercules were in Greek myths. Where did they come from?*

**THE PLAYBOY BUNNY.** When Hugh Hefner was a little boy, one of his prized possessions was "a blanket with bunnies all over it." Apparently, he never outgrew it—when he started *Playboy* magazine, he used the same bunny as his symbol.

**THE JOLLY GREEN GIANT.** In the early 1920s, the Minnesota Valley Canning Company introduced a new, large variety of peas to the American market. They called the peas "green giants," and because the law required it to protect their trademark, they put a picture of a Green Giant on the label. Where did they get the original art? They lifted it from *Grimm's Fairy Tales*. Oddly enough, the original giant was white, not green; he looked like a dwarf, not a giant; and he wasn't jolly—he was scowling. His image eventually softened, and he became such a powerful symbol that the company changed its name to the Green Giant Co.

**BETTY CROCKER.** The Washburn Crosby Company, a Minneapolis flour maker, got so many letters asking for baking advice that in 1921, they made up a character to write back to consumers. They picked the name "Betty" because it sounded "warm and friendly," and "Crocker" was picked to honor a former company director. To come up with a signature for Betty (so she could sign "her" letters), the company held a contest for its women employees. The winner—which is still used today—was submitted by a secretary.

**THE QUAKER OATS MAN.** In 1891, seven oatmeal millers combined to form the American Cereal Company. One of the seven was Quaker Mill of Ravenna, Ohio, which had trademarked the Quaker man 14 years earlier. So when the American Cereal Company changed its name to Quaker Oats in 1901, the Quaker man was revived as its symbol. The real Quakers weren't too happy about this, by the way. They tried to get Congress to prohibit manufacturers from using religions' names on their products.

**The average American eats 10 lbs. of chocolate a year.**

# FAST FOOD FACTS

*Fascinating factoids about fast food.*

There are more than 55,000 fast food restaurants in the U.S.

When Colonel Sanders started selling chicken in the late '50s, he was 65 years old. His only goal was to make $1,000 a month.

Two-thirds of the eateries in the U.S. serve fast food. And two-thirds of the people who go out to eat get their meals at fast food restaurants.

Fast food fries are usually sprayed with sugar, which gives them their brown coloring when cooked.

Domino's offers 10 different toppings for its pizza. That means you can get 3.9 million different combinations of pizzas there.

Pepsico, Pepsi's parent company, is one of the world's largest fast food restaurateurs. Among its holdings: Kentucky Fried Chicken, Taco Bell, and Pizza Hut. All serve Pepsi, of course. Pepsico also owns Frito-Lay.

Every day, approximately 46 million Americans eat at fast food restaurants.

Colonel Sanders wasn't particularly fond of Kentucky Fried Chicken after he sold it. He called the "extra-crispy" chicken "a damn fried doughball stuck on some chicken," and he said the KFC gravy was "pure wallpaper paste."

Wendy's was named after the daughter of the company's founder, Dave Thomas.

Thomas claims his square burgers are designed for grill efficiency. Others say it's "a marketing ploy." The four corners hang out over the edge of the bun, making the burger look bigger.

Regional fast food numbers:
#1. The Midwest; 30.5% of the population eats fast food at least once a week.
#2. The South; 30.4%.
#3. The West Coast; 23%.
#4. The East Coast; 16.5%.

There are 525 McDonald's eateries in Japan.

# THOREAU'S THOUGHTS

*Thoughts from Henry Thoreau, the outspoken American iconoclast of the 19th century.*

"Distrust any enterprise that requires new clothes."

"It is a characteristic of wisdom not to do desperate things."

"If Christ should appear on Earth, he would be denounced as a mistaken, misguided man, insane and crazed."

"It takes two to speak the truth—one to speak, and one to listen."

"Simplify, simplify."

"The mass of men lead lives of quiet desperation."

"What men call social virtues, good fellowship, is commonly but the virtue of pigs in a litter, which lie close together to keep each other warm."

"Blessed are they who never read a newspaper, for they shall see Nature, and through her, God."

"It is only when we forget all our learning that we begin to know."

"Do not be too moral. You may cheat yourself out of much life."

"Aim above morality. Be not simply good, be good for something."

"You cannot kill time without injuring eternity."

"The highest condition of art is artlessness."

"What man believes, God believes."

"A man is rich in proportion of the number of things he can afford to let alone."

"Business! I think there is nothing—not even crime—more opposed to poetry, to philosophy, to life itself, than this incessant business."

"There are a thousand hacking at the branches of evil to one who is striking at the root."

"Not until we are lost—in other words, not until we have lost the world—do we begin to find ourselves."

# THE TRUTH ABOUT SPIRO T. AGNEW

*You'd think that if a Vice President of the U. S. was accused of taking bribes—and had to resign because of it—we'd all remember the incident in detail. That's not the case with Spiro Agnew; his resignation in 1973 was quickly overshadowed by Watergate. But hey—let's not forget the guy. He's part of American history.*

**AGNEW'S CAREER**

• In 1962, he ran for Baltimore County Executive. He was elected, and served until 1966.

• In 1966, he ran for governor of Maryland as a Republican. As it happened, the Democrats nominated a reactionary who stood no chance of being elected. Agnew won.

• In 1968, ghetto riots hit Baltimore. "Agnew met with the leaders of the state's black moderates," reported *Time* magazine, "and before the TV cameras, dressed them down for not controlling the rioters. The incident established Agnew as a hard-liner on race and caught the eye of Richard Nixon."
The result: Nixon picked him as his running mate.

• In 1969, Agnew emerged, said *U.S. News & World Report*, as "one of the most controversial Vice Presidents the United States has seen in many a day." He was a strident moralist and a "law and order" man whose trademark was violent verbal attacks. His speeches were peppered with phrases like "parasites of passion," and "nattering nabobs of negativism."

• He was reelected with Nixon in 1972, and looked like the heir apparent to the Presidency. Then it all collapsed. In 1973, the *Wall Street Journal* learned that Agnew was under investigation in Maryland for having taken kickbacks from building contractors while he was both county executive and governor.

• On Oct. 10, 1973, after months of negotiating, Agnew resigned. He appeared in court and pled "No Contest" to income tax evasion—which the judge pointed out was equivalent to a guilty plea. It was part of an extensive plea-bargaining process that enabled him to avoid jail. The Government insisted, however, that they be allowed to make their case aginst him public.

**In 1976, the theme song from the TV show "Happy Days" hit #5 on the *Billboard* charts.**

## THE GOVERNMENT'S EVIDENCE

One of several contractors who admitted paying bribes to Agnew was named Lester Matz. Here's a part of the government's report on one of the incidents he recaled. It took place in 1969, a few months after Agnew had become V.P.:

"Matz called the Vice President's office in Washington and set up an appointment to meet with Mr. Agnew. On a piece of yellow legal-sized paper, Matz calculated the sum then 'owed' to Mr. Agnew for work received by Matz's company from the State of Maryland. He met with Mr. Agnew, showed him the calculations, and briefly reviewed them for him. He then handed him an enveloped containing approximately $10,000 in cash....Mr. Agnew placed this envelope in his desk drawer.

"Matz also told the Vice President that the company might 'owe' him more money in the future....They agreed that Matz was to call Mr. Agnew's secretary when he was ready to make the next payment and to tell her that he had more 'information' for Mr. Agnew. This was to be a signal to Mr. Agnew that Mr. Matz had more money for him.

"After this meeting, Matz returned to Baltimore and told [an associate] of the payment. He also told [him] that he was shaken by his own actions, because he had just made a payoff to the Vice President of the United States."

## AGNEW'S STATEMENT IN COURT

In a cleverly worded statement, Agnew made it seem as though he was denying the charges against him.

**For example:** The government said he took kickbacks. As Agnew explained it: "I admit that I did receive payments during the year 1967 which were not expended for political purposes, and...that contracts were awarded by State agencies in 1967 and other years to those who made such payments, and that I was aware of such awards....I stress, however, that no contracts were awarded to contractors who were not competent to perform the work, and in most instances State contracts were awarded without...payment of money by the contractor."

Careful reading of the text, however, shows that he was really saying something like: "Sure I took money, but not all the time, and only from good contractors."

**According to *Billboard*: Elvis was the #1 artist of the '50s, #2 in the '60s, & #13 in the '70s.**

# ELEMENTARY, MY DEAR STEVE

*Can you match wits with the world-famous sleuth, Leslie Boies? Here are more mysteries for you to solve. Answers are on p. 454.*

It was a dark, rainy night. Leslie Boies, the celebrated solver-of-mysteries, was driving north from Thomasville on a narrow country road in her 1957 DeSoto coupe. Her faithful companion, Steve, was at the wheel. It was a critical situation—they had to reach the little town of Montez before sunrise if they were going to save Raymond Redel, the famous chair designer, from his nefarious son-in-law.

Suddenly they came to a crossroads...and they discovered that the signpost had been knocked down. Steve hopped out to take a look. One of the arrows on the sign said "Montez, 23 miles"...But there was no way to tell which road it had been pointing to.

"We're lost, Leslie," Steve exclaimed forlornly.

"I declare, Steve, sometimes you are so dense," Leslie sighed. Then she informed Steve how to tell which road was the right one.

**How did Leslie know which way to go?**

**2.** Steve was lounging around the apartment, reading the paper. "Hey, Les," he called, "There's a town I was reading about where nobody ever shaves himself—they all let the barber do it."

Leslie walked in, practicing yo-yo tricks she planned to perform in the upcoming Detective's Follies. "Well, Steve, if that's true, then who shaves the barber?"

Steve looked puzzled. "Maybe there are two barbers in town."

Leslie shook her head. "No, my uncle lives there and I know there's only one."

Steve shrugged. "I give up."

**Who does shave the barber?**

**3.** Steve came home one day and found Leslie hard at work on a new murder case.

"Sorry to bother you, Honey, but I'm a little perplexed about something. I could use your help to get it resolved."

Leslie looked up, and focused affectionately on Steve "How can I help my faithful companion?" she offered.

"Well, on the way home today, I ran into two women."

Leslie's expression darkened. "Ye-e-s?"

"Well, they looked exactly alike, so I asked if they were twins. They said no, but they had the same mother and father, and they were born on the same day in the same year. When I asked how that was possible, they just laughed and walked away. Were they putting me on?"

Leslie smiled. "Nope. They were telling the truth."

**How was that possible?**

**4.** It was late in the evening. Renowned detective Leslie Boies was studying fingerprint technology when Inspector Gordon Van Gelder of the St. Martin's Police arrived. Steve, a lanky 6-footer she called her "pet guy," let the Inspector in.

Inspector Van Gelder knew Leslie too well to beat around the bush. "Here's the scoop," he said. "A guy named Mingo's been murdered, and I can't figure out how it was done. He and his pal, Arnie, went into Noona's Bar down on 9th St. together and each ordered a Scotch on the rocks. Arnie had to get home, so he drank his fast. But Mingo stayed and nursed his awhile, drinking it slowly. And then he just keeled over and died.

"I know the drinks and the glasses were exactly the same. No one slipped anything into Mingo's drink, and Arnie—who's fine, by the way—definitely didn't doctor Mingo's drink at all. So I can't understand how one of them could have died and the other walked away healthy. The lab report will probably tell me what happened, but I'd sure like to figure it out before then. Can you help?"

Leslie smiled indulgently, reached for a pad and a pencil, and jotted down a few words. "Arrest the bartender, Inspector," she said, handing him the paper. "This will tell you how he did it."

After Van Gelder left, Steve turned to his companion. "Well, are you going to to tell me how it happened?"

"Why, it was elementary, my dear Steve," she replied, winking at him.

**How was the murder committed?**

**When Bugs Bunny first appeared in 1935, he was called "Happy Rabbit."**

# YOGI SEZ

*Gems from Yogi Berra, Hall of Fame catcher for the New York Yankees.*

"It's deja vu all over again."

[Explaining a loss]
"We made too many wrong mistakes."

"The game's not over 'til it's over."

"You give 100% in the first half of the game, and if that isn't enough, in the second half you give what's left."

[On quotes like these]
"I really didn't say everything I said."

[Asked why he hadn't been to a favorite restauarant lately]
"It's so crowded, nobody goes there anymore."

"If people don't want to come out to the ballpark, nobody's going to stop them."

[On being honored with a "Yogi Berra Night" ]
"I want to thank all you people for making this night necessary."

[Asked, during spring training, what his hat size was]
"I don't know. I'm not in shape yet."

"You've got to be careful if you don't know where you're going, because you might not get there."

"We have deep depth."

[On seeing a Steve McQueen movie]
"He must have made that before he died."

"I never blame myself when I'm not hitting. I just blame the bat and if it keeps up, I change bats...After all, if I know it isn't my fault that I'm not hitting, how can I get mad at myself?"

[On meeting King George IV]
"Nice to meet you, King."

"Baseball is ninety percent mental. The other half is physical."

"It gets late early out there."

# NICKNAMES

*What would you call celebrities if you knew them personally? According to Carl Sifakis in* The Dictionary of Historic Nicknames, *you might know them by names like these:*

**Johann Sebastian Bach.** In his lifetime, the great composer's music was considered so boring and out of date that even his own family called him "The Old Wig."

**Humphrey Bogart.** If you were a Hollywood acquaintance, you night have known him as "Whiskey Straight."

**Claudette Colbert.** The Oscar-winning actress worried so much about the way she looked during filming that her cameramen dubbed her "The Fretting Frog."

**Christopher Columbus.** Historians call him a great explorer, but his own crew wasn't so kind. When his quest for riches led them to insect-infested tropical islands instead of gold and silver, they christened him "The Admiral of the Mosquitoes."

**Davy Crockett.** No one who knew Davy believed a word of his outrageous stories about his exploits in the wild. Acquaintances called him "The Munchausen of the West"—a name inspired by Baron von Munchausen, the popular fictional character of the late 1700s, whose trademark was absurdly exaggerated claims about his own life.

**Wyatt Earp and Bat Masterson.** The heroes of Western legends and prime-time TV shows were apparently as interested in other pursuits as they were in law and order. On various occasions they owned saloons, gambling establishments, and even a brothel or two. In their home, Dodge City, Kansas, they were known as "The Fighting Pimps."

**Dwight David Eisenhower.** In his hometown of Abilene, Kansas, the other kids knew him as "Ugly Ike."

**U.S. families fight more about money than anything else. 2nd place: kids; 3rd place: chores.**

**Billy Graham.** In his early days, the famous crusading evangelist was known as "The Preaching Windmill" because of "his exuberant arm flailing."

**Sam Houston.** The most celebrated hero in Texas' fight for independence from Mexico during the 1830s is known today as "The Father of Texas." But Indians who knew him called him "Big Drunk."

**Robert F. Kennedy.** America remembers him as RFK, or Bobby. Lyndon Johnson always called him "The Little Shit."

**Spiro T. Agnew.** Nixon's vice president was known by adversaries as "Spiro T. Eggplant."

**Abraham Lincoln.** "Honest Abe's" nickname didn't come from politics—it came from his youthful efforts as "a judge and referee at cockfights."

**Richard Nixon.** Nicknames haven't been kind to the ex-prez. When he was in college, he was so humorless that classmates called him "Gloomy Gus." And he spent so much time studying that he was dubbed "Iron Butt." When he ran for Congress in 1950, he earned the title "Tricky Dick."

**Leo Tolstoy.** The author of *War and Peace* is considered one of the greatest novelists in history. But people who knew him as a child—even his own family and close friends—called the troubled youth "Crybaby Leo."

**Henri de Toulouse-Lautrec.** The famous French painter suffered through childhood accidents that gave him the appearance of a dwarf—but not in every way. When he lived in a brothel, the prostitutes, amused by the contrast in size between "his large male member" and the rest of his body, dubbed him "the Teapot."

**Warren G. Harding.** Probably should have been called "The Rodney Dangerfield of Politics," but in 1920 when he was elected president, Rodney wasn't around yet. Instead, he was called "Everybody's Second Choice," because he was nominated as a compromise candidate in a "smoke-filled room."

**Last roundup: In 1962 "Chief," the last U.S. Cavalry horse, was retired.**

# MT. RUSHMORE

*Here's Charles Panati's version of how the four big faces got there, from* Extraordinary Origins of Everyday Things.

**HOW IT GOT ITS NAME.**

"The full story of the origin of Mount Rushmore begins 60 million years ago, when pressures deep within the earth pushed up layers of rock. The forces created an elongated granite-and-limestone dome towering several thousand feet above the Dakota prairie lands. The first sculpting of the mountain was done by nature. The erosive forces of wind and water fashioned one particularly protuberant peak, which was unnamed until 1885.

"That year, a New York attorney, Charles E. Rushmore, was surveying the mountain range on horseback with a guide. Rushmore inquired about the impressive peak's name, and the guide, ribbing the city lawyer, answered, 'Hell, it never had a name. But from now on we'll call the damn thing Rushmore.' The label stuck. And later, with a gift of five thousand dollars, Charles Rushmore became one of the earliest contributors to the presidential memorial."

**THE MEMORIAL**

"The idea to transform a gigantic mountaintop into a colossus of human figures sprang from the mind of a South Dakota historian, Doane Robinson. In 1923, Robinson presented to the state his plan to simultaneously increase South Dakota's tourism, strengthen its economy, and immortalize three 'romantic western heroes.' [Ed. note: The original plan was to sculpt the heads of Kit Carson, Jim Bridger, and John Colter.] A commission then sought the skills of renowned sculptor John Gutzon de la Mothe Borglum, an authority on colossi.

"Idaho born, Borglum started as a painter, then switched to sculpture, and his fame grew in proportion to the size of his works. The year Doane Robinson conceived the idea for a Mount Rushmore memorial, Borglum accepted a commission from the United Daughters of the Confederacy to carve a head of General Robert E. Lee on Stone Mountain in Georgia.

"Mount Rushmore, though, beckoned with the greater challenge. Borglum opposed sculpting Western heroes. The notion was provincial, he argued. A colossus should capture prominent figures. In a letter dated August 14, 1925, Borglum proposed the faces of four influential American presidents."

**THE SCULPTURE.**

"Construction on the 6,200-foot-high wilderness peak was fraught with dangers. And the mountain itself was inaccessible except by foot or horseback, which necessitated countless climbs to lug up drills and scaffolding. But for Borglum, two features made the remote Rushmore peak ideal. The rocks faced southeast, ensuring maximum sunlight for construction, and later for viewing. And the peak's inaccessibility would protect the monument from vandals.

"Bitter winters, compounded by a chronic shortage of funds, continually threatened to terminate construction. Weathered surface rock had to be blasted away to expose suitably firm stone for sculpting. The chin of George Washington, for instance, was begun thirty feet back from the original mountain surface, and Theodore Roosevelt's forehead was undertaken only after 120 feet of surface rock were peeled away.

"Borglum worked from a scale model. Critical 'points' were measured on the model, then transferred to the mountain to indicate the depth of rock to be removed point by point.

"In 1941, fourteen years after construction began—and at a total cost of $990,000—a new world wonder was unveiled. There stood George Washington, whom Borglum selected because he was 'Father of the Nation'; Abraham Lincoln, 'Preserver of the Union'; Thomas Jefferson, 'The Expansionist'; and Theodore Roosevelt, 'Protector of the Working Man.'

"The figures measure sixty feet from chin to top of head. Each nose is twenty feet long, each mouth eighteen feet wide, and the eyes are eleven feet across. 'A monument's dimensions,' Borglum believed, 'should be determined by the importance to civilization of the events commemorated.'

"Gutzon Borglum died on March 6, 1941, aged 74. The monument was essentially completed. His son, also a sculptor, added the finishing touches."

**From *Roadside America*:** "The Black Hills can get foggy....Many a tourist Dad has been known to blow his top after driving umpteen miles...only to find he can't see those giant faces, goddammit."

# THE BIRTH OF KLEENEX

*Feel a sneeze coming on? If you're like most Americans, you reach for a kleenex without even thinking about it. But that wasn't always true. In fact, not so long ago there was no such thing. Here's how they were invented.*

## MILITARY SUPPLIES

The Kimberly-Clark Corporation originally designed the product that evolved into Kleenex tissues for *military* use.

• It started in 1914. World War I was being fought in Europe, and the cotton soldiers needed for bandages was starting to run out.

• So Kimberly-Clark devised a product called Cellucotton—an absorbent, soft paper that could be used to dress wounds.

• It was so effective that the army looked for other uses. And they found one: They used it as an air filter for soldiers' gas masks.

## PEACETIME PROBLEM

Kimberly-Clark got too enthusiastic about their new material and overproduced it. After the war, they had warehouses full of Cellucotton left over; they *had* to find a new way to sell the stuff.

• Their clever solution: They marketed it as a modern women's tool for cleaning off makeup, and a "sanitary cold cream remover."

• Calling it Kleenex Kerchiefs, they hired movie stars to endorse it as a secret path to glamour. It was a big success.

## SURPRISE SOLUTION

But Americans found another use for the product. Kimberly-Clark was inundated with letters that informed them the Kleenex Kerchiefs were great for nose-blowing.

•Men, in particular, wanted to know why Kleenex had to be a woman's product. And women griped that men were stealing their Kleenex to sneeze into.

• During the 1920s, Kimberly-Clark introduced a pop-up box that always left one tissue sticking out of the box, waiting to be grabbed.

• But the question remained—were people buying Kleenex as a cold cream remover, or a nose-blower? A survey showed that 60% of the people used it as the latter. So that's what K-C emphasized, and that's how we think of it today.

# ROCK ME, SUE ME

*It's not all peace and love in the rock 'n' roll world. It's big bucks... and as the stakes get higher, the lawsuits get bigger. Here are a few.*

**GHOSTBUSTERS**

The "Ghostbusters" theme song, by Ray Parker, Jr. sounded a lot like Huey Lewis and the News' "I Want a New Drug." And sure enough, it turns out that the film's producers originally wanted Lewis, himself, to pen their theme song. When he refused, they hired Parker and requested something similar to Lewis's hit. Lewis sued for copyright infringement, and the case was settled out of court.

**HEY, HEY, HEY**

The Beatles' version of "Kansas City" was written by Jerry Leiber and Mike Stoller—or at least that's the way the song was credited when it came out in 1964. But it turned out the Beatles had recorded a medley of "Kansas City" and "Hey, Hey, Hey," a Little Richard composition that originally appeared on the B-side of his 1956 hit "Good Golly Miss Molly." It took Little Richard about 20 years to figure out what had happened, but when he did—and took it to court—it paid off in big numbers: $500,000.

**MY SWEET LORD**

George Harrison's "My Sweet Lord" casually borrowed the melody of the Chiffons' 1963 hit "He's So Fine," written by Ronald Mack. One strange aspect of the case: Ronald Mack was dead by the time his estate pressed charges and won. Another: Although Harrison had to pay, he was absolved of plagiarism. It was, according to the judge, "unconscious plagiarism."

**STAIRWAY TO GILLIGAN'S ISLAND**

Led Zeppelin, the biggest-selling band of the 1970s, were known among music experts for stealing songs from old blues artists and then crediting themselves. Their first hit, "Whole Lotta Love," was virtually a note-for-note recreation of Willie Dixon's "I Need Love." And "How Much More" was a direct lift of Howling Wolf's "Killing Floor."

But when someone messed with one of *their* tunes, it was time for legal action. A San Francisco-based band called Roger and The Goosebumps recorded a hilarious parody of the group's "Stairway to Heaven," matching Zep's melody with the lyrics of the theme song to "Gilligan's Island." Led Zepplin quickly had its lawyers block the song's release."It was a real blow," said one of the Goosebumps later. "We were getting airplay all over the country—I think we had a hit on our hands." Later, the same band did an equally funny take-off of the Beatles' "Fool on the Hill," called "Fudd on the Hill," sung in an Elmer Fudd voice. Thankfully, the Beatles didn't sue.

**SURFIN' USA**

The Beach Boys' big hit of 1963 sounded vaguely familiar to Chuck Berry...and it should have; he wrote the melody. Brian Wilson had appropriated it from Berry's 1958 tune, "Sweet Little Sixteen." Berry's publisher sued on his behalf, and won. The result: Berry owns 100% of the rights to both his own tune and Wilson's.

**OLD MAN DOWN THE ROAD**

The strangest case of an artist being sued for copyright infringement must be the one involvng John Fogerty's 1984 comeback hit, "The Old Man Down The Road."

He was sued for copying himself.

The story: "Old Man Down the Road" bore more than a little resemblence to "Run Through the Jungle," a tune Fogarty had previously written and recorded with Creedence Clearwater Revival, The problem: Fogarty no longer owned the rights to his original song, and there was bad blood between him and Saul Zaentz, the man who did.

Zaentz owned Fantasy Records, the label Creedence Clearwater Revival had recorded on. He and Fogerty had been embroiled in a long, bitter lawsuit over royalties that Creedence said were still owed to them. And when Fogerty included a tune on his solo album (the same one with "Old Man" on it) called "Zaentz Can't Dance," Saul sued him for defamation of character. Fogerty had to change it to "Vanz Can't Dance."

The highlight of the "Old Man" case was Fogerty's appearance in court, where he demonstrated to the jury how he composes tunes. They must have enjoyed it; he won.

**In high school, Robin Williams was voted "Least Likely to Succeed."**

# LOST IN SPACE

*This show still has a cult following; Why? Don't ask us. We've never even been able to figure out why the Robinsons didn't just push that whining SOB Dr. Smith out the airlock and forget him.*

## HOW IT STARTED

After producing everything from documentaries to comedies in the '50s, filmmaker Irwin Allen discovered kids' science fiction/adventure films in the '60s. He made *The Lost World* (1960), *Voyage to the Bottom of the Sea* (1961), and Jules Verne's *Five Weeks In a Balloon* (1963). All were successful. But special-effects films are hard to finance, so Allen decided to move to TV.

His first effort was a popular 1964 adaptation of *Voyage to the Bottom of the Sea.* His second was to be a live-action version of a comic book called *Space Family Robinson* (Swiss Family Robinson in space). But while Allen was still making the 2-hour pilot in 1964, Walt Disney, who owned the rights to the name, decided that Allen couldn't use it. So Allen changed it to "Lost In Space."

It was supposed to be a serious space adventure show, like "Star Trek" (no kidding), but when Allen showed it to CBS executives for the first time, he got a rude shock. One of the men who was there that day recalls: "Irwin, who has absolutely no sense of humor, thought he was making a very serious program. But in the viewing room, the network executives who were watching the pilot were absolutely hysterical, laughing . . . Irwin got furious and wanted to stop the showing...But his assistant kicked him under the table and whispered, 'Never mind. They love it.' " And they did. CBS bought the show and ran it for 3 years, from 1965 to 1968. Allen went on to make films like *The Poseidon Adventure* and *Towering Inferno*, for which he is known as "The Master of Disaster."

## INSIDE FACTS

### You Bet Your Life

The man who financed "Lost In Space" was "the one, the only... GROUCHO!" Marx and Irwin Allen were good friends. Groucho included a photo of himself and Allen in his book, *The Groucho-Phile*. The caption: "I taught him everything he knows about 'disaster' pictures. This picture was taken either at his wedding or mine."

**Saved By the Mail**
Dr. Smith (Jonathan Harris) was originally meant to be killed off after 6 weeks. In fact, he was such a "minor" character that his contact stated that he couldn't be billed higher than 7th in the credits! But fan mail was overwhelmingly in favor of keeping him.

**Adventures of Zorro**
Dr. Smith's popularity was particularly frustrating to Guy Williams (John Robinson), who—guaranteed top billing—assumed he'd be the star. Instead, he rarely got *any* important dialogue. "I must be getting paid more per word than Lawrence Olivier," he groused.

**Special Effects**
Irwin Allen was notoriously cheap. For example, the dome on the frog alien's space ship in the episode "The Golden Man" was actually a giant champagne glass from a Marilyn Monroe film, salvaged by the director from the 20th Century Fox junk pile. Originally, the space ship in the episode was budgeted at $10,000. But when Allen was told the cost, he hit the roof. "Let the frog walk," he screamed. So the director had to scrounge and get it for free.

**TV Robotics**
• The Robot (no name) bore a striking resemblance to Robby, the famous robot from the film *Forbidden Planet* (1956). No coincidence. He was created by Bob Kinoshita, Robby's co-designer.
• Lights flashed on the robot in synchronization with his voice. An electronic innovation? No. A little actor was inside, pressing a telegraph key in the left claw as he spoke.
• The actor in the robot saw out via the robot's plastic collar. Viewers couldn't see him in the shell, because he was in black-face.

**Phony Numbers**
The Robinsons traveled on planet surfaces in a vehicle with the official-looking call numbers "277-2211 IA" painted on it. Actually, the 7 digits are 20th-Century Fox's phone number. And the IA is producer Irwin Allen's initials.

**Surprise!**
Every member of the cast learned the show was cancelled by reading about it in the newspapers.

**The opposite sides of a dice cube always add up to 7.**

# NOTABLE & QUOTABLE

*Memorable comments from memorable personalities.*

## JOHN WAYNE

• "Westerns are closer to art than anything else in the motion picture business."

• "I don't feel we did wrong in taking this great country away from [the Indians]. There were great numbers of people who needed new land and the Indians were selfishly trying to keep it for themselves."

• [About liberated women] "They have a right to work wherever they want to—as long as they have dinner ready when you get home."

• "There's been no top authority saying what marijuana does to you. I really don't know that much about it. I tried it once, but it didn't do anything to me."

## J. EDGAR HOOVER

• "Justice is incidental to law and order."

• "We are a fact-gathering organization only. We don't clear anybody. We don't condemn anybody. Just the minute the F.B.I. begins making recommendations on what should be done with its information, it becomes a Gestapo."

## AL CAPONE

• "Don't get the idea that I'm one of those goddamn radicals. Don't get the idea that I'm knocking the American system."

• "Vote early and vote often."

• "When I sell liquor, it's called bootlegging; when my patrons serve it on silver trays on Lake Shore Drive, it's called hospitality."

• "I'm like any other man. All I do is supply a demand."

• "[Communism] is knocking at our gates, and we can't afford to let it in....We must keep America whole and safe and unspoiled. We must keep the worker away from Red literature and Red ruses; we must see that his mind remains healthy."

**The leaves of an adult oak tree give off 7 tons of water every day.**

# DINER LORE

*As Richard Gutman said in* American Diner: *"One nice thing about a diner is that anyone who shares American values and American ways of doing things can function there."*

## ORIGIN OF THE LUNCHWAGON

The year was 1872.

The city was Providence, Rhode Island.

Thousands of late-night factory workers had a problem—every restaurant in town closed promptly at 8:00 p.m., and they couldn't get anything to eat when their shifts let out.

The solution was provided by an enterprising pushcart peddler named Walter Scott. He outfitted a horsedrawn wagon with a stove and storage space and drove around the streets selling sandwiches, boiled eggs, and coffee for a nickel. The wagon only provided shelter for Scott—his customers had to stand out on the street. But it was a welcome service and an instant success. Before long, "after hours lunchwagons" were operating all over town.

## INDOOR SEATING

Fifteen years later, an enterprising worker named Sam Jones introduced the first custom-made, walk-in lunchwagon—complete with a kitchen, a counter, and stools. It seated four to five people, and it, was immediately successful. Walk-in lunchwagons became popular all over the Northeast; soon they were being made in factories.

## THE DINER EVOLVES

By 1910 dozens of lunchwagons—many of them rundown eyesores—were rumbling around the streets of most New England cities. Although they were only allowed to operate between dusk and dawn, many were staying on the streets until noon—which outraged many "respectable" citizens. Cities began cracking down on them, forcing the wagons off the streets by 10:00 A.M.

Lunchcart owners didn't like the idea of closing up when there was plenty of business around, so they came up with a way to skirt the rules—they just picked a good site where they could set up their lunchcarts permanently. Then they took off the wheels and

**The Western hero most often portrayed in films: Buffalo Bill. 2nd place: Billy the Kid.**

hooked up to power, water, and gas lines and expanded their kitchens. Now they were officially called "street cafes," and they could operate all day and all night. They were the original 24-hour diners.

## DINER FACTS

• The term *diner* originated with manufacturer Patrick J. Tierney, who called his prefab early-1900s restaurants "dining cars." Salesmen shortened them to "diners."
• Tierney was proud that, in 1911, his company built the first diner with an indoor toilet.
• Contrary to popular belief, diners were never converted from railroad dining cars. Rather, in the late '30s manufacturers were so impressed by the streamlined look of modern locomotives that they imitated the style. They called these diners "Streamliners."
• Diners reflect technological advances. When, in the late '30s, materials like stainless steel, Naugahyde, and Formica became available, diner-makers put them to use. So what we call a "classic" diner was actually "state of the art" in its time.
• At their peak in the late '40s, there were some 7,000 diners. Today there are only 2,000.

## DINER DIALOGUE (from the film, *Five Easy Pieces*)

**Jack Nicholson:** "I'd like a plain omelette—no potatoes on the plate—a cup of coffee, and a side order of wheat toast."
**Waitress:** "I'm sorry, we don't have any side orders here."
**Nicholson:** "No side orders? You've got bread and a toaster of some kind?"
**Waitress:** "I don't make the rules."
**Nicholson:** "Okay, I'll make it as easy for you as I can. I'd like an omelette—plain—a chicken salad sandwich on wheat toast—no mayonnaise, no butter, no lettuce, and a cup of coffee."
**Waitress:** "A Number Two, chicken salad sandwich—no butter, no mayo, no lettuce, and a cup of coffee. Anything else?"
**Nicholson:** "Yeah. Now all you have to do is hold the chicken, bring me the toast, give me a check for the chicken salad sandwich, and you haven't broken any rules."
**Waitress:** "You want me to hold the chicken, huh?"
**Nicholson:** "I want you to hold it between your knees."

**Examining one strand of your hair can enable a scientist to tell your sex, age, and race.**

# DINER LINGO

*Diner waitresses and short order cooks have a language all their own—a sort of restaurant jazz, with clever variations on standard menu themes. Here's a little collection of some of the best.*

**Burn the British:** Gimme an English muffin
**Draw one in the Dark:** A black coffee
**Balloon Juice:** Seltzer
**An M.D.:** A Dr. Pepper
**Hold the hail:** No ice
**Wreck 'em:** Scrambled eggs
**Sweep the kitchen:** A plate of hash
**Adam and Eve on a raft:** Two poached eggs on toast
**A spot with a twist:** A cup of tea with lemon
**Bossy in a Bowl:** Beef stew
**A Blonde with Sand:** Coffee with cream and sugar
**Break It and Shake It:** Add an egg to a drink
**A Stack of Vermont:** Pancakes with maple syrup.
**Million on a Platter:** A plate of baked beans
**A White Cow:** A vanilla milkshake
**Let it Walk:** It's to go
**Noah's Boy on Bread:** A ham sandwich
**A Murphy:** A potato
**Nervous Pudding:** Jello
**Paint a Bow-wow Red:** Gimme a hot dog with ketchup
**Eve with a lid:** A piece of apple pie
**Burn one, take it through the garden, and pin a rose on it:** Gimme a burger with lettuce and onion
**Mike and Ike:** Salt and pepper shakers
**Angels on Horseback:** Oysters rolled in bacon and placed on toast
**Cow Paste:** Butter
**Lighthouse:** Bottle of ketchup
**Hounds on an Island:** Franks and beans
**Frog Sticks:** French fries
**Houseboat:** A banana split
**Wax:** American cheese
**Fry Two, let the sun shine:** 2 fried eggs with unbroken yolks
**Throw it in the Mud:** Add chocolate syrup
**Hug One:** Squeeze a glass of orange juice
**Life Preservers:** Doughnuts
**Put out the lights and cry:** An order of liver and onions
**One from the Alps:** A Swiss cheese sandwich
**Put a Hat on It:** Add ice cream
**A Splash of Red Noise:** A bowl of tomato soup

**Americans watch more TV in January and February than any other time of year.**

# WILL POWER

*A will is the last chance the deceased has to drive the living nuts. Here are a few true-life examples of slightly offbeat wills.*

**THE DECEASED:** Ms. Eleanor Ritchey, the unmarried granddaughter of the founder of Quaker State Oil (Philip John Bayer).

**THE BEQUEST:** Ms. Ritchey died in 1968, with an estate worth around $12 million. According to Scott Bieber in *Trusts and Estates* magazine: "Under her will, she left over 1,700 pairs of shoes and 1,200 boxes of stationery to the Salvation Army. The rest of her estate went to the dogs." Real dogs, he means—a pack of 150 strays that Ritchey had adopted as pets. The will set up a trust that permitted the mutts to live in the lap of luxury for up to 20 years. At the end of that period—or on the death of the last of the dogs, whichever came first—the remainder of the estate went to Auburn University.

**WHAT HAPPENED:** In 1984, Musketeer, the richest dog in America and the last of the original 150, went to that great kennel in the sky. Auburn got its money.

**THE DECEASED**: Patrick Henry, American patriot.

**THE BEQUEST:** Everything he owned was left to his wife—as long as she never married again. If she did, she forfeited the whole thing. "It would make me unhappy," he explained, "to feel I have worked all my life only to support another man's wife!"

**WHAT HAPPENED:** She remarried anyway.

**THE DECEASED:** Charles Millar, famed Canadian lawyer.

**THE BEQUEST:** According to Thomas Bedell in *Having the Last Word*, his will "consisted mainly of practical jokes. He willed shares in the Ontario Jockey Club to 2 crusaders against gambling. To 3 men who hated one another, he left equal shares of the same house. And part of his estate was promised to the Toronto mother giving birth to the largest number of children in the decade after his birth."

**WHAT HAPPENED:** The public either loved or hated it. News-

**If you're an average American, you're carrying $27.**

papers called it "the Stork Derby." Moralists tried to invalidate the will on the grounds that it promoted promiscuity. But in the end, a half a million dollars was split between a quartet of women who had each had 9 kids in the 10 ensuing years.

**THE DECEASED:** Robert Louis Stevenson, author of *Treasure Island*, etc.
**THE BEQUEST:** In addition to his normal earthly goods, Stevenson tried to leave his birthday. He willed it to a good friend who'd complained that since she was born on Christmas, she never got to have a real birthday celebration.

**THE DECEASED:** Felipe Segrandez, the sole survivor of the wreck of the Spanish ship *Santa Cecilia*. At the time he made out his will, he was a castaway on an island somewhere west of Africa.
**THE BEQUEST:** His will divided his estate between his relatives. It was written in his own blood, sealed in a bottle, and tossed into the ocean.
**WHAT HAPPENED:** The bottle was found on a South African beach by a prospector and was forwarded to Spanish authorities. Unfortunately, they couldn't execute the will; it was found in 1934, but had been written 178 years earlier, in 1756.

**THE DECEASED:** An attorney in France.
**THE BEQUEST:** $10,000 to "a local madhouse." The gentleman declared that "it was simply an act of restitution to his clients."

**THE DECEASED:** An Australian named Francis R. Lord.
**THE BEQUEST:** One shilling to his wife "for tram fare so she can go somewhere and drown herself."
**WHAT HAPPENED:** The inheritance was never claimed.

**THE DECEASED:** Sandra West, wealthy 37-year-old Beverly Hills socialite.
**THE BEQUEST:** Her estate was worth about $3 million, most of which she left to her brother—provided he made sure she was buried "in my lace nightgown and my Ferrari, with the seat slanted comfortably."

**WHAT HAPPENED:** That's how they buried her, surrounding the Ferrari with concrete so no one would be tempted to dig it up and drive it away.

**THE DECEASED:** A woman in Cherokee County, North Carolina.
**THE BEQUEST:** She left her entire estate to God.
**WHAT HAPPENED:** The court instructed the county sheriff to find the beneficiary. A few days later, the sheriff returned and submitted his report: "After due and diligent search, God cannot be found in this county."

**THE DECEASED:** Edgar Bergen, famed ventriloquist.
**THE BEQUEST:** $10,000 to the Actor's Fund of America—so they could take care of his dummy, Charlie McCarthy, and put him in a show once a year.
**WHAT HAPPENED:** They went along with it.

**THE DECEASED:** A rich, unmarried New Yorker. Died: 1880.
**THE BEQUEST:** He left everything to his nephews and nieces, with the exception of 71 pairs of pants. He wrote: "I enjoin my executors to hold a public sale at which these trousers shall be sold to the highest bidder, and the proceeds distributed to the poor. No one purchaser is to buy more than one pair."
**WHAT HAPPENED:** The auction took place. Each person who bought a pair of pants, upon examining their purchase, discovered "a $1,000 bill sewn into a pocket."

**THE DECEASED:** A merchant.
**THE BEQUEST:** Quoted in *To Will or Not to Will:* "My overdraft at the bank goes to my wife—she can explain it. My car goes to my son—he will have to go to work to keep up the payments....I want six of my creditors for pallbearers—they have carried me so long they might as well finish the job."

# ONE GOOD YAWN DESERVES ANOTHER

*Wonder why you cover your mouth when you yawn? Charles Panati did, and here's what he said about it in his book,* Extraordinary Origins of Everyday Things.

**THE POLITE YAWN**

"Today, covering the mouth when yawning is considered an essential of good manners. But the original custom stemmed not from politeness but from fear—a fear that in one giant exhalation the soul, and life itself, might depart the body. A hand to the lips held back the life force."

**THE DEADLY YAWN**

"Ancient man had accurately observed (though incorrectly interpreted) that a newborn, struggling to survive, yawns shortly after birth (a reflexive response to draw additional oxygen into the lungs). With infant mortality extraordinarily high, early physicians, at a loss to account for frequent deaths, blamed the yawn. The helpless baby simply could not cover its mouth with a protective hand. Roman physicians actually recommended that a mother be particularly vigilant during the early months of life and cover any of her newborn's yawns."

**THE CONTAGIOUS YAWN**

"Today it is also considered good manners when yawning to turn one's head. But courtesy had nothing to do with the origin of the custom, nor with the apology that follows a yawn. Ancient man had also accurately observed that a yawn is contagious to witnesses. Thus, if a yawn was dangerous to a yawner, this danger could be 'caught' by others, like the Plague. The apology was for exposing friends to mortal danger."

**WHAT GOES HERE?**

Since we've got a space at the bottom of the page, we'll throw in a recommendation for a favorite bathroom book: *Rules of Thumb*, by Tom Parker. Includes 896 bite-size, bizarre rules for living, about everything from ostrich eggs to "Getting Emotionally Involved."

**Genghis Khan is said to have killed over a million people in *one hour* in the year 1221.**

# THE SHOWER SCENE

*Facts about one of the most chilling scenes in movie history.*

Alfred Hitchcock has provided filmgoers with some of the cinema's most thrilling moments, but most movie historians agree that in terms of pure shock value, the shower scene in *Psycho* tops the list.

It is probably the most famous single scene in film history.

It's admired for its masterful editing (approximately 65 edits in 45 seconds), its skillful use of music (Bernard Herrman's screeching violins) and its shocking conclusion, where the movie's apparent protagonist (played by Janet Leigh) is suddenly butchered to death in a shower.

• Although there's practically no graphic violence in the scene, it has literally scared some people out of taking showers—including Janet Leigh, who says in her autobiography that *she* refuses to take them anymore.

• Amazingly, Hitchcock later claimed he had made the film as a *joke*.

• The screenplay was adapted from Robert Bloch's novel of the same name in 1959 (by Joseph Stefano, who later created TV's "The Outer Limits"), and was shot on the set of the "Alfred Hitchcock Presents" television series.

**FACTS:**

Since *Psycho*'s release in 1960, film students have dissected every frame of film in the shower scene. Among the interesting details:

• It took seven days to shoot the 45-second scene.

• By far, the most difficult shot was of Marion Crane's (Janet Leigh's) open-eyed stare as she lay dead outside the shower. At first Hitchcock attempted to get special contact lenses for Leigh, but time constraints prevented it. Instead, Hitchcock used an ingenious three-shot method: (1) a close-up of Leigh's eye from a still photograph, which cuts away to (2) a shower spigot and running water and then back to "live action" of (3) Leigh staring, wide-eyed, on the bathroom floor . . . trying desperately not to blink. It is one of the film's many legends that if you look closely, you can see Leigh blink (Mrs. Hitchcock said she saw it).

• Another legend has it that a stand-in model was used for Leigh—but she denies that. Leigh says the only model used was when her body is carried out in a sheet by police in a later scene.

• The blood washing down the drain was really chocolate sauce.

• Only one shot in the entire shower scene montage shows a knife entering the body and no blood is seen in the shot.

• Some shots use as little as eight frames of film (i.e., one-third of a second).

• Anthony Perkins (as Norman Bates) did not actually act in the scene. He was on Broadway at the time of the shooting, starring in a play; a stand-in filled in as "Mom."

• Mixed-up priorities: According to Hitchcock, studio executives were more concerned about having a toilet flushing onscreen than they were about the implicit violence.

• Janet Leigh refused to let her daughter (actress Jamie Lee Curtis) watch the movie as a child when it appeared on TV.

• Hitchcock got the movie past censors by first submitting a script with many more horrible scenes, knowing that by allowing them to be cut he would get more leverage on the others.

## JANET LEIGH ON THE SHOWER SCENE:

"What I was to wear in the shower scene gave the wardrobe supervisor migraines. I had to appear nude, without being nude. She and I pored over striptease magazines, hoping one of their costumes would be the answer. . . . There was an impressive display of pinwheels, feathers, sequins, etc., but nothing suitable for our needs. Finally, the supervisor came up with a simple solution: flesh-colored moleskin. . . . So each morning for seven shooting days and seventy-one setups, we covered my private parts, and we were in business."

"For sundry reasons, we had to do [the scene] over and over. At long last a take was near completion without a mishap. Abruptly I felt something strange happening around my breasts. The steam from the hot water had melted the adhesive on the moleskin, and I sensed the napped cotton fabric peeling away from my skin. What to do?...I opted for immodesty...and made the correct judgment. That was the printed take."

# A FOOD IS BORN

*These foods are fairly common, but you've probably never wondered where they came from. Here are the answers anyway.*

**FROZEN CONCENTRATED ORANGE JUICE.** During World War II, the U.S. government wanted an easy-to-carry, powdered orange juice for soldiers in the field. They commissioned the Minute Maid Company to develop it, but the effort only succeeded a few weeks before the war ended—so the powder was never produced. However, as a by-product of their research, Minute Maid discovered that o.j. could be concentrated and frozen. When the war was over, they took advantage of the discovery and marketed it.

**McDONALD'S FILET-O-FISH SANDWICH.** The first successful non-burger "entree" in McDonald's history was a concession to organized religion. In the early '60s, the McDonald's in Cincinnati lost sales every Friday because the large Catholic population couldn't eat meat—and McDonald's had nothing else to offer. The owner asked Mac chairman Ray Kroc for permission to expand the menu. Kroc resisted at first ("Let 'em eat burgers, like everyone else!"), but ultimately supported research into selling a fish sandwich. McDonald's researchers decided to use codfish, but didn't call it that for two reasons: One, they were legally allowed to call it the much classier "North Atlantic Whitefish," and two, Kroc's childhood memories of cod liver oil were too unpleasant. After successful test-marketing, the fish sandwich went on the McDonald's menu permanently in 1963.

**LIFESAVERS.** In 1912 a Cleveland candymaker named Clarence Crane decided to make a mint to sell in the summer. Until then, most mints were imported from Europe; Crane figured he could cut the price by making them in the U.S. He had the candy manufactured by a pill-maker—who discovered that his machinery would only work if it punched a hole in the middle of each candy. So Crane cleverly called the mints LifeSavers.

**There are no living relatives to William Shakespeare.**

**A-1 STEAK SAUCE.** The Royal Chef for England's King George IV (1820-1830) whipped up this sauce as a treat for His Majesty, a devoted epicure. How did George like it? "Absolutely A-1," he reputedly declared. The sauce became so popular around the Court that when the chef—a gentleman named Brand—retired from his position, he started a company specifically to manufacture it. After World War I, an American company licensed it and distributed it in the States. It's still the biggest-selling sauce of its kind.

**CAESAR SALAD.** The name of this unique salad doesn't refer to the Roman conqueror, but to the man who created it—a Tijuana restaurateur named Caesar Cardini. Here's one account of its origin: "Cardini started several restaurants in Tijuana, Mexico in the early '20s. He devised the salad in 1924 during the Fourth of July weekend at Caesar's Place. He served it as finger food, arranging the garlic-scented lettuce leaves on platters. Later, he shredded the leaves into bite-sized pieces. The salad became a hit with the Hollywood movie stars who visited Tijuana, and soon was a specialty of such prestigious restauants as Chasen's and Romanoff's."

**MAXWELL HOUSE COFFEE.** In the 1880s, a young Tennessean named Joel Cheek became obsessed with the idea of roasting the perfect blend of coffee. After years of experiments, he came up with the blend he liked. Then, in 1892, he persuaded the owners of Nashville's ritzy Maxwell House Hotel to serve it exclusively. Cheek was so encouraged by the clientele's enthusiastic response to the coffee that he named it after the hotel.

**BISQUICK.** The first instant biscuit mix was inspired by a train ride. In 1930, an executive of General Mills was traveling by train and ordered some biscuits in the dining car. He expected them to be cold and stale, since it was long past the usual dinner hour. But instead, they were hot and fresh—and they arrived almost instantly. He inquired how this was possible, and was told that the bread dough had been mixed in advance and stored in the refrigerator. The executive thought it was a great idea. He worked with General Mills chemists and created a similar product—but one that could be kept in a box, unrefrigerated. It was so popular when it was introduced in the '30s that it revolutionized American baking habits.

**The sound of E.T. walking was made by someone squishing her hands in Jello.**

# PRIME-TIME PROVERBS

*More words of wisdom from* Prime Time Proverbs, *by Jack Mingo and John Javna.*

**ON EXISTENCE**
"I reek, therefore I am."
**—Diane Chambers,**
***Cheers***

"There's more to life than sitting around in the sun in your underwear playing the clarinet."
**—Lt. Larry Casey,**
***Baa Baa Black Sheep***

**ON THE GOOD LIFE**
"I'm a lucky guy—I mean, life has been good to me. I've got a good job, good health, a good wife, and a fantastic barber."
**—Ted Baxter,**
***The Mary Tyler Moore Show***

**ON THE LEGAL SYSTEM**
"This is America. You can't make a horse testify against himself."
**—Mr. Ed,**
***Mr. Ed***

**Venus Flytrap:** "I'm not gonna sit here and let her lie!"
**Lawyer:** "You have to. This is a court of law."
***—WKRP in Cincinnati***

**ON INDIVIDUALITY**
**Frank Burns:** "Don't you understand? The man is not normal."
**Hawkeye Pierce:** "What's normal, Frank?"
**Frank:** "Normal is everybody doing the same thing."
**Trapper McIntyre:** "What about individuality?"
**Frank:** "Well, individuality is fine. As long as we do it together."
***—M*A*S*H***

**ON WOMEN**
"It's been proven through history that wimmin's a mystery."
**—Popeye,**
***The Popeye Cartoon Show***

**ON LOVE**
"Love makes you do funny things. It made me get married."
**—Buddy Sorrel,**
***The Dick Van Dyke Show***

"Love's the only thing in life you've got to earn. Everything else you can steal."
**—Pappy Maverick,**
***Maverick***

# THE MINI-SKIRT SAGA

*Today, when practically anything goes in fashion, people have forgotten how revolutionary the mini-skirt was in its day. In the mid-'60s, when it caught on, it was more than a fashion—it was a philosophy, a political statement, a news event. Here are some facts to remind you.*

**HISTORY.**
The mini-skirt was created by an English seamstress named Mary Quant. As a girl, Mary hated the straightlaced clothes grown-ups wore. So when she got older, she made unconventional clothes for herself.

In 1955, she opened the world's first boutique in London, selling "wild and kinky" handmade clothes, like the ones she wore. She used bright colors, lots of plastic, and kept hemlines shorter than normal (though they weren't minis yet). Her fashions caught on with hip Londoners. They became known as "mod" (for modern) clothes, and Mary became a local celebrity.

In 1965, young girls in London were beginning to wear their dresses shorter than ever. Taking a cue from them, Quant began manufacturing skirts that were outrageously short for the time. She called them "mini-skirts." They took off like wildfire.

Later that year, respected French designer Andre Courreges brought the mini-skirt and go-go boots (his own creation) to the world of high fashion. This made the mini a "style" instead of a "fad" and inspired influential women—movie stars, models, heiresses—to shorten their skirts. But the largest American clothing manufacturers weren't sure whether to hop on the mini bandwagon until the day in 1965 that Jackie Kennedy appeared in public with a shortened hemline. After that, it was full speed ahead.

The mini fad lasted for less than a decade. But it permanently altered the concept of what was acceptable in women's attire, and helped break down traditional barriers for women in other areas of society.

**The Meaning of the Mini-Skirt, Part I**
In 1965, Mary Quant, creator of the mini-skirt, was asked to reveal the meaning of the mini-skirt. Her reply: "Sex."

**The Meaning of the Mini-Skirt, Part II**

"Without a doubt, the pill bred the mini, just as it bred the topless bathing suit by Rudi Gernreich in 1964. They were intended to prove that women were in control of their destiny and could choose whom they wished to mate with."

—*In Fashion*, by Prudence Glynn

## THE MINI-SKIRT — INTERNATIONAL CONTROVERSY

Today, the mini-skirt is a fashion, not a political issue, but in the '60s, it was a major controversy. Here's how some people reacted:

- **In the Vatican:** Women in mini-skirts were not allowed to enter Vatican City.
- **In the Malagasy Republic:** An anti-mini-skirt law went into effect in 1967. Violators were subject to ten days in jail.
- **In the Congo:** In 1967 police arrested three hundred women wearing mini-skirts, which were banned.
- **In Venezuela:** Churches in Caracas put up signs telling people to give up their minis or "be condemned to hell."
- **In Egypt:** Women in minis were subject to a charge of indecent behavior. This law was passed because two women wore mini-skirts in the center of the city and caused a two-hour traffic jam.
- **In Zambia:** Gangs of youths roamed the streets assaulting girls in mini-skirts and forcibly lowering their hemlines. After a week, the war against mini-skirts was declared officially over when women went on television and said they "realized their mistake."
- **In Greece:** Anyone wearing a mini-skirt was jailed.
- **In the Philippines:** A congressman proposed that mini-skirts be banned. But the proposal was withdrawn when a congresswoman threatened to retaliate by outlawing elevator shoes.
- **In Rio De Janeiro:** In 1966, a sixty-three-year-old man on a bus was overcome when a young woman wearing a mini-skirt crossed her legs in the seat next to him. He bit her on the thigh and was sentenced to three days in jail.
- **In the U.S.A.:** Disneyland outlawed mini-skirts—the gatekeepers measured the distance from the woman's knee to her hemline and restricted her entrance until she ripped out the hem.

In most schools during the '60s, if the hem of a dress didn't touch the floor when a girl was kneeling, it was considered a mini, and the guilty party was sent home. "And don't come back until you look respectable, young lady."

**Copernicus was the first person to butter his bread.**

# THE ORIGIN OF DRACULA

*Dracula first appeared in 1897 in a book written by Irish author Bram Stoker.* Extraordinary Origins of Everyday Things *says:*

The nineteenth-century Irish writer Bram Stoker came serendipitously upon the subject matter for his novel *Dracula* while engaged in research at the British Museum. He discovered a manuscript of traditional Eastern European folklore concerning Vlad the Impaler, a fifteenth-century warrior prince of Walachia. According to Romanian legend, the sadistic Prince Vlad took his meals al fresco, amidst a forest of impaled, groaning victims. And Vlad washed down each course with his victims' blood, in the belief that it imbued him with supernatural strength.

Vlad's crimes were legend. On red-hot pokers, he impaled male friends who had fallen from favor, and women unfaithful to him were impaled, then skinned alive. Imprisoned himself, he tortured mice and birds for amusement. His mountaintop retreat, known as Castle Drakula, suggested the title for Stoker's novel.

Although Stoker had found his model for Dracula, it was a friend, a professor from the University of Budapest, who suggested a locale for the fiction by relating lore of the vampires of Transylvania. The novelist traveled to the area and was...impressed with its dark, brooding mountains, morning fogs, and sinister-looking castles.

Dracula was an immense success when published in 1897, wrapped in a brown paper cover. And the novel was responsible for reviving interest in the Gothic horror romance, which has continued into the present day in books and films.

**EEAGH! TWO AWFUL VAMPIRE RIDDLES**

**"How can you spot a Vampire jockey?"**

"He always wins by a neck."

**"Why aren't Vampires good gamblers?"**

"Because they always make sucker bets."

# CHURCHILL SPEAKS

*Words of wisdom from the quotable Sir Winston Churchill.*

"History will be kind to me, for I intend to write it."

"Although I am prepared for martyrdom, I prefer that it be postponed."

"If you have an important point, don't try to be subtle or clever. Use a pile driver. Hit the point once. Then come back and hit it again. Then hit it a third time—a tremendous whack."

"It is a mistake to look too far ahead. The chain of destiny can only be grasped one link at a time."

"In war you can only be killed once, but in politics, many times."

"I have taken more out of alcohol than alcohol has taken out of me."

"A fantatic is one who can't change his mind and won't change the subject."

"Eating words has never given me indigestion."

"I like a man who grins when he fights."

"I am always ready to learn, although I do not always like being taught."

"The inherent vice of Capitalism is the unequal sharing of its blessings; the inherent vice of Socialism is the equal sharing of its miseries."

"A hopeful disposition is not the sole qualification to be a prophet."

"We are all worms, but I do believe I'm a glow worm."

"It is a fine thing to be honest, but it is also important to be right."

"Never turn your back on a threatened danger and try to run away from it. If you do that, you will double the danger. But if you meet it promptly and without flinching, you will reduce the danger by half. Never run away from anything. Never!"

# WHO WAS THAT MAN?

*Some songs leave you wondering who they're about. Here are the stories behind a few, from* Behind the Hits, *by Bob Shannon and John Javna.*

**I WRITE THE SONGS; BARRY MANILOW**

Most people associate this tune with Barry Manilow, because his version sold millions of records. But it actually has nothing to do with him. He didn't write it—Bruce Johnston, one of the Beach Boys, did. And Johnston didn't write it about Manilow—or himself. He was inspired by someone he considers a truly great songwriter.

***Who was that man?***

Johnston says: "I guess it's pretty obvious that I wrote the song about Brian Wilson."

Wilson, the leader of the Beach Boys, really *has* written songs the whole world sings. For example: "Good Vibrations," "In My Room," "Fun, Fun, Fun," "I Get Around," "Surfer Girl," "Help Me Rhonda," and so on. Good choice.

**KILLING ME SOFTLY WITH HIS SONG; ROBERTA FLACK**

Roberta Flack didn't write this song; a poet and folksinger named Lori Lieberman did.

**The Story.** One evening in 1972, Lori went to L.A.'s Troubador to see a singer who had earned the nickname "The Hudson River Troubador" when he sailed from Maine to New York with Pete Seeger, trying to call attention to pollution. She was impressed by what she saw and heard. "I thought he was just incredible," she recalled. "He was singing songs that I felt pertained to my life at that time. I was going though some difficult things, and what he was singing about made me think, 'Whoa! This person knows me! I don't understand.' Never having met him, how could he know me so well? I went home and wrote a poem and showed it to the two men I was working with at the time."

Those two men, Norman Gimbel and Charles Fox, thought the poem could be adapted into a great song. They quickly reworked it and gave it back to Lieberman to record on her own album.

In its original form it was ten minutes long—too long for radio play—so it was edited and released as a single. It got a little airplay, but never sold. It did, however, get included on a tape of music created especially for airline headsets.

**How It Became a Hit:** On a flight from Los Angeles to New York, Roberta Flack plugged in her personal headphones and began leafing through the in-flight magazine to see what songs were included on the 10 channels of music that were available. Her main interest was to see if any of her recordings were among the offerings. They weren't.

But Flack happened to notice the listing for a song she'd never heard. The title seemed interesting, so she tuned it in. By the time she reached New York she knew she had to record it. "When I heard it," Flack said, "I absolutely freaked. In New York, I started calling people, asking how to find the guys who wrote that song."

Flack felt she had stumbled on an "uncut diamond," a song that she could restructure and improve and make her own. It became the most important project in her life, and she spent eight months on it. "Roberta came out with the most wonderful version," says Lieberman. "Killing Me Softly" was released in January; it became the top-selling song in the nation by February, and won three Grammy awards for Flack.

***Who was that man?***

The gentle "killer" was folksinger Don McLean. He had just completed his second album, "American Pie," and his rendition of the title song was the performance that inspired Lieberman. McLean says: "After she announced it, somebody called me up and said, 'Hey, somebody's written a song about you.' The first question I asked was, 'Is it any good?' "

## YOU'RE SO VAIN; CARLY SIMON

This is probably old news by now, but it's worth repeating. Carly Simon's first big hit created a controversy. As soon as it was released, people began speculating about its subject. Who was "so vain"? Was it Mick Jagger? Her husband, James Taylor?

***Who was that man?***

Simon wanted to keep an air of mystery around the song, so she was reluctant to reveal her secret. But producer Richard Perry wasn't so shy. "It's about a compilation of men," he said, "but primarily Warren Beatty."

**39% of Americans think that the best way to get rich is to win a lottery.**

# WORDPLAY

*More origins of common phrases.*

**KEEP THE BALL ROLLING**
*Meaning*: To keep things going, to maintain momentum.
*Background*: Comes from the presidential election of 1840, which was won by Whig party candidate William Henry Harrison. The election campaign included the usual pamphlets, buttons, banners, and one unique item—a giant 6-foot paper ball with all the Whig slogans written on it (e.g., "Tippecanoe and Tyler Too!"). Harrison's supporters took it from town to town, rolling it down the streets shouting "Keep the ball rolling!"

**GET UP ON THE WRONG SIDE OF BED**
*Meaning*: To start the day feeling bad, or to wake up in a bad mood.
*Background*: Reflects a long-standing cultural bias against the left side of the body. The phrase was originally "get out of bed the wrong way"—which meant with your left foot first, or while you were lying on your left side—a sure sign, people believed, that things were destined to go wrong that day. The phrase evolved into "get up on the wrong side of bed."

**BEAT AROUND THE BUSH**
*Meaning*: To avoid dealing with the main issue.
*Background*: In the Middle Ages, people trapped birds for food by dropping a net over a bush and beating the ground around it with a club. As frightened birds perched in the bush tried to fly away, they were caught in the net. Someone who kept beating around the bush after the birds were trapped never got to the point of the activity—actually getting the birds and eating them.

**BARK UP THE WRONG TREE**
*Meaning*: To focus on the wrong object or idea.
*Background*: A hunting term. In Colonial days, pioneers used hounds to trap raccoons and possums. The dogs would chase the animals up trees, then sit and bay at the tree trunk. Occasionally, the hound would get fooled and the hunter would find his pet barking "up" the wrong tree.

# THE FABULOUS '60S

*More miscellany from the pop decade, courtesy of Gordon and John Javna's great bathroom reader,* 60s!

### WAR GAMES

One of the forgotten footnotes of the Vietnam war is the toys it inspired. In 1961 JFK committed our first troops to Vietnam...and in 1962, toys relating to Vietnam began to appear. "We've discovered through dealer interviews and consumer mail that our customers are demanding toys about Vietnam," explained the sales manager of a major toy company. Among the big sellers:

• **The Mattel "Guerilla Gun."** In 1963, Mattel painted its Dick Tracy Submachine guns camouflage green and packaged each one with a poncho, toy hand grenades, and a beret. They immediately sold 2 million of them, twice as many as they had when the product was just a Dick Tracy gun.

• **The Green Beret hobby kit.** Aurora Plastics marketed a plastic assemble-it-yourself model of a Green Beret holding a machine gun and tossing a hand grenade. "Inspired by the great motion picture *The Green Berets*, starring John Wayne," it said on the box. No mention of the real war, though.

• **"Viet Nam, a Game for Interested Americans."** The next best thing to being there—an educational board game for people who liked role-playing.

### WHO CARES ABOUT THE CEREAL?

In 1965 kids discovered an animated TV commercial for a brand-new cereal. It actually had a cast of characters the way cartoons did: lovable old Cap'n Crunch, his crew of kids, his faithful pet, Seadog, and the villains, archenemy Magnolia Bulkhead and Jean LaFoot, the barefoot pirate. The kiddie videophiles loved the commercials and, of course, made their parents buy the cereal. It quickly became the most popular new cereal of the decade, giving its manufacturer, Quaker Oats, the sweet taste of success.

What consumers didn't know: Cap'n Crunch was carefully

planned out as a TV promotion *before the cereal even existed.* Quaker hired Jay Ward, creator of Bullwinkle, to come up with a cartoon character and produce one-minute commercials—cereal serials—of Cap'n Crunch sailing the high seas, keeping the world safe for breakfast. Then, when they were satisfied with the ads, Quaker produced the actual cereal. It became the best-selling new cereal of the decade.

## WHO DUNNIT?

The first James Bond film, *Dr. No,* came out in 1963. But Ian Fleming's books were already selling well in America by then. Here's how it happened: In 1961, a well-known intellectual was asked by a reporter from *Life* magazine to name his favorite books. The man, who was known to read a book a day, quickly supplied a list of 10 of them. Most were scholarly works . . . except one—*From Russia with Love,* a James Bond thriller.

This was the only book on the list that most Americans would even consider buying. And they did. The guy had so much influence that James Bond became an overnight sensation in bookstores.

Who was the man whose list started the Bond craze?

President John F. Kennedy.

## MACHINE AGE MAN

They sang it on TV in 1962: "Here he comes, here he comes, greatest toy you've ever seen, and his name is Mr. Machine. . . ." Mr. Machine was a plastic wind-up robot with a top hat, who clunked and whirred, and walked mechanically. Manufactured by the Ideal Toy Company in 1962, he became one of the most popular toys of the early sixties.

But kids and their parents never realized that Mr. Machine was more than a toy—it was actually a comment on the condition of modern man.

It was created by Marvin Glass, a neurotic toy designer who considered himself something of a philosopher. One day Glass was having a typical argument with his ex-wife. Just before she hung up, she screamed at him: "You're nothing but a machine!" Glass pondered the comment. Maybe she was right, he thought. . . . Maybe the 20th century had turned all of us into machines. Inspired, Glass designed his homage to modern life, Mr. Machine.

# LUNACY

*We've heard enough about moons and Junes to last a lifetime. But the joke is that some of the old fables about the power of the moon might actually be true.*

**MOON CHILD:**
- The average menstrual cycle for women is 29.5 days—precisely the same as a lunar month.
- The human gestation period is 9 months. But whose months? The average birth occurs 265.5 days after conception—which happens to be the exact equivalent of 9 lunar months.

**STUDIES SHOW THAT:**
- More children are born after new and full moons than at any other time.
- More boys are born after a full moon, and more girls are born after a new moon.
- People who are experiencing a lot of stress have an increase in pulse rates during a full or new moon.
- Surgeons have found that around the full or new moons, their patients bleed more.
- When full and new moons occur, more people are admitted into mental hospitals and hospital emergency rooms are busier.
- There's an increase in certain crimes (rape, robbery, assault) during a full moon.

**THE WORD**
- "Lunacy" refers to the Roman moon goddess, Luna.
- In ancient times, people thought that exposure to the moon could "affect the mind."
- People were advised not to sleep with moonlight shining on their faces, or they would become "moonstruck" (crazy).
- The word *lunacy* is probably derived from ancient observations that during a full moon, mad people became more frenzied.
- The term *lunatic fringe* was coined by Teddy Roosevelt, who was describing some of his followers in the Bullmoose Party during the 1912 presidential election.

**From the bottom of a well, you can actually see the stars during the daytime.**

# THE GUMBY STORY

*He's the "Clayboy of the Western World," an American icon. But what does he stand for, and where did he come from? Now it can be told.*

**A STAR IS BORN.** Gumby was created in the mid-'50s by Art Clokey, a filmmaker who had learned "stop-motion animation" (film is shot one frame at a time and the inanimate subject is moved between shots) at the University of Southern California, working with a world-famous expert.

- After graduating, Clokey experimented with his "stop-motion" techniques in an art film he called *Gumbasia.* The stars of the film were geometric clay forms ("It was cheaper than getting actors") that metamorphized to the rhythm of a jazz soundtrack.
- Clokey took *Gumbasia* to a Hollywood producer, hoping to make feature films. Instead, the producer decided Clokey ought to make a kids' TV show. He put up the money for a pilot, and Clokey created the star—a clay character named Gumby. NBC then commissioned several 6-minute films.
- Gumby made his first appearance on "The Howdy Doody Show" in 1956. Then in March, 1957 he got his own NBC program.
- Beginning in 1958, "The Adventures of Gumby" was offered as a syndicated show. By the mid-'60s, he was everywhere.

**GUMBY: PERSONAL DATA**

- His name came from a type of sticky clay soil found in Michigan, known as "gumbo."
- The shape of his head was inspired by a photo of Clokey's father. In it, the senior Clokey had a cowlick that looked to his son like "the bump of wisdom that Buddhists have." So Art passed it on to Gumby.
- According to Clokey: "His green color represents the chlorophyll found in plants, while his bluish tint reflects the sky. He's got his feet on the ground and his head in the sky."
- His pal, Pokey, is orange because, says Clokey, "Pokey represents the critical, doubting, more earthy side of life."
- His voice was supplied by Dick Beals. Pokey's voice was supplied by Clokey himself.

## HIS FALL AND RESURRECTION

Gumby's popularity lasted through the '60s and into the early '70s. But by the late '70s, he was washed up; TV stations had dropped the show, and toymakers had stopped manufacturing Gumby toys.

• Art Clokey was nearly broke. His house was about to be foreclosed on, and the new toy product in which he had invested heavily—something called Moody Rudy—was proving to be a bomb. Worse, his daughter had recently been killed in a car accident. Life was not going Art's way.

• In 1979, he went to Hong Kong to take a look at the Moody Rudy manufacturing facilities. While he was there, he decided to visit Satya Sai Baba, an Indian holy man he'd once seen in a film.

• As journalist Sean Elder describes it: "On that day in 1979, Clokey and his wife, Gloria, were among the faithful hundreds sitting outside Baba's ashram, awaiting...a glimpse of the Master. Once or twice a day Baba would make the rounds, pouring ash from his hand onto objects that the devout held up to be blessed: books, photographs, religious statues. That afternoon, Sai Baba found Clokey in the lotus position, holding a small likeness of Gumby. Ash poured forth from his hand onto Gumby's sloping head, and the master moved on. 'Then I went home,' says Clokey, 'and things began happening.' "

## THE GUMBY REVIVAL

• It started at the Pasadena Art Center, where Clokey gave a talk on animation. The Gumby-philes who attended enjoyed it so much that they set up some screenings of Gumby films (remember, it was pre-video, and they hadn't been seen on TV for years) in the auditorium of the Beverly Hills Library.

• This was sold out for two weeks in a row—which prompted the owners of a chain of movie theaters to send Clokey around the country, appearing with his Gumby films. He was a hit everywhere.

• Inspired by the Gumby revival, a couple of cadets painted a Gumby sign and flew it during the 1980 Army-Navy football game. This, in turn, was spotted by the producer of "Saturday Night Live," who decided it would be a kick to dress Eddie Murphy in a Gumby suit. Suddenly Gumby was a star again.

• Clokey is clear about who's responsible for his turn in fortunes—Satya Sai Baba. "He's the epitome of cosmic creation in human form," he explains. "He taught me that Gumby is me, and since we're all alike, Gumby is everyone."

# EARTH TRIVIA

*A few fascinating facts about the planet to help you while away the time:*

The earth isn't round. It's slightly flattened on the top and bottom.

❖

There are over 300,000 miles of coastline on the planet.

❖

The longest mountain range in the world is the Andes, in South America. It is 4525 miles long. Next longest: The Rockies, followed by the Himalayas, the Great Dividing Range in Australia, and the Trans-Antarctic Mountains.

On a mountain, the temperature drops about 3-1/2° for every 984 feet you climb.

❖

The atmosphere extends about 5,000 miles above the earth. It consists of five separate layers: the exosphere, thermosphere, mesosphere, stratosphere, and troposphere.

❖

The troposphere is the life-supporting layer closest to the earth. It is also the smallest—only10 miles high.

❖

There are about a million earthquakes every year. Most are so small they don't even register.

❖

The deepest lake in the world is the U.S.S.R.'s Lake Baikal. Its size: 30 miles wide by 400 miles long. Its depth: over a mile (approx. 6,360 feet ). "It's so deep," says one source, "that all five of the Great Lakes could be emptied into it."

❖

The largest lake (or inland sea) in the world is the Caspian Sea, on the border of Iran and the U.S.S.R.

❖

About 20% of the Earth's surface is desert. However, most deserts are not sand (only about 15% are). Deserts are frequently bare rock or gravel.

The Sahara Desert takes up about 1/3 of Africa. It is almost as big as the continental United States.

❖

If you could take all of the salt out of the ocean and spread it on land, you'd have a five hundred-foot layer of salt covering the Earth's surface.

**You can only see a rainbow in the morning or late in the afternoon.**

# THE STORY OF LAYLA

*Several B.R.I. members wrote and asked for the inside story on this classic Eric Clapton tune—one of the most popular rock songs of all time.*

Eric Clapton could play the blues as few other guitarists could—a talent which both satisfied and tortured him. Unlike some of his fellow British "bluesmen," Clapton was keenly aware that he was a white musician imitating an essentially black art form. This created a terrible conflict; playing the blues was his first love, but was he really entitled to practice his craft? In order to reconcile the feelings, Clapton became a blues purist. He believed that you had to suffer in order to be able to play the blues—so he was miserable a lot of the time. He was particularly unhappy when he wrote his most famous composition, "Layla."

**THE BIRTH OF LAYLA**

The real "Layla's" real name was Patti Boyd—or more accurately, Patti Boyd Harrison. She was the wife of Beatle George Harrison when Eric Clapton began pursuing her.

• Harrison first met her on the set of *A Hard Day's Night* in 1964. A stunning nineteen-year-old blonde model, she was only supposed to make a brief appearance in the film and leave; instead, she and George fell in love and eventually married.

• George and Eric were close friends. They'd known each other since the days when the Beatles and the Yardbirds (Eric's group at the time) were becoming popular. As they both became superstars, they hung out together more and more. They even contributed to each other's recordings. Eric played a magnificent solo on "While My Guitar Gently Weeps"; George co-wrote and played on Cream's "Badge." George wrote "Here Comes the Sun" while sitting in Eric's garden; he wrote "Savoy Truffle" specifically for Eric, who was having dental problems but still couldn't resist chocolates. George joined Eric when he toured with a band called Delaney and Bonnie and Friends, etc.

• George didn't realize, however, that over the years Eric had quietly fallen in love with his wife. Eric told Patti (but not George) about his feelings, but she wouldn't hear anything of it. She remained dedicated to the man who had written "Something" for her.

• Already a tortured soul, Eric was plunged into despair. In an outburst of emotion, he wrote "Layla." Later, when people asked him who he was singing for, all he would say was, " 'Layla' was about a woman I felt really deeply about and who turned me down, and I had to pour it out in some way."

• You may be wondering how "Patti" became "Layla." The answer: Clapton lifted the name "Layla" from a Persian love story called "Layla and Mashoun." The tale had little similarity to the Eric/Patti/George love triangle. Clapton just liked the title. The song was recorded and released in 1970, but it flopped. The reason: the record was attributed to Derek and the Dominoes; no one knew it was Clapton, so it didn't get airplay.

• Eric, who had poured his heart and soul into the record, threw in the towel. He gave up music and took up heroin. "I basically stayed in the house with my girlfriend for two and-a-half years," he told *Rolling Stone* magazine, "and we got very strung out. Dying from drugs didn't seem to me then to be a terrible thing."

• Ironically, during this low point in his life, "Layla" was re-released and became one of the all-time FM favorites...and then struck gold as a Top 10 single.

• In 1974, Clapton kicked the heroin habit and re-emerged on the music scene with "I Shot the Sheriff," his first #1 song.

• A happy ending for Eric: Patti eventually divorced George and, in a secret ceremony in Tucson, Arizona, in 1979, married Clapton. The ultimate irony: Patti and Eric later joined George in a recording of the Everly Brothers' old hit, "Bye, Bye Love."

## UNRELATED MORBID TRIVIA

*From Fred Worth's Hollywood Trivia:*

• George Reeves, the star of TV's "Superman," was buried wearing the grey double-breasted suit he wore when he played Clark Kent.

• Bela Lugosi, who played the vampire Dracula in many films, was buried in his Dracula cape.

# BATMAN ON TV

*Holy bonanza! In the summer of 1989,* Batman *became one of the biggest-grossing films of all time. But the Batman TV series in 1966 was just as much of a smash on the small screen.*

## HOW IT STARTED

Back in 1939, cartoonist Bob Kane created Batman as a stablemate for the popular DC Comics character, Superman. A skilled detective who kept his identity hidden under a cape and mask, this "Batman" hunted down criminals in the night . . . and murdered them. He was an instant smash.

After his comic book success, Batman became a radio series, then made the jump to movie serials in the late '40s.

By 1965, pop art was big and a comic book revival was on, and the time was right for Batman to make a bat-leap onto TV. As it happened, ABC was hard up for anything that would bolster its sagging ratings. So when Douglas Cramer suggested the idea to network executives, they agreed to give Batman a shot. What could they lose? William Dozier, who had never even heard of Batman, was hired to produce the series, and he recruited "the most bizarre thinker I knew," Lorenzo Semple, to develop scripts. Then fate lent a hand. As production for the series was beginning in fall 1965, Columbia Pictures released four hours of old Batman movie serials under the title *An Evening With Batman and Robin.* It played to packed houses at college campuses around the country and ignited "Batmania." Dozier rushed production to take advantage of this good fortune. And Batman premiered in January of 1966. Holy ratings! It shot up to #1 immediately, becoming an instant cult classic.

## INSIDE FACTS

### Holy Bat-Craze

TV ignited a Batman merchandise boom. In 1966, over 60 manufacturers made more than 500 Batman products and sold more than $60 million worth of them . . . making Batman the biggest fad America had ever seen. Suddenly consumers could buy Batbath bubble soap, Batman peanut butter, Batman greeting cards, Batman pajamas, and so on. The fad was repeated 23 years later, in 1989.

**Who Is That Masked Man?**
The actors chosen to play the Dynamic Duo were virtual unknowns. Adam West (Batman) had co-starred for a season in a 1961 TV series called "The Detectives," but other than that, had endured 7 years of bit parts in TV shows and Italian Westerns before becoming an "overnight success." Burt Ward (Robin) had even less experience, and was flat broke when he got the part. To celebrate, he and his new bride cashed in 25¢ worth of Coke bottles and bought 8 chicken wings.

**Top Priorities**
When ABC broke into the middle of a "Batman" episode to announce the emergency landing of the Gemini 8 spacecraft, they were flooded with irate phone calls. Holy priorities! Apparently, Bat-fans cared more about the fictional exploits of the Caped Crusader than the real-life ones of the astronauts.

**Follow that Car**
The TV Batmobile was a modified Lincoln Continental, customized by George Barris for the show at a cost of $30,000. Despite the impressive fireball that burst from the rear of the car upon ignition, it ran on plain old gasoline.

**Guardian Angel**
Aunt Harriet, Bruce's kindly old relative, was not in the original comic book. She was added to the Wayne household by Dozier to parry charges of homosexual overtones in the show (3 men living together). "She watches everything," said a network representative.

**So Bad, He's Good**
In 1966, Frank Gorshin was nominated for an Emmy for his performance as the Riddler, making him the most critically acclaimed villain on TV.

**Status**
Viewers will spot plenty of familiar faces in "Batman" reruns. "Batman" was the show it was "in" to be "on"; and guest stars included Joan Collins, Milton Berle, Liberace, Vincent Price, Cliff Robertson, Otto Preminger, Zsa Zsa Gabor, Burgess Meredith, et al.

# NAZI OR NOT?

*These celebrities have been accused of being Nazis. But were they? Or are they just the victims of nasty rumors?*

**THE ACCUSED:** Errol Flynn, swashbuckling screen idol of the '30s and '40s.

**THE CHARGE:** Flynn actively worked as a Nazi spy.

**THE EVIDENCE:**

• *Exhibit A*: Flynn was apparently a rabid anti-semite.

• *Exhibit B*: One of Flynn's closest friends, Dr. Hermann Erben, was unmasked as a Nazi spy after the war. He and Flynn traveled extensively together (e.g., during the Spanish Civil War, they went to Spain and posed as journalists), and when Erben was booted out of America by the U.S. Government, Flynn smuggled him back into Mexico.

• *Exhibit C*: During the war, the U.S. Government had Flynn under surveillance, calling him a potential subversive.

• *Exhibit D*: He insisted that the 1941 film *Dive Bomber* be shot on location at the San Diego naval base. His accusers say it was to give "Japanese military planners a look at American defense installations and aircraft carriers."

**THE DEFENSE:** Flynn died in 1959, and the charge was made 21 years later by author Charles Higham, in his book *Errol Flynn: The Untold Story*.

• Ex-spy Erben denies Flynn had ever worked with him.

• Flynn's Hollywood cohorts scoff at the charges, saying that at worst, Flynn was guilty only of standing by a pal.

• It has been pointed out that although he was watched, Flynn was never picked up by the government

• Flynn's daughters sued Higham for libel. "We're hoping... we might discourage authors like Higham from writing about people who aren't even alive to defend themselves," explained one. The California Supreme Court refused to hear the case.

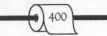

**NAZI OR NOT?** The evidence is too thin to convict anyone, but it's an intriguing possibility.

**Women are 37% more likely to go to a psychiatrist than men are.**

**THE ACCUSED:** Charles Lindbergh, the first man to fly solo nonstop across the Atlantic. A national hero.

**THE CHARGE:** Lindbergh was either America's "number one Nazi sympathizer," as many politicians charged, or worse. FDR is quoted as having told Henry Morganthau, his secretary of the Treasury, in 1940: "If I should die tomorrow, I want you to know this. I am absolutely convinced Lindbergh is a Nazi."

**THE EVIDENCE:**

- *Exhibit A*: In 1938, Lindbergh accepted a medal from Adolf Hitler, and publicly expressed his admiration for Germany.
- *Exhibit B*: Returning to America, he began making speeches in favor of the U.S. staying out of any European conflict at all costs. This was—coincidentally?—a policy priority for the German government as well.
- *Exhibit C*: He became a central figure in the America First Committee (stay out of Europe, take care of America first), tirelessly giving speeches and radio addresses directed not only at keeping America out of World War II, but at preventing the U.S. from supporting Britain.
- *Exhibit D*: When "interventionist" politicians attacked him as a Nazi, his political allies urged him to repudiate fascism and Hitler. He refused to do so.
- *Exhibit E*: Pre-war cables from the German consulate in Washington described his efforts as a wonderful propaganda tool, and urged the Nazi government not to publicly support his position, lest he be branded a traitor.
- *Exhibit F*: In an October, 1941 speech he blamed the British and the Jews for the public pressure to get America into the war. "The leaders of the British and Jewish races...for reasons which are not American, wish to involve us in the war," he said.

**THE DEFENSE:** When America went to war, Lindbergh wrote in his diary: "I have always stood for what I thought would be to the best interest of this country, and now we are at war I want to take part in it, foolish and disastrous as I think the war will prove to be. Our decision has been made, and now we must fight to preserve our national honor and our national future." He got a job working with Ford Motor Company, developing bomber manufacturing capacity. And in 1944, he went to Germany to help the U.S. study their rocket-building facilities.

**NAZI OR NOT?** Yes and no. He considered himself a patriotic American and joined in the war effort (even though he disagreed with it). But his sympathies clearly lay with the Nazis. Even in his diaries, he never criticized Hitler or fascism. And the prospect of a Nazi-dominated Europe was a positive one to him; he admired their efficiency and orderliness. When the war was over, he still maintained we should never have become involved. Confronted with the sight of a concentration camp, he merely said it was no worse than America had treated the Japanese, and added: "Judge not, that ye not be judged."

**THE ACCUSED:** Gary Cooper.

**THE CHARGE:** Cooper was a " strong Nazi sympathizer." This allegation, too, was made by Charles Higham in his book, *Cary Grant: The Lonely Heart*.

**THE EVIDENCE:**

• *Exhibit A:* In 1938, Cooper visited Germany.

• *Exhibit B:* While there, he met with high government officials and may even have had a secret meeting with Hitler.

• *Exhibit C:* Hitler's favorite movie was Cooper's *Lives of the Bengal Lancers*.

**THE DEFENSE:**

• According to Cooper's wife at the time, the charge is "a despicable, bald-faced lie." She says Cooper never went to Germany in 1938.

• Origin of the rumor, according to the ex-wife: she and Gary accompanied her mother and stepfather to Germany in 1939. It was a special favor to FDR, with whom her stepfather was friends.

• Says the ex-wife: "It was shortly after Lindbergh said what he did about the power of the German Air Force. FDR wanted to know about Germany's finances, and my stepfather made contact with a Goering—not Hermann Goering, but his half-brother…to look at some plants."

**NAZI OR NOT?** The evidence is embarrassingly scanty. Unless more turns up, there's no case at all.

**From age 5 to age 15, an American kid will see about 13,500 people killed on TV.**

# THE BIRDS

*Some inside dope on one of Alfred Hitchcock's spookiest films.*

Alfred Hitchcock's 1963 film *The Birds* was a milestone: no one had ever tried to work with so many animals at once; and no one has ever used live animals so effectively in a suspense film.

Much of the credit goes to Hollywood's #1 bird expert, Ray Berwick. He was familiar with the Daphne DuMaurier short story on which *The Birds* was based, but never imagined anyone would try to film it. Then, one morning at 6:30, he got a call telling him to be at Hitchcock's office in an hour. He walked in on a *Birds* production meeting, where he was told that $250,000 had already been spent on mechanical birds that didn't work. Could they use live birds? Not even Berwick was sure. But he agreed to try.

## BERWICK'S APPROACH

• Although thousands of untrained birds—sparrows, finches, buntings, seagulls, and ravens—were ultimately used, Berwick only trained 100-150 ravens, blackbirds, and seagulls for the film.

• Of the trained birds, only 25 or 30 were well-trained; that's all they needed. Birds, says Berwick, have a tendency to follow leaders, so the well-trained birds lead the others wherever the director wants them to go.

• The small birds weren't trained—and they didn't have to be. In one convincing scene, for example, they were just "dumped down a chimney."

• According to Berwick: Once the wild birds were tame, they lost their fear of humans and actually became "the birds," attacking members of the cast and crew.

• Hitchcock wanted to include an owl among his feathered fiends, but had to cut the owl's scene because it looked comical.

## BEHIND THE SCENES

Years after the film was released, Berwick revealed the secret of making seagulls look as though were attacking humans:

• He taught the birds to land on people's heads whenever people were standing still. And each time they performed that stunt

**If you ate Frosted Flakes as a kid, there's a 50% chance you're still eating them.**

successfully, they were fed.

• In the film, the audience saw what *looked* like people running down a street being chased by seagulls; in reality, the seagulls were flying along *with* the people, waiting for the people to stop moving so the birds could perform their trick.

• As soon as the director yelled "Cut!" the actors stopped running and the birds landed on their heads—and received their food rewards.

• **Postscript:** After the film was completed, the seagulls that had been used in the film were taken to the Pacific shore and set free. According to Berwick, trained seagulls will forget what they've been taught in about a week, if no one's working with them. But for the first week after the birds were released, there were strange reports of seagulls landing on people's heads at the beach. No one believed the reports, of course—except the people who'd worked on *The Birds*. And they weren't about to explain it to anyone.

## ADVENTURES IN CINEMAGIC

In one carefully crafted scene, co-star Tippi Hedren was rowing across a lake when a seagull seemed to swipe her across the head—leaving her bloodied. Here's how Hitchcock's crew did it:

• They ran two tubes up Hedren's dress: one, which went to her forehead, spurted "blood" ; the other, which went to the top of her head, was attached to an air compressor.

• Then they released the gull, which was one of the birds trained to land on people's heads.

• The gull started to land on Hedren's head. But at the moment it touched her, the air compressor was turned on. The burst of air scared the bird into flying away.

• At the same moment, the "blood" squirted through the other tube, making it seem as though the bird had attacked. A complicated stunt, but clever and effective.

## AFTERMATH

Hitchcock and Berwick made a lot of enemies in pet shops wth *The Birds*. After the film was released, sales of pet birds plummeted.

• Turnabout: Years later, Berwick was also responsible for a bird "boom" when he brought Fred the cockatoo to the screen in the TV show "Baretta."

# STRANGE LAWSUITS

*More examples of the American legal system gone slightly nuts.*

**THE PLAINTIFFS:** Michael and Geraldine S., of Bridgehampton, New York.

**THE DEFENDANT:** The Hampton Day School.

**THE LAWSUIT:** The S. family was angry that their 6-year-old son Philip, a first-grader, wasn't getting any homework. So they sued the school for $1,500.

**THE RESULT:** The jury rejected the S.'s claim and "ordered them to hand over the $975 in tuition they had refused to pay the school."

**THE PLAINTIFF:** Andrew Freese, a 23-year-old silver miner.

**THE DEFENDANT:** The state of Idaho.

**THE LAWSUIT:** Freese objected to the slogan on the Idaho license plate, "Famous Potatoes," because it forced him to advertise potatoes against his will. "This imposition has been borne by the long-suffering citizens of Idaho for the last 12 years," he said in his complaint. He added that mentioning only potatoes discriminated against Idaho's other major products, like lumber...and silver.

**VERDICT:** Unknown.

**THE PLAINTIFFS:** The family of Tomontra Mangrum, a 15-year-old West Palm Beach girl.

**THE DEFENDANT:** Marlon Shadd, a 17-year-old West Palm Beach boy.

**THE LAWSUIT:** Tomontra claimed she was stood up by Marlon on prom night. "I talked to him a few days before, and he said he already had his tux and the tickets," she told reporters. "I was very upset when he didn't show up." Marlon, on the other hand, insisted he'd called off the date a week before the prom. "I told her I fractured my ankle," he said. Tomontra's mother filed suit against Shadd, seeking $49.53 for the cost of the shoes, flowers, and hairdo her daughter had gotten for the prom. Shadd's mother tried to

**28% of American men think they're handsome.**

settle out of court: "I offered her the money. You know what she tells me? She tells me the boy has to be punished."
**VERDICT:** Pending.

**THE PLAINTIFF:** Lori C.
**THE DEFENDANT:** Jack Lee C.
**THE LAWSUIT:** When Jack met his future bride at a party, he told her his parents had been killed in an auto accident some ten years before. After they were married, Lori "became suspicious when her husband started waving guns around at home. She investigated and found that Jack had shot his parents to death, but was cleared on insanity grounds." She not only sued for divorce, she asked for an additional $20,000 for "emotional distress."
**THE VERDICT:** Settled out of court.

**THE PLAINTIFF:** Virginia N., a dental hygenist from Naperville, Illinois.
**THE DEFENDANT:** James L., her former employer.
**THE LAWSUIT:** Ms. N. charged that Mr. L. forced his employees to hug him each day before leaving work. She asserted that if she had been informed that to hug and be hugged was part of the job description, she "would not have taken the job." She also said that whenever she tried to "dash from work hugless," her employer complained bitterly. Did she quit or was she fired?
**VERDICT:** Pending.

**THE PLAINTIFF:** Randall Dale Adams.
**THE DEFENDANT:** Filmmaker Errol Morris.
**THE LAWSUIT:** Adams was convicted of murder in 1977. Ten years later, Morris made a film about the Adams case and as he did, he became convinced that Adams was innocent. The movie, *The Thin Blue Line*, presented the case for Adams's innocence so effectively that he was released from prison. Morris's reward? When Adams got out of jail, he sued the filmmaker for $60,000 for using his story.
**VERDICT:** Settled out of court. Adams dropped the suit, and Morris agreed that Adams should receive full rights to any further commercial uses—notably films or books—of his life.

**75% of Americans say they like to doodle.**

# PRIME-TIME PROVERBS

*More words of wisdom from* Prime-Time Proverbs.

**ON CHANGING**
"Some of us change, some of us mutate."

**—Joyce Davenport, *Hill Street Blues***

**ON HELPING**
**New Yorker** (Victim): "Lemme get this straight—you're saying that you saw me in trouble, so you came over for no reason, with nothing in it for you, and saved my life?"
**Good Samaritan:** "Yep."
**Victim:** "You're sick!"

***—Barney Miller***

**ON GRATITUDE**
**Radar O'Reilly:** "How can I ever thank you?"
**Hawkeye Pierce:** "Well, you can give us your firstborn."
**B.J. Hunnicut:** "And an order of fries."

**—M*A*S*H**

**ON NICE GIRLS**
**Jack Tripper:** "She's pure and wholesome and virtuous. Whatever happened to girls like that?"
**Janet Wood:** "They all go out with guys like you."

***—Three's Company***

**Sue Ann Nivens:** "Mary, what do you think turns on a man?"
**Mary Richards** (exasperated): "Sue Ann, I haven't the slightest idea."
**Sue Ann:** "I know that, dear. I was just trying to make your day."

***—The Mary Tyler Moore Show***

**ON NUCLEAR WAR**
**Agent 99:** "Oh, Max, what a terrible weapon of destruction."
**Maxwell Smart:** "Yes. You know, China, Russia, and France should outlaw all nuclear weapons. We should insist upon it."
**99:** "What if they won't?"
**Smart:** "Then we may have to blast them. That's the only way to keep peace in the world."

***—Get Smart***

**ON EXERCISE**
"Relaxation helps you live longer. Don't exercise, it could kill you."

**—Roger Addison, *Mr. Ed***

# SEE EUROPE IN THE U.S.

*Tip from the B.R.I. travel director: Want to see Europe? Why bother? As fast as you can think up places to visit overseas, we'll find you a nicer, more sanitary, air-conditioned domestic version as an alternative.*

**THE LEANING TOWER OF PISA**
May we suggest a trip to Niles, Illinois.? There, out in front of the local YMCA, is a half-scale replica, with a gift store at the bottom and an observation deck on top. And after you've taken some souvenir photos of your family holding up the Leaning Tower, why not head for a day under the Eiffel Tower? No, not the one in France. Of course, we're referring to the Eiffel Tower at the King's Island Theme Park near Cincinnati, Ohio.

**THE STATUE OF DAVID**
Why spend 10 billion lira for a cold-water hotel to stay to see this? It doesn't even move, and what else is there to do, once you've seen it? Wouldn't you rather see an exact replica inside Caesar's Palace in Atlantic City, N.J., at the Ringling Brothers Museum of Art in Sarasota, Fla., or in Sioux Falls, S.D., where it is dedicated to Tom Fawich, inventor of the four-door automobile? You bet you would.

**THE LAST SUPPER**
By all accounts the original Last Supper is peeling and dingy. No need to head to Rome—not only does America have carloads of Last Suppers to see, we've got them made out of such an ingenious variety of materials that even Leonardo himself would've been hard-pressed to match them.

- See one crafted from gourd seeds at the Gourd Museum in Angler, N.C.
- See one made of butterfly wings at the Christ Only Art Gallery, Eureka Springs, Ark.
- There are life-sized versions made of wood at Kissimmee, Florida's Woodcarving Museum, of plaster in Rhyolite, Nev., and a bas-relief in Yucca Valley, California's Desert Christ Park.

• The best one, though, is the larger-than-life stained glass Last Supper in Glendale, California's Forest Lawn Cemetery. This window comes complete with narration...and back-lighting to show the coming of evening to the Holy Land.

**STONEHENGE**

America has two! There's one in North Salem, N.H., but the best (in the world) is in Mary Hill, Wash. It is full-sized and complete, not just a ruined pile of dusty rocks like the original. And the parking lot is big enough for a car to do "doughnuts" in, something the fun-loving ancient Druids would've appreciated.

**THE BLARNEY STONE**

With all the trouble in Ireland, you'd be much better off visiting the Blarney Stones in either Shamrock, Texas, or in Irish Hills, Michigan. The latter is heartily recommended, due to its proximity to both the Michigan International Speedway and The Prehistoric Forest dinosaur park. Let 'em match that in Erin.

**AFRICA**

You can visit Cleopatra's Needle in New York City, Cleopatra's Barge in Las Vegas, and the Rosicrucian Egyptian Shrine in San Jose, California.

• What about actual pyramids? Well, Bedford, Indiana, tried to construct a replica out of limestone (along with a replica of the Great Wall of China) but ran out of funds. But don't pack your bags for Giza yet. Not before you visit the aptly designed Pyramid Supper Club in Beaver Dam, Wisconsin, and sample their specialty after-dinner drink, the "Yummy Mummy."

• After drinks in Wisconsin, why not travel to the Oyotunji African Village near Sheldon, S.C.? There, King Adefunmi I, Ooni of Life, will treat you to a splendid afternoon of traditional Nigerian garb and customs. And remember this: If happy exhaustion catches up with you after your long day, it won't be from a tsetse-fly bite.

**GREECE**

Tourist disappointment with polluted Athens is well-chronicled. But don't whine about missing history, when a trip to Nashville, Tennessee, will place you in front of a full-scale, clean version of

**Watch out for German shepherds—they bite more people than any other breed of dog.**

the Parthenon. And in Greece you can't visit Loretta Lynn's Dude Ranch and motocross attractions after your day of pointless rubble-rousing.

• If that doesn't sate your Grecian yearning, spend the weekend at the Greek Spongers' Village in Tarpon Springs, Florida.

### INDIA

From the quiet rolling hills of West Virginia, suddenly there bursts forth the spectacular Hari Krishna Palace of Gold in the town of New Vrindavan. This tremendous palace recreates the mystical buildings and gardens of India—sans untouchables—in a truly fabulous manner. Now you know what gets done with all that money the Krishnas raise in airports.

• The illusion of India is not yet complete, the Krishnas say, but will be by the time they finish the adjoining Krishnaland theme park, complete with live elephants to transport guests from the Temple of Understanding to the Diety Swan Boat rides. All this is forecast to cost $50 million.

### DENMARK

There are a number of "little Denmarks" in the United States, but there is none better than Solvang, Calif. Danish windmills and thatched roofs appear as one drives through the warm countryside of Southern California. Is Solvang better than Denmark? Is Denmark 30 minutes from the beautiful beaches of Santa Barbara? Does Denmark have MTV? Case closed.

### SWITZERLAND

Sugarcreek, Ohio, and the surrounding towns one up this land of neutral nebbishes. If Switzerland is so proud of its cheeses, how come they don't have the world's largest cheese wheel, like they do at Heine's Place (in nearby Berlin, Ohio)? And don't believe the Swiss travel brochures if they tell you that Switzerland is the home of the world champion of Steinstossen, or stone-tossing, because he lives in Sugarcreek. (Stone-tossing is a big deal in Switzerland. Isn't that exciting?) Sugarcreek has gas stations that look like ski chalets, the world's largest cuckoo clock and, if that weren't enough, John F. Kennedy's Navy footlocker is exhibited in the town museum.

**Every time Beethoven sat down to write music, he poured ice water over his head.**

# MORE FAMOUS CHEATERS

*The culprits here are a small-time trio of crooks and a big-time corporation.*

**CULPRITS:** Clifford Irving and friends.

**CIRCUMSTANCES:** In 1971, billionaire Howard Hughes was the most famous recluse alive. For fifteen years he had refused to give interviews, refused to be photographed, refused even to be seen in public. So when a little-known author named Clifford Irving stepped forward as co-author of Hughes's authorized autobiography, it created a sensation. Irving had proof—letters scrawled in Hughes's own handwriting, checked and verified by the world's leading handwriting experts, attesting to the fact that the project was genuine.

*Life* magazine paid Irving an enormous sum for the magazine rights. "We've checked this thing out. We have proof," a Time, Inc. spokeman declared. Then McGraw-Hill gave Irving $650,000 for the right to publish the book, and the author delivered a 1050-page manuscript with Hughes's own notes in the margins.

Then the scheme fell apart. Irving had guessed that Hughes would remain aloof rather than becoming embroiled in a messy public confrontation. But he guessed wrong. In 1972 Hughes publicly disavowed the book; at the same time, Swiss authorities found out that Irving's wife, Edith, had been depositing checks made out to Hughes. Further investigation revealed that while Irving was in Mexico supposedly interviewing the rich hermit, he was actually having an affair with a German actress.

**VERDICT:** The Irvings and an accomplice named Dick Suskind were arrested and tried on various charges, ranging from conspiracy to breaking Swiss banking laws. They were convicted.

**AFTERMATH:** First of all, they had to give the money back. Then Clifford served 17 months in prison; he was paroled in 1974. Edith served 2 months in a U.S. jail and 14 in a Swiss one. Suskind served 5 months. When it was over, the Irvings got a divorce. Edith

More Hollywood films have been made about boxing than about any other sport.

remarried and moved to Spain. Suskind moved to Spain, too. Irving moved to Easthampton, Long Island and started writing again. In 1982 he published a moderately successful novel called *Tom Mix and Pancho Villa*.

**CULPRIT:** General Motors, America's auto manufacturing giant.

**CIRCUMSTANCES:** In the '30s, General Motors was looking for ways to expand its bus manufacturing business. So, along with Greyhound, Standard Oil, Firestone Tires, and several other corporations, they formed a company to buy municipal streetcar systems and dismantle them.

They started in 1932 with a few small urban public transportation systems—the streetcar lines in Kalamazoo, Michigan; Saginaw, Michigan; and Springfield, Ohio. When that worked, they moved on to bigger cities.

In 1936, they "engineered the conversion of New York City's stretcars to GM buses." Later, they moved on to Los Angeles.

As anti-trust lawyer Bernard Snell tells it: "In December 1944, [a company] financed by GM and Standard Oil...purchased the local system, scrapped its electric transit cars, tore down its power transmission lines, ripped up the tracks, and placed GM diesel buses fueled by Standard Oil on Los Angeles' crowded streets."

**VERDICT:** "In April of 1949," says *Environmental Action*, "a Chicago federal jury convicted GM of criminally conspiring with Standard Oil and Firestone to replace electric transportation with buses and to monopolize sale of buses. GM was fined $5,000."

**AFTERMATH:** While once there was a "vibrant public transportation" system of non-polluting electric trolleys and streetcars in America, we now have buses spewing tons of carbon monoxide into the air, doing their part to make urban air unbreathable. And, of course, General Motors has a lucrative bus business.

**Footnote:** The head of GM once said, "What's good for General Motors is good for America." Would he still think so? By the summer of 1989, Los Angeles—with its abnormally heavy dependence on cars—had the worst quality air in the U.S. It was so bad that L.A. was forced to adopt an emergency plan to cut down on pollution. Ironically, the measures suggested included: "Cleaner-running buses," and "cleaner fuel for all buses." Plus: "The use of electric cars will be encouraged."

# FOOTBALL NAMES

*Football fans know these names by heart. But they probably don't know how the teams got them. Here are the stories behind some famous names; info from* Name That Team!

**Los Angeles Rams.** When they were founded in Cleveland in 1937, the team's owner resisted public pressure to call his club the Indians, after the local baseball team. Instead, he named them after a college football team—the Fordham Rams. In 1945, the Rams became the first N.F.L. franchise to switch cities when they moved to L.A.

**Cleveland Browns.** When the Rams left Cleveland, a new N.F.L. franchise took its place, and a contest was held to pick a new name. The winner was the "Panthers" ...but the owners found out there was already a semipro Ohio football team called the Panthers—and they stunk. So another contest was held. This time the winner was "Brown Bombers," inspired by boxing champion Joe Louis. The name was then shortened to "Browns," probably because the coach's name was Paul Brown.

**Houston Oilers.** The owner of the team made all his money in oil, and picked the name "for sentimental reasons."

**Los Angeles Raiders.** Originally located in Oakland, California, the team was first called the "Metropolitan Oakland Area Football Club." That was too unwieldy, so the Oakland Chamber of Commerce held a contest to find a new one. The winner: the "Oakland Senors." The team's reaction: "Forget it." The owners came up with "Raiders" on their own.

**Green Bay Packers.** The club was named for the Indian Packing Company, which sponsored the team when it was formed in 1919. Ironically, the company went out of business during the Packers' first season. But the team was a success; they joined the N.F.L. two years later.

**New Orleans Saints.** The team was admitted to the N.F.L. on November 1, 1966—which happens to be All Saints' Day. But the team probably got its name from the classic New Orleans jazz tune, "When the Saints Go Marching In."

**Philadelphia Eagles.** When they first began playing, in 1924, they were a pathetic club called the Frankford Yellowjackets (Frankford was the section of Philly they played in). The team went belly-up during the Depression, and two local businessmen bought it for $2500. F.D.R. had just been elected President; his two major economic programs—the New Deal and the National Recovery Act—used an eagle as their symbol. The team's new owners adopted the New Deal eagle as their symbol, too.

**Phoenix Cardinals.** Originally the Chicago Cardinals. They got their name when the team's owner bought a batch of second-hand jerseys from the University of Chicago. Someone commented they looked like the University's maroon shirts, and the owner replied defensively that they weren't maroon—they were "cardinal red." The name stuck.

**Washington Redskins.** They started out as the Duluth (Minnesota) Eskimos in 1928. In 1932, because they were having a tough time surviving, they moved to Boston. Their new home was the stadium owned by baseball's Boston Braves (now the Atlanta Braves), so they changed their name to the Boston Braves as well. But the arrangement didn't work out; the following season, the football team moved across to Fenway Park, home of the Boston Red Sox. To avoid offending the Red Sox (by keeping the name of the local rivals), the football team changed its name from Braves to Redskins. In 1938, the Redskins moved to Washington.

**New York Giants.** When the team was formed in 1925, they played in the Polo Grounds—home of the New York Giants baseball team. Owner Timothy Mara was a Giants fan already, so he named his team after them.

**Chicago Bears, Detroit Lions,** and **New York Jets.** All derived their names from local baseball teams—the Chicago Cubs, Detroit Tigers, and New York Mets.

# VONNEGUT SAYS…

*A few thoughts from novelist Kurt Vonnegut, Jr.*

"What passes for culture in my head is really a bunch of commercials."

"Laughing or crying is what a human being does when there's nothing else he can do."

"It strikes me as gruesome and comical that in our culture we have an expectation that a man can always solve his problems. This is so untrue that it makes me want to laugh—or cry."

"People don't come to church for preachments, of course, but to daydream about God."

"The canary bird in the coal mine theory of the arts: Artists should be treasured as alarm systems."

"People need good lies. There are too many bad ones."

"Thinking doesn't seem to help very much. The human brain is too high-powered to have many practical uses in this particular universe."

"We are healthy only to the extent that our ideas are humane."

"Beware of the man who works hard to learn something, learns it, then finds himself no wiser than before."

"Any reviewer who expresses rage and loathing for a novel is preposterous. He or she is like a person who has put on full armor and attacked a hot fudge sundae."

"I can think of no more stirring symbol of man's humanity to man than a fire engine."

"There is no reason why good cannot triumph as often as evil. The triumph of anything is a matter of organization. If there are such things as angels, I hope they are organized along the lines of the Mafia."

"Say what you will about the sweet miracle of unquestioning faith. I consider a capacity for it terrifying."

"We are what we pretend to be."

**The $ Barometer:** ***Citizen Kane*****, considered the best movie ever made, was a box office flop.**

# 96 TEARS

*"96 Tears" is as popular today as it was when it was first released in 1966. Here's the story behind the song, from* Behind the Hits.

One of the all-time classic rock tunes is a simple song called "96 Tears." The band responsible for it, Question Mark and the Mysterians, were the embodiment of a number of rock phenomena: They were the ultimate "garage band"; they were living proof that anyone could be discovered and become a star; and finally, they were the classic one-hit wonder, a band that zoomed to the top and suddenly disappeared.

**THE MYSTERY**

Maybe you had to be there to appreciate this, but part of the excitement about "96 Tears" when it originally hit the airwaves in 1966 was trying to figure out who'd recorded it. They called themselves "Question Mark and the Mysterians." But who were they, really? Why wouldn't they reveal their true identities? It gave the deejays something to talk about when they played the record ("Friends, I have it on authority that Question Mark is actually Bob Dylan"), and it lent a little glamour to an otherwise ordinary garage-band tune. As a matter of fact, it's more interesting not to know who recorded "96 Tears." Does the name Rudy Martinez mean anything to you? That's Question Mark's real name.

**BACKGROUND**

The band's members were actually five young guys from Mexico whose families had all migrated to work in Michigan's Saginaw Valley. They took their group name from a Japanese alien-invasion movie, and they adopted their pattern of secrecy from their lead singer. Rudy always sported dark glasses and called himself "Question Mark." Early in the band's career, he wanted everyone else to go incognito, too; he suggested that the group be called XYZ, and that each member be referred to only by initials. Maybe he'd seen too many James Bond movies.

The band played around the Saginaw area for a few years in the mid-'60s, developing a repertoire that included an original number called "Too Many Teardrops," a poem that Rudy had written and

**Left in the dark: there's no sun at the North Pole for 186 days each year.**

set to very simple music. The rest of the group liked the tune, but not the title. They wanted to call it "69 Tears." But they decided they'd never get it onto the radio with a title like that. So they eventually began calling it "96 Tears" instead.

## THEIR BIG BREAK

Like millions of other garage bands in the '60s, Question Mark and the Mysterians wanted to make a record. But no big label would talk to them, so they contacted a woman named Lilly Gonzales, who owned a little outfit in Texas called Pa-Go-Go Records. They told her they had some good songs, and she set them up with a recording session in a Bay City, Michigan, studio. (Actually, it wasn't a real studio—it was a converted living room).

They hauled their instruments—guitar, bass, drums, and Farfisa organ—to the studio, and played a few tunes. Then Pa-Go-Go pressed 500 records and sent them back to the band to distribute to deejays in the area.

The boys carried their discs around, asking jocks to listen...and surprisingly, several did. Particularly Bob Dell at WTAC in Flint and Tom Shannon at CKLW in Detroit, who played "96 Tears" regularly.

Then a funny thing happened. Executives at a national label that was almost bankrupt, Cameo Records, heard "96 Tears" on CKLW, and picked it up for distribution. They began selling it in other parts of the country. And suddenly, it took off. The song was recorded in February. By October, seven months later, it achieved the ultimate rock 'n' roll fantasy—#1 in America.

## A PERFECT ENDING

The band broke up, according to lead guitarist Robert Balderrama, because its anonymous lead singer, Question Mark, "was on kind of an ego trip." Figure that one out.

## IRRELEVANT ASIDE

In 1989, the Federal government financed a study on tuxedos to find out how to tax them. In a 54-page report, they revealed thought-provoking data like: "There are two major types of tuxedos—basic black tuxedos and fashion tuxedos." Their "principal findings" were that a rental tux lasts an average of 1.9 years, while the privately owned tux might last as long as 3.7 years.

**John Wayne appeared in 153 movies. In all but 11 of them, he was the star.**

# THE ORIGIN OF FRANKENSTEIN

*The original Frankenstein's monster wasn't Boris Karloff—it was (believe it or not) a character created by a 19-year-old author named Mary Shelley...more than 170 years ago.*

## BACKGROUND

In the summer of 1816, 19-year-old Mary Wollstonecraft Shelley and her 24-year-old husband, the poet Percy Bysshe Shelley, visited Switzerland. "It proved a wet, uncongenial summer," she wrote some 15 years later, "and incessant rain often confined us for days to the house."

To pass the time, the Shelleys and their neighbors—28-year-old Lord Byron, his 23-year-old personal physician, and his 18-year-old lover—read German ghost stories aloud. They enjoyed it so much that one day, Byron announced, "We will each write a ghost story." Everyone agreed, but apparently the poets, unaccustomed to prose writing, couldn't come up with anything very scary.

Mary was determined to do better. "I busied myself to think of a story," she recalled, "One which would speak to the mysterious fears of our nature and awaken thrilling horror." Yet she couldn't come up with anything. Every morning, her companions asked: "Have you thought of a story?" "And each morning," she wrote later, " I was forced to reply with a mortifying negative."

## A FLASH OF INSPIRATION

One evening Mary sat by the fireplace, listening to her husband and Byron discuss the possibility of reanimating a corpse with electricity, giving it what they called "vital warmth."

The discussion finally ended well after midnight, and Shelley retired. But Mary, "transfixed in speculation," couldn't sleep.

"When I placed my head on the pillow," she recalled, " I did not sleep, nor could I be said to think. My imagination, unbidden, possessed and guided me, gifting the successive images that arose in my mind with a vividness far beyond the usual bounds of reverie. I saw—with shut eyes but acute mental vision—I saw the pale student of unhallowed arts kneeling beside the thing he had put together....I saw the hideous phantasm of a man stretched out, and then, on the working of some powerful engine, show signs of life and stir with an uneasy, half-vital motion.

"Frightful must it be; for supremely frightful would be the effect of any human endeavor to mock the stupendous mechanism of the Creator of the world. His success would terrify the artist; he would rush away from his odious handiwork, horror-stricken. He would hope that, left to itself, the slight spark of light which he had communicated would fade; that this thing would subside into dead matter; and he might sleep in the belief that the silence of the grave would quench forever the transient existence of the hideous corpse which he had looked upon as the cradle of life. He sleeps; but he is awakened; the horrid thing stands at his bedside, opening his curtains, and looking on him with yellow, watery eyes...."

## THE PERFECT HORROR STORY

At this point, Mary opened her eyes in terror—so frightened that she needed reassurance it had all just been her imagination. She gazed around the room, but just couldn't shake the image of "my hideous phantom." Finally, to take her mind off the creature, she went back to the ghost story she'd been trying to compose all week. "If only I could contrive one," she thought, "that would frighten people as I myself had been frightened that night!" Then she realized that her vision was, in fact, the story she'd been reaching for.

As she recounted: "Swift as light and as cheering was the idea that broke in upon me. 'I have found it! What terrified me will terrify others; and I need only describe the spectre which had haunted my midnight pillow.' On the morrow I announced I had thought of a story. I began the day with the words, 'It was on a dreary night in November,' making only a transcript of the grim terrors of my waking dream."

## THE NOVEL

The first version of Frankenstein was a short story. But Mary's husband encouraged her to develop it further, and she eventually turned it into a novel. It was published anonymously in 3 parts in 1818. "Mary," notes one critic, "did not think it important enough to sign her name to the book....And since her husband wrote the book's preface, people assumed he had written the rest of the book as well....It was not until a later edition of *Frankenstein* that the book was revealed as the work of a young girl."

# HOW PANTYHOSE HATCHED

*Today, you can find pantyhose in every supermarket, clothes store, department store, drug store, and so on. Surprisingly, they've only been around since the mid-'60s.*

In the early '60s, women were still wearing traditional stockings with garter belts, as they had since 1939, when DuPont first introduced nylons.

But as the mini-skirt caught on, stockings became impossible to wear. Whenever a woman sat down, the tops of her stockings showed. It was embarrassing. But what could she do instead?

Hosiery manufacturers looked desperately for a solution to the problem. They tried all kinds of bizarre things—stocking glue (roll it onto the top of your leg, and the stocking will stick there—no garters needed), decorating the tops of the stockings (so it looked like they were meant to be seen), even girdles with stockings already attached. But the only alternative that really made sense was a new kind of sheer tights called pantyhose. And they were much more expensive than stockings. Would women pay for them?

Enter Mary Quant, the creator of the mini-skirt. She added patterns to tights and—accompanied by a huge publicity campaign—introduced them as an integral part of the mini-skirt outfit. It was not only the solution to embarrassing stocking problems, she said, but an essential element of the "mini-look." Since it was in fashion, woman gladly paid the price.

Once the market for pantyhose was established, manufacturers developed ways to cut prices. Soon, undecorated pantyhose were cheaper than traditional stockings, and—since they were more convenient—they quickly replaced the old-fashioned kind. By the early '70s, 95% of all women's hosiery sold was pantyhose.

**FASHION FLOP:** In the mid-'60s, Coty tried cashing in on the colored pantyhose craze by offering "Body Paint." Why bother wearing expensive pantyhose, they asked, when you can paint your legs? The "mini, kicky, bare-as-you-dare fashion" was packaged in a paint can, and came complete with a roller and paint tray. There were four colors: Blue, green, mauve, or "flesh." It bombed.

**Plywood emits formaldehyde—it's one of the home's biggest indoor polluters.**

# BY GEORGE!

*George Burns was always a popular performer. But by lasting longer than his compatriots, he's become an elder statesman, too.*

"Too bad that all the people who know how to run the country are driving taxicabs and cutting hair."

"By the time you're eighty years old, you've learned everything. You only have to remember it."

"I must be getting absent-minded. Whenever I complain that things aren't what they used to be, I forget to include myself."

"The most important thing in acting is honesty. If you can fake that, you've got it made."

"I don't believe in dying—it's been done. I'm working on a new exit. Besides, I can't die now—I'm booked."

"I smoke cigars because at my age, if I don't have something to hold onto, I might fall down."

"Retirement at 65 is ridiculous. When I was 65, I still had pimples."

"Happiness? A good cigar, a good meal, a good cigar, and a good woman—or a bad woman; it depends on how much happiness you can handle."

"If you live to the age of a hundred, you've got it made, because very few people die past the age of a hundred."

"I don't worry about getting old. I'm old already. Only young people worry about getting old."

"I was married by a judge. I should have asked for a jury."

"Happiness is having a large, loving, caring, close-knit family in another city."

"Critics are eunuchs at a gang-bang."

"To be perfectly honest, I don't think acting is very hard. They say the most important thing to be able to do is laugh and cry. Well, if I have to cry I think of my sex life, and if I have to laugh, I think of my sex life."

# THE THREE STOOGES

*There's nothing like the sound of a good "Nyuk, nyuk, nyuk" to make a Three Stooges fan smile. Even if you don't like them, you have to be impressed by their enduring popularity.*

**HOW THEY STARTED.**

There are so many different stories about the Stooges' origin that it's hard to know which is correct. Probably none of them. Anyway, here's one that sounds good.

• There was a vaudevillian named Ted Healy, a boyhood friend of Moe and Shemp Horwitz. One night in 1922, some acrobats working for him walked out just before a show. Desperate, he asked Moe to fill in temporarily, as a favor.

• Moe, in turn, got his brother Shemp out of the audience, and the 3 of them did an impromptu routine that had the audience in stitches. Moe and Shemp loved the stage, so they changed their names from Horwitz to Howard and hit the road with their friend as Ted Healy and the Gang (or Ted Healy and his Stooges, depending on who tells the story).

• In 1925, the trio was on the lookout for another member and spotted Larry Fine (real name: Louis Feinberg) playing violin with the "Haney Sisters and Fine." Exactly why they thought he'd be a good Stooge isn't clear, since he'd never done comedy before, but he joined as the third Stooge anyway.

• They traveled the vaudeville circuit for years under a variety of names, including Ted Healy and his Racketeers, his Southern Gentlemen, his Stooges, etc. Then they wound up in a Broadway revue in 1929, which led to a movie contract.

• In 1931, Shemp quit and was replaced by his younger brother, Jerry. At the time, Jerry had a full head of hair and a handsome mustache—but Healy insisted he shave them both off...hence the nickname "Curly."

• Three years later, after a bitter dispute, the boys broke up with Healy. They quickly got a Columbia film contract on their own, and The Three Stooges were born.

• Over the next 23 years, they made 190 short films—but no features. For some reason, Harry Cohn, head of Columbia Pictures, wouldn't allow it (despite the Stooges' popularity and the fact they were once nominated for an Oscar).

• Between the '30s and the '50s, the Stooges made four personnel changes: In 1946, Curly suffered a stroke and retired; Shemp then returned to the Stooges until his death in 1955; he, in turn, was replaced by Joe Besser (Joe) and Joe DeRita (Curly Joe).

## INSIDE FACTS.

### Two-Fingered Poker

One day backstage in the '30s, Larry, Shemp and Moe were playing cards. Shemp accused Larry of cheating. After a heated argument, Shemp reached over and stuck his fingers in Larry's eyes. Moe, watching, thought it was hilarious...and that's how his famous poke-in-the eyes routine was born.

### Profitable Experience

By the mid-'50s, the average budget for a Three Stooges' episode—including the stars' salaries—was about $16,000. Depending on the time slot, Columbia Pictures can now earn more than that with one showing of the same film...in one city.

### So What If He's Dead?

The last four Stooges episodes featuring Shemp were filmed after he died. The films' producer, Jules White, brought in a Shemp "double" who was only seen from behind.

### The Stooges' Resurrection

By the mid-'50s the demand for short films had petered out. So in 1957, Columbia unceremoniously announced they weren't renewing the Stooges' contracts. Moe and Larry were devastated. After 23 years, what else could they do? Moe was rich from real estate investments, but Larry was broke—which made it even harder. They decided to get a third Stooge (Curly and Shemp were dead) and go back on tour. Joe DeRita, "Curly Joe," was selected. They started making appearances in 3rd-rate clubs, just to have work.

Meanwhile, Columbia, looking for a way to get a few bucks out of its old Stooge films, released them to TV at bargain prices. They had no expectations, so everyone (particularly Moe and Larry) was shocked when, in 1959, the Stooges emerged as the hottest kids' program in America. Suddenly the Stooges had offers to make big-time personal appearances and new films. And they've been modern American cult heroes ever since.

**In 75% of American households, women manage the money and pay the bills.**

# A BIZARRE GENIUS

*Great geniuses are often said to be "born ahead of their time." William James Sidis, on the other hand, seems to have been born out of his time completely; on the wrong world, in the wrong dimension. Perhaps someday the world will understand Sidis's strange genius. Probably not.*

William James Sidis was born in 1898. His father, Boris Sidis, taught psychology at Harvard and was considered one of the foremost psychologists of his day. Boris argued that traditional approaches to childrearing obstructed the learning process. The elder Sidis was determined not to make that mistake with his son.

- He started by stringing words together with alphabet blocks above the child's crib.
- He eschewed the usual "googley-goo" babytalk that adults lapse into around infants, speaking instead to the child the same way he would speak to an adult. If the boy showed any interest in a subject, Boris encouraged his curiosity and study.

The effect of all this on the boy was astounding. By the time he was two, Willie was reading literature meant for adults; by age four he was typing letters in French and English; at age five he wrote a treatise on anatomy and dazzled everyone with a mathematical expertise few adults could match.

## HIGHER EDUCATION

William Sidis graduated from Brookline High School when he was eight years old. When he applied to Harvard, the entrance board suggested he take a few years off to let his personality catch up to his intellect.

- Willie spent the time between high school and college reading books in French, German, Latin, Greek, Russian, Turkish, and Armenian.
- The boy entered Harvard at age eleven, becoming the youngest student ever to attend the school.
- Later that year, he gave a speech in front of the Harvard Mathematical Society on the subject of "Four-Dimensional Bodies." After the speech, Professor Daniel Comstock of MIT told reporters that

**The first baseball team to put numbers on their uniforms: the N.Y. Yankees, in 1929.**

the boy would someday be the greatest mathematician of the century.

## DOWNHILL

From that moment on, William Sidis's world was never the same. Reporters followed his every move. He was a celebrity. His classmates treated him differently.

- The boy kept to himself, walking to his classes alone.
- At some point, Sidis realized his intellect was not admired—it was stared at. He wasn't merely intelligent—he was a freak.
- Within a year, at age 12, he suffered a nervous breakdown. He was taken to his father's Psycho-therapeutic Institute and treated.
- A few months later, Willie was back at Harvard, studying as diligently as ever. He graduated cum laude at the age of sixteen.
- In 1918, he began teaching mathematics at Rice University in Texas. But the annoyance of constant media attention finally took its toll. Quitting his teaching post, the young man moved back to Boston and, after a notorious arrest at a socialist march, disappeared from sight.
- In 1924, a reporter found him in New York City, working in a Wall Street office for menial pay. Sidis told the reporter that he was not the boy-wonder he once was. (Although this was probably not true. At one point, Sidis's knowledge of mathematics led him to completely rework his employer's statistical tables in his spare time, for amusement.) He wanted anonymity and a menial job that made no demands on him. Soon afterwards, he dropped out of sight again.

## A STRANGE OBSESSION

- As an adult, Sidis had one great passion, a passion that has intrigued psychologists and writers for years. Sidis spent hours every day in search of streetcar transfers. He would chase them through windy lots, chisel them from icy sidewalks, and rescue them from rainy gutters. During his lifetime, he collected over two thousand of them, all different.
- In 1926, he published a book on the subject of his hobby. The book, *Notes on the Collection of Transfers*, is—to say the least—esoteric. Sidis filled it with page after page of detailed information on how the transfers are interpreted, how to use them to their best advantage, and techniques used by the devoted "peridromophile"

(his term for someone who collects streetcar transfers) to find abandoned transfers.

• For those with merely a passing interest in the subject, he provided a chapter of bad streetcar jokes.

• Sidis used the pseudonym "Frank Folupa" to throw the press off the track, but it did not work. The book was quickly ascribed to him and once again, Sidis had to flee from the curious eyes of the press, losing himself in the crowded streets of New York City.

• Sidis managed to stay out of view for many years after that. In 1937, a writer working for *The New Yorker* magazine found him in a rundown rooming house in South Boston.

• Sidis told the reporter that he was no longer a mathematical genius. "The very sight of a mathematical formula," he claimed, "makes me physically ill." When the *New Yorker* article appeared, Sidis sued for invasion of privacy. Acting as his own attorney, Sidis offered to take an I.Q. test to prove just how normal he was. The suit was thrown out of court.

• Again the world forgot about him—until 1944, when, at the age of 46, William James Sidis died of a cerebral hemorrhage.

No one can explain his life. But one thing is certain: he knew more about streetcar transfers than anyone in history. And for this, we salute him.

## ANOTHER "UNUSUAL" COLLECTOR

George Wahlert, of New York, has what he believes to be the world's largest collection of Apollo 11 memorabilia. He hasn't got any moon rocks or lunar modules yet, but he does have stamps, plates, mugs, cups, plaques, medals, flags, towels, curtains, T-shirts, hats, pencils, spoons, watches, clocks, models, lunchboxes...and even a bedspread—all commemorating the first flight to the moon.

How did George become hooked on the subject? Apollo 11 landed on the moon on his birthday.

Now he has enough stuff to fill a museum.

Would he like to go to the moon someday? He already has his Pan Am ticket.

He even bought two acres of moon land, and has a moon deed to prove it. "There's probably a lunar rover parked on my property right now," he says.

**When they grow up: 1 in 100 American boys, and 1 in 150 girls, will become lawyers.**

# MACK THE KNIFE

*A classic tune with a classy history. From* Behind the Hits, *by Bob Shannon and John Javna.*

Bobby Darin's version of "Mack the Knife" was the #1 song of 1959. But few people who enjoyed it then—or have since—had any idea of its strange 30-year history.

## THE SHARK BITES...

"Mack" debuted in Germany in 1929, in the Kurt Weill / Bertolt Brecht production of the *Threepenny Opera*, a scathing social commentary with parallels to the rise of Adolf Hitler. It was then known as "The Ballad of Mac the Knife" and was a song about MacHeath, the central character of the play. It was quite candid about Mac's bloody escapades.

The Nazis didn't particularly like Weill; he, Brecht, and Weill's wife, Lotte Lenya—who had created the role of Jenny in the original play—fled to the United States.

## NEVER A TRACE OF RED

But it wasn't until the early '50s that the *Threepenny Opera* was performed here—and when it was, "The Ballad of Mac the Knife" became a very different song. In the conservative atmosphere of the times, the German lyrics were considered too violent to be translated literally. So an American named Marc Blitzstein was assigned to rewrite it.

## MACKIE'S BACK

By 1956, millions of Americans had heard the melody of "Mac the Knife"...but they still hadn't heard either the German *or* American version of the lyrics—because the Dick Hyman Trio had recorded it as an instrumental. Hyman called it "Moritat," and it sold over a million copies.

Around that time, Louis Armstrong also recorded it, using Blitzstein's lyrics. But when Satchmo sang the song, he made a mistake in the list of characters near the end; he added singer/actress Lotte Lenya's name to the roll-call of ladies who'd succumbed to "Mackie." It was this version that got to Bobby Darin.

**According to polls, America's all-time favorite foreign movie star is Brigitte Bardot.**

## DARIN'S "MACK" ATTACK

An up-and-coming rock 'n' roll singer who had already scored with "Splish Splash," "Queen of the Hop," and "Dream Lover," Darin was hesitant about "Mack the Knife." He recorded it as part of an album called "That's All," but never envisioned it as a single. His friend Dick Clark agreed, telling Darin that it could never be a hit—it was too different. Besides, about twenty different versions of the song had already been recorded in 1956.

But Darin didn't have the last word on the subject. His record label, Atco, decided to release it as a single over his objections. To his surprise, "Mack the Knife" rocketed up the charts immediately. It was not only the most popular record of the year—selling over two million copies—but also won the Grammy for "Record of the Year." Darin was named "Best New Artist," although he'd been around the Top 10 for a while, and the song transformed him into a Frank Sinatra-type entertainer.

## MACKIE'S BACK...AGAIN

In all, between 1956 and 1960 "Mack the Knife" appeared in the Top 40 seven times. The most memorable of these was the last one, by Ella Fitzgerald. Her version—a tribute to Satchmo and Darin—was recorded live at a concert in Berlin, and she forgot the words. It wasn't a problem, though. Ella is one of the all-time great improvisers, and the Germans had no idea what the English meant. She just made up the lyrics, which was all anyone had been doing since the original English translation anyway.

• **Final note:** The song keeps going and changing. In the late '80s, Frank Sinatra attempted a version of "Mack the Knife." He didn't start with Weill's, or Armstrong's or Darin's version, though—instead, he copied Ella's.

## ABOUT BOBBY DARIN:

- His real name was Walden Robert Cassotto.
- He picked the named "Darin" out of a phone book.
- While he was a scuffling young singer, he and Connie Francis fell in love. Her father chased him away. She never got over it; Darin went on to marry teenage heartthrob Sandra Dee.
- Darin's first big hit, "Splish Splash," was written by the mother of a popular New York deejay, Murray the K.
- His congenitally weak heart gave out in 1973; he died at age 37.

**The oldest tree in the world is the macrozamia tree of Australia. It lives for 7,000 years.**

# BODY PARTS

*Some interesting facts about the human body.*

How much blood is running through your body right now? If you're an average person, about 6 quarts.

☞

If you've got a normal head of hair, you have about 100,000 hairs on it.

• But if you're a redhead, you've probably got only about 90,000. For some reason, redheads have less hair than other people.

• Blondes, on the other hand, have more hair on their heads.

☞

Your brain weighs 3 pounds. It contains 14 billion cells.

☞

A human hair grows at an average rate of 8 inches a year.

☞

At birth, an infant has 350 bones.

• As the child grows, many bones fuse with other bones.

• So by the time the child is grown, his or her body contains only 206 bones (give or take a few—not every bone does what it's supposed to).

☞

Your heart will probably beat 36 million times this year.

Your eye measures about an inch in diameter.

• It weighs around a quarter of an ounce.

• If you're a man, your eyes are slightly bigger than the average woman's.

☞

If your sense of smell isn't working, you can't taste an onion.

☞

The normal adult has 656 muscles.

• 42% of an average male's body weight is muscle.

• 38% of an average female's body weight is muscle.

☞

As an infant grows, the body part that grows least is the eye. While the rest of an adult body is 20 times bigger than it was at birth, the eye is only 3-1/4 times bigger.

☞

The average adult gets 7-1/2 hours of sleep every night.

• As we age, we need less sleep—until we hit our 60s, when the need starts to increase again.

# LILY TOMLIN SAYS...

*Comments from a great comedienne.*

"No matter how cynical you get, it's impossible to keep up."

"There will be sex after death; we just won't be able to feel it."

"The trouble with the rat race is that even if you win, you're still a rat."

"For fast acting relief, try slowing down."

"If truth is beauty, how come no one has their hair done in the library?"

"Why is it when we talk to God, we're said to be praying—but when God talks to us, we're schizophrenic?"

"If you read a lot of books, you're considered well-read. But if you watch a lot of TV, you're not considered well-viewed."

"The best mind-altering drug is truth."

"If something's true, you don't have to believe in it."

"You are what you think.... Geez, that's frightening."

"Sometimes I worry about being a success in a mediocre world."

"I had a friend who was getting married. I gave her a subscription to *Modern Bride*. The subscription lasted longer than the marriage."

"If love is the answer, could you rephrase the question?"

"What most distinguishes us humans from lower animals is our desire to take drugs."

"Sometimes I feel like a figment of my own imagination."

"We're all in this alone."

"What goes up must come down...but don't expect it to land where you can find it—Murphy's Law applied to Newton's."

"Our ability to delude ourselves may be an important survival tool."

# "LET'S DO THE TWIST"

*Looking back 30 years, past slam-dancing and Flashdancing and* Dirty Dancing, *it's hard to believe how significant—and scandalous—the tame Twist was when it first appeared. It's considered nostalgic fun today, but it was a powerful force in its time. It helped change American society in the '60s, and its impact is still being felt. Here's a quick retrospective.*

**ITS ORIGIN**

Everyone knows that "Mr. Twister" is Chubby Checker. "You know," he said, "I taught the world how to dance as they know it today. I'm almost like Einstein creating atomic power. Whatever dances came after the Twist, it all started here."

But "The Twist" was not originally done by Chubby Checker. The original version was written and recorded by a rhythm and blues performer named Hank Ballard.

• In the '50s, Ballard was a popular R&B singer who toured with his band, the Midnighters. The band often danced while they played, and one night . . . . "I was just watching them go through their routines, seeing them twisting their bodies," Ballard recalls, "and the lyric just came to me—'Twist.' " He wrote the rest of the lyrics to go along with their movements, taking the melody from an old R&B song, "What'cha Gonna Do."

• In 1959 he recorded the song and it was released as the flip side of "Teardrops on My Letter." He thought it should be the hit side, but couldn't convince his record company. "They thought it was just another mediocre record," he sighs.

• Ballard and his group tried to popularize the dance as they toured the country, and when they got to Baltimore it finally caught on. There, a deejay named Buddy Dean (who hosted a TV dance party) watched Baltimore teenagers Twisting up a storm. "He saw these kids doing the dance," says Ballard, "so he called up Dick Clark and told him to come over and see them."

• Clark, hosting "American Bandstand" in nearby Philadelphia, liked what he saw. He played the song on his show, and was impressed by the audience response, so he offered Ballard a chance to introduce the dance on "Bandstand." It would have been Ballard's big break, but it fell through. Instead, Clark got someone to do a new version. "He was trying to find someone to emulate my voice," Ballard says.

## ENTER CHUBBY CHECKER

Clark found just the right person—Ernest Evans, an expert at mimicking other singers. Ernest changed his name to Chubby Checker at the suggestion of Clark's wife ("He looks just like a little Fats Domino—let's call him Chubby Checker"), and the new version of "The Twist" was released.

• Chubby copied Ballard's version exactly—it's almost impossible to tell the difference between them.

• With Dick Clark pushing it, Checker's record became a #1 smash in 1960, and the dance became a teenage craze. Then, like all fads, it died down.

• In 1962, however, adults discovered it. Society celebs like Zsa Zsa Gabor were photographed twisting at the Peppermint Lounge . . .and suddenly the dance was bigger than ever. Chubby's version of "The Twist" zoomed back up the charts to #1 again. It is still the only record ever to reach #1 in two different years. It was on the charts for 8 months, longer than any other #1 record in history.

• Twist records were released by the carload. Joey Dee and the Starliters hit #1 with "The Peppermint Twist"; young Rod McKuen sang "Oliver Twist"; Ray Charles put out a Twist album; Chubby did "Let's Twist Again"; Sam Cooke did "Twistin' the Night Away"; even Frank Sinatra got into the act. Everyone in America, it seemed, was doing the Twist. Except Hank Ballard.

## AS A DANCE

The "Twist" made social dancing accessible to everyone; it was the first dance that anybody—young or old, athletic or uncoordinated, etc.—could do. There was nothing special to learn, no need to take lessons, and no need to practice. Instructions for the Twist could be summed up in one sentence. "It's like putting out a cigarette with both feet," explained Chubby Checker, "and coming out of a shower and wiping your bottom with a towel to the beat of the music. It's that simple."

• It was the first modern dance that people did without touching each other. Practically every popular dance since 1960 (except

**A monkey was once tried and convicted for smoking a cigarette in South Bend, Indiana.**

disco) is a direct outgrowth of the Twist.

• And finally, after howling about the immorality of rock 'n' roll in the late '50s, parents gave up their protests in 1962 and joined in . . .doing the Twist. It was the first time adults accepted rock. Until then, it was associated with juvenile delinquency.

**AS A MERCHANDISING BOOM**

While the Twist was *the* popular dance, Twist merchandise sold like hot cakes. You could get "twist" anything.

• Clothes became "Twist clothes" if you put fringes on them (fringes would fly out when you twisted);

• A "Twister chair" was so twisted that you couldn't sit on it;

• "Twist cigars" (bent stogies) were available;

• You could even eat a misshapen hot dog called a "Twistfurter." "The Twist has now danced its way onto the dinner table," announced its manufacturer.

**AS A SCANDAL. Some examples of the international furor caused by the Twist:**

**1961**: The Associated Press reported a scandalous scoop. "Under a secret service guard," AP claimed, "Mrs. Jacqueline Kennedy slipped out of Palm Beach last night and for an hour and a half danced the Twist in a Fort Lauderdale nightclub." AP turned out to be wrong—Jackie was home all night. AP had to publish a public apology. . .its first since it announced the end of World War II prematurely.

**1962:** Tampa, Florida, banned the Twist in its community centers.

**1962:** The United Arab Republic banned the Twist.

**1962:** Red Chinese newspapers castigated "ugly displays" of young people doing the Twist in Maoming Cultural Park in China.

**1962:** The Twist was banned by the Buffalo, New York, diocese in parish, school, and Catholic Youth Organization events.

**1962:** The South African foreign minister deplored the fact that South African youth were doing the Twist, calling it a "strange god from the United States."

**1963:** The Twist was East Germany's most popular dance, despite the fact that the Communist Party had denounced it.

**1963:** The South Vietnamese government said the Twist "was not compatible with the anti-Communist struggle," and banned it.

**There have been 69 movies featuring the character Zorro.**

# MUHAMMAD ALI SPEAKS

*The great boxer was also known as a talker. A few of his comments:*

"Pleasure is not happiness. It has no more importance than a shadow following a man."

"Everybody's negotiable."

"I'm so fast I could hit you before God gets the news."

"When you're as great as I am, it's hard to be humble."

"A nation is only as good as its women."

"My toughest fight was with my first wife."

[Explaining his retirement] "There are more pleasant things to do than beat up people."

"I'll beat him so bad he'll need a shoehorn to put his hat on."

"There are no pleasures in a fight, but some of my fights have been a pleasure to win."

"It's just a job. Grass grows. Birds fly. Waves pound the sand. I beat people up."

"I'm not only the greatest, I'm the double greatest."

"When you can whip any man in the world, you never know peace."

"No one knows what to say in the loser's room."

"Wars on nations change maps. Wars on poverty map change."

"The man who views the world at 50 the same as he did at 20 has wasted 30 years of his life."

"I fear Allah, thunderstorms, and airplane rides."

"I'm one black man who got loose."

"Christianity is a good philosophy if you live it, but it's controlled by white people who preach it but don't practice it. They just organize it and use it any which way they want to."

"I just *said* I was the greatest—I never thought I was."

**At one time, Hawaiian women were forbidden by law to eat coconuts.**

# AMERICA'S NOSTRADAMUS

*If you read the* National Enquirer *at the checkout counter of your local supermarket, you've seen that people like Jeanne Dixon are always trying to predict the future. They rarely get it right, of course. But in 1900 John Watkins did. In an article written for* The Ladies' Home Journal, *he looked a century into the future and foresaw subways, air-conditioning, Satellite TV, and lots more. No one has ever come close to this prognosticating feat—except maybe Nostradamus. Here's a small excerpt from Watkins' amazing 1900 article.*

**BACKGROUND.** John Elspeth Watkins was a Philadelphia newspaperman whose predictions were recently rediscovered by two Indiana professors. They call him "The Seer of the Century," and note that he was lucky enough to see many of his predictions come true before dying in the '40s.

What's amazing about these predictions? Remember what was going on in 1900: Production on primitive autos had just begun; they were still just a novelty. People lived in squalor and ill health, and died young. There was no such thing as an airplane. There was no radio; the first feature movie hadn't yet been made; the telephone had been invented a scant 25 years earlier. It was a whole different world—yet somehow, Watkins described ours in detail.

"These prophecies," he wrote in his introduction, "will seem strange, almost impossible."

It's a fascinating measure of how things have changed to realize that our way of life seemed like science fiction to the average American of 1900.

## EXCERPTS FROM WATKINS' PREDICTIONS

**"Man Will See Around the World.** Persons and things of all kinds will be brought within focus of cameras connected electrically with screens at opposite ends of circuits, thousands of miles at a span. American audiences in their theatres will view upon huge curtains before them the coronations of kings in Europe or the progress of battles in the Orient. The instrument bringing these distant scenes to the very doors of people will be connected with a giant telephone apparatus transmitting each incidental sound into its appropriate place. Thus the guns of a distant battle will be heard to boom when seen to blaze, and thus the lips of a remote actor or singer will be heard to utter words or music when seen to move."

**"The American Will Be Taller by from one to two inches.** His increase in stature will result from better health, due to vast reforms in medicine, sanitation, food, and athletics. He will live fifty years instead of thirty-five as at present—for he will reside in the suburbs."

**"Hot and Cold Air from Spigots.** Hot or cold air will be turned on from spigots to regulate the temperature of a house as we now turn on hot or cold water from spigots to regulate the temperature of the bath....Rising early to build the furnace fire will be a task of the olden times. Homes will have no chimneys, because no smoke will be created within their walls."

**"No Mosquitoes nor Flies.** Boards of health will have destroyed all mosquito haunts and breeding grounds, drained all stagnant pools, filled in all swamp-lands, and chemically treated all still-water streams. The extermination of the horse and its stable will reduce the house-fly."

**"Ready-Cooked Meals Will Be Bought from establishments similar to our bakeries of today.** Such wholesale cookery will be done in electric laboratories...equipped with electric stoves, and all sorts of electric devices, such as coffee-grinders, egg-beaters, stirrers, shakers, parers, meat-choppers, meat-saws, potato-mashers, lemon-squeezers, dishwashers, dish-dryers and the like. All such utensils will be washed in chemicals fatal to disease microbes."

**"There will Be No Street Cars in Our Large Cities.** All traffic will be below or high above ground when brought within city limits. In most cities it will be confined to broad subways or tunnels, well lighted and well ventilated, or to high trestles with "moving-sidewalk" stairways leading to the top. These underground or overhead streets will teem with automobile passenger coaches and freight wagons, with cushioned wheels. Subways or trestles will be reserved for express trains. Cities, therefore, will be

**The Boy Scouts were founded in 1910.**

free from all noises." [Ed. note: not quite.]

**"Photographs Will Be Telegraphed from any distance.** If there be a battle in China a hundred years hence snapshots of its most striking events will be published in the newspapers an hour later. Even today photographs are being telegraphed over short distances. Photographs will reproduce all of Nature's colors."

**"Automobiles Will Be Cheaper Than Horses are today.** Farmers will own automobile hay-wagons, plows, harrows, and hay-rakes. A one-pound motor in one of these vehicles will do the work of a pair of horses or more.... Automobiles will have been substituted for every horse vehicle now known.... The horse in harness will be as scarce, if, indeed, not scarcer, then as the yoked ox is today."

**"Everybody Will Walk Ten Miles.** Gymnastics will begin in the nursery, where toys and games will be designed to strengthen the muscles. Exercise will be compulsory in the schools. Every school, college, and community will have a complete gymnasium.... A man or woman unable to walk ten miles at a stretch will be regarded as a weakling."

**"There Will Be No Wild Animals except in menageries.** Rats and mice will have been exterminated. The horse will have become practically extinct.... The automobile will have driven out the horse. Cattle and sheep will have no horns. They will be unable to run faster than the fattened hog of to-day. Food animals will be bred to expend practically all of their life energy in producing meat, milk, wool, and other by-products. Horns, bones, muscles and lungs will have been neglected."

**"Submarine boats** submerged for days will be capable of wiping a whole navy off the face of the deep. "

**"To England in Two Days.** Fast electric ships, crossing the ocean at more than a mile a minute, will go from New York to Liverpool in two days. The bodies of these ships will be built above the waves. They will be supported upon runners, somewhat like those of the sleigh. These runners will be very buoyant. Upon their undersides will be apertures expelling jets of air. In this way a film of

**Until 1857, foreign coins were considered U.S. money if they were made of a precious metal.**

air will be kept between them and the water's surface. This film, together with the small surface of the runners, will reduce friction against the waves to the smallest possible degree." [Ed. note: Wow! He's predicting hydrofoils.]

**"Telephones Around the World.** Wireless telephone and telegraph circuits will span the world. A husband in the middle of the Atlantic will be able to converse with his wife sitting in her boudoir in Chicago. We will be able to telephone to China quite as readily as we now talk from New York to Brooklyn. By an automatic signal they will connect with any circuit in their locality without the intervention of a 'hello girl.' "

**"Automatic instruments reproducing original airs exactly will bring the best music to the families of the untalented.** In great cities there will be public opera-houses whose singers and musicians are paid from funds endowed by philanthropists and by the government. The piano will be capable of changing its tone from cheerful to sad. Many devices will add to the emotional effect of music."

**"How Children Will Be Taught.** A university education will be free to every man and woman. Several great national universities will have been established. Children will study a simple English grammar adapted to simplified English, and not copied after the Latin. Time will be saved by grouping like studies...Medical inspectors regularly visiting the public schools will furnish poor children free eyeglasses, free dentistry, and free medical attention of every kind. The very poor will, when necessary, get free rides to and from school and free lunches between sessions." [Ed. note: An incredible, revolutionary concept in 1900.]

**"Oranges...in Philadelphia.** Fast-flying refrigerators on land and sea will bring delicious fruits from the tropics and southern temperate zone within a few days. The farmer of South America, South Africa, Australia, and the South Sea Islands, whose seasons are directly opposite to ours, will thus supply us in winter with fresh summer foods which cannot be grown here. Scientists will have discovered how to raise here many fruits now confined to much hotter or colder climates."

**All the Zodiac symbols are animals, except one—Libra.**

# LEAVE IT TO BEAVER

*The Cleavers and their clan are classic TV creations—from June, who wore pearls while she vacuumed...to the rotten Eddie Haskell...to Beaver Cleaver, the quintessential '50s innocent.*

**HOW IT STARTED.**

By 1957, shows like "The Danny Thomas Show" and "Father Knows Best"—sitcoms that portrayed modern American family life from an adult point of view—were hits. But Bob Mosher and Joe Connelly, who'd written together since 1942 (their major credit was over 1500 "Amos 'n' Andy" TV and radio scripts) came up with a new twist—a family sitcom that centered on the kids, not the parents. They called the program "Wally and Beaver" and modelled the characters after their own children. The stories they proposed were based on real-life occurrences in their own households.

When the pilot was filmed in 1957, it featured a slightly different cast than the one America eventually came to know: Barbara Billingsley (June) and Jerry Mathers (Beaver) were in it, but Hugh Beaumont (Ward Cleaver) and Tony Dow (Wally) were not.

CBS liked it anyway, and bought it for the 1957-58 season. Beaumont and Dow were hired to join the permanent cast, and production began.

However, the producers made one last change—they gave their show a new title. "Wally and the Beaver" didn't work, they said, because "it sounded like a show about a boy and his pet." Instead, they appropriated the title of a 1954 sitcom, "Leave It to Larry," and altered it slightly.

"Beaver" ran from 1957 to 1963. Surprsingly, though, it was never a huge hit. In its six seasons on the air, it didn't place among the Top 25 shows of a year even once.

## INSIDE FACTS

### Meet the Beave

At age 8, Jerry "Beaver" Mathers was already a professional actor, with TV appearances and a major film role (in Alfred Hitchcock's *The Trouble With Harry*) under his belt. But he was so fidgety when he was auditioning for the role of Beaver that the producers asked him what the trouble was. He blurted out: "I gotta go to my scout meeting." Rather than disqualifying him, that won Jerry the job. His honesty and "little boy" qualities were exactly what they were looking for in their main character.

**Big Boys Don't Cry**

After the pilot, "Beaver's" producers began searching for a new actor to play Ward. One day, Jerry Mathers was called in to read with Hugh Beaumont, who'd befriended him when they co-starred in a religious film. In one scene, tears had been required, but Jerry just couldn't do it. Beaumont gave the boy invaluable advice: "Cover your face with your hands and laugh—it'll sound the same." It worked. So now, here was the man who'd been so kind to him, reading for the part of his father. When Jerry got home that night, he prayed Beaumont would get the part of Ward. And he did.

**Those Pearls**

June Cleaver caused a nation of TV-viewing kids to wonder why their moms didn't wear pearls while doing the laundry, too. The secret: Barbara Billingsley wore them in each episode not for aesthetics or even character development, but because the ex-model had a very skinny neck.

**But Don't Flush It!**

The first "Beaver" episode ever filmed, "Captain Jack," wasn't the first one aired—because it was censored! It included scenes of Wally and Beaver keeping a pet alligator in their toilet tank, and showing a toilet on camera was against CBS policy. It was finally shown as the 4th episode.

**Monstrous Copy**

After "Beaver," Mosher and Connelly created another family sitcom—"The Munsters"! Oddly enough, several "Munsters" episodes re-worked Beaver plots, with child werewolf Eddie Munster filling in for the Beave.

**Historic Coincidence**

Two events make Oct. 4, 1957 a historic date to remember: on that day, both "Leave It to Beaver" and Russia's first satellite, Sputnik 1, were launched.

# THE GREAT ROCKEFELLER

*John D. Rockefeller, one of the most famous Americans who ever lived, is a hero to some, a villain to others. Here are some facts about his life that you may not have heard before, excerpted from* Everybody's Business.

## HIS PARENTS

"Rockefeller, born in 1839, seems to have inherited his character in equal portions from his con artist father and his stern, Calvinist mother."

**The Father:** "William Avery Rockefeller, was a tall, effusive, barrelchested man who amassed great sums of money first by flimflamming the Iroquois Indians near his home in upstate New York and later by selling patent medicines, including an elixir he claimed could cure cancer."

- "He gave medical consultations to the gullible country folk for $25—a good two months' wages."
- "In 1849 he was indicted for the rape of a young woman who had worked in the Rockefeller household...."
- "He moved his family to Cleveland in 1853 so that he could take advantage of the settlers streaming west in covered wagons with their life savings."
- "He often went away for long periods, and finally he disappeared altogether. Years later, a reporter working for Joseph Pulitzer discovered that the elder Rockefeller survived to the age of 96 and spent his last 40 years living under an assumed name in South Dakota in a bigamous marriage with a woman 20 years his junior."

**The Mother:** "The task of setting the children on the path of righteousness fell to the mother, Eliza Davison Rockefeller, described as a 'thin, hatchet-faced woman with flaming red hair and equally stark blue eyes.' "

- "A devout Baptist, she studied the Bible and filled young John with maxims he carried through life, such as 'Willful waste makes woeful want.' "

## ROCKEFELLER GOES INTO BUSINESS

"Upon graduating from high school in 1855, Rockefeller chose to

go into business rather than to college."
• "He got a job as a bookkeeper with a Cleveland commodity merchant for $3.50 a week—10% of which he faithfully donated to the Baptist church."
• "After three years he had saved $800 and he decided to start his own commodity business with a partner, Maurice Clark."
• "Needing another $1,000, he turned to his father, who had promised each of his children that amount when they turned 21. John was only 19-1/2, but his father agreed to lend him the money at 10% interest until he came of age. 'I cheat my boys every chance get,' the father liked to say. 'I want to make 'em sharp.' "

## ROCKEFELLER DISCOVERS OIL

"Commodity prices rose sharply during the Civil War, and the new firm of Clark & Rockefeller made impressive profits. But a development even more far-reaching than the war was emerging around Titusville, Pennsylvania, where Edwin Drake had drilled the world's first successful oil well in 1859."
• "Oil was established as the cheapest, most efficient of illuminants, and...quickly started to replace candles and whale oil. The 'oil regions' sprouted derricks overnight, and dozens of refineries sprang up, first in Pittsburgh and New York and then...Cleveland."
• "In 1863 an acquaintance of Clark came to the partners with a proposition to start a refinery. Rockefeller dipped into his savings and invested $4,000 as a silent partner. At first he saw it as an unimportant sideline, but as the oil boom continued he began to devote more of his attention to it. In 1865, at the age of 26, he bought out the others and took control of the business."
• "His refinery was already the largest in Cleveland, and he was determined to expand. Around this time a startled bystander happened to see Rockefeller in his office, jumping into the air, clicking his heels, and rejoicing to himself, 'I'm bound to be rich! Bound to be rich! Bound to be rich!' "

## ROCKFELLER DESTROYS HIS COMPETITION

"Rockefeller now set out to control the oil industry. He realized that the big money in oil would not be made at the well, since prices collapsed every time someone struck a new find."
• "The key to his success, Rockefeller saw, was to control the refining and transportation of oil. Borrowing heavily from Cleveland

banks, he expanded his refining capacity and leased all the available tank cars from the railroads, leaving his competitors with no way to ship their oil out of Cleveland."

• "Next he negotiated an agreement with the Lake Shore Railroad to give him secret rebates on the crude oil he shipped from the oil regions to Cleveland and the refined oil he sent from Cleveland to the East Coast....With his freight advantage secure, Rockefeller formed a new company in 1870, called Standard Oil."

• "In the same year several railroads came up with a new plan: they would secretly combine with the largest refiners in each major refining center, to the benefit of both parties. Freight rates would go up, but the refiners in the scheme would get their money back through rebates on their shipments and additional 'drawbacks' on the shipments of other refiners who were not in on the arrangement. Rockefeller saw it as a way to get rid of his bothersome competitors in Cleveland: they could either collapse their businesses into his, in exchange for stock, or they would be bankrupted by the rebate scheme."

## BROTHERLY LOVE

"Rockefeller's younger brother, Frank, was a partner in a firm competing with Standard Oil. John D. told him: 'We have a combination with the railroads. We are going to buy out all the refiners in Cleveland. We will give everyone a chance to come in....Those who refuse will be crushed. If you don't sell your property to us, it will be valueless.' Frank did not sell, and he went bankrupt. He remained bitter for the rest of his life and eventually moved his two children's bodies from the family burial plot in Cleveland so they would not have to spend eternity in the company of John D. Rockefeller."

## GOOD MR. ROCKEFELLER

"Rockefeller looked back on this period with great piety. 'The Standard was an angel of mercy,' John D. told a biographer late in life. It was a situation, he explained, of 'the strongest and most prosperous concern in the business...turning to its less fortunate competitors...and saying to them, "We will stand in for the risks and hazards of the refining business....Come with us, and we will do you good." ' "

## ROCKEFELLER WANTS IT ALL

"Within three months, Rockefeller bought up all but 3 of his 25 competitors in Cleveland. Standard Oil controlled one-quarter of the nation's refining capacity, but he was not satisfied."

• "Rockefeller raised his sights and convinced more independent refiners in New York, Philadelphia, Pittsburgh, and the oil regions to come into the Standard combine. He did it with such secrecy that almost no one knew about his oil monopoly until it was a fait accompli."

• "By 1880 Rockefeller was refining 95% of the nation's oil."

• "At the time, American companies were prohibited from owning shares in other companies in other states. To get around this restriction, Rockefeller devised an 'oil trust,' which owned shares in each of the component companies—pretending all the while that the companies were independent."

• "He lavished bribes and 'deals' on state legislators."

• "He drove his competitors out of business by undercutting their prices until they gave up, and he expanded his power by buying oilfields across the country."

## CHANGING HIS IMAGE

Rockefeller was one of the most powerful men in the world when, in a 1911 anti-trust action, the Supreme Court forced Standard Oil to divide itself into into 31 different companies—but it wasn't as big a blow as it seemed to the public—because behind the scenes, Rockefeller held the bulk of the stock in all of them.

• With the aid of a publicist named Ivy Lee, the Rockefellers began a concerted effort to change his image. The Rockefeller Foundation was created; at Lee's behest, Rockefeller began giving away nickels (to children) and dimes (to adults) on the street; newspapers were encouraged by Lee to cover John D.'s golf games instead of his business practices.

• The effort was so effective that when he died in at age 97, John D. Rockefeller was known as a philanthropist by most Americans.

• His obituaries did little to contradict the image. Ivy Lee had seen to it that they were rewritten to include only data supplied by an "authorized" biographer.

**About 70% of Americans who go to college do it just to make more money.**

# ELEMENTARY, MY DEAR STEVE

*Once again, here's the famous woman sleuth, Leslie Boies, with a few simple mysteries for you to solve.* *Answers on page 454.*

Leslie Boies, beautiful blonde detective, was reading a report on the "Penge Bungalow Case" to her faithful companion, Steve.

"Mrs. Krojanker was making biscuits in the kitchen and accidentally dropped her diamond ring into some coffee," she read. "Strangely enough, though, the diamond didn't get wet."

"Wait a minute," Steve interjected. "How is that possible?"

"It's elementary, Steve," Leslie replied.

**What happened?**

**2.** "You know, Steve," Leslie said, "Once, I was captured and almost bumped off by my arch-enemy, Fritz von Springmeyer."

Steve was surprised. "I didn't know that."

"Yes, the only thing that saved me was his gang's code of honor. They had a tradition—they always gave their captives an even chance to escape death. They took two pieces of paper, wrote "death" on one and "freedom" on the other. Then they told me to pick one. Now, I knew that that von Springmeyer couldn't afford to let me live, so he'd probably written "death" on both papers. But I thought fast, and they had to free me."

Steve was stumped. "How'd you, do it, Les?"

**How *did* she do it?**

**3.** Leslie and Steve were having coffee, discussing Leslie's latest case. The famous detective happened to glance down and saw there was a fly in her coffee.

"Yuck! Waiter!" she called, "Take this coffee away and bring me a fresh cup."

The waiter took her coffee away, and returned with more.

Leslie took a sip. Then she exploded angrily—"Waiter, this is the same cup of coffee I had before!"

**How did she know?**

# THE NUT BEHIND GRAPE NUTS

*To appreciate this story, first read "The Birth of a Flake" on page 294. Then come back and read this.*

One of the guests in John Kellogg's Battle Creek sanitarium (The San) was a feeble 37-year-old named Charles W. Post, who arrived there in 1891. His story is told in the strangely fascinating book, *The New Nuts Among the Berries*:

Born in Springfield, Illinois in 1854, Post had wandered in search of success until, at age 37, he had become a well-to-do real estate salesman and blanket manufacturer in Fort Worth, Texas. He had also become a sick man, although we do not know the nature of his illness.

We do know that Dr. Kellogg promptly put Post in a wheelchair, and that after a few months Post hadn't enough cash left to remain a San resident; he had to become an outpatient. So he and his wife and daughter lived in a rented room in town, while Mrs. Post sewed suspenders to pay her husband's medical bills.

By the end of 9 months, Post was getting desperate. He still felt sick, and now he was destitute to boot. He pleaded with Dr. Kellogg to keep him on as a patient. He had spent quite a little time around the San's experimental kitchen. He knew that Kellogg had a new cereal coffee, called Minute Brew, and begged to help promote and sell the coffee in exchange for treatment and a little share of the profits. Post was coldly refused. John Harvey was not a loose man with money. And he did not believe in sharing profits with anyone....Why take Post in?

So Post studied the powers of the mind, took up Christian Science, determinedly repeated to himself, "I am well," got out of his wheelchair and went to work. He had studied the economics of The San and liked what he saw. So with his gift of persuasion, he raised some money and by 1892 established his small La Vita Inn on a plot of 10 acres. Here diet and mental healing were combined, and at prices much lower than those of The San. Meat was allowed to lure those who wanted it. But despite these and other inducements, Mrs. Post still had to go on sewing suspenders.

Post got some of Kellogg's overflow, some of his malcontent clients, and some of his employees. He talked up his own powers to heal with faith and hypnosis. But things were still so slow that he went back to Kellogg and offered to pray for San patients for only $50 a week. The answer was the usual no.

So now Post began writing a book—*I Am Well! The Modern Practice of Natural Suggestion as Distinct from Hypnotic or Unnatural Influence*.....The book featured amazing stories of instant cures—no waiting around for months and taking all those enemas. In some cases of bad teeth, dyspepsia, or troubled bladder, one could hope for same-day service. He also knocked out a pamphlet, *The Road to Wellville*, which he gave away. In both the book and the pamphlet he criticized Kellogg, making the Doctor his certain enemy.

Later on, the San magazine, *Good Health*, would say that Post had spent a lot of time around the San kitchen. The clear implication was that Post had borrowed some of the formulas for his products. *Good Health* quoted Kellogg as saying, "Let him see everything that we are doing. I shall be delighted if he makes a cereal coffee and wish him every success. The more he sells of it the less coffee will be consumed, and this will be of great benefit to the American people."

In January of 1895, the year Dr. Kellogg discovered and launched the cereal flake, C.W. Post put out [a coffee substitute he called] Postum Cereal Food Coffee. The original marketing tool was a handcart which was pushed through the town of Battle Creek.

Soon Post took samples to Grand Rapids, Michigan. Almost without capital, he told wholesale grocers they could pay him if and when they sold their Postum. He talked newspapers into ad credit on the strength of the line, "It Makes Red Blood." By the end of the year, his sales amounted to over $250,000. In three years, they tripled.

**American law: Less than 50% of the lawsuits filed actually go to court.**

Steadily Post opened wider and wider markets, using ads for which he invented such ailments as "coffee neuralgia" and "coffee heart." Postum could cure them, he said. "Lost Eyesight Through Coffee Drinking" was another of his gambits. And they worked; 50 years later Postum was still being sold as the answer to "coffee nerves." He ploughed a fortune into advertising, using every cent of profit and borrowing more. He began to take ads in the New York Magazine of Mysteries, offering spot cash to get testimonials of cures.

Largely because sales of Postum fell off in summer, Post came up with a cereal to try and take up the warm-weather slack....It was broken into rock-hard bits crumbled from sheets of baked wheat. He called it Grape Nuts, and he pulled out all the stops to announce its curative properties. According to ads which first ran in 1898, it was almost a specific for appendicitis. It tightened up loose teeth, fed the brain through what was implied to be almost a direct pipeline, and quickly disposed of tuberculosis and malaria. Of course, it worked better when consumed with a certain amount of faith; so Post put a copy of *The Road to Wellville* in each package. By 1901, C.W. Post was netting a million dollars a year.

In 1904, C.W. Post [scandalized the religious community of Battle Creek when he] divorced his suspender-sewing wife and married his typist. He was in his fifties; she was in her twenties. He also introduced a new cereal called "Elijah's Manna." Actually, it was corn flakes, which he had appropriated from Kellogg. But the cereal was unsuccessful until he changed its name to "Post Toasties." Then it became the cornerstone of Post Cereals, and later, General Foods.

In 1914, having tried to build his own city in Texas, and having failed to make it flourish by setting off explosions to bring rain, C.W. Post became depressed. In his Santa Barbara, California, home, he fired one of his own fine rifles into his head.

## UNRELATED ASIDE

When Harry Truman was told there were ghosts in the White House, he replied: "I'm sure they're here and I'm not half so alarmed at meeting up with any of them as I am at having to meet the live nuts I have to see every day."

# WHAT'S THE BEEF?

*What's the real difference between Burger King and McDonald's? Not what you'd think. An examination by Mike Wilkins.*

For years, Americans have watched as the world's two largest and most successful hamburger chains—Burger King and McDonald's—battled it out over supposed differences:

- Flame-broiling vs. frying
- *Doing It All For You* vs. *Having It Your Way*
- Whoppers vs. Big Macs.

And so on. To the uninitiated, these distinctions may seem like advertising hyperbole...But the fact is, the differences between McDonald's (10,000 restaurants, $13 billion in sales) and Burker King (4,500, $1.5 billion) are quite real.

## BACKGROUND

**McDonald's**

The mythology of the birth of the McDonald's chain is fairly well known. In 1954, Ray Kroc, a fifty-year-old paper cup and milk-shake-mixer salesman (actually owner of the company that made them), visited the McDonald Brothers' bustling restaurant in San Bernardino, California in 1954, after they placed a large order for his mixers. Impressed with their volume of business and the simplicity of their limited menu operation, he struck a deal for franchise rights, opened his first restaurant in Des Plaines, Illinois in 1955, and built McDonald's into the burger behemoth it is today.

**Burger King**

Surprisingly, Burger King also began with a visit to the original McDonald's. In 1952—two years before Kroc arrived—Keith Cramer, owner of a small Florida drive-in restaurant, made a pilgimage to watch the McDonald brothers in action. He was so impressed that he adapted their methods and began franchising his "Insta-Burger King" concept. A year later, the enterprise was taken over by franchisees Jim McLamore and David Edgerton. At first, Burger King was concentrated in the Southeast. But in 1967 it was acquired by Pillsbury, which began to expand the chain nationawide. With Pillsbury's economic muscle behind it, Burger King could challenge McDonald's in head-to-head competition. Their ad strategy: Burger King encouraged consumers to compare the "differences" between the two giants.

None of the ads, however, pinpointed the *real* differences.

## WHAT'S THE DIFFERENCE?

The biggest difference between Burger King and McDonald's is this: McDonald's cooks their hamburgers using a batch process. Burger King cooks theirs using a machine-paced assembly process.

- Check it out: Next time you go into one of these restaurants, watch how the burgers are cooked. McDonald's fries their hamburgers on a large platen, in batches, or groups, of up to twelve. Two or more batches may be on the platen at one time, in various stages of cooking. When the guy in the back says "Quarter Pounders Up," a whole batch is ready at the same time.
- Burger King is built around its "continuous chain broiler." Raw hamburgers are placed at one end, and 80 seconds later they come out the other end, cooked. This machine-paced assembly process is common in most industrial manufacturing processes. It turns hamburger production into an assembly line, much like the type Henry Ford introduced to automobiles in the early 1900s.

## IT'S BIGGER THAN IT LOOKS

As simple as this distinction (broiled vs. fried) seems, it is, in fact, at the core of each chain's operation, and is responsible for the corporate culture of each.

- For example: When hiring workers, McDonald's makes a big point about joining the McDonald's team, of the many incentives for doing good jobs, of its nonsalary benefits. Most McDonald's have a framed picture of the "Crew Member Of The Month" on a wall near the cash registers. McDonald's holds an Olympic-style competition to reward the best workers from around the country at each aspect of its food preparation. Not long ago, its advertising featured successful people who had once worked at McD's. When ordering, look at the McD uniforms. Many of the workers have pins or special nametags that signify profiency or accomplishment at a task.
- Go to Burger King and all you see is a "Help Wanted" sign. There are no incentives to join the "Burger King Pit Crew" and the

non-salary benefits are much less than those offered by McDonald's. (Total compensation was nearly $1 per hour greater at McDonald's in 1984.)

## TEAMWORK VS. ASSEMBLY LINE

How does this relate to production methods? In a batch process, the speed of delivery is dependent upon the worker. At McDonald's, 12 burgers are made at one time. They are hand-seared after 20 seconds on the grill, turned at 60 seconds, and pulled at 100. When they come off the grill, workers must quickly add condiments, wrap and shelve them. If there are two batches going in different stages of cooking, it means that speed is even more essential to keep the production moving. And this means that the crew must all be motivated, or the process gums up. People must be willing and able to help in another's area in case of backup. Teamwork and a sense of team must be present. Thus the motivational and non-salary rewards.

At Burger King, on the other hand, no matter how fast the burgers are prepared once they are cooked, the rate-limiting step is the cooking itself. One burger at a time comes off the chain broiler at the rate of eight per minute, maximum. The machine paces the process. (Again, in slow times this is not entirely accurate because at these points in the day, BK keeps an inventory of already cooked patties in a steam tray at the end of the broiler. That is why BK sometimes has to microwave its burgers.) As long as you can do your part of the assembly process in 7.5 seconds per burger (adding pickles and onions in 7 seconds is easy even if you're not very motivated—try it someday), that's all that is required. If you get excited and love your work, and can do it faster, so what? You still have to wait for the machine to spit out the next patty. This means that Burger King saves money on wages and hiring expense, by not paying for all the motivation-inspired cross-talk.

## HAVE IT WHOSE WAY?

Batch processing also means less room for individual differences in members of the batch. Twelve burgers come up, 12 burgers are all done exactly the same. At Burger King, since one patty comes out at a time, each can be made to individual order. Thus the *Have It Your Way* point of difference (vs. *We Do It All For You*) harped on by Burger King stems directly from the difference in production methods.

Also, batch processing means that twelve burgers will be ready (or 10 Quarter Pounders, or 6 Macs, since 12 patties = 6 Macs), whether or not customers are ready for them. During rush hour this is not a problem, but at other times it can be—especially in a business that promises fresh food. McDonald's and Burger King throw old food out—after 10 minutes in McDonald's case. That is what those cards with the numbers are doing on the McDonald's food shelves. When the minute hand gets to that number, all food in front of the card gets pitched.

## WASTE NOT...

Since a product may stay in the bin nine minutes, keeping it warm is a problem. That is why McDonald's uses those Styrofoam containers, especially for its larger sandwiches. Styrofoam is much more expensive (and less ecologically sound) than the cardboard Burger King uses. Burger King doesn't need to keep finished burgers warm as long, so it doesn't spend for the fancy packaging. A McDonald's restaurant spends about 1¢ per revenue dollar more on paper costs than does a Burger King. That adds up to a yearly $15 million savings systemwide for BK.

• As one might guess, McDonald's throws away much more food than Burger King does. In fact, in the seedy Tenderloin area of San Francisco, the derelicts paint stars on the wastecans of the nearby restaurants and stores. The only four-star can in the neighborhood? McDonald's.

## BATCHES MEAN BUCKS

How can McDonald's stay on top—or even competitive—with its system? The answer is that, when it is running right, the batch process allows for much greater throughput and faster speed of service. And speed is one big reason for the popularity of fast food in the first place. If an item is waiting in a bin, it obviously takes less time to serve than one made "your way."

• The batch process can deliver 300 burgers an hour vs. 200 for the continuous chain broiler.

• Speed standards given to individual restaurants by each headquarters bear this out. At side-by-side locations, the standard for a McDonald's is up to twice as fast as for a Burger King (a customer wait of, say, 90 seconds vs. three minutes).

• This difference may not be that noticeable per individual customer, but it means that McDonald's can do twice the dollar volume at peak than can a similarly sized Burger King.

Even customer flow is regulated by the speed of the broiler. Once the steam tray and bin reserves are gone, Burger King simply cannot serve more than eight burgers per minute. This accounts for at least some of the tremendous difference in the dollar volume per store between the two chains ($1.5 Billion over 4,500 stores, vs. $13 billion over 10,000). McDonald's is systemically better equipped to handle crowded areas. It is only during off-peak times when Burger King comes close in dollar volume, and is actually more efficient because of less waste, paper, and salary expenses.

So there you have it. An enormous "hidden" difference at the heart of the two chains. Next time you hear either of them make a claim about their service or products, check to see if it's based on their methods of production. Chances are, it will be.

**UNRELATED INFO:**

These were the #1 songs in America during the first week of each of the following years, according to *Billboard* magazine:

- 1958: "At the Hop," by Danny and the Juniors
- 1960: "El Paso," by Marty Robbins
- 1963: "Go Away Little Girl," by Steve Lawrence
- 1965: "Downtown," by Petula Clark
- 1966: "The Sounds of Silence," by Simon and Garfunkel
- 1967: "Kind of a Drag," by the Buckinghams
- 1969: "Crimson and Clover," by Tommy James & the Shondells
- 1971: "Knock Three Times," by Dawn
- 1972: "American Pie," by Don McLean
- 1973: "You're So Vain," by Carly Simon
- 1974: "The Joker," by the Steve Miller Band
- 1975: " Lucy In the Sky," by Elton John
- 1976: "Saturday Night," by the Bay City Rollers
- 1979: "Too Much Heaven," by the Bee Gees
- 1980: "Please Don't Go," by KC & the Sunshine Band
- 1982: "I Can't Go for That," by Hall & Oates
- 1983: "Down Under," by Men At Work

**On the average: You can get about 6 glasses of wine from a standard-size bottle.**

# ELEMENTARY MY DEAR STEVE: SOLUTIONS

PAGE 247

**1.** A man with the hiccups was cured when the bartender scared him. The man—who happened to own a carnival—was very grateful, and when he died, he left the bartender his Funhouse.

**2.** If the nightwatchman had a dream that the 5:30 train crashed, that meant he was sleeping on the job. It turned out well for the night watchman; he was such a sound sleeper that he was able to get a job demonstrating mattresses for department stores.

PAGE 358–359

**1.** Remember, they had just come from Thomasville. All they had to do was reposition the signpost so that the "Thomasville" arrow was correct. That way, the road to Montez was obvious. They got their in time, and thwarted the evil son-in-law just as he was breaking into the wall-safe

**2.** No one shaves the barber—she's a woman. Good barber, too.

**3.** They're two of three triplets. Leslie made Steve promise never to see them again.

**4.** The poison was in the ice cubes. Arnie luckily saved his own life when he gulped down his drink and left before the ice melted. Mingo wasn't so lucky. The bartender, it turned out, was working for a used car dealer on the side, and wanted Mingo's '64 Mustang convertible.

PAGE 445

**1.** She dropped her ring into a bag of dry, ground coffee.

**2.** She quickly grabbed one of the pieces of paper, and ripped it up. Then she said, "I've chosen my fate. Let us see which one is left." The paper that was left said "death," which meant she'd chosen "freedom." Von Springmeyer was forced by the rest of the gang to let Leslie go.

**3.** Leslie had a sweet tooth, and always put sugar in her coffee. When she tasted the coffee, it was sweet.

**"The Star Spangled Banner" became America's national anthem in 1931.**

*Uncle John's*

# THIRD BATHROOM READER

# THANK YOU

*The Bathroom Readers' Institute sincerely thanks the people whose advice and assistance made this book possible.*

Eric Lefcowitz
Larry Kelp
John Javna
Derek Goldberg
Michael Goldberger
John Dollison
Jim Morton
Michael Brunsfeld
Richard Kizu-Blair
Gordon Van Gelder
Stuart Moore
Fifth Street Computers
Jay Nitschke
Penelope Houston
Bob Shannon
Jack Mingo
Patty Glikbarg
Robin Kipke Alkire
Lyn Speakman

The city of Domme
"Weird Brain"
Antiques and Collecting magazine
Harry L. Rinker
Ron Barlow
Michael Dorman
Vince Staten
Anita Sethi
Dan Simon
Bill Batson
David Davis
Duane Dimock
Sandra Konte
The EarthWorks Group
Reddy Kilowatt
Rocky
Bob Migdal
Lenna Lebovich
The Sharp Fax Machine

# UNCLE JOHN'S MAILBAG

*Our first two Bathroom Readers brought in lots of mail with interesting stories and comments...Here's a random sample:*

**Gentlemen:**
If you recall, several weeks ago, astronomers discovered rings around Uranus. Well, after spending several hours engrossed in your book, so did I!

—*John M., Fort Mill, South Carolina*

**Fellow Bathroom Readers:**
Whenever I have a relative or guest at my house, they always come out of the bathroom and ask me why there is a stack of magazines on the back of the toilet. When I answer them, they just chuckle and call me "silly."

I'm glad to see there's finally an offical bathroom reader's publication that I can leave on the toilet so people can answer the question for themselves. Keep up the good work!

—*Duane J., Palm Bay, Florida*

**Dear Uncle John:**
I was beginning to think that Excremeditation was a dying cultural phenomenon, a lost art. Uncle John's Second Bathroom Reader is the simmering potpourri in the Great Outhouse of Life.

—*F. Lee S., Charlottesville, Virginia*

**Dear B.R.I.:**
We would like to sit down and be counted. We read the first book in the bathroom, but since we're traveling for a year, we read the second book out loud to each other while driving. We enjoyed driving on Route 66...which we didn't even know existed until we read your book...And, hey, whatever happened to Burger Chef, Burger Queen, and Jack-in-the-Box? Any chance you'll write about them in a future edition?...FYI: Your books make great housewarming gifts! We are waiting with our pants around our ankles for book #3!

—*Amy & Rex Y., Athens, Michigan*

**Dear Uncle John:**
I was reading the Bathroom Reader when I noticed I was out of toilet paper. Unfortunately, I had to make the most out of what I had. Will you please send me a copy of pages 38-39? Thanks.

*Arnie P., Seattle, Washington*

**Dear B.R.I.:**
I'd like to admit that one day I read the Bathroom Reader in 20° weather in an outhouse. Thanks, you guys helped me keep my mind off the cold.

*—Robert W., Old Tappan, New Jersey*

**Dear Uncle John:**
Thanks a ton. Now my husband *lives* in the john.

*—Renee G., Los Angeles, California*

**Dear Uncle John:**
Info on Kelsey—

1. My nickname is Kelley.
2. I'm 14 years old.
3. I love to read (especially on the pot).

*—Kelsey B., Cedar Rapids, Iowa*

**Dear Sirs:**
After reading your book, I had to take time out from the "business at hand" to write this letter. Having been a bathroom reader for many years, I found your book to be very "moving." There's a lot of very good information to "pass" on to others.

*—Jim B., Canyon Country, California*

**Dear Uncle John:**
Who is that guy on the back cover of both your books? Is it you? And what's he doing with the clipboard? I've just got to know—I read both your books cover-to-cover, and have spent hours staring at that picture, "passing" the time.

*—Glenn W., Montpelier, Vermont*

*Glad you asked, Glenn. He's not Uncle John; he's Larry Kelp, a music critic at an urban newspaper. Of course, he's busy recording data about America's bathroom reading habits. Keep up the great work, Lar!*

# THE PAPER CHASE

*At the B.R.I., we get a lot of questions about toilet paper. Heck, we even get them written on toilet paper. Recently, one of our "field representatives" discovered a couple of selections that should satisfy even the most finicky T.P. afficianado. The first is this piece adapted from a self-published book called* The Vanishing American Outhouse, *by Ronald Barlow It should unroll a few mysteries.*

## YESTERDAY'S PAPER

"Toilet paper is a fairly modern invention. Today's thoughtfully perforated product was patented by an Englishman named Walter J. Alcock, in the early 1880s. At first there was little demand for toilet paper by the roll. British pharmacy owners stocked this item under their counters and out of sight; T. P. was an affront to Victorian sensibilities.

"But Mr. Alcock was undaunted by the public's reserve and promoted his product religiously. His singleminded missionary zeal eventually paid off. By 1888 toilet paper fixtures (roll-holders) were stocked in most hardware stores, and today Alcock's original factory exports two-ply tissue to a world-wide market."

★ ★ ★

## BEFORE PAPER

"What did folks use before paper was in wide circulation? Affluent Romans used sponges, wool, and rosewater. The rest of the world grabbed whatever was at hand, including shells, sticks, stones, leaves, hay, or dry bones. Royalty in the Middle Ages was fond of silk or goose feathers (still attached to a pliable neck) for this delicate clean-up task."

★ ★ ★

## NO CORNY JOKE

"Rural Americans traditionally relied on corncobs instead of T.P. James Whitcomb Riley wrote a poem commemorating the experience:

*The torture of that icy seat could make a Spartan sob,*
*For needs must scrape the gooseflesh with a lacerating cob.*

Riley's family privy must have had an outdated supply of corncobs because old timers tell me that fresh ones are not all that uncomfortable. The term: 'rough as a cob' could perhaps apply to produce left out in the sun and rain for a year or so, but not to the supply of month-old corncobs used in privy confines. Guests often had a choice of colors, even before the invention of toilet paper. According to privy folklore, red cobs outnumbered white ones by a two to one ratio. The modus operandi was to use a red cob first and then follow up with a white one to see if another of the red variety was necessary."

★ ★ ★

## T.P. BY MAIL

"Mail order catalogs came into general outhouse use in the late 1880s. Prior to that time they consisted of less than a dozen pages and could not compete with newspapers, dress patterns and other *uncoated* paper stock. Concerned mothers routinely removed the 'female undergarment' and 'personal hygiene' sections of these catalogs before consigning them to the outhouse. By the early 1930s most magazines and mail-order catalogs had converted to slick clay-coated pages and fell into general disuse as a T.P. substitute.

"The following letters, adapted from Bob Sherwood's 1929 book, *Hold Everything*, illustrate how important the thick semi-annual Sears catalogs were to many country households:

***The Letter***

Dear Sears & Roebuck:

Please find enclosed money order for one dollar ($1.00) for which please send me ten packages of your Peerless Toilet Paper.

Yours sincerely, Abner Bewley, Sr.

***The Reply***

Dear Sir:

We acknowledge receipt of your order with enclosure of $1.00 in payment for ten packages of Peerless Toilet paper. We assume you have taken this price from one of our old catalogs. On account of the recent increase in the cost of manufacturing this article, the price is now listed at $1.50 for ten packages. On receipt of an

**Americans eat about 22 pounds of tomatoes every year—mostly in ketchup and tomato sauce.**

additional fifty cents, we will forward at once.

Very respectfully, SEARS & CO.

**The Back-Fire**

Gentlemen:

I am in receipt of your reply to my letter ordering ten packages of Peerless Toilet Paper.

If I had had one of your old catalogs, I would not have needed any toilet paper.

Please send me your latest catalog, and return my money.

Yours Sincerely, Abner Bewley, Sr.

P.S. After thinking the matter over you had better send two catalogs, as we have a very large family."

★ ★ ★

## FOREIGN PAPER

"There are enough different varieties of toilet paper to inspire a major collection. (Smithsonian...are you listening?)

• One can write very easily in pen and ink on modern day Czechoslovakian toilet issue, which is of the consistency of writing paper. My son's college roommate just sent him a long letter on some of this 'poor man's stationery.'

• German-made bathroom tissue is light gray in color and rather coarse textured. The brand used on railway trains is imprinted 'Deutsche Bundesbahn' on every single sheet.

• In England, museum-going tourists are quick to notice that each square of paper is plainly marked 'Official Government Property.'

• In some Scandinavian restrooms the extra heavy roll is simply too large to carry away.

• Mexico solved her paper pilfering problem in airport and bus station 'baños' by not supplying any at all. Be prepared and bring your own, or you'll be forced to borrow from an adjacent stall-holder.

• Upscale European consumers are switching to a new luxury brand of paper; the pre-moistened, perfumed squares, sealed separately in foil envelopes, are not unlike the 'wet wipes' mothers buy in American supermarkets.

★ ★ ★

## AUTOMATIC WIPE

According to a 1988 article in *The San Diego Union*, fully 11.5% of all Japanese homes are now equipped with deluxe flush toilets which have built-in hot-water cleansing and hot-air drying mechanisms; these features preclude the need for any sort of tissue at all.

What are the chances of a Japanese-owned electronic-potty-maker locating its manufacturing facilities in San Diego, or some other U.S. city? 'Almost nil,' stated a spokesman. 'Only the quality control standards in Japan are strict enough to produce these devices without fear of public-liability lawsuits.' "

★ ★ ★

## RECOMMENDED READING

*The Vanishing American Outhouse* is an oversized paperback full of color photos of outhouses, and goes where no man has gone before in its detailed study of American outhouse history. To order a copy, send $15.95 plus $1.50 for postage and handling to: Windmill Publishing Co., 2147 Windmill View Rd., El Cajon, CA 92020.

## TWINKIE POWER

• It's been estimated that the cake in a Twinkie will outlast the wrapper—which is made of plastic, and probably takes about 200 years to decompose. But according to William Poundstone in *Bigger Secrets*, that's just a rumor. He says that the Continental Baking Company, makers of America's favorite cremed cake, pulls unsold boxes of Twinkies off grocery store shelves every four days. Believe it or not.

• When James A. Deware invented the Twinkie in 1930, he called it, "The best darn-tootin' idea I ever had." How good was it? A Continental Baking Company executive claims that one man lived for 7 years solely on a diet of Twinkies and Cutty Sark.

# COMMON PHRASES

*What do these familiar phrases really mean? Entymologists have researched them and come up with these explanations.*

**SIAMESE TWINS**
***Meaning:*** Identical twins who are physically attached.
***Background:*** Eng and Chang Bunker were always close—in fact, the twin brothers from Siam were born joined at the liver. P.T. Barnum hired the Bunkers and exploited them on the carnival and sideshow circuit during the mid-1800s. Though the brothers were really three-quarters Chinese, Barnum thought "Siamese" had a more exotic ring, and coined the term we still use today. (Side note: Eng and Chang lived long lives, married twin sisters and fathered more than twenty children).

**LONG IN THE TOOTH**
***Meaning:*** Old.
***Background:*** Originally used to describe old horses. As horses age, their gums recede, giving the impression that their teeth are growing. The longer the teeth look, the older the horse.

**TO GO BERSERK**
***Meaning:*** To go mad, or to act with reckless abandon.
***Background:*** Viking warriors were incredibly wild and ferocious in battle, probably because they ate hallucinogenic mushrooms in pre-battle ceremonies. They charged their enemies recklessly, wearing nothing more than bearskin, which in Old Norse was pronounced "berserkr" or "bear-sark."

**TO FACE THE MUSIC**
***Meaning***: To deal with a troubling situation.
***Background***: All actors have experienced stage fright, but eventually they must stand upon the stage and face the audience and orchestra (the music).

**A-OKAY**
***Meaning:*** All correct, or all systems working.
***Background:*** NASA engineers added 'A' onto "OKAY" because the 'O' sound sometimes got lost in radio static.

**Toto's real name was Terry.**

# EDIBLE NAMES

*Like fast food? Try this list. You still may not know what you're eating, but at least know what's it's named after.*

**McDONALD'S.** Named after two brothers who were scenery movers in Hollywood during the 1920s—Richard and Maurice ("Mac") McDonald. They started the first modern fast food joint in San Bernardino, California after World War II and sold out to Ray Kroc for $2.7 million in 1961.

• Sidelight: They gave up the rights to use their own names, so when they wanted to open another fast food restaurant, they had to call it "Mac's." Kroc was so incensed they were competing with him that he opened a McDonald's across the street from "Mac's" and drove the McDonald brothers out of business.

**ARBY'S.** Forest and Leroy Raffel wanted to open a fast food restaurant called Big Tex, in Akron, Ohio...but someone else already owned the name. So they settled for Arby's—R.B.'s—after the first initials of *R*affel *b*rothers.

**TACO BELL.** No, it has nothing to do with mission bells. The chain was founded in 1962 by Glen W. Bell.

**JACK IN THE BOX.** There was a huge, square metal ventilation unit on the roof of Robert Peterson's restaurant. It was really ugly, but he couldn't remove it...So he covered it up instead, disguising it as a jack-in-the-box. Then he changed the name of his restaurant, making it seem as though the whole thing had been planned.

**HARDEE'S.** Founded by Wilbur Hardee, who opened the first Hardee's in Greenville, North Carolina in 1960.

**BOB'S BIG BOY.** In 1937, local orchestra members told 19-year-old Bob Wian they wanted "something different"; so the young owner of the ten-stool Bob's Pantry served up the "Big Boy" double-decker hamburger. It became so popular that Bob changed the name of his eatery to match it.

**In Italy, a whole year's salary is the proper amount to pay for an enagement ring.**

**PIZZA HUT.** Frank Carney, a 19-year-old engineering student at the University of Wichita, opened a pizza parlor in 1958 with his older brother Dan. It was in a rented, hut-shaped building with a sign that only had room for eight letters and a single space. Pizza Hut was the perfect name because it described the restaurant *and* fit the sign.

**CHURCH'S FRIED CHICKEN.** George W. Church, who'd previously sold incubators and run a chicken hatchery, founded the chain after he retired.

**DAIRY QUEEN.** In 1938, Sherb Noble put together a 10¢ All-You-Can-Eat promotion for his Kankakee, Illinois store. He offered a brand new kind of "semi-frozen" ice cream called "Dairy Queen," and was dumbfounded by the public's response—they bought 16,000 servings of it in two hours. Two years later, Noble opened a food stand that sold nothing but Dairy Queen.

**KENTUCKY FRIED CHICKEN.** "Colonel" Harlan Sanders had a restaurant in Corbin, Kentucky. His speciality was fried chicken.

**WHITE CASTLE.** In 1921, Walter Anderson needed money to open his fourth hamburger stand. He borrowed the money—$700—from a local real-estate and insurance salesman named Billy Ingram, who suggested that the restaurant be called the "White Castle," symbolizing cleanliness and strength. Since it was Ingram's money, Anderson humored him.

**WENDY'S.** Dave Thomas, an executive at Kentucky Fried Chicken, decided to open his own chain of fast food restaurants in 1969. The first one was located in Columbus, Ohio. It was named for Thomas's third daughter, Wendy.

**NOW THAT YOU'RE HUNGRY...**
**SOME NUTRITION INFO**

• From *Best Worst And Most Unusual*: "If one is really starving, consider licking some postage stamps. The glue is a mixture of cassava (the source of tapioca) and corn...starchy but nutritious."

# OH, ZSA ZSA!

*Sure, you've read about her in the National Enquirer (only while you're waiting in line at the supermarket, of course). But what do you really know about Zsa Zsa Gabor? You might surprised to learn that a century ago, while she was still a young lady, she was quite beautiful and...yes, we admit it—pretty clever. A few words from, and about, this national institution.*

**WHAT ABOUT ZSA ZSA?**

"She not only worships the golden calf, she barbecues it for lunch."

—*Oscar Levant*

"I feel a little like Zsa Zsa Gabor's fifth husband. I know what I'm supposed to do, but I'm not sure how to make it interesting."

—*Senator Al Gore, the 24th speaker at a political dinner*

"As a graduate of the Zsa Zsa Gabor School of Creative Mathematics, I honestly do not know how old I am."

—*Erma Bombeck*

**ZSA ZSA SAYS...**

- "I'm a marvelous housekeeper...Every time I leave a man, I keep his house."
- "You never really know a man until you've divorced him."
- "Macho does not prove mucho."
- "A man in love is incomplete until he has married. Then he's finished."
- "I want a man who's kind and understanding. Is that too much to ask of a millionaire?"
- "I never hated a man enough to give him his diamonds back."
- "Husbands are like fires. They go out when unattended."
- "I know nothing about sex because I was always married."

**...BUT THEY'RE NOT ALL BIMBOS**

"I will do anything to initiate world peace."

—*Jayne Mansfield*

**Confederate General Robert E. Lee didn't own slaves. He didn't believe in it.**

# TRAVELS WITH RAY

*Perplexing adventures of the brilliant egghead Ray "Weird Brain" Redel. Answers are on page 672.*

Only a few men in modern history have been known specifically for their ability to think. There's Albert Einstein, Buckminster Fuller, and of course the most famous of all, Ray "Weird Brain" Redel. As I'm sure you've heard, "Weird Brain" 's reputation for solving word problems inspired friends to spring practical jokes on him constantly. Everyone wanted to be the one to say he or she had stumped him.

A few years ago, "Weird Brain" and I went to Egypt together for the International Smart Guys Conference. After listening to boring highbrow discussions for two days, we escaped to the local marketplace. It was refreshing to wander through the crowd, listening to people bark prices at each other instead of scientific theories.

Suddenly, a man in a white suit appeared before us, clutching something in his hand. He staggered and groaned and pointed to the object in his hand. I felt as though I was in a Hitchcock movie. The man managed to gasp, "*If you feed it, it will live. If you give it water, it will die.*" Then he swooned.

Alarmed, I looked for the police. But Ray just reached into his pocket, pulled out something, and tossed it to the prostrate man. "Here, Humphrey," he said—for the "dying" man was really "Weird Brain" 's Hollywood drinking buddy, Humphrey Bogart—"Nice try, but I think this is what you want."

**What did "Weird Brain" toss Bogart?**

The next day, we decided to do a little sightseeing. The cab driver offered to suggest a destination. "Sure," I said, "where should we go?" The driver grinned and said in broken English, "*It has a bed, but never sleeps; and has a mouth, but never eats.*" "Weird Brain" yawned. "Casey," he told the driver, who was New York Yankees manager Casey Stengel, an old pal, in disguise—that one's so old everyone knows it. But if it'll make you happy, take us there.

**Where did Casey take us?**

# BONEHEAD ADS

*Businesses spend billions of bucks on ads every year—but some of them backfire. A few amusing examples:*

## SAY WHAT?

*Translating U.S. ad slogans into other languages doesn't always work.*

• In China, a Coca-Cola ad used Chinese symbols to sound out "Coca-Cola" phonetically. The soda company withdrew the ad after learning the symbols "Co" "Ca" "Co" " La" meant "Bite the wax tadpole."

• In Brazil, an American airline advertised that its planes had "rendezvous" lounges, not realizing that in Portuguese "rendezvous" means a place to have sex.

• "In Taiwan," according to a book called *The Want Makers*, "Pepsi's 'Come Alive with the Pepsi Generation' was reportedly translated on billboards as 'Pepsi brings your ancestors back from the dead.'"

• "In French Canada, Hunt-Wesson attempted to use its 'Big John' brand name by translating it into French as 'Gros Jos,' a colloquial French phrase that denotes a woman with huge breasts."

• When the gringos at General Motors introduced the Chevrolet *Nova* in Latin America, it was obvious they didn't know their Spanish. Ads all across Latin America heralded the arrival of the new, reliable *Nova*, which in Spanish means "Doesn't go."

## SMELL IT LIKE IT IS

*Two of the most ludicrous Scratch'n'Sniff ads ever:*

• In June, 1977, the Rolls-Royce Motor Car Company introduced a campaign entitled "This, In Essence, Is Rolls Royce." Apparently, the company's executives hired scientists to analyze the smell inside a Rolls. They came up with a scent strip that was supposed to smell like leather upholstery.

• In 1989, BEI Defense Systems ran a Scratch'n'Sniff ad for its Hydra 70 weapons system in *The Armed Forces Journal*. It pictured two battling helicopters; when scratched, it gave off the smell of cordite, the odor left in the air after a rocket explosion.

# CELEBRITY HYPOCHONDRIACS

*Everyone's at least a little afraid of getting sick, but some people take it to extremes. Here are some of history's most famous hypochondriacs:*

**THE CELEBRITY:** Howard Hughes

**THE SYMPTOMS:** When he was a little boy, the billionaire-to-be's mother fussed over every change in Howard's physical and emotional conditions. One result: Hughes developed a low tolerance to pain.

• After crashing one of his planes in Hollywood in 1946, Hughes began to display an irrational fear of dust and germs. He used Kleenex tissues on everything, and refused to touch doorknobs or let other people use his bathroom. (He once spent 26 straight hours in the bathroom; he also suffered from severe constipation).

• His fastidiousness got out of hand when he wrote out nine-step instructions to his housekeepers on how to open a can of fruit. He became a virtual recluse.

• One of the most bizarre manifestations of his obsession with health was a urine collection, purportedly for medical testing.

• Ironically, towards the end of his life, Hughes lost all pretenses of hygiene. He stopped taking care of himself—letting his hair and fingernails grow outrageously long—and stopped eating; he weighed only 93 pounds when he died.

**THE CELEBRITY:** Charles Darwin

**THE SYMPTOMS:** The father of the theory of evolution, staunch believer in the "survival of the fittest," apparently wasn't such a hardy specimen himself. Darwin was a life-long hypochondriac who suffered from stomach aches, chronic insomnia and fatigue.

• In 1849, he began a daily diary which included a running commentary on the state of his health. He kept it up for six straight years.

• In one entry, he wrote gloomily, "It has been a bitter mortification for me to digest the conclusion that the 'race is for the strong' and that I shall probably do little more but be content to admire the strides others made in science." He lived forty-one years after making that statement.

• Some have speculated that Darwin's ailments were brought about by the stress of his "heretical" theories; others have claimed they were an easy solution to meeting social obligations.

**THE CELEBRITY:** Napoleon Bonaparte

**THE SYMPTOMS:** Napoleon had a lifelong fear and hatred of medicine. As a student, he studied anatomy but was too squeamish to continue. He reportedly claimed, "I believe in the doctor, not medicine."

• The "Little Emperor" suffered a plethora of maladies, most of them the result of stress, including: skin disorders, ulcers, dysuria (difficulty urinating) and a nervous cough.

• To combat his hypochondria, Napoleon took steaming hot baths, sometimes 1-1/2 hours long. He also developed meticulous grooming habits, including gargling with brandy and water, and showering himself with eau-du-cologne.

• One doctor's report of Napoleon from the battlefields of Russia said, "The constitution of the Emperor was highly nervous. He was very susceptible to emotional influences...divided between the stomach and the bladder."

• Some scholars even doubted the diagnosis of Napoleon's death (stomach cancer) during his exile in St. Helena, claiming he died of hysteria brought on by boredom.

**THE CELEBRITY:** Alfred Lord Tennyson

**THE SYMPTOMS:** According to one of Tennyson's friends, the poet laureate of England worried "more about his bowels and nerves than about the Laureate wreath he was born to inherit."

• Throughout his life, Tennyson was beset by seizures, fits and trances, which including seeing animals floating across his field of vision.

• An admitted hypochondriac, Tennyson was obsessed with going bald and blind. Among the treatments he sought was a radical form of water therapy called hydropathy, which included being rolled naked into wet blankets and then plunged into water.

• Three of his major poems, "In Memoriam," "The Princess" and "Maud" alluded to his preoccupation with mental illness.

**Home-Sweet-Home: One-fifth of Americans spend their vacations at home.**

• In reference to his hypochondria, Tennyson was once quoted as saying, "I'm black-blooded like all Tennysons." He lived past 80.

**THE CELEBRITY:** H.L. Mencken

**THE SYMPTOMS:** The irascible essayist, one of the most respected American journalists of the 20th century, rationalized his hypochondria by once stating "the human body is a complex organism in a state of dubious equilibrium. It is almost unthinkable for all parts of it be operating perfectly at any one time."

• Mencken suffered an obsessive-compulsive need to continually wash his hands.

• Among his real-or-imagined maladies was a chronic sore throat (which resulted in three operations), hives, low blood pressure, lumbago, sinus infections, ulcers and hemorrhoids. He also suffered from terrible allergies, which, Mencken wrote, "I accept philosphically as a reasonable punishment for my errors."

• For years, Mencken kept a medical diary of his hay fever, which included log entries of his temperature, the weather conditions and the medicine he was taking. He also subjected himself to many new miracle cures, which lead him to describe himself as a "sort of laboratory animal" for medical experimentation.

**THE CELEBRITY:** Florence Nightingale

**THE SYMPTOMS:** The woman who revolutioned modern nursing was also a confirmed hypochondriac; she suffered from migraine headaches, chronic coughs, breathlessness, fainting and nervous distress.

• After her heroic deeds in the Crimean War, Nightingale became convinced that her heart trouble placed her in imminent danger.

• Starting in 1859, she became a virtual recluse, confined to bed and sofa, where she continued to write letters and books about nursing.

• Though she often claimed she was on the edge of death, Nightingale lived a long life. She died in 1910, at the age of 90.

**AND DON'T FORGET...**Michael Jackson. The thriller of pop and dance music is often seen in public wearing a surgical mask. Once, he tried to buy a germ-free hyperbaric oxygen chamber to sleep in, but the manufacturer refused to sell it to him.

**People in the Southern U.S. watch more TV than people in any other region.**

# BOMBS AWAY!

*Sitcoms don't have to be dumb...but they usually are. Here are the premises of some of the dumbest and most obscure sitcoms flops ever. Yes, they really aired on national TV.*

**MY LIVING DOLL** (1964-65) An Army psychiatrist who lives with his sister brings home a gorgeous woman one day, explaining that she's got severe mental problems and needs constant care. He neglects to explain that she's not really a person at all—she's a robot who's so lifelike and sexy that men lust after her. She calls the psychiatrist "Master," and she'll do anything (yes, anything) he tells her to. So what does he do? What would you do? Well, all he wants is to teach her good manners. That's more than enough to make this show unbelievable.

**MONA McCLUSKEY** (1965) A Hollywood star makes 40 times as much money as her husband, an Air Force sergeant (he gets $500 a month, she gets $5000 a week). But the guy won't let her spend any of her dough—they live on his salary or nothing. Well, she's so in love that she agrees: She moves into a two-bedroom apartment and then spends all her time trying to figure out ways to secretly use her own money. The show lasted longer than the marriage would have—seven months.

**IT'S ABOUT TIME** (1966-67) Two astronauts accidentally break through the time barrier and wind up in a prehistoric era. There they coexist with a bunch of Neanderthals until they fix their space capsule—and then they head for L.A. But whoops! A couple of cavemen hitch a lift into the present. Intelligently, the astronauts hide the Neanderthals in an apartment and try to teach them about modern life. This inanity could only come from the fertile mind that also gave us "Gilligan's Island" and "The Brady Bunch."

**RUN BUDDY RUN** (1966-67) A couple of goofy assassins try to catch and kill a guy who accidentally overheard their secret plans in a Turkish bath. Some fun.

**The U.S. is home to 2/3 of the world's lawyers.**

**THE SECOND HUNDRED YEARS** (1967-68) The cryogenics sitcom. A 33-year-old prospector is frozen alive in an avalanche in 1900. Sixty-eight years later he thaws out. Surprise! He's still 33 and full of pep. He goes to live with his son, who's now older than ol' dad, and his grandson, who's the same age. In fact, he and his grandson look exactly alike. What a coincidence!

**THE GIRL WITH SOMETHING EXTRA** (1973-74) Sally Field gave up her nun's habit and stopped flying. Now she's got ESP. And she's married to John Davidson. She says she can read his mind, but how can she be sure there's really something in it? The premise sounds like a *National Enquirer* story.

**THE WAVERLY WONDERS** (1978) Among television critics, this show is already a legend. Who thought it up? Is he still allowed into Hollywood? Joe Namath was the star, playing a basketball coach/history teacher at a small Wisconsin high school. Joe didn't know anything about history, as you might imagine. And his players didn't know anything about basketball. So what's the joke? The inept teacher? The inept basketball team? The inept TV network?

**APPLE PIE** (1978) The ultimate absurdity in family sitcoms. It broke all sitcom records for brevity too, lasting exactly two weeks. The plot: In 1933, a hairdresser decided she wanted a family. So she advertised for one in the local paper. The result: a collection of weirdos that rivals *King of Hearts*—a con-man "husband," a "son" who thinks he's a bird, a "grandpa" who's barely still moving, and a "daughter" who likes to tap dance around the house.

**TURNABOUT** (1978) A husband and wife, in an idle moment, wish they could switch places. They're only kidding around, but they speak in the presence of a magic Buddha statue—and Buddha *doesn't* kid around. Overnight, their spirits switch bodies—the man becomes a cosmetics exec in a woman's body, and the woman becomes a male sports reporter.

**MR. MERLIN** (1981-82) Merlin the Magician shows up in the 1980's as a garage mechanic. Merlin the Mechanic. Next time you tell a repairman he's a real wizard, think twice. You might be inventing a sitcom.

**The U.S. Department of Defense spends about $6,000,000 on recruiting—every day.**

# PRIME-TIME PROVERBS

*Here are some more TV quotes from the book* Primetime Proverbs, *by Jack Mingo and John Javna.*

**ON LOVE**

"Ah—love— the walks over soft grass, the smiles over candlelight, the arguments over just about everything else..."

**Max Headroom,**
***Max Headroom***

"I'm looking for a serious commitment—someone who'll stay the night."

**—Stewardess,**
***Married...With Children***

**THE FACTS OF LIFE**

"There's an old Moroccan saying—trust in God, but tie your camel tight."

**—Annie McGuire**
***Annie McGuire***

"There are three things you don't get over in hurry—losing a woman, eating bad possum, and eating good possum."

**—Beau La Barre**
***Welcome Back, Kotter***

"Reservations are the condoms in the birth of new ideas."

**—Twiggy Rathbone**
***Heavy Metal***

**ON SEX**

"If sex were fast food, you'd have an arch over your head."

**—Carlotta Winchester,**
***Filthy Rich***

[After his first time] "I'm so excited. It's like discovering America, or a third arm or something. This is the greatest thing that ever happened to me. I should have started this ten years ago. I mean, the hell with television."

**—Billy Tate,**
***Soap***

"I haven't had much experience saying 'No' to a woman. The closest I've ever come is, 'Not now, we're landing.' "

**—Sam Malone,**
***Cheers***

**ON WOMEN**

**Dwayne Schneider:** "A woman is like a bathtub full of water— once you get it hot, it doesn't cool off too fast."
**Barbara Cooper:** " And once it does, it has a ring."

***—One Day at a Time***

# FAMILIAR NAMES

*Some people achieve immortality because their names become commonly associated with an item or activity. You already know the names—now here are the people.*

**Giovanni Casanova.** A European diplomat. At age 16, his "immoral behavior" got him expelled from a seminary. Later, he was so notorious as a lover that his name became synonymous with seduction.

**Count Paul Stroganoff.** A 19th-century Russian diplomat. He funded archaeological expeditions, supervised a Russian educational district, and ate huge amounts of the sauce now named after him.

**Daniel Elmer Salmon.** A veterinary surgeon. He first identified the rod-shaped bacteria, *salmonella*, that causes food poisoning.

**Adolphe Sax.** A Belgian musical-instrument maker. In the early 1840s, he turned the music world on its ear with his invention, the *saxophone*.

**Ambrose Everett Burnside.** A Union General in the Civil War. His full side-whiskers (to complement his moustache) were so distinctive that they were called "burnsides." Over time, the word has been transformed into *sideburns*.

**James Smithson.** An English chemist. It took ten years of debate before Congress accepted his bequest for a Washington, D.C. *Smithsonian Institution*, for "the increase and diffusion of knowledge among men."

**Oliver Fisher Winchester.** An American men's shirt manufacturer. His special talent was improving on others' inventions, notably the Winchester repeating rifle invented by Benjamin Henry.

**Mr. and Mrs. Legrand Benedict.** After complaining that there was nothing new being served by New York restaurants, this "high society" couple cooked up the idea of *eggs benedict*.

**According to M magazine, 84 percent of bicyclists think about sex while cycling.**

**Rudolph Boysen.** An American horticulturist. After years of experimentation breeding hybrid berries, he finally came up with a *boysenberry*.

**John Montague.** The 4th Earl of Sandwich. A compulsive gambler who would not leave any game to dine, he had his valet serve him a piece of cold meat placed between two slices of bread.

**Captain Bo.** A legendary English fighter. His exploits inspired other combatants, who used a variation of his name, *boo*, as a bloodcurdling war cry.

**Julius Caesar.** The Roman Emperor was allegedly the first person delivered via *caesarian section*, through his mother's abdominal wall.

**James Thomas Brudenell.** The 7th Earl of Cardigan. The button-up sweater is named after him.

**Thomas "Stonewall" Jackson.** A Confederate General in the Civil War. He is credited for "standing like a stone wall" against Union troops at the first battle of Bull Run. Today we call similar holding actions *stonewalling*.

**John Macadam.** An Australian chemist. He discovered the *Macadamia nut*.

**Vidkun Quisling.** Leader of Norway in 1940. His surname became synonymous with *traitor* after he collaborated when they occupied his country.

**Joseph Pulitzer.** A newspaper publisher. His will created and funded the Pulitzer Prize for journalism.

**Josh Billings**. A 19th century humorist. He popularized a bantering comedy style which became known as *joshing*.

**Charles Moncke.** A British blacksmith. He is credited with inventing the monkey wrench (which the British call a "spanner").

**Canada owns more U.S. real estate than Japan.**

# ASSORTED MANIACS

*You've heard of pyromaniacs and kleptomaniacs, but chances are you've never heard of these loonies. Do you know a...*

**Coprolalomaniac:** Someone who compulsively uses foul language.

**Doromaniac:** Someone who compulsively gives presents.

**Cresomaniac:** Someone suffering from delusions of wealth.

**Timromaniacs:** Someone obsessed with postage stamps.

**Emetomaniac:** A person who always feels like throwing up.

**Ablutomaniac:** Someone obsessed with taking baths.

**Hellenomaniac:** Someone who compulsively uses Greek or Latin words.

**Ailuromaniac:** A person obsessed with cats.

**Philopatridomaniac:** Someone who's always homesick.

**Dromomaniac:** A compulsive traveler.

**Phagomaniac:** Someone who constantly craves food.

**Xenomaniac:** Someone obsessed with foreign customs.

**Oniomaniac:** A person who compulsively buys things.

**Klazomaniac:** Someone who always feels like shouting.

**Micromaniac:** Someone suffering from delusions of a shrinking body.

**Titillomaniac:** A compulsive scratcher.

**Erythromaniac:** Someone who's always blushing.

**Catapedamaniac:** Someone who always feels like jumping from high places.

**Chionomaniac:** Someone obsessed with snow.

**Theomaniac:** Someone who's sure he or she is God.

**Nudomaniac:** A person obsessed with nudity.

**Ichthyomaniac:** Someone who's just crazy about fish.

**Arithomaniac:** Someone who compulsively counts objects.

**Cynomaniac:** Someone obsessed with dogs.

**Onychotillomaniac:** A person who constantly picks his or her nails.

**Bruxomaniac:** Someone who grinds his or her teeth all the time.

**Lycomaniac:** Someone suffering from delusions of being a wolf.

**There are three museums in the world which only exhibit footwear.**

# VIEWER'S CHOICE

*Hollywood producers often use sneak previews to shape the way their movies end. Here are some examples of the ways preview audiences have influenced the final versions of recent films.*

**COCKTAIL**
Initial tests by the Disney Company revealed that audiences found this Tom Cruise vehicle a snooze. So Disney executives decided to shoot more footage—including bar scenes of Cruise mixing drinks and dancing up a storm in front of bikini-clad bathing beauties and presto!—they had a hit. *Cocktail* went on to gross $160 million.

**PRETTY IN PINK**
In the original ending of the film, Molly Ringwald ended up with her awkward friend Duckie (Jon Cryer) instead of the slick and wealthy Blaine (Andrew McCarthy). When preview audiences disapproved, director John Hughes re-filmed the ending to conform to their wishes, including a romantic liason between Ringwald and McCarthy.

**LITTLE SHOP OF HORRORS**
In both the original film and off-Broadway musical production, the "Little Shop Of Horrors" ended with Audrey, the people-eating plant, munching down the lead characters. During preview tests for the 1986 film version of the musical, however, audiences expressed their displeasure that Rick Moranis and Ellen Greene became plant food. The cast and crew flew back to England to film an entirely new—and happy—ending where the plant was killed instead.

**FIRST BLOOD**
Preview audiences were asked to vote on whether Rambo, played by Sylvester Stallone, should die at the end of movie. Two endings had already been filmed. One showed Rambo shot by his enemy, Richard Crenna (which was how the 1972 novel on which the movie is based, ended). The other showed an emotionally-drained Rambo being led away by Crenna alive. Audiences were split on

the decision, but apparently the producers made the correct choice by letting Rambo live. The sequels, *Rambo: First Blood Part II* and *Rambo III*, were box-office bonanzas.

## THE BIG CHILL

Lawrence Kasdan's cult movie about '60s college pals reuniting in the '80s originally had a different ending—a flashback to the group's hippie days at the University of Michigan. Preview audiences, however, refused to accept the actors dressed up as college-age kids and the ending was cut.

***An exception to the rule:***

## STAR WARS

Marketing research for the 1976 mega-hit was conducted by the staff of Twentieth Century Fox. It concluded that "you can't use war in the title," and that "robots could turn off the mass majority of moviegoers." Director George Lucas ignored the advice and obviously the force was with him—*Star Wars* is one of the top-grossing films of all time.

## MISCELLANEOUS MOVIE FACTS:

• **Bizarre Movie Titles:** *Betta, Betta in the Wall, Who's the Fattest Fish of All* (United States, 1969), *She Ee Clit Soak* (United States, 1971), *Recharge Grandmothers Exactly!* (Czechoslovakia, 1984), *I Go Oh No* (Taiwan, 1984), *Egg! Egg?* (Sweden, 1975), *Phfft* (United States, 1954), and *Film Without Title* (East Germany, 1947).

• **Sound Stomachs:** To create the language of the mutants in *Island of Lost Souls* (United States 1932), sound-man Loren L. Ryder recorded a mixture of animal sounds and foreign languages, then played them backwards at alternating speeds. The effect: the sound induced nausea—audiences vomited in the theaters.

• **The Amazing van der Zyl:** Sometimes beautiful movie actresses don't have beautiful voices to go with their good looks. Enter Nikki van der Zyl, the voice of the James Bond Girls. In *Doctor No* (1962) Miss van der Zyl is the voice of all but two women in the film. She also dubbed the neanderthal grunts for Racquel Welch in *One Million Years BC (1962)*. Of course, the films don't credit her.

# QUAYLE QUIPS

*Vice President Dan Quayle may not be articulate, but he's quotable. Here are some of his more memorable remarks.*

"What a waste it is to lose one's mind. Or not to have a mind. Do I mean that?"

"Republicans understand the importance of the bondage between parent and child."

"We're going to have the best-educated American people in the world."

*When asked by state* GOP *chairman to consider running for Congress:* "I'll have to check with my dad."

"Hawaii has always been a very pivotal role in the Pacific. It is in the Pacific. It is part of the United States that is an island that is right here."

*On his decision to join the National Guard in 1969:*
"Well, growing up in Huntington, Indiana, the first thing you think about is education."

*On which vice president he might model himself after:*
"I don't know if there's one that comes to mind."

"It's rural America. It's where I come from. We always refer to ourselves as real America. Rural America, real America, real, real America."

*On the ethics of his admission into law school:*
"I deserve respect for the things I did not do."

*On the Holocaust:*
"An obscene period of our nation's history."

"Verbosity leads to unclear, inarticulate things."

*On the meaning of Thanksgiving:*
"The first would be our family. Your family, my family—which is composed of an immediate family of a wife and three children, a larger family with grandparents and aunts and uncles. We all have our family, whichever that may be."

*At the Inauguration:*
"I'm not used to going in front of President Reagan, so we went out behind the Bushes."

**Dan Quayle's favorite film is "Ferris Bueller's Day Off."**

# DISNEY STORIES: SNOW WHITE

*"Snow White and the Seven Dwarfs" was Walt Disney's first full-length cartoon feature, and it was nearly his last. Hollywood, appalled at the money he was pouring into it, dubbed it "Disney's Folly." It premiered in L.A. on December 21, 1937—and received a standing ovation. It also received a special Academy Award—"a full-size Oscar and seven little ones." Of course, the Disney version and the Grimm fairy tale were substantially different. Here are some examples of how the tale was changed.*

## THE DISNEY VERSION

Snow White's stepmother, the Wicked Queen, is jealous of Snow White's beauty. So she sends Snow White to the forest with one of her hunters. He's supposed to kill the young Princess and bring her heart to the queen as proof the girl is dead...but he can't do it. He lets Snow White go free, kills a wild boar and brings the boar's heart to the Queen instead.

• This trick almost works. But the queen consults her magic mirror and learns that Snow White is still alive.

• Meanwhile, Snow takes up residence with the seven dwarfs.

• One day, the wicked queen shows up looking like a hag and offers Snow White a poison apple. The dwarfs catch the queen in the act, but they're too late; Snow White dies. The dwarfs chase the queen to a rocky cliff where she falls to her death.

• A handsome Prince shows up and kisses the dead princess. Snow White is revived; she and the Prince live happily ever after.

## THE ORIGINAL VERSION

• To small children, Disney's version is nightmarish enough. We can only wonder what children would think of the gruesome goings-on in the original fairy tale.

• The Queen doesn't ask for Snow White's heart—she wants the princess's lungs and liver. When the hunter brings her the boar's innards, the Queen—thinking they're Snow White's—has them boiled in salt and eats them.

**Pigs killed off the dodo bird.**

• In the original story, the Queen tries to kill Snow White three times. The first two attempts fail. Since the Queen uses the same disguise all three times, we have to assume Snow White, although pretty, is a little short in the brains department.

• The dwarfs—who don't have cute names like Sneezy and Grumpy—do put Snow White in a glass coffin. But the Prince doesn't wake her with a kiss. In fact, kissing her never enters his mind. He just thinks she's pretty (albeit dead), and wants to keep her around his castle.

• On the way back to the castle, servants carrying the casket trip and drop it. This dislodges the poison apple from Snow White's throat and she's revived.

• In this tale, the Queen makes it back to her castle after apparently killing Snow White. A little later, she's invited to a wedding. The wedding, it turns out, is Snow White's. When the Queen arrives, Snow and the Prince have a pair of red-hot iron shoes waiting in the fireplace. The Queen is forced to wear the shoes and dance until she drops dead.

## SAMPLE PASSAGES (FROM THE ORIGINAL)

"The Queen summoned a huntsman and said, 'Take the child out into the forest. I never want to lay eyes on her again. You are to kill her and bring me back her lungs and liver as proof of your deed'...The cook was ordered to boil [the boar's organs] in salt, and the wicked woman ate them and thought that she had eaten Snow White's lungs and liver."

*The Queen receives an invitation to Snow White's wedding. She's stunned, because she was sure Snow White was dead.*

"The evil woman uttered a loud curse and became so terribly afraid that she did not know what to do. At first she didn't want to go to the wedding celebration. But she couldn't calm herself until she saw the young queen. When she entered the hall, she recognized Snow White...and she was so petrified with fright that she couldn't move. Iron slippers had already been heated over a fire, and they were brought over to her with tongs. Finally, she had to put on the red-hot slippers and dance until she fell down dead."

**It was illegal in Nazi Germany to name your horse "Adolph."**

# JUST YOUR TYPE

*Have you ever wondered why the letters on a typewriter are arranged so strangely? Here's the answer:*

**BUILT FOR SPEED**

In 1872, Charles Latham Sholes and two partners developed a bizarre-looking machine they called the "Type-Writer." It wasn't the original typewriting machine, but it was the first to go beyond the experimental stage.

However, shortly after Sholes and his partners started selling it, they ran into a problem: The machine couldn't keep up with quick-fingered typists; the keys would jam if they were struck too closely in succession. Sholes spent long hours in his workshop, but still couldn't find a way to quicken the machine's keystrokes.

**NOT SO FAST**

One day in his lab, the desperate inventor had a brainstorm—a clever idea which still affects typists today. Since he couldn't speed up the machine to accomodate typists, he decided to slow down typists to accommodate the machine. He set out to design the most inconvenient, awkward, and confusing arrangement of typewriter keys possible.

After weeks of research, Sholes settled on what is now called the QWERTY keyboard (after the first six letters of the typewriter's third row). With this new keyboard, Sholes was confident everyone would have to "hunt and peck"—and even an expert typist would be slowed enough to use his machine. He marketed a model with the altered keyboard as a "groundbreaking advancement," boasting that a typist could now type the word "typewriter" without having to leave the third row.

Today we type on high-speed machines that Sholes couldn't have imagined in his wildest dreams. But we still use the keyboard he devised to save his primitive machine.

**SWEET DREAMS...**Where did the term *lollipop* come from? According to *How Did They Do That*: "George Smith, who invented the candy on a stick in the early 1900s, had other money-making interests: Lolly Pop was one of the finest racehorses of the time."

# CARTOON CORNER

*A few facts about the origins of your favorite cartoon characters.*

**THE FLINTSTONES.** This half-hour cartoon, introduced in 1960, was TV's first animated sitcom...and the first prime-time cartoon show ever. Hanna-Barbera Studios originally planned to take a standard sitcom—"a young couple with a kid and a dog"—and transpose it to prehistoric times. But that wound up too much like "Blondie." So Joseph Hanna turned it into a prehistoric "Honeymooners" instead, complete with an Art Carney-type next-door neighbor.

The original stars were Fred and Wilma Flagstone; the program was going to be called "Rally 'Round the Flagstones." But Mort Walker, creator of the comic strip "Hi and Lois," objected. Pointing out that Hi and Lois's last name is Flagston, he insisted that "Flagstone" was too similar to his creation, and asked Hanna-Barbera to change the name.

Receiving this news, one furious Hanna-Barbera producer suddenly had a vision of a Stone Age man rubbing two stones together to make fire—two flint stones. And that became the new name. Footnote: "The Flintstones" was the first cartoon ever to rank among the Top 20 shows of a year, ranking at #18 in 1960.

**MIGHTY MOUSE.** In 1939, DC comics introduced Superman; by the early 1940s, Superman was so popular that the comics had been joined by a Superman radio show and a series of animated cartoons. Paul Terry, a veteran cartoon-maker (Terrytoons), decided to capitalize on the Superman craze. So in 1942, he introduced an invulnerable flying rodent (dressed in a Superman-style costume, complete with a red cape) named Super Mouse. The public loved it. A year later, anxious to avoid a lawsuit, Terry changed Our Hero's name to Mighty Mouse.

**ROCKY AND BULLWINKLE.** In 1948 Jay Ward and his partner, Alex Anderson, decided to create a cartoon series especially for TV—which had never been done. For their stars, they had in mind an animal duo—a smart little creature (the hero) and a big dumb one (the sidekick). They proposed two shows:

• "Crusader Rabbit," featuring a rabbit and his towering, dimwitted tiger buddy.

• "Frostbite Follies," featuring a flying squirrel and a big, dumb moose.

The first one they developed, "Crusader Rabbit," was immediately successful...so they didn't bother working out the second one. Then, in the mid-1950s, Ward sold his rights to "Crusader" and started work on a new cartoon show that adults would appreciate, too. He went back to the squirrel and moose concept.

He'd already picked the name Bullwinkle for the moose. It was inspired by a car salesman in Berkeley, California, where Ward lived. "Every day I'd drive by this sign, Bullwinkle Chevrolet or something," he recalled several decades later, "and I'd think to myself, 'If I ever do another cartoon character, I'm gonna name it Bullwinkle.'" The name Rocky for the little squirrel was a takeoff on tough-guy, macho names. Ward worked on the show for several years. It finally debuted as "Rocky and His Friends" in 1959.

**GOOFY.** Mickey Mouse's pal made his screen debut in the 1932 cartoon Mickey's Review, as Dippy Dawg. (At the time, "dippy" was popular slang for "someone foolish or slightly mad.") The inspiration: country folks whom Pinto Colvig, Goofy's voice, had known in Oregon. Over the next 6 years Dippy Dawg became a regular character, but his name was changed to Dippy, then Dippy the Goof, and finally Goofy (although for a while in the '40s, his name changed again, to Mr. Geef). His first-ever appearance as Goofy was in the 1939 short, *Goofy and Wilbur*.

**TWEETY BIRD.** Created by Bob Clampett, a Warner Brothers animator. The inspiration for Tweety's wide-eyed stare and little body was a nude baby photograph of Clampett himself. The canary's famous phrase, "I tawt I taw a puddy-tat," originated in a letter Clampett wrote to a friend on MGM stationery. He drew a surprised baby bird pointing at Leo the Lion, saying "I tink I taw a titty-tat!" Clampett's friend wrote back that he got "quite a kick" out of the "titty-tat" gag. (It was a little off-color for the times). "Titty-tat" was turned into "Puddy-tat" for the big screen.

**MEL BLANC.** Believe it or not, the man who provided Bugs Bunny's voice was allergic to carrots.

**The New York League for the Hard of Hearing says 50% of D.J.s suffer hearing damage.**

# MYTH AMERICA

*You may have believed these myths all your life; after all, they were taught to us as sacred truths. But here's another look...*

## REMEMBER THE ALAMO

**The Myth:** The defenders of the Alamo fought for justice, political freedom, and independence.

**The Truth:** It was as much an issue of slavery as it was independence. In the 1820s Texas was a part of Mexico, and much of its land was being settled by slave-owning farmers and ranchers from the southern U.S. But in 1830, the Mexican government passed a law outlawing slavery. Soon after, American settlers revolted, and the Alamo was defended—at least in part because American settlers wanted to keep their slaves.

## BAR-B-COW

**The Myth:** Mrs. O'Leary's cow kicked over a lantern while being milked and started the Great Chicago Fire of October 8, 1871.

**Background:** The cow was merely a scapegoat . . .or scapecow. Michael Aherns, a reporter whose newspaper account first broke the legendary cow story, later admitted he made the whole thing up to boost his paper's circulation.

**The Truth:** The fire did start somewhere near the O'Leary house, but the Chicago Fire Department never found the real cause of the blaze.

## THE FATHER OF OUR COUNTRY

**The Myth:** George Washington was the first president of the United States.

**The Truth:** Washington was the first to serve as America's president under the Constitution of 1789, but the United States was a sovereign nation 13 years before the Constitution was written. In 1777, the Congress adopted the Articles of Confederation, which were ratified by the states in 1781. Later in 1781, this new legislative body convened and elected John Hanson as "President of the U.S. in Congress assembled." Hanson had been a member of the Maryland assembly and the Continental Congress, where he played a key role in convincing Maryland, the only state against the Articles of Confederation, to ratify them. Washington himself sent Hanson a letter of congratulations on his "appointment to fill the most important seat in the United States." However, Hanson and the *seven* other presidents who served before George Washington have been forgotten.

## THOREAU-LY SURPRISING

**The Myth:** Henry David Thoreau was a recluse who spent his Walden years in solitude, far from civilization.

**The Truth:** During his two years at Walden, Thoreau kept a pretty busy social schedule. He made frequent trips to the nearby town of Concord to spend time with friends and enjoy some of his mother's home cooking. In addition, he often played host to whole groups of visitors in his "secluded" cabin. Ralph Waldo Emerson was a frequent visitor, as was Bronson Alcott, who dropped by weekly. One day, April 1, 1846, Thoreau had about 30 people over for a meeting. According to Walter Harding's *The Days of Henry Thoreau*, "hardly a day went by that Thoreau did not visit the village or was not visited at the pond."

**The Myth:** Thoreau spent an extended period of time in prison for refusing to pay poll taxes which would support the Mexican War of 1846 and slavery.

**The Truth:** Thoreau did do jail time for his act of civil disobedience—one night of it. He was bailed out the following morning by an unidentified woman rumored to be his Aunt Maria, or Ralph Waldo Emerson in disguise. Legend has it Thoreau begged to stay in jail, but the jailer would have none of it.

## CHARGE!

**The Myth:** Teddy Roosevelt commanded his hardy band of Rough Riders on their charge up Cuba's San Juan Hill in the Spanish-American War.

**The Truth:** Contrary to the popular image of the courageous cavalry charge on horseback, the cavalry unit was on foot; their horses had accidentally been left in Florida. And Roosevelt wasn't even on San Juan Hill. He did take part in the charge on nearby Kettle Hill, but only watched from there as Colonel C. Wood led the Rough Riders up San Juan Hill.

**One out of five American families doesn't have a bank account.**

# REEL GANGSTERS

*If you're an old movie buff, you've probably seen classic gangster films like* Scarface, Little Caesar, *and* Public Enemy. *Here's some behind-the-scenes trivia about how the films were made.*

## BIG AL IS WATCHING YOU

*Scarface* (1932) was the best known of all early gangster films. Director Howard Hughes and screenwriter Ben Hecht modeled the main character, Tony Camonte (played by Paul Muni), after Chicago mobster Al Capone. Capone heard about it. And just to make sure *Scarface* was to his liking, he sent some of his own men to monitor the filming, as "advisors."

How do you spell relief? Capone enjoyed the film so much he bought a print of it and threw a huge party for Hawks in Chicago.

## THE UN-NATURAL LOOK

Edward G. Robinson's portrayal of vicious killer Caesar Enrico Bandello in *Litte Caesar* (1930) made him a star. But he actually hated firing guns; in fact, every time he shot one in the film, he shut his eyes. Director Mervin LeRoy wanted a "cold and unblinking" killer, so he taped Robinson's eyelids open.

## RIGHT GUY, WRONG PART

James Cagney was brought to Hollywood by Darryl Zanuck, and was immediately miscast as a smooth character in *The Millionaire*. One day Zanuck was watching unedited cuts of the film, wondering why Cagney wasn't working out. A scene ended; Cagney turned to the camera, sneered, and said, "For God's sake, who wrote this crap?" Zanuck realized the tough-talking Cagney was perfect for the gangster roles he was having such a hard time casting. It made Cagney's career.

In the most famous 1930s gangster scene, Cagney (*Public Enemy*, 1931), smashed half a grapefruit in Mae Clark's face. It wasn't in the script. Cagney and Clark staged it as a practical joke to shock the film crew, but director William Wellman liked it and left it in. Later in life, Cagney wasn't able to finish a meal in a restaurant without being offered a free half-grapefruit.

**At the wedding of Ronald Reagan's daughter Patti: 134 guests and 180 security personnel.**

# FIT FOR A KING

*A few thoughts from Maring Luther King, Jr., winner of the Nobel Peace Prize and one of the greatest leaders of the 20th Century.*

"Human salvation lies in the hands of the creatively maladjusted."

"I live each day under a threat of death. I know I can meet a violent end."

"Philanthropy is commendable, but it must not cause the philanthropists to overlook the circumstances of economic injustice which make philanthropy necessary."

"He who passively accepts evil is as much involved in it as he who helps to perpetrate it."

"Freeedom is never voluntarily given by the oppressor; it must be demanded by the oppressed."

"War is a poor chisel to carve out tomorrows."

"All progress is precarious, and the solution of one problem brings us face to face with another problem."

"Nothing pains some people more than having to think."

"We will have to repent in this generation not merely for the vitriolic words and actions of the bad people, but for the appalling silence of the good people."

"Injustice anywhere is a threat to justice everywhere."

"The means by which we live have outdistanced the ends for which we live."

"Our scientific power has outrun our spiritual power. We have guided missiles and misguided men."

"A man has no right to live until he has found something to die for."

"Shallow understanding from people of goodwill is more frustrating than absolute misunderstanding from people of ill-will."

# MARS ATTACKS

*On October 30, 1938, over a million-and-a-half listeners tuned in to the most famous radio broadcast of all-time—*War Of The Worlds*, a dramatization of* H.G. *Wells' classic science fiction novel about a Martian invasion. Here's what happened.*

## HERE THEY COME

The radio version of *War of the Worlds* was just an elaborate Halloween joke played by actor Orson Welles and the regulars of "Mercury Theatre on the Air." But it caused a nationwide panic. Some terrified families fled from their homes; others prepared for a full-scale Martian war.

## ON THE SPOT

Welles insisted on making the broadcast of *War of the Worlds* as realistic-sounding as possible. At first, the announcements that Martians had landed came in the form of news bulletins interspersed between live big-band remotes. Gradually the tone of the broadcast became more hysterical. Some of the bulletins ("We take you now to Washington for a special broadcast on the national emergency...") sounded particularly unnerving to a nation on the verge of World War II.

## I CAN'T LOOK

Since the show had no sponsors, there were only a few interruptions to announce that the show was a dramatic presentation. Listeners tuning in mid-broadcast heard frightening "on the scene" descriptions of the attacking Martians. "Good heavens, something's wriggling out of the shadow like a grey snake. Now it's another one, and another. They look like tentacles to me. There, I can see the thing's body. It's large as bear and it glistens like wet leather. But that face...it's indescribable. I can hardly force myself to look at it. The eyes are black and gleam like a serpent. The mouth is V-shaped with saliva dripping from its rimless lips that seem to quiver and pulsate."

Although he was oblivious to the hysteria his program was stirring up, Welles was still clever enough to give the show a happy ending—the Martians are conquered and calm is restored. Welles concluded the broadcast by saying, "And if your doorbell rings and nobody's 'there,' that was no Martian...it's Halloween."

## THE PANIC

By the time the broadcast was completed, millions of Americans were convinced that a Martian invasion had occurred. Police switchboards were flooded from coast to coast by calls from terrified listeners. Among the reactions:

- One New Jersey resident mistook a water tower for the Martians and blasted it with a shotgun.
- Twenty families from one apartment building evacuated their homes with wet towels on their faces to avoid deadly Martian rays.
- Pennsylvania's governor offered troop support to New Jersey, where the invasion was supposedly taking place.
- A woman paged her husband at a Broadway play to warn him of the attack—and many audience members fled with him.
- A husband in Pittsburgh came home to find his wife with a bottle of poison in her hand, saying "I'd rather die this way than that."

Despite the hysteria, no deaths resulting from the broadcast have ever been documented.

## FALL OUT

- Police stormed CBS studios after the broadcast and held the cast and crew for questioning (Mercury employees hid the tape of the show, fearing that it would be confiscated). After a few hours of intense grilling, the police let everybody go.
- Welles became an instant nationwide celebrity. The day after the broadcast, he seemed as incredulous as anybody about all the hoopla: "I'm extremely surprised to learn that a story, which has become familiar to children through the medium of comic strips and many succeeding novels and adventure stories, should have had such an immediate and profound effect upon radio listeners."
- In 1947, the citizens of Ecuador had a similar hysterical reaction to Radio Quito's dramatization of the Mercury script. Once again, panic-stricken residents fled into the streets. Later, when a mob of terrified listeners found out the broadcast wasn't real, they burned down the radio station (Ecuador's oldest) in anger. One radio station employee died in the blaze.

# DICK NIXON, FOOTBALL COACH

*Judging from Watergate, you might say strategy wasn't Richard Nixon's strongest suit. But that didn't keep Nixon from trying to "coach" two football teams—the Washington Redskins and the Miami Dolphins—while he was serving as president.*

## BACKGROUND

• Nixon was an acknowledged football freak, an armchair quarterback who often peppered his speeches with allusions to the game.
• He once referred to Congress as "a fourth-quarter team," adding, "in the last quarter, we have to score a lot of points."
• The White House used the code name "Operation Linebacker," for a secret Pentagon strategy in Vietnam during Nixon's presidency. Nixon's personal code name was "Quarterback."

## COLLEGE DAYS

• Nixon was never much of a football player. He made the freshman squad at Whittier College in California, but later in his college career was only allowed to practice with the team and sit on the bench.
• He later recalled: "I played on the C team...and I didn't even make that."
• In 1969, a few days before being inaugurated, he finally received a varsity letter from Whittier.

## THE COACH AND THE PREZ

• George Allen, who coached the Redskins during Nixon's tenure at the White House, had previously been Whittier's football coach.
• The two met at a college sports banquet in 1952 and became very close. Allen, who spoke often to the president, publicly praised him, saying, "The president thinks football is a way of life. He is a competitor."
• Allen, like Nixon, wasn't known for his scruples. Once, while he was coach of the Redskins, Allen traded away a draft choice he didn't have. Football officials fined him $5,000.

**40% of the pure water you use in your house is flushed down the toilet.**

## PEP TALK

• In November, 1971, President Nixon visited the Redskins at their practice camp in Virginia. He gave them a pep talk: "I've always said that in life, as well as in sports, politics, and business, what really makes a team or a country is when it has lost one, it doesn't lose its spirit. I think this team has the spirit it takes. I think government has it. You're going to go on and win."

• The president was wrong. Washington lost the National Football Conference championship game that season to the San Francisco 49ers, partly due to Nixon's playmaking.

• Late in the second quarter of the game, with the Redskins on the verge of a touchdown, Coach Allen ran a play that Nixon had especially requested—a flanker reverse with Roy Jefferson. The play resulted in a 13-yard loss, throwing the Redskins from the 49ers' 8-yard line to the 21-yard line. The Skins had to settle for a field goal.

• When the 49ers won the game, 24-20, many sportwriters claimed Nixon's play had been the turning point of the game.

## SWITCHING SIDES

• Following the Redskins' loss to the 49ers, Nixon quickly switched allegiances to the Miami Dolphins, claiming he had followed the team from his vacation home in Key Biscayne, Florida.

• The Dolphins defeated the Baltimore Colts, 21-0, for the American Football Conference title. That night, their coach, Don Shula, received a 1:30 am phone call from the president. "I thought it might be some nut calling," Shula later recounted. "But his aide said, 'Is this Mr. Shula?' Then he said, 'The president is calling.' I thought it might be a hoax. I was listening to make sure it was his voice."

## SINKING THE DOLPHINS

• Shula would soon regret Nixon's interest.

• Somehow it became public knowledge that the President had suggested the Dolphins run a specific play for their star wide-receiver, Paul Warfield, against the Dallas Cowboys in the upcoming Super Bowl. "I think you can hit Warfield on that down-and-in pattern," Nixon told Shula.

• The Dolphins failed to complete the play three times in the 1972 Super Bowl, which the Cowboys won handily, 24- 3.

• After the game, Warfield complained that the Cowboys had keyed on him thanks to Nixon. "They had two weeks to prepare and they made sure that under any circumstances we wouldn't be able to catch that pass," he said.

## NO BONES ABOUT IT

• More than a few Cowboys fans took umbrage at Nixon's support of the Dolphins. The Bonehead Club of Dallas, a group of Dallas businessmen, awarded their annual "Bonehead of the Year Award" to Nixon two days prior to the Super Bowl.

• Nixon accepted the award "in the spirit in which it is given . . . in good humor."

## CSONKA'S COMPAINT

• Larry Csonka, the Dolphins' star running back, wasn't all that pleased with Nixon's playmaking either. He later complained, "President Nixon may identify with football players, but I don't identify with him, and I haven't met a player yet who does. The man upset me with his role as superjock. Here he is, the one man in the world who has, at his fingertips, all the information and influence to make a lot of people's lives better. But what's he doing calling football players on the telephone and giving pep talks to teams? It just brainwashes people more, makes people think football is a lot more important to them than it really is. He's either hung up on the violence or else he's pulling off a master con job on a lot of sports fans. He's implying that he's one of them and he's hoping to get their votes in return."

## KILMER'S COMPAINT

• Despite his coaching ineptitude, Nixon kept meddling with the Redskins the following season.

• Billy Kilmer, the Redskins' quarterback, became so frustrated that he told the *Washington Post*, "He's really hurting us. He calls all the time. He told some guy from Cleveland he met in New York that Cleveland had a good team but they had quarterback problems. Then Cleveland got all psyched up and they were much harder to beat. I think I'm going to ask George Allen to tell the president not to talk about the game until after we've played it."

## POSTSCRIPT

• By 1978, both Nixon and Coach Allen had lost their jobs. But unlike the ex-President, Allen had landed a new one as the head coach of the Rams.

• Surfacing to express confidence in his old pal, Nixon fearlessly predicted that Allen would coach the Rams to the Super Bowl.

• "I'm not saying they will win the Super Bowl," he told the *Los Angeles Herald Examiner* in 1978, "but I think he'll get them there at least."

• Not exactly. Allen was fired early in the season; the Rams lost in the playoffs. Nixon was later spotted in Yankee Stadium, rooting for the New York Yankees. Apparently, he'd become a baseball fan.

## AD-VERSARIES: WOULD YOU BUY A USED CAR FROM THESE GUYS?

• **Mr. Clean versus Mr. Bush:** In 1985, Procter & Gamble took a poll to see how many people could identify Mr. Clean, the genie character used as a trademark for one of their cleaning products. 93% of consumers could identify him. That year, *People* magazine also took a poll and found that only 56% of the same shoppers could identify then-Vice President George Bush.

• **TV Time:** The average American teenager will see some 350,000 TV commercials by the time he or she graduates from high school.

### Obsolescent Ads

• **Planned:** During the 1984 Super Bowl, Apple Computer showed a commercial that depicted a procession of robot-like people marching off a cliff. The idea: Most computer buyers pick the same old thing, but choosing an Apple is daring to be different. The widely-praised ad, which cost over $500,000 to produce, was intentionally never shown again.

• **Un-Planned:** In 1989, Pepsi paid Madonna a whopping $5 million for one two-minute commercial featuring her new hit "Like A Prayer." Ironically, the ad was abruptly cancelled by Pepsi after a month when consumers confused the commercial with Madonna's video of the same song, which featured "sacreligious" images like burning crosses.

# SPACE JUNK

*Since Sputnik I was launched in 1957, nearly four thousand satellites have been put into orbit. Many just exploded; others have been deliberately blown up. As a result, there are literally billions of pieces of man-made debris now circling the earth...a veritable junkyard in space. So here's some "space junk" trivia.*

Seven U.S. Delta rockets and a French observation satellite have exploded in space.

In 1961, Cuban premier Fidel Castro charged that a chunk of a U.S. spacecraft had fallen on Cuba and killed a cow.

In 1962, a 21-lb. fragment of Soviet Sputnik IV landed at the intersection of Park and North 8th Streets in Manitowoc, Wisconsin.

In 1978, a Soviet satellite came crashing back to Earth, contaminating hundreds of square miles of Canadian territory with radiation. What caused the crash? Scientists' best guess: the satellite collided with space junk, which caused it to go off its orbit.

Lost and never found: Astronaut Ed White lost a white glove during the Gemini 4 flight in 1965; George "Pinky" Nelson lost two minature screws while attempting to repair a satellite on a space shuttle mission in 1984.

In 1981, a Soviet navigation satellite exploded into 135 pieces after colliding with space debris.

Over 7,000 objects floating in space are being tracked from earth; only five percent are satellites.

Dodging space junk is a dangerous occupation. A 0.5 millimeter metal chip could puncture a space suit and kill an astronaut walking in space. A particle as small as ten millimeters could damage and possibly even destroy an orbiting space vehicle.

Before it blew up in 1986, the space shuttle Challenger was hit by a flake of paint measuring 0.2 millimeters, which damaged a window during one of its missions.

**Americans make $500 million worth of illegal long distance phone calls annually.**

# JUST SAY NO-HIT!

*Although quite a few public figures dabbled in pyschedelics during the late '60s and early '70s, few played major league baseball. Dock Ellis did...and pitched a no-hitter on LSD.*

## BACKGROUND

Dock Ellis was a premier pitcher from 1968 through 1979, winning 138 games while playing for the Pittsburgh Pirates, New York Yankees, Oakland Athletics, Texas Rangers and New York Mets. Of all his achievements, which include pitching in two World Series, his biggest was the no-hitter he pitched as a Pittsburgh Pirate against the San Diego Padres on June 12, 1970.

Fourteen years later, Ellis revealed he had accomplished this feat while under the influence of LSD.

## A LONG STRANGE TRIP

Apparently, Ellis took the dose at noon and then realized he had to pitch at 6:05 p.m. that night. "I was in Los Angeles and the team was playing in San Diego, but I didn't know it," Ellis told the *Pittsburgh Press* in 1984. "I had taken LSD. I thought it was an off-day."

## THE ACID TEST

The game was the first in a twi-night doubleheader between the Pirates and the Padres. Despite the powerful effects of the LSD, Ellis pitched brilliantly for nine innings, allowing no hits (he walked eight and hit a batter). "I can only remember bits of pieces of the game," Ellis later recounted. "I was psyched. I had a feeling of euphoria." According to one source, Ellis believed the ball was talking to him, telling him what pitches to throw.

## THE AFTERMATH

Ellis didn't dare admit what he'd done. In fact, he never pitched on psychedelics again. Years later, Ellis was treated for drug dependency and became the coordinator of an anti-drug program in Los Angeles.

# FABULOUS FAKES

*There are plenty of little lies and hoaxes in the newspapers every day—from President Reagan pretending to light the White House Christmas tree, to votes of confidence for baseball managers about to be fired. But some hoaxes capture the public's imagination, and fool the experts at the same time. Here are some classics.*

## THE PILTDOWN MAN

**THE DISCOVERY:** In 1912, the remains of the fabled "missing link" between man and ape were found at an English excavation site. The exciting discovery included nine pieces of a skull and a jawbone.

**THE HOAX:** Charles Dawson was a British lawyer and amateur archeologist when he "discovered" the remains of the half-ape/half-man in a pit at Piltdown Common near Sussex, England. Dawson claimed the fossils were proof that human life had origins in England—a notion that appealed to British sensibilities.

In 1915, Dawson made a similar discovery two miles away from the first, proving the "Piltdown Man" was part of a race of people. The problem was, no one could get close enough to the bones to either prove or disprove Dawson's theory—he kept them locked up and only provided plaster cast models of the fossils.

**THE UNMASKING:** Dawson died in 1916, but it wasn't until 1953 that scientists finally got a chance to test the authenticity of the bones. They quickly proved the "Piltdown Man" was a fraud and concluded that Dawson probably bought the bones in an auction and tried to pass them off as "the missing link" as a practical joke.

## THE CARDIFF GIANT

**THE DISCOVERY:** In 1869, workers digging near a well in Cardiff, New York discovered the petrified remains of a ten-foot tall man. Newspapers dubbed him "the Cardiff Giant" and hailed the discovery as the paleontogical "find of the century." "Cardiff Giant fever" swept the country.

**THE SCHEME:** The Cardiff Giant was the brainchild of a cigar manufacturer named George Hull, from Binghamton, New York.

**Young Guns: The average age of U.S. Military personnel is 25.**

Hull bought a 5-ton block of gypsum in Iowa and had it shipped to Chicago, where two marble cutters, with him as their model, spent three months carving out a likeness of a naked man.

According to Stephen Jay Gould in *Natural History* magazine: "Hull made some crude and minimal attempts to give his statue an aged appearance. He chipped off the carved hair and beard because experts told him that such items would not petrify. He drove darning needles into a wooden block and hammered the statue, hoping to simulate skin pores. Finally, he dumped a gallon of sulfuric acid all over his creation to simulate extended erosion." Hull then had the statue buried in Cardiff (in the backyard of a friend who was in on the hoax), where it was not-so-accidentally "discovered" by two unsuspecting workmen hired to dig a well there.

**THE UNMASKING:** A Yale paleontologist named O.C. Marsh exposed the fraud a few weeks later. After giving the Cardiff Giant the once-over, he declared that the Giant "was of very recent origin and a decided humbug." Shortly thereafter, under intense pressure, Hull confessed to his fraud.

**AFTERMATH:** Hull had managed to sell the rights to the Cardiff Giant—for $30,000 to a consortium of businessmen—before revealing the hoax. Although the Cardiff Giant was no longer the acknowledged "Eighth Wonder of the World," people still paid 50¢ apiece to see it. P.T. Barnum later made a copy of the fake and also put it on exhibition in New York City. Reportedly, his model outdrew the original when both were on display at the same time. The original Cardiff Giant is still on display at the Farmer's Museum in Cooperstown, New York.

## THE ORANGE MOONMEN

**THE DISCOVERY:** In 1835, a New York *Sun* writer named Richard Adams Locke broke the stunning news that a British astronomer had seen furry, orange creatures living on the moon. The public was fascinated.

**THE HOAX:** Locke claimed that British astronomer Sir John Herschel had been trying out a new telescope when he noticed bison grazing on the moon. Supposedly, Herschel also saw blue goats, tropical forests and white beaches. Locke made the moon sound like a vacation spot. And the most amazing revelation was...there were apparently orange humanoid creatures, sporting leather wings, living on the lunar surface.

**THE UNMASKING:** Locke's chicanery was quickly exposed. Herschel disavowed the story and Locke owned up. He made up the entire thing to satirize an astronomer from Scotland who'd been claiming that he had discovered plant life on the moon.

## BATS IN THE BELLE-FRY

**THE DISCOVERY:** During the Civil War, Ida Mayfield, a beautiful belle from Louisiana, became the toast of New York society. She was among the most beautiful, well-bred women in the city, and married Ben Wood, a newspaper magnate and congressman. She wore the finest gowns and jewels, danced with the Prince of Wales, was presented to Empress Eugenie of Austria, and entertained President Cleveland. Then, during the financial panic of 1907, she disappeared without a trace.

**THE HOAX:** Ida Mayfield was really Ellen Walsh, the penniless daughter of an immigrant textile worker, using a borrowed dress, the name of respected Louisiana family, and her innate charm. Wood never knew her real identity.

**THE UNMASKING:** In 1931, Ida Mayfield was found blind, deaf and shrunken. She was 94 years old, and living in a dingy New York hotel room, wearing a "dress" made only of two hotel towels pinned together. Her room was a mess of yellowed newspapers, letters and boxes, all scattered in disarray. She was judged incompetent and was made a ward of the court.

However, when they opened the boxes, they found securities worth hundreds of thousands of dollars. A diamond and emerald necklace was hidden in a box of crackers. And to top it off, fifty $10,000 dollar bills were contained inside a pouch tied around her waist. When collectors took this from her, she died.

## FABULOUS FAKES ADDENDUM:

In 1708, English writer Jonathan Swift was so sick and tired of an astrologer that he wrote and published a fake obituary about the man, whose career subsequently took a dive.

# DEFINITIONS

*How's your vocabulary? In the first two Bathroom Readers we included some obscure words and their meanings, so you could impress your friends and neighbors. Here's another batch.*

**Labrose:** Thick-lipped

**Xenoepist:** Someone with a foreign accent

**Nosocomephrenia:** Depression resulting from prolonged stay in the hospital

**Hebetate:** To become stupid or boring

**Palpebrate:** To wink

**Quakebuttock:** A coward

**Glock:** To swallow in large gulps

**Brumous:** Foggy or misty

**Noyade:** Mass execution by drowning

**Ergophile:** A workaholic

**Weener:** A trustworthy or believable person

**Phrontistery:** A place to study

**Crurophilous:** Liking legs

**Dactylgram:** Fingerprint

**Valgus:** Knock-kneed or bow-legged

**Fample:** To feed a child

**Thuften:** Having webbed toes

**Errhine:** Causing sneezing

**Sphragistics:** The study of engraved seals

**Subrahend:** The amount subtracted

**Cygnet:** A young swan

**Misocapnist:** Someone who dislikes tobacco smoke

**Culch:** Meat scraps

**Recrement:** A bodily secretion that is re-absorbed

**Dentiscalp:** A toothpick

**Sorbile:** Drinkable

**Glabella:** The space on your forehead between your eyebrows

**Vespertilonize:** To turn into a bat

**Misodoctakleidist:** Someone who dislikes practicing the piano

**Deglutible:** Capable of being swallowed

**Spasmatomancy:** Fortune-telling based upon body twitches

**Bonnyclabber:** Sour, coagulated milk

**Peen:** The end of a hammer opposite the striking end

**Opsigamy:** Marriage late in life

**Hesternal:** Having to do with yesterday

**Shoding:** The part in a person's hair

**The chairman of Hyundai is called "The Chairman," even by his wife and kids.**

# BLACK AND WHITE

*In 1972, Three Dog Night hit #1 on the pop charts with a tune called "Black and White" ("The ink is black, the page is white..."). Here's the amazing true story behind it.*

## LEGAL HISTORY

In 1896, in a decision called *Plessy v. Ferguson*, the United States Supreme Court ruled that racial segregation was constitutional—as long as blacks were given facilities which were "separate but equal" to those provided to whites. This ruling was the basis for institutionalized segregation in America.

Fifty-eight years later, the NAACP and a group of black families, with the support of Attorney General Herbert Brownell, sued the Topeka, Kansas school system, claiming that segregation was discriminatory and violated their constitutional rights. In an historic decision known as *Brown v. the Board of Education*, the court ruled in their favor, unanimously overturning the *Plessy* verdict. "In the field of public education, the doctrine of 'separate but equal' has no place," the court ruled.

During the months following the decision, more than 150 school districts integrated. Others fought the decision, and eventually lost. But the decision's impact was not merely on schools. It was one of the turning points of the Civil Rights movement, and marked an awakening of black activism that changed the face of American culture forever.

## A SONG IS BORN

To jubilant Americans like Earl Robinson, an activist-songwriter who composed "Joe Hill," the *Brown v. Board of Education* ruling was a triumph. He and David Arkin, actor Alan Arkin's father, wrote "Black and White" to commemorate the event. It was a modern folk song.

"It was done in the '50s to celebrate a Supreme Court decision on segregation in the schools," Robinson says. "It was a famous decision, and this was kind of a celebration song, written actually, with children in mind, and no ideas whatsoever about it going popular."

Robinson was a performer himself, and sang the song whenever he gave concerts ("The first place it was performed was in Elizabeth Irwin High School in the New York area, by the junior high school class there"). Thus it was passed around among New York folksingers , until it landed in...Guyana?

Robinson says: "In the late '50s, I got a call from CBS, which wanted to use my song, 'The Ink Is Black'—which isn't the title—for a documentary film they were making. It seems there was some kind of a Peace Corps that was working in French Guyana, and CBS wanted to clear the song because it was being used by them there, to teach the French Guyanese how to speak English! In the film, they showed a blackboard with a pointer, so you would hear [sings] 'The Ink Is Black...' and they'd point to the words as it went along. That became a theme song for this whole film, which was about how the American group was helping them build a recreation hall."

## BACK TO AMERICA

"So then Sammy Davis Jr. got ahold of it through a publisher of mine, and he sang it and pressed 5,000 copies for the Anti-Defamation League of B'nai B'rith, which he was strongly connected with—and this was kind of like a flash in the pan. Pete Seeger also recorded it. He did it with a bunch of kids, and I wasn't too impressed, although I was happy that Pete did it.

"Anyway, it kept on being sung around, spreading slowly, by word of mouth until I got called on the phone in the early '70s. Someone told me, 'Three Dog Night is singing your song, did you know that?' I didn't even know who the Three Dogs were, to tell you the truth. I had no concept of it. You know, they told me later, when I went to attend a concert where they were singing, that they had heard the song in Holland, over a radio, where it was being sung by a Jamaican group. Now, I remembered this Jamaican group, but we paid very little attention to them because very little royalties were coming in from them. But the guys in Three Dog Night told me that they knew immediately it was going to be a hit when they heard it." And it was. Six weeks after it was released, it reached #1 in the nation. But virtually none of the millions of fans who bought it had any idea of what it was really about.

# REAL ADS

*Some ad characters—Charmin's Mr. Whipple, for instance—are so believable that we forget they're simply actors playing parts. Just to remind us, here's some inside info on a few of them.*

**THE STAR:** Clara Peller in "Where's the Beef?"
**BACKGROUND:** Joe Sedelmaier, a producer of commercials, was filming a scene in a Chicago barbershop when he discovered that nobody had hired a manicurist. He sent an assistant to a local beauty shop to find one and she returned with Clara Peller, an octogenarian manicurist who had worked in a nearby salon for 35 years. She looked at Sedelmaier and said gruffly: "How ya doin', honey?" Sedelmaier realized he had found a "natural." "She's a counterpart to all those sweet little old ladies," he explained.
**THE AD:** In 1984, Sedelmaier convinced Wendy's Old Fashioned Hamburgers to design an ad campaign around Peller, who growled the catchy phrase, "Where's the beef?" Almost immediately, Wendy's sales jumped 15%. The slogan "Where's the beef?" entered the popular lexicon when Presidential candidate Walter Mondale used the phrase against his Democratic rival, Gary Hart, in the primary campaigns.

Meanwhile, the 82-year-old Peller became an instant cult star with a national fan club. She ended up making $500,000 for the Wendy's ad, plus merchandising. Before she passed away in 1987, Peller said "I made some money, which is nice for an older person, but Wendy's made millions because of me."

**THE STAR:** Jim Varney in "Hey, Vern!"
**BACKGROUND:** John R. Cherry III, a Nashville ad executive, was searching for an innovative ad campaign to publicize an amusement park that, in his words, was "so bad we couldn't show it on television." His solution: a fictional character named Ernest P. Worrell, a nosy country bumpkin with a penchant for injuring himself, who continually harasses an off-screen character named Vern.

To fill Ernest's silly shoes, Cherry picked Jim Varney, who'd appeared on the TV show "Fernwood 2-Night," as a "mobile home daredevil." Ironically, Varney was a trained Shakespearean actor.

**THE AD:** Although the amusement park closed after three months, Ernest was an immediate success. Sensing Ernest's potential, Cherry and Varney cleverly decided to license the character to any company that wanted him—rather than identifying Ernest with one particular product. Eventually, the duo collaborated on over 3,000 Ernest commercials (sometimes filming as many as 20 a day) plugging everything from Toyota cars to Snickers bars. In 1987, Ernest made it to the movies in "Ernest Goes To Camp," a $4 million feature that outdrew its competition, the $45 million "Ishtar." Since then, two other features, "Ernest's Christmas" and "Ernest Goes To Jail"—both huge box-office successes—have been released. No doubt more are on the way.

**THE STAR:** David Leisure in "You Have My Word On It."
**BACKGROUND:** David Leisure was an unemployed actor when an ad agency chose him to star in a series of Isuzu TV ads that were based on the character of "The Liar," popularized by Jon Luvitz on "Saturday Night Live." After auditioning several candidates, the agency hired Leisure "because he could lie like a pro." Leisure's previous biggest screen role had been as a Hare Krishna in the film "Airplane!"
**THE AD:** The ads featured Leisure playing Joe Isuzu, a car salesman who made outlandish claims about Isuzu cars while the words "he's lying" appeared under him. The campaign caught the public's imagination and Isuzu car sales jumped 18%. Meanwhile, the character became a household name. In the 1988 Presidential race, Michael Dukakis compared George Bush's tax promises to Joe Isuzu.

**THE STAR:** Dick Wilson in "Don't Squeeze The Charmin."
**BACKGROUND:** In 1964, Proctor and Gamble was looking for an actor to portray Mr. Whipple, an uptight supermarket manager who (for some strange reason never fully explained) begged his shoppers to stop squeezing Charmin toilet paper. Dick Wilson, an ex-vaudevillian, won the role over 80 potential Mr. Whipples. The first ads were filmed in Flushing, New York.
**THE AD:** Mr. Whipple caught on; Charmin became the bestselling toilet paper in the country. One 1970s survey found that more people recognized Mr. Whipple than Jimmy Carter. Unfortunately, Wilson became typecast. "When I go through the toilet paper section," he told People magazine, "I get some very strange looks."

# MOORE TO COME

*In a recent poll, TV critics called "The Mary Tyler Moore Show" one of the 5 best sitcoms ever. As the first program to feature a single career woman competing on equal terms with men, it was certainly among the most influential. Here are some interesting facts about the show:*

## HOW IT STARTED

From 1961 to 1965, Mary Tyler Moore co-starred in the popular TV program "The Dick Van Dyke Show." But after she left the show, her career didn't fare too well. She tried movies, and wound up in films like *Change of Habit*, with Elvis Presley (she played a nun). She gave Broadway a shot (a musical version of *Breakfast At Tiffany's*), and the play closed before opening night. People began to notice that she'd never made it on her own, and suspected that she'd just been lucky on TV. She needed to do something to prove herself.

Then in 1969 she was invited to co-star with Dick Van Dyke in a TV special called "Dick Van Dyke and the Other Woman." Van Dyke's previous TV special, which co-starred singer Leslie Uggams, hadn't done well. But the Moore-Van Dyke show got high ratings, and Mary got the credit. The result: she received an offer from CBS that was too good to pass up; if she'd star in a new sitcom for them, they'd give her total creative freedom in developing it—plus part-ownership of the series. If it succeeded, she'd be rich. She accepted the offer.

Moore chose her new character carefully. She didn't want to be a housewife because she'd been "married" in "The Dick Van Dyke Show" (and wanted to avoid typecasting). She didn't want to be another sitcom "widow." So she decided to become a divorcee. Her writers created a pilot in which a recently-divorced woman (Mary) struggled with a career as an associate TV producer, and CBS loved it—except for the divorce. America wasn't quite that liberated yet. The network requested a change, saying they were afraid viewers would assume she had "divorced" Van Dyke. So the part was re-written to make Mary a refugee from a love affair. That was fine with CBS. The series debuted in Sept. 1970, and was a hit from the start. For three years in a row, it was among the Top 10 TV shows in America.

**According to a Yale study, you think better in the winter than in summer.**

## SCOREBOARD

• The *Mary Tyler Moore Show* was the most honored show in Emmy history. It received 27 awards, including three for best comedy show, one for directing, and five for writing. Moore, Ed Asner (Lou Grant), and Valerie Harper (Rhoda Morgenstern) received three Emmys each; Ted Knight (Ted Baxter) and Betty White (Sue Ann Nivens) received two apiece; and Cloris Leachman (Phyllis, the land-lady) was presented with one.

• Even more impressive, the show spawned more successful spinoffs than any other sitcoms: *Rhoda*, *Phyllis*, and *Lou Grant*. In the 1975 season, two of the spinoffs placed in the Top Ten of the Year (*Phyllis* was #6, *Rhoda* was #8), outstripping even *Mary*, which ranked at #19.

## REVENGE

Ironically, the only major cast-member who never received an Emmy for his work on the *MTM Show*—Gavin Macleod (Murray)—went on to the biggest TV success of all of them. He wound up as captain of the *Love Boat*, which ranked in the Top 5 several years in a row—higher than Mary or any of its spinoffs ever got. Amazing, but true.

## HOME SWEET HOME

Remember that quaint house at 119 North Weatherly, where Mary supposedly had her apartment? It was owned by a University of Minnesota humanities professor. She was initially delighted to let MTM Productions shoot its exterior for use on the show (the interior scenes were done in the studio).

But when the program became popular, doorbell ringers began showing up regularly, asking for Mary, Rhoda, and Phyllis. The professor's life was so disrupted that she refused to let MTM film the outside of her house anymore. When MTM ignored her wishes and showed up to film the outside of her house anyway, the professor hung banners reading "Impeach Nixon" out of the windows that were supposed to be Mary's. That stopped the film crew.

Soon after, Mary "moved" to a high rise.

**ANGLERS TAKE NOTE:** In Tennessee and Washington, it's illegal to fish with a lasso.

# JOCKS IN POLITICS

*Are all jocks dumb? Not necessarily. Some wind up making laws, starting revolutions, even running countries. A few examples:*

**George Bush.** Right after World War II, Yale had the best baseball team in the East; it won the Eastern Division NCAA championships twice. Bush was the team's starting first baseman, and was even named captain in his senior year (1948). Five members of the Yale team signed pro contracts after graduation. Bush supposedly thought about going pro, too.

**Mario Cuomo** (governor of New York). Tried professional baseball for a single season, then quit. In 1952, he played with a minor league team in the lowly Class D Georgia-Florida League. His record: A .244 batting average, with one homer in 254 at bats. His strength, according to a scouting report was that he would "run right over you."

**Fidel Castro.** A star pitcher at the University of Havana in the 1940s. Cuba once had a minor league team (the Havana Sugar Kings) and when Castro took over the country, he enthusiastically supported it. In fact, Premier Castro once pitched an inning in the minors, striking out 2 batters—on called strikes (after which he left the mound and shook the umpire's hand). In another game, his team was losing in the 9th inning—so he declared that the game would go into extra innings. They played until Castro's team won.

**Jack Kemp** (former New York congressman, secretary of HUD). Spent 13 years as a pro quarterback, leading the AFL's Buffalo Bills to championships in 1964 and 1965. He used his standing as a local Buffalo hero to run for Congress—and won.

**Bill Bradley** (U.S. senator from New Jersey). Star of the Princeton University "Cinderella" basketball team in 1965, Rhodes Scholar who returned to the U.S. and signed with the New York Knicks. He was a starting guard on their world championship 1970 and 1973 teams. In 1978, he was elected senator; and in the '80s, he was the architect of major tax reform legislation.

# SECRET RECIPES

*Here's some fascinating data we found in a wonderful book called* Big Secrets *by William Poundstone.*

## TWINKIES

In 1976, the *Snack Food Yearbook* reported "[Twinkies inventor James] Deware says [the Twinkies] formula is a secret...He always refers to [the filling] as a creamed filling, emphasizing the need to add the 'ed.' " So what's really in the filling? Among other things:

- Sugar and corn syrup. (40%)
- Shortening content (25%). Here's what's written on the label: "partially hydrogenated vegetable and/or animal shortening (contains one or more of the following: soybean oil, cottonseed oil, palm oil, beef fat, lard)." Hydrogenated vegetable shortening is oil turned into a wax-like solid. Beef fat is...well...the fat from beef.
- Skim milk (7%). The "nutritional" part.
- Butter flavoring (1%).

## KENTUCKY FRIED CHICKEN

The Colonel's "secret recipe" is a special combination of eleven herbs and spices, right? Not even close. In a laboratory analysis, the "eleven herbs and spices" were revealed to be a sum total of zero herbs and only four spices, namely salt, pepper, flour, and Monosodium Glutamate (MSG).

## OREOS

What's the creme filling in America's favorite sandwich cookie? Mostly sugar and shortening, with hydrogenated coconut oil the favored shortening. Lard is also used occasionally, but not beef fat.

## COCA-COLA

Does Coca-Cola, which is made with coca leaves, have any cocaine in it? Trace amounts, almost certainly. Even if 99.99999999 percent of the cocaine from the coca leaves was removed, millions of cocaine molecules would remain floating in each can of Coke. Regardless, Coca-Cola is still 99.5% sugar water.

**In a single year, over 200,000 pounds of barnacles collect on the bottom of a steamship.**

# INVASION! PART I

*European history is full of invasions. But since it became a nation in 1776, the U.S. has rarely been the target of foreign attacks. In fact, we could only think of five of them. Here's one.*

**THE INVADERS:** The British.

**THE DATE:** August 24, 1814.

**BACKGROUND:** During the early 1800s, relations between Britain and America were strained. One reason: the English had broken their promise to leave Canada after the Revolutionary War. Another: the British fleet had begun seizing American ships that were headed for France (which was at war with England).

Ultimately, the dispute over free trade led to open conflict—on June 18, 1812 President James Monroe declared war. (Historians call it the War of 1812). Two years of fighting ensued. In 1814, the U.S. mounted a particularly destructive attack on the British stronghold in York, Canada, burning down several government buildings. The British decided to retaliate.

**THE INVASION:** Under the command of British General Robert Ross, 4,000 British troops sailed through Chesapeake Bay, headed for Washington. There was virtually no resistance. British soldiers marched into America's capital and burned down government buildings—including the Capitol, the Library of Congress, and the White House.

President James Madison and his wife, Dolly, were warned of the attack and managed to escape, taking only the White House drapes, Gilbert Stuart's famous portrait of George Washington, and some fine china with them. Ravenous British soldiers raided the White House and polished off all the food they could find. Then, using rockets and gunpowder, they incinerated the place. That night, a drenching thunderstorm put out the fire, but not in time to save the young nation's symbol of power.

**AFTERMATH:** Later that year, the Treaty of Ghent was signed between the two nations, ending the War of 1812. Conquered territories were returned and hostilities ceased. Four years later, on January 1, 1818, the Madisons moved into the newly restored White House. No foreign power ever occupied it again.

# WORD PLAY

*Here are some more origins of common phrases.*

**SON OF A GUN**
***Meaning:*** An epithet.
***Background:*** In the 1800s, British sailors took their wives along on extended voyages. When babies were born at sea, the mothers delivered them in a partitioned section of the gundeck. Because no one could be sure who the *true* fathers were, each of these "gunnery" babies was called a "son of a gun."

**PUT UP YOUR DUKES**
***Meaning:*** Raise your fists and get ready to fight.
***Background:*** In the early 1800s, the Duke of York, Frederick Augustus, shocked English society by taking up boxing. He gained such admiration from boxers that many started referrring to their fists as the "Dukes of York," and later, "dukes."

**HAVING AN AXE TO GRIND**
**Meaning:** Having a hidden agenda.
**Background:** The expression comes from a story told by Benjamin Franklin. A man once praised Franklin's father's grindstone and asked young Benjamin to demonstrate how the grindstone worked. As Franklin complied, the stranger placed his own axe upon the grindstone, praising the young boy for his cleverness and vigor. When the axe was sharpened, the man laughed at Franklin and walked away, giving the boy a valuable lesson about people with "an axe to grind."

**NO BONES ABOUT IT**
***Meaning:*** Without a doubt.
***Background:*** The *Oxford English Dictionary* traces this phrase to a 1459 reference to eating stew. Stew-eaters had to be careful not to swallow bones. If a bowl of stew had no bones in it, one could eat it without hesitation. Bone appetit.

**People in the Soviet Union don't chew gum.**

## UPPER CRUST

***Meaning:*** Elite.

***Backround:*** In the Middle Ages, nobility and royalty were served the choice part of a loaf of bread, the upper crust, before it was offered to other diners.

## HIS NAME IS MUD

***Meaning:*** Fallen into ill-repute or disrespect.

***Backround:*** John Wilkes Booth, the man who assassinated President Lincoln, broke his leg as he escaped the scene of the crime. Samuel Mudd, a country doctor who hadn't heard of the assassination yet, treated Booth's injury. When he received news of the assassination the following day, Mudd notified the authorties that his patient might have been the assassin. But the doctor had a second surprise coming—he was arrested as a conspirator and sentenced to life in prison.

President Andrew Johnson, Lincoln's successor, commuted Mudd's sentence after the doctor helped stop a yellow fever outbreak at the jail. However, Mudd's family was still trying to clear his name as recently as the 1980s.

## MEET A DEADLINE

***Meaning:*** Finish a project by an appointed time.

***Backround:*** The phrase originated in prisoner-of-war camps during the Civil War. Because resources were scarce, the prison camps were sometimes nothing more than a plot of land surrounded by a marked line. If a prisoner tried to cross the line, he would be shot. So it became known as the "deadline."

## TOE THE LINE

***Meaning:*** To behave or act in accordance with the rules.

***Backround:*** In the early days of the British Parliament, members of Parliament wore swords in the House of Commons. To keep the Members from fighting during heated debates, the Speaker of the House of Commons forced the Government and Opposition party to sit on opposite sides of the chamber. Lines, two sword-lengths plus one foot apart, were drawn in the carpet. Members were required to stand behind the lines when the House was in session. To this day, when a member steps over the line during a debate, the speaker yells: "Toe the Line."

**UPS ships 12 million packages daily. 20 million a day around Christmastime.**

# AMAZING COINCIDENCES

*How many bizarre coincidences have you experienced in your life? We'll bet that none of them were as weird as these.*

## PSYCHIC LINC

Abraham Lincoln's eldest son, Robert Todd Lincoln, was on the scene of *three* separate presidential assassinations.

• First, he was summoned to his father's side after his father was mortally wounded at Ford's Theatre in 1865.

• The second occurred in 1881, when Lincoln was Secretary of War under President Garfield. Lincoln went to Union Station in Washington to inform the president he could not travel with him due to work overload. By the time Lincoln arrived, Garfield had been shot by Charles Guiteau.

• The third assassination occurred 20 years later in 1901, when Lincoln accepted an invitation from Presdent William McKinley to meet him at the Pan-American Exposition in Buffalo, New York. When Lincoln entered the festival he noticed a crowd had gathered—William McKinley had just been mortally wounded by Leon Czolgosz.

## WHAT ABOUT HYMN?

In 1950, *Life* magazine reported that 15 people barely missed disaster by an intricate stroke of luck. The 15, members of a church choir in Beatrice, Nebraska, were supposed to meet at 7:15 pm for practice. Each one got delayed...each for a different reason! For example, one had car trouble, another was finishing house chores, another was catching a radio show, etc. Whatever the reason, they were all lucky to be late: The church was destroyed in an explosion at 7:25.

## BASIC TRAINING

A distraught architect threw himself in front of a train in the London Underground in a suicide attempt. Luckily, the train stopped inches from his body; in fact, it had to be jacked off its tracks to allow his removal. When questioned, however, the driver informed officials he hadn't stopped the train. An investigation revealed that one of the passengers, unaware of the suicide attempt, had independently pulled the emergency brake. Postscript: London Transport officials considered prosecuting the passenger for illegal use of the emergency brake but ultimately decided against it.

## GEORGE, BY GEORGE

George D. Bryson, a businessman from Connecticut, decided to change his travel plans and stop in Louisville, Kentucky, a place he'd never visited before. He went into a local hotel and made preparations to check into Room 307. Before he could do so, a hotel employee handed him a letter addressed to his exact name. It turned out the previous occupant of Room 307 was another George D. Bryson.

## NUMBER, PLEASE

In 1983, a woman told British Rail authorities about a disturbing vision she had of a fatal train crash involving an engine with the numbers 47 216. Two years later, a train had a fatal accident, similar to one the woman had described. The engine number, however, was 47 299. Later, someone noticed that the number had previously been changed by nervous British Rail officials. The original number: 47 216.

## WHAT'S THE GOOD WORD?

Several secret code words were devised by Allied military commanders during their preparations to invade Normandy in World War II. Among them: "Utah," "Neptune," "Mulberry," "Omaha," and "Overlord." Before the invasion could begin, however, all of these words appeared in a crossword puzzle in the *London Daily Telegraph*. After interrogating the puzzle's author, an English school teacher, authorities became convinced that it was sheer, inexplicable coincidence.

## THE MOST AMAZING

On three separate occasions—in the years 1664, 1785, and 1860—there was a shipwreck in which only one person survived the accident. Each time that one person was named Hugh Williams.

# TRAVELS WITH RAY

*Perplexing adventures of the brilliant egghead Ray "Weird Brain" Redel. Answers are on page 672.*

One weekend Ray "Weird Brain" Redel, the man who inspired Rodin's statue "The Thinker," decided to go backpacking at Yosemite National Park. "I've been pushing this old brain too hard," he told me as we set off for the mountains.

"I don't see how you can tell," I muttered.

At that, "Weird Brain" slapped his forehead. "Here's proof," he groaned. "I just realized I've forgotten something terribly important."

"Did you forget to turn off the stove at home?" I grumbled.

"No, no, nothing like that. I just forgot to bring something."

I was getting exasperated. "What? What did you forget to bring?"

He glared at me. "Don't use that tone of voice. You want to know what I forgot? Figure this out: *It has cities, but no houses; it has forests but no trees; it has rivers but no fish.*"

I smiled. "Well, why didn't you say so. Let's just get another one."

**What did "Weird Brain" forget?**

When we finally got to Yosemite, "Weird Brain" ran into an old friend—a photographer named Ansel Adams.

"Anse, m'boy, what are you doing around here?" he asked the shutterbug.

"Well, Weirdo, I think Yosemite's the best place to enjoy my favorite thing in nature."

"Which is..."

Adams smiled, and I could tell he was testing "Weird Brain"'s fabled ability to solve riddles. "*What can pass before the sun without making a shadow?*" he asked. "That's what I love best.

**What was Adams saying he loved?**

# BATHROOM NEWS

*Here are a few of the stories we flushed out during the past year.*

## JUST WHAT WE NEEDED

October, 1989: A North Carolina company has introduced "Talking Tissue," a novelty gadget which fits the standard toilet paper dispenser. Each time you pull the tissue, you hear one of four recordings: "Yuk-yuk," "Stinky-stinky," "Nice one-nice one," or alarm bells. Batteries not included.

## DOWN IN THE DUMPS

January, 1990: A man in Lawrence, Kansas, spent a night underneath an outhouse after he fell through the seat trying to retrieve his wallet. He was rescued by Sheriff Loren Anderson, who said the man wasn't injured, "but in a pretty ugly mood."

## UNCLE SAM SAT HERE

November 6, 1989: Archaeologists recently discovered Uncle Sam's toilet six feet under Ferry Street in Troy, New York. The site is where 19th century meatpacker Sam Wilson used to live (see *Uncle John's Second Bathroom Reader* for more info). During the War of 1812, Sam labelled his meat-crates "U.S.," which led American soldiers to joke that they were being fed by Uncle Sam. A developer is building a supermarket and a park on the site, but Uncle Sam's bathroom floor and house foundation will be preserved for visitors to view.

## RIGHT BACK AT YA

January, 1990: Over 20 toilets and urinals in the King County, Washington, Court House erupted after being flushed. Apparently, a plumber who was making repairs mistakenly switched an air compressor with a water line.

## SINGAPORE STAKE OUT

June, 1989: Undercover agents arrested six men for not flushing urinals in Singapore public restrooms.

In a separate investigation, Singapore courts fined a man $75 for urinating in an elevator. Police nabbed him in the elevator after the *urine detector* locked the elevator doors. A hidden video camera recorded the whole event and the footage was later used as evidence.

## THE JOHN POLICE

December 19, 1989: Police employees in Concord, California, filed a $30 million lawsuit against the Concord Police Department after they found a hidden camera installed above a urinal in the men's room. Police Chief George Straka explained that the surveillance was necessary to catch the culprit who had clogged the urinal a few times, causing it to flood the chief's office downstairs.

## HIGH-TECH TOILETS

October 29, 1989: "New high-tech toilets from Japan can do it all, including check your health. Here are a few features of some of the latest models:"

• No paper is needed. The push of a button sends a jet of cleansing water upward. A control panel allows the user to adjust the angle, pressure and temperature of the stream. Drying blasts of hot air and mists of perfume follow seconds after. As the commercial for the Toto Ltd. *Toto Queen* says, "Even your bottom wants to be washed."

• The "intelligent bowl" automatically drops a strip of litmus paper into the bowl. Optical sensors analyze urine levels of protein, sugar and other substances. Blood pressure and pulse data are measured if the user inserts his finger in the blood pressure device on the side of the toilet. All test results are revealed on a display screen beside the toilet.

## POTTY-PARITY

Setpember, 1989: The American Society of Interior Designers honored Sandra Rawls, an assistant Professor at the University of Missouri, Columbia, for her research which revealed that women's restrooms need more toilets, because women need more time than men. The states of California, New York and Virginia have listened to Rawls's advice and have intoduced so-called "potty-parity" laws.

# THE SIMPUL SPELLING MOOVMENT

*At the turn of the century, Andrew Carnegie spent over $200,000 in an attempt to simplify spelling. Here are a few of the details of that forgotten episode in American history.*

**E-Z DUZ IT:** In 1906, millionaire industrialist Andrew Carnegie was approached by Melvin Dewey, the head of the New York libraries, and Brander Matthews, a Columbia University professor, with a revolutionary plan to simplify spelling. Carnegie was enthusiastic. He believed that easier spelling could lead to world peace. Together, the threesome formed the Simplified Spelling Board; their expressed goal was to convince authorities to begin changing the spelling of 300 words.

Among the words targeted were though (tho), confessed (confest), dropped (dropt), through (thru), kissed (kist), fixed (fixt), enough (enuf), prologue (prolog), thoroughfare (thorofare) and depressed (deprest).

**ENUF ALREDDEE:** Theodore Roosevelt was an instant convert to the simplified spelling plan. On August 29, 1906, he ordered the U.S. Printer to use the new spelling on all executive branch publications. For an instant, it looked as if simplified spelling would be instituted nationwide.

Roosevelt's plan met instant oppostion. It even made front-page news—both here *and* abroad. In England, the *London Times* ridiculed the American president with a headline reading "Roosevelt Spelling Makes Britons Laugh."

Congress was equally outraged by Roosevelt's decree. In late 1906, they debated the idea on the floor of the House. Sensing an embarrassing political defeat, Roosevelt quickly withdrew his support for the plan.

**WEL, THATZ THAT:** Carnegie was deeply disappointed. Eventually he dropped his financial support for the Simplified Spelling Board, writing, "I think I hav been patient long enuf...I have a much better use of $25,000 a year."

**It's illegal to have a pet dog in Iceland.**

# GREAT NEWSPAPER LEADS

*The first paragraph in a newspaper story is called the "lead." Technically, it's supposed to answer five questions: Who? What? Where? When? and Why? Here are some of the greatest leads in newspaper history.*

"John Dillinger, ace bad man of the world, got his last night—two slugs through his heart and one through his head. He was tough and he was shrewd, but he wasn't as tough and shrewd as the Federals, who never close a case until the end. It took 27 of them to end Dillinger's career, and their strength came out of his weakness—a woman."

—Jack Lait for the *International News Service*, July 23, 1934

"Death and destruction have been the fate of San Francisco. Shaken by a trembler at 5:13 o'clock yesterday morning, the shock lasting 48 seconds, and scourged by flames that raged diametrically in all directions, the city is a mass of smouldering ruins."

— *The San Francisco Call, Chronicle and Examiner*, April 19, 1906

"In the darkness of night and in water two miles deep the *Titanic*, newest of the White Star fleet and greatest of all ocean steamships, sank to the bottom of the sea at twenty minutes past two o'clock yesterday morning. The loss of the *Titanic*—costliest, most powerful, greatest of all the ocean fleet—while speeding westward on her maiden voyage will take rank in maritime history as the most terrible of all recorded disasters at sea."

—*New York Herald*, April 15, 1912

"Steel-nerved Alan B. Shepard Jr., rode a rocket into space today, exclaimed 'What a beautiful sight' as he looked down on the earth, and then dropped to a safe landing in the Atlantic ocean. To the wiry, 37-year-old navy commander, the historic adventure obviously was no more frightening than many earlier flights he had made

**In 1936, a cabin on the Hindenburg airship cost $750 for a trans-Atlantic flight.**

in experimental aircraft. 'It's a beautiful day,' he told marines on the helicopter that plucked his space capsule out of the water after a soaring flight 115 miles above the earth and 302 miles southeast from the Cape Canaveral launching pad. Then his nonchalance gave way to excitement as he declared: 'Boy, what a ride!' "

—Ralph Dighton for the *Associated Press*, May 5, 1961

"War broke with lightning suddeness in the Pacific today when waves of Japanese bombers attacked Hawaii this morning and the United States Fleet struck back with a thunder of big naval rifles. Japanese bombers, including four-engine dive bombers and torpedo-carrying planes, blasted at Pearl Harbor, the great United States naval base, the city of Honolulu and several outlying American military bases on the Island of Oahu. There were causalities of unstated numbers."

—*The New York Times*, December 8, 1941

**OTHER NEWS:**

Here are some items from a great "bathroom reader" called *News Of the Weird*.

• An Alaskan assemblyman authored legislation to punish "public flatulence, crepitation, gaseous emission, and miasmic effluence," with a $100 penalty.

• Firefighters in Thurston, Washington slept through a fire in their own station. A passing police officer noticed the blaze and called in the alarm.

• In 1986, firefighters used wire cutters and pliers to free a San Jose, California woman from a tight pair of designer jeans.

• In the 1988 Massachusetts Democratic primary, Herbert Connolly dashed from a late campaign appearance to the polling place to cast his ballot. He got there fifteen minutes late, and lost his seat on the Governor's council. The final tally: 14,716 to 14,715.

• The Internal Revenue Service fined George Wittmeier $159.78 for not paying all of his taxes. He was a penny short on his return.

**Only one of the Seven Wonders of the Ancient World still exists—the Sphinx.**

# FLAKE-OUT

*When financial analysts say baseball cards are a better investment than the stock market, you know collecting has become a way of life. But cereal boxes? It's strange but true. Here are some examples.*

**CORN FLAKES.** One of the most collectible cereal boxes is the 1984 Kelloggs' Miss America commerative Corn Flakes Box. The box features Vanessa Williams, the first black Miss America, with a congratulatory endorsement on the back panel that claims the limited edition box is "a lasting reminder that America remains the land of opportunity…and we must continue to promote the American dream and encourage all Americans to freely pursue life, liberty and happiness." Ironically, the box was recalled immediately after *Penthouse* magazine published pictures of Williams in the buff.

**WHEATIES.** In the 1950s Wheaties stopped using athletes on their boxes and started using Walt Disney figures. Within a year, sales went down 15%. General Mills had a huddle, kicked Disney out, and recalled their sports stars. But the Disney boxes are valuable today.

**SWISS MIX.** The psychedelic generation of the late 1960s didn't miss out on cereal boxes—pop-artist Peter Max designed a surreal cereal box for an imported Swiss Mix cereal called LOVE. It's now collectible.

**WHEAT AND RICE HONEYS.** A pair of 1969 Wheat and Rice Honeys boxes featuring the Beatles in "Yellow Submarine" recently sold for $7000.

**COUNT CHOCULA.** In 1981, General Mills released a cereal called Count Chocula. The box featured a cartoon Count Dracula in front with a Bela Lugosi Dracula in the background. The "Bela" Dracula was wearing a six-point star pendant. A religious group objected to what they felt was a "Star of David" and the box was recalled. Today collectors pursue it religiously.

**Moose are very nearsighted. Some try to mate with cars.**

# PARDON ME

*The Constitution gives our president the power to grant pardons. This doesn't mean he can overturn guilty verdicts—it only gives him the authority to remove the legal penalties. You hardly ever hear about presidential pardons, but they're granted all the time. Here are a few of the more interesting ones.*

## RICHARD NIXON

The most famous pardon in U.S. history occurred on September 8, 1974, when Gerald Ford granted Richard Nixon "a full, free, and absolute pardon" for any crimes connected with the Watergate scandal. The decision was extremely controversial. A Gallup Poll conducted after the pardon found that 56% of the American public thought Nixon should have been brought to trial for Watergate.

An August, 1983 article in *Atlantic* magazine by journalist Seymour Hersh alleged that Ford and Nixon had cut a deal for a pardon before the latter's resignation on August 9, 1974. According to the article, Nixon made a threatening phone call to Ford on September 7—one day before the pardon—to make sure the deal was still on. Ford "really resented it," an unnamed Ford aide told Hersh.

## ARMAND HAMMER

Armand Hammer, multi-millionaire head of Occidental Petroleum, was pardoned by George Bush in August, 1989, for making an illegal $54,000 contribution to Nixon's 1972 re-election campaign. Hammer was found guilty and placed on a year's probation for the offense—making a political contribution in the name of another person—in March, 1976. He was fined $3,000.

## GEORGE STEINBRENNER

In January, 1989, George Steinbrenner, shipbuilder and ex-owner of the New York Yankees, was pardoned by Ronald Reagan. Steinbrenner had been convicted of making an illegal $100,000 contribution to Richard Nixon's re-election campaign in 1972.

**Every year, Mexico City sinks about 10 inches.**

Steinbrenner was fined $15,000 in 1974 and later suspended for two years by Baseball Commissioner Bowie Kuhn after pleading not guilty to the charges. Kuhn lifted the suspension in March 1976 after 16 months had been served.

## TOKYO ROSE

In one of his last official acts as president in 1977, Ford pardoned Iva Toguri D'Aquino (aka, Tokyo Rose), who had served six years in jail for making pro-Japanese propaganda broadcasts during World War II. D'Aquino, an American citizen of Japanese descent, had gone to Japan to visit a sick aunt in July, 1941, just before war broke out between the two countries. Unable to return to the U.S., she was recruited by Japanese authorities to try to demoralize American troops. According to the *New York Times*, "For the G.I.s in the South Pacific, the broadcasts were as much a part of the routine as Spam. In between familiar selections of American music there was the voice of a woman telling American servicemen that their wives and girlfriends were being taken over by the civilians who remained behind and that there was really no point in fighting on any further because the Japanese were going to win anyway. The G.I.s began calling her Tokyo Rose. To most soldiers and sailors the broadcasts were a pleasant joke."

D'Aquino was indicted for treason and was sentenced to 10 years in prison beginning in 1949 (she was released in 1956 for good behavior). She also paid a $10,000 fine.

## DRAFT RESISTERS

On January 21, 1977, in his first act as president, Jimmy Carter issued an unconditional presidential pardon to Vietnam draft resisters. Prior to Carter's proclamation, Gerald Ford had granted a limited amnesty to Vietnam draft resisters in 1974 if they swore allegiance to the U.S. and agreed to perform two years of public service. 21,700 people took advantage of Ford's program. Carter's unconditional pardon—which excluded deserters and veterans with less-than-honorable discharges—affected between 100,000 and 500,000 people.

## ...AND TWO PARDONS REFUSED

• Samuel A. Mudd, a physician who aided assassin John Wilkes Booth, (he set his broken leg after the assassination) pleaded for a pardon for his inadvertant role in the death of Abraham Lincoln. Mudd was paroled in 1869 from a life sentence, but was never pardoned. In 1988, his grandson, Dr. Richard Mudd, gave up a 61-year campaign to clear his name after the Reagan White House refused to grant one.

• In 1914, journalist George Burdick, a writer for the *New York Tribune*, broke a story about prominent officials who were going to be indicted for smuggling. A Federal grand jury demanded to know his sources, but Burdick refused to reveal them. President Wilson stepped in and offered a full pardon, but Burdick refused. This set a precedent—no one had ever refused a pardon before. Eventually, the Supreme Court upheld Burdick's right to refuse Wilson's pardon, arguing it preserved the privilege against self-incrimination. The case was widely regarded as a major victory for freedom of the press. Burdick never revealed his source.

## ODDS & ENDS

• In 1795, George Washington issued the first presidential pardon to two instigators of the Whiskey Rebellion. They'd led a mob that attacked and burned a tax collector's home on July 17, 1794.

• During the War of 1812, President James Madison announced amnesty for pirates and smugglers "in the vicinity of New Orleans who helped fight the British."

• Abraham Lincoln pardoned over 10,000 Confederate soldiers for their role in the Civil War. His successor, Andrew Johnson, issued a full pardon in 1865 to all Confederates, except leaders, as long as they took an oath of allegiance to the United States. Then in 1868, Johnson granted an unconditional amnesty to "all persons engaged in the late rebellion."

• During his two terms as president, Ronald Reagan granted 380 pardons. Among the offenses for which people were pardoned were tax evasion, possession of untaxed whiskey, possession with intent to distribute cocaine, illegal transfer of machine guns, and copyright infringement.

# NAME & PLACE

*Would you want to live in Hell Station, Accident, or Dildo? You can. Here are the strange names of some real places.*

**Frozen Run, West Virginia:** A man saved his own life by wrapping himself in the skin of a recently killed buffalo. His friends had to thaw it to get him out.

**Preacher's Head, New Mexico:** A rock resembling the face of a serious-looking man overlooks the town.

**Dildo, Newfoundland:** Coincidentally, it's the birthplace of Shannon Tweed, *Playboy* magazine's 1982 Playmate of the Year.

**Anxiety Point, Alaska:** Sir John Franklin, a British explorer, was afraid that bad weather would prevent his team from reaching a point on the Alaskan coast. They made it, and left this permanent reminder of his nervousness.

**Nipple Mountain, Colorado:** One formation on the mountain is named "Clara's Bird's Nipple."

**Chilly Buttes, Idaho:** A cold place in the winter.

**Chicago, Illinois:** From the Algonquin word meaning "onion-place."

**Hell Station, Michigan:** Locals say it freezes over every winter.

**Art, Texas:** As one resident explained, "Well, it's not for Arthur or Artesian, and far as I know people here weren't ever especially arty. We've heard they picked it just because they wanted a real short name."

**Sacul, Texas:** A reverse spelling of (John) Lucas, an early settler in the area.

**Lake Italy, California:** The lake is shaped like a boot.

**Accident, Maryland:** In 1774, surveyors marked off a parcel of land by mistake. They decided to immortalize the error.

# YOU BET YOUR LIFE

*To a generation of viewers who only know the Marx Brothers from their films, it may come as a surprise that Groucho was also a radio and TV star...as the host of a quiz show called "You Bet Your Life," which aired from 1950 to 1961.*

## HOW IT STARTED

In 1947, radio was the most popular entertainment medium in America. Groucho Marx was no longer a movie star, but he did a guest spot on *The Bob Hope Show* that turned into a hilarious ad-lib free-for-all. The act impressed a successful radio producer named John Guedel, who happened to be in the audience that night. When it was over, Guedel approached Groucho and asked him if he could ad-lib like that all the time. Groucho replied that he'd done it all his life.

Guedel was excited. He thought Groucho's talent was wasted with scripts—he ought to do a show in which he was allowed to interact with "real people," ad-libbing. Groucho, who'd hosted four different radio shows and had bombed every time, was open to anything. But when Guedel suggested a quiz show, Groucho balked. He said he had to think about it.

Groucho wondered if he could live with himself as a game-show host...and decided he could. ("What the hell, nothing else had worked.") So he made an audition tape. But no network was interested. So Guedel, convinced that America would love tuning in to the real Groucho, took the tape directly to a sponsor and got it on the air that way. Within a few years Guedel looked like a genius and Groucho's career was revived—"You Bet Your Life" was one of America's top 10 radio shows.

At that time, TV networks were snapping up popular radio programs and adapting them to television. Everything from "Burns and Allen" and "The Jack Benny Show," to "Gangbusters" and "The Lone Ranger" wound up on the tube. Naturally, Groucho was approached about bringing his show to TV. CBS and NBC both wanted it—but in the ensuing battle for Marx's talents, CBS head William Paley offended Groucho by referring to the fact that they were both Jewish and that Jews should stick together. NBC head Robert Sarnoff was also Jewish. Groucho chose NBC.

## INSIDE INFO

### Stiff Upper Lip.

Without his mustache, Groucho was unrecognizable to the public; he could walk the streets without being stopped by fans. For radio and TV he refused to use the phony mustache he wore in his movie days ("That character is dead," he said). But he did agree to grow a real mustache.

### TV or Not TV?

When Groucho's show moved to TV, NBC wanted to add all kinds of visual gimmicks "to make it more interesting." They also wanted to resurrect his movie persona. But Groucho insisted on keeping things simple, as they had been in the radio format. No funny walks, no costumes. Just Groucho in a business suit, sitting in front of a curtain with his guests. It turned out to be a good idea: From the time the show debuted in 1950 to the time it was cancelled 11 years later, "You Bet Your Life" was the most consistently popular game show on TV.

### Nobody Loses.

Groucho wasn't comfortable with some aspects of being a game show host. He complained, for example, that he felt bad when people had to leave the show broke. He said, "Can't we ask them a simple question, like who's the President of the U. S., or who's buried in Grant's Tomb?" So that became part of the show. Whenever someone lost, Groucho asked the easiest question possible, and the contestant got a few bucks as a consolation.

### Close Encounters.

In 1973, NBC started burning original negatives of the 250 reels of *You Bet Your Life* to make space in their warehouse. Fortunately, someone thought to call the show's producer, John Guedel, and ask if he wanted a few negatives as souvenirs; they'd already burned 15 of them. A shocked Guedel stopped the destruction and made a deal with NBC to take over syndication of *The Best of Groucho*. In 1973, a Los Angeles TV station aired reruns at 11:00 p.m. as a favor to Groucho. The ratings were so good that stations all over the country picked it up, and the show was revived.

**Video Mania: On average, Americans rent over 6 million videos a day.**

# GROUCHO & GUESTS

*No one could ad-lib like Groucho. Here are a few spontaneous remarks from "You Bet Your Life."*

**Groucho:** "What's it like in South Carolina?"
**Woman:** "Oh, it's wonderful, Goucho, Southern hospitality and wonderful folks."
**Groucho:** "Well, we want you to feel at home here, Marie, so we'll pay you in Confederate money."

**Groucho:** "How did you meet your wife?"
**Man:** "A friend of mine."
**Groucho:** "Do you still regard him as a friend?"

**Groucho** (to husband & wife with arms around each other): "How long have you been married?"
**Wife:** "Two and a half years, Groucho."
**Groucho:** "Why are you holding on to each other? Are you afraid if you let go, you'll kill each other?"

**Groucho:** "What are you gonna do with your money?"
**Man:** "I'm gonna make my wife happy, Groucho."
**Groucho:** "What are you gonna do—get a divorce?"

**Groucho:** "You don't mind if I ask you a few questions, do you?"
**Woman:** "If they're not too embarrassing."
**Groucho:** "Don't give it a second thought. I've asked thousands of questions on this show, and I've yet to be embarrassed."

**Woman** (explaining herself): "I'm afraid you don't follow me."
**Groucho:** "Even if I did, you'd have nothing to be afraid of."

**Groucho** (to the father of triplets): "Do you have a job?
**Man:** "Yeah."
**Groucho:** "What is it?"
**Man:** "I work for the California Power Company."
**Groucho:** "My boy, you don't work for the California Power Company. You *are* the California Power Company."

**Groucho:** "What's your husband's name?"
**Woman:** "Milton August."
**Groucho:** "What's his name in September?"

**In Helsinki, Finland, police rarely give parking tickets—they deflate tires.**

# BANNED IN THE U.S.A.

*Censorship is a big issue for bathroom readers. After all, we don't want anyone telling us what we can read in here...or if we can read in here at all! So we've included a few tidbits on censorship in this edition, to remind us all to sit down and be counted.*

AND STAY OUT!

Bring us your tired, your wretched...etc.? Not in the early '50s. In 1952, at the height of our Cold War hysteria, a provision was added to the Immigration and Nationality Act of 1952 to keep certain "undesirable" people from entering the U.S. The law, known as the McCarran-Walter Immigration Act, was vetoed by then-President Harry S Truman, but overriden by Congress. Usually, "undesirable" meant "suspected Commies," although the 33 provisions included categories for people who engaged in espionage, polygamy and "deviant sexual behavior."

But the bill was actually a political tool, designed to keep people with controversial views (like John Lennon) out of the country. In 1984 alone—32 years after the act was passed—8,000 people from 98 different countries were banned from the U.S.A. under the auspices of the bill, because of their political beliefs.

WHO'S WHO?

Among the people banned from the U.S.A. since 1952 were actors, singers, writers, and politicians. Two examples:

• *Gabriel García Márquez*, Colombian author and winner of the Nobel Prize. Márquez, a critic of U.S. foreign policy, was denied a visa in 1963. Eight years later, he was allowed in temporarily to accept an honorary degree from Columbia University. The terms of Márquez's restricted visa included the stipulation that an FBI agent would accompany him everywhere he went.

• *Pierre Trudeau*, future Prime Minister of Canada. He was denied entry because he had participated in an economic conference in Moscow in 1952 and was labeled a "Communist sympathizer." Trudeau was eventually allowed to travel in the U.S. after immigration officials interviewed him in Montreal and gave him "clearance."

Postscript: Congress finally repealed the law in January, 1990.

# DISNEY STORIES: SLEEPING BEAUTY

*In 1959, Walt Disney released Sleeping Beauty, an adaptation of the classic fairy tale. It took 6 years and $6 million (an incredible sum at the time) to finish. But it was a disappointment at the box office, taking in just $5.3 million that year. Since then, it has grossed almost 5 times that much. Of course, the Disney version and the original story were substantially different. Here are some examples of how the tale was changed.*

## THE DISNEY VERSION

A King and a Queen in a faraway kingdom throw a party for their newborn daughter. They invite everyone from miles around...except a Wicked Witch, who's really upset about it. She shows up anyway, and casts this spell on the baby: On her 15th birthday, the young Princess will prick her finger on a spinning wheel spindle and die.

• A Good Fairy attending the party softens the curse, changing it to 100 years of sleep instead of death.

• The King tries to avoid the curse by burning every spinning wheel in the kingdom. No luck; on her 15th birthday, the Princess discovers a tower chamber where an old woman is working a spinning wheel. The Princess tries her hand at it, pricks her finger, and falls asleep. So does everyone else in the kingdom.

• Thick, impenetrable brambles grow around the castle. 100 years later, a young Prince shows up.

• The Witch throws the Prince into her dungeon. When he escapes, the Witch turns herself into a dragon and attacks him. The Prince slays her, enters the castle, and kisses the Princess, who wakes up (along with the rest of the people in the castle). The Prince and Princess live happily ever after.

## THE ORIGINAL VERSION

• Disney's version of Sleeping Beauty is based loosely on Charles Perrault's telling of this ancient fairy tale. But Disney only tells half the story.

• In the original, the Wicked Witch disappears from the story after casting her spell. No brambles grow up around the castle.

• The Prince just happens to arrive at exactly the moment Sleeping Beauty is supposed to wake up. The Prince secretly marries her, and they have two children—a daughter (Aurora) and son (Day). It isn't until his father dies and he becomes king that the Prince invites Sleeping Beauty to his castle.

• The Prince's mother, it turns out, is an Ogress. While he's away at war, the Queen Mother orders the chef to slaughter and cook the daughter, then the son, and eventually Sleeping Beauty herself. The chef can't bring himself to do it—he hides the trio and serves other animals instead.

• Eventually the Queen Mother discovers the truth. She orders Sleeping Beauty and her children to be thrown into a cauldron of carnivorous reptiles. In the nick of time, the new King arrives home and the Queen Mother leaps into the cauldron herself.

## SAMPLE PASSAGE (FROM THE ORIGINAL)

"The Prince—now the King—had no sooner left than the Queen Mother sent her daughter-in-law and the children to a country house in the wood so that she might more easily gratify her horrible longing. She followed them there a few days later, and one evening she said to her head cook, 'I will eat little Aurora for dinner tomorrow.'

"'Oh no, Madam,' the cook exlaimed.

"'Yes, I will.' said the Queen Mother, and she said it in a voice of an Ogress longing to eat fresh meat. 'And I want her served with my favorite sauce.'

"The cook, seeing that an Ogress isn't someone to trifle with, took his knife and went up to Aurora's room. She was about four years old, and she came jumping and laughing toward him, threw her arms around his neck, and asked him if he had any candy for her. He burst into tears, dropping the knife; then he went into the farmyard and killed a little lamb, which he served up with such a delicious sauce that the Ogress assured him she'd never eaten anything so tasty. Meanwhile, he carried Aurora to his own home and gave her to his wife to hide, so the Queen Mother wouldn't find her."

**Mr. Green Jeans's nickname in real life was "Lumpy."**

# THE AUSTRALIAN BEATLES

*When Beatlemania and the British Invasion hit the U.S. in the mid-sixties, many musicians suddenly found themselves out of work. Here's the story of a creative solution that turned into one of the all-time great rock'n'roll hoaxes.*

It was rock 'n' roll news in 1965. A new band had arrived in America. Direct from the outbacks of Australia—Armstrong, Australia, aborigine country—came the "Down Under" continent's answer to the Beatles! The Strange brothers, Miles, Niles and Giles, known professionally as the Strangeloves. They were strange, indeed. They dressed in loud striped outfits and wore native hats. And the three didn't look at all alike. But that, they explained, was because they had the same mother and different fathers.

The boys had rhythm, too. Playing jungle drums, they brought back the old Bo Diddley beat with a great song called "I Want Candy," which took off like a frightened kangaroo, hopping up the American charts into the Top 10. The Strangeloves toured three times with the Beach Boys, who thought the brothers were the most insane people they'd ever met. They appeared on Radio Caroline in England. And they had the time of their lives on NBC-TV's "Hullabaloo." An unbelievable feat for a group that didn't exist. They were real people, of course, but they weren't named Strange. And they weren't from Australia. The Strangeloves came straight from the Brill Building in New York City.

The Brill Building was rock'n'roll's Tin Pan Alley in the early '60s. It was the home of songwriters like Ellie Greenwich and Jeff Barry, Carole King and Gerry Goffin, and Neil Sedaka and Howie Greenfield, who had been the source of hundreds of hit songs in the early sixties. But in 1965, no one wanted to hear American groups. So songwriters/producers Bob Feldman, Jerry Goldstein, and Richard Gotterher got the idea to put together a fake "British Invasion" act. They donned bizarre costumes, learned their accents from a Britisher named Doug Moody, and the Strangeloves were born. After writing "I Want Candy" and recording it for their record label, Bang Records, the act went on tour. First stop, the dome at Virginia Beach, where Feldman recalls, "There were 3,000 kids with banners saying, 'Welcome to the U.S., Strangeloves.' And the mayor gave us the key to the city and there we were. We had to go through with it!"

The Beach Boys knew the truth; nobody else did, except the Strangeloves' immediate families. In fact, the group turned down a $10,000 offer to appear on "The Ed Sullivan Show" because Richard didn't want his elderly Jewish grandmother to see him on TV in a wild leopard-skin outfit. The Strangeloves' "Australian" accents, filtered through their native Brooklynese, must have sounded pretty authentic. They eventually appeared with almost every major British act and they never got caught. But the ruse did lead to some unexpected close calls. One time on a local Pittsburgh dance show, host Clark Race unexpectedly brought out a boomerang and handed it to Miles (Feldman), who was supposedly a champion thrower. As Bob was about to throw it, Clark stopped him and said, "Miles, that's not the way to hold a boomerang." Bob looked right into the camera and said, "Clark, that's why I'm the champion and you're not." "Miles" then proceeded to throw it. He hit the cameraman on the shoulder, barely missing his head, and knocked him to the floor. As the cameraman fell, his camera went with him.

At nearby Kennywood Park, the Strangeloves were hired without a backup band. They had their jungle drums with them and wowed the crowd with a 45-minute version of "Shout." Bob then went for some fun on an amusement park ride called "The Magic Carpet Ride," forgot to hug his knees as instructed, and fell over the top. He was carried to the infirmary where they tended to his injured shoulder...but he found out that he couldn't even drop his pose there! The head nurse was from Sydney, Australia, and she recognized him. As Bob tells it, "She said, 'You're one of those Strange boys, aren't you?'...Now I had to cry out in pain with an accent, too!"

Mercifully, the Strangeloves' pose only lasted until 1966.

**The song sung most often in America is "Happy Birthday to You."**

# DUMB SCIENCE

*Ever wonder what scientists do in their laboratories all day? Here are a few real-life examples.*

**THE EXPERIMENT:** James McConnell, head of the University of Michigan's Planaria Research group, wanted to see if memory "can be eaten and reused." So he trained a batch of worms, ground them up, and fed them to a second group of untrained worms.
**THE CONCLUSION:** According to McConnell, it worked. The untrained worms demonstrated behavior he'd taught the ground up worms. Minor problem: He never got the same results again.

**THE EXPERIMENT:** A scientist named Spalding brilliantly theorized that a baby chick's instinct to follow a mother hen originates in its brain. In an 1873 experiment, he removed the brains of baby chicks and placed the chicks a few yards from a mother hen.
**THE CONCLUSION:** Spalding's groundbreaking paper, "Instinct," tells us: "Decerebrated chicks will not move towards a clucking or retreating object."

**THE EXPERIMENT:** To test the rumor that Coca-Cola is an effective spermicide, Harvard University researchers added sperm samples to test tubes, each containing a different type of Coke.
**THE CONCLUSION:** A minor success. Diet Coke was the most effective, followed by Classic Coke, New Caffeine-Free, and in last place, New Coke. Researchers suggest that levels of acidic pH and perhaps some secret formula components were the determining factors. In any event, a Coca-Cola official was quoted to say: "We do not promote Coca-Cola for medical purposes. It is a soft drink."

**THE EXPERIMENT:** Are rats psychic? In 1974, two parapsychologists named Craig and Treuriniet decided to find out. They put rats in a lab maze with only two exits—one leading to freedom, the other to death. (They would kill the rats).
**THE CONCLUSION:** Half chose the correct path; half didn't. Unsatisfied with the results, Craig and Treuriniet theorized a correlation between the rat's psychic powers and phases of the moon.

# HONESTLY, ABE

*Abraham Lincoln, our 16th president, was surprisingly quotable. Here are a few of his better-known sayings.*

"The best way to destroy your enemy is to make him your friend."

"God must love the common man, he made so many of them."

"No man is good enough to govern another man without that other's consent."

"It's been my experience that people who have no vices have very few virtues."

"No matter how much cats fight, there always seems to be plenty of kittens."

"People who like this sort of thing will find this the sort of thing they like."

"Public opinion in this country is everything."

"Human action can be modified to some extent, but human nature cannot be changed."

"A man's legs must be long enough to reach the ground."

"Those who deny freedom for others deserve it not for themselves."

"My father taught me to work, but not to love it. I never did like to work, and I don't deny it. I'd rather read, tell stories, crack jokes, talk, laugh—anything but work."

"Tact is the ability to describe others as they see themselves."

"The things I want to know are in books; my best friend is the man who'll get me a book I ain't read."

"The man who is incapable of making a mistake is incapable of anything."

"The ballot is stronger than the bullet."

"As I would not be a slave, so I would not be a master. This expresses my idea of democracy."

"The best thing about the future is that it comes only one day at a time."

# YOU BE THE JUDGE

*Blowin' In The Wind is one of the best-known folk songs in American history. It was written by Bob Dylan, of course . . . or was it? Here's an analysis from the book* Behind the Hits, *by Bob Shannon and John Javna.*

This appeared in *Newsweek* on November 4, 1963. . ."There is a rumor circulating that Dylan did not write "Blowin' in the Wind," but that it was written by a Millburn, New Jersey high school student named Lorre Wyatt, who sold it to the singer. Dylan says he did write the song, and Wyatt denies authorship, but several Millburn students claim they heard the song from Wyatt before Dylan ever sang it." Who is really responsible for the song? Here is all the info we could find...what do you think?

**CLUE #1**

Dylan comes to New York in autumn of 1960, or February of 1961 (there are two stories), to visit Woody Guthrie at Greystone Hospital. He continues to visit through 1963.

• "In the autumn of 1960, Dylan quit the University of Minnesota and decided to visit Guthrie at Greystone Hospital, in New Jersey."—Nat Hentoff, in the *New Yorker*, 1964.

• "In February 1961, Dylan came East, primarily to visit Woody Guthrie at Greystone Hospital in New Jersey. The visits have continued..."—liner notes to "The Freewheelin' Bob Dylan," in 1963.

**CLUE #2**

Lorre Wyatt is doing volunteer work at Greystone at the same time Dylan is visiting it, from Autumn 1960, to Spring 1963.

• Among activities listed for Wyatt in his 1963 high school yearbook: "Folksinging at Hospitals, 1, 2, 3."

• "Lorre's sense of humor, musical ability, and strong desire to help people have made him a welcome sight to the ill and mentally retarded children at Kessler Institute and Greystone Hospital."—liner notes from "A Time To Sing," an album released in 1963 by a Millburn High School folksinging group called the Millburnaires.

## CLUE #3

Both Dylan (according to many sources), and Lorre Wyatt (according to Millburn High graduates whom we interviewed) are hanging out in Greenwich Village in 1961 and 1962. So the two might have met in either Greystone or the Village. Or both.

## CLUE #4

Although "The Freewheelin' Bob Dylan," the LP on which "Blowin' In the Wind" first appears, will not be released until May 1963, Dylan actually records the song on July 9, 1962 (according to Columbia Records). This would seem to indicate that the song is legitimately his—but there is one irregularity.

## CLUE #5

The song is not published and copyrighted in Dylan's name until July 30, 1962—three weeks after Dylan records it. This is highly unusual; the normal procedure is for a songwriter to write a song, get it published, and then record it. Hypothetical situation: Dylan learns the song from Wyatt, takes it into a recording session, and gets such a favorable reaction that he takes credit for it. After learning from Wyatt that he hasn't published it, Dylan has his own publisher, M. Witmark and Sons, do it in his name. Alternative hypothesis: Dylan just never bothers with the legal details until a few weeks after recording it. Would he take his own songs that lightly?

## CLUE #6

A December 1962 issue of *The Miller*, the Millburn High School newspaper, mentions that Wyatt had written the song in the summer.

• "Last summer Lorre, an amateur folk singer and guitarist, put together a melody that had come to him in snatches."

• The article then adds: "He began writing lyrics to it in early autumn, inspired by Student President Steve Oxman's welcoming speech [in September of 1962]." This, of course, is at odds with the fact that Dylan recorded the song in July. However, we contacted Oxman, and he explained that the article had things reversed—his speech was inspired by the already existing song.

## CLUE #7

According to *The Miller*, Wyatt sells the song to Dylan for $1000. He donates the money to CARE in memory of his deceased mother. "Blowin' in the Wind," says the paper, "a song written by senior Lorre Wyatt, and expressing the singer's own philosophy concerning the world's problems, is now the property of a well-known folksinger. Recently, the singer heard 'Blowin' In the Wind' while in New York and bought the song and the rights to it for one thousand dollars. Shortly after this, Lorre donated the money to CARE. When asked why, he replied, 'Just listen to the words in the song, and I think you'll understand.' "

## CLUE #8

The Chad Mitchell Trio records "Blowin' in the Wind" for Kapp Records in early 1963.

• *The Miller* says this in its February 2, 1963 issue: "The Chad Mitchell Trio has added 'Blowin' In the Wind,' a song written by MHS senior Lorre Wyatt, to its latest album, 'Chad Mitchell in Action.'. . .The publicity department at Kapp Studios said, 'Lorre has created a beautiful ballad. A song of this nature takes longer to write and to become well-known, but it has a greater meaning and a richer melody than most of today's popular rock and roll tunes.'"

• However, when the record comes out, the song is credited to Dylan on the label.

## CLUE #9

The Millburnaires, of which Wyatt is a member, record an album in April of 1963. It is called "A Time to Sing." "Blowin' in the Wind" is on the album, and is credited to Wyatt. The Millburnaires make a deal with Riverside Records to release the LP nationally.

## CLUE #10

"The Freewheelin' Bob Dylan" is released on Columbia Records on May 27, 1963.

## CLUE #11

Here is what Lorre says in the liner notes on the back of the Millburnaires' album: "Did you ever stop to ask yourself why the hate, the greed, the hunger—the fear?...No, they're not 'pretty' questions, but they're ones that must be asked. But we must do more than just ask: we must do something about them. It is our duty to God, ourselves, and to our fellow man. 'None is so blind as he who will not see.' The biggest criminals are people like you and I, who see things that are wrong, and know that they're wrong, and yet do nothing about them. How many times can a man turn his head and pretend that he just doesn't see?"

### CLUE #12

From the liner notes of "Freewheelin':" "The first of Dylan's songs in this set is 'Blowin' in the Wind.' In 1962, Dylan said of the song's background: "I still say that some of the biggest criminals are those that turn their heads away when they see wrong and they know it's wrong."

### CLUE #13

The Millburnaires' album is re-released nationally in the fall of 1963 as "Teenage Hootenanny" but gives no credits for authorship of "Blowin' in the Wind." It does have Wyatt's liner notes about "criminals," though.

### CLUE #14

Dylan in his "Biograph" LP: "It was just another song that I wrote and got thrown into all the songs I was doing at the time. I wrote it in a cafe across the street from the Gaslight. Although I thought it was special, I didn't know to what degree. I wrote it for the moment."

### CLUE #15

Interviews with Millburn students and teachers reveal that many recall the song being sung by the Millburnaires in a school performance in either the fall of 1962 or the spring of 1963. It was definitely introduced as Wyatt's song, and it was before the Dylan album was released. Sample interview (with Bill McCormick, M.H.S. history teacher): "[What people understood], was that one of the contingencies of the buyout was that, whatever monetary arrangements were made, it was to the effect that [Wyatt] had sold all rights and was not to ever claim that it was his. I shouldn't say it was common knowledge, but that was the hot rumor back 10, 12, 15 years ago, whatever." Ray Fowler, engineer on the

Millburnaires' LP: "Everyone I talked to at the time, said that Wyatt wrote the song."

**CLUE #16**

When columnist Mike Royko contacted Lorre in 1974 and asked him if he'd written "Blowin' in the Wind," Wyatt's answer was, "I don't want to talk about it." Royko: "[I told him that] all he had to do was deny writing "Blowin' in the Wind" and the matter would be closed for good. Did Wyatt deny writing it? He said, 'No comment.'" Royko contacted Anthony Scaduto, who wrote a Dylan biography, and asked what he thought. Scaduto said he believed the Wyatt story was phony, and that Dylan wrote "Blowin' in the Wind."

**Did Dylan write Blowin' in the Wind? You be the judge.**

✔ ✔ ✔

## WORKING GIRL

*Mary Tyler Moore, head of the MTM TV production company, is one of the world's wealthiest women. Some interesting facts about her:*

- At age 18, she landed her first TV role. It didn't exactly make her a star. She played "Happy Hotpoint," a tiny elf with pointy ears. She jumped out of an icetray in a Hotpoint refrigerator ad and said, "Hi, Harriet. Aren't you glad you bought a Hotpoint?"
- She finally landed a regular part in a prime time series in 1959. It was on *Richard Diamond*, and she played Sam, the sexy switchboard operator. The only catch: all they ever showed of her was her legs.
- She kept auditioning. But all she could get were bit parts. Then she got a call from her agent. "He told me, 'Get over to Carl Reiner's office. He wants to talk to you about playing Dick Van Dyke's wife. I said 'No, I may just as well stay home. I'm not going to get it.'" He finally convinced her to go, and she got the part.
- With her husband, she created MTM Enterprises, which owned TV shows like "Newhart," "WKRP in Cincinnati," and "Rhoda."
- She said: "Three things help me get through life successfully: An understanding husband, an extremely good analyst, and millions and millions of dollars."

# ELVIS-O-RAMA

*Here's some info from Vince Staten's irreverent guidebook,* Unauthorized America.

## ALL SHOOK UP

"Elvis hated Robet Goulet.

"Detested him.

"Any time he saw Goulet on TV, he became violently angry. Unfortunately, in the days when Mike Douglas and Merv Griffin ruled the airwaves, Goulet was on TV a lot. Elvis shot up the TV with Goulet on it several times, usually in his suite at the Las Vegas Hilton Hotel. The most famous time Elvis pulled a derringer out of his boot and fired it into the set, sending sparks everywhere."

"Elvis didn't limit his gunplay to shooting up TV sets. He shot up lots of small appliances and a few large ones. In February 1974, he fired at light switch in his Vegas suite. The bullet penetrated the wall and just missed his girlfriend at the time, Linda Thompson. She came running into his room trembling, but Elvis was able to soothe her by saying, 'Hey now, hon, just don't get excited.'

"From then on he confined his shooting to the TV and the chandelier, explaining to his boys, 'We're in the penthouse. Nobody's gonna get hit as long as you shoot straight up.'"

## THE FIRST SWIVEL

"The question of the ages is: what did he shake, and when did he shake it? Let's face it, his swivel hips were the one thing that set him apart from the other young singers of his day. They didn't call him Elvis the Pelvis for nothing.

"So when and where did he first shake his hips while singing?

"Country music legend Webb Pierce says it happened July 30, 1954, on a country music package tour that played Overton Park in Memphis. 'Elvis told me that it was the first time he had ever sung before a big crowd and that he was real scared. He said he thought he was gonna faint out there on stage, so he started flapping his legs, just to keep from passing out. Then he noticed the crowd was reacting to it, so he just kept doing it.'"

# PRIME-TIME PROVERBS

*Here are some more TV quotes from the book* Primetime Proverbs, *by Jack Mingo and John Javna.*

**ON POLITICS**
"When I was in third grade, there was a kid running for office. His slogan was: 'Vote for me and I'll show you my weewee.' He won by a landslide."

—Dorothy,
***The Golden Girls***

**ON "FREE LOVE"**
"You American girls have such big breasts all the time…So please, give us the number of your apartment so we can go up there and have sex with you now!"

—Dan Aykroyd
(The Wild and Crazy Guy),
*Saturday Night Live*

**ON PETS**
[To his dog] "You're glad to see me every minute of your life. I come home, you jump around and wag your tail. I go to the closet, I come out, you jump around and wag your tail. I turn my face away and turn it back, you wag your tail. Either you love me very much or your short-term memory is shot."

Dr. Harry Weston,
—*Empty Nest*

"The only good cat is a stir-fried cat."

—**Alf, *ALF***

**COP TALK**
**Witness** [refusing to testify because he doesn't want to "get involved"]: "Mr. Friday, if you were me, would you want to get involved?"
**Sgt. Joe Friday:** "Can I wait a while?"
**Witness:** "Huh?"
**Friday:** "Before I'm you."

—*Dragnet*

**Killer:** "You made a mistake, and I'm not going to pay for it."
**Sgt. Joe Friday:** "You're going to use a credit card?"

—*Dragnet*

**ON LINGUISTICS**
"Due to the shape of the North American elk's esophagus, even if it could speak, it could not pronounce the word *lasagna.*"

—**Cliff Clavin, *Cheers***

"You must always keep abreast of other tongues."

—**Batman, *Batman***

# OH SAY CAN YOU SEE?

*A Bathroom Reader's dilemma: What would do if you heard the National Anthem right now? Stay seated? Stand? Well, no one's watching. Hum it to yourself while you read this, and do whatever you want.*

**THE PRISONER**

During the War of 1812, British troops marched on Washington, D.C. and burned down the White House. Then, with their sights set on Baltimore, they sailed up the Chesapeake River, taking a civilian prisoner with them—a Dr. William Beanes, who'd supposedly helped arrest 3 English soldiers in Washington.

**THE RESCUE.**

The next day Francis Scott Key, a prominent young lawyer from Washington, met with British military commanders on the Chesapeake Bay and persuaded them to release Beanes (who'd actually *assisted* wounded British soldiers). But the Brits wouldn't let Key go until the planned bombardment of Baltimore's Fort McHenry was over. So he was detained on the British boat overnight.

**THE DEFENSE**

During the night, Key got a first-hand look at the raging battle. He assumed that the British would take Baltimore, as they had Washington. But in the morning, he awoke to find that the American flag was still flying over Fort McHenry. Inspired by the American defense, he jotted down an emotional poem.

**THE SONG**

On his way back to shore, Key wrote the words down on an envelope. The next day, he showed the poem to his wife's sister. She found it so inspiring that she took it to a printer, made handbills, and circulated the poem around Baltimore. The next week, the *Baltimore American* newspaper became the first to publish it.

Surprise: the words were set to the melody of a *British* song called "Anacreon in Heaven." Another surprise: It didn't become the National Anthem until 1931—after being voted down in 1929 because it's a British tune, and a poor marching song.

# CUSTOM-MADE

*You know these customs. Now, here's where they came from.*

## CLINKING GLASSES AFTER A TOAST

Nobles and knights were sometimes assassinated by enemies who'd poisoned their wine. So when they got together socially, each poured a little of his own wine into everyone else's goblet, as a precaution. That way, if one man poisoned another, he poisoned everyone—including himself...Over the years, the tradition of exchanging wine has been simplied into this gesture of friendship.

## SPLITTING THE WISHBONE

In ancient Rome, soothsayers used the bones and entrails of birds to predict the future. In fact, one Latin term for "soothsayer," *auspex*, means "one who looks at birds." The soothsayer would " throw the bones" (a precursor of throwing dice) or dissect the bird to receive insight. Nowadays, we just break the wishbone, hoping to get the larger—and luckier—piece.

## BUTTONS ON COAT SLEEVES

Researchers credit this to Napoleon Bonaparte. Apparently, while inspecting some of his troops, he spotted a soldier wiping his nose on his jacket sleeve. Disgusted, Napoleon ordered all new shirts and jackets for his army—this time with buttons on the sleeves.

## WEARING BLACK FOR MOURNING

Until King Charles VIII died in the late fifteenth century, Europeans in mourning wore white (for hope or renewal). But when Anne Brittany, Charles' widow, went into mourning, she donned black. The result: a funeral fashion that continues today.

## THROWING RICE & EATING CAKE AT WEDDINGS

For the Romans, wheat was a symbol of fertility. In fact, the Latin term for wedding, *conferreatio*, means "eating wheat together." Weddings began with the bride holding wheat sheaves and ended with the married couple eating wheat cakes. Over the years, wheat sheaves and wheat loaves have been replaced by throwing rice and serving multi-tiered cakes.

# RADIO STUNTS

*Radio stations will do practically anything for a little publicity. Three cases in point...*

In 1990, WKRL in St. Petersburg, Florida introduced an all-Led Zeppelin format by playing the song "Stairway to Heaven" for 24 hours straight. According to *Pulse* magazine: "Two hours into the marathon the police showed up...Evidently a lot of listeners had called them thinking the DJ had a heart attack or was being held up at gunpoint." After 12 days of playing nothing but Led Zeppelin songs, the station decided to add another group to their format: Pink Floyd.

In 1988, the Baltimore Orioles opened their season by losing 21 straight games—a major league record. Ten games into the losing streak, Bob Rivers, a disc jockey at WIYY in Baltimore, vowed to stay on the air until the Orioles won their first game. At first it seemed like a fun idea...but then the Orioles kept losing.

Rivers kept his word—he stayed on the air 24 hours a day, sleeping only between songs. His plight made international headlines. But 258 hours later, the ordeal was finally over: the Orioles defeated the Chicago White Sox, 9-0. After playing the Who song "I'm Free," Rivers went home for some well-deserved rest.

In 1982, WSAN in Allentown, Pennsylvania announced a contest—three randomly drawn contestants would climb on top of a WSAN billboard...and live there. The one who stayed there the longest would win a mobile home. Sleeping bags and portable toilets were provided by WSAN; the rest was up to the contestants.

On September 20, 1982 the marathon began. Three men perched on a billboard off Interstate 22 in Allentown. Even through freezing winter temperatures, none would give up. Newspapers worldwide picked up the story. In March, 1983, one of the contestants was busted for selling marijuana. The two remaining billboard-sitters stayed until May 4, 1983, seven months after the contest began. Finally, WSAN declared both men winners. Each received a mobile home, a car, clothes and a free vacation. The third guy was awarded free rent for a year, a color TV and a three month supply of Big Macs.

**That's a mouthful: Over 200 different languages are spoken in the African country of Zaire.**

# THE HAYS OFFICE

*From 1922-1945, Will H. Hays—the acknowledged "czar" of Hollywood—wielded an iron hand over the Motion Pictures Producers and Directors Association (MPAA). As the moral guardian of American moviegoers, he alone decided what did and didn't make it to the screen.*

## BACKGROUND

Films have been censored from the beginning. In 1894, just two weeks after Edison introduced the Kinescope in Atlantic City, New Jersey, residents complained about the primitive scenes in *Dulorita in the Passion Dance*. In 1897 a New York judge closed a film that depicted a bride preparing for her wedding night, calling it "an outrage upon public decency."

By the time America entered the "Roaring Twenties," however, religious groups had upped the ante, calling for a boycott if certain moral standards were not upheld. In 1921, when popular comic Fatty Arbuckle was accused of raping and killing an actress named Virginia Rappe, America was scandalized. Arbuckle was later acquitted of the charges (although his career was ruined), but the damage was already done.

## THE CZAR

To forestall public criticism, Hollywood named Will Hays as "chief censor." He was the perfect man for the job. One contemporary commentaror called him "as indigenous as sassafras root. He is one of us. He is folks."

Hays had been a rising star in the Republican Party, serving as the party's chairman in 1918. He was even briefly nominated for president in the 1920 Republican Convention and later served as Postmaster General under President Warren G. Harding.

By 1924, Hays had issued a Code of Standards which stipulated what kind of films could and could not be made. It prevented 67 books and plays from becoming films that year.

## THE FORBIDDEN

In 1927, Hays issued a pamphlet called "Don'ts and Be Carefuls," which included 11 subjects "to be avoided" and 26 to "handle with care." Among the "avoided" were:

**Mark Twain, Charles Dickens, and Thomas Edison never graduated from high school.**

• "Scenes of actual childbirth—in fact or in silhouette."

• "Branding of people or animals."

• "Excessive or lustful kissing, particularly when one character is a 'heavy.' "

• Also banned: revealing dresses, lingerie and shots which showed a woman's inner thigh.

Several years later, the Hays Office issued amended codes including 43 words that were banned, including "broad," "cripes," "fairy," "hot" (as applied to a woman) and the phrase "in your hat."

## THE PRODUCTION CODE

Despite pressure from the Hays Office, motion pictures became increasingly racy in the early 1930's due to diminishing Depression-era receipts. One Catholic group threatened a nationwide boycott, saying, "The pesthole that infects the entire country with its obscene and lascivious moving pictures must be cleansed and disinfected."

Enter Joseph Breen, appointed by Hays to enforce a strict 1934 Production Code. Among the rules of the code were: no machine guns, no gambling, no graphic killings, no dying policeman, no exposed bosoms, no excessive drinking, no lace lingerie and no drugs.

Without the Production Code Seal, a film was virtually dead in the water. Anyone distributing or exhibiting a film without the seal could be severely fined.

## CHANGES

Rather than risk not getting the Production Seal refused, most movie companies made whatever changes the "Hays Office" recommended. Among the decisions were:

• Forbidding Walt Disney to show a cow's udder in a cartoon.

• Altering a Joan Crawford film title from *Infidelity* to *Fidelity*.

• Removing all references to the city of Chicago in *Scarface* and forcing producer Howard Hughes to add "Shame of the Nation" to the title.

• Ruling that adultery could not be directly mentioned in the 1935 screen adaptation of *Anna Karenina*, starring Greta Garbo—despite the fact that adultery was the subject of the book it was based on.

# BODY PARTS

*A few fascinating facts about your body to entertain you while you pass the...uh...time.*

Your brain weighs around three pounds. All but ten ounces is water.

☛

It takes 200,000 frowns to make a permanent wrinkle.

☛

While you're resting, the air you breathe passes through your nose at about four miles per hour. At this rate, you breathe over 400 gallons of air every hour.

☛

If you stub your toe, your brain will register pain in 1/50 of a second.

☛

It takes about 150 days for your fingernails to grow from your cuticles to your fingertips.

☛

The cartilage in your nose doesn't stop growing. Expect it to grow 1/2 inch longer and wider as you age.

☛

New freckles generally stop appearing after age 19 or 20.

Bone is about four times stronger than steel. It can endure 24,000 pounds of pressure per square inch.

☛

The average adult has about 18 square feet of skin.

☛

To say one word, you use over 70 muscles.

☛

Your brain uses less power than a 100-watt bulb.

☛

Women have a more developed sense of smell than men do.

☛

The average man shrinks a little more than one inch between the ages of 30 and 70. In the same period of time, the average woman shrinks two inches.

☛

There are over 200 taste buds on each of the small bumps on your tongue.

**In 1989, Americans bought over 7,000 Harlequin romance books...every hour.**

# LUCY THE RED

*Everyone loved Lucy. When she died in 1989, newspaper obituaries mourned the passing of the brilliant red-headed comedienne. But few mentioned her brief affiliation with the Communist party in 1936...and the way it almost destroyed her career.*

## BACKGROUND

In the early 1950s, during the height of Senator Joe McCarthy's "red menace" witch-hunts, an appearance before McCarthy and the House Un-American Activities Committee (HUAC) could ruin anybody—especially a Hollywood celebrity. At the time, "I Love Lucy" was the number one television show in the country. But that didn't make Lucy exempt from scrutiny. In 1953, Lucille Ball's political beliefs became a nationwide controversy.

## REVELATION

In 1953, in his popular newsparer gossip column, Walter Winchell reported this shocking news: Lucille Ball, "America's sitcom sweetheart," had been a "commie!" Lucy denied it, of course; and Desi emotionally proclaimed, "The only thing red about Lucy is her hair. And that's not even real!"

## THE INVESTIGATION

On September 4, 1953, Ball was asked to explain to the House Un-American Activities Committee (HUAC) why she had registered as a Communist on March 19, 1936.

William A. Wheeler, an investigator for HUAC, flew to Hollywood for Lucy's testimony. In the transcripts later released, Ball explained that she had registered as a Communist "to appease an old man," namely, her grandfather Fred C. Hunt, an ardent socialist.

"How we got to signing a few things," she told Wheeler, "or going among some people that thought differently, that has happened to to all of us out here in the last ten or twelve years, and it is unfortunate, but I certainly will do anything in the world to prove that we made a bad mistake."

But why had Ball voted for the Communist candidate in a primary election? While not really denying she had, Ball claimed she "had really racked my brain...and all I remember was something like a garage and a flag, like a voting day."

As for her political leanings, Ball was more conclusive. "I am not a Communist now," she testified. "I never have been. I never want to be. Nothing in the world could ever change my mind."

## THE AFTERMATH

Both the Congress and the country forgave Lucy's "mistake." After her testimony, Representative Donald J. Jackson of California revealed that the committee had known of her Communist party registration for over a year and only divulged it to quell growing rumours that Lucy was a red.

Letters of sympathy poured in from all over the nation. But a few people, including J. Edgar Hoover, apparently had their doubts.

## THE FBI

According to Jack Anderson's 12/7/89 column in the *Washington Post*, Hoover kept an open file on Lucy and her husband Desi Arnaz. Among the contents:

• Lucy went to great lengths to "make her grandfather happy." Besides registering as a Communist Party member, she signed a nominating petition of the Communist candidate for the California State Assembly in 1936. She was also named as a member of the Communist party's State Central Committee in California, although Lucy later denied any knowledge of her membership.

• In testimony before the State Legistative Committee on Un-American Activities in 1943, a Hollywood writer claimed to have attended Communist Party meetings at 1344 North Ogden Drive in Hollywood—Lucy's address at the time. According to Anderson, "The writer said Ball was not there but approved of the meeting."

• In 1951, the Communist newspaper, the *Daily Worker*, alleged that Lucy had once been more outspoken in her opposition to McCarthy but had been warned to keep quiet.

• While many movie people were pilloried for less, Lucy escaped unscathed. "My conscience has always been clean," she told a press conference after her testimony in 1953. "And I have great faith in the American people. They have been very good to me in the past and I'm sure they will be now."

# PIGS IN SPACE

*We honor astronauts like Neil Armstrong and John Glenn for their pioneering feats in space. But animals have been the real "guinea pigs" of flight since the first balloon took off in the 1700s.*

## UP, UP, AND AWAY

One month before the first manned balloon flight, a sheep, duck and a chicken were loaded onto a ballon and launched in Versailles, France on September 19, 1783. They survived the eight minute, two mile flight, achieving a peak altitude of 1,700 feet. The event was witnessed by King Louis XVI and Marie Antoinette.

## FLYING PIGS

- On October 30, 1909, the first pig flew on an airplane. The stunt was inspired by the expression "pigs might fly," a phrase commonly used to express skepicism about flying. Lord Barbazon of England, wanting to put the expression to rest, kept a pig in a basket during an airplane flight.
- On February 18, 1930 the first cow flew from St. Louis. In a publicity stunt, the cow was milked during the flight. The milk was parachuted to the ground in sealed paper cartons.

## A DOG'S LIFE

- The first living creature to orbit the Earth was a Russian dog named Laika, who was launched in a Russian satellite on November 3, 1957. The satellite orbited the Earth 2,370 times before burning up—with Laika aboard—during re-entry.
- The first animals to orbit Earth and survive were two dogs named Belka and Strelka on Sputnik 5, which was launched August 19, 1960.

## MONKEY BUSINESS

- The U.S. also sent up animals before sending a human into space. On May 28, 1959, two monkeys named Able and Baker were launched 300 miles into space from Cape Canaveral, Florida. They were recovered alive the next day in the Caribbean.

**American cheese hails from England.**

# ROCK NAMES

*Where do rock groups get their outrageous names? From movies, books, and medieval torture devices. Some examples:*

**ABBA:** An acronymn of the first letters of the band's four members, Agnetha Ulugeus, Bjorn Ulugeus, Benny Anderson and Annifred Anderson.

**The Bay City Rollers:** Came up with their name by sticking a pin in a map of the world. It landed on Bay City, Michigan.

**The Beatles:** A tribute to Buddy Holly's Crickets. The "a" was added by John Lennon, who later explained that it came to him in a dream.

**Buffalo Springfield:** Members of the legendary L.A.-based group were stumped for a name. A member of the band was looking out their manager's window at a construction site in Hollywood, when he spotted a steamroller with the brand name "Buffalo Springfield."

**The Doors:** Jim Morrison got the band's name from Aldous Huxley's book *The Doors Of Perception*, which dealt with Huxley's experimentation with psychedelic drugs.

**Duran Duran:** Named after a character in the film *Barbarella*, starring Jane Fonda.

**The Grateful Dead:** The name of an Egyptian prayer which band member Jerry Garcia spotted in a dictionary.

**Iron Maiden:** A medieval torture device.

**Jefferson Airplane:** Slang for a roach clip.

**Jethro Tull:** Named after the 18th century British inventor of the seed drill.

**A housefly can carry germs as far as 15 miles from the original source.**

**Led Zeppelin:** Based on a comment by the late Who drummer Keith Moon, who jokingly remarked that an early live appearance of the band "went down like a lead balloon."

**Lynard Skynard:** Inspired by Leonard Skinner, a teacher who once suspended the original band members from high school for having long hair.

**Manhattan Transfer:** After the 1920 novel by John Dos Passos.

**Pink Floyd:** An amalgam of two American blues artists, Pink Anderson and Floyd Council.

**The Ramones:** After Phil Ramone, the name Paul McCartney adopted for himself when the Beatles were the Silver Beatles.

**The Rolling Stones:** Taken from Muddy Waters' song, "Rolling Stone Blues."

**Sha Na Na:** Supposedly the doo-wop lyrics from "Get A Job," a 1957 hit by the Silhouettes.

**Steely Dan:** Based on the name of a dildo in William Burrough's novel, *The Naked Lunch*.

**The Thompson Twins:** There are no Thompsons or twins in the band, which took its name from characters in the Belgian comic book, *Tintin*.

**Three Dog Night:** It is a practice of Australian aborigines to sleep with three dogs on particularly cold nights.

**UB40:** Named after the British unemployment benefit form.

**The Velvet Underground:** Lou Reed lifted the name from a title of a cheap paperback novel.

**The Yardbirds:** A tribute to legendary be-bop saxophonist Charlie "Yardbird" Parker.

# MYTH AMERICA

*Here we are again: You may have believed these stories since you were a kid—after all, they were taught as sacred truths. Well, it's time to take another look...*

**TEA TIME**

**The Myth:** The Boston Tea Party was held because the British imposed a tax on tea.

**The Truth:** The exact opposite is actually true. The British did impose the Townsend Act, which taxed a number of goods—including tea—quite heavily. However, the tax on tea didn't really affect the colonists—they drank a smuggled, less expensive Dutch tea (John Hancock was a big Dutch tea smuggler).

To undercut the American tea-smuggling operation, the British rounded up between 15 and 20 million pounds of surplus tea, passed the Tea Act which eliminated taxes on British tea, and priced their huge supply below the price of the smuggled Dutch tea.

Colonists responded to this British interference by dumping the British tea before it was unloaded. That was the event called the Boston Tea Party.

**FOR WHOM THE BELL TOLLS**

**The Myth:** Alexander Graham Bell invented the telephone.

**Background:** About 15 years before Bell uttered the famous words, "Mr. Watson, come here; I want you," German scientist Phillip Reis had developed a crude working telephone. And about five years before Bell's historic race to the patent office, an Italian scientist named Antonio Meucci offered the patent office a rough description of a telephone's structure and principles. But nothing ever came of it.

**The Truth:** Bell wasn't the first to develop the device—but he was the first to patent it...barely. Many scientists were working on a telephone at the same time; one of them—Elisha Gray—arrived at the U.S. Patent Office with a model telephone just two hours *after* Bell. In fact, some say Gray's telephone was better than Bell's and more like the one we use today. By the time Bell received his patent, so many people claimed the telephone as their own invention

**The Write Stuff: Famous storyteller Hans Christian Anderson couldn't spell.**

that Bell had to defend the patent in court. In fact, the case went all the way to the *Supreme Court*. The verdict: the high court was divided in his favor, allowing him to the rights to the phone.

## FULTON'S FOLLY

**The Myth:** Robert Fulton invented the steamboat.

**The Truth:** Twenty years before Fulton built his first steamboat, *Fulton's Folly*, in 1807, James Rumsey had a steamboat chugging up the Potomac and John Fitch had one traveling the Delaware. In some states, Fitch even secured exclusive rights to run passenger and freight steamboat trips. So why does Fulton get the credit for the invention 20 years later? Rumsey and Fitch died broke, while Fulton had a knack for promotion and fund-raising. But Fulton did fail to make one key sale—to Napoleon Bonaparte, who thought the idea of steamships impractical. Some historians say the little conqueror's bad decision might have saved the English.

## FORD FACTS

**The Myth:** Henry Ford produced the first automobile.

**The Truth:** Karl Benz and Gottlieb Daimler, two German engineers who went on to form Mercedes-Benz, each developed working gasoline engine automobiles in 1885. The first American car was built by Charles and J. Frank Duryea in 1893. By then, Benz already had a model, the Velo, ready for sale to the general public.

**The Myth:** O.K., if Ford didn't invent the car, at least he invented the auto assembly line.

**The Truth:** No, chalk this one up to Ransom E. Olds, creator of the Oldsmobile. Olds introduced the moving assembly line in the early 1900s and boosted car production by 500%. The previous year, the Olds Motor Vehicle Company had turned out 425 cars. The year after they made over 2,500 of them. Ford improved Olds's system by introducing the conveyor belt, which moved both the cars *and* needed parts along the production line. The belt cut Ford's production time from a day to about two hours. A significant contribution, but not the original.

# WHO'S ON FIRST?

*The Abbott and Costello baseball routine "Who's On First?" is considered a landmark in the history of comedy.*

Abbot and Costello's recording of "Who's On First?" became the first gold record placed in the Baseball Hall of Fame in Cooperstown, New York.

• "The Baseball Scene," as it was known before it was given the title "Who's On First?" was a burlesque standard long before Abbot and Costello popularized it. In fact, Abbott and Costello each performed it with other vaudeville partners before teaming up in 1936.

• When the duo first performed the routine on radio's "The Kate Smith Hour," they were forced to change the ending from "I don't give a damn!" / "Oh, that's our shortstop" to "I don't care" / "Oh, that's our shortstop." President Roosevelt was listening; he enjoyed it so much that he called them personally to offer congratulations after the show.

**HERE'S THE ROUTINE**

**BUD**: You know, strange as it may seem, they give baseball players peculiar names nowadays. On the St. Louis team Who's on first, What's on second, I Don't Know is on third.

**LOU:** That's what I want to find out. I want you to tell me the names of the fellows on the St. Louis team.

**BUD:** I'm telling you. Who's on first, What's on second, I Don't Know is on third.

**LOU:** You know the fellows' names?

**BUD:** Yes.

**LOU:** Well, then, who's playin' first?

**BUD:** Yes.

**LOU:** I mean the fellow's name on first base.

**BUD:** Who.

**BUD:** The fellow's name on first base for St. Louis.

**LOU:** Who.

**BUD:** The guy on first base.

**LOU:** Well, what are you askin' me for?

**BUD:** I'm not asking you. I'm telling you. Who is on first.

**LOU:** I'm askin' you, who is on first?

**BUD:** That's the man's name.

**LOU:** That's whose name?

**BUD:** Yes.

**LOU:** Well, go ahead and tell me.

**BUD:** Who?

**LOU:** The guy on first.

**BUD:** Who.

**LOU:** The first baseman.

**BUD:** Who is on first.

**LOU:** (*Trying to stay calm*) Have you got a first baseman on first?

**BUD:** Certainly.

**LOU:** Well, all I'm trying to find out is what's the guy's name on first base.

**BUD:** Oh, no, no. What is on *second* base.

**LOU:** I'm not askin' you who's on second.

**BUD:** Who's on first.

**LOU:** That's what I'm tryin' to find out.

BUD: Well, don't change the players around.

**LOU:** (*starting to get angry*) I'm not changin' anybody.

**BUD:** Now take it easy.

**LOU:** What's the guy's name on first base?

**BUD:** What's the guy's name on *second* base.

**LOU:** I'm not askin' you who's on second.

**BUD:** Who's on first.

**LOU:** I don't know.

**BUD:** He's on third. We're not talking about him.

**LOU:** (*begging*) How could I get on third base?

**BUD:** You mentioned his name.

**LOU:** If I mentioned the third baseman's name, who did I say is playing third?

**BUD:** (*starting all over again*) No, Who's playing first.

**LOU:** Stay offa first, will ya?
**BUD:** Please, now what is it you'd like to know?
**LOU:** What is the fellow's name on third base?
**BUD:** What is the fellow's name on second base.
**LOU:** I'm not askin' ya who's on second.
**BUD:** Who's on first.
**LOU:** I don't know.
**BUD & LOU:** (*together*) Third base!
**LOU:** (*tries again*) You got an outfield?
**BUD:** Certainly.
**LOU:** St. Louis got a good outfield?
**BUD:** Oh, absolutely.
**LOU:** The left fielder's name.
**BUD:** Why.
**LOU:** I don't know. I just thought I'd ask.
**BUD:** Well, I just thought I'd tell you.
**LOU:** Then tell me who's playing left field.
**BUD:** Who's playing first.
**LOU:** Stay outa the infield!
**BUD:** Don't mention any names there.
**LOU:** (*firmly*) I wanta know what's the fellow's name in left field.
**BUD:** What is on second.
**LOU:** I'm not askin' you who's on second.
**BUD:** Who is on first.
**LOU:** I don't know!
**BUD & LOU:** (*together*) Third base! (*Lou makes funny noises*)
**BUD:** Now take it easy, man.
**LOU:** And the left fielder's name?
**BUD:** Why?
**LOU:** Because.
**BUD:** Oh, he's center field.
**LOU:** Wait a minute. You got a pitcher on the team?
**BUD:** Wouldn't this be a fine team without a pitcher?
**LOU:** I dunno. Tell me the pitcher's name.

**Indians in the Andes mountains have 3 quarts more blood than people living at sea level do.**

**BUD:** Tomorrow.
**LOU:** You don't want to tell me today?
**BUD:** I'm telling you, man.
**LOU:** Then go ahead.
**BUD:** Tomorrow.
**LOU:** What time?
**BUD:** What time what?
**LOU:** What time tomorrow are you gonna tell me who's pitching?
**BUD:** Now listen, who is not pitching. Who is on—
**LOU:** (*excited*) I'll break your arm if you say who is on first.
**BUD:** Then why come up here and ask?
**LOU:** I want to know what's the pitcher's name!
**BUD:** What's on second.
**LOU:** (*sighs*) I don't know.
**BUD & LOU:** (*together*) Third base!
**LOU:** You gotta catcher?
**BUD:** Yes.
**LOU:** The catcher's name.
**BUD:** Today.
**LOU:** Today. And Tomorrow's pitching.
**BUD:** Now you've got it.
**LOU:** That's all. St. Louis got a couple of days on their team. That's all.
**BUD:** Well, I can't help that. What do you want me to do?
**LOU:** Gotta catcher?
**BUD:** Yes.
**LOU:** I'm a good catcher, too, you know.
**BUD:** I know that.
**LOU:** I would like to play for St. Louis.
**BUD:** Well, I might arrange that.
**LOU:** I would like to catch. Now Tomorrow's pitching on the team and I'm catching.
**BUD:** Yes.
**LOU:** Tomorrow throws the ball and the guy up bunts the ball.

**BUD:** Yes.

**LOU:** So when he bunts the ball, me, bein' a good catcher, I want to throw the guy out at first base. So I pick up the ball and I throw it to who?

**BUD:** Now that's the first thing you've said right!

**LOU:** *I don't even know what I'm talkin' about!*

**BUD:** Well, that's all you have to do.

**LOU:** I throw it to first base.

**BUD:** Yes.

**LOU:** Now who's got it?

**BUD:** Naturally.

**LOU:** Naturally.

**BUD:** Naturally.

**LOU:** I throw the ball to naturally.

**BUD:** You throw it to Who.

**LOU:** Naturally.

**BUD:** Naturally, well, say it that way.

**LOU:** That's what I'm saying!

**BUD:** Now don't get excited, don't get excited.

**LOU:** I throw the ball to first base.

**BUD:** Then Who gets it.

**LOU:** He'd better get it.

**BUD:** That's it. All right now, don't get excited. Take it easy.

**LOU:** (*beside himself*) Now I throw the ball to first base, whoever it is grabs the ball, so the guy runs to second.

**BUD:** Uh-huh.

**LOU:** Who picks up the ball and throws it to What. What throws it to I Don't Know. I Don't Know throws it back to Tomorrow. A triple play!

**BUD:** Yeah, could be.

**LOU:** Another guy goes up and it's a long fly ball to center. Why? I don't know. And I don't give a damn!

**BUD:** What was that?

**LOU:** I said, I don't give a damn!

**BUD:** Oh, that's our shortstop.

**One out of every seven birds in the world is a finch.**

# STRANGE LAWSUITS

*Tired of being sprayed by department store employees? Are headless cartoon characters terrorizing your children? Don't take the law into your own hands. Take 'em to court.*

**THE PLAINTIFF:** Deborah Martorano.

**THE DEFENDANT:** Bloomingdale's Department Store.

**THE LAWSUIT:** Martorano claimed she was wrongfully sprayed with perfume by a store employee. On April 30, 1984, she was shopping for a blouse on her lunch hour when a roving perfume-demonstrator approached her and squirted her with fragrance. Martorano's lawyer claimed his client, a lifelong asthma and allergy sufferer, spent 10 days in a New York hospital recovering from "respiratory distress" resulting from the unsolicited spritz.

**VERDICT:** She accepted a $75,000 settlement from the store.

**THE PLAINTIFF:** John Moore.

**THE DEFENDANT:** Regents of the University of California.

**THE LAWSUIT:** Moore claimed one of his organs was pirated. In 1976, University of California-Los Angeles Medical Center doctors removed Moore's spleen in a successful effort to cure his cancer. Doctors later found that the spleen possessed unique cancer-fighting cells; experiments with the cells led to a new discovery worth an estimated $3 billion. Moore, who was never told that his ex-organ had commercial value, sued for part of the profits.

**VERDICT:** In 1990, 14 years after the operation, Moore lost the case.

**THE PLAINTIFF:** The estate of an unidentified 34-year-old co-pilot.

**THE DEFENDANT:** Gates Lear Jet Corporation.

**THE LAWSUIT:** The estate claimed that a jet's windshield wasn't thick enough. In 1987, an 11.5 pound loon crashed through the windshield of a state-of-the-art jet during takeoff, killing the loon and the co-pilot. The man's estate contended that the windshield should have been "birdproofed." It was, Gates Lear said, but

**One in five American men have spent at least a night in jail.**

only for birds weighing up to four pounds.
**VERDICT**: A Michigan circuit court awarded the man's estate $1.5 million in compensatory damages.

**THE PLAINTIFF:** McDonald's.
**THE DEFENDANT:** McDharma's Natural Fast Foods.
**THE LAWSUIT:** McDonald's hadn't a clue that McDharma's, a 15-employee vegetarian restaurant where cashiers wear T-shirts, shorts, and sandals, even existed until the three-year-old Santa Cruz, California eatery sought its own national trademark. McDonald's had nothing against the top-selling "Brahma Burger," a burger made of beans, nuts, seeds, grains, and soy, but objected to the McDharma's use of the trademarked "Mc." "It's such a joke," McDharma's co-owner Bernie Shapiro said, "and they're the only ones taking it seriously."
**VERDICT:** McDharma's was forced to drop the "Mc," but instead of removing the two letters from their sign, McDharma's painted a red circle with a slash over them. McDonald's sued again; McDharma's eventually removed the "Mc." However, McDharma's received a handful of offers for franchises.

**THE PLAINTIFF:** Mr. and Mrs. Lonnie and Karen B.
**THE DEFENDANT:** The Walt Disney Corporation
**THE LAWSUIT:** The couple claimed that they were falsely arrested for shoplifting while they and their daughters, Lindsay, 6, and Melissa, 2, were visiting Disneyland. They were detained for questioning. Apparently, while they waited, Lindsay caught sight of several actors dressed as Disney characters who had taken their costume headpieces off...and she freaked out. The couple sued for damages, claiming their daughter suffered nightmares and had to undergo therapy as a result of the experience.
**THE VERDICT:** Pending.

**MISC. DID WE MENTION THIS?**

From the book *George Washington Had No Middle Name*: "A biography of George Armstrong Custer, by James Warner Bellah, reads in its entirety: 'To put it mildly, this was an oddball.' "

**In the Olympics, men and women compete together in rifle shooting.**

# LATE NIGHT WITH DAVID LETTERMAN

*A few words from America's favorite gap-toothed talk show host.*

"This warning from the New York City Department of Health Fraud: Be suspicious of any doctor who tries to take your temperature with his finger."

"Martin Levine has passed away at age 75. Mr Levine had owned a movie theater chain here in New York. The funeral will be held on Thursday at 2:15, 4:20, 6:30, 8:40, and 10:50."

"A professor at Johns Hopkins has come forth with an intriguing thought about a perennial question: He says that if an infinite number of monkeys sat typing at an infinite number of typewriters, the smell in the room would be unbearable."

"Interesting survey in the *Journal of Abnormal Psychology*. New York City has a higher percentage of people you shouldn't make any sudden moves around than any other city in the world."

"Tip to out-of-town visitors: If you buy something here in New York and want to have it shipped home, be suspicious if the clerk tells you they don't need your name and address."

"Every year when it's Chinese New Year here in New York, there are fireworks going off at all hours. New York mothers calm their children by telling them it's just gunfire."

"New Jersey announced today that they were adopting a new license plate slogan: 'Try Our Creamy Thick Shakes.'"

"Someone did a study of the three most often heard phrases in New York City. One is, 'Hey, taxi.' Two is, 'What train do I take to get to Bloomingdales?' And three is, 'Don't worry. It's just a flesh wound.' "

"High insurance rates are what really killed the dinosaurs."

# MONKEE BUSINESS

*The Monkees were one of the most popular bands in the world, but weren't allowed to play on their own records—until they went on strike. Here's the inside story, from* Behind the Hits, *by Bob Shannon and John Javna.*

From the outside, everything looked great for the Monkees in 1967. In one year they had leaped from semi—or total—obscurity to overnight superstardom. They had a hit TV series, two #1 singles ("Last Train to Clarksville," and "I'm A Believer"), and two #1 albums ("The Monkees," and "More of the Monkees"). The only problem was the Monkees weren't allowed to play on their own records. Why not? Because Don Kirshner, the musical supervisor of the Monkees, said so. It was...well...embarrassing. Here they were, pretending to be a real group, when in fact they had almost nothing to do with "their" music. Critics made fun of them. Even worse, teenyboppers idolized them for something they weren't doing. And to add insult to injury, Kirshner made more money from their records than they did. They each got a 1.5% royalty, but Kirshner got 15%! They had their pride, after all.

Trouble had been brewing for some time between Kirshner and the group, particularly Mike Nesmith, who wasn't even allowed to play guitar on the songs he *wrote*. That was Kirshner's studio policy; the Monkees just sang vocals while studio musicians played on the tracks. But what the hell, Kirshner reasoned, he was getting results—hits—and that was his job. So what if Nesmith had to stand by and watch Glen Campbell put the guitar licks on his own song, "Mary Mary"? This was the only way management could be sure it was right. The bottom line was what counted, after all. Nesmith, a genuinely creative individual, just stewed.

"Essentially, the big collision I had with Don Kirshner was this," said Nesmith; "he kept saying, 'You can't make the music; it would be no good, it won't be a hit.' And I was saying, 'Hey, the music isn't a hit because somebody wonderful is making it, the music is a hit because of the television show. So, at least let us put out music that is closer to our personas, closer to who we are artistically, so

**Legendary lawman Wyatt Earp was kicked out of California for horse-stealing.**

that we don't have to walk around and have people throwing eggs at us,' which they were."

Eventually the feud came to a showdown in early '67 at Kirshner's suite at the Beverly Hills Hotel. Kirshner had just handed the four Monkees some new demos (including "Sugar, Sugar," a bubblegum hit later for Kirshner's Archies) that they would be putting vocals on. Nesmith stepped forward and demanded that musical control be give to the Monkees. When Kirshner refused, Nesmith angrily smashed his fist through the wall, declaring, "That could have been your face!" Then the Monkees went off to record some original material *without* Kirshner's approval.

What happened next is a little unclear. While the Monkees were working out their own songs, Kirshner appears to have approached Davy Jones, one of the members of the group, and talked him into going into the studio without the rest of the Monkees. Jones put the vocals on several tunes, one of which was "A Little Bit Me, A Little Bit You." But the Monkees weren't doing the backing vocals. Who was it? Eric Lefcowitz, author of *The Monkees Tale*, speculates, "Kirshner was quoted once as saying that Neil Diamond and Carole King had sung back-up vocals on some Monkees songs, and I think that if you listen closely to 'A Little Bit Me,' you can hear them. It sounds like Neil Diamond to me." And why would Jones record without the rest of his group? "I don't know, of course," Lefcowitz says, "but Davy Jones hadn't ever had the chance to sing lead before. This was *his* session. Maybe that had something to do with it."

Whatever. The important thing is that in a power play, Kirshner recorded and released "A Little Bit Me, A Little Bit You" without even telling the Monkees he was doing it! That was the last straw. Monkees' producers Bert Schnieder and Bob Rafelson wanted hits, but they weren't going to put up with that from anyone. They fired Kirshner, and yanked the single out of American record stores. Then they re-released it with a Monkees' original—Nesmith's "The Girl I Knew Somewhere"—on the B side. Finally the Monkees could smile. They were out from under Kirshner...and a song they'd actually played on made the Top 40—"The Girl I Knew Somewhere" reached #39 on the charts.

**Layne Hall of New York, age 109, has been driving 75 years—without an accident.**

# GIVE US A HAND

*You probably can't put a finger on the origins of these common gestures, but here's some info you might find handy.*

## THE FINGER

It doesn't matter what you call it—"the bird," "the finger," or the "freeway salute"— the middle finger is among the most well-known symbols in America. Believe it or not, the gesture can be traced to the ancient Romans, who called it the "finger without shame" or *digitus impudicus*. Psychologists say it's a symbol of phallic aggressiveness.

## THE RING FINGER

Over two-thousand years ago, Greek physicians believed that a special "vein of love" connected this finger to the heart. It logically became the finger to be "bound" by an affair of the heart.

## CROSSING FINGERS

Ever cross your fingers for good luck? Historians suggest this popular gesture comes from the pre-Christian belief that a cross symbolizes perfect unity. The intersection point of the fingers was said to possess a mystical quality which would hold the wish until it was fulfilled.

## THUMBS UP OR THUMBS DOWN

This symbol wasn't always used to rate new movies or hitch rides. According to popular lore, it was a matter of life or death. Roman emperors would use "thumbs up" to spare a defeated gladiator's life, and "thumbs down" to order his death.

## THUMBING YOUR NOSE

You've done it before—touching your thumb to the tip of your nose and extending your fingers like a fan. It's understood as an insult all over the world, but what does it mean? Some folklorists say it's a mock military salute. Others maintain that it's a graphic suggestion that someone stinks.

# THE GREAT *TITANIC*

*You've probably heard of the Titantic. We had, but we didn't really know much about it. So this piece by Eric Lefcowitz was particularly interesting.*

## BACKGROUND

Steamships were the most viable means of trans-Atlantic travel when the White Star Company decided to build the world'd largest ship, the *Titanic* in 1912. Its proposed measurements—900 feet (3-1/2 city blocks) long and 11 stories high—were enough to make it front-page news. But size wasn't all it had to offer. The company announced a breakthrough in steamship design; with 16 watertight compartments and a double bottom, the *Titanic* would be "unsinkable." If water got through the first hull, spokesmen explained, the second one would still keep the boat afloat.

The construction of the Titanic captured the public's imagination. Newspapers billed it as a "floating Camelot." By the time it was ready to sail, the whole world was watching.

## THE VOYAGE

On April 12, the *Titanic* left for its maiden voyage from Southhampton, England to New York. Accommodations varied: There were cramped, low-cost quarters in the bowels of the boat for arriving immigrants; and there were luxurious upper-deck suites for the upper class. A one-way luxury ticket cost an incredible $4,350.

Fatal mistake: The captain, intent on breaking the world's record with the fastest trans-Atlantic journey ever, ignored warnings about icebergs.

The result: On April 15, four days, 17 hours, and 35 minutes later, the "unsinkable" Titanic hit an iceberg in the North Atlantic. It was 350 miles from Newfoundland. In the darkness of night, the mighty boat plunged into water two miles deep.

It was the most dramatic ship disaster of all-time; 1,512 passengers were killed.

## TITANIC FACTS

• The *Titanic*'s band played on deck as the ship was sinking. The song they played was "Autumn," a popular British waltz.

**Noble ladies of Greece and Rome carried the tiny Maltese dog (3-6 lbs.) in their robe sleeves.**

• There was lifeboat space for only 1,200 of the 2,227 passengers.

• Only 705 people, most of them women and children, survived the disaster. They were picked up by the Cunard liner *Carpathia*.

• Among the rich and famous who went down with the ship were John Jacob Astor and Benjamin Guggenheim.

• Unlike the 1898 disaster of the French ship, *La Bourgogne*—where women and children were trampled by hysterical passengers attempting to get on lifeboats—chivalry and honor prevailed on the *Titanic*; most of the women and children survived. However, a greater proportion of first-class passengers survived than lower-class travelers, including immigrants, who were on the lower decks.

• The *California*, a freighter only 10 miles away, saw eight distress flares fired from the *Titanic* but did not respond, figuring they had been set off in celebration.

• Several changes in sea travel regulations occurred after the disaster. Every ship was required to have enough lifeboats to accommodate every passenger. The International Ice Patrol was also organized.

• Only one ship has struck an iceberg since the *Titanic* sank—it happened during World War II.

• A song called "The Wreck of the *Titanic*" became popular shortly after the disaster. Sample lyrics: "Oh, they built the ship *Titanic* to sail the ocean blue. And they thought they had a ship that the water couldn't get through. But an iceberg on the wave, Sent it to its watery grave. It was sad when that great ship went down."

## DISCOVERING THE WRECK

*Still controversial:* For years people searched for the most famous wreck of all-time. Finally, in 1985, the *Titanic* was discovered by a U.S./French exploratory team. To keep potential looters away, its location wasn't divulged. But in 1987, the French members returned to the site and—contrary to the wishes of the U.S. team, who thought the site should be preserved out of respect to the dead—salvaged 800 artifacts from the wreck. In response, the U.S. Senate, whose members agreed the site should be left alone, passed a resolution banning the display of the recovered *Titanic* items for profit in the United States.

# WEIRD COINCIDENCES

*A reader sent us this list of the bizarre similarities between the assassinations of Lincoln and Kennedy. It's hard to believe, but they're true. Rod Serling, where are you?*

Abraham Lincoln was elected in 1860, and John Kennedy in 1960, 100 years later.

Both Lincoln and Kennedy mentioned having premonitions of death before their assassinations.

Lincoln's secretary, named Kennedy, warned him not to go to the theater that fatal night. Kennedy's secretary, named Lincoln, tried to talk him out of going to Dallas.

Both men died of bullet wounds to the head.

Both were killed as they sat beside their wives.

Both were ardent proponents of civil rights.

John Wilkes Booth, Lincoln's assassin, was born in 1839, and Lee Harvey Oswald, Kennedy's assassin, was born in 1939, exactly 100 years later.

The names John Wilkes Booth and Lee Harvey Oswald each contain 15 letters.

Booth shot Lincoln in a theater and fled to a warehouse. Oswald shot Kennedy from a warehouse and fled to a theater.

Both Presidents were succeeded by vice-presidents named Johnson. Andrew Johnson followed Lincoln, and Lyndon B. Johnson followed Kennedy.

Andrew Johnson was born in 1808, and Lyndon B. Johnson was born in 1908, 100 years later.

Both were killed on Friday.

Both Johnsons were Democrats, southern, and former senators.

The names Kennedy and Lincoln each contain seven letters.

The names Andrew Johnson and Lyndon Johnson each contain 13 letters.

Both Booth and Oswald were killed before reaching trial.

**According to a recent study, about 20% of men and 6% of women sleep naked.**

# SATURDAY NIGHT LIVE

*The original version of Saturday Night Live, which ran from 1975 to about 1980, was a milestone in modern TV. Some say its hip, bold, innovative humor hasn't been matched since then. Here's how it got on the air.*

## HOW IT STARTED

In early 1975, NBC executives were looking to improve Saturday night ratings in the 11:30-1:00 a.m. time slot. "Tonight Show" reruns were getting stale, and research showed that viewers were constantly changing channels, indicating that a restless audience was looking for something new. . . and not finding it. "The problem," Producer Lorne Michaels explained a few years later, "was that no one in TV was accurately expressing what was going on. Carol Burnett sketches were dealing with the problems of another generation—divorce, Valium, crab-grass, adultery. It used to drive me crazy to see Bob Hope doing a sketch about marijuana and acting drunk."

When Michaels and NBC vice president Dick Ebersol suggested a 90-minute variety show featuring "rock'n'roll, satire, changing hosts, and a cast of unknown regulars who'd done almost no TV," NBC brass shocked them by accepting. Michaels also proposed going "live," sensing that the young, hip, late-nite crowd would be drawn to the "anything goes" atmosphere of such a format. "I felt that American kids knew TV as well as French kids knew wine and that there was such a thing as good TV."

Michaels began casting. He recruited some of the best young talent available, including Dan Aykroyd, Chevy Chase, Gilda Radner, and John Belushi. On Oct. 11, 1975, unaware of the profound effect they were about to have on an entire generation of American youth, the Not Ready for Prime Time Players appeared for the first time on "Saturday Night Live."

## INSIDE INFO

**Peanuts.** The Not Ready For Prime Time Players' starting weekly salaries in 1975 were $750 per week.

**Employment Opportunity.** Four of the original eleven writers on SNL had just graduated from college, and the show was their first post-college job.

## THE ORIGINAL CAST

• On his 21st birthday Bill Murray was in a Chicago jail (busted with eight lbs. of marijuana on him). After his release, jobless and penniless, he decided to try comedy. He joined his brother (Brian Doyle-Murray) at the Second City comedy troupe. There he found his niche; soon afterwards, SNL called and offered him a spot.

• John Belushi was the last cast-member hired for SNL. Lorne Michaels had sincere reservations about unleashing such a volatile, "on-the-edge" talent in front of a live camera, but after seeing John's "Samurai Pool Hustler," how could he resist? "Everyone in the group wanted him," Dick Ebersol said, "but we heard horrendous tales of his being a discipline problem." Said writer Michael O'Donoghue: "He wanted to grab the world and snort it."

• An experienced writer with "The Smothers' Brothers Show," Chevy Chase was originally hired only to write for SNL. But he wanted to act. One night, after dinner with Lorne Michaels, Chase took off down the street, threw himself into the air, and landed in "the biggest puddle I'd ever seen. We figured," says Michaels, "that if he wanted it that badly, we might as well give him a shot." But he'd only signed a one-year contract, so after the first season he left.

• Dan Aykroyd was hired for the show at the last minute, and for a while had to commute between Canada and the U.S. on his motorcycle.

• Laraine Newman auditioned for SNL in a hospital room, where Dick Ebersol was recuperating from an illness.

• Jane Curtin was hired out of a Boston improv group. There were equally talented applicants for the spot, but says Dick Ebersol, "we thought we needed someone who was white bread."

• The best physical comedian in the troupe, Gilda Radner was the first person hired for SNL. She was also from Second City.

• The only cast member without formal comic training (though he had formal music training at Julliard), Garrett Morris was first hired as a writer. When Michaels saw him acting in *Cooley High*, Morris was added to the cast.

# FROG FACTS

*Kermit the Frog says, "It's not easy being green." Maybe this is what he means.*

There are around 2,600 different species of frogs. They live in every continent except Antarctica.

Frogs don't drink water—they absorb water through their skin.

Every species of frog as its own special mating call, made only by the males. The call has two parts—"a whine," which the whole species uses, and a "chuck" which is the individual frog's calling card. Females listen to the chuck carefully—the larger, more desirable frogs make longer, deeper chucks. The drawback: bats, which eat frogs, also listen for long, deep chucks.

One expert reports "A frog from Ethiopa has teethlike protusions and eats snails—shells and all."

An Australian frog hatches its offspring in its stomach, then spits out fully developed frogs—sometimes more than 20 at once.

The skin of some poisonous frogs is so toxic that it will kill any creature that bites it. Only 1/100,000 of a gram of skin poison from one species is enough to kill a man.

Have you ever heard of flying frogs? They do exist, but they don't really fly—they can't gain height in the air. Instead, they glide. Top speed: 24 kilometers per hour, fastest of all amphibians.

According to an expert, "One frog in Colombia is so toxic that local Indians merely wipe their arrows across its skin to poison the tips."

Reputedly, there's a frog in Australia that excretes a hallucenogenic slime. Natives lick it to get high.

Film for frog-fans: *Frogs*, a ludicrous 1972 horror flick starring Ray Milland. "Thousands of frogs overrun a remote, inhabited island off the southern U.S. coast, devouring any human who gets in their way." An absolutely ribbeting film.

# THE NAME IS FAMILIAR

*Some people have achieved immortality because their names have become product brand names. You already know the names—now here are the people.*

**King C. Gillette.** William Painter—the man who invented the bottle cap—suggested that Gillette, a traveling salesman, invent something that people could use a few times and throw away. In 1895, while cursing his dull razor, Gillette realized that disposable razors would be a perfect invention. Devising a thin enough blade was the problem; Gillette tinkered with 700 blades and 51 razors before getting it right in 1903. Within three years, he was selling over 500,000 blades annually.

**Sir Joseph Lister.** Even before the mouthwash that bears his name was invented, Lister fought germs; he campaigned against filthy hospitals and against doctors who performed surgery in their street clothes. When St. Louis chemist Joseph Lawrence invented the famous mouthwash, he named it 'Listerine' both to honor and to take advantage of Lister's well-known obsession with cleanliness.

**Clarence Birdseye.** Brooklyn-born "Bob" Birdseye was the first person to figure out how to freeze fresh food and still preserve its taste and nutrition. Birdseye's insight came from an Arctic expedition; he observed that Caribou meat, quickly frozen in the sub-zero temperatures, retained its flavor when cooked months later. He returned to America and worked for years to develop a quick-freezing process. When he succeeded in 1929, he sold his invention for the then-enormous sum of $22 million; Birdseye foods still bears his name.

**Charles Fleischmann.** An Austrian native who first visited the United States during the Civil War, he found our bread almost as appalling as our political situation. At the time bread was mostly home-baked, using yeast made from potato peelings, and its taste was unpredictable. The next time he came to America,

Fleischmann brought along samples of the yeast used to make Viennese bread. In 1868, he began to sell his yeast in compressed cakes of uniform size that removed the guesswork from baking. In 1937, yeast sales reached $20 million a year. After Prohibition ended, Fleischmann and his brother Maximillian found another use for their yeast—Fleischmann's distilled gin.

**William and Andrew Smith.** The makers of the Smith Brothers Cough Drops were the sons of Poughkeepsie, New York restauranteur and candymaker James Smith. In 1870, one of Smith's customers gave him a recipe for a "cough candy." Smith made a batch and quickly sold it all. People in the windswept Hudson Valley—plagued by constant colds during the long winters—clamored for more... And so the Smith family became America's cough drop kings. When copycat "Smith" cough drops appeared, the bearded brothers introduced the famous box that bears their pictures, as a means of guaranteeing authenticity.

**John B. Stetson.** While traveling out west in the 1850s, Stetson became adept at trapping animals and sewing the skins together, making them hats for sun protection. When he returned to Philadephia, he started a hat business for $100; his mainstay, "The Boss of the Plains" hat, became the classic symbol of the Wild West.

**William Scholl.** As apprentice to the local shoemaker, "Billy" Scholl's work led him to two conclusions: feet were abused, and nobody cared. So, in a burst of idealism, Scholl appointed himself the future foot doctor to the world. Strangely enough, it actually happened. By the time he became a M.D. at 22, Dr. Scholl had invented and patented his first arch support; in fact, he held over 300 patents for foot treatments and machines for making foot comfort aids. And his customers seemed to appreciate it—a widow once wrote him that she buried her husband with his "Foot-Eazers" so he would be as comfortable as he was in life. Until he died, in his eighties, Dr. Scholl devoted himself to saving the world's feet, adhering always to his credo: "Early to bed, early to rise, work like hell, and advertise."

**A parking space in one New York City "condo garage" sells for $29,000.**

# FULLER IDEAS

*Buckminster Fuller, an architect, inventor, scientist, mathematician, philosopher, and we don't know what else, was considered one of the most original thinkers of the 20th century.*

"Faith is much better than belief. Belief is when someone *else* does the thinking."

"If nature had wanted you to be a specialist she'd have had you born with one eye with a microscope fastened to it."

"Either war is obsolete or men are."

"Don't oppose forces, use them."

"It struck me that nature's system must be a real beauty, because in chemistry we find that the associations are always in beautiful whole numbers—there are no fractions."

"Politics is an accessory after the fact."

"People should think things out fresh and not just accept conventional terms and the conventional way of doing things."

"God to me…is a verb, not a noun, proper or improper."

"I am a passenger on the spaceship Earth."

"The most important thing about Spaceship Earth—an instruction booklet didn't come with it."

"If we do more with less, our resources will be adequate to take care of everybody."

"The end move in politics is to pick up a gun."

"When I'm working on a problem, I never think about beauty. I think only how to solve the problem. But when I have finished, if the solution is not beautiful, I know it is wrong."

"You can't reorder the world by talking to it."

"We are not going to be able to operate our spaceship Earth successfully nor for much longer unless we see it as a whole spaceship and our fate as common. It has to be everybody or nobody."

# CLOSE CALLS

*Four presidents—Abraham Lincoln (1865), James Garfield (1881), William McKinley (1901) and John F. Kennedy (1963)— have lost their lives to assassins. Others have barely escaped assassination attempts. Here are the most famous "close calls" in American history.*

**THE ATTEMPT:** On January 30, 1835, President Andrew Jackson was in the Capitol rotunda, attending funeral services for Congressman Warren B. Davis of South Carolina. He was approached by Richard Lawrence, a 35 year-old house painter, who drew two revolvers and pointed them at the president...but both guns misfired. Jackson was so incensed that he rushed at Lawrence and started to beat him with his cane.

**THE MOTIVE:** Lawrence had approached Jackson a week before on the White House grounds and begged the president for money. Jackson thought he was a "harmless lunatic" and dismissed him.

**THE SENTENCE:** Lawrence was tried by prosecutor Francis Scott Key, author of "The Star Spangled Banner." He pled insanity, claiming he was the King of England, but the verdict was "guilty." He later died in a mental institution.

**THE ATTEMPT:** On October 14, 1912, former President Theodore Roosevelt was campaigning for a third term in Milwaukee, Wisconsin, running as the Progressive Party candidate. Roosevelt was approaching an automobile on his way to a speech when a New Yorker named John Schrank pulled a revolver, pointed it between two spectators, and pulled the trigger. Roosevelt staggered but didn't fall. Although there was no blood, Roosevelt's handlers begged him to go to the hospital. Roosevelt refused. "I shall deliver this speech or die," he reportedly said. And that's what he did; he delivered a fifty-minute speech to a cheering throng at the Milwaukee Auditorium. When he pulled the 100-page speech out of his vest, however, he noticed a bullet hole in it. A bullet had penetrated four inches into his body, right under his right nipple. Finally, after the speech was completed, Roosevelt consented to go to the hospital where he was treated for shock and loss of blood.

**THE MOTIVE:** Schrank claimed that William McKinley, who'd been assassinated in 1901, had revealed in a dream that Teddy Roosevelt was behind his death...and that Schrank should avenge him. Schrank had stalked Roosevelt from New Orleans to Chicago and then to Milwaukee to accomplish this.

**THE SENTENCE:** Schrank was later found guilty of attempted murder, and was sent to an insane asylum where he spent 32 years. He died in 1943.

**THE ATTEMPT:** In 1933, Guiseppe Zangara wanted to kill a president—it didn't matter which one. As it happened, Franklin D. Roosevelt had just defeated Herbert Hoover in the 1932 election and was the new president-elect. So he became Zangara's target.

Roosevelt had just finished giving a speech in Chicago when Zangara approached the podium and fired his revolver five times. One shot hit Anton Cermak, Chicago's mayor; another wounded a spectator seriously. Three others were hit—but Roosevelt was untouched. Reportedly, the mortally wounded Cermak told FDR "better me than you." He died two days after FDR's inauguration.

**THE MOTIVE:** Zangara was a brick-layer who had emigrated from Italy. He was a self-professed anarchist and had previously considered killing Hoover and Calvin Coolidge.

**THE SENTENCE:** Zangara was found guilty of murder and sentenced to the electric chair. In jail, he wrote his autobiography, which ended with "I go contented because I go for my idea. I salute all the poor of the world." On the day of his execution in Florida, Zangara became enraged when he saw that no photographers were present. He reportedly said, "No pictures? All capitalists are a lousy bunch of crooks."

**THE ATTEMPT:** On November 1, 1950, Harry S Truman was taking a nap at the Blair House, his temporary quarters while the White House was being restored. Outside, three policeman and a Secret Service agent were on guard when two men approached the Blair House from different directions, in an attempt to kill Truman. The first, Oscar Collazo, tried to shoot an officer, but the gun didn't fire. He eventually shot the guard in the leg and ran for the steps. Meanwhile, the other conspirator, Griselio Torresola, approached and fired at an officer, Leslie Coffert, who was hit but managed to shoot Torresola in the head. Both Coffert and Torresola died later.

**THE MOTIVE:** Collazo, who suffered slight injuries, later stood trial. He claimed that he and Terresola—both of whom were Puerto Rican—were fighting for Puerto Rico's independence, and hoped to get attention for their cause by assassinating Truman.

**THE SENTENCE:** He was found guilty and sentenced to death. In a surprise move, Truman commuted Collazo's sentence to life in prison eight days before he was scheduled to die.

**THE ATTEMPT:** On September 5, 1975, Lynette "Squeaky" Fromme drew a Colt .45 loaded with four bullets and aimed it at President Gerald Ford during a campaign stop in Sacramento, California. Fromme managed to squeeze the trigger but the firing chamber was empty. She was wrestled to the ground by Secret Service agents.

**THE MOTIVE:** Fromme, a follower of Charles Manson, had once declared, "I'll die for Charlie; I'll kill for him, I'll do whatever is necessary."

**THE SENTENCE:** She was tried under the post-JFK-assassination law that made any attempt on a president's life a Federal offense. She was found guilty and imprisoned. On December 24, 1987, Fromme escaped from a West Virginia prison, after hearing a rumor that Manson was dying and wanted to see her. Two days later she was apprehended on a country road.

**THE ATTEMPT:** On September 22, 1975, a few weeks after Fromme's attempt on Ford's life, another woman in California attempted to kill the president. The woman was Sarah Jane Moore, a 45-year old police and FBI informant, who, only the day before, had been interrogated by the police for threatening the president's life (they confiscated her .44 gun). Moore's shot at Ford was deflected by a bystander in the crowd who knocked her arm as she pulled the trigger of her .38. The shot ricocheted off a concrete wall and slightly injured a nearby cab driver.

**THE MOTIVE:** Moore later claimed, "it was kind of an ultimate protest against the system."

**THE SENTENCE:** She was convicted and jailed. Like Fromme, Moore made a jail break in 1979 but was later apprehended.

**THE ATTEMPT:** On March 29, 1981, John Hinckley arrived in Washington, D.C. after a three-day cross-country bus trip from Los Angeles. The next day he checked out of his hotel, went over the Washington Hilton and waited for President Reagan to come out after a speech to union representatives. When Reagan emerged from the hotel, Hinckley drew out a .22 caliber "Saturday Night Special" and fired six Devastator bullets. One shot ricocheted off a waiting limousine and struck Reagan, who later recovered.

**THE MOTIVE:** Apparently, it was a "gift of love" to actress Jody Foster. Hinckley left a note to Foster which said "there is a definite possibility that I will be killed in my attempt to get Reagan...I'm asking you to please look into your heart and at least give me the chance with this historical deed to gain your respect and love."

**THE SENTENCE:** On June 21, 1982, Hinckley was found "not guilty" of attempting to assassinate the president for reasons of insanity and was admitted to St. Elizabeth's Hospital in Washington.

**P.S.** There is no precedent for letting attempted assassins out of jail. None have ever been released from custody alive.

## A LITTLE MORE PRESIDENTIAL TRIVIA

**From Sid Frank and Arden Davis Melick's book *Presidents: Tidbits and Trivia*:** "On April 10, 1865, Washington crowds, overjoyed at the news of Robert E. Lee's surrender, surged around the White House, cheering and calling for the President to make a speech.

"Abraham Lincoln appeared, quieted the throng, and promised to make a few remarks. But first, he said, turning toward the members of a band which was at the scene, he had a request. He would like the band to play 'Dixie.'

" 'Dixie?' The Confederate song? Why 'Dixie?' The crowd stirred restlessly. Was this another of Lincoln's jokes?

" ' "Dixie," ' he said, 'is one of the best tunes I have ever heard, and now we have captured it.' A mighty cheer went up from the crowd and the band played 'Dixie.' "

**Check a map: Reno, Nevada is west of Los Angeles, California.**

# TRAVELS WITH RAY

*Perplexing adventures of the brilliant egghead Ray "Weird Brain" Redel. Answers are on page 672.*

One morning, "Weird Brain" Redel, the most renowned thinker of our time, called and asked if I wanted to go to the gym with him and lift weights. I have to admit that weight-lifting isn't really my bag, but the prospect of spending a few hours with a brilliant man like "Weird Brain" was too good to pass up. I agreed.

When we got there, I discovered that our trainer for the day was Charles Atlas—the guy I used to see on the back of comic books. Wow!

But even Mr. Atlas, who taught thousands of people how to keep bullies from kicking sand in their faces, couldn't resist trying push "Weird Brain" around with a little weightlifter's riddle. "Okay Brain," he said to his old buddy, "try this one: *Light as a feather, Nothing in it, But a big guy can't hold it for more than a minute.*"

"Weird Brain" rolled his eyes and said, "Charlie, you ask me that every time I come to the gym. It's the same answer as last week."

**What WAS the answer?**

When my friend, "Weird Brain" Redel returned from the month-long Western Hemisphere Egghead Conference in Panama, I picked him up at the airport.

"I hope you brought your 1953 Chevy panel truck," he said.

"Of course I did," I replied; "You asked me to on the phone. But I don't understand why."

"Well," "Weird Brain" explained, "As you know, I had my new pre-sotonic-zorperator along, and the only thing I could find that was big enough and padded enough to ship it in was..." I saw that horrible gleam in his eye, and I knew he was going to answer me in a riddle. "Was *what?*' I shuddered. He replied: "*The man who made it didn't want it, the man who bought it didn't use it, the man who used it didn't know it.*"

**What did "Weird Brain" use for a shipping crate?**

# INVASION! PART II

*Most invasions of the U.S. aren't any big deal, except as foot-notes in history...and as excellent bathroom reading (although we're sure that wasn't on anyone's mind at the time). Take these invasions, for example:*

**THE INVADERS:** Pancho Villa and his guerilla army.

**THE DATE:** March 9, 1916.

**BACKGROUND:** Many folk heroes—Emiliano Zapata and Albert Obregon, for instance—emerged during the Mexican revolution in 1910. But the most notorious was a former cattle rustler named Francisco "Pancho" Villa. To the people of Chihuahua, Mexico's largest state, he and his guerilla army of 40,000 men seemed like Robin Hood, stealing from rich landlords and giving to the poor.

At first, the U.S. government supported Villa and his outlaw army. But after the war was won, Washington was forced to ally itself with a single faction of the splintered Mexican revolutionary movement...and it chose Villa's rival, Venustian Carranza. Villa was furious. He felt betrayed, and decided to retaliate against the U.S.

**THE INVASION:** Villa led an army of 1500 guerrillas across the border and attacked the 13th U.S. Cavalry in Columbus, New Mexico. During the raid, Villa's men killed 18 Americans, burned down several buildings, and stole a quantity of weapons. But as they retreated across the border into Mexico, 50 of Villa's troops were killed by U.S. Army personnel.

**AFTERMATH:** The American public was seething. U.S. president Woodrow Wilson responded to the attack by ordering John J. "Black Jack" Pershing to cross the Mexican border and capture Villa. The so-called "Punitive Expedition" was a dismal failure; the nimble Villa eluded Pershing's troops. Months later, the American army gave up and retreated emptyhanded. Pershing later claimed the campaign had given his men field experience for future battles in World War I.

Villa was assassinated in Parral, South Chihuahua in 1923.

**THE INVADERS:** Eight Nazi terrorists.

**THE DATES:** June 13 and June 17, 1942.

**BACKGROUND:** In early 1942, German U-boats were a menacing presence in the waters off the East Coast. Fearing a secret Nazi invasion, the U.S. ordered the approaches to harbors in New York, Boston, and Portland, Maine to be mined.

U.S. authorities had no inkling, however, that the invasion being planned by Nazi strategists involved only eight men—specially trained terrorists with instructions to bomb selected factories and bridges and shake the confidence of the American public.

**THE INVASION:** On the night of June 13, four Nazi agents rowed a collapsible boat from a German U-boat to a beach in Amagansett, Long Island. Fortunately for the U.S. John C. Cullen, a 21-year-old second class seaman in the Coast Guard, stumbled onto the four Germans while patrolling the beach. The nervous Nazis claimed to be shipwrecked fisherman.

Cullen was suspicious, particularly when the group's leader, Johann Dasch, tried to bribe Cullen with $300 to shut up. Cullen took the money and rushed back to Coast Guard headquarters to tell his superiors. The FBI instantly rushed in and found a cache of weapons and explosives that the Germans had buried on the beach. An extensive search was conducted but the agents had already fled.

Four days later, another Nazi foursome landed without detection on the beach of Ponte Vedra, Florida.

**AFTERMATH:** Dasch, leader of the Nazi mission, was unnerved by his run-in with Cullen. The Nazi spy convinced his partner E.P Burger to abandon their intricately conceived plan. The duo traveled to Washington, D.C., and turned themselves in to the FBI.

Thanks to Dasch's information, FBI officials tracked down the other six Nazis before they could carry out their mission. Dasch and Burger were sentenced to jail (Truman later commuted their sentences and sent them back to Germany, where Dasch wrote a book about the mission). The other six were executed within a month of their capture, before the public was informed.

**BEN FRANKLIN SPEAKLIN':** "Our Constitution is in actual operation; everything promises that it will last; but in this world nothing is certain but death and taxes."

# DISNEY STORIES: CINDERELLA

*In 1949, Uncle Walt released the musical cartoon version of Cinderella, which "combined realism with caricature." The people—Cinderella, her family, and the Prince, were drawn from life; the animals were just cartoon characters. Of course, the Disney version and the original story were substantially different. Here are Jim Morton's examples of how the tale was changed:*

## THE DISNEY VERSION

Cinderella is horribly mistreated by her mean step-mother and step-sisters. She's stuck dreaming while she scrubs floors.

• When the Prince holds a ball for the women of the Kingdom, trying to find a wife, Cinderella isn't allowed to go—she has to finish her chores. But Cinderella's Fairy Godmother appears. With her magic wand (bibbety, bobbety, boo), the Fairy turns a pumpkin into a coach and makes a beautiful gown for the girl. She warns Cinderella to be home by midnight; that's when the spell wears off.

• When the Prince sees Cinderella he immediately falls in love, and spends the entire evening with her. Cinderella loses all track of time; before she knows it, the clock strikes twelve. She flees the palace, leaving behind only a glass slipper.

• The Prince searches his Kingdom for the woman whose foot fits the glass slipper. The step-sisters try to squeeze into it, but can't. When Cinderella tries it on, the Prince realizes she's the one he's looking for. They marry and live happily ever after.

## THE ORIGINAL STORY

• Most people don't realize there are two popular versions of Cinderella (it's actually a very old folktale, and there are dozens of variations all over Europe). Disney's film is a remarkably accurate retelling of Charles Perrault's version. But what about kids who don't have the Perrault fairy tales around the house and turn, instead, to the Brothers Grimm version? Boy, are they in for a surprise!

• The differences between the Perrault and the Grimm versions are startling. The Grimm tale is so gruesome it approaches Grand Guignol, and has more in common with Alfred Hitchcock's *The Birds* than it does with the Disney film.

• There is no Fairy Godmother in the Grimm story. Cinderella is helped by two pigeons, who bring her a gown and slippers, and help with her chores. The slippers in the Grimm version are gold, not glass. (In other versions, the slippers are made of fur.)

• It's not a ball, but a three-day festival, that Cinderella attends. So the Prince has three chances to find her, and narrows the search down to one household—he doesn't have to try the shoe on every woman in the kingdom. (Cinderella doesn't lose her slipper by chance, either. On the third day of the festival, the Prince, after losing Cinderella on two previous occasions, has the palace stairway coated with pitch.)

• When the Prince tries the gold slipper on Cinderella's stepsisters, the shoe is too small. The first step-sister cuts her big toe off to get her foot into the slipper. The second step-sister cuts her heel off to fit into the slipper. Each time, the blood on the slipper (pointed out by the two pigeons) betrays the women. Finally the Prince tries the slipper on Cinderella, and of course, it fits.

• Cinderella and the Prince marry, and at Cinderella's wedding, the pigeons appear once more and peck out the eyes of the two step-sisters. Gruesome.

## SAMPLE PASSAGE (FROM THE GRIMM VERSION)

*The Prince brings the gold slipper to Cinderella's house, and the step-sister tries it on first.*

"The oldest took the shoe into a room to try it on, and her mother stood by her side. However, the shoe was too small for her, and she could not get her big toe into it. So her mother handed her a knife and said, 'Cut your toe off. Once you become Queen, you won't have to walk anymore.'

"The maiden cut her toe off, forced her foot into the shoe, and went out to the Prince. He took her on his horse as his bride, and rode off. But they had to pass the grave where the two pigeons were sitting on the hazel tree, and they cried out: *'Looky, look, look, At the shoe that she took; There's blood all over, and her foot's too small. She's not the bride you met at the ball.'* "

# FILM TERMS

*Every business has its slang. Here are some of the terms movie people use, some of which you've probably seen on screen.*

**Annie Oakley:** A free ticket to a movie screening.
**Apple Box:** A box that actors stand on while filming a scene.
**Best Boy:** Assistant to the head gaffer (see gaffer).
**Clapsticks:** The wood sticks that are struck together to signify the beginning of filming a scene.
**Click Track:** Audible click used in musical scoring.
**Dolly Shot:** Wheeling the camera on tracks for motion in a film shot.
**Dope Sheet:** Storyboards (see storyboards) used in animation films.
**Final Cut:** The last edited version of a film ready for release.
**Gaffer:** Electrician on a film set.
**The Grip:** Head fix-it person on the set.
**Juicer:** Electrician in charge of the main power source.
**Lap Dissolve:** Editing together two shots, one fading in, the other fading out.
**Matte Shot:** Film editing technique where foreground and background images are placed together to form one shot.
**Oater:** A Western.
**Outtake:** Footage not used in final cut.
**P-O-V:** Acronym for point-of-view. Camera is positioned to simulate a character's line of sight.
**Rear Projection:** Cost-cutting filming technique where actors stand in front of a projection on a translucent screen.
**Rushes:** Daily screenings of footage from a work-in-progress.
**SFX:** Acronymn for sound effects.
**Sky Pan:** Huge floodlights used for large areas to be lit.
**Slate:** Board used with clapsticks (see left column) to identify scenes during editing.
**Splice:** Editing two pieces of film together.
**Space Opera:** Slang for science fiction film.
**Storyboards:** Sketches drawn to depict, shot-for-shot, the action to be filmed.
**Swish Pan:** Rapid camera movement causing a blurring sensation.
**Weenie:** A plot device that is considered to be a gimmick.
**Walla Walla:** Background noise in a scene.

# CARTOON CORNER

*Miscellaneous facts about your favorite cartoon characters.*

**DAFFY DUCK**

Daffy first appeared in the 1937 cartoon, "Porky's Duck Hunt." According to animator / director Chuck Jones in *Chuck Amuck*, he and his co-workers were looking for a voice to complete this new character—"a duck who enjoyed being nutty." While they were brainstorming, someone did an impression of their boss, producer Leon Schlesinger, who had a heavy lisp. Pressed for time, the crew impulsively decided to use that voice.

It wasn't until later that it occured to them what they'd done. Schlesinger would have to screen the cartoon and approve the new character—lisp and all. He wasn't going to think it was funny to hear his own voice coming from the duck.

Expecting to be fired, the animators wrote out their resignations and took them to the cartoon's first screening. Schlesinger arrived, the lights were dimmed, and at the producer's cry of "Roll the garbage!" Daffy Duck lit up the screen. A few minutes later, the lights went back on and all eyes focused on Schlesinger. His reaction? Jones recalls: "He said, 'Jesus Crithe, that's a funny voithe! Where'd you get that voithe?' "...He didn't have a clue!

**FELIX THE CAT**

You may find it hard to believe, but Felix was the first cartoon superstar—the Mickey Mouse of the silent film years. In 1919 he appeared in a short called "Feline Follies," and was so popular that Pat Sullivan's production studio could barely keep up with the demand. They turned out 26 cartoons a year—one every two weeks. Among Felix's early achievements:

- In 1922 he appeared as the New York Yankees' lucky mascot.
- In 1923, he shared the screen with Charlie Chaplin.
- In 1927, a Felix doll was Charles Lindbergh's companion on his historic trans-Atlantic flight.
- In 1928, he became the first image ever to appear on TV. When the first experimental television broadcast occurred, the subject was a Felix doll.

So what happened? Why didn't Felix remain popular? Like a lot of movie-industry people, Felix's owner, Pat Sullivan didn't believe in "talkies." So silent star Felix the Cat was eclipsed by the new talking cartoons.

### YOGI BEAR

When Hanna-Barbera produced Jellystone's smarter-than-the-average-bear, New York Yankees catcher Yogi Berra threatened to sue them. The grounds: Among other things, defamation of character. Although everyone in America made the connection between Yogi and Yogi, a Hanna-Barbera executive producer swore "it was just a coincidence." He said the character was inspired by Ed Norton (Art Carney), the next-door neighbor in "The Honeymooners."

### HUEY, LOUIE, & DEWEY

This is one of the greatest "naming" stories we've ever heard. It comes from a fascinating book called *Cartoon Monickers*, by Walter M. Brasch.

"One day in the late 1930s, Harry Reeves, a gagman working on the Donald Duck cartoons, burst into the work area of Jim Carmichael, a layout man, proclaiming, 'Jim, we've got three new characters. Donald's nephews. And we're gonna work them into a lot of screwy situations with the duck. But we haven't got name for 'em. Got any ideas for naming three cute li'l ducks?"

"Carmichael recalls that he 'wasn't too interested that morning in the nomenclature of three cute li'l ducks, so I glanced at the front page of the newspaper...Thomas E. Dewey was doing something political in New York, and Huey P. Long was blabbering in New Orleans. So, off-handedly, I said, 'Why don't you call them Huey and Dewey?' A friend, Louie Schmitt, was passing in the hall and gave a big hello. Inspired, I said, 'Hell, call the little clunkers Huey, Louie, and Dewey.' Harry leaped up, yelping 'That's it!' "

### POPEYE

The sailor man was a popular comic strip character before he made his screen appearance—in an early '30s Betty Boop cartoon. A few years later, in 1936, he won an Oscar for *Sinbad the Sailor*. If the dialogue between Popeye and Olive Oyle often seems informal, it's because a lot of it was ad-libbed.

**Spectators drink more than 1,800 gallons of mint julips at each Kentucky Derby.**

# THE OLD BALL GAME

*Baseball's unofficial anthem, "Take Me Out To The Ballgame," is one of the best-known songs in America. But only a few trivia buffs know the story behind it. Here it is:*

**THE WORDS:** In the summer of 1908, a vaudevillian named Jack Norworth was riding the New York City subway when he noticed an advertisement that read "Baseball Today—Polo Grounds." He'd never been to a baseball game, but he knew the sport was getting popular...and it hit him that a baseball song might fit into his act. Inspired, he jotted down some lyrics about a woman named Katie who was crazy about baseball games.

**THE MUSIC:** Norworth rushed to the office of a music-publisher friend named Albert von Tilzer. Von Tilzer had never seen a baseball game either, but he quickly set the words to music.

**THE FLOP:** Norworth was convinced he had a hit...But when he sang "Take Me Out To The Ballgame" during his vaudeville act in Brooklyn that night, the crowd seemed bored. No one complained ...but no one paid much attention to it, either.

**THE HIT:** So Norworth tried a different approach; he turned the song into a "Nickelodeon slide show"—a sort of turn-of-the-century MTV. Slide shows, featuring sing-along lyrics and illustrations (in this case, photos of pretty Miss Katie Casey at a Polo Grounds game), were shown at movie theaters between films. Audiences "followed the bouncing ball," and sang along. Norworth's ploy worked. "Take Me Out To The Ballgame" became a hit. Ironically, it wasn't until *after* the song was popular that Norworth finally went to an "old ballgame."

**THE MISSING LINK:** Everybody knows the chorus to "Take Me Out To The Ballgame." But here are the verses: *Katie Casey was baseball mad. Had the fever and had it bad. Just to root for the hometown crew, Ev'ry sou, Katie blew. On a Saturday her young beau, Called to see if she'd like to go. To see a show but Miss Kate said "No I tell you what you can do..."*

# LOOSE ENDS

*What would a Bathroom Reader be without flushing out some new information on toilets?*

## TOILET ART

Two toilets have figured prominently in the art world:

• Marcel Duchamp rocked the art world in 1917 when he made a urinal into sculpture by turning it upside down and signing it "R. Mutt." The piece, entitled "The Fountain," upset an art committee's dignified sensibilites—they refused to exhibit it. According to the *New York Times*, however, the work "is now considered a masterwork," although it exists only in a photograph taken by Alfred Stieglitz.

• Another "art toilet" surfaced in 1985 when a three-hole outhouse seat was discovered to have been "painted" by famed artist Willem de Kooning in 1954. Apparently, de Kooning splattered some paint on the seat to make it resemble a marble surface as a joke for a party he was throwing in a rented home in Bridgehampton, New York. An art dealer spotted the 22" X 99" toilet seat in an auction, and bought it for $50. Theoretically, the three-seater could be worth millions, which is how much de Kooning's regular work sells for.

## LOOK OUT BELOW

Gene Gordon of Fort Worth, Texas was in his backyard in late 1987 when he heard a loud bang in his house. He checked it out, and found a large hole in his roof and chunks of blue ice melting in his attic. After an investigation, it was determined that the ice originated from an airplane toilet. Apparently, blue cleaning fluid had leaked from the airplane's toilet, frozen in mid-air, and dropped to earth.

## THE BOTTOM LINE

• In 1985, Lockheed Corporation charged the U.S. government $34,560 for 54 toilet seats (or about $600 a piece) for the Navy's P-3C Orion anti-submarine planes. When government officals told

Lockheed that the same seat could be purchased by mobile-home owners for $25, the price was lowered to $100 apiece.

• The most expensive toilet ever made was the one developed for the space shuttle. The price tag for NASA's waste collector: $3,000,000.

## LOO-SELY SPEAKING

The popular British slang for *toilet* is the "loo." Where did the term come from? One theory suggests its roots are in a pay toilet with an L-shaped handle followed by two O-shaped coin slots—spelling out the word "loo." A more plausible explanation: it derives from the phrase "gardyloo," which Scottish people shouted before throwing trash out of the window and onto the street. Another longshot: it's a pun on the words "water closet" and "Waterloo."

## EXPENSIVE TOILET PAPER

Billy Edd Wheeler, the country songwriter who penned "Coward of the County" for Kenny Rogers, also wrote a little gem of a book called *Outhouse Humor* (published by August House).

Here's a sample joke from the volume:

"At a filling station near Bland, Virginia, before they got indoor plumbing, customers had to use the outhouse if they wanted to go to the bathroom.

Actually, they had two outhouses under one roof, with side doors, but they were separated in the middle only by a partition built about a foot off the floor, and running up to about six feet...similar to the rows of stalls in restrooms in airports.

One time two men were in this outhouse at the same time. After one man finished going he noticed there wasn't any toilet paper left on the spool, so he pecked on the wall and said, 'Hey bud, would you kindly share some of your paper with me? This one's empty over here.' The voice came back from the other side: 'Sorry, pal, but there ain't much left over here, either. I'm afraid there's just enough for me.'

A few minutes passed. There was another peck on the wall, and the first man said, 'Uh, buddy...you ain't got five ones for a five, have you? Or maybe two fives for a ten?' "

**Among American cash crops, marijuana outranks corn in yearly value.**

# BLUE SUEDE SHOES

*And now, the mystery of the most famous pair of shoes in rock 'n' roll history.*

Pop culture is full of contradictions. Stories about the beginnings of fads, products, books and songs are fun to tell, but you can't be sure if they're true. To illustrate the point, here are two versions of the origin of the rock'n'roll classic, "Blue Suede Shoes," each told by believable sources. One, Carl Perkins, wrote the tune. The other, Johnny Cash, has been a friend of Perkins' since the days when "Blue Suede" was recorded. If anyone should know the story, Carl should. But Johnny Cash seems to be pretty sure about his version, too. We'll never know exactly which of these stories is true.

**STORY A—*"Blue Suede Shoes," according to Carl Perkins*:** On December 4, 1955, a Jackson, Tennessee musician named Carl Perkins played at a local dance tht changed his life. "[I was] playin' a club in my hometown," he remembers, "for a high school sorority dance. A beautiful girl was dancin' with a boy who had on a pair of blue suede shoes...He said, 'Uh-uh, don't step on my suedes!' "

Carl couldn't believe it—this kid was with a gorgeous girl, but all he cared about were his shoes! What a nut! When the dance ended, Perkins went home and went to sleep. And then at 3:00 A.M. he suddenly awoke with a song in his head. He jumped out of bed, grabbed the first piece of paper he could find—which happened to be a brown paper potato sack—and wrote down the lyrics to "Blue Suede Shoes."

**STORY B—*"Blue Suede Shoes," according to Johnny Cash*:** Carl Perkins and Johnny Cash were part of Sam Phillips' fabled Sun Records stable, which included Jerry Lee Lewis, Roy Orbison, and a certain Mr. Elvis Presley. One night, Cash, Presley and Perkins were performing in Amory, Mississippi. Cash and Perkins had already done their shows and Presley was onstage. In the wings, Cash told Perkins that he really had a "feel for the 'bop' kind of song," and asked why didn't he record one? Perkins said he'd tried, but he could never come up with the right song. So Cash gave him an idea for a tune. He told Carl a story about his Air Force days. His sergeant, Cash said, was a black man named C. V. White, who was always immaculately dressed. White would come into Cash's room and ask how he looked. After Cash replied, White would say, "Just don't step on my blue suede shoes," and leave the room. Cash would yell after him that those were Air Force regulation shoes, not blue suede, and White would say, "Tonight when I get to town they're gonna be blue suede, man!" Perkins exclaimed, "That's a great idea for a bop song!" He grabbed a pencil and before Elvis was offstage, Perkins had written it.

**FOR THE RECORD**

• The original intro was "One for the money, two for the show, three to get ready and go, man, go." As they were recording, Perkins said "Go, cat, go" instead. The record producer asked, "This word 'cat,' what did you mean?" Perkins: "I have no idea where it came from." "Cat" was actually a slang word for "black person."

• Released on New Year's Day, 1956, "Blue Suede" took about three months to break out of the South. By March it was headed for the top of all three music charts (Pop, Country, R&B). But as Perkins was driving to appear on "The Perry Como Show," where he was to make his first national appearance and receive his gold record for "Blue Suede," he got into a serious car accident that killed one of his brothers and put him in the hospital. His interrupted career was never the same again.

**THE TOP FIVE—Week of April 21, 1956**

1. **Heartbreak Hotel**
   —*Elvis Presley*
2. **Hot Diggity Dog/Jukebox Baby**
   —*Perry Como*
3. **Poor People of Paris**
   —*Les Baxter*
4. **Blue Suede Shoes**
   —*Carl Perkins*
5. **Lisbon Antiqua**
   —*Nelson Riddle & His Orchestra*

# PRIMETIME PROVERBS

*Here are some more TV quotes from the book* Primetime Proverbs, *by Jack Mingo and John Javna.*

ON GOD

"God don't make no mistakes —that's how he got to be God."

—Archie Bunker,
***All in the Family***

"Well, I certainly don't believe God's a woman, because if He were, men would be the ones walking around wearing high heels, taking Midol, and having their upper lips waxed."

—Julia Sugarbaker,
***Designing Women***

Archie Bunker: "All the pictures I ever seen, God is white."
George Jefferson: "Maybe you were looking at the negatives."

—***All in the Family***

ON BOOZE

"Never cry over spilt milk. It could've been whiskey."

—Pappy Maverick,
***Maverick***

"Oh, I just adore beer. It's so... so...democratic."

—Kookie's Girlfriend,
***77 Sunset Strip***

ON THE ARMY

"What other job lets you die for a living?"

—Hawkeye Pierce,
**M*A*S*H***

THE RICH

"He's got a purse the size of an elephant's scrotum, and it's just as hard to get your hands on."

—Edmund Blackadder,
***Blackadder II***

[*To Mama's rich boyfriend*]
"It's a pleasure to meet a man of your charming credit rating."

—Kingfish,
***Amos'n'Andy***

SKEWERED SAYINGS

"You've buttered your bread, now sleep in it."

—Gracie Allen,
***The George Burns and Gracie Allen Show***

"People in stucco houses should not throw quiche."

—Sonny Crockett,
***Miami Vice***

**Your place or mine? The waiting list for an apartment in Poland is 20 years.**

# BEWITCHED

*From 1964 to 1972, Elizabeth Montgomery starred in TV's "Bewitched" as Samantha Stevens, the perky blonde housewitch who could take care of household chores with a twitch of her nose.*

## HOW IT STARTED

In 1942, Veronica Lake starred in the title role of a movie comedy called *I Married a Witch*. The plot: an upright, middle-class American guy discovers his bride is literally an enchanting young woman.

In 1958, Kim Novak played a witch with her sights set on future husband James Stewart in the romantic comedy, *Bell, Book and Candle*.

In 1963, William Dozier and Harry Ackerman, two executives at Screen Gems TV, decided to make a suburban family sitcom with a "brand new" twist: The husband unwittingly marries a pretty, young witch. Well it was new for TV, anyway.

They wrote the pilot script and took it to Tammy Grimes, an English actress who'd been starring in Broadway's "The Unsinkable Molly Brown." Grimes had a TV contract with Screen Gems, didn't like the script, but she refused to say whether she'd do the show or not. "Why not rewrite it," she suggested, infuriating Dozier. But he obliged; commissioning a new script.

While he was waiting, Dozier got a call from an old friend he'd been dying to work with—Liz Montgomery. Liz, it seems, had fallen in love with a TV director named William Asher and the two of them wanted to spend all their time together—so they were interested in a TV show in which she could star, while he directed. Dozier immediately decided that Montgomery would make the perfect witch, but he couldn't offer her the part in "Bewitched" ("I couldn't even mention it,")—he was already committed to Tammy Grimes.

Fortunately, Grimes didn't like the new script either. She held out for a show in which she played the part of a befuddled English heiress. (It went on the air as "The Tammy Grimes Show," and lasted about two months.) Montgomery, meanwhile, took the part of Samantha, and "Bewitched" became the hottest new show of 1964. It was in the Top 10 for five straight years.

## JUST KIDDING

When filming for the show began, Liz Montgomery was eight months pregnant. So Asher (by now her husband, as well as the director), had to shoot the first five shows without her, adding in her parts later. A few weeks after the baby was born, Montgomery was out on the set making up for lost time.

## THE NOSE KNOWS

Some people can wiggle their ears. Elizabeth Montgomery can wiggle her nose. (It's not as easy as it looks—try it.) "Bewitched" 's producers put the trick to good use by making Sam's nose her magic wand. No one else on the show could do it, so they had to settle for hand gestures, or—in the case of Tabitha (the daughter), moving her nose with her finger.

## MOON SHOT

Agnes Moorhead, who played Sam's mother, Endora, was invited to Cape Kennedy by NASA to witness the Apollo 12 moon flight in 1969. She was the honorary "technical advisor," since, as Endora, she had been on the moon herself. "I distinctly remember," she said, "being on the moon at least 7 times over the past 6 years."

## WHICH WITCH?

Moorhead didn't particulary like being known as "the witch." That was understandable. She was 57 and had been performing for over 50 years when she first appeared as Endora. She had starred in almost 100 films, won an Emmy, and was nominated for 5 Oscars. She died of lung cancer in 1974, ten years later.

## DARRIN'S LUCK

Viewers often ask why there were two different actors playing Darrin Stephens, Samantha's husband. Here's why: After 5 seasons as Darrin, actor Dick York had to withdraw from the series because of serious back pains. It turns out that in 1959, while working on a film with Gary Cooper, he sustained a back injury, tearing all the muscles loose from his spine. Over the years the pain got worse and by the time York got to "Bewitched," the injury had become so debilitating that he missed 14 episodes of the show.Then one day he had a seizure; he was rushed to the hospital and never returned to "Bewitched" again. He was replaced by Dick Sargent.

# FAMOUS LAST WORDS

*When you gotta go, you gotta go. Here are some final quotes from people who really knew how to make an exit.*

"I'll be in hell before you've finished breakfast, boys...Let her rip!"

**—"Black Jack" Ketchum,** ***murderer, before being hanged***

"The Countess Rouen sends her compliments but begs to be excused. She is engaged in dying."

**—The Countess Rouen,** ***in a letter read by her attendant to her guests***

"Go away...I'm alright."

**—H. G. Wells,** ***writer***

"God bless...God damn. . ."

**—James Thurber,** ***writer***

"If this is dying, I don't think much of it."

**—Lytton Strachey,** ***writer***

"Four o'clock. How strange. So that is the time. Strange. Enough."

**—Sir Henry Stanley,** ***explorer***

"You sons of bitches. Give my love to mother."

**—"Two Gun" Crowley,** ***sitting on the electric chair***

"Now comes the mystery."

**—Henry Ward Beecher,** ***preacher***

"Oh God, here I go."

**—Max Baer,** ***boxer***

"Friends applaud, the Comedy is over."

**—Ludwig van Beethoven**

"All my possessions for a moment of time."

**—Elizabeth I,** ***Queen of England***

"And now, in keeping with Channel 40's policy of always bringing you the latest in blood and guts, in living color, you're about to see another first—an attempted suicide."

**—Chris Hubbock,** ***newscaster who shot herself during broadcast***

"Drink to me."

**—Pablo Picasso**

"Why yes— a bullet-proof vest."

**—James Rodgers,** ***murderer, before the firing squad, asked if he had final request***

**Lip Service: Reuters News Service gave its founder a 17-word obituary.**

# ASTEROIDS

*At the B.R.I. Science Department, we have a saying: A day without Bathroom Reading is like a pain in the asteroid. Ah, but what do we really know about asteroids? Read on...*

## BACKGROUND

• Asteroids are collections of rocks and dust half a mile or more in diameter. Scientists theorize they are leftover fragments from the Big Bang.

• Most asteroids orbit the sun in a large belt between Mars and Jupiter. Over a billion fragments reside in the belt, ranging from dust-sized particles to Ceres, an asteroid 637 miles in diameter.

• How do asteroids escape the asteroid belt? Through the Kirkwood Gap, named for Daniel Kirkwood, an American astronomer. He discovered that the belt was separated into two different regions by a mysterious gap. Asteroids that enter the gap shift into an orbit closer to Earth's. One out of five asteroids end up crossing Earth's orbit.

## A MISS IS AS GOOD AS 500,000 MILES

On March 23, 1989, a huge asteroid passed within half a million miles (approximately twice the distance from the Earth to the Moon) of hitting the Earth. If the asteroid, which was traveling at 46,000 miles an hour, had actually crashed into Earth, it would have had a devastating impact, equivalent to exploding 20,000 one-megaton hydrogen bombs.

Scientists later calculated that the asteroid missed the Earth by six hours in its orbit. If it had hit Earth, the crater would have been 10 miles long and one mile deep.

## ASTEROIDS IN THE PAST

• The first scientific finding that proved asteroids were not pieces of alien spacecraft occurred in 1803 in northern France.

• In 1908, an asteroid the size of a small building crashed near the Stony Tunguska River in Siberia. Its force was later measured to be equal to 12 megatons of TNT.

• In 1984, a Japan Air Lines flight saw a mushroom-like cloud 70,000 feet tall and 200 miles wide. The flight landed at a U.S. base in Anchorage, Alaska for fear it had flown through radiation, but no traces were found. Eventually, scientists concluded that the airliner may have passed through a cloud created by an exploding meteor.

• Scientists have found evidence of a huge asteroid collision around 100 miles off the coast of New Jersey from 34 million ago.

• An asteroid named Icarus came within four million miles of hitting Earth in 1968. This "near miss" prompted the notion that nuclear missiles could be deployed to deflect oncoming asteroids. In 1982, a scientific conference in Colorado concluded that a one-kilometer asteroid could be diverted by the using a nuclear device only half the power of the atomic bomb dropped on Hiroshima.

## THE ODDS

• According to the *New York Times*, there are more than 80 asteroids of at least one kilometer that could threaten the Earth. Other scientists estimate there are over 1,000 asteroids with orbits that could collide with Earth's.

• Despite the danger, scientists say the chances of a giant asteroid colliding with Earth in our lifetime are relatively small—it only happens once every 100,000 years or so.

## THE EFFECTS

• Scientists have argued that asteroid impacts in the past may have caused the Earth's magnetic field to reverse, triggering the ice age and ultimately continental drift, the breaking up of the continents 80 million years ago.

• The biggest recorded asteroid hit Earth 66 million years ago and spread lava over India. Some scientists have argued that its enormous impact eventually wiped out the dinosaurs by enveloping the Earth in dust and smoke, causing the Earth to cool.

• The dinosaur/asteroid theory arose after the discovery of the element iridium in the same geologic layers that existed when the dinosaurs disappeared. Iridium is abundant in asteroids.

**On average, Salt Lake City citizens consume more Cracker Jacks than any other Americans.**

# IT'S THE LAW

*Believe it or not, these laws are real.*

In Logan County, Colorado, it's illegal to kiss a sleeping woman.

It's illegal to ride a camel on Nevada highways.

In North Carolina motels, it's a crime to move twin beds together or to make love on the floor.

In Miami, Florida, it's unlawful to imitate an animal.

Women in Morrisville, Pennsylvania, are required by law to purchase a permit before wearing lipstick in public.

Laws in Indianapolis, Indiana, and Eureka, Nevada, make it a crime to kiss if you wear a moustache.

New York City law entitles its horses to a 15 minute "coffee-break" after each two hours of work.

Children are prohibited from doing handstands on Denver, Colorado sidewalks—it might frighten horses.

It's a crime in Zion, Illinois to offer a cigar to a dog, cat, or any pet. No mention of cigarettes or pipes.

Laws in Boston, Massachusetts prohibit sleeping in "day clothes."

If your horse is ugly, the law prohibits you from riding it down a street in Wilbur, Washington.

In Minnesota, it's illegal for a woman to be dressed-up as Santa Claus on city streets.

Kansas law prohibits catching fish with your bare hands.

Arkansas law prohibits schoolteachers with "bob" hairdos from getting raises.

Don't even think about it—*Bull throwing* is illegal in Washington D.C.

You're breaking the law if you're wearing "form-fitting" pants in Lewes, Delaware.

A law in Hartford, Connecticut, prohibits the teaching or education of a dog.

# OPEN & CLOTHED

*A few interesting tidbits about clothing.*

## BLUE FOR BOYS, PINK FOR GIRLS

The blue comes from an ancient superstition—the pink is sort of an afterthought.

According to *How Did They Do That?*, "The choice of blue dates back to ancient times, when evil spirits purportedly plagued young children but could be warded off with certain colors: blue, emblematic of the heavens, had an immanent power to dispel satanic forces (Many Arabs in the Mideast continue to paint their doorways blue.) Since it was of paramount importance to protect little boys, they were clothed in blue, while little girls were left to fend for themselves. Only much later did parents, somewhat guilty about the girls' lack of identity, assign them precious pink."

## SUPERMAN'S CLOTHING

Every time George Reeves, TV's Superman, donned his costume for a public appearance, he risked kicks in the shins, fists in his back, and other assaults by young admirers eager to prove how strong the "Man of Steel" really was.

One afternoon in Detroit in 1953, the costume almost cost Reeves his life. He was making an appearance at a department store when a young fan pulled out his father's loaded .45 Army Colt and pointed it directly at Reeves's chest. Miraculously, Reeves talked the kid into putting it down. He assured the boy that Superman could stand the force of the shot, but "when bullets bounce off my chest, they might hurt you and others around here."

## CHARLIE CHAPLIN'S TRAMP OUTFIT

In 1914, director Mack Sennet told Chaplin to "get into a comedy makeup." He scouted the dressing room and came up with baggy pants and derby belonging to the enormously overweight comedian, Fatty Arbuckle, a cutaway jacket from Roscoe Conklin, and a pair of size-14 shoes from Ford Sterling. They were so big that the only way to keep them on was to wear them on the wrong feet. The cane was the only thing Chaplin actually owned.

**On July 22, 1972, a lady in Rome gave birth to quindecaplets—10 girls and 5 boys.**

# KUNG PHOOEY

*Is it serious philosophy or TV gobbledygook? You be the judge of these quotes from TV's only "Buddhist" western, "Kung Fu."*

"Grasshopper, look beyond the game, as you look beneath the surface of the pool to see its depths."

***—Master Po***

"The caterpillar is secure in the womb of the cocoon. And yet—to achieve its destiny—it must cast off its earthbound burden...to realize the ethereal beauty of the butterfly."

***—Master Po***

**Master Po:** "What have I told you, Grasshopper?"
**Caine:** "That life is a corridor and death merely a door."

"The blossom below the water knows not sunlight. And men, not knowing, will find me hard to understand."

***—Caine***

"Will shooting guns and making bombs make you men and not dogs?"

***—Caine***

"Seek always peace...We are all linked by our souls, and if one is endangered so are all."

**—Caine**

"To seek freedom, a man must struggle. To win it, he must choose wisely where and when he struggles, or it is like spitting in the wind."

***—Caine***

**Caine:** "Master Kan, what is it to be a man?"
**Master Kan:** "To be a man is to be one with the Universe."
**Caine:** "But what is the Universe?"
**Master Kan:** "Rather ask: what is *not* the Universe?"

"Remember always—a wise man walks with his head bowed, humble like the dust."

***—Master Po***

"The power to hope cannot be taken away with guns or fences."

***—Caine***

"Perceive the way of nature and no force of men can harm you. Do not meet a wave head-on, avoid it. You do not have to stop force; it is easier to redirect it."

***—A monk***

**There are twice as many heart attacks in winter as in summer.**

# DON'T LOOK NOW

*Here's a look at a few of the movies that have been banned in the U.S. over the last 75 years.*

**SPIRIT OF '76** (1917). A silent propaganda film made to enlist public support for America's entry into World War I. The film reenacted Revolutionary War events, like Paul Revere's ride and the signing of the Declaration of Independence.

One scene depicted British soldiers attacking women and children. Although the scene was realistic, England was America's ally in the war effort, so it was considered treasonous. Authorities seized the movie, alleging (erroneously) that the movie had been financed by Germans. The film's producer, Robert Goldstein—who later became an executive at 20th Century Fox—was convicted of violating the Espionage Act and was sentenced to jail (his sentence was later commuted by Woodrow Wilson).

**THE NAKED TRUTH** (1924). A silent movie about a man who gets venereal disease and marries. His brain is affected by V.D. and he kills his wife. Nudity, not subject matter, got this film banned in Newark, New Jersey due to a brief scene in which a male and female were shown partially naked.

Note: one of the main figures in the controversy, William J. Brennan (head of Newark's Public Safety Department), was the father of future Supreme Court Justice, William J. Brennan, Jr. Brennan upheld the censorship by refusing to see it and review the case. *The Naked Truth* was also banned in New York.

**THE MAN WITH THE GOLDEN ARM** (1955). Banned in Maryland for depicting drug use. The film, directed by Otto Preminger, was about a card shark (played by Frank Sinatra) who becomes a drug addict. The Maryland Board of Censors suggested that United Artists cut the scene of Sinatra being injected by a drug pusher. According to the *Historical Dictionary of Censorship in the United States*, the state of Maryland "was the only locality that attempted to censor this film: It was exhibited across the United States and Western Europe without problems, and even won a scientific and cultural award in the Netherlands." United Artists sued and a judge reversed the order.

**TITICUT FOLLIES** (1969). A documentary on the horrible conditions in a state prison for the criminally insane in Bridgewater, Massachusetts. Scenes included a forced nose-feeding of an inmate on a hunger strike.

Producer and director Frederick Wiseman received permission to make the film as long as he protected the privacy of the film's subjects. However, when the documentary was shown commercially, the state of Massachusetts filed suit, contending the film had violated their contract and the inmates' privacy. Massachusetts won, and the Supreme Court refused to hear an appeal. The result: The documentary was put under permanent court restrictions. Selected audiences were allowed to view the film as long as profits were put into a trust fund for the inmates.

Wiseman later commented, "There was no evidence introduced at the trial that the film was not an honest portrayal of the conditions...if [then State Attorney General Elliot] Richardson and the other politicians in Massachusetts were genuinely concerned about the privacy and dignity of the inmates of Bridgewater, they would not have allowed the conditions that are shown in the film to exist. They were more concerned about the film and its effect on their reputations than they were about Bridgewater."

**CINDY AND DONNA** (1970). The Sheriff of Pulaski Country, Kentucky went to see this X-rated film at a drive-in. After staying for the entire motion picture, the Sheriff arrested the manager of the theatre and confiscated the film. The manager was convicted of exhibiting an obscene film. He appealed to the Supreme Court, which overturned the conviction on the grounds that no warrant had been served.

**CARNAL KNOWLEDGE** (1971). This film starring Jack Nicholson, Art Garfunkle, Candice Bergen, and Ann-Margaret was a critically-acclaimed drama about two college friends who take different roads in life; one straight, the other a swinger. The state of Georgia ruled that the film was obscene. In 1974, the Supreme Court found that it was not obscene. William Rehnquist delivered the opinion, stating, "the subject of the picture is, in a broad sense,

**Americans eat over 7 billion quarts of popcorn a year. 10% of it is eaten at movie theaters.**

sex...(but) the camera does not focus on the bodies of the actors at such times."

**DEEP THROAT** (1972). The most-banned film in United States history (25 states brought it to trial) starred Linda Lovelace and Harry Reems. The X-rated skin flick was first ruled obscene in Georgia. Lovelace later denounced her role in the film, which made millions at the box-office.

**CALIGULA** (1980). *Penthouse* publisher Bob Guccione produced this screen version of Gore Vidal's novel about the bloody reign of the Roman Empire's fourth Caesar. The film, starring Malcolm McDowell, Sir John Gielgud, and Peter O'Toole (all of whom later officially "disassociated" themselves from the final product),showed explicit sex and violence, earning an X rating. It was banned in Boston and Atlanta, but a judge in Boston refused to uphold an obsenity claim, ruling the subject was related to historical facts. The Supreme Court ruled in 1984, agreeing that the film was not obscene. "Caligula" became the largest-grossing X-rated film ever produced independently, although critics hated it, and at least one of the actresses tried to sue the producer for talking her into performing in an X-rated scene.

## THE WINDY CITY

Chicago is the "Big Banned" of America when it comes to motion pictures. Among the censorship battles that have taken place there:

• Chicago censors denied licenses to show newsreels criticizing Nazi Germany before WWII. They also banned Charlie Chaplin's "The Great Dictator," a parody of Hitler, for fear of upsetting the large German population of the city.

• They banned newsreels which showed scenes of Chicago policemen shooting at union protestors.

• They refused to issue a permit for the movie *Anatomy of a Murder* because the words "rape" and "contraceptive" were used.

• They deleted scenes of a buffalo giving birth in Walt Disney's "Vanishing Prairie," the 1954 Academy Award-winning documentary.

# STENGEL-ESE

*Legendary New York Yankees and Mets manager Casey Stengel offers a few confusing words of wisdom.*

*To a hitter with the bases loaded:* "Let him hit 'ya; I'll get you a new neck."

"There are three things you can do in a baseball game. You can win, or you can lose, or it can rain."

"Now all you fellers line up alphabetically by height."

"You have to have a catcher, because if you don't, the pitch will roll all the way back to the screen."

"They say you can't do it, but sometimes it doesn't always work."

"Look at that guy. Can't run, can't hit, can't catch. Of course, that's why they gave him to us."

*On two 20-year-old players:* "In 10 years, Ed Kranepool has a chance to be a star. In 10 years, Greg Goosen has a chance to be 30."

"We're in such a slump that even the ones that are drinkin' aren't hittin'."

"Good pitching will always stop good hitting, and vice versa."

"I love signing autographs. I'll sign anything but veal cutlets. My ballpoint pen slips on veal cutlets."

"The secret of managing a club is to keep the five guys who hate you away from the five who are undecided."

"The Mets have come along slow, but fast!"

"Being with a woman all night never hurt no professional ballplayer. It's staying up all night looking for a woman that does him in."

"I'll never make the mistake again of being 70 years old."

"They say some of my stars drink whiskey, but I have found that the ones who drink milkshakes don't win many ball games."

"Most ball games are lost, not won."

**The fourth most common language in the U.S. is sign language.**

# MYTH AMERICA

*1992 is the 500th anniversary of Columbus's historic voyage. So it's a good time to clear up a few myths about him.*

**THE MYTH:** Columbus proved the Earth was round.
**THE TRUTH:** The ancient Greeks knew the world wasn't flat two thousand years before Columbus was born. Pythagoras came up with the theory in the in sixth century B.C., and Ptolemy proved it in the second century A.D. Before Columbus even left on his first voyage to the New World, he studied globes and maps depicting a round planet. He had a hard time finding funding for his voyage, not because his contemporaries thought he would sail off the earth's edge, but because they thought the Orient was too far to reach by sailing west.

**THE MYTH:** He was the first European to discover North America.
**THE TRUTH:** Columbus never even set foot on the North American continent. The closest he ever came was the islands of the Caribbean and South America. The America whose "discovery" we celebrate is actually a tiny island near San Salvador, which was already inhabited anyway. Even Columbus wouldn't take credit for discovering a new continent—he died thinking he he had reached India. Actually, the Vikings were the first Europeans to reach North America, around 1000 A.D.

**THE MYTH:** Columbus was a friend to the Indians.
**THE TRUTH:** Sad to say, that's not even close. Take his Haitian exploits for example: According to historian Howard Zinn, Arawak Indians who didn't honor Columbus and his crew with regular contributions of gold "had their hands cut off and bled to death." After two years, half of Haiti's 250,000 inhabitants were dead "through murder, mutilation, or suicide." Many of the native Indians who survived were enslaved and brought back to Spain. "Let us in the name of the Holy Trinity, go on sending all the slaves that can be sold," Columbus wrote.

# MILITARY DOUBLE-TALK

*What is the Pentagon spending our money on this year? See if you can figure it out. Try to match these official U.S.military terms with their civilian meanings.*
*Answers on page 674.*

1. "Interlocking slide fastener."
2. "Portable hand-held communications transcriber."
3. "Weapons system."
4. "Hexiform rotatable surface compression unit."
5. "Special weapon."
6. "Habitability improvements."
7. "Vertically deployed anti-personnel device."
8. "Aerodynamic personnel decelerator."
9. "Wood interdental stimulator."
10. "Universal obscurant."
11. "Kinetic kill vehicle launcher."
12. "Missionized crew station."
13. "Radiation enhancement weapon."
14. "Interfibrous friction fastener."

**A.** Neutron bomb

**B.** Hammer

**C.** Parachute

**D.** Toothpick

**E.** Cockpit

**F.** Smoke from smoke bombs

**G.** Steel nut

**H.** Anti-satellite weapon

**I.** Bayonet

**J.** Pencil

**K.** Zipper

**L.** Atomic bomb

**M.** Furniture

**N.** Bomb

**Forty percent of Americans have never visited a dentist.**

# YOU BE THE JUDGE

*On July 20, 1969, Neil Armstrong became the first human being to set foot on the moon. But his famous comment, "That's one small step for man, one giant leap for mankind" has caused some controversy. Did he write the words himself...or did someone at NASA slip him the line? No one knows for sure, but here are some clues that may help you decide for yourself.*

**CLUE #1**

The quote doesn't make sense. Apparently, Armstrong meant to say "one small step for a man" instead of "one small step for man." What are the odds that he would have misquoted himself? (Armstrong claims he said "one small step for a man" but the "a" dropped out during transmission).

**CLUE #2**

In 1983, Armstrong told *Esquire* that he made the words up after—not before—landing on the Moon. With all the pressure and details to take care of, how likely is it that he could have come up with such an eloquent phrase?

**CLUE #3**

The quote—with the correct "a" included—appeared on a NASA press blackboard only minutes after Armstrong uttered the words. Did NASA know in advance about the quote?...And if so, doesn't that contradict Armstrong's own testimony?

**CLUE #4**

Armstrong is often described as the archtypical "strong and silent type." Many thought the words didn't sound like something he'd ordinarily say. Wouldn't Armstrong have asked a writer to help coin a phrase for such a momentous event?

**CLUE #5**

Space flight is a highly regimented process. Would NASA allow an

**Ho, Ho, Ho: Americans use as many artificial Christmas trees as real ones.**

astronaut to write the history of the space agency's finest hour with just anything that came into his mind? Don't forget—billions of people were watching and listening.

### CLUE #6

One writer, Oriana Fallaci, tried to prove Armstrong would not have been allowed to improvise on the spot. She bet astronaut Pete Conrad that he wouldn't be allowed to say "It may be a small step for Neil, but it's a big step for a little fellow like me" during the Apollo 12 mission. But Conrad did say the words (he claims Fallaci never paid up the $500 bet).

### YOU BE THE JUDGE

No one's ever proven whether or not Armstrong authored the phrase. Buzz Aldrin, his Apollo moonwalking partner, has defended Armstrong. So has every NASA official. What do you think?

★ ★ ★

### MORE JUNK ABOUT SPACE JUNK

• After only a handful of human visits, the moon is already littered. Apollo astronauts left behind a space buggy, camera equipment (worth $5,000,000) and the two golf balls that Alan Shepard hit.

• On the average, more than three man-made objects crash into Earth each week.

• In 1969, five crewmen on a Japanese freighter in the Sea of Japan were seriously injured after debris from a Soviet spacecraft crashed into their ship.

• Thus far, the most famous object to fall to earth was the 78-ton U.S. Skylab, which caused a world scare during the days leading up to its reentry. Despite an international scare, the debris from Skylab did not kill anybody; instead it exploded over the Indian Ocean and the Australian Outback. The debris from Skylab was considered public domain; i.e., finders, keepers. A 17-year truck driver named Stan Thornton won a $10,000 prize from the *San Francisco Examiner* by being the first person to turn in a piece of Skylab.

# EDISON ENLIGHTENS

*Thomas Edison was a genius inventor who gave us the electric light, the phonograph, and movies. He also gave most of the credit for his accomplishments to hard work, not brilliance. Some of his ideas:*

"Genius is one percent inspiration and ninety-nine percent perspiration."

"The chief function of your body is to carry your brain around."

"We don't know a millionth of one percent about anything."

"Restlessness and discontent are the first necessities of progress."

"I am glad that the eight-hour day had not been invented when I was a young man. If my life had been made up of eight-hour days I do not believe I could have accomplished a great deal. This country would not amount to as much as it does...if the young men had been afraid that they might earn more than they were paid."

"I am long on ideas, but short on time. I expect to live to be only about a hundred."

"The inventor tries to meet the demands of a crazy civilization."

"I never did anything worth doing by accident, nor did any of my inventions come by accident; they came by work."

"Everything comes to him who hustles while he waits."

"To my mind the old masters are not art; their value is in their scarcity."

"Not only will atomic power be released, but someday we will harness the rise and fall of the tides and imprison the rays of the sun."

"There is no substitute for hard work."

"When down in the mouth remember Jonah—he came out all right!"

"The English are not an inventive people; they don't eat enough pie."

# RECYCLING FACTS

*Here are some fascinating facts from the EarthWorks Group's handy new book, "The Recycler's Handbook."*

Some 94,000 cans are recycled every minute in America.

• Americans use 100 million steel and tin cans every day. We recycle about 5% of them...which means we dump more than 30 billion into landfills every year.

• Americans use enough corrugated cardboard in a year to make a bale the size of a football field and the height of the World Trade Center. About 40% of it is recycled.

• If Americans recycled half our newsprint every year, we'd need 3,200 fewer garbage trucks to collect municipal trash.

• Americans throw away enough used motor oil every year to fill 120 supertankers. It could all be recycled.

• According to the EPA, we create enough garbage every year to fill a convoy of 10-ton garbage trucks 145,000 miles long—more than halfway from here to the moon.

• About 70 million car batteries are recycled in the U.S. each year. The other 15-20%, with 165,000 tons of lead, go to landfills.

• To make plastics, the U.S. uses about a billion barrels of petroleum by-products each year. How much is that? Enough to fill over 56,000 olympic-sized swimming pools.

• According to the Glass Packaging Institute, we now use around 41 billion glass containers a year—an average of about 165 per person. How much of that is recycled? About 30%...which means nearly 30 billion glass containers go into landfills.

• Every year, Americans dispose of 1.6 billion pens, 2 billion razors and blades, and 18 billion diapers. They're all sitting in landfills somewhere.

• In 1988, about 9 million automobile bodies—more than American automobile plants produced that year—were recycled.

**New York City has been host to only 27 ticker-tape parades, total.**

# COLLEGE NAMES

*We know the names—Cornell, Harvard, Stanford...*
*Here's where a few of them come from.*

**Brown University.** Nicholas Brown, a member of a wealthy Rhode Island shipping family, gave a $5,000 endowment to Rhode Island College in 1804. By that time, Brown's family had given the school more than $160,000, and officials decided a name-change was in order.

**Cornell University.** Samuel Morse invented the telegraph, but it was Ezra Cornell who put it to work. He devised a practical method of stringing insulated wires along telephone poles, and provided the first telegraph service to the cities of the northeast. His initial donation of land and $500,000 put the school on its feet.

**Stanford University.** Amasa Leland Stanford, a robber baron who got himself elected governor of California and a U.S. senator, founded the university in memory of his son, Leland Jr., who died of typhoid fever at the age of 15.

**Johns Hopkins University.** Humbled by his own poor education, Johns Hopkins, a wealthy Baltimore merchant and banker, willed $7,000,000 to found the now famous university and hospital.

**Duke University.** Once there was a school in North Carolina called Trinity College. Then, in 1925, a wealthy tobacco, textiles and utilities magnate named James B. Duke gave them $107 million. Suddenly, the name Duke had a certain ring to it.

**Harvard University.** In 1638 John Harvard, a wealthy Massachusetts settler, left half his estate—$1,480—to a two-year-old local bible college. It was the largest gift to the new school at that point; the school repaid the favor by calling itself Harvard College.

**Brigham Young University.** Named after one of the founding fathers of the Church of Jesus Christ of Latter Day Saints (the Mormons).

# SPACE NAZIS

*Whatever happened to the scientists who supplied Hitler's war machine with its advanced weaponry? Many of them moved to the U.S. at our government's invitation, to join our space program.*

Following the defeat of Germany at the end of World War II, the United States began Project Paperclip, a secret program that employed "ex"-Nazis in U.S. scientific efforts. Many of the scientists smuggled into America by our government had committed war crimes—but U.S. officials didn't care. In fact, information about their past was deliberately covered up to circumvent laws that prohibited Nazi collaborators from entering the country.

## CODE NAME: OVERCAST

According to Linda Hunt's 1985 exposé in the *Bulletin of the Atomic Scientists*, the scheme "grew from the notion that German and Austrian scientists were part of the spoils of the war which had been won against Nazi Germany." Initially, the top secret program, whose code name was Overcast, called for temporary immigration of "Nazi experts in rocketry, aircraft design, aviation, medicine, and other fields," writes Hunt. "But by early 1946, the War Department found their skills too valuable to lose and pushed for a revised program that would allow them to stay in the United States."

## SEAL OF APPROVAL

In early 1946, Overcast was renamed Project Paperclip and the operation was approved by President Harry S. Truman. According to official policy, "No person found...to have been a member of the Nazi Party and more than a nominal participant in its activities or an active supporter of Naziism or militarism shall be brought to the U.S."

But government agencies ignored these regulations. Records of the German scientists' Nazi backrounds were routinely altered and sometimes deleted altogether. As a result, perpetrators of some of the most heinous war crimes in World War II soon became full-fledged American citizens. From 1945 to 1952, 765 German scientists were admitted to the U.S. All of them were committed Nazis.

**If a black cat crosses your path in Japan, it's considered good luck.**

## CASE HISTORIES

***Arthur Rudolph.*** Designed the Saturn 5 rocket used in the Apollo moon landings. During World War II, he was the operations director of the Mittelwerk factory at the Dora-Nordhausen concentration camp in Germany, where 20,000 workers were tortured to death. At first, Rudolph denied to U.S. officials that he had witnessed any incidents of abuse at the camp, but later admitted seeing 12 prisoners hanged from a crane ("I do know that one lifted his knees after I got there," Rudolph testified).

An earlier 1945 military file had concluded that Rudolph was "100% Nazi, dangerous type, security threat!!!" This appraisal was ignored, however, and Rudolph was allowed to become a U.S. citizen. In 1984, while under investigation for his war record, Rudolph fled to West Germany.

***Wernher von Braun.*** Instrumental in many areas of NASA's Apollo program. In 1947, von Braun was labeled an "SS officer" and "potential security threat" to the United States. But several months later, a new security evaluation, specifically rewritten to allow von Braun to emigrate, claimed "no derogatory information is available...like the majority of members, he may have been a mere opportunist." Von Braun was subsequently allowed to come to the U.S., despite the fact that his V-2 rocket had been used to bombard London during World War II. He became an American celebrity and was even showcased as a role model for American children during the 1950s and early 1960s.

***Kurt Blome.*** A high-ranking Nazi scientist who was put on trial at Nuremberg in 1947 for conducting human experiments. Although he was acquitted there, it was generally accepted that the charges had basis in fact: During a 1945 interrogation by the U.S. military, Blome admitted that he had been ordered in 1943 to experiment with plague vaccines on concentration camp prisoners.

Two months after his Nuremberg acquittal, Blome was being interviewed in Camp David, Maryland, for information about biological warfare. He supplied technological details and names of Nazi collaborators in his experiments.

In 1951, the U.S. Army Chemical Corps chose to ignore Blome's background when it hired him to work on chemical warfare for "Project 63," the U.S.'s secret effort to hire Germans scientists before the Russians got to them. Nowhere in Blome's files did it mention his arrest or trial at Nuremberg.

***Hermann Becker-Freysing*** and ***Siegfried Ruff.*** Both Becker-Freysing and Ruff (and 21 others) were charged at the Nuremberg War Crimes trials for participating in cruel medical experiments on Dachau concentration camp inmates. Before the trials began, however, both were contacted by the Army Air Force Aero Center in Heidelberg, Germany. According to the *Bulletin of the Atomic Scientists*, Becker-Freysing and Ruff were paid "to write reports or conduct laboratory tests for the Army Air Force's use that were based on wartime experiments which Nuremberg prosecutors later charged had been conducted on concentration camp victims." Becker-Freysing was later found guilty and sentenced to 20 years in jail for conducting seawater experiments on prisoners at Dachau. Ruff was acquitted for conducting experiments that killed over 80 Dachau inmates who had been locked in a chamber that simulated high altitude pressure.

***Konrad Schaefer.*** Schaefer was charged in the Nuremberg trials for his role in Becker-Freysing's sea water experiments. According to the charges, Schaefer oversaw experiments on Dachau concentration camp inmates who were starved and then force-fed sea water that had been chemically altered to make it drinkable. Like Becker-Freysing and Ruff, Schaefer was paid by the Aero Center to inform the Army and Air Force about his experiments.

In 1949, Schaefer was allowed to enter the United States in spite of the fact he had admitted to having been tried at Nuremberg (he was acquitted, despite evidence that he had attended planning meetings for the experiments.) Ironically, when Schaefer was sent back to Germany in 1951, it was not because of his war crimes—the Air Force simply could not find a job for him.

## OBJECTIONS

In 1947, the *Bulletin of the Atomic Scientists* ran one of the first exposes on Project Paperclip. The two authors of the piece, Hans Bethe and H.S. Sack argued against the immigration of the ex-Nazi scientists: "Is it wise, from a long-range point of view, or even compatible with our moral standards, to make this bargain? Would it not have been better to restrict the stay of these scientists in this country to the absolute minimum? For it must be borne in mind that many of them, probably the majority, are diehard Nazis, or at least worked wholeheartedly with the Nazis; otherwise they would not have held their high posts so vital for the Nazi war machine."

## JUSTIFICATION

Addressing the moral argument about using war criminals, Bosquet Wev, the director of the Joint intelligence Objectives Agency said in a 1947 memorandum: "The best interests of the United States have been subjugated to the efforts expended in 'beating a dead Nazi horse'...the return of these scientists to Germany would present a far greater security threat to the United States than their retention."

## DENUNCIATION

In December, 1946, Albert Einstein, Norman Vincent Peale and other prominent Americans issued protests to the American government concerning Project Paperclip. But the issue quickly died down, since little information was made public.

## THE END OF PAPERCLIP

Project Paperclip came to an end in 1957 after 11 years. Ironically, the government of West Germany began to complain of a "brain drain" of its best scientists. Since that time, writes Linda Hunt, many of imported ex-Nazi scientists "have received the highest honors bestowed by the military on civilians and have risen to top positions at NASA and other governmental agencies and in private industry."

***And Now for Something Completely Different...***

"What kind of animals were the dinosaurs? Up until the last decade, many scientists would have answered with confidence: Dinosaurs were huge, slow-moving, cold-blooded reptiles of the past... Today some paleontologists offer radically different views: Dinosaurs were active, perhaps even warm-blooded animals, comparable to modern mammals and birds." —*National Geographic*, 1978

**Blue is America's favorite color.**

# DISNEY STORIES: PINOCCHIO

*The original Pinocchio was written by an Italian educator named Carlo Lorenzini (using the name Carlo Collodi) in 1883. It was adapted by Disney at a cost of $2.5 million and released in 1940. Although it contains "some of the finest art and animation sequences every produced," it wasn't a big hit. Of course, the Disney version and the original story were substantially different. Here are Jim Morton's examples of how the tale was changed.*

## THE DISNEY VERSION

• Geppetto, a kindly old wood carver, makes a marionette named Pinocchio. Then he wishes (on a star) that the puppet were a real boy, so he could have a son.

• A talking bug named Jiminy Cricket is appointed Pinocchio's conscience. He follows Pinocchio on a series of adventures.

• Pinocchio is accosted by a fox and a cat—two humorous con artists—is sold to Stromboli, and sent to Pleasure Island, where dumb, selfish boys are turned into beasts. Pinocchio narrowly escapes being turned into a donkey.

• He's eventually reunited with Geppetto in the belly of a whale; Geppetto was swallowed while he was out looking for Pinocchio.

• Pinocchio helps the wood carver escape, and for his unselfishness, he's turned into a real boy. Jiminy Crickett beams and sings.

## THE ORIGINAL VERSION

• Disney follows the main themes of the book, but skips over the grim moments from the original story.

• For example: When Pinocchio hides his gold coins in his mouth, the cat attempts to force Pinocchio's mouth open with a knife. Pinocchio bites the cat's paw off and spits it out. While he's running away, Pinocchio meets a zombie girl. Then the fox and cat hang him by the neck, trying to make him spit out the gold.

• The biggest difference between the Disney Version and the book is Jiminy Cricket. In the book, the cricket has no name. It appears early in the story and is promptly smashed with a hammer by Pinocchio. Later in the tale, the cricket's ghost pops up as a sort of insect Obi Wan Kenobi, offering Pinocchio guidance (rarely heeded) as he goes on his journeys.

• Also in the original, on Pleasure Island (called Playland in the book), Pinocchio does turn into a donkey and is sold at the market. He's forced to perform in a circus before going lame. Then he's sold to a man who plans to use Pinocchio's skin to make a drum. The man tries to drown Pinocchio, but fish eat the donkey skin off him, revealing the puppet inside.

• Pinocchio does rescue Geppetto, but from the belly of a shark, not a whale. This deed alone isn't enough to turn Pinocchio into a boy. The puppet works from sunrise to sundown every day for five months before his wish is finally granted.

## SAMPLE PASSAGES (FROM THE ORIGINAL)

"'Why are you sorry for me?' Pinocchio asked the cricket.

"'Because you are a puppet, and—what is worse—you have a wooden head,' the cricket replied.

"At these last words, Pinocchio lost his temper and, seizing a mallet from the bench, threw it at the cricket.

"Perhaps he did not mean to hit him, but unfortunately the mallet struck the cricket right to the head. The poor insect had scarcely time to cry 'Cri-cri-cri,' and there he was, stretched out stiff, flattened against the wall."

• • •

*The fox and cat are trying to rob Pinnochio.*

"'Ah-ha, you rascal! So you hid your money under your tongue! Spit it out at once!'

"Pinocchio did not obey.

"'Oh, so you can't hear? Then we'll make you spit it out.'

"And one of them seized the puppet by the end of his nose, and the other by his chin, and they pulled without mercy, one up, the other down, to make him open his mouth; but it was no use.

"Then the smaller assassin drew a horrid knife and tried to force it between his lips, like a chisel, but Pinocchio, quick as lightning, bit off his hand and spat it out. Imagine his astonishment when he saw that it was a cat's paw."

**The heads of a two-headed snake will fight over food—even though they share one stomach.**

# THE ARCHIES

*When you were a kid, were* Archie *comics part of your bathroom reading? Here's a new Archie story from* Behind the Hits, *by Bob Shannon and John Javna.*

If you grew up in post-World War II America, the chances are you've read at least one *Archie* comic book in your life. As Maurice Horn says in *The World Encyclopedia of Comics*, "Archie, like Batman, Superman, and a small handful of others, has transcended comic books into pure Americana. There will, it often seems, always be an Archie. It is inevitable as death and taxes."

## THE '40s & '50s: ARCHIE'S EARLY DAYS

Archie Andrews, a red-headed, freckle-faced creation of cartoonist Bob Montana, first appeared in *Pep* comic books in 1941. He was portrayed as the "typical" American teenager of the '40s, and he was so popular that within a year he had his own comic book. His audience increased. He starred in a radio show. By the '50s, a whole cast of characters—and more comic book titles—had evolved.

Now Archie and his pals from Riverdale High were the "typical" American teenagers of the '50s. Maybe you remember that Archie had a red jalopy and a big crush on rich and snooty Veronica Lodge; Jughead Jones wore a strange-looking beanie and loved hamburgers; Betty, Veronica's best friend and rival, was hopelessly in love with Archie; Moose was a super-strong but super-dumb athlete; and so on. They all hung out at Pop's Malt Shoppe when they weren't in school under Mr. Weatherbee's watchful eye.

## ARCHIE IN THE '60s

But as popular as the Archie clan was in the '40s and '50s, the '60s was their golden decade. With the help of the cartoon show that premiered on CBS in 1968, sales of everything connected to Archie characters, from lunch boxes to comic books, skyrocketed. For example, best-selling comics normally sold about 300,000 copies a month in the '60s; in 1969, at the height of the cartoon show's popularity, *Archie* comics sold over a million a month!

## ARCHIE ANDREWS, ROCK STAR

Included in this fantastic marketing windfall was a scheme to merchandise the Archie characters as a Monkees-style rock 'n' roll group. The Monkees had already proven TV's effectiveness in selling records to American kids. Now the people behind the Archie TV show wanted to cash in on the same appeal. They hired the man behind the Monkees' hits, Don Kirshner, as "music supervisor," and he began putting together a session group to make records as the Archies. Since the stars of this TV series were animated, Kirshner didn't have to put up with what he must have regarded as prima donna actors again (his association with the Monkees ended on unfriendly terms). For this job, he could just hire anonymous studio singers.

## DANTE'S INFERNO

Enter Ron Dante, an out-of-work jingle and demo singer whose only previous hit ("The Leader of the Laundramat") had been credited to the Detergents. Says Dante, "[Kirshner] was casting for the Archies, and he was listening to a lot of singers. I heard that a musician friend of mine was playing on the session, and I just happened to fall by and say, 'Why don't you try me?' I auditioned for it because I had just written a Broadway show that bombed, and my career in Broadway had gone down the drain. So I said, 'I think I'd better jump back into records and take anything I can get my hands on,' and that was the beginning of it. I went and auditioned; I sang for about a half-hour.

"The next day, they called me and said, 'All right, you're gonna do the season's music.' We must have done a hundred tunes that first season. Over the years, I must have done about three or four hundred songs for the Archies. I auditioned with songs like 'Bang Shang-A-Lang' and 'Truck driver,' and I said, 'Here I go again.'"

## HOW SWEET IT IS

The Archies released an album in 1968, and had a moderate hit with "Bang Shang-A-Lang" that year. But their second single—"Sugar Sugar"—was a smash. It became the biggest-selling record of 1969, with total sales of over four million. It was even covered by Wilson Pickett, who turned it into a Top 25 hit as a soul song. The Archies had two more Top 40 singles in the next year. But a proposed Archies tour was not to be. "They wanted me to dye my hair and put freckles on and go out as Archie," Dante says, "and I said, 'Oh boy, is this a career move, or what?' "

**In anonymous surveys, 40% of Americans confessed cheating on their taxes.**

# GROUCHO GOSSIP

*How did the Groucho Marx and his brothers get into show business? And where did they get those funny names? Now it can be told. From Cult TV by John Javna.*

Julius Henry Marx (Groucho's real name) wasn't happy when his mother pushed him into becoming a vaudevillian. His dream was to become a doctor. But soon he, two brothers and a friend were touring backwater theaters as the Four Nightingales.

## WISECRACKS

They were less than successful. During a performance in Texas, the entire audience left the theater to catch an escaped mule. When they returned, the angry brothers dropped their regular act and ad-libbed a routine mocking the patrons instead. They expected boos, but they got laughter. It changed the Marx brothers' act forever: they learned they could make fun of people and get away with it.

## NAME GAME

Years later, another piece fell into place. Julius and his brothers were playing poker with a friend who was making fun of a popular comic character named "Knocko the Monk." The friend made up a similar name for each of them. Leo became Chicko because he chased women constantly. Adolph became Harpo (he played the harp). Milton became Gummo (because he liked to chew gum?). And Julius, who groused constantly, became Groucho.

## LUCKY BREAK

The Marx Brothers might never have become stars if it hadn't been for a lucky accident. One night in 1924, a major play-opening was cancelled in New York. Reviewers, left with nothing else to see that night, showed up at the opening of a new Marx brothers' vaudeville act instead. They expected to find a typically boring variety act—but the surprised reviewers loved the Marx Brothers. Their rave reviews made Groucho and his family instant celebrities and Broadway stars...which led to Hollywood.

# BANNED BOOKS

*It can't happen here? Guess again. Each year, the American Booksellers Association holds a "Banned Books Week" to call attention to the issues surrounding censorship. Here are some books that were banned, or nearly banned, during the 1980s.*

**The Diary of Anne Frank**, by Anne Frank. In 1983 members of the Alabama State Textbook Committee wanted the book rejected because it was "a real downer."

**Lord of the Flies**, by William Golding. In 1981 the book was challenged by a high school in Owen, North Carolina because it was "demoralizing inasmuch as it implies that man is little more than an animal."

**Biology**, by Karen Arms and Pamela S. Camp. In 1985 the Garland, Texas textbook selection committee complained of "overly explicit diagrams of sexual organs."

**The American Pageant: A History of the Republic**, by Thomas A. Bailey and David M. Kennedy. In 1984 officials in the Racine, Wisconsin School District complained the book contained "a lot of funny pictures of Republicans and nicer pictures of Democrats."

**Zen Buddhism: Selected Writings**, by D.T. Suzuki. In 1987 the school system of Canton, Michigan was informed that "this book details the teaching of the religion of Buddhism in such a way that the reader could very likely embrace its teachings and choose this as his religion."

**1984**, by George Orwell. In 1981 the book was challenged in Jackson Country, Florida because it was "pro-communist and contained explicit sexual matter."

**Slugs**, by David Greenburg. In 1985 an elementary school in Escondido, California banned the book for describing "slugs being dissected with scissors."

**A Light In the Attic**, by Shel Silverstein. In 1986 the popular children's book was challenged at an elementary school in Mukwonago, Wisconsin because it "gloried Satan, suicide and cannibalism, and also encouraged children to be disobedient."

**The Crucible**, by Arthur Miller. In 1982 citizens of Harrisburg, Pennsylvania complained about staging a play with "sick words from the mouths of demon-possessed people. It should be wiped out of the schools or the school board should use them to fuel the fire of hell."

**Slaughterhouse Five**, by Kurt Vonnegut. In 1985 complaints were made in an Owensboro, Kentucky high school library because the book had "foul language, a section depicting a picture of an act of bestiality, a reference to 'Magic Fingers' attached to the protagonist's bed to help him sleep, and the sentence: 'The gun made a ripping sound like the opening of the fly of God Almighty.' "

**Meet the Werewolf**, by Georgess McHargue. In 1983 the school district of Vancouver, Oregon claimed the book was "full of comments about becoming a werewolf, use of opium, and pacts with the devil."

**Album Cover Album**, by Roger Dean. (A book of album covers). In 1987 the Vancouver, Washington school district objected to a photo of the "Statue of Liberty with bare breasts as exemplary of several photos that were pretty raw toward women."

**The Amazing Bone**, by William Steig. In 1986 a parent in Lambertville, New Jersey complained to the local school library about "the use of tobacco by the animals" in this fantasy.

**The Haunting Of America**, by Jean Anderson. In 1985 an elementary school in Lakeland, Florida claimed it "would lead children to believe in demons without realizing it."

**SIDENOTE:** Lewis Caroll's **Alice's Adventures In Wonderland** was banned in China in 1931. Authorities objected that "animals should not use human language, and that it was disastrous to put animals and human beings on the same level."

**An automatic spaghetti-spinning fork was patented in 1950.**

# DON'T QUOTE ME ON THAT

*You'd be surprised how many famous quotes were never actually said by the people they're attributed to. Here are some classic examples.*

**The Quote:** "Play it again, Sam." —*Humphrey Bogart*
**The Truth:** The real line from *Casablanca* is "You played it for her, you can play it for me. If she can stand it, I can—Play it." Dooley Wilson (Sam) didn't really play it. In real life, Wilson couldn't play the piano; the accompaniment was dubbed in afterwards.

**The Quote:** "Elementary, my dear Watson." —*Sherlock Holmes*
**The Truth:** Arthur Conan Doyle wrote four novels and 56 short stories that feature his detective; Holmes doesn't say it in any of them. Basil Rathbone, an actor who portrayed the sleuth in films of the 1930s and 1940s, was the one who made the line famous.

**The Quote:** "I cannot tell a lie." —*George Washington*
**The Truth:** Washington's biographer, Mason Weems, fabricated the whole cherry tree incident six years after Washington's death.

**The Quote:** "Hold on, Mr. President!" —*Sam Donaldson*
**The Truth:** The aggressive White House television reporter claims he never said it at any of the presidential press conferences he covered, although it is the title of a recent book he wrote.

**The Quote:** "Win one for the Gipper." —*George Gipp*
**The Truth:** Knute Rockne, the Notre Dame football coach to whom dying player George Gipp allegedly spoke his final words, was known for embellishing the truth to inspire his players. Experts believe that Rockne—who first told the story a long eight years after Gipp's death—made it up.

**In the United States, there are four times more astrologers than astronomers.**

**The Quote:** "You dirty rat!" —*James Cagney*
**The Truth:** Cagney denied ever saying this in any of his movies.

**The Quote:** "Go west, young man." —*Horace Greeley*
**The Truth:** A man named John Babsone Soule first wrote it in an article for Indiana's *Terre Haute Express* in 1851. Greeley reprinted the article in his *New York Tribune*, but gave full credit to Soule.

**The Quote:** "On the whole, I'd rather be in Philadelphia."
—*W.C. Fields*
**The Truth:** Fields' alleged epitaph first appeared as a joke in a *Vanity Fair* magazine around 1950, after his death.

**The Quote:** "The government is best which governs least."
—*Thomas Jefferson*
**The Truth:** Historians can't find evidence that the founding father ever said it.

**The Quote:** "There are three kinds of lies: lies, damn lies, and statistics." — *Mark Twain*
**The Truth:** In his autobiography, Twain credited this saying to Benjamin Disraeli.

**The Quote:** "Judy, Judy, Judy." —*Cary Grant*
**The Truth:** The line comes from a popular impersonation of Grant by comedian Larry Storch.

**The Quote:** "War is hell." —*William T. Sherman*
**The Truth:** The Union general really said, "There is many a boy here today who looks on war as all glory, but, boys, it is all hell."

**The Quote:** "He who hesitates is lost." —*Joseph Addison*
**The Truth:** The original line from his play *Cato*, is, "The woman that deliberates is lost."

# AIN'T THAT A SHAME

*Here's an interesting commentary on old-time rock, from* Behind The Hits, *by Bob Shannon and John Javna.*

One of the more sordid aspects of rock'n'roll's early history was "cover artists," the white guys who imitated black artists who created the songs, the arrangements, and the harmonies. But the worst part wasn't that the cover artists were imitators—the worst part was that they copied the black artists' records while the original version was still new. So the cover versions competed with—and usually did better than—the originals. The difference between them was often minor; one rendition sounded like it was done by white singers, the other sounded like it was done by black singers. So lily-white radio stations pushed the songs done by by "acceptable" (white) artists. And these artists became stars.

**MR. RIPOFF**

A good example is Pat Boone. Pat, a pious fellow, got onto the charts doing cover versions of the El Dorados' "At My Front Door" (Pat: #7; the El Dorados: #17), the Charms' "Two Hearts (Pat: #16), Little Richard's "Tutti Frutti" (Pat: #12, Richard: #17), and a bunch more. Little Richard was so incensed by Boone's cover version of "Tutti Frutti" that he purposely made the follow-up, "Long Tall Sally," too fast for Boone to sing. Nonetheless, Boone figured out how to adapt "Long Tall Sally" to his style, and gave Richard a run for his money. Little Richard's version did beat Boone's, but only by one place on the charts (Richard: #7, Pat: #8).

**WHITE BUCKS**

There was also a huge difference in the attitudes of the artists toward their songs. To the originators, the songs were a part of life. To the rip-off artists, it was just business. Take, for example, one of Pat Boone's biggest hits, "Ain't That a Shame"—which actually belonged to Fats Domino. Fats, who was an established artist, wrote this song from a personal experience.

"I usually record my songs like things that people say everyday," Fats says. "Like 'Ain't That A Shame.' I was passin', walkin' down the street and I saw a little lady beatin' a little baby, you know, spankin' a baby. And I heard somebody say, 'Ain't that a shame.' "

In 1956, Fats released the song and it went to #10. Not bad, except that Pat Boone covered it right away, and his version went to #1, obviously taking some sales from Fats.

Pat, however, didn't really identify with the tune. In fact, he objected to it because the grammar was bad.

## PROPER ENGLISH

" 'With 'Ain't That A Shame,' I balked," Boone says. "I said, 'Look, I just transferred to Columbia University, I'm an English major. I don't want to record a song called 'Ain't That A Shame.' I mean, 'ain't' wasn't an accepted word. It is now in the dictionary, but I was majoring in English and I felt that this was going to be a terrible thing if it was a hit. I tried to record it, 'Isn't That A Shame,' and it just didn't work."

Boone continues: "And I must say that I was complimented...I would go to radio studios, walk in, and the deejays were astonished to see that I was white."

Maybe they'd been listening to Fats' record.

## THE STONES

The Rolling Stones have written some great original music, but they've also liberally "used" other people's music from the very beginning of their recording careers. "Stoned," the flip side of their first British hit ("I Wanna Be Your Man"), for example, was a copy of a 1964 hit called "Green Onions." An album cut called "Prodigal Son," which is credited to Jagger/Richards, is virtually a note-for-note copy of an old blues tune by Furry Lewis. Even the guitar licks are the same.

The Stones' first American Top 10 record, "Time Is On My Side," is another imitation, a note-for-note copy of the original version by New Orleans singer Irma Thomas. Even Mick Jagger's "rap" in the middle of the song is lifted from Irma's rendition. "Time On My Side" should have been the successful follow-up to her Top 20 tune, "I Wish Someone Would Care," but before Irma's record had a chance, the Stones' version was already rocketing up the charts. "I really liked the song, and I put my heart and soul into it," Irma says. "Then along comes this English group that half-sings it and gets a million-seller. And after that I stopped doing it."

**America has more senior citizens than teenagers.**

# BODY LANGUAGE

*Here are some fascinating facts about the human body.*

## IT'S A GAS

• An average person releases nearly a pint of intestinal gas by flatulence every day. Most is due to swallowed air. The rest is from fermentation of undigested food.

• Burping while lying on your back is a lot harder than burping while you're sitting or standing.

• The two things that make farts smell, *skatole* and *indole*, are commonly used in making perfumes.

• Your stomach produces a new lining every three days. Reason: It keeps stomach acids from digesting your stomach.

## TAKE A BREATHER

• The average person breathes 70 to 80 million gallons of air in a lifetime.

• A newborn's first breath requires 50 times the suction of an ordinary breath.

• You inhale over 3,000 gallons of air every day.

• An infant breathes about three times faster than a 20-year-old.

• On the average, a person who smokes a pack of cigarettes a day will die at 67, seven years earlier than the average nonsmoker.

## THE EYES HAVE IT

• Most men's pupils get 1/3 bigger when looking at pictures of sharks, but shrink in reaction to pictures of babies.

• 33% of the population has 20/20 vision.

• The muscles in the average eye move up to 100,000 times in a day.

• Every time you blink, you wash irritating contaminants out of your eyes.

• 1 out of every 500 people have one blue eye and one brown eye.

• You can't keep your eyes open when you sneeze.

## DON'T SWEAT IT

• One square inch of your skin has over 600 sweat glands and 90 oil glands.

• In a hot climate, a person can perspire up to 3 gallons of sweat a day.

**In a UCLA study, 87% of the people researchers smiled at smiled back.**

# SHARK !!!

*Some fascinating factoids about the ocean's most feared predator.*

Sharks lived more than 400 million years ago—200 million years before dinosaurs existed.

Shark skin is covered with small teeth-like denticles which can tear human skin on contact. It was once used as sandpaper by coastal woodworkers.

In a single year, a shark goes through more than 20,000 knife-like teeth.

Unlike other fish, sharks lack air bladders and consequently have to keep moving to avoid sinking and drowning.

To a shark, a swimmer in a black wetsuit looks a lot like a seal or sea lion.

Sand Tiger shark embryos fight to the death inside the mother's womb until only one shark is alive at birth.

In May 1945, fishermen off Cuba caught the largest Great White shark on record—measuring over 21 feet and weighing 7,302 pounds.

The Great White shark has no natural enemies and it never gets sick.

Sharks have no bones in their body—only cartilage.

Three times as many people are killed by lightning as are killed by sharks.

A plankton-eating Whale shark caught off Pakistan measured over 41 feet and weighed over 33,000 pounds.

Sharks have three eyelids on each eye to protect against the thrashing of its prey.

Don't swim or dive with cuts—some types of shark can smell one part of blood in 100 million parts of water.

An attacking shark can sometimes be confused and diverted by a hard blow to the nose, or a poke in the eye or nostrils.

Sharks live only in salt water, except for the mysterious Bull sharks, sometimes found swimming miles up rivers.

**Napoleon Bonaparte was afraid of cats.**

# SITUATION TRAGEDY

*Ever wish your family could be more like the Partridge Family or the Nelsons? It turns out, there were no families like that.*

Back in the "golden age" of TV, situation comedies presented audiences with the image of an ideal Middle Class America. Parents were patient, neighbors were nice, and kids were neat (even their bedrooms were spotless). In reality, however, many of the child actors in these "perfect" TV families had less-than-perfect lives offscreen.

## FATHER KNOWS BEST

From 1954-63, the "white-bread" Anderson family of Springfield, U.S.A., could do wrong. But two of the main actors ran into trouble after the show went off the air.

• Billy Gray (who played the son, Bud) spent 45 days in jail on marijuana charges and later dropped out from society. He told *TV Guide*, "I look back at the show and see it as a lie, a lie that was sold to the American people."

• Like Gray, Lauren Chapin (who played the youngest daughter, Kathy) also had drug troubles. She became addicted to heroin and speed, and did jail time for forging a check.

## THE PATTY DUKE SHOW

Many people were shocked when Patty Duke revealed in her autobiography, *Call Me Anna: The Autobiography of Patty Duke*, that she had suffered from severe manic-depression during her TV sitcom days. She wrote, "I hated being less intelligent than I was, I hated pretending that I was younger than I was."

• From 1963-66, Duke starred in the popular series, but gradually the stress of playing two roles—herself and her look-alike cousin—caught up with her; she became depressed, anorexic and eventually an alcoholic and drug addict.

• To make matters worse, her managers, John and Ethel Ross, were not only physically and emotionally abusive (they wouldn't allow Duke to watch her own show) but, according to Duke, embezzled her savings as well.

## THE PARTRIDGE FAMILY

• The happy-go-lucky Partridge Family was a favorite of pre-teens in the early 1970s.

• After the show ended, Danny Bonaduce, the cherubic bass player, developed drug problems. By age 21, he had squandered $350,000 in savings on his cocaine habit. In 1985 he was arrested for possession of cocaine, but the charges were dismissed after drug counseling. In 1989, Bonaduce resurfaced as a DJ in Philadelphia, claiming "My only reponsibility is not to promote drugs." Within a year, Bonaduce was busted again, this time for purchasing crack.

• Susan Dey, who was 16 when the show began, later claimed to have suffered from severe anxiety which resulted in anorexia and bulimia.

## THE ADVENTURES OF OZZIE AND HARRIET

• For 14 years, 1952-66, Americans tuned in to "The Adventures of Ozzie and Harriet." The Nelsons were a real-life family, which certainly added to their appeal, but it didn't exclude them from real-life problems.

• Fans of Ricky Nelson were shocked when his autopsy revealed that he had been freebasing cocaine just prior to the plane crash that killed him on December 31, 1984 in DeKalb, Texas.

## FAMILY AFFAIR

In 1976, Annissa Jones, who played "Buffy" on the series "Family Affair" was found dead of an overdose after a party in Oceanside, California. The coroner reported that Jones had "the largest combination of drugs in any cases I've ever encountered." Toxological tests showed massive amoungs of cocaine, Quaaludes and barbituates. Jones was 18.

# NAME & PLACE

*Planning to move? Why not make your home in Sodom... or Elephant's Playground? Or any of these other strangely-named places:*

**Sodom, Vermont**: Its name was changed to Adamant, VT in 1905, by people who shuddered at the thought of having their incoming mail addressed to Sodom.

**Mount Derby, Colorado:** It's hat-shaped.

**Coffee-Los Lake, Maine:** Locals, who like to call nearby Telos Lake "tea-less lake," thought they should have a "coffee-less lake" too.

**Einanuhto Hills, Alaska:** From the Aleut word meaning "three breasts."

**Phoenix, Arizona:** Traces of an Indian or pre-Indian village were found at the site. Town founders, taking the name from the mythological bird who rises form the ashes, hoped their new town would rise from the village's ruins.

**Bosom, Wyoming:** A town with two peaks.

**Mistake Peak, Arizona and Mistaken Creek, Kentucky:** Wrong peak, wrong creek.

**Elephant's Playground, California:** Home of large boulders in a meadow.

**"Gotham City":** In England, during the reign of King John, Gotham villagers all feigned lunacy to discourage the king from establishing a hunting lodge nearby that would lead to an increase in taxes. The name now means a city overrun by madness. Washington Irving coined the phrase in a description of New York in 1807.

**Bimble, Kentucky:** From the names of Will and Rebecca Payne's prize oxen—Bim and Bill.

**Portland, Oregon**: The two men who named the city couldn't decide—Portland (like the Maine city)...or Boston? A coin flip settled the debate in favor of Portland.

**The most popular American dog names are Rover, Spot, and Max—in that order.**

# COMMON PHRASES

*In the first two* Uncle John's Bathroom Readers, *we gave you the origins of some familiar phrases. Here are a few more.*

SECOND STRING

***Meaning:*** Replacement or backup.

***Background:*** You might have caught William Tell without an apple, but not without a second string. In medieval times, an archer always carried a second string in case the one on his bow broke.

IN THE LIMELIGHT

***Meaning:*** The center of attention.

***Background:*** In 1826, Thomas Drummond invented the limelight, an amazingly bright white light, by running an intense oxygen/hydrogen flame through a lime cylinder. At first, the intense light was used in lighthouses to direct ships. Later, theatres began using the limelight like a spotlight—to direct the audience's attention to a certain actor. If an actor was to be the focal point of a particular scene, he was thrust into the limelight.

MAKE THE GRADE

***Meaning:*** To fulfill expectations, or succeed.

***Background:*** In railroad jargon, the term "grade" refers to the slope of the hill. When a train reaches a plateau or mountaintop, it has "made the grade."

FLASH IN THE PAN

***Meaning:*** Short-lived success.

***Background:*** In the 1700s, the pan of a flintlock musket was the part which held the gunpowder. If all went well, sparks from the flint would ignite the charge, which would then propel the bullet out the barrel. However, sometimes the gun powder would burn without igniting a main charge. The flash would burn brightly but only briefly, with no lasting effect.

# ELVIS: STILL DEAD?

*Here's a piece about the Phantom of the Rock World, Elvis. It's taken from Vince Staten's irreverent guidebook,* Unauthorized America.

"In 1988, for some reason, people all across America got the idea that Elvis wasn't really dead, that he had faked his death to get a little peace and quiet, and that he had actually spent the previous eleven years enjoying himself, wandering the country, seducing fat waitresses who knew who he was but decided not to tell until the *Weekly World News* called.

"He was spotted in Georgia and in Germany; in Texas and in Tennessee. But the majority of the sightings centered in the Kalamazoo, Michigan area."

## INSIDE SOURCES

"The Elvis Is Alive mania began the last week in May, 1988 when the *Weekly World News* broke the story: After faking his tragic death [in 1977], exhausted idol Elvis Presley was secretly flown to Hawaii, where he began his new life under the name John Burrows.

"The newspaper quoted from a new book, *Is Elvis Alive? The Most Incredible Elvis Presley Story Ever Told*, by author Gail Brewer-Giorgio, who—just coincidentally—also wrote the novel *Orion*, about a rock star who faked his own death. The Elvis book came complete with an audiocassette tape of conversations with Elvis *after* his death."

## ELVIS SPEAKS

"'Everything worked just like it was meant to be,' E said on the secret tape. 'There was an island I had learned about a long time ago. I must have spent a year there. I really needed the rest.'

"Voice analyst Len Williams of Houston verified that the voice on the tape was Elvis's, and that the tape had been edited. Brewer-Giorgio shrugged that one off, saying it was edited to take out the voice of the person talking with Elvis."

## PROGRESS REPORT

"So how has Elvis been since his death? 'It's been enjoyable, but it's been a constant battle, growing a beard and this and that, to keep from being recognized…I'm hoping that a lot of people out there are not disappointed with me. I mean, I didn't mean to put anybody through any pain. It's taken a lot to have to do what I had to do. But in the long run it's going to pay off.'"

## MORE ON TAPE

"The tape was supposedly made in 1981. Elvis said he hadn't had a sleeping pill in three years and didn't like the films about him. He said he plans to come out when 'the time is right.'"

## HE'S BACK

"Soon America's tabloids were swamped with tales from chubby waitresses who had lived with Elvis and pimply-face teenagers who saw someone who looked like him at the local hamburger heaven.

"In the June 28, 1988, issue of the supermarket tabloid *Weekly World News*, amid such headlines as 'Space Aliens Graveyard Found!' and 'Man Keeps Wife's Body in Freezer for 23 Years!' and 'Cheeseburger Kills Space Alien!' was this shocker:

I'VE SEEN ELVIS AND HE'S ALIVE AND WELL!
Woman spots Presley at a Kalamazoo Burger King"

## EYEWITNESS ACCOUNT

"The diligence of *Weekly World's* reporters had turned up an eyewitness, Louise Welling, fifty-one, a Kalamazoo, Michigan housewife, who said she saw Elvis twice; in September she had gone to Felpausch's grocery in suburban Vicksburg, Michigan, after church, and spotted him in the next checkout lane. He was buying a fuse. 'He was dressed in an all-white jumpsuit and holding a motorcycle helmet,' she said. 'He'd lost weight, and he didn't have sideburns.'

"She spotted him a second time two months later at the J. C. Penney entrance of the Crossroads Mall. And in May her children saw Elvis in a red Ferrari at a Burger King drive-through window."

## TOUGH QUESTIONS

"Was Elvis Alive?

"And if so, why hadn't he had a hit lately?

"I conducted my own investigation.

"The first thing I had to answer was: why Kalamazoo?

"Why did Elvis Presley, Tupelo, Mississippi native and longtime Memphis, Tennessee resident pick Kalamazoo for his hideaway?

"I had no clue. I didn't even know where Kalamazoo was."

## THE INVESTIGATION

"To help unravel the mystery, I sent for the Kalamazoo Chamber of Commerce's newcomer guide. I assume Elvis must have done this in those hectic last days before his death...What was it about Kalamazoo, I kept asking myself?...the annual Michigan Wine & Harbor Festival in September?...the Kellogg Bird sanctuary? The NASA/Michigan space center?

"Terrific stuff, sure, but nothing Elvis would have cared about.

"I couldn't find any plausible explanation until I spotted a short paragraph on the back of the Kalamazoo County 'come and see our corner of Michigan' brochure. It leaped out at me: 'Kalamazoo County...is the world headquarters of the Upjohn Company, and you can take a fascinating tour of their pharmaceutical production facility.'

"Bingo."

## DRUG STORE COWBOY

In the last 7 months of his life, Elvis had 5,300 uppers, downers, and painkillers prescribed for him.

## ELVIS LIVES AGAIN

"Just when you thought it was safe to read a supermarket tabloid again, the *National Examiner* was back on the Elvis Lives story. E had been spotted living on a farm near Cleveland, Alabama. He'd been glimpsed at the local pharmacy and at the Dogwood Inn in Oneonta, Alabama. He was using the name Johnny Buford during his Alabama sojourn."

# GOLDWYNISMS

*Samuel Goldwyn was one of Hollywood's great movie producers. He was also famous for murdering the English language—sort of the Yogi Berra of the film world. In Hollywood, his sayings were called Goldwynisms. Here are some classic examples:*

"All this criticism—it's like ducks off my back."

"Too caustic? To hell with the cost—we'll make the movie anyway."

"We've all passed a lot of water since then."

*Asked about the message of one of his films:* "I'm not interested in messages. Messages are for Western Union."

"I'm willing to admit that I may not always be right...But I'm never wrong."

"Tell me, how did you love the picture?"

"I want a movie that starts with an earthquake and works up to a climax."

"I'll believe in color television when I see it in black and white."

"Don't let your opinions sway your judgment."

"Let's have some new clichés."

"These days, every director bites the hand that laid the golden egg."

"In two words: im possible."

"This music won't do. There's not enough sarcasm in it."

"Let's bring it up to date with some snappy 19th century dialogue."

"If you can't give me your word of honor, will you give me your promise?"

"A verbal contract isn't worth the paper it's written on."

"Anyone who goes to see a psychiatrist ought to have his head examined."

"The most important thing in acting is honesty. Once you've learned to fake that, you're in."

"If I could drop dead right now, I'd be the happiest man alive."

**The island of Cyprus has one movie theater for every eight of its inhabitants.**

# TISSUE TALK

*According to Harry L. Rinker, "all toilet paper is not created equal." Rinker should know—believe it or not, he collects the stuff. Here's "Rinker on Collectibles," a column excerpted from* Antiques and Collecting *magazine.*

If you have traveled abroad or used an outhouse, you are aware of one basic truth—all toilet paper is not created equal. What a perfect excuse to collect it.

**BEGINNER'S NOTE**

On the surface, collecting toilet paper need not be an expensive hobby. Select pilfering from public restrooms and friends' bathrooms will provide enough examples to begin a collection. Of course, if you travel abroad to obtain examples, the costs increase considerably. However, I discovered that once my friends found out that I have a toilet paper collection...their personal contributions rolled in.

**GETTING STARTED**

I became aware of the collectible potential of toilet paper in the late 1970s when I learned about a woman who was appearing on the Women's Club lecture circuit talking about the wide assortment of toilet paper that she encountered during her travels. She charged a fee for her presentation and did not seem to lack bookings. She obviously was cleaning up.

After resisting the urge to follow suit for almost a decade, I simply gave up and began my own toilet paper collection. My initial beginnings were modest. I wrote to several German friends and asked them to send me some examples of German toilet paper. Udo, my friend in Hamburg, outdid himself. Among the examples he sent was toilet paper from the German railroad.

A close examination of the light gray textured paper revealed that each sheet was stamped "Deutsche Bundesbahn." This says something about a nation's character. The German railroad administration is so concerned about a roll of toilet paper that they find it necessary to stamp their name on every sheet. The ridiculousness of the German railroad administration is surpassed by the English government. When you use the public restrooms at government museums throughout England, you quickly notice that each sheet of toilet paper is marked "Official Government Property." What a subtle way to recognize that your tax dollars are at work.

## GI T.P.

The U.S. military now issues its field troops camouflage toilet paper. It seems the Viet Cong used mounds of used white stuff to track our troop movements during the Vietnam War. What happened to the good old, collapsible GI shovel?

## THE RULES

Since toilet paper collecting is in its infancy, now is an excellent time to create rules concerning how to validly accumulate this important new collectible. For example, how many sheets are necessary to have a valid example? Ideally, I suggest four to six; but, a minimum of two, one to keep in mint condition and the other to record the time and place of acquisition, will do in a pinch.

Do you collect single sheets or the entire roll? This is a tough one. I started out by collecting sheets. Then I began thinking about the potential value of wrappers and added them to my collection. Since I had gone that far, I figured why not save the entire roll. When I realized that same rolls were packaged in units of four to six, I was forced to save the entire package. My collection, which originally was meant to be confined to a shirt box, now occupies several large boxes.

## TALKIN' TOILETS

Toilet paper collecting provides an engaging topic for cocktail parties and other social gatherings. Everyone has a toilet paper story to tell. I remember the time I had to use the facilities in the basement of the Moravian Archives in Herrnhut, East Germany. The nature of the call required my immediately locating a toilet with no regard to the toilet paper status. Later examination revealed no toilet paper, but rather an old railroad time schedule booklet with some of the pages torn out. As I tore a sheet loose, the ink on the paper came off in my fingers. You can imagine the rest. I should have saved an example, but I wasn't thinking of toilet paper collecting at the time.

**The number one use of gold in the United States: Class rings.**

## BE A T.P. CONNOISSEUR

I think everyone should be required to use a farm or camp outhouse at some point in his or her life. The stories of corn cobs and Sears catalogs are true. I know. I remember the concern espressed by my rural relatives when Sears switched to glossy paper stock. I have a number of old catalogs in my collection.

As my toilet paper collection grew, I became fascinated with the composition and variety of designs and patterns of toilet paper. When I first visited Germany in the late 1960s, their extremely coarse gray toilet paper had the quality of sandpaper. It was rough, but you had confidence the job was getting done. In 1987 I found that German toilet paper tastes now matched the Americans' desire for soft, almost tissue-like paper. The significance of this shift and what is says about the development of the German character should not be overlooked.

## FAVORITE THINGS

As with all my collections, I have some favorite examples, among which are a half roll of toilet paper that a friend brought me from England that has a surface texture equivalent to wax paper and a German aluminum foil package that contains toilet paper moistened and perfumed to act and smell like a wash and dry. I have a special box in which I put translucent examples, those you can see through when held up to the light. Their use gives real meaning to the phrase "doubling up."

## HELLO OUT THERE

Thus far, I have been unsuccessful in locating other serious toilet paper collectors. They exist; there are collectors for everything. If I can locate them, I would be glad to discuss swapping duplicates.

Meanwhile, you can help. The next time your travels in the U.S.A. or abroad bring you into contact with the unusual during a period of daily meditation, save a few examples and send them to me (care of *Antiques and Collecting* magazine, 1006 S. Michigan Avenue, Chicago, Illinois 60605). Is there the making of a future museum collection here? Time will tell.

# SAY GOODNIGHT, GRACIE

*George Burns and Gracie Allen were two of the only performers to successfully jump from vaudeville to radio to TV. Their sitcom, "The George Burns and Gracie Allen Show," aired from 1951 to 1958. It's been seen continuously in reruns for the last three decades.*

## HOW IT STARTED

George was a small-time vaudevillian and Gracie was jobless and broke when they met in 1924. Gracie went to a New Jersey club to watch a friend of hers perform. Also on the bill: a duo called "Burns and Lorraine." Gracie thought the dancer (Burns) would make a good partner and approached him about working together. George figured he had nothing to lose. At age 27, he had been a flop at everything he'd tried.

In their original act, Gracie was the "straight man," and George got the funny lines. But even as a "straight man," Allen got more laughs than Burns. So he rewrote the act, creating the daffy character that made Gracie famous. It was a selfless, professional gesture for which she always admired him. It was also a canny one—the new act was a hit. By the end of the '20s, the pair were vaudeville headliners. By 1932 they had their own radio show, which grew in popularity until they had a weekly audience of 45 million people.

Then, in the late '40s, George decided radio was on its way out (though not everyone realized it), and he decided to jump to television. Gracie, on the other hand, steadfastly refused to be a part of a TV show. George figured she was just afraid to see how she looked on the small screen—which he considered ridiculous. Some radio stars disappointed their fans with they way they looked, but Burns and Allen didn't have to worry. "Gracie," said George, "looked even better" than she sounded. So he offered her a deal. If she did a test shot on-camera and didn't like the way she looked, he'd forget all about television. She agreed, and he got his way.

Next question: what was the show going to be about? There were hours of meetings with CBS, and according to Burns, he finally asked why they couldn't do their radio program on TV. "Why give us a new look," he asked, "when nobody's seen the old one yet?"

**Tallest man on record: Robert Wadlow— 8 feet 11 inches. He died at age 22, still growing.**

It made sense. The radio series had featured Burns and Allen as themselves, and Blanche and Harry Morton as their next door neighbors. So did the TV series.

## NAME & RANK

• George Burns's real name is Nat Birnbaum. He was born in New York City to a poor, Orthodox Jewish family. Trying to make it in show business before he met Gracie, he'd been "a singer, a dancer, a yodeling juggler, did a roller skating act, an act with a seal, worked with a dog...You name it, I did it."

• As a youth in San Francisco, Gracie hung around theaters, dreaming of becoming an actress. When she graduated from high school, she joined an Irish act as a "colleen," and headed for Broadway. It didn't work—the act fell apart when they got to New York. When she met George she was taking odd jobs just to keep eating, and was seriously considering giving up and going back home.

## LOST TREASURE

The first 50 TV shows B&A did were live. It wasn't until their third season that the program was saved on film, so the reruns we watch today actually begin in 1953, not 1951. What did we miss? George says he appeared in an entire episode with his fly open.

## HEADACHES

It's not easy being a scatterbrain. Despite her three decades in show business, Gracie suffered from severe stage fright...not to mention camera fright. And her concentration on her work was so intense that she frequently suffered from debilitating migraine headaches. She seldom had time to rest in bed, so she had their home decorated in subdued shades of green, pink, and brown to soothe herself.

## SAY GOODNIGHT, GRACIE

• In 1958, Gracie retired. She died in 1964 of heart problems.

• George tried going solo, teamed up with comedienne Carol Channing, and even did a sitcom called "Wendy and Me," with Connie Stevens as a daffy blonde (a bomb). Nothing worked until 1975, when he won an Oscar for *The Sunshine Boys*. After that he became one of America's most venerated—and visible—actors.

# GRACIE ALLENISMS

*Gracie Allen was one of America's funniest comediennes for 40 years. Here are some of her classic TV lines.*

"This recipe is certainly silly. It says to separate two eggs, but it doesn't say how far to separate them."

**Harry von Zell:** "You're sending your mother an empty envelope?"
**Gracie:** "I wanted to cheer her up. No news is good news."

"I read a book twice as fast as anybody else. First I read the beginning, and then I read the ending, and then I start in the middle and read toward whichever end I like best."

"There's so much good in the worst of us, and so many of the worst of us get the best of us, that the rest of us aren't even worth talking about."

**Gracie:** "Every time I bake a cake, I leave it in five minutes too long and it burns."
**Harry von Zell:** "So?"
**Gracie:** "So today I put in one cake, and I put in another five minutes later. When the first one starts to burn, I'll know the second one's finished."

**Gracie:** "You can't give up, Blanche. Women don't do that. Look at Betsy Ross, Martha Washington—they didn't give up. Look at Nina Jones."
**Blanche Morton:** "Nina Jones?"
**Gracie:** "I never heard of her either, because she gave up."

**Harry von Zell:** "Gracie, isn't that boiling water you're putting in the refrigerator?"
**Gracie:** "Yes, I'm freezing it."
**Harry:** "You're freezing it?"
**Gracie:** "Um-hmmm, and then whenever I want boiling water, all I have to do is defrost it."

**Gracie:** "Something smells good."
**Peter:** "It's Mr. Morton's ribs."
**Gracie:** "Really? George only puts cologne on his face."

**George:** "What's that?"
**Gracie:** "Electric cords. I had them shortened. This one's for the iron, this one's for the floor lamp."
**George:** "Why did you shorten the cords?"
**Gracie:** "To save electricity."

# ALL-AMERICAN SPORTS

*Football and basketball are American creations, right? Well, sort of. Here's where "our" sports really come from.*

## FOOTBALL

**Historical Origin:** Football is a hybrid of soccer and rugby, two sports imported by British colonists. Rugby, which allows players to pick up the ball and run with it, was adapted by the British from a 2nd century Roman game called "harpastum." Soccer originated in Florence, Italy, in the mid-1500s.

**American Origin:** Harvard University is credited with establishing American football, which was introduced on the campus in 1869 as "The Boston Game." In 1875, Harvard beat Yale in the first U.S. intercollegiate game; there were 15 players on each team. The 11-man team with a quarterback was added five years later.

• Football got so violent that, in 1905, 18 men died from injuries sustained on the field. There was a public outcry to ban it, but a football enthusiast named President Theodore Roosevelt stepped in. He called an emergency meeting of college football officials and instituted safety measures that enabled football to survive.

## BASKETBALL

**Historical Origin:** 16th century Aztecs played "ollamalitzli," a basketball-like game: Players tried to "shoot" a rubber ball through a stone ring on a stadium wall and the team that scored first won. Ollamalitzli "professionals" didn't play for huge contracts and shoe endorsements. The player who scored the goal won all of the audience's clothes. And the losing team's captain was...beheaded.

**American Origin:** In 1891 James Naismith, a gym teacher at the Young Men's Christian Association Training School in Springfield, Massachusetts created a game for his bored students. He hung two peach baskets on opposite ends of the gym, chose two 9-man teams, and told each team to try to score without running, or kicking the ball. Kids spread the new game to other schools.

• Two initial differences: An unlimited number of players could play at the same time (even 100), and baskets still had bottoms in them. Every time someone scored, they had to stop and get the ball out. It took two decades to come up with an open-bottom net.

# PUBLIC ENEMY #1

*In the '20s and '30s, gangsters like Machine Gun Kelly, Pretty-Boy Floyd, and Baby-Face Nelson literally shot their way into the headlines. All of them became legendary figures, but one captured the public's imagination more than any other—John Dillinger. Here is his story.*

## BACKGROUND

During the Depression, the American public developed an insatiable appetite for crime-buster stories. John Dillinger seemed to be the perfect romantic criminal—handsome, dapper, arrogant and audacious.

In reality, Dillinger's life was less romantic than his image. Born in Indianapolis in 1902, he was a chronic drifter. He enlisted in the U.S. Navy in 1923 after being dropped by his girlfriend, and five months later, deserted to take up armed robbery. His first prison sentence soon followed—ten years at the Indiana State Reformatory for a grocery store stick-up in Mooresville, Indiana. Twice Dillinger tried to escape. He failed both times.

Then, in 1933, he was released on parole. Three weeks later he robbed a factory manager in Illinois. One week after that, he pulled off his first bank robbery—$3,000 from a Daleville, Indiana bank. Seeing that crime could (at least temporarily) pay, Dillinger formed a gang. Within three weeks they robbed $10,000 from a Montpelier, Indiana bank and $28,000 in Indianapolis.

Dillinger was captured in Dayton, Ohio but his gang stormed the jail, killed the sheriff and freed their boss. Two days later they stole an arsenal of machine guns and bullet-proof vests from an Auburn, Indiana police station. Now Dillinger was officially Public Enemy Number One, according to the FBI.

## THE HUNT

A nationwide manhunt ensued. By this time, Dillinger's antics were a nationwide obsession. *Time* magazine ran an article called "Dillinger Land," which included a board game listing all of his crimes.

Dillinger's gang moved onto Wisconsin, where they heisted $28,000 from a bank in Racine. In early 1934, they robbed an East

Chicago, Indiana bank, killing a bank guard in the process. Once again, Dillinger was captured—this time in Tuscon, Arizona. Dillinger was flown to Indiana to be tried for the bank guard murder.

A month later, in perhaps his most outrageous exploit, he broke out of jail again—by carving a look-alike pistol out of a washboard, which he used to threaten the sheriff, Mrs. Lillian Holley. To add insult to injury, he used the sheriff's car to escape.

Over 600 FBI agents were now assigned to capture Dillinger. But backed by a gang of bandits that included Baby Face Nelson, Dillinger eluded FBI agents. In St. Paul, Minnesota, the FBI cornered the gang but allowed Dillinger to escape through the back door. On May 15, Congress asked for the public's help—offering a $25,000 reward for his capture.

## THE CAPTURE

Finally, on July 22, 1934, the FBI got their man. Thanks to a tip from Anna Sage, the so-called "Woman In Red," the FBI learned that Dillinger planned to attend a movie in Chicago that night with Sage (who ran a local brothel) and his new girlfriend, a waitress named Polly Hamilton. The trio went to see *Manhattan Melodrama* (starring Clark Gable and William Powell) at the Biograph Theater.

Sage wore a red dress for identification. When Dillinger emerged from the theater, Melvin Purvis, the head of the FBI's manhunt, lit a cigar as a signal to waiting agents. The two women disappeared. Sensing something suspicious was going on, Dillinger reached into his pocket for his pistol. Before he could fire, the FBI killed him in a volley of gunfire.

## DILLINGER FACTS

- Reportedly, several people dipped their handkerchiefs in his blood outside the Biograph Theatre for a future souvenir.
- After Dillinger's death, the Chicago morgue opened its doors, so the public could view the corpse of "public enemy number one."
- FBI Chief J. Edgar Hoover kept a plaster facsimile of Dillinger's death mask at the FBI in one of his offices. Alongside it was Dillinger's straw hat and the unsmoked cigar he was carrying on the night of his death.

# DISNEY STORIES: THE LITTLE MERMAID

*Disney Studios' 1989 cartoon, The Little Mermaid, was adapted from a story by the Brothers Grimm. Of course, the Disney version and the original story were substantially different. Here are Jim Morton's examples of how the tale was changed.*

## THE DISNEY VERSION

A young mermaid, infatuated with humans, saves a Prince from drowning and immediately falls in love with him. But she realizes that there's no way he'll ever love her unless she can walk on land, so she goes to the evil Sea Witch and asks for help.

• The Witch agrees to help...but with certain conditions: The mermaid must give up her voice; and the Prince must fall in love with her within a week. The mermaid agrees without hesitation.

• When it looks like the Little Mermaid may actually win the prince's love in time, the Sea Witch uses the mermaid's voice to trick him. He falls in love with the witch instead, and—still under her spell—agrees to marry her.

• The Little Mermaid and her animal friends stop the wedding in the nick of time. Enraged by the interruption, the Witch tries to drown the Prince, but he kills her first.

• The Little Mermaid gets her wish to walk on land, and she joins the Prince she loves. They live happily ever after.

## THE ORIGINAL VERSION

• The Little Mermaid does save the prince from drowning, and does go to the Sea Witch for help. But the similarities end there.

• The Sea Witch doesn't magically steal the mermaid's voice—she cuts her tongue out.

• When the Little Mermaid shows up at the prince's door, he says she reminds him of the girl who saved him from drowning. It sounds promising, but apparently the prince isn't too good with faces—while he's visiting a neighboring kingdom, he meets a princess and decides she's the one who saved him. So he decides to marry her, ruining the mermaid's chance for true love and eternal life. (In this version mermaids don't have souls, so they can't go to heaven when they die. Only humans can).

• The Little Mermaid gets one last chance to save herself. Her sisters go to the Sea Witch and trade their hair for a magic dagger. If the mermaid kills the prince with the dagger before sunrise, she can be a mermaid again.

• She goes to kill the prince while he's sleeping, but she can't do it. Instead, she jumps into the ocean, and she dissolves into sea foam.

## SAMPLE PASSAGES (FROM THE ORIGINAL)

"'You must pay me,' said the Witch; 'and it is not a trifle that I ask. You have the finest voice of all here at the bottom of the water; you think you can use it to enchant the Prince, but you have to give it to me.'

"'But if you take away my voice,' said the Little Mermaid. 'What will remain to me?'

"'Your body,' replied the Witch; 'your graceful walk, and your eyes should be enough to capture a human heart. Well, have you lost your nerve? Put out your little tongue, and I'll cut it off.'

"...And she cut off the little mermaid's tongue. Now the Princess was dumb; she could neither sing nor speak."

• • •

*The Little Mermaid's sisters show up carrying a knife.*

"'The witch has given us a knife; here it is...Before the sun rises you must thrust it into Prince's heart, and when the warm blood falls on your feet, they will grow together again into a fishtail...Hurry up! Either he or you must die before the sun rises! ...Kill the Prince and come back! Hurry up!'

"And they vanished beneath the waves. The Little Mermaid drew back the curtain and saw the beautiful bride lying with her head on the Prince's breast. She bent down and kissed his brow...Then she looked at the sharp knife in her hands, and again looked at the Prince, who in his sleep murmured his bride's name ...The knife trembled in the mermaid's hand. But then she threw it far away into the waves—they turned red where it fell, and it seemed as though drops of blood spurted up out of the water. Once more she looked at the Prince; then she threw herself into the sea, and felt her frame dissolving into foam."

# ALFRED HITCHCOCK PRESENTS

*Alfred Hitchcock was one of the first Hollywood greats to lend his name to a TV show. His acclaimed anthology series ran from 1955 to 1965.*

## HOW IT STARTED

How did Alfred Hitchcock, one of the best-known film directors in the world, wind up on TV at a time when most Hollywood greats were avoiding it? Good advice, that's how. His friend and former agent, Lew Wasserman, was the head of MCA, a burgeoning "entertainment conglomerate" that was itching to get into TV. Wasserman thought Hitch was the perfect vehicle. First, he was a "name." Second, he traditionally made a cameo appearance in each of his enormously successful films, so people knew what he looked like. And third, a major magazine publisher had just contracted with Hitchcock to produce *The Alfred Hitchcock Mystery Magazine*, reinforcing his public image as master of suspense/mystery. Wasserman's immortal comment, uttered at a meeting in early 1955: "We ought to put Hitch on the air."

Wasserman then had to convince Alfred, who was unsure about getting involved. He feared it would hurt his image as a filmmaker, since the movie world looked down on the small screen. But he also trusted Wasserman, who offered him full creative control and advised that he get involved while the medium was young. Hitchcock agreed, and the show was bought by CBS. His appeal was so great that neither the network or sponsor needed a pilot—it simply went on the air. The success secured his place as the personification of "mystery and suspense" in American culture.

## INSIDE FACTS

### Good E-E-Evening

Hitchcock's lead-ins and closing comments often had nothing to do with the episode being aired. They were actually shot 24 at a time, 4 times a year, and spliced into completed episodes.

**Cher, Tom Cruise, Richard Chamberlain, and Greg Louganis are dyslexic.**

**Crime Does Pay**

The ownership of each episode of "Alfred Hitchcock Presents," after showing on TV once, reverted to Alfred Hitchcock. In 1964, he traded the rights to the series (along with ownership of *Psycho*) to MCA for 150,000 shares of the company's stock. This made him MCA's 4th largest shareholder, and an extremely wealthy man.

**Unlikely Source**

The Hitchcock theme song was actually a classical piece chosen by Alfred himself. It is Gounod's "Funeral March of a Marionette."

**Just Kidding**

Sponsors weren't happy with Alfred's constant put-downs of their commercials, until they discovered that the audience liked the companies better for having a sense of humor (which they didn't really have). Then they stopped hassling him about it.

**Un-Sawn Episode**

The only episode of *Hitchcock Presents* which was never shown was called "The Sorcerer's Apprentice." It was a story about a retarded boy who watched a magician saw a man in half and then killed someone trying to duplicate the trick. CBS refused to allow it on TV, saying it was too morbid.

**Guest Star**

In 10 years, Alfred Hitchcock actually directed only 20 out of the 362 episodes of the show.

**Doodling**

Hitchcock, who was once a commercial artist, drew the famous sketch of his profile that appeared on the show.

**Buried Treasure**

Most of the story ideas for the program came from short stories and novels. Hitchcock believed that if an author had a really good idea, he wouldn't use it in a TV script—he'd save it and use it in his own work. One year, his staff read more than 400 novels before they found 32 stories they could use.

**Two cultures in the world don't use fire—Andaman islanders and Pygmies.**

# GOOD E-E-EVENING

*Before each episode of "Alfred Hitchcock Presents," the "Master of Suspense" offered a few pearls of wisdom, like these.*

"There is nothing quite so good as a burial at sea. It is simple, tidy, and not very incriminating."

"We seem to have a compulsion these days to bury time capsules in order to give those people living in the next century or so some idea of what we are like. I have prepared one of my own. I have placed some rather large samples of dynamite, gunpowder, and nitroglycerin. My time capsule is set to go off in the year 3000. It will show them what we are really like."

"The paperback is very interesting, but I find it will never replace a hardcover book—it makes a very poor doorstop."

"These are bagpipes. I understand the inventor of the bagpipes was inspired when he saw a man carrying an indignant, asthmatic pig under his arm. Unfortunately, the man-made sound never equalled the purity of the sound achieved by the pig."

"When I was a young man, I had an uncle who frequently took me out to dinner. He always accompanied these dinners with minutely detailed stories about himself. But I listened—because he was paying for the dinner. I don't know why I am reminded of this, but we are about to have one of our commercials."

"The length of a film should be directly related to the endurance of the human bladder."

"In each of our stories, we try to teach a little lesson or paint a little moral—things like Mother taught: 'Walk softly and carry a big stick'; 'Strike first, ask questions after'—that sort of thing."

"I seem to have lost some weight and I don't wish to mar my image. I cannot reveal exactly how much weight. I can only say that had I lost ten more pounds, I would have had to file a missing persons report."

# INVASION! PART III

*This wasn't exactly an invasion—but in 1942, the Japanese did attack California...sort of. Actually, the reaction was more memorable than the invasion itself.*

**THE INVADERS:** A Japanese submarine.

**THE DATE:** February 23, 1942.

**BACKGROUND:** On December 7, 1941, Japan attacked Pearl Harbor. The U.S. responded by declaring war on Japan. Did Japan plan to attack the West Coast next? Californians watched the skies warily.

**THE INVASION:** About three months after America entered World War II, a Japanese submarine surfaced near the town of Goleta, California, eight miles north of Santa Barbara. It hurled 15 shells at refineries owned by the Bankline Oil Company, and disappeared. It escaped, despite an all-out search launched by the Navy and Air Force.

The shelling was the first attack on the U.S. mainland since 1918 when a German U-boat fired shells at Cape Cod. There was minimal damage—estimated at $500—and there were no injuries. However, reports that an airplane hangar was spotted on the submarine's rear deck caused jitters in Southern California. People began preparing for an imminent air attack.

**AFTERMATH:** Two days later, on February 25, shaky nerves gave way to general hysteria in Los Angeles. Early that morning, authorities believed they spotted an enemy plane. Assuming L.A. was under attack, they dispatched Army planes to defend them. The city was blacked out and air-raid alarms went off while local Army officials tried to locate equipment they'd lent to Paramount Pictures for a war movie.

According to the *San Francisco Chronicle*, authorities tried to blow the "enemy plane" out of the sky. They reported: "Anti-aircraft guns pumped thousands of rounds of ammunition toward an objective presumed fixed in the piercing beams of uncounted searchlights."

Then red-faced officials realized it was a false alarm; the object in question turned out to be the planet Venus.

**At last count, there were only ten Rolls Royces in the Soviet Union.**

# THE BASEBALL MYTH

*According to traditional baseball lore, our national pastime was invented by Abner Doubleday, in Cooperstown, New York. Was it? Not even close. Here's the truth.*

## THE MISSION

At the turn of the century, baseball was becoming a popular pastime...and a booming business. Albert G. Spalding, a wealthy sporting goods dealer, realized that the American public would be more loyal to a sport that had its origins in the U.S. than one with roots in Europe. So it became his mission to sell baseball to America as an entirely American game.

## THE COMMISION

In 1905, Spalding created a commission to establish the origin of baseball "in some comprehensive and authoritative way, *for all time*." It was a tall order for any historian, but Spalding was no historian—and neither were the friends he appointed to his blue-ribbon commission.

Spalding gave six men honorary positions: Alfred J. Reach, head of another sporting goods company (known by many as the "Business Genius of Base-Ball"), A.G. Mills, the third president of the National League; Morgan G. Bulkeley, first president of the National League; George Wright, a businessman; and Arthur P. Gorman, a senator who died before the study was completed. James Sullivan, president of an amateur athletic union, functioned as secretary for the commission.

## THE SUBMISSIONS

In 1907, the Special Baseball Commission issued the Official Baseball Guide of 1906-7, a report which A.G. Mills said "should forever set at rest the question as to the origin of baseball." What research had the group compiled in almost three years? Their files contained just three letters—one from Henry Chadwick, an Englishman who had helped popularize baseball; one from Spalding himself; and one from James Ward, a friend and supporter of Spalding.

In his letter, Chadwick pointed out the obvious similarities between baseball and a game called "rounders," a popular sport in England as well as Colonial America. Rounders was played on a diamond with a base on each corner. A "striker" with a bat would stand beside the fourth base and try to hit balls thrown by a "pecker." If he hit the ball fair, the striker could earn a run by "rounding" the bases. If the striker missed the ball three times, or if his hit was caught before touching the ground, he was "out." After a certain number of outs, the offensive and defensive teams switched. Ring a bell? It didn't with Spalding and his men. The commission, which selected Chadwick's letter to represent the "rounder's contingent," quickly dismissed it because Chadwick was born in England.

In deference to Spalding, James Ward supported the theory of American origin, though his letter stated that "all exact information upon the origin of Base-Ball must, in the very nature of things, be unobtainable." His testimony amounted to no more than a friendly opinion.

Spalding's letter vehemently argued "that the game of Base-Ball is entirely of American origin, and has no relation to, or connection with, any game of any other country." On what evidence did he base this argument, as well as the Doubleday/Cooperstown theory? On the letter of a mystery man named Abner Graves, a mining engineer from Denver, who claimed to recall Doubleday inventing the game of baseball *sixty-eight* years earlier (Graves was over eighty years old when he gave his account).

## THE OMISSION

In his report, Spalding stated that Graves "was present when Doubleday first outlined with a stick in the dirt the present diamond-shaped field Base-Ball field, including the location of the players on the field, and afterward saw him make a diagram of the field, with a crude pencil on paper, memorandum of the rules of his new game, which he named 'Base Ball.'" However, none of this romantic imagery was actually in the Graves letter—no stick and no "crude pencil diagram of the rules"—Spalding made the whole thing up. Nor was Graves present at the first game, as Spalding claimed. Graves stated in his letter, "I do not know, nor is it possible to know, on what spot the first game was played according to Doubleday's plan." Graves' letter simply recounted the rules of the game, and how he thought Doubleday "improved" an *already existing game* called Town Ball. Spalding cleverly embellished and promoted the old miner's tale to make it the stuff of legends.

Spalding was also clever enough to know that Doubleday, a famous Civil War general, was "legend material" and would be an effective marketing tool in selling the Doubleday/Cooperstown myth. "It certainly appeals to an American's pride to have had the great national game of Base Ball created and named by a Major General in the United States Army," wrote Spalding.

## DOUBLEDAY AND BASEBALL

- No record associated Doubleday and baseball before 1905.
- Doubleday entered West Point September 1, 1838, and was never in Cooperstown in 1839.
- Doubleday's obituary in the New York Times on January 28, 1893, didn't mention a thing about baseball.
- Doubleday, himself a writer, never wrote about the sport he supposedly invented. In a letter about his sporting life, Doubleday reminisced, "In my outdoor sports, I was addicted to topographical work, and even as a boy amused myself by making maps of the country." No mention of baseball.

## BASEBALL IN EARLY WRITTEN RECORDS

The game of "baseball" was well documented long before its purported invention in 1839.

- In 1700, Revered Thomas Wilson, a Puritan from Maidstone, England, wrote disapprovingly about some of the events taking place on Sunday. "I have seen Morris-dancing, cudgel-playing, baseball and cricketts, and many other sports on the Lord's Day."
- In 1774, John Newberry of London published a children's book named *A Little Pretty Pocket-Book*. The 30-page book presents a number of games, each one with a rhyme and woodcut illustration. One of the games in the book is "BASE-BALL," which is described in the following rhyme:

BASE-BALL
The Ball once struck off,
Away flies the Boy
To the next destin'd Post
And then Home with Joy.

The accompanying illustrations depicts some young boys playing what is clearly a hit-the-ball-and-run kind of game. Posts mark separate bases at the corners (posts were used as bases in American baseball well into the 1860s). One boy is tossing the ball; another is waiting to strike the ball, while waiting beside a base; at a different base, another boy is poised to make a dash for "home."

Other early written references to baseball include the following:

- A 1744 book describes a rounders-like game as "base-ball."
- So does an 1829 London book called *The Boy's Own Book.*
- The acclaimed author Jane Austin refers to "baseball" in her 1798 novel, *Northanger Abbey.*
- C.A. Peverlly, in *The Book of American Pastimes*, published in 1866, clearly affirms that baseball came from the English game of rounders.

## AT THE TIME

- Francis C. Richter said Spalding "...was the greatest propagandist and missionary the game ever knew and spent more time, labor, and money in spreading the gospel of Base Ball than any other man of record."
- The *New York Times* said: "The canny sports writer now refers to Abner with his tongue in cheek." *The Sun* of NewYork called it "a popular and harmless legend."

## NUTS TO YOU

*The average American eats about nine pounds of peanuts per year.*

- Americans eat about 800 million pounds of peanut butter each year, enough to spread across the Grand Canyon's floor.
- The peanut wasn't popular in America until the late 1800s, when the Barnum Circus began selling them under the Big Top.
- Arachibutyophobia is the fear that peanut butter will stick to the roof of your mouth.
- One of Elvis Presley's favorite foods was a fried peanut butter and banana sandwich; Chef Julia Child loves peanut butter on corn chips.

# LANDSLIDE LYNDON

*In 1964, Republicans claimed that Democratic Presidential nominee Lyndon B. Johnson had a sordid past that included stealing his senate seat in 1948. It turns out they were right. This wonderful piece was contributed by B.R.I. member Michael Dorman.*

**THE RACE BEGINS**

In 1948, while serving as a relatively obscure member of the House of Representatives, Lyndon Johnson entered the race for a vacant Texas seat in the Senate. Four other candidates were campaigning for the position in the Democratic primary. The most prominent among them was Coke Stevenson, who had served two terms as governor of Texas.

Since the Republican party fielded only token candidates in those days in Texas, victory in the Democratic primaries was equivalent to election. In the first primary for the Senate seat, Stevenson led the balloting with 477,077 votes—71,460 more than Johnson, who finished second. But because the remaining votes were divided among the other three candidates, Stevenson failed to win a majority of all ballots cast. Under Texas law, a second (or runoff) primary between Stevenson and Johnson was required to choose the winner of the Senate seat.

**MR. BIG**

During the period between the first and second primaries, Johnson forged a political alliance with a notoriously corrupt southern Texas political boss named George P. Parr. For almost four decades, Parr and his father before him had ruled as virtual feudal barons over a five-county area of oil-rich, sagebrush country just north of the Mexican border. Their subjects—thousands of Mexican-Americans—lived in terror of the Parr political machine.

Year after year, the frightened citizens trudged to the polls and voted the straight Parr ticket. This solid bloc of votes, guaranteed to any politician who won Parr's favor, could tip the balance in a close statewide race.

In the runoff, the initial returns from the five counties controlled by Parr gave Johnson 10,547 votes and Stevenson only 368. But Stevenson had run strongly in other parts of the state. When the statewide returns were tabulated, they showed Stevenson defeating Johnson by the razor-thin margin of 112 votes out of a total of almost 1 million cast.

## HEADS I WIN, TAILS YOU LOSE

It was then that George Parr reached into his bag of political tricks and produced for Lyndon Johnson what came to be known as "the miracle of Box 13." After all the statewide returns were in and Johnson appeared to be the loser, Parr's election officials in Precinct (Box) 13 in the town of Alice suddenly claimed they had discovered some additional votes that had not previously been counted. Johnson's campaign manager, John Connally (who would later serve as Governor of Texas and U.S. Secretary of the Navy and Secretary of the Treasury), rushed to Alice to confer with the officials who would count the ballots that had supposedly been found. Former Governor Stevenson—fearing that Parr was in the process of trying to steal the election for Johnson—also hurried to the scene to protect his interests. He took with him two aides, James Gardner and Kellis Dibrell, who had formerly been FBI agents.

The ballot box from Precinct 13 was put away, purportedly for safekeeping, in a bank vault. The hitch was that the bank, along with almost everything else in the area, was controlled by George Parr.

It was not until six days after the election that Parr's officials submitted their revised tally of the votes from Box 13. They claimed they had found 203 ballots that had not previously been tabulated. Of those, they maintained, 201 had been cast for Johnson and only 2 for Stevenson. Thus, if these supposed ballots were allowed to stand, Johnson would win the primary by 87 votes.

By the time the additional votes were tabulated, a subcommittee of the Texas Democratic Executive Committee—assigned to count and certify the statewide ballots—had already issued a report declaring Stevenson the winner. But within hours after the subcommittee's declaration of what were assumed to be the final results, Johnson's aides announced that they expected the tabulation of the additional votes from Box 13 to change the outcome.

With the claim that the 201 newly discovered votes for Johnson would give him the victory, the situation in Parr's territory grew tense. Former Governor Stevenson and his aides demanded to see the list of registered voters in Precinct 13 so that they could check whether fraudulent ballots had been cast. Like the supposed ballots, the list of voters had also been locked in the bank vault. Bank officers, some of whom served as election officials for Parr, initially refused to allow Stevenson's men to see the list. Stevenson's aides had intended to examine it, note the names of the supposed voters, and then check whether such persons actually existed and had voted. Rumors swept Parr's territory that he and his henchmen were prepared to resort to gunplay, if necessary, to prevent inspection of the voting list. Standing by was his force of heavily armed *pistolero* sheriff's deputies. Stevenson appealed for help from the state capital in Austin, asking that a force of Texas Rangers be dispatched to the scene to prevent violence and ensure an honest count of the ballots. State officials responded by sending one of the most famous Texas Rangers of all time, Captain Frank Hamer, the man who had tracked down the notorious Bonnie Parker and Clyde Barrow and led the posse that killed them in a blazing Louisiana gun battle.

**BULLETS AND BALLOTS**

On the morning after Hamer's arrival, a showdown loomed in Wild West fashion on the street outside the bank. Five of Parr's henchmen, with loaded rifles at the ready, stood ominously across the street from the bank. A dozen others, with *pistolas* conspicuously displayed, formed a semicircle directly in front of the bank. Former Governor Stevenson, fearing Parr's men might try to shoot him and his aides and then claim self-defense, ordered his assistants to take off their coats before approaching the bank—to make clear they were carrying no concealed weapons.

Then, minutes before the bank was scheduled to open, Captain Hamer led Stevenson and his aides toward the bank. He halted a few feet from the semicircle of Parr men, stepped out in front of Stevenson's group, and stood there for a few moments to make sure everyone present recognized him.

In a scene that could have come right out of *High Noon*, Hamer crossed the street and set himself squarely in front of the five

**About half of Nicaragua's population is younger than 18.**

riflemen. He pointed his finger to the far end of the street and ordered, "Git!"

The men grumbled and swore for a few seconds, but then obeyed. Hamer next crossed back to the semicircle of men in front of the bank, surveyed the group silently at first, then barked, "Fall back!" The men cleared a path for Hamer, Stevenson and his aides to enter the bank.

## LOOK, BUT DON'T TOUCH

Tom Donald, a Parr aide who ran the bank and also handled political chores for the local organization, opened the door. Stevenson and his assistants entered, but Hamer would not let the *pistoleros* inside. A short time later, Democratic party officials with responsibility for counting the votes and certifying the election results arrived. One of them, H. L. Adams, demanded that Donald open the bank vault and hand over the election records, since the Democratic party was entitled to serve as custodian of its own primary race documents. But Donald, acting on George Parr's orders, refused to comply.

"I will permit you to see the voting list, but not to handle it," he said. All he would agree to do was remove the voting list from the vault, hold it up, and allow the Stevenson men and party officials to view it from across a wide table. Stevenson and his aides began taking down names and immediately spotted several oddities. The persons whose ballots had been belatedly "found" had all signed their names in what seemed to be the identical handwriting.

Furthermore, their names appeared in ink that differed in color from all other names on the rolls. As if those facts were not suspicious enough, the "late" voters had somehow managed to cast their ballots in alphabetical order. Since voters usually show up at the polls in haphazard fashion, there seemed no reasonable explanation of why all these citizens would have appeared alphabetically.

After Stevenson and his men had recorded the names of only 17 voters, however, a telephone rang and was answered by Parr aide Donald. He listened for a minute, then folded the voting list and put it back in the bank vault. "That's all," he said.

Frustrated but determined to plod ahead, Stevenson's men began trying to locate the 17 persons whose names they had noted.

They quickly discovered that four of them could not have voted: the foursome had long been buried in a local cemetery. Another man whose name appeared on the list was found alive, in a distant Texas city. He denied even being in Parr's county on election day, much less voting there. A local housewife whose name appeared on the list said she had not voted and was not even qualified to vote. After a dogged investigation, Stevenson's aides were unable to find a single person from among the 17 who had actually voted.

**AND THE WINNER IS...**

Stevenson and Democratic party officials went into court, charging that Parr had tried to steal the election for Johnson. They asked the courts to take speedy action to prevent such a theft from receiving official sanction. But Johnson and his forces took court action of their own, seeking to certify Johnson as the winner of the election. They accused Texas Ranger Captain Hamer of entering into a conspiracy with Stevenson, various Democratic party officials, and others to have the belatedly "found" votes set aside as fraudulent. And they asked the court to bar any further recount of the votes. While the rival court actions were pending, the Texas Democratic Executive Committee met in Fort Worth to consider which candidate to certify as the winner. On the first ballot there was a 28-28 deadlock between Stevenson and Johnson. A second ballot produced identical results. Then Johnson, his campaign manager, John Connally, and his lawyer, John Cofer, left the room where the meeting was taking place, after being promised no additional votes would be taken until they returned. They made arrangements to have a member of the executive committee who had not been present for the prior votes flown to Fort Worth from Amarillo, almost 350 miles away. They did not return to the executive committee meeting until the previously absent member, C. C. Gibson, arrived.

On the next ballot, Gibson voted to certify Johnson as the winner—making the tally 29 to 28. The committee then adjourned its meeting.

Although winning the Democratic primary run off guaranteed election in Texas, there was still the formality of a general election. The slate certified by the Texas Democratic Executive Committee was ordinarily listed on the ballot for the general election alongside token slates of candidates fielded by the Republicans and minority parties. In many races, the Republicans did not even bother to nominate candidates. But in any event, it would be necessary for the winners of the Democratic nominations to go through the motions of running in general election campaigns.

Responsibility for printing the official general election ballots rested with Paul Brown, the Texas secretary of state. At the time of the tight, controversial Democratic Executive Committee meeting, Brown was already facing the deadline for ordering the printing of the ballots. But he could not do so until he knew the outcome of the Johnson-Stevenson contest. Once the committee voted to certify Johnson, Brown ordered the ballots printed with Johnson's name as the official Democratic candidate for the Senate.

Former Governor Stevenson then went into the United States district court in Dallas and filed a new lawsuit seeking to overturn the certification of Johnson as winner by both the Democratic Executive Committee and Secretary of State Brown. Federal Judge T. Whitfield Davidson, in whose court the case was filed, had left Dallas for a weekend of relaxation at a farm he owned near Marshall, Texas. Stevenson drove all night to reach Davidson's farm and asked him to sign a court order preventing, at least temporarily, what the former governor contended was the "theft" of the election.

## A BLANK SLATE

Judge Davidson, after reading the legal petition presented by Stevenson, agreed to sign the order. It instructed that all election returns and ballots from George Parr's territory be seized, pending court examination. It also barred Secretary of State Brown from printing the general election ballots until the court examination was completed. A hearing on Stevenson's suit was set for September 21.

Immediately after learning of the court order, Secretary of State Brown rushed to the print shop where the ballots were to be produced. He discovered the ballots were about to begin rolling off the presses. At the last moment, he ordered Johnson's name stricken and the ballots printed without a Democratic senatorial candidate listed.

Johnson and his forces soon counterattacked. They tried to persuade a federal appeals court to overturn Davidson's order, but the best they could do was get the appeals court to set a hearing on the matter for October 2—eleven days after Davidson's own hearing. Meanwhile, Davidson appointed a San Antonio attorney, William R. Smith, to conduct an investigation of the purported vote theft for the court. Smith was empowered to go to Parr's territory, take possession of the election records, subpoena witnesses, and gather evidence on all facts related to the run off election.

Smith lost no time in hurrying to the scene, taking with him federal marshals to help in the investigation. But when they arrived, they discovered that the election records were missing and that the Parr lieutenants whose testimony was wanted had mysteriously gone to Mexico—beyond the reach of the court—on what they claimed was urgent business. The ballot boxes were ultimately found, but all they contained were old newspapers and other trash.

## JUSTICE TO THE RESCUE

Thus, when the hearing opened on September 21 in Judge Davidson's court, the most critical evidence was absent. The voting list, the ballots, and other election materials were gone. Johnson's team of attorneys, including both John Cofer and a friend of Johnson's named Leon Jaworski (later Watergate special prosecutor), seized the opportunity to claim that Stevenson had no case.

"This plaintiff [Stevenson] lost his race for United States senatorial nominee in a Democratic primary, over which only the regular Democratic officials have jurisdiction," Cofer told Judge Davidson. "This court has no jurisdiction. He [Stevenson] has no civil rights [that are being violated], as pleaded in his petition. He is merely a poor loser."

The judge, however, had little patience for such an argument. Banging his gavel to silence Cofer, Davidson denied his request to throw the case out of court. "This plaintiff, Mr. Stevenson, has alleged he has been robbed by fraud of a seat in the United States Senate," the judge said. "Not a shred of evidence has been submitted to disprove his claim. He...is entitled to a hearing in open court. And that hearing he shall have. This court will decide on the merits of his petition."

Davidson was wrong. He would not have a chance to conclude his hearing or decide the case on its merits. Lyndon Johnson had retained a noted Washington lawyer, Abe Fortas, to file a petition with U.S. Supreme Court Justice Hugo Black asking him to order Davidson's hearing halted. (Fortas himself would later serve a controversial term on the Supreme Court, on appointment from his former client, then-President Lyndon Johnson.) Fortas's petition to Justice Black did not deal with the merits of the election fraud charges, but merely contended that the issues in the case should be resolved by the Democratic party and not by the federal courts. Justice Black signed an order forbidding Judge Davidson to proceed further with the hearing or otherwise consider Stevenson's case.

## ORDER IN THE COURT

Justice Black was empowered to issue such an order on his own because the full Supreme Court was not in session at the time. Theoretically, the full court ultimately could have reversed his ruling. But the effect of the order was to halt Judge Davidson's consideration of the case indefinitely. Since the general election was quickly approaching, there would be little time for the full court to hear arguments and reverse Black's decision in time to allow Stevenson to get his name on the general election ballot.

Black's court order was flown from Washington to Texas and presented to Judge Davidson by a federal marshal. Davidson reluctantly halted his hearing. "This court has no choice but to submit to the mandate from the Supreme Court, although, in my opinion, Mr. Justice Black has acted hastily and probably illegally," Davidson said.

For all intents, Justice Black's order put an official seal on what many considered Johnson's theft of the Senate seat—with a major assist from George Parr. Time ran out on Stevenson's further efforts to win court consideration of the vote-fraud charges. Secretary of State Brown ordered Johnson's name listed on the ballot as the official Democratic Senate nominee. Johnson then easily swept to victory in the general election.

## SENATOR JOHNSON

When he returned to Washington as senator, he had a new

nickname—"Landslide Lyndon"—derived from his 87-vote "victory" in the race against Stevenson. Within a few years, he would become the Senate majority leader and be considered the second most powerful man in Washington. Some said he was the most powerful, because President Dwight D. Eisenhower was in the White House at the time and was considered by many a weak chief executive. In 1960 Johnson would be elected vice president on John F. Kennedy's ticket; he would become president upon Kennedy's assassination in 1963 and win his own presidential election a year later.

## THE COURSE OF HISTORY

Thus there is strong reason to speculate that the entire history of the United States might have been radically different if George Parr and his cohorts had not "stolen" the 1948 election for Johnson. If Stevenson had been declared the winner of the senatorial primary, Johnson would have remained in the House for at least several more years. He could not have become Senate majority leader when he did and thus probably would not have been the vice presidential candidate in 1960. As a result, he would not have become president. He himself observed many times that only a fluke could have put him or anyone else from the South or Southwest in the White House under the political conditions prevailing in the United States in the 1950s and 1960s. Actually, in his case, it took two flukes: the first was the purported "theft" of the Senate election, the second was President Kennedy's assassination.

Meanwhile, George Parr continued delivering one-sided majorities at the polls for his pet candidates. Johnson was a major beneficiary of such election manipulation. Another beneficiary was John Connally, who was elected governor of Texas with help from Parr.

## NO JOY IN PARRVILLE

During the early 1970s Parr was indicted on charges of failing to list on his tax returns income of more than $287,000. In March 1974 he was found guilty and sentenced to 10 years in prison. By the time his final appeal was turned down, Parr was 74 years old. He had been convicted of other crimes in the past but had served only one prison term.

He was due to appear in court for a hearing. When he did not show up, he was listed as a fugitive. Federal marshals were sent to hunt for him, and they found him slumped over the steering wheel of his car in a pasture near his palatial home. He was dead, with a bullet wound in his head. A .45-caliber pistol and an M-14 military rifle lay on the car seat. A local justice of the peace ruled the death a suicide, apparently prompted by Parr's reluctance to serve any prison time at his advanced age.

By the time of Parr's death, Lyndon Johnson lay in his own grave. There were those who felt the story of the theft of the 1948 Senate election should be buried along with them.

✓ ✓ ✓

**TV TIME: ALL IN THE FAMILY**

• "All in the Family"'s twelve-and-a-half season run was second only to "Ozzie and Harriet" (which ran fourteen) among TV sitcoms.

• The original title of the show was "Those Were the Days"—hence the name of the theme song.

• The theme was performed with only a piano and two voices (Archie's and Edith's) because Norman Lear had only $800 in his budget to record it and that was the cheapest way to go.

• When Gloria gave birth to "Joey" in 1975, the event inspired another first—the "Joey" doll, billed as the first "anatomically correct male doll."

• Rob Reiner wore a toupee for his role as the long-haired Mike Stivic—he's actually as bald as his father, Carl Reiner. Even without hair, however, fans recognized him on the street wherever he went and yelled "Meathead" after him. He hated it.

• In 1974, Carroll O'Connor went on strike for more money. At first it seemed that his demands couldn't be met—so, according to *TV Guide*, the show's writers came up with an emergency plan to have Archie attend a convention, where he would be mugged and murdered. That way the show could continue with the rest of the cast. O'Connor settled for $2 million per year.

• Edith Bunker was so important to Americans that when she "died" of a stroke in 1980, *Newsweek* ran a half-page obituary, as they would have for a real world leader.

# TRAVELS WITH RAY

*Perplexing adventures of the brilliant egghead Ray "Weird Brain" Redel. Answers are on page 672.*

On occasion, "Weird Brain" Redel, the celebrated thinker, would host a party at his plush home in the Hollywood hills. Of course, everyone who "mattered" in Tinseltown wanted an invitation. But "Weird Brain" had his own agenda... and his own friends. Some were well-known socialites, like Grace Kelly and Prince Ahmed Faroul; some were big brains like Einstein, and others were just...well, people like me.

One starry evening "Weird Brain," Al Schweitzer and Al Einstein were deeply engrossed in a discussion about biology with Jayne Mansfield. Jayne had them enthralled. "Well," she said, "you big, silly brains talk all the time about evolution and that sort of thing. That's so cute." She gave Einstein a peck on the forehead, leaving a big lipstick smear. "OOO, why, I'll bet you don't even know what a duckling becomes when it first takes to water."

"Of course we do, Miss Mansfield," Al Schweitzer interjected, "—a semi-mature aquatic web-toed aviant."

"No, honey," Jayne cooed. "That's not it." And when she explained it to them, the smartest guys in the world had to admit Jayne was right.

**What DID she say?**

Later that evening, "Weird Brain" and a few physicist buddies were discussing their newest discoveries. One little bearded guy with a German accent, dressed in a white smock that made him look as if he had just left Dr. Frankenstein's laboratory, volunteered some startling data. "I have stumbled upon something," he intoned, "that comes once in a minute, twice in a moment, but not once in a thousand years."

The eggheads gasped. How was this possible? "Weird Brain" reached over and gave the guy's beard a tug. It came off...revealing Peter Lorre. "Okay, Pete, enough jokes. Tell them what you mean."

**What did Lorre have in mind?**

# FAMOUS CHEATERS

*In the last Bathroom Reader, we introduced a feature called "Famous Cheaters." Here's another installment.*

**BACKGROUND:** In the mid-50s, quiz shows, like "Tic Tac Dough," "21," and "The $64,000 Question," were the hottest thing on TV. The public couldn't get enough of them. ("The $64,000 Question" was the only show to beat "I Love Lucy" in the annual ratings, ranking as the #1 program of 1955.) Network executives loved them, too, because they were cheap to produce, and extremely profitable. By 1958, over 24 game shows were on the air. The competition grew increasingly fierce.

**QUIZ CROOKS:** Unknown to the public, a number of shows, including "The $64,000 Question," had begun rigging the competition to increase their entertainment value and improve their ratings.

It turned out that answers were often provided to preferred contestants—such as Charles Van Doren, an assistant English professor at Columbia University, who'd been making $5,500 a year. In 1956, the 29-year-old Van Doren became an overnight celebrity thanks to his appearances on the show "21." After knocking off the champion Herb Stempel, Van Doren went on to win $129,000. The media dubbed him "the quiz whiz." Soon after he appeared on the cover of *Time* magazine and was hired by NBC's "Today" show for $50,000.

**THE ACCUSATION:** Stempel was bitter at being defeated by Van Doren. He complained to several New York newspapers that "21" was fixed. There were no immediate reactions to Stempel's revelations, but in 1958 a contestant on CBS's game show "Dotto"—where contestants connected dots to reveal celebrity faces—claimed to have found an opponent's notebook with answers in it.

**THE INVESTIGATION:** In response to growing speculation, the House Committee on Legislative Oversight investigated allegations that quiz shows were fixed. Among the first witnesses to come forward was actress Patty Duke, who had won $64,000 on "The

$64,000 Question." Duke claimed that the show's associate producer, Shirley Bernstein (the sister of conductor Leonard) had secretly given her the correct answers before the show.

But the most damaging revelations were made by Van Doren. In a dramatic confession on November 2, 1959, before the U.S. Senate, he admitted that all his "21" victories had been fixed. Van Doren claimed that producer Albert Freedman "told me that Herbert Stempel, the current champion, was an unbeatable contestant because he knew too much. He said that Stempel was unpopular, and was defeating opponents right and left to the detriment of the program. He asked me if, as a favor to him, I would agree to an arrangment whereby I would tie Stempel and thus increase the entertainment value of the program."

Van Doren appeared remorseful. "I would give almost anything I have to reverse the course of my life in the last three years...I was involved, deeply involved, in a deception." He immediately resigned from his teaching post at Columbia and was fired at NBC's "Today Show" as well.

**THE RESULT:** The nation was shocked by Van Doren's testimony: *Life* magazine wrote that it had "exposed a nation's sagging moral standards." Then-president Eisenhower was quoted as saying "it was a terrible thing to do to the American people." The *Washington Post* ran an editorial saying "it will render very little service to the public to make Charles Van Doren a scapegoat. It is an industry, not an individual, that stands in need of redemption." Almost immediately all game shows—even honest ones—were removed from the air. Congress passed legislation making quiz show fraud punishable by law.

## MISCELLANEOUS

• Charles Van Doren later became an executive with *Encyclopedia Brittanica.* He refused to discuss the scandal after his congressional testimony.

• Dr. Joyce Brothers won $64,000 fielding questions on boxing; Barbara ("Get Smart") Feldon won $64,000 answering questions on Shakespeare. Consolation Prize: Anyone who made it to the big $64,000 question and blew it, still got to drive home in a new Cadillac.

# REAL PEOPLE

*Some rock songs are about real people, though most of us never know it. Here are three examples:*

**BAD, BAD LEROY BROWN, by Jim Croce**

Jim Croce met the man who inspired "Leroy Brown" while he was in the Army, stationed at Fort Dix, New Jersey. He and Croce were both going to school to learn how to become telephone linemen. Croce recalls: "He stayed there about a week and one evening he turned around and said he was really fed up and tired. He went AWOL, and then came back at the end of the month to get his paycheck. They put handcuffs on him and took him away. Just to listen to him talk and see how 'bad' he was, I knew someday I was gonna write a song about him."

**THE SULTANS OF SWING, by Dire Straits**

The Sultans of Swing was a jazz band that Mark Knopfler, leader of Dire Straits, happened to see at a pub one night.

Knopfler: "My brother Dave was living somewhere in Greenwich and we went out to the pub—I think it was called the Swan...and we had a game of pool and a couple of pints. There was a jazz band playing and there was nobody in there except us and a couple of kids in the corner. They did a couple of requests. I asked them for 'Creole Love Call,' and it was great. There are loads of bands like that. They're postmen, accountants, milkmen, draftsmen, teachers. They just get together Sunday lunchtimes, nighttimes, and they play traditional jazz. It's funny, because they play this New Orleans music note-for-note...in Greenwich, England."

**PEGGY SUE, by Buddy Holly**

This was Buddy Holly's first solo record, and one of the most famous "girl-name" records in rock history. But although Buddy made Peggy Sue famous, she wasn't in love with him—she was Cricket drummer Jerry Allison's girlfriend. Later Jerry and Peggy Sue tied the knot, and Buddy celebrated with a tune called "Peggy Sue Got Married." By the time they got divorced, Buddy was dead.

**Take a plane: A cab ride from Los Angeles to New York costs $6,000.**

# MAGAZINE ORIGINS

*They're American institutions now, but once they were just someone's ideas. Here's a quick look at the origins of a few U.S. mags.*

***Reader's Digest.*** A young Minnesotan named DeWitt Wallace realized that modern Americans didn't have time to get all the latest information. They needed quick, easy access to it, and he could provide it in a magazine. Why didn't people just tune in to radio or TV? It was 1920.

On October 15, 1921 DeWitt Wallace and Lila Acheson were married. They also sent out several thousand mimeographed fliers asking people to subscribe to their new digest. When they returned from their honeymoon, more than 1,000 subscriptions were waiting. *Reader's Digest* was born.

***Time.*** In 1923, two Yale friends—Britt Hadden and Henry Luce—also created a sort of "digest." They scoured dozens of newspapers for important news and synopsized it in "approximately 100 short articles, none of which are over 400 words." The first issue (March, 1923), financed by wealthy Yale acquaintances, was a bomb. So they changed directions, hiring a news staff and developing the pointed, pun-filled, opinionated writing style that's now the standard in American magazines. That worked; *Time* flew.

***Fortune.*** Started in February 1930 as a way to use the excess material being produced by *Time*'s business department.

***Newsweek.*** It looks and sounds like *Time* magazine? That's because it was started by a man who'd worked at *Time*, and whose fondest wish was to drive *Time* "out of business." Thomas Martyn started it on February 17, 1933. Today it's owned by the *Washington Post*.

***TV Guide.*** TV was becoming an American institution in 1952 when Philadelphia publisher Walter Annenberg spotted an ad for a magazine called *TV Digest*. Was there really a market for it? His staff said yes...so he decided to start a national TV magazine with regional listings. He bought up the half-dozen regional TV magazines that had already sprung up and consolidated them into a single new publication. The Apr. '53 debut issue featured Lucy's baby.

# SOLUTION PAGE

TRAVELS WITH RAY, PAGE 467

• Ray tossed Bogart a pack of matches. The answer to Bogart's riddle was "Fire." And since he was pointing to a cigarette, "Weird Brain" figured he wanted a light. Bogie, furious, jumped up and challenged "Weird Brain" to a drinking match. They tied three times, then both passed out.

• Casey was talking about a river, of course. I assume it was the Nile, though Casey kept calling it the "Vile."

TRAVELS WITH RAY, PAGE 515

• A map. We bought another one, but got lost anyway, and stumbled into the valley full of prehistoric creatures...but that's another story.

• The wind. Never leaves a shadow, as far as I know.

TRAVELS WITH RAY, PAGE 580

• "Your breath," Charlie guffawed.

• "Weird Brain" shipped his scientific equipment in a coffin. "I hope that doesn't mean my idea is dead, nyuk-nyuk-nyuk," he said. I told him he'd been hanging around the 3 Stooges too long.

MILITARY DOUBLE-TALK, PAGE 607

1-K, 2-J, 3-N, 4-G, 5-I, 6-M, 7-A, 8-C, 9-D, 10-F, 11-H, 12-E, 13-L, 14-B

TRAVELS WITH RAY, PAGE 667

• "You big brains are so-o-o-o goofy," Jayne giggled. "The first thing a duckling becomes when it takes to water is...wet." Not even Einstein could argue with that.

• Lorre was talking about the letter M, a letter he was quite fond of. "M" was the title of the film that made him a star.

*Uncle John's*

# FOURTH BATHROOM READER

Selections from "Prime Time Proverbs" Copyright © 1989 by Jack Mingo and John Javna. Reprinted by permission of the authors.

"The Monster Mash," "Surprise Hits," "Instant Hits," "Songwriter Stories," and "First Hits" originally appeared in *Behind the Hits*. Copyright © 1986, by Bob Shannon and John Javna. Reprinted by permission of the authors.

"Economy Class Syndrome" originally appeared in *The Airline Passenger's Guerrilla Handbook*. Copyright © 1989 by George Albert Brown. Reprinted by permission of Slawson Communications, San Marcos, California.

"Pun For The Money" originally appeared in *Get Thee To A Punnery*, published by Wyrick & Company. Copyright © 1988 by Richard Lederer. Reprinted by permission of the publisher.

"The Press and the Prez" and "In the News" originally appeared in *If No News, Send Rumors: Anecdotes of American Journalism*. Copyright © 1989 by Stephen Bates. Reprinted with permission of St. Martin's Press.

"The Compass in Your Nose" and "Zz-zz-zz" originally appeared in *The Compass In Your Nose and Other Astonishing Facts About Humans*. Copyright © by Marc McCutcheon. Reprinted by permission of Jeremy P Tarcher, Inc., Los Angeles.

"What's In a Name" originally appeared in The Best Baby Name Book in the Whole World, Copyright © 1984 by Bruce Lansky. Reprinted by permission of the publisher, Meadowbrook Press.

# THANK YOU

*The Bathroom Readers' Institute sincerely thanks the people whose advice and assistance made this book possible, including:*

John Javna
John Dollison
Jack Mingo
Phil Catalfo
Ross Owens
Eric Lefcowitz
Mike Litchfield
Fritz Springmeyer
Lyn Speakman
Catherine Dee
Lenna Lebovich
Melanie Foster
Dayna Macy
Megan Anderson
Emma Lauriston
Denise "Hi Ho!" Silver
Nenelle Bunnin
Sharilyn Hovind
Ann Krueger Spivack
Audrey Baer Johnson
Gary the proofreader
Penelope Houston
Mike Goldberger
Gordon Van Gelder
Jay Nitschke
Mike Brunsfeld
Tia Kratter
Zoila Zegovia
Thomas Crapper
Jeff Stafford
The EarthWorks Group
...and all the bathroom readers

This page is for Emergency Use Only.

# UNCLE JOHN'S BATHROOM LEADER

*The Bathroom Reader offers a special "Bowl Me Over" salute to Lyndon Baines Johnson—probably the only president who actually conducted affairs of state while seated on the pot.*

## GETTING IT BACKWARDS

According to Doris Kearns Goodwin, in her biography, *Lyndon Johnson and the American Dream*, "Few Presidents have permitted the kind of intimacy between themselves and their staffs that Johnson encouraged. When he had to go to the bathroom in the middle of a conversation, it was not unusual for him to move the discussion there. Johnson seemed delighted as he told me of 'one of those delicate Kennedyites who came into the bathroom with me and then found it utterly impossible to look at me while I sat there on the toilet.' "

" 'You'd think he had never seen those parts of the body before. For there he was, standing as far away from me as he possibly could, keeping his back toward me the whole time, trying to carry on a conversation. I could barely hear a word he said. I kept straining my ears and then finally I asked him to come a little closer to me. Then began the most ludicrous scene I had ever witnessed. Instead of simply turning around and walking over to me, he kept his face away from me and walked backward, one rickety step at a time. For a moment I thought he was going to run right into me. It certainly made me wonder how that man had made it so far in the world.' "

## THE EARLY DAYS

LBJ's habit of making the most of his "down time" actually began in the 1930s—long before he was elected president. According to biographer Robert Caro, the 24-year-old Johnson, a secretary to a Texas Congressman, bullied the other officeworkers while seated on the pot:

"The toilet in the office was set in a short corridor between its two rooms. Johnson would sit down on it, and there would come a call: "L.E.! [L.E. Jones, Johnson's assistant] L.E.!" L.E. would say,

'Oh, God,' because he hated this. At first, he attempted to stand away from the door, but Johnson insisted he come right into the doorway, so he would be standing over him, and L.E. would stand with his head and nose averted, and take dictation...The tactic was, indeed, 'a method of control'...those who observed it, knew it was being done to humiliate [Jones], and to prove who was boss."

## ONE-MAN SHOW

Though a big believer in bathroom business, Johnson would not tolerate it from his staff. According to Caro, he wouldn't allow them to go to the bathroom at all while they worked: 'If he caught you reading a letter from your mother, or if you were taking a crap, he'd say, "Son, can't you *please* try a little harder to learn to do that on your own time?" '

## IN THE NEWS

People in Johnson's inner circle weren't his only victims—even members of the press got a taste of his bathroom manner. Steven Bates describes CBS reporter/White House correspondent Robert Pierpont's lunch with LBJ: "After they had eaten...the President told Pierpont to stay for coffee. By about 3:00 p.m. the conversation had become an LBJ monologue. Pierpont tried again to leave. Johnson stood up and said it was time to cross the hall.

"Pierpont followed Johnson into a bedroom. The President started undressing, handing each piece of his clothing to a valet. LBJ stripped naked, continuing his monologue the whole time. He put on a pajama top and walked into a bathroom, 'speaking loudly, over the sound of passing water.' Then LBJ put on the pajama bottoms and got into bed. He talked for another fifteen minutes, then said good-bye—three hours after the conversation had begun."

## CONSTITUENT SERVICE

Even *voters* occasionally saw Johnson in the altogether. Caro describes a typical scene during LBJ's 1948 campaign for the U.S. Senate: "Rooms in many small-town hotels had only hand basins, with communal toilets at the end of the hall. These bathrooms were small and hot, and it was cooler if the door was left open, so often Johnson left it open. Not a few voters therefore saw the candidate for the U.S. Senate sitting on the toilet, and described that sight to relatives and friends."

# MYTH CONCEPTIONS

*At the BRI, we love "facts" that aren't true. Here's some info that may surprise you.*

**Myth:** The Great Wall of China is visible from the moon.
**Truth:** No manmade objects are visible from that far out in space. According to astronomers, it's about as visible as a popsicle stick from 240 miles away.

**Myth:** Alligator shirts have alligators on them.
**Truth:** They're crocodiles—René Lacoste, a French tennis star known as *le crocodile*, invented them in the 1920s.

**Myth:** The sardine is a species of fish.
**Truth:** The word "sardine" actually refers to any breed of small fish—including herring and pilchard—that's been stuffed into a sardine can.

**Myth:** S.O.S. stands for "Save Our Ship."
**Truth:** It doesn't stand for anything—it was selected as a distress signal because it's easy to transmit in morse code: 3 dots, 3 dashes, 3 dots.

**Myth:** I.O.U. stands for "I owe you."
**Truth:** Originally the borrower wrote "I Owe Unto," followed by the lender's name.

**Myth:** Thumb sucking causes buck teeth.
**Truth:** An old wive's tale. Thumb sucking may even be beneficial. Some researchers believe that it aids the development of facial muscles and bones.

**Myth:** Karate is a Japanese martial art.
**Truth:** It actually started in India and spread to China—before reaching Japan. It first became popular in Okinawa in the 1600s, when officials prohibited Okinawans from possessing weapons.

**Poll Results: Only 29% of married couples agree on most political issues.**

**Myth:** Thomas Edison invented the lightbulb in 1879.

**Truth:** The first incandescent bulb was invented by Sir Humphrey Davy in 1802. But the filaments he used burned out quickly. Edison pioneered the use of carbonized cotton filaments—making the bulbs practical for the first time.

**Myth:** Your ears are the things you see on the side of your head.

**Truth:** Technically, the human ear is located inside the skull, and stops at the end of the ear canal. The parts you can see are called the *pinnas*.

**Myth:** You can judge the nutritional content of an egg by the color of its shell.

**Truth:** Eggshells don't tell you anything about the egg—but they do tell you about the hen that laid it: white eggs are laid by hens with white earlobes; brown eggs are laid by chickens with red earlobes.

**Myth:** The Egyptians were master embalmers.

**Truth:** The dry climate deserves most of the credit. In fact, as Egyptian embalming methods "advanced" over time, corpses began deteriorating more quickly.

**Myth:** Fortune cookies were invented in China.

**Truth:** They were invented in the U.S. in 1918 by Charles Jung, a Chinese restaurant owner, to amuse customers while they waited for their food. Only later were they served *after* the meal.

**Myth:** The French poodle originated in France.

**Truth:** The breed was created in Germany around the 16th century. Called *puddel,* or "splash" dogs, they were bred to retrieve ducks. They didn't become popular in France until years later.

**Myth:** According to the Bible, Angels have wings.

**Truth:** Nowhere in the Bible does it say that angels have wings. The idea didn't become popular until painters and sculptors began adding them.

**There are three times as many cows as people in Montana.**

# THE WHOLE DOUGHNUT

*"Doughnuts," says Michael Lasky in his book* Junk Food, *"are the ultimate junk food. Fortified with globs of sugar and then fried in oceans of hot grease, they have found a niche in our stomachs."*

Doughnuts originated in 16th-century Holland. They were cooked in oil, and were so greasy that the Dutch called them *olykoeks*, or "oily cakes."

The Pilgrims, who'd lived in Holland, brought the cakes with them when they came to America. Their version: a round doughy ball about the size of a nut—a *doughnut*.

The origin of the doughnut hole: Captain Hanson Gregory, a 19th-century Maine sea captain, was eating a doughnut while sailing through a storm. Suddenly the ship rocked violently and threw him against the ship's wheel—impaling his cake on one of its spokes. Seeing how well the spoke held his cake, Gregory began ordering all of his cakes with holes in them.

Doughnuts were popularized in the U.S. after the Salvation Army fed doughnuts—cooked in garbage pails and served on bayonets—to troops during World War I. Soldiers got so hooked on them that they were called "doughboys."

The French have a doughnut they call *pet de nonne,—"Nun's Fart."* According to legend, a nun living in the abbey of Marmoutier was preparing food for a religious feast. Suddenly she farted, and the other nuns laughed at her. She was so embarrassed that she dropped the spoonful of dough she was holding into a pot of boiling oil—accidently making a doughnut.

Doughnut-dunking was first popularized at the Roseland Ballroom in the '20s, when actress Mae Murray slipped and accidentally thrust a doughnut into a cup of coffee.

The *glazed* doughnut is almost three times as popular as any other type of doughnut.

**Attention caffeine addicts: Hawaii is the only U.S. state where coffee is grown.**

# WEIRD BOARD GAMES

*When you think of board games, you probably think of Monopoly or Risk. But there are plenty of bizarre board games you've never heard of. Here are a few examples. (No kidding—these games were really sold.)*

**Dr. Ruth Westheimer's Game of Good Sex.** Based on her sexual advice talk shows. Couples play the game trying to accumulate Arousal Points in quest of Mutual Pleasure. Two to four couples could play but only consenting adults—over 21—were allowed to buy it.

**Mafia.** The purpose: to gain control of Sicilian airports, real estate, construction projects, banks, and drug trade. The rules call for each "family," assisted by henchmen, to move around a map of Sicily selling heroin and eluding the police. The Italian-made board game caused considerable controversy in its native country.

**Is The Pope Catholic?** In 1986, two Boston-based entrepreneurs manufactured this game. Players move around the board trying to attain the rank of pope. Among the obstacles (or temptations) along the way: nipping at holy wine and squandering the church's money on candy. Small miracles help players out. A winner is declared when a cloud of white smoke is sent by the Convocation of Cardinals, signaling the election of a pope.

**Twinkies and Trolls.** The proprietors of "Buddies," a well-known gay bar in Boston, invented this game, which they described as "a lighthearted reflection of gay life and the gay lifestyle." Players come out of the closet, visit their first gay bar and the "baths" in New York, San Francisco, Provincetown, and Ft. Lauderdale. The object is to amass as many "Twinkies" (gay slang for young, attractive preppies), and avoid "Trolls" (old, ugly gay men).

**Class Struggle.** Bertell Ollman was a Marxist professor at New York University when he invented this game. The object is to win the revolution, and each player represents a different class of society. Ollman later wrote a book about his experiences in marketing the game. It was called *Class Struggle Is The Name Of The Game: True Confessions Of A Marxist Businessman.*

**Gender Bender.** Makes players answer questions as if they were members of the opposite sex.

**Trump: The Game.** Developed by real estate tycoon Donald Trump. Like Monopoly, the object is to make the most money. But unlike Monopoly, the smallest denomination is $10 million...and each bill bears Trump's face. Trump explained: "I wanted to teach business instincts. It's great if they can learn that from a game instead of having to go out and lose your shirt." That, of course, was before Trump lost his own shirt.

**NUKE: The Last Game on Earth.** Developed by two architects, Chris Corday and Steve Weeks. The game gives players the chance to be world leaders, deciding the fate of the world. If they can't work out their problems, the world is destroyed.

**Civil War.** In 1989, Naji Tueini, a Lebanese entrepreneur, successful marketed this game based on his country's internal turmoil. It rewards strategy such as "reselling products sent as international assistance" and "taking hostages," but docks points for getting stuck in a fall-out shelter during heavy bombardment. It was translated into English and French.

**It's Only Money.** In 1989, more than 25 major companies (like Porsche, Seagrams, Revlon and Mastercard) paid $30,000 apiece to have their products promoted in this game. Each company got a storefront" on the board where players (or "shoppers") browsed in a bustling shopping mall, trying to avoid crowds on the escalators. The game's creator, Eric S. Medney, described the game as delivering "corporate messages to the entire family while they're having fun."

**Bankruptcy.** The object is to acquire as many companies as possible without going bankrupt. If you do declare bankruptcy, however, you have to play Russian roulette with a toy gun included with the set. If the gun pops, you're out. The inspiration for the game? Victor Smith, its creator, explained: "I was on the edge of bankruptcy when the idea hit me."

# TAMMY FAYE

*Remember when Tammy Faye Bakker was in the news every day? In case you're feeling nostalgic, here are some of the things she's said.*

We were raising money to be missionaries in the Amazon. Can you imagine me in the Amazon! All day long trying to keep my false eyelashes from falling off and my nails from breaking. The only way I would have fit in is that I like jewelry just as much as the natives."

"I'm a good cook. In the evening, I make mostly chicken or tuna sandwiches, or we'll go out for pizza."

"There's times I just have to quit thinking, and the only way I can quit thinking is by shopping."

"We prayed and asked God to give us the money to buy a trailer. We took this meeting in West Virginia, a tiny church up in the mountains. God began to bless and move. We started praying for the trailer in that meeting and people put $100 bills in the offering for us. We were embarrassed because we had been putting $20 and $30 in the bank. Now God was performing a miracle and giving us the most money we had ever had in our lives.... The next week, we purchased the most beautiful 30-foot Holiday Rambler trailer."

"I wear wigs all the time, and Jim never knows who I'm going to be."

"One day while eating supper, little Chi Chi, who liked lima beans, ate some and ran into another room.... When the dog didn't return, I wondered. Jim had seen the dog fall over on the carpet and not get up. Jim went and checked Chi Chi and then gently said, 'Tammy, Chi Chi is dead.'...I prayed and prayed and prayed. 'O Jesus, please raise Chi Chi from the dead.' I expected Jim to bring Chi Chi home any minute.' "

"No matter what they print, no reporter has ever seen me with black tears running down my face, 'cause I always use waterproof mascara."

"My shoppin' demons are hoppin'."

# IN THE NEWS

*In his book,* If No News, Send Rumors, *Stephen Bates tells hundreds of fascinating stories about the news media. It's an excellent bathroom reader. Here are a few excerpts.*

In the early 1700s the price of a newspaper, twopence a copy, was steep. As later gentlemen callers would bring flowers or candy, a man of the era would sometimes bring a newspaper as a gift when calling on a woman, so that she could read of the latest Indian raids, runaway slaves, and pirate attacks.

Early Newspapers were often passed from person to person. Some papers contained one or more blank pages, which a subscriber could fill in with his own news before sending the newspaper on to friends.

A 1987 computer analysis found that these words most frequently appear in the New York Post headlines (in descending order): Cop, Kill, Judge, Wall Street, Death, No, Slay, U.S., Soviet, Court.

The choice for the lead story in *USA Today*'s September 15, 1982 inaugural edition was based on an informal survey undertaken by the newspaper's founder, Al Neuharth. Bashir Gemayel, president-elect of Lebanon had been murdered, and most *USA Today* editors assumed that story would lead the paper, as it did other papers across the country. But Monaco's Princess Grace had died in a car crash, and Neuharth suspected her death was, for most Americans, the more important story.

To find out, he visited a bar and a political gathering. In both places, nearly everyone was talking about Princess Grace. When Neuharth mentioned the Lebanon assassination, people shrugged. The next morning, *USA Today*'s lead story was headlined, "Princess Grace dies in Monaco. Gemayel ended up on an inside page.

When he learned that crucial work on the atom bomb had taken place nearby, the city editor of the *Nashville Tennessean* told a photographer to go out to the research facility and get two pictures—one of a whole atom, and one after it was split.

In the '60s *Rolling Stone* offered a free roach clip to every new subscriber. In the '80s its standard employment contract allowed the magazine to test employees for drug use.

In October, 1967, a major anti-war protest was held in Washington, D.C. Crowd estimates varied widely, in part reflecting the publications' political viewpoints:

*Washington Post:* 50,000
*Time:* 35,000
*Wall St. Journal:* 2,500

On several occasions, William Randolph Hearst's New York *Journal* suggested that President McKinley should be killed. One editorial, for instance, declared that "If bad institutions and bad men can be got rid of only by killing them, then the killing must be done."

For such remarks, the *Journal* was vilified when the president was assassinated in 1901. "The journalism of anarchy," the *Brooklyn Eagle* editorialized, "shares responsibility for the attack on President McKinley." Hearst's enemies spread the false story that McKinley's assassin had been arrested with a copy of the *Journal* in his pocket.

Stung by the criticism, the Journal changed the name of its morning edition to the *American*. Bad feelings remained, though, and five years later the McKinley issue helped defeat Hearst in his campaign for governor of New York.

A *Los Angeles Times* article in 1972 read "70-Car Fog Pileup." In fact, sixty-nine cars had crashed. An editor changed it, reasoning that sixty-nine was a smutty number.

*Washington Post* reporter Carl Bernstein nearly wasn't around to cover the Watergate scandal. Bernstein had asked executive editor Ben Bradlee to make him the full-time rock critic. Bradlee agreed, but the job had ended up going to someone else.

Resentful, Bernstein decided to leave the *Post*. He wrote to *Rolling Stone* and asked if he could replace the departing Hunter S. Thompson as political writer. Bernstein was waiting was waiting for a reply when he was assigned to cover the break-in at the Democratic National Committee's Watergate offices.

# POP QUIZ

*So you think you know popular culture. Here's a chance to find out. Some of the answers are in sections of this book and previous* Bathroom Readers*—all of them are on page 892.*

**CLASSIC TOYS**

1. On the Japanese Barbie, these are even bigger, rounder and more voluptuous than the on the American Barbie. What are they?

2. What do the inventions of Silly Putty and the Slinky have in common?

3. What gives crayons their distinctive smell?

4. Where was the inventor of the Ant Farm when he came up with the idea?

**STYLE**

5.Who invented the Hawaiian shirt and why?

6. What animal is on the alligator shirt?

**ON THE SCREEN**

7. Where did Art Clokey get the idea for the bump on Gumby's little green head?

8. Who almost got the role of Dorothy in the *Wizard of Oz?* Which comic did they write the Wizard's lines for?

9. Who was first choice for the main character in *Casablanca?*

10. Which three of the Stooges were brothers?

11. How much older was Vivian Vance than Lucille Ball?

12. How did *Our Gang*'s Alfalfa die?

**MUSIC**

13. Before it had words, what was the working title of the Beatles' song, *Yesterday?*

14. How many record choices did you get on the first jukebox?

15. The average number of grooves on a 45 RPM record? How does that compare with the number of grooves on a 33 RPM record?

**ART VS. REAL LIFE**

16. Which are there more of in the world: plastic lawn flamingos or real flamingos?

17. Which lasted longer—the TV show M*A*S*H or the real Korean War?

18. The subject of Andy Warhol's first pop paintings was the thing he loved most. What was it?

# MODERN MYTHOLOGY

*A hundred years ago, Americans identified with Uncle Sam, Paul Bunyan, and Johnny Appleseed. Today, there are a new crop of cultural heroes, like these characters:*

**The Campbell's Soup Kids.** Grace Gebbie Wiederseim grew up in Philadelphia in the mid-1800s. One morning when she was a young girl, she stood in front of her parents' mirror and drew a picture of herself. She liked it so much she saved it.

In 1904, Grace was a successful illustrator and the wife of a Campbell's Soup advertising executive. One afternoon he asked her to help create an advertising campaign for Campbell's. She pulled out her childhood self-portrait...and used it to create Dolly Drake and Bobby Blake—the Campbell's Soup Kids.

**Poppin' Fresh (The Pillsbury Doughboy).** In 1965 the Pillsbury Company hired ad exec Rudy Pera to design an advertising campaign for their new refrigerated dough product...But he had trouble thinking of anything that would make the brand stand out. One day he began playfully pounding on a container of the dough, hoping to drum up ideas. "I imagined what could pop out," he recalls. "A dough man? A dough baker? A *dough boy*?" Polls taken more than 20 years later show that the Pillsbury Doughboy is the most popular ad character in the U.S.—more popular than Ronald McDonald, Tony the Tiger, or Morris the Cat.

**Mr. Zig Zag.** During the 1850s the French army recruited Algerians to help fight in the Crimean war. One of them is still famous today—even though his name has been forgotten; his face is on the cover of Zig Zag rolling papers.

**Ronald McDonald.** Willard Scott, weatherman on NBC's *Today Show*, was the first McClown. Here's the story he tells:

"The folks at the NBC television station in Washington—WRC TV—had signed on a national kiddie show [called "Bozo the

Clown"], and they tapped me to star in the thing. That's how I got to be Bozo the Clown...I did a lot of personal appearances as Bozo—at shopping malls, local fairs, that sort of thing. After a while a local McDonald's restaurant asked me to appear at an opening, and before too long my Bozo was a regular fixture at area franchises. When WRC dropped [the show], McDonald's didn't much like the idea of having to drop a successful promotion. They were hooked on clowns...And so—you guessed it—Ronald McDonald was born...Actually, he came very close to being christened Donald McDonald, but Ronald sounded just a touch more natural, so we went with that."

**Rudolph the Red-Nosed Reindeer.** In 1939, Montgomery Ward hired Robert May to write a Christmas poem for their department store Santas to give away during the holiday season. He came up with one he called *Rollo the Red-Nosed Reindeer*. Executives of the company loved it, but didn't like the name Rollo. So May renamed the reindeer Reginald—the only name he could think of that preserved the poem's rhythm. But Montgomery Ward execs rejected that name, too. Try as he might, May couldn't come up with another name that fit—until his four year-old daughter suggested *Rudolph*.

**Teenage Mutant Ninja Turtles.** Peter Laird, a 29-year-old artist, was the staff illustrator for the gardening page of a Massachusetts newspaper in 1983. His job didn't pay very well, and he was looking for ways to make extra money on the side...so a local comic magazine editor suggested he work with Kevin Eastman, a 20 year-old short-order cook and amateur cartoonist, to drum up ideas for a new comic book. Laird decided to give it a shot. One night he and Eastman were experimenting with karate themes. Eastman drew a picture of a turtle wearing a Ninja mask. They both liked the idea, and stayed up all night developing a storyline. By morning the one "Ninja Turtle" had expanded to four *Teenage Mutant* Ninja Turtles—Leonardo, Raphael, Michaelangelo, and Donatello.

Why name them after Renaissance artists? Laird explained: "The characters should have have had Japanese names, but we couldn't come up with convincing ones."

Nuns have the longest life expectancy of any demographic group in the U.S.

# AT THE OSCARS

*Here are a few lesser-known stories about the Academy Awards ceremonies*

## THAT LITTLE GOLD STATUE

• According to legend, the Oscar was named in 1931 when a secretary at the Academy saw the statuette and exclaimed, "Why, he reminds me of my Uncle Oscar!" A reporter overheard the remark and used it in a story, and the name stuck.

• In 1942, gold and bronze were being used in the war, so Oscars were made out of plaster. (Actor Barry Fitzgerald accidentally decapitated his plaster Oscar while practicing his golf swing indoors).

• When Dustin Hoffman accepted his Oscar in 1979, he described the statuette for the audience: "He has no genitalia and he's holding a sword."

## HOSTS WITH THE MOST (OR LEAST)

• At the 1947 Oscar ceremony, Ronald Reagan supplied live narration for "Parade of Stars," a silent compilation of Oscar-winning films. Oblivious to the fact that the film was running upside down, backwards, and showing on the ceiling instead of on a screen, Reagan kept reading: "This picture embodies the glories of our past, the memories of our present, and the inspiration of our future."

• Comedian Jerry Lewis was the host in 1958 when the Oscar ceremony actually finished 20 minutes earlier than expected. No one realized the show was ending early until they were well into the closing number, "There's No Business Like Show Business." Lewis shouted "Twenty more times!" and tried to drag out the finale by grabbing a baton and conducting the orchestra. Actors onstage paired up and started dancing. Meanwhile, the audience started to get up and leave. Dean Martin danced by the podium and grabbed a leftover Oscar.

A few minutes later Lewis picked up a trumpet and started trying to play it. That's when NBC turned its cameras off. Eventually, NBC had to plug the hole with a short film on *pistol shooting*.

**The ice covering Antarctica is an average of 6500 ft. thick.**

## NO-SHOWS

*Not everyone shows up for Oscar night:*

• Robert Rich won the Best Screenplay Oscar in 1956 for *The Brave One*, but never claimed his award. That's because there *was* no Robert Rich. The winner was actually Dalton Trumbo, one of the notorious "Hollywood Ten," a group of writers who had been blacklisted for their left-wing views. Trumbo managed to sneak himself onto the nomination list by using "Robert Rich" as a pseudonym.

• In 1970 the Academy decided to give Orson Welles an honorary Oscar—presumably to make up for the fact that they'd snubbed him for *Citizen Kane* in 1941. When he didn't show up to accept it, the Academy announced he was out of the country. Actually, he was just a few miles away, watching the whole thing on television.

• That same year George C. Scott refused a Best Actor Oscar for his title role in the movie *Patton*. Instead of attending the ceremony, he says he watched a hockey game on TV, then went to bed.

• In 1979, 79-year-old Melvyn Douglas was nominated as Best Supporting Actor for *Being There*. His chief competition was child star Justin Henry, who played the contested child in the divorce drama, *Kramer vs. Kramer*. Douglas didn't show up for Oscar night, and told reporters: "The whole thing is absurd, my competing with an 8-year-old." Although Henry did show up, Douglas still won.

## AND THE WINNER IS...

• In 1984, F. Murray Abraham won the Oscar for Best Actor. (He played the jealous composer Antonio Salieri in the movie *Amadeus*.) Until then, Abraham's most prominent screen role had been as a leaf in a Fruit of the Loom underwear commercial.

• In 1946, *The Razor's Edge* failed to win the Oscar for Best Picture...But it *was* named the year's best by the National Association of Barbers.

• Humphrey Bogart wasn't thrilled at winning an Oscar for *African Queen*: "Hell," he remarked, "I hope I'm never nominated again. It's meat and potatoes roles for me from now on."

• Playwrite George Bernard Shaw was livid about winning the Best Screenplay Oscar for *Pygmalion.*"It's an insult," he railed. "To offer me an award of this sort is an insult, as if they have never heard of me before...and it's very likely they never have."

• The nameplate on Spencer Tracy's first Oscar was mistakenly made out to *Dick* Tracy.

## WINNERS, PART II

*The ultimate Oscar winner/loser story involved a little-known Polish director named Zbignew Rybcyznski, who was nominated for Best Animated Short in 1983:*

• Presenter Kristy McNichol tried to pronounce his name as a nominee, but giggled and gave up halfway through. When Rybcyznski won, McNichol tried again. This time she called him "Zbigniewski Sky."

• Rybcyznski made his acceptance speech through an interpreter but they were cut off when the orchestra struck up the theme from "Loony Tunes."

• Co-presenter Matt Dillon tried to ease Rybcyznski off the stage, but the director held his ground by shaking Dillon's hand and kissing McNichol. He added some final words but the interpreter lost them in the translation. They came out, "On the occasion of the film like *Gandhi*, which will portray Lech Walesa and Solidarity."

• Later in the evening, Rybcyznski stepped out for a cigarette. He tried to return to his seat, but a guard wouldn't let him back in. The guard didn't believe that Rybcyznski, who was dressed in a tuxedo and tennis shoes, was a guest. Rybcyznski got angry, kicked the guard, and wound up in jail.

• The director asked for attorney Marvin Mitchelson, who specializes in palimony cases, because he was the only Hollywood lawyer he could think of.

• Mitchelson took the case, but on the following conditions: "First, bring me an interpreter; and then tell me how to pronounce his name." The charges were dropped.

• Rybcyznski's conclusion: "Success and defeat are quite intertwined."

# PRIME TIME POLITICIANS

*You see politicians on TV all the time—but not usually in shows like "The Dukes of Hazard" and "The Beverly Hillbillies." Here are a few actors who followed Ronald Reagan's footsteps into politics.*

**The Race:** U.S. Congress (Virginia), 1984.

**Candidate:** Nancy Kulp (Democrat). Played Jane Hathaway, the sour-faced bank secretary on "*The Beverly Hillbillies*," for nine seasons.

**Political Background:** Worked for Adlai Stevenson in the 1952 presidential race against Eisenhower; elected to the Screen Actor Guild's Board of Directors in 1982. She also worked with the Democratic State Committee of Pennsylvania.

**The Race:** Kulp ran unopposed in the primary and won the Democratic nomination. But Buddy Ebsen, who played Jed Clampett on "The Beverly Hillbillies," campaigned against her in the general election. He taped a radio ad for Kulp's opponent, Bud Shuster, which said: "I dropped [Nancy] a note to say, 'Hey Nancy, I love you dearly buy you're too liberal for me—I've got to go with Bud Shuster.' " Shuster beat Kulp by 117,203 to 59,449.

**The Race:** Mayor of Carmel-by-the-Sea, California, 1986.

**The Candidate:** Clint Eastwood (no party affiliation).

**Political Background:** Eastwood wanted to expand his Carmel restaurant, the *Hog's Breath Inn.* City Hall refused to let him. So, in true *Dirty Harry* style, he took them on and ran for mayor.

**Outcome:** He defeated incumbent mayor Charlotte Townshend by 2,166 votes to 799. He held the $200-a-week post for two years.

**The Race:** U.S. House of Representatives (Iowa), 1986.

**The Candidate:** Fred Grandy, Republican. Played Burl "Gopher" Smith for nine years on *The Love Boat*.

**Political Background:** Grandy was David Eisenhower's roommate at Exeter Academy and later was best man at Eisenhower's wedding to Julie Nixon. He also served as a speechwriter for Congressman Wiley Mayne (R-Iowa). A Harvard graduate fluent in both French and Arabic, Grandy wanted to dispel his image as the dimwitted Gopher. Even so, he told *People* magazine, "If there were no Gopher, there would be no Fred Grandy for Congress."

**Outcome:** Grandy's opponent, Clayton Hodgson, criticized him for not living in Iowa's Sixth district (Grandy had lived in Iowa as an orphan at 12), and aired tapes of Grandy on NBC's "Tonight Show" describing Iowa as the "only place in the world where people still use 'by golly' in a sentence." Still, Grandy won the election in 1986 by 3,000 votes.

**The Race:** U.S. House of Representatives (Georgia), 1988.

**The Candidate:** Ben Jones (Democrat). Jones played Cooter, the auto mechanic on *The Dukes of Hazard*, for seven seasons.

**Political Background:** Worked on Jimmy Carter's 1980 presidential campaign. Lost his first bid for Congressman Pat Swindall's House seat in 1986, but ran again in 1988. Reason for getting involved: "I awoke naked in a tattoo parlor in Talladega, Alabama. I knew it was time to change my lifestyle. So I went into politics."

**Outcome:** *The Washington Post* described the race as "perhaps the nastiest, most personal congressional campaign in the country." Swindall was facing a perjury indictment for lying about his involvement with an undercover cop posing as a drug money launderer. He tried to portray the four-time married Jones as a wife-beater, alluding to charges of battery against an ex-wife, for which he had been fined $50. Jones' defense: "I'm not your typical political candidate; I've seen the insides of jails." Nevertheless, he captured 60% of the vote and defeated Swindall.

**The Race:** Mayor of Palm Springs, California, 1988.

**The Candidate:** Sonny Bono (Republican). Bono and his ex-wife Cher, had a variety T.V. show in the '70s and several hit songs.

**Political Background**: None.

**The Race**: Although he faced opposition ("Clint's a big star," commented outgoing Palm Springs mayor, Frank Bogert. "Sonny's a big nothing.") Bono won the election easily. But in 1990 his opponents started a petition drive to recall him after he dropped out of an AIDS walk-a-thon. It failed.

# SURPRISE HITS

*Some of pop music's most popular records have become hits through totally unexpected circumstances—discovered by deejays in a 25¢ bin, featured on ads years after their first release, picked as TV themes. These flukes are the equivalent of winning the "pop lottery." Here are a few classic examples:*

## GET TOGETHER—THE YOUNGBLOODS

**Background:** The Youngbloods first album was released in 1967 on RCA records. It included the song "Get Together," which was released as a single. Unfortunately, the song only reached #62 on the national charts—a flop, as far as RCA was concerned. The record was quickly forgotten.

**The Surprise:** To promote Brotherhood Week in 1969, the National Conference of Christians and Jews put together a package of public service messages for TV announcers and radio deejays to read on the air. They decided to include a record for stations to use as background music, and the one they picked—without informing the Youngbloods—was "Get Together."

**The Hit:** After a week of national radio and TV exposure, the record started becoming popular. Radio stations began playing it...and RCA cashed in by re-releasing it. In the summer of 1969, two years after it was first released, "Get Together" hit #1, sold about 2 million copies, and made the Youngbloods stars.

## "HANKY PANKY"—TOMMY JAMES & THE SHONDELLS

**Background:** In 1963, a Niles, Michigan high school student named Tommy Jackson made a record called "Hanky Panky" with his band, the Shondells. It became a regional hit in parts of Michigan, Illinois, and Indiana. Then it disappeared.

**The Surprise:** A year and a half later, a Pittsburgh, Pennsylvania, deejay named Bob Livorio found a copy of "Hanky Panky" in a pile of 25¢ records. He began playing it on the air. When it became popular with his audiences, rival deejays dug up their own copies of the record...and a "Hanky Panky" war was on. A local record company bought the rights to the record and distributed it to Pittsburgh record stores. In 3 weeks, "Hanky Panky" was the city's #1 song.

Meanwhile, Tommy Jackson—whose band had broken up when

he graduated from high school the year before—didn't know anything about this. He was at his family's house one evening when he got a phone call from a Pittsburgh deejay named "Mad Mike" Metro. As Tommy recalls it: "He said, 'Your record's #1. Can you come to Pittsburgh?' I said, 'What record? Who is this? What's your name?' I thought it was one of my friends pulling my leg. Finally, the guy started to sound official, and I started hearing radio noises in the background. I said, 'My god! He's telling the truth!' "

**The Hit:** When Tommy Jackson—now Tommy James—arrived in Pittsburgh, kids went wild. By this time "Hanky Panky" had gotten a lot of publicity in the record industry, and major companies were eager to distribute it nationally. The winner: Roulette Records, which bought it for $10,000. The record repeated its success on a national level, becoming the #1 song in America...and Tommy James became one of pop's biggest stars."I don't think that kind of stuff can happen anymore," Tommy muses. "We're talking an absolute Cinderella story!"

### "HUMAN NATURE"—MICHAEL JACKSON

**Background:** Steve Porcaro was a studio musician and a member of the group Toto. One day his little daughter came home from school upset about a fight she'd had with some of her playmates. "Why do they do that?" she asked.

"It's just human nature," her father replied.

He realized that phrase might make a good title for a song....So he went into Toto's recording studio and made up a melody—which he put onto a tape cassette, singing nonsense syllables and occasionally throwing in the phrase, "It's just human nature." Then he left the cassette lying around and forgot about it.

**The Surprise:** About this time, Quincy Jones was looking for songs to use on Michael Jackson's new album, "Thriller." He asked David Paitch—also a member of Toto and one of the most respected songwriters in the music business—to submit material for Jackson. Paitch went into Toto's studio, picked up a used cassette, and recorded three songs. Then he sent the cassette to Quincy Jones.

Jones didn't feel any of Paitch's tunes were right for "Thriller"... but just before he turned off the tape recorder, he realized there was an extra song on the cassette—Steve Porcaro's scratch vocal of "Human Nature." It turned out that without realizing it, Paitch picked up the tape with Porcaro's song on it. Jones decided "Human Nature" was perfect for Jackson. Porcaro, who had no idea anyone had the tape, was astonished.

**The Hit:** All the song needed now was lyrics. Jones contacted songwriter John Bettis, who wrote the words in two days. Not only was "Human Nature" included on "Thriller," the biggest-selling album in history, it was also released as a single. It reached #7 on *Billboard's* charts, and sold over a million copies.

## TIME IN A BOTTLE—JIM CROCE

**Background:** "Time In a Bottle" was a "throwaway" tune on a Jim Croce album. The producers didn't even bother putting the finishing touches on it because, as one of them said, "No one is ever gonna hear it."

**The Surprise:** Producers of a 1973 TV movie called "She Lives"—about a woman dying of cancer—heard Croce's album and liked "Time in a Bottle." They decided to make it the movie's theme.

**The Hit:** "The next day," Croce's record producer recalls,"we got a call from our record company telling us that they had 50,000 orders for the album, just in the Midwest. People had fallen in love with the song. It was just instantaneous. I think they sold something like 200,000 albums in the next two weeks That's why 'Time in a Bottle' was released as a single—because of that show." About three months later, the song hit #1.

## "OH HAPPY DAY"—THE EDWIN HAWKINS SINGERS

**Background:** Edwin Hawkins assembled the 46-member Northern California State Youth Choir in mid-1967. A few months later, he needed to raise funds for the choir's trip to a convention. So he picked out 8 members of the choir and recorded an album (which included "Oh Happy Day") in the basement of his church. He was delighted when the choir sold 600 copies of it.

**The Surprise:** Two years later, a San Francisco rock promoter happened to find the album in a warehouse while flipping through a stack of gospel records. He gave it to a popular deejay named Abe "Voco" Kesh, who played the record on the air.

**The Hit:** Kesh played "Oh Happy Day" so often that it became an S.F., then a national hit. Sales jumped from 1,000 to over a million.

# PUN FOR THE MONEY

*"There's something irresistible about bad puns," notes BRI member Michael McDonald. "For some reason, the worse a pun is the more we like it." Well, here are some real groaners from* Get Thee to a Punnery, *by Richard Lederer See if you can fill in the* punch *lines:*

**THE STORY:** An ancient jungle king tyrannized his subjects and forced them to build him one elaborate throne after another—first of mud, then bamboo, then tin, then copper, then silver, and so on. When the king became tired of each throne, he would store it in the attic of his grass hut. One day the attic collapsed, and the thrones crashed down upon the chief's head and killed him.
**The moral:** *"People who live in grass houses* ________________________."

**THE STORY:** A congregation decided to paint the walls of the church. They were doing an admirable job until they began to run out of paint, so they decided to thin the stuff in order to complete their task.

Shortly after the job was finished, the rains descended from the heavens, and the paint began to peel from the walls of the church. And a thunderous voice boomed from above:
*"Repaint, and* ______________________________"

**THE STORY:** In an ancient kingdom, the castle was surrounded by a treacherous swamp called the Yellow Fingers. Whenever the king would ask his lords and knights to cross the Yellow Fingers, they would reply:
*"Let your pages* ______________________________"

**THE STORY:** Mrs. Wong, a Chinese woman, gave birth to a blond-haired, blue-eyed Caucasian baby. When the doctor asked Mr. Wong to explain the astonishing occurrence, he replied:
*"It takes two Wongs* ___________________________"

**THE STORY:** In days of old when knights were bold, people were a lot smaller than they are today, so much smaller, in fact, that many knights rode upon large dogs when they couldn't get horses. One dark and stormy night, as the rain blew about, a squire entered a pet store in order to purchase a large dog for his master, the Black Knight. Unfortunately, all the shopkeeper could offer the squire was one undersized, mangy mutt. Commented the squire: "*I wouldn't send a knight* ________________________"

**THE STORY:** In Baghdad, a worthy young man named Abdul found a beautiful urn. When he began to polish the urn, out came a magnificently bearded genie, who introduced himself as Benny. Benny granted Abdul the obligatory three wishes and bid him goodbye. Abdul knew that if he could shave Benny's beard, the genie would have to return to the urn and grant him three more wishes. Wielding a magic razor, Abdul shaved off Benny's beard, and, sure enough, Benny flew back into the enchanted vessel.
**The Moral:** "*A Benny shaved* ____________________"

**THE STORY:** A Frenchman and a Czechoslovakian went out hunting for bear. When the two had not returned after four days, their friends, fearing the worst, went out searching for them. The group came to a clearing, and, sure enough, they saw a mother and father bear each with a bloated belly. Slashing open the belly of the female, the distraught friends found therein the remains of the Frenchman. Their darkest fears confirmed, the group looked at the other bear and guessed:
"*The Czech.* ____________________."

**THE STORY:** A witch doctor kept the members of his tribe in subjugation by means of his powerful magic. Whenever one of the tribespeople tried to revolt against the witch doctor, the tyrant uttered a magic incantation and turned the person into an apple. One night a group of the doctor's subjects sneaked into his hut, opened his book of magic recipes, and learned the apple incantation. When the doctor awoke, the people turned him into an apple. But the magic book warned that if the apple ever dried out and changed significantly in weight, it would change back into a doctor, who would take his revenge. So every day they would place the apple on a scale to make sure that its weight remained the same.
**Moral:** "*A weigh a day* ________________________."

General George Patton was dyslexic.

# THANKS... BUT NO THANKS

*If you've written a manuscript but can't find a publisher, take heart. Even the best writers get rejection slips. For example, a newspaper editor once told Rudyard Kipling: "I'm sorry, Mr. Kipling, but you just don't know how to use the English language." Here are some other notable rejection letters from editors to authors.*

**Manuscript:** *Madame Bovary*, by Gustave Flaubert
**Editor's Comment:** "You have buried your novel underneath a heap of details which are well done but utterly superfluous."

**Manuscript:** *Remembrance of Things Past*, by Marcel Proust
**Editor's Comment:** "My dear fellow, I may perhaps be dead from the neck up, but rack my brains as I may I can't see why a chap should need thirty pages to describe how he turns over in bed before going to sleep."

**Manuscript:** *The Diary of Anne Frank*, by Anne Frank
**Editor's Comment:** "The girl doesn't, it seems to me, have a special perception or feeling which would lift that book above the 'curiosity' level."

**Manuscript:** *Atlas Shrugged*, by Ayn Rand
**Editor's Comment:** "The book is *much* too long. There are too many long speeches...I regret to say that the book is unsaleable and unpublishable."

**Manuscript:** *Ulysses*, by James Joyce
**Editor's Comment:** "We have read the chapters of Mr. Joyce's novel with great interest, and we wish we could offer to print it. But the length is an insuperable difficulty to us at present. We can get no one to help us, and at our rate of progress a book of 300 pages would take at least two years to produce."

**The first advertisement to discuss body odor was a 1919 ad for the deodorant Odo-Ro-No.**

***Manuscript:*** *The Postman Always Rings Twice*, by James M. Cain
**Editor's Comment:** "I think it is only a matter of time before you reach out into more substantial efforts that will be capable of making some real money as books."

**Manuscript:** *Lord of the Flies*, by William Golding
**Editor's Comment:** "It does not seem to us that you have been wholly successful in working out an admittedly promising idea."

**Manuscript:** *And to Think That I Saw It On Mulberry Street*, by Dr. Seuss
**Editor's Comment:** "Too different from other [books for] juveniles on the market to warrant its selling."

**Manuscript:** *Ironweed*, by William Kennedy
**Editor's Comment:** "There is much about the novel that is very good and much that I did not like. When I throw in the balance the book's unrelenting lack of commerciality, I am afraid I just have to pass."

**Manuscript:** *Kon-Tiki*, by Thor Heyerdahl
**Editor's Comment:** "The idea of men adrift on a raft does have a certain appeal, but for the most part this is a long, solemn and tedious Pacific voyage."

**Manuscript:** *Lady Chatterly's Lover*, by D.H. Lawrence
**Editor's Comment:** "For your own good, do not publish this book."

**Manuscript:** *Animal Farm*, by George Orwell
**Editor's Comment:** "It is impossible to sell animal stories in the USA."

**Manuscript:** *The Blessing Way*, by Tony Hillerman
**Editor's Comment:** "If you insist on rewriting this, get rid of all that Indian stuff."

**RANDOM QUOTE:** "A man can be happy with any woman as long as he does not love her." —Oscar Wilde.

# THE KING AND I

*You may have already seen the famous photos of Elvis Presley and Richard Nixon in the Oval Office. Here's the inside story behind that meeting—taken directly from the memos of the White House staff.*

Even Elvis was a fan. He thought J. Edgar Hoover was "the greatest living American"...and Nixon "wasn't far behind." On December 21, 1970, Elvis dropped by the White House unannounced, asking to see the President. He brought this letter with him:

**DEAR MR. PRESIDENT:**

First, I would like to introduce myself. I am Elvis Presley and admire you and have great respect for your office. I talked to Vice President Agnew in Palm Springs three weeks ago and expressed my concern for our country. The drug culture, the hippie elements, the SDS, Black Panthers, etc. do not consider me as their enemy or as they call it, the establishment. I call it America and I love it. Sir, I can and will be of any service that I can to help the country out. I have no concerns or motives other than helping the country out. So I wish not to be given a title or an appointed position. I can and will do more good if I were made a Federal Agent at Large and I will help out by doing it my way through my communications with people of all ages. First and foremost, I am an entertainer, but all I need is the Federal credentials. I am on this plane with Senator George Murphy and we have been discussing the problems that our country is faced with.

Sir, I am staying at the Washington Hotel, Room 505-506-507. I have two men who work with me by the name of Jerry Schilling and Sonny West. I am registered under the name of Jon Burrows. I will be here for as long as it takes to get the credentials of a Federal Agent. I have done an in-depth study of drug abuse and Communist brainwashing techniques and I am right in the middle of the whole thing where I can and will do the most good.

I am glad to help just so long as it is kept very private. You can have your staff or whomever call me anytime today tonight, or to-

**The British pound got its name because it was originally equal to the value of a pound of silver.**

morrow. I was nominated this coming year one of America's Ten Most Outstanding Young Men. That will be in January 18 in my home town of Memphis, Tennessee. I am sending you the short autobiography about myself so you can better understand this approach. I would love to meet you just to say hello if you're not too busy.

Respectfully,

Elvis Presley

**P.S.** I believe that you, Sir, were one of the Top Ten Outstanding Men of America also. I have a personal gift for you which I would like to present to you and you can accept it or I will keep it for you until you can take it.

*Dwight Chapin, the White House Appointments Secretary, met with Elvis. He wasn't sure what to do—did Nixon want to speak with the King? Was he a Presley fan? Did he even know who the singer was? Chapin passed the buck and wrote a memo to H.R. Haldeman, White House Chief of Staff:*

**DEAR H.R.:**

Attached you will find a letter to the President from Elvis Presley. As you are aware, Presley showed up here this morning and has requested an appointment with the President. He states that he knows the President is very busy, but he would just like to say hello...I think that it would be wrong to push Presley off on the Vice President since it will take very little of the President's time and it can be extremely beneficial for the President to build some rapport with Presley.

*Haldeman approached Nixon about meeting with Elvis, and Nixon agreed. Here are the official White House notes describing the meeting:*

**DECEMBER 21, 1970**

The meeting opened with pictures taken of the President and Elvis Presley. Presley immediately began showing the President his law enforcement paraphernalia including badges from police departments in California, Colorado, and Tennessee. Presley indicated that he had been playing Las Vegas and the President indicated that he was aware of how difficult it is to perform in Las Vegas.

The President mentioned that he thought Presley could reach young people, and that it was important for Presley to retain his credibility. Presley responded that he did his thing by "just singing." He said that he could not get to the kids if he made a speech on the stage, that he had to reach them in his own way. The President nodded in agreement.

Presley indicated that he thought the Beatles had been a real force for anti-American spirit. He said that the Beatles came to this country, made their money, and then returned to England where they promoted an anti-American theme. The President nodded in agreement and expressed some surprise. The President then indicated that those who use drugs are also those in the vanguard of anti-American protest. "Violence, drug usage, dissent, protest all seem to merge in generally the same group of young people."

Presley indicated to the President in a very emotional manner that he was "on your side." Presley kept repeating that he wanted to be helpful, that he wanted to restore some respect for the flag which was being lost. He mentioned that he was just a poor boy from Tennessee who had gotten a lot from his country, which in some way he wanted to repay. He also mentioned that he is studying Communist brainwashing and the drug culture for over ten years. He mentioned that he knew a lot about this and was accepted by the hippies. He said he could go right into a group of young people or hippies and be accepted which he felt could be helpful to him in his drug drive. The President indicated again his concern that Presley retain his credibility.

At the conclusion of the meeting, Presley again told the President how much he supported him, and then, in a surprising, spontaneous gesture, put his left arm around the President and hugged him.

* * *

During a 1958 visit to Venezuela, Vice President Richard Nixon was spit upon by a protester. After Secret Service agents grabbed the man—Nixon kicked him in the shins. He admitted in his book *Six Crises* that "nothing I did all day made me feel better."

# OLD NEWS IS GOOD NEWS

*Are your newspapers piling up in the garage? Here's some recycling info from* The Recycler's Handbook, *written by the EarthWorks Group.*

If you're one of the millions of Americans who are recycling your newspapers, here's some good news: You're making a big difference.

Not only are you saving natural resources and landfill space, you're helping to change the way the paper industry works.

Until recently, newspaper publishers believed that recycling was just a fad—that we'd "get over it." Now it's clear that Americans are committed...So they're going to give us what we want.

## RECYCLING NEWS

• Every day Americans buy about 62 million newspapers...and throw out around 44 million of them. That means the equivalent of about 500,000 trees is dumped into landfills every week.

• If we recycled just half our newsprint every year, we'd need 3,200 fewer garbage trucks to collect our trash.

• If you recycled the *New York Times* every day for a year, you'd prevent 15 pounds of air pollution. That doesn't sound like much, but it adds up. If everyone who subscribes to the *New York Times* recycled, we'd keep over 6,000 *tons* of pollution out of the air.

• According to *Clean Ocean Action*, recycling a 36" tall stack of newspaper saves the equivalent of about 14% of the average household electric bill.

• Top uses for recycled newsprint: More newsprint, paperboard. Also, construction paper, insulation, egg cartons, animal bedding.

## PILES OF PAPER

• One of the results of America's new enthusiasm for recycling is a "newspaper glut." More paper on the market means lower prices. This is bad for collection programs, but good for mills.

• Of the 25 newsprint mills in the U.S., only ten of them can recycle. Most of our newsprint is manufactured in Canada, and only two of the 42 newsprint mills there are set up to recycle. However, many have announced plans to recycle; some are beginning.

• It may be a while before mills catch up to the public. It takes about 18 months and $40-80 million to retool a mill to recycle.

• Does this mean we shouldn't bother recycling? No, no, no. Mill-owners and newspapers have been waiting to see if recycling is a legitimate trend before they make major investments. But because we've kept the pressure up, they're making the necessary adjustments.

## SIMPLE THINGS YOU CAN DO

### 1. Find a Recycling Center

• It should be easy. Most recyclers accept newspaper, including curbside programs, recycling centers, charity paper drives, etc.

### 2. Recycle

• Ask your recycling center or curbside service if newspapers should be tied or left loose.

• If they should be tied, put them in bundles about 10" thick, so they're easy to carry. Tying tip: Lay the string in an empty box with the ends draping out over the sides. Put the paper in the box and make the knot.

• If they should be left loose, store the papers in brown grocery bags or cardboard boxes.

• Don't worry about pulling out all the glossy inserts, but don't *add* any junk mail or magazines to the pile. Try to keep the paper dry.

• If you're taking the newspaper to a recycling center, you may be asked to empty out the bags or cut the strings holding the bundles; some recyclers prefer just the newspaper.

• Don't recycle newspaper you've used for birdcages, for housebreaking your dog, or for painting or art projects.

## FOR MORE INFORMATION

**"Read, Then Recycle."** American Newspaper Publishers Association, The Newspaper Center, 11600 Sunrise Valley Drive, Reston, VA 22091; (703) 648-1125. *A free pamphlet.*

**Dog food bags can't be recycled; they have plastic linings inside.**

# ABOUT JAMES DEAN

*What was "The Rebel Without a Cause" really like?*

Dean was fascinated with death. He wrote poems about dying, and often drew pictures of himself hanging by a noose from the ceiling of his apartment. During one trip to his home town, he had a local funeral parlor photograph him lying in a casket.

★

His main body of work consisted of several TV appearances and only three motion pictures—*East of Eden*, *Rebel Without a Cause*, and *Giant*.

★

While filming *Giant*, Dean annoyed his coworkers by walking around with unfurled pastries hanging out of each nostril.

★

Once on the set he even urinated in full view of the public. His explanation: "I figured if I could piss in front of those 2,000 people, man, and I could be cool....I could get in front of the camera and do just anything, anything at all."

★

Dean didn't have any front teeth; he had to wear a special bridge to fill in the gap. He liked to startle people by smiling at them with his teeth out.

★

Dean had several gay roommates while living in Hollywood. When asked whether he was bisexual, he reportedly responded: "Well, I'm certainly not going through life with one hand tied behind my back!" He also avoided the military draft by registering as a homosexual.

★

In late 1955 Dean filmed a TV commercial on auto safety for teenagers. One of his lines: "Drive safely, the life you save may be mine..." A few weeks later, he was killed in a car wreck.

★

Dean's last words before he slammed into Donald Gene Turnupseed's 1950 Ford Tudor near Cholame, on California Highway 466: "That guy up there has to stop, he's seen us..."

★

Dean really did say, "Live fast, die young and leave a good-looking corpse."

**Two animals—Rin Tin Tin and Lassie—have stars on Hollywood's walk of fame.**

# STRANGE LAWSUITS

*Here are more of the BRI's "worst and weirdest" true-life lawsuits.*

**THE PLAINTIFF:** The Karolinska Institute in Stockholm, Sweden

**THE DEFENDENT:** Olaf Olavson

**THE LAWSUIT:** In 1910 Olavson was desperate for cash, so he sold his body to the Karolinska Institute (to be used for medical research after he died). But in 1911 he unexpectedly inherited a fortune and decided to "buy himself back." To his surprise, the institute wouldn't cooperate.

When Olavson flatly refused to donate his body, the institute actually sued for breach of contract.

**THE VERDICT:** Not only did Olavson owe his body to the Institute...he actually owed them money as well. The judge decided that since he'd had two teeth removed without the Institute's permission, Olavson had illegally tampered with their property.

**THE PLAINTIFF:** Joyce and David W., of Berlin Heights, Ohio

**THE DEFENDENT:** Natalina Pizza Co. of Elyria, Ohio

**THE LAWSUIT:** The couple said a frozen pizza they bought on April 26, 1986 had made them "violently ill," caused "emotional distress," and led to the death of their dog, Fluffy.

Although the expiration date on the pizza was April 18, "it was labeled edible for human consumption seven days after that date"...so the pair ate a few pieces. They claimed it was "spoiled, rotten, rancid, and moldy," and made them so sick they had to seek medical help. Fluffy didn't die from eating pizza; the couple ran him over in the driveway as they headed for the hospital.

They sued the pizza company for $125,000.

**THE VERDICT:** Not reported.

**THE PLAINTIFFS:** The Cherry Sisters, an Iowa singing group

**THE DEFENDENT:** The Des Moines *Register*

**THE LAWSUIT:** At the turn of the century, the *Register* ran a scathing review of the Cherry Sisters' act. Their reporter wrote that

"Their long, skinny arms, equipped with talons at the extremeties...waved frantically at the suffering audience. The mouths of their rancid features opened like caverns, and sounds like the wailings of damned souls issued therefrom."

Outraged and humiliated, the singers sued for libel.

**THE VERDICT:** The judge asked the sisters to perform their act for him in court...and then ruled in favor of the newspaper. It was, as one historian says, "a landmark libel case."

**THE PLAINTIFF:** Sarah, a 27-year-old woman with 46 personalities

**THE DEFENDENT:** Mark Peterson, of Oshkosh, Wisconsin

**THE LAWSUIT:** Peterson, who dated Sarah, was accused of deliberately drawing out the personality of Jennifer, described as "a gullible 20-year-old who he thought would have sex with him."

He was charged with rape. During the trial, he took the stand and testified he didn't know Sarah had multiple personalities. "I thought she was talking about her brothers and sisters," he said.

**THE VERDICT:** After deliberating for six hours, the jury found him guilty.

**THE PLAINTIFF:** Edith Tyler

**THE DEFENDENTS:** A restaurant in Flagstaff, Arizona

**THE LAWSUIT:** Tyler, a patron of the restaurant, ordered stuffed cabbage. She was appalled when she dug into it and found that it "apparently contained a used rubber prophylactic." She sued for $150,000.

**THE VERDICT:** Settled out of court.

**THE PLAINTIFF:** Tom H., a 24-year-old resident of Boulder, Colorado

**THE DEFENDENTS:** His parents

**THE LAWSUIT:** The young man, who'd spent a lot of time in mental institutions, blamed his parents for screwing him up. He sued them for "psychological malparenting." It was, he explained, a healthy alternative to following through on his "desire to kill his father."

**THE VERDICT:** He got no money.

**THE PLAINTIFFS:** Eric Hubert, Jeffrey Stabile, Jr., Christopher Drake

**THE DEFENDENT:** Disneyland

**THE LAWSUIT:** In 1988, the men were slow-dancing with each other at a Disneyland concert when a security guard allegedly approached them and told them that "touch dancing is reserved for heterosexual couples only." They sued, claiming their civil rights had been violated.

**THE VERDICT:** They agreed to drop the suit "in exchange for a pledge from Disneyland that the park would not discriminate based on sexual orientation."

**THE PLAINTIFF:** Wah-Ja Kim, a 58-year-old acupuncturist from Monterey, California

**THE DEFENDENTS:** William Hall, her ex-husband, and Jeannie Westall, his friend

**THE LAWSUIT:** In December 1983 Kim dropped in at Hall's condominium and got into an argument with Westall. During the fight, Westall allegedly bit off Kim's right pinkie. Kim sued for $1 million in damages, claiming that "she could not effectively stick pins in her patients' bodies without her little finger." She also said the loss posed a spiritual problem, since "the Confucianism of her native Korea demands 'that every human being should have a perfect, whole body to join our ancestors and carry on in the next life.' "

**THE VERDICT:** A jury awarded her $55,000.

**THE PLAINTIFF:** Relatives of a recently deceased man

**THE DEFENDENT:** A Vallejo, California cemetary

**THE LAWSUIT:** At the end of a funeral, cemetary employees realized the coffin they were about to lower into the ground was too wide for the hole. They tried turning the coffin on its side, but mourners stopped them. Then the employees tried breaking off the handles; it didn't work. Finally, "they tried to force it by jumping up and down on the lid." The coffin broke, and the funeral had to be stopped. Relatives sued for $500,000.

**THE VERDICT:** Settled out of court.

**The film *Total Recall* contained 55 paid references to 31 products.**

# WHAT'S THE WORD?

*Here are some unusual origins of common words, provided by BRI member John Dollison.*

**Addict.** Slaves known as *addicts* were given to Roman soldiers to reward performance in battle. Eventually, a person who was a slave to anything became known as an addict.

**Appendix.** In Latin it means "the part that hangs." A human appendix hangs at the end of the large intestine; appendices come at the end of books.

**Bistro.** In the 1812 campaign against Napoleon's armies, Russian soldiers pushed all the way into the outskirts of Paris. They became known for shouting "bistro"—"hurry up"—at slow-moving waiters in sidewalk cafes.

**Quakers.** During a run-in with the law, George Fox, founder of the Society of Friends, told the British judges hearing his case to "tremble at the word of God." One of them laughed back at Fox, calling him a "quaker." The nickname stuck.

**Atlas.** It was once a tradition for map-makers to include a scene of the Greek god Atlas carrying the Earth on his shoulders in their map books. In time the books themselves came to be known as *atlases*.

**Avocado.** A South American Indian word for testicle.

**Escape.** In Latin, *escape* means "out of cape." The ancient Romans would often avoid capture by throwing off their capes when fleeing.

**Oklahoma Sooners.** Before opening the Oklahoma Territory to settlers, the United States government sealed the borders temporarily to allow everyone a fair chance to claim the free land. Some settlers broke the law and entered before the deadline—getting there *sooner* than anyone else.

**People removed at the last minute from the Sgt. Pepper cover: actor Leo Gorcey, Gandhi, and Hitler.**

**Posh.** Originally stood for "Port-outbound, Starbord-home." Clever passengers traveling through the Suez canal in the 1800s ordered cabins on the left side of the ship for the trip out and cabins on the right side for the return voyage. This kept their staterooms in the shade both ways. The desirable accommodations were recorded as "P.O.S.H." in ship records.

**Kangaroo.** During a trip to Australia Captain Cook, the British explorer, asked a tribesman the name of the large animals he saw hopping about. The tribesman replied "kangaroo"...which means "I don't know."

**Pandemonium.** Coined in the 1600s by the English author John Milton in his book *Paradise Lost.* Pandemonium is the capital of Hell, where Satan and other demons plan their adventures.

**Noon.** Derived from the Latin word for ninth. The word "noon" originally meant the 9th hour after sunrise, or 3:00 pm.

**Best Man.** It was traditional in Scotland for a prospective groom to kidnap the woman he wanted for his wife. His friends would help him. The largest and strongest was called "the best man."

**Sincere.** *Sine Cera* means "without wax" in Latin. Legend has it that Roman stone carvers would pass off hollow columns (used for building) as solid by filling them with wax. In time *sine cera* came to refer to anything that was authentic or pure.

**Coconut.** Portugese explorers thought the three holes on the shell made the coconut resemble a human. They named it *coco*—"smiling face."

• • •

**BAD JOKE DEPARTMENT:**

**Q:** How many psychiatrists does it take to change a lightbulb?

**A:** One...But the lightbulb has to want to change.

# CHEWING GUM

*Does your chewing gum lose its flavor on the bedpost overnight? Not if it's in a glass of water, according to* The Whole Pop Catalog. *Here are some other bits of gum trivia from the book.*

"Every year, nearly two billion dollars worth of chewing gum is sold in America alone. That's enough to give 300 pieces a year to every American over the age of three."

"Even our most primitive ancestors engaged in recreational chewing. Along with human bones and other prehistoric artifacts, archaeologists at some sites have discovered well-chewed wads of tree resin."

"The first mass-produced gum (made of spruce resin) was manufactured by John Curtis in 1848."

"Clove gum was one of America's most popular flavors during Prohibition; patrons of speakeasies used it to hide the smell of alcohol on their breath. Today the most popular flavor is mint."

"The first bubble gum was invented by Frank Fleer in 1906—but never made it to market. It was so sticky that the only way to remove it from skin was with vigorous scrubbing and turpentine."

"It took Fleer more than twenty years to fix the recipe. In 1928 the 'new improved' gum was introduced as Dubble Bubble gum. It became the largest selling penny candy within just a few years."

"Why is bubble gum pink? Pink was the only food coloring on the shelf the day the first commercial batch of Dubble Bubble was made."

"New York Central Railroad once employed a full-time gum removal man to clean discarded gum from Grand Central Station. He harvested an average of seven pounds a night. The wad grew to fourteen pounds on holiday weekends."

"On June 3, 1965, the Gemini IV astronauts chewed gum in outer space. And according to NASA, when the astronauts were finished with the gum they swallowed it."

**There are an estimated 4,000 sunken ships off the coast of New England.**

# MYTH AMERICA

*Here's a batch of historical "truths" that aren't true.*

## TORY, TORY, TORY

**The Myth:** The vast majority of American colonists supported the rebellion during the Revolutionary War.

**The Truth:** According to President John Adams, at the beginning of the war only about a third of the people were on the side of the revolution. Another third were on the side of the British, and the rest didn't care either way. After a while, the ratio changed as British supporters were terrorized, publicly humiliated and finally attacked. Many fled to Canada.

## FOOLED AGAIN

**The Myth:** Abraham Lincoln said: "You can fool all the people some of the time and some of the people all of the time, but you can't fool all of the people all of the time."

**Background:** Claims that Lincoln said it did not surface until more than 50 years after he was supposed to have said it. The remark was not recorded in any newspapers in Lincoln's time.

**The Truth:** Some researchers attribute the remark to circus showman P.T. Barnum.

## ASLEEP AT THE WHEEL

**The Myth:** John F. Kennedy was a hero in World War II; when his tiny PT-109 patrol boat was rammed and sunk by a destroyer, he singlehandedly saved three members of his own crew.

**Background:** In his (ghost-written) book *PT-109*, Kennedy presented this version of the events that night. Yet, while he apparently showed great endurance and courage after his boat sank, there's some question as to whether the incident might have been avoidable in the first place.

**The Truth:** At least one Kennedy biographer argues that Kennedy's own negligence may have doomed his boat. According to a number of the ship's crew members, Kennedy and most of the crew were sleeping when PT-109 was rammed—not attacking the destroyer as Kennedy later claimed. Naval experts point out that it is unlikely for a ship as small and quick as PT-109 to be outmaneuvered by a ship as large as a destroyer, unless the crew is caught off guard.

## SWAN SONG

**The Myth:** General Douglas MacArthur coined the saying "Old soldiers never die; they just fade away."

**The Truth:** He was just quoting a British Army song from World War I.

## SO HIGH, SOLO

**The Myth:** Charles Lindbergh was the first person to fly nonstop across the Atlantic Ocean.

**The Truth:** He was the *67th* person to fly nonstop across the Atlantic. The first nonstop flight was made by William Alcock and Arthur Brown in 1919, eight years before Lindbergh's flight. Lindbergh's was famous because he did it *alone*.

## IN THE GROOVE

**The Myth:** Thomas Edison invented the phonograph to bring music to the masses.

**Background:** When Edison first played "Mary Had a Little Lamb" on his crude recording device, he knew he was onto something commercially significant. But he didn't have a clue what it was.

**The Truth:** He was actually trying to create the first telephone answering machine. The problem he saw with the phone was that, unlike the telegraph, you couldn't leave messages for people. Edison came up with an idea and—to his shock—it worked the first time he tried it. Still, it became clear that the machine wasn't suited for telephones. So Edison began marketing phonographs to businesses, believing that it was only suitable as a dictating machine. It took fifteen years and the successes of other manufacturers for him to be convinced that people would buy the machines for home music.

**Mother Jones was Mary Harris Jones, a crusader for the rights of laborers.**

# KISSING

*This won't help you kiss any better, but it will give you something to talk about afterwards.*

## HOW KISSING EVOLVED

• One theory: it evolved from sniffing, a form of greeting still used by animals. In some languages "kiss me" translates literally as "smell me."

• Another theory: it's a holdover from breast feeding.

## PROCEED WITH CAUTION

• Europeans of the Dark Ages took kissing very seriously. French women who kissed men other than their husbands were considered guilty of adultery, and Italian men who kissed women in public had to marry them.

• The Great Plague that struck London in 1665 killed thousands—and put kissing out of style. The "substitute" kisses Londoners developed to avoid actually kissing someone—tipping hats, waving hands, and bowing—are still used as greetings today.

• Concerned about the moral and hygienic dangers of kissing, a group of Kansas men founded the Anti-Kissing League in 1909. Members took vows never to kiss their wives again.

## SCREEN KISSES

• Thomas Edison filmed the first movie featuring an onscreen kiss in 1896. The "film"—called *The Kiss*—was a 30-second clip starring May Irwin and John C. Rice. It played in nickelodeons.

• Ronald Reagan's ex-wife gets the credit for the longest kiss in Hollywood history. In the 1940 film *You're in the Army Now,* Jane Wyman's kiss with Regis Toomey lasts more than 3 minutes.

• In the mid-1980s Rock Hudson kissed Linda Evans on TV's "Dynasty." Soon afterward he died of AIDS, setting off a nationwide debate on the safety of kissing. Today the Screen Actor's Guild requires film companies to notify actors in advance if their roles require "deep kissing."

**The average homebuyer looks at eight houses before finding the right one.**

## KISSING FACTS

• According to Dr. Joyce Brothers, American women kiss an average of 79 men before marrying.

• Longest kiss on record, according to the *Guiness Book of World Records:* 130 hours, 2 minutes. Bobbie Sherlock and Ray Blazina set the record at a charity "Smoochathon" held in Pittsburgh, Pennsylvania in 1979.

• The Japanese did not kiss at all before coming in contact with Westerners.

• Do you kiss your wife goodbye in the morning? Some studies have shown that you'll outlive people who don't by as much as five years.

• In the Middle Ages, where you kissed someone depended on their social status. You kissed equals on the mouth, and superiors on the hand, knee, or feet (the more "superior" they were, the lower you kissed). You didn't have to kiss inferior people at all; they kissed you.

• Studies conducted in the 1950s showed that more than 250 colonies of bacteria are transmitted from one person to another during an average kiss. The good news: most are harmless.

• • •

## FROM OUR WRONG # DEPARTMENT:

In 1940 A. Douglass Thompson, a Tennessee paper boy, was delivering his papers when he was attacked and bitten by a neighborhood dog. Thompson had it taken to the pound. It was released to its owner a few days later.

But the owner of the dog, Gertrude Jamieson, was so upset at Thompson for impounding her pet that she began harassing him with obscene phone calls several times a day. She kept it up—for 43 years. Finally in 1983, at the age of 85, she stopped calling Thompson (who by now was age 59)—but not because she had forgiven him. The only reason she stopped calling was because she had suffered a minor stroke and was confined to a hospital room without a telephone.

**Horses use 17 muscles to twitch their ears. Humans use only 9.**

# RUTH'S TRUTHS

*Babe Ruth did more than hit home runs. He gave a few interviews, too.*

(Responding to a comment that he made more money than President Hoover): "I had a better year than he did."

"I have only one superstition. I make sure to touch all the bases when I hit a home run."

"A man ought to get all he can earn. A man who knows he's making money for other people ought to get some of the profit he brings in. Don't make any difference if it's baseball or a bank or a vaudeville show. It's business, I tell you. There ain't no sentiment to it. Forget that stuff."

"Don't quit until every base is uphill."

"Gee, it's lonesome in the outfield. It's hard keeping awake with nothing to do."

"Hot as hell, ain't it, Prez?" (His greeting to President Calvin Coolidge, during a game at the Washington ball park.)

" I hit big or I miss big. I like to live as big as I can."

"If I'd just tried for them dinky singles, I could've batted around six hundred."

"It's hell to get older."

"I've heard people say that the trouble with the world is that we haven't enough great leaders. I think we haven't enough great followers. I have stood side by side with great thinkers—surgeons, engineers, economists; men who deserve a great following—and have heard the crowd cheer me instead...I'm proud of my profession. I like to play baseball. I like fans, too...But I think they yelled too loudly and yelled for the wrong man."

"What I am, what I have, what I am going to leave behind me—all this I owe to the game of baseball, without which I would have come out of St. Mary's Industrial School in Baltimore a tailor, and a pretty bad one, at that."

"You need a certain number of breaks in baseball...and every other calling."

**In 1991 General Motors was #1 on the Fortune 500 list—but 485th in profitablilty.**

# THE SOUND OF MUZAK

*You hear it in the elevator, in your dentist's office, at the supermarket—even in the reptile house of the Bronx Zoo. Here's the inside story on the music you love to hate:*

## ORIGIN

General George Squier was the head of the U.S. Signal Corps in World War I. During the war he discovered a way to transmit music over electrical lines. When the war was over, he showed his discovery to a Cleveland, Ohio utility. The company liked his invention, and in 1922 helped Squier set up the Wired Radio Company.

• Their plan: provide an alternative to radio by broadcasting music to households through their power lines (for a fee).

• Squier changed his company's name to *Muzak* in 1934. Why? He liked Kodak's name, and wanted something that sounded similar.

## MUZAK AT WAR:

Squier overlooked one thing when he started his business: households receiving radio broadcasts free of charge would not see any reason to pay a monthly fee for Muzak's wire broadcasts. This made it tough to attract customers. However, events during World War II helped keep the company in business:

• To combat assembly line fatigue, the British government began broadcasting the BBC in defense factories.

• When production at these plants increased as much as 6%, the U.S. government hired Muzak to pipe sound into U.S. plants. Their productivity rose 11%.

• Studies showed that even cows and chickens increased productivity when "functional" music played in the background.

• Seeing this, the company switched its focus to increasing productivity for business customers. Today it broadcasts via satellite to

180 different Muzak "stations" around the country—and into the ears of more than 100 *million* "listeners" worldwide.

## MIND CONTROL

If you thought Muzak just played songs at random, think again:

### At Work

• To maximize Muzak's uplifting potential, the company gives each of its songs a "mood rating" that ranges from "Gloomy" (minus three) to "Ecstatic" (plus eight). An overall "stimulus value" is determined for each song.

• Broadcasts are divided into 15 minute "segments": 14 minutes of songs with 1 minute of silence at the end. The "stimulus value" of a segment increases with each song.

• To revive sluggish workers, Muzak plays speedier segments between 10:00 and 11:00 am.

• The songs slow down again at 1:00 pm. Why? To calm employees after lunch.

• By 3:00 pm the music picks up pace—to energize workers at the end of the day.

### At the Supermarket

The broadcasts Muzak provides to supermarkets are *always* slow-paced—studies have shown that shoppers who listen to slow music spend more time shopping...and as much as 35% more money.

## MUZAK FACTS

• President Dwight D. Eisenhower played Muzak in the White House—and Lyndon Johnson liked it so much he bought a local Texas franchise. He even had Muzak speakers installed in the trees of the LBJ ranch.

• Neil Armstrong listened to Muzak during the Apollo XI voyage to the moon.

• During the fall of Saigon in 1975, State Department staffers evacuated the American embassy compound with Muzak playing in the background.

• No surprise: 90% of Muzak "listeners" say they like the stuff. Andy Warhol claimed it was his favorite music.

# FAMILIAR NAMES

*Some people achieve immortality because their names are associated with common items or activities. You already know the names—now here are the people*

**Atoine de la Mothe Cadillac.** A French explorer, Cadillac founded Detroit in 1701.

**Ernesto Miranda.** Miranda was arrested in 1963 for stealing $8 from a Phoenix, Arizona bank employee. He confessed, but the U.S. Supreme Court threw out his conviction—the police had not advised him of his rights. To avoid the same mistake, police now read the *Miranda Warning* to people they arrest.

**Alexander Garden.** A South Carolina botanist born in 1730. The Royal Society of Botany in London named a newly discovered tropical plant, the *gardenia*, in his honor in 1755.

**Captain William Lynch.** A Virginia farmer during the Revolutionary War, Lynch organized bands of townspeople to dispense justice to outlaws and British collaborators. These bands became known as "Lynch Mobs," and hanging someone without a trial became known as "Lynching."

**Ludwig Doberman.** A German dog breeder in the late 1800s. He is the "father" of Doberman Pinschers.

**Henry Deringer.** An American gunsmith of the 1840s, Deringer invented a tiny pistol that he named after himself. Imitators copied his guns—and misspelled his name. Today derringer is still spelled with two r's.

**Thomas and William Bowler.** The Bowlers, English hatmakers in the 1860s, made a brimmed hunting hat for one of their customers. It became known as a "bowler" hat.

**Thomas Derrick.** A notorious hangman in England during the 17th century, Derrick designed a hoisting apparatus for the gallows—which he used to execute more than 3,000 people. The apparatus—and the crane that resembles it—are both called derricks.

**Annual event: About 650,000 Americans invite dogs to birthday parties thrown for their own dogs.**

**Charles Henry Dow and Edward D. Jones.** Journalists at the turn of the century, Dow and Jones created the first index of U.S. stock prices—the Dow-Jones Average. It later appeared in the newspaper they founded, *The Wall St. Journal*.

**Captain Fudge.** Though his first name has been forgotten, Captain Fudge was a captain in the British Navy in the 1600s. His wild tales about his seafaring adventures earned him the nickname "Lying Fudge." Sailors of the day referred to his storytelling as "fudging it."

**Dr. Thomas Lushington.** Lushington was a heavy-drinking English chaplain in the 1600s. His reputation as a drunk was so great that the *City of Lushington*, a London drinking club, was named in his honor more than 200 years after his death. The club's inebriated clientele inspired the word *lush*.

**Mr. Scheuster.** Like Captain Fudge, Scheuster's first name has been forgotten. He was a crooked criminal lawyer in New York in the 1840s, whose name inspired the term *shyster*.

**Admiral Edward "Old Grog" Vernon**. Old Grog was famous for pacing his ship's deck in a grogram cloak—that's how he got his nickname. But he was also famously cheap. When he began watering down the rum he served to his sailors, they christened the weakened spirit "Grog."

**E.A. Murphy, Jr.** Murphy was not an optimist. An American engineer in the 1940s, he was the first to utter the words "Anything that can go wrong *will* go wrong"— Murphy's Law.

**John Taliaferro Thompson.** A general in the U.S. Army in the 1920s. He was one of the inventors of the Thompson sub-machine gun in 1921. Though the "Tommy Gun" never really caught on with the military as Thompson had hoped, by the late 1920s it was a big hit with the mob.

**Antionette Perry.** A popular stage actress whose career spanned from 1905 to 1949. The Tony awards are named in her honor.

**Sequoya.** Sequoya—who also used the name George Guess—was an Indian scholar who developed a system of writing for his native Cherokee language. Sequoia redwood trees are named after him.

# IFS AND BUTTS

*Warning: The Surgeon General has determined that reading about cigarettes is not harmful to your health.*

Richard Joshua (R.J.) Reynolds—one of the fathers of the cigarette industry—hated cigarettes. He preferred chewing tobacco and would not allow smokes in his house.

Though Turkish tobacco is popular all over the world, 7th century Turks hated smokers. One punishment: smokers were led through town on muleback—with their pipes shoved up their noses.

In 1989, Reynolds introduced Uptown, a menthol brand designed specifically for blacks. Within days of its introduction, civil rights groups and anti-smoking organizations lit into Reynolds. Two months later, Uptown was dumped.

Who's the camel on the package of Camel cigarettes? Old Joe, a camel in Barnum and Bailey's circus. R.J. Reynolds had his personal secretary photograph him in 1913. The package is an exact copy of the photo.

Unlucky promotion: R.J. Reynolds paid Amelia Earhart to take Lucky Strikes with her on her ill-fated trip across the Atlantic.

Kent cigarette filters were originally made from the same material as WW II gas masks.

In the late 1980s, R.J. Reynolds spent $300 million developing Premier, a high-tech "smokeless cigarette" that came with a 4-page set of instructions. Smokers were supposed to light the "carbon heat source" at the tip and suck flavorings out of the "flavor capsule." It flopped.

If you were a tobacco farmer in the 1930s and 40s, you wouldn't have had to fight in World War II. Pres. Roosevelt declared tobacco "an essential crop" at the outbreak of the war—exempting tobacco growers from the draft.

# THE DUSTBIN OF HISTORY

*They were VIPs in their time...but they're forgotten now. They've been swept into the Dustbin of History.*

**FORGOTTEN FIGURE:** Lord Cornbury (Edward Hyde), colonial governor of New York from 1702 to 1708.

**CLAIM TO FAME:** Edward Hyde, a cousin of Queen Anne, was appointed governor of New York in 1702. When colonists went to welcome him, they found him rocking on his porch, knitting a doily and wearing one of his wife's dresses.

Things got weirder when he threw his first dress ball. Not only was he decked out in a formal gown; he also charged an admission fee, and insisted that his guests all feel his wife's ears...which he had described in a long poem as "conch shells."

For many years, he was the was the talk of New York—especially when it turned out he had taken the governorship to escape creditors in England. Then in 1708 he was caught embezzling public funds.

**INTO THE DUSTBIN:** Cornbury was confined to debtor's prison until his father died, when he inherited a title and returned to England. No monuments to his rule were built, but he did leave his family name on land along the Hudson: Hyde Park.

**FORGOTTEN FIGURE:** Lucy Page Gaston, 1860-1924, American anti-tobacco reformer.

**CLAIM TO FAME:** After legendary prohibitionist Carrie Nation, she was the most famous American female reformer of her time. In 1899 she founded the Chicago Anti-Cigarette League, which became the National Anti-Cigarette League two years later. For a while the movement she inspired was a real threat to the tobacco industry, as cigarette sales dipped by 25%.

By 1920 she was so well-known that she became a candidate in the Republican presidential race, vowing to "emancipate" the country from smoking. But she won few votes, and Warren

Harding, a smoker, was nominated.

**INTO THE DUSTBIN:** In June, 1924, Gaston was hit by a trolley while crossing a street. She was taken to a hospital, but did not respond well to treatment. That's when doctors discovered she was terminally ill. She died two months later—of throat cancer.

**FORGOTTEN FIGURE:** Luise Rainer, a film star of the '30s.

**CLAIM TO FAME:** She was the first person ever to win two consecutive Academy Awards—for Best Actress in 1936 (for *The Great Ziegfield) and* in 1937 (for *The Good Earth*).

In 1936, nominations were still carefully controlled by movie studios. Rainer's first nomination was engineered by MGM to help develop her career. (It was only her second film, and it was a relatively small part.) No one thought she would actually *win* the Oscar. That's why everyone voted for her.

The following year, voting was opened up for the first time to thousands of actors, writers, etc. Rainer, who was well-liked for not acting like a "star," beat out Greta Garbo and Barbara Stanwyck.

**INTO THE DUSTBIN:** For some reason, MGM forced Ranier into a quick series of throwaway roles; two years and five insignificant pictures later, she was a has-been. Her downfall led gossip columnist Louella Parsons to coin the term "Oscar jinx."

**FORGOTTEN FIGURE:** Smedley Butler, America's most famous soldier—a U.S. Marine and two-time Medal of Honor winner, nicknamed "Old Gimlet Eye."

**CLAIM TO FAME:** Once called "the finest fighting man in the armed forces" by Teddy Roosevelt, Butler was renowned for personal bravery, tactical brilliance, and the ability to inspire his fellow soldiers. He joined a Marine force in China during the Boxer rebellion, and helped carry a wounded comrade 17 miles through enemy fire back to their camp. He was promoted to captain—at age 18. He later served in Cuba, Nicaragua, Panama, Honduras, and Haiti.

Butler served in France during World War I—not at the front, but as commander of a troop depot, Camp Pontanezen. Ironically, his greatest fame came from this post. The camp was practically buried in mud; and the troops were short of food and blankets. But somehow, Butler scrounged a huge supply of slats used for trench floors and created walkways and tent floors to keep the troops out of the mud.

The grateful soldiers never forgot him; as one said, "I'd cross hell on a slat if Butler gave the word."

After the war, Butler was regarded as presidential material (he didn't run). He was also a popular figure on the lecture circuit.

In the early '30s, he was approached by men claiming to be associated with the American Legion. They wanted him to organize a fighting force to overthrow Franklin Roosevelt—and said there was $300 million available to fund the insurrection. Butler played along and eventually learned he was being courted by the American fascist movement. He divulged the plot before the Un-American Activities Committee in 1934, but nothing much came of it; the story was hushed up because several prominent figures were involved.

**INTO THE DUSTBIN:** Butler retired from the Corps in 1931, but continued to speak out on military and foreign-policy issues. He died in 1940.

**FORGOTTEN FIGURE:** William Walker, American journalist, physician, lawyer, and soldier of fortune.

**CLAIM TO FAME:** Walker is the only native-born American ever to become president of a foreign nation. From July 1856, to May 1857, he was self-appointed dictator of Nicaragua, a nation he took over with a hand-picked force of mercenaries who called themselves "The Immortals."

Walker's success made him a hero throughout the U.S., where the notion of "Manifest Destiny" was gaining wide acceptance. Crowds cheered his exploits, newspapers hailed his triumphs. But a coalition of Central American nations, financed in part by Cornelius Vanderbilt, overthrew Walker. On May 1, 1857, he and his troops fled back to the U.S.

Walker made three more attempts to win control in Central America. Finally, in the fall of 1859, he and his men attacked Honduras and were captured by British and Honduran troops.

**INTO THE DUSTBIN:** Walker surrendered to the British, expecting he would again be returned to the States. But he was turned over to the Hondurans instead, and was executed by a firing squad on September 12, 1860.

He was so hated by Nicaraguans that he became a symbol of "Yankee Imperialism." He is still remembered there.

**U.S. Highway facts: Odd numbered highways move north and south, Even go east and west.**

# HOW LONG?

*See if you can guess the average lifespan of the following things (answers on page 892).*

**1. The American male in 1900:** A. 32.4 years B. 46.3 years C. 66.3 years

**2. American male in 1990:** A. 67.3 years B. 72.1 years C. 78.6 years

**3. The American female in 1900:** A. 48.3 years B. 52.8 years C. 60.1 years

**4. American female in 1990:** A. 68.4 years B. 74.8 years C. 79.0 years

**5. Beer:** A. 3-5 weeks B. 12-18 months C. 3 months

**6. Freeze-dried fish squares (Stored at 70° F):** A. 25 years B. 12 months C. 72 months

**7. Facelifts:** A. 1-3 years B. 6-10 years C. 10-18 years

**8. U.S. Patents:** A. 17 years B. 70 years C. Unlimited

**9. Lightning Bolts:** A. 1-7 microseconds B. 45-55 microseconds C. 11 seconds

**10. Cockroaches:** A. 40 days B. 6 months C. 7 years

**11. Bras:** A. Up to 9 months B. Up to 2 years C. Up to 5 years

**12. Ballistic missiles:** A. 10-15 months B. 10 - 15 years C. 100-150 years

**13. Snowflakes:** A. From 7 minutes to several centuries B. From 30 seconds to 4 days C. From 1 minute to 9 months

**14. Televisions:** A. 7-10 years B. 10-15 years C. 15-18 years

**15. Skywriting:** A. 45-60 seconds B. 5-7 minutes C. 45 minutes

**16. A professional football (when used in an NFL game):** A. 6 minutes B. 30 minutes C. One hour

**17. Moonbeams:** A. 1.3 Seconds B. 12 minutes C. 1 hour

**18. A dollar bill (in circulation):** A. 3.8 months, or 900 folds B. 18 months, or 4,000 folds C. 2.5 years, or 10,000 folds

# JOIN THE CLUB

*Every time you drive into a town, you see signs with info on Rotary, Kiwanis, or Elk's club chapters. How did they come up with those names? Here are some answers.*

**The Benevolent and Protective Order of Elks:** The group started out in the 1860s as "The Jolly Corks," a drinking club for vaudevillians. Members changed the name to the Elks after they saw a stuffed elk in Barnum's Museum in New York City.

**Kiwanis International:** Founded as The Benevolent Order of Brothers in 1914 by Allen S. Browne, a Detroit businessman. A year later the group changed its name to Kiwanis, borrowing from the Canadian Indian expression "nun keewanis." They believed that it meant "we trade." Actual translation: "we have good time/ we make noise."

**The Rotarians:** When a group of Chicago businessmen founded a service organization in 1905, they decided to make the meetings convenient for everyone by *rotating* the meeting place from one member's office to another. They couldn't think of a name for it—so they just named it the *Rotary* Club.

**The Shriners:** During a visit to France in 1867, Walter M. Fleming, a New York doctor, went to see an Arabian musical comedy. At the end of the performance, the cast initiated the audience into a "secret society." Fleming liked the idea—and in 1872 he formed the Ancient Arabic Order of the Nobles of the Mystic Shrine... commonly known as the *Shriners*.

**The Freemasons:** The group traces its roots back to 17th century guilds of English "freestone mason" guilds of highly skilled craftsmen who carved the ornate stonework used to build monasteries, palaces and cathedrals.

**The Lion's Club:** Adopted when the group was founded in 1917. It stands for what members consider "the true meaning of citizenship: **L**iberty, **I**ntelligence, and **O**ur **N**ation's **S**afety."

**Vital stats: 42% of U.S. men and 31% of U.S. women say they clean their belly buttons every day.**

# CLASSIC MOVIES: BEHIND THE SCENES

*You've seen the films—now here are the stories.*

**PRIDE OF THE YANKEES (1942).** The film biography of New York Yankee first baseman Lou Gehrig starred Gary Cooper...who'd never played baseball in his life. He couldn't run, couldn't field, and couldn't throw.

• The studio hired an expert to teach him baseball fundamentals, but it didn't do any good. Doubles still had to be used whenever Gehrig was supposed to be out in the field.

• Cooper had a knack for batting, though; he was able to meet the ball solidly, with a fairly convincing swing. Unfortunately, he was right-handed and Gehrig had been left-handed.

• Director Sam Woods's solution: He filmed Cooper hitting right-handed and flipped the film so the actor appeared to be batting from the left side.

• That meant other details had to be reversed. For example: Special mirror-image Yankee uniforms had to be designed. And new ballpark billboards that were printed backwards were erected, so the signs would be readable.

• After all that trouble, Wood wouldn't take any chances casting an actor as Babe Ruth. He signed the Babe to play himself.

**SINGIN' IN THE RAIN (1952).** For years Arthur Freed, the producer of this classic musical, wanted to name a film—any film—"Singin' in the Rain" (after the popular 1920's song)...and this was his chance. It didn't matter to him that there were no rain scenes originally planned for the movie...or that its star and director, Gene Kelly, thought he was nuts.

• When Freed insisted, Kelly gave in and choreographed the film's main dance sequence around the song.

• But the splashing footsteps that audiences heard in the "Rain" dance routine weren't all Kelly's. To enhance the "puddle" effect, a young dancer sloshed through a series of water-filled buckets off-screen. (The dancer was Gwen Verdon, who later starred in *Damn Yankees*.)

• During the dance, Kelly looked joyful. Actually, he was miserable. He had a terrible cold and was afraid that prancing around in all that water would give him pneumonia.

• He was also unhappy about his 19-year-old female co-star, Debbie Reynolds. She'd never sung or danced before, and he had to tutor her for every number.

**KING KONG (1933).** Merian C. Cooper, the film's producer, wanted to include a scene audiences would never forget. As Paul Boller reports in his excellent book, *Hollywood Anecdotes*: "Late one afternoon in February 1930, as he was leaving his office in mid-town Manhattan, Cooper heard the sound of an airplane, glanced out of the window, and saw a plane flying close to the New York Life Insurance Building, then the city's tallest building. At once it flashed into his mind: 'If I can get that gorilla logically on top of the mightiest building in the world, and then have him shot down by the most modern of weapons, the airplane, then no matter how giant he was in size, and how fierce, that gorilla was doomed by civilization.' "

• "By the time RKO came to make the picture, Cooper had had to move Kong, first to the new Chrysler Building, and then, finally, to the Empire State Building, which, when completed in 1931, was the tallest structure in the world."

• King Kong, of course, was a model. He was actually 18" tall.

**HIGH NOON (1952).** Gary Cooper starred as a sheriff who had to face a band of outlaws by himself. Cooper, who was 50 years old, was praised for the convincing way he made his character seem pained and worried. Actually, it wasn't all acting. Right before filming began, Cooper was hospitalized for a hernia. During the filming, he was troubled by a hip injury. After the film was finished, he went right back to the hospital—this time to have a duodenal ulcer removed.

• He had other reasons to look worried: He thought his co-star, Grace Kelly, was too inexperienced, and that the movie was dull.

• Kelly *was* inexperienced—*High Noon* was only her second movie—but that's why the director had hired her. He wanted the character to seem innocent and naive.

• The movie *was* dull, too. It bombed in its first preview and had to be completely re-edited. Editor Elmo Williams shortened it, sped up the pace, and transformed it from a turkey to a classic. Cooper won an Oscar for Best Actor.

**THE GRAPES OF WRATH (1940).** The film that made Henry Fonda a star was adapted from one of the most controversial novels in America's history. The book was denounced—and even banned—in many communities as "subversive."

• Author John Steinbeck insisted that 20th Century Fox guarantee the studio would "retain the main action and social intent" of his book.

• Before agreeing, Fox hired detectives to check the accuracy of Steinbeck's portrayal of life in migrant camps. The report: conditions were even worse than Steinbeck had suggested.

• Fox was worried the film's pro-labor message might provoke a response from banks and agri-business (the novel's two villains). So they filmed it under tight security, with unusual secrecy.

• They posted armed guards at the studio door. None of the actors was given a complete script; they had to read from mimeographed sheets instead. The sheets were collected at the end of each day; no one was allowed to leave the set with a script. During shooting, the film was given a false title—*Highway 66*—so the crew could film wherever they pleased without creating a controversy.

• The cast and director John Ford went out of their way to make sure the public knew the film was "apolitical," and it won two Oscars.

**AND NOW A SHORT FEATURE FROM THE BOOK,**
***Hollywood Anecdotes*, by Paul Boller:**

"For the opening of Pinocchio (1940) Walt Disney's publicity department decided to hire eleven midgets, dress them in Pinocchio outfits, and have them frisk about on top of the theater marquee on opening day. At lunchtime, food and refreshments were passed up to the marquee, including a couple of quarts of liquor. By three o'clock that afternoon things had gotten out of hand and an amused crowd in Times Square was regaled by the spectacle of eleven stark-naked midgets belching noisily and enjoying a crap game atop the Broadway marquee. Police with ladders removed the gamblers in pillowcases."

**CLASSIC BLOOPERS**

• In *The Invisible Man*, the title character is supposed to be naked, but the footprints he leaves are of shoes instead of bare feet.

• If you look closely in the famous chariot race scene in *Ben Hur* (1959), you'll see a red sports car driving by the Coliseum in the distance.

• In *El Cid*, a 1961 movie extravaganza about an 11th century Spanish hero, a costly crowd scene was spoiled by an extra wearing sunglasses.

• *The Green Berets* features a dramatic shot of the sun...setting in the east.

• In another crowd scene, this time from the 1982 epic *Gandhi*, one of the peasants is sporting Adidas tennis shoes.

**MOVIE NOTES**

• A South Korean movie theater owner decided that *The Sound of Music* was too long, so he shortened the movie himself—by cutting out all of the songs.

• Why was the computer in *2001* named HAL? The director claimed the name is a hybrid of the two principal learning systems Heuristic and Algorithmic. However, a number of critics have pointed out that if you replace each initial in HAL with the letter that succeeds it, you wind up with the well-known name of a real-life computer...IBM.

• The shortest shooting schedule for a full-length, commercial film was two days...for Roger Corman's 1959 classic, *Little Shop of Horrors*.

**George Reeves, TV's Superman, needed three people to help him out of his costume.**

# THE COMPASS IN YOUR NOSE

*What do you know about your body? Here's some fascinating info from a book called,* The Compass in Your Nose, *by Marc McCutcheon*

## THE COMPASS IN YOUR NOSE

### Magnetic Attraction

- All humans have a trace amount of iron in their noses, a rudimentary compass found in the ethmoid bone (between the eyes) to help in directional finding relative to the earth's magnetic field.
- Studies show that many people have the ability to use these magnetic deposits to orient themselves—even when blindfolded and removed from such external clues as sunlight—to within a few degrees of the North Pole, exactly as a compass does.
- Though no one knows how this "sixth" sense is processed by the brain, more than two dozen animals, including the dolphin, tuna, salmon, salamander, pigeon, and honeybee, have been found to have similar magnetic deposits in their brains to help them in navigation and migration.

### The Off-Duty Nostril

- Nostrils switch on and off every three to four hours, so that one is always smelling and breathing while the other closes down and rests.

### Whose Nose?

- Women have a better sense of smell than men due to higher levels of the female hormone estrogen.
- Interestingly, a woman can detect the odor of musk—a scent associated with male bodies—better than any other odor.

### Scent-sational

- The sex/scent connection is a powerful one. About 25 percent of people with smell disorders—due to either head injuries, viral infections, allergies, or aging—lose interest in sex.

**The comic strip "Dick Tracy" was originally called "Plainclothes Tracy."**

## HAIR TODAY, GONE TOMORROW

### Get Growing

• On the scalp, each hair grows continuously for 3 to 5 years, then enters a resting phase. After about 3 months of "resting," the hair falls out; a new hair starts growing 3 to 4 months later. Ninety percent of the scalp is always in the growing phase.

• Eyebrow hairs stay short because their growing phase only lasts for 10 weeks. Eyelashes are replaced every 3 months. A person will grow about 600 complete eyelashes in a lifetime.

• "Beards grow faster than any other hair on the body, and blond beards grow fastest of all. The average beard grows about 5-1/2 inches in a year—or about 30 feet in a lifetime. The longest beard on record was grown by Hans Langseth of Kensett, Iowa." When he died in 1927 his beard measured 17-1/2 feet.

### Baldness

• One out of every five men begin balding rapidly in their 20s. Another one out of five will always keep their hair. The others will slowly bald over time.

• As a general rule, the more hair a man has on his chest at age 30 the less hair he'll have on his head at age 40.

• Women typically lose as much as 50 percent of their hair within 3 months of childbirth. This partial and temporary balding is caused by severe fluctuations of hormones.

### Hair Growth and Loss

• The average hair grows half an inch per month, with the fastest growth generally occurring in the morning hours. Hair sprouts fastest of all when you're in love, which may also be due to fluctuations of hormones.

• A loss of about 70 hairs per day is typical, but emotional stress (including falling out of love), illness, malnourishment, and anemia can more than double this amount.

### Goosebumps

• The goosebumps that break out on our skin when we're cold represent little more than the body's effort to erect the coat of fur our ancestors lost over 100,000 years ago. Raised body hair provides added insulation.

## ONLY SKIN DEEP

### Sags, Lines, and Wrinkles

• Collagen—the skin's network of protein fibers—breaks down and becomes less pliable with age, causing sags, lines, and wrinkles to form on the face, neck, and hands. Any expression that manipulates the skin deeply and consistently will promote wrinkling (it takes about 200,000 frowns to create one permanent brow line), but exposure to sunlight and cigarette smoke hastens the process.

### Dead Skin and Where It Goes

• The body constantly sheds dead skin cells and replaces them with new ones. Thousands of these cells are lost, for example, every time we shake hands or swing a baseball bat. By the time we reach age 70, we'll have shed 40 pounds of dead skin.

• Of the dust floating around in the average house, 75 percent is made up of dead skin cells.

## HEAR, HEAR

### Human versus Animal Hearing

• Vampire and fruit bats can hear pitch as high as 210,000 hertz, ten times higher than humans. The dolphin's hearing is even more sensitive, with an acuity of 280,000 hertz.

• The best overall long-distance hearing, on the other hand, belongs to the fennec, a small African fox. Its oversized ears enable it to hear the movements of another animal up to one mile away.

### The Future of Ear Wiggling

• The ability to wiggle the ears is a vestige of evolution, a throwback to a time when our ancestors could "cock," or adjust, the ears to aid in hearing. The musculature for ear cocking has gradually diminished over the eons through genetic reprogramming. Most of us have lost the ability to move the ears at all in such a manner.

## ON ANOTHER SUBJECT...

### Doo-wop Mysteries Of Life:

How can you tell if a singer is singing "Bom-Bom," or "Bomp-bomp"? And is there any way to be sure that it's "Dip-dip" rather than "Dit-dit"?

# ABE LINCOLN, WARTS AND ALL

*We've all heard so much about Abraham Lincoln that it's easy to assume we know everything important about him. Actually, most of us know almost nothing. For example, did you know...*

## THE REAL ABE

• Some photographs of Lincoln show him with a mole on the right side of his face—but other photos show it on the left. The reason: few full-length pictures of Lincoln existed when he was running for president. So when photographers needed one, they put Lincoln's head onto other people's bodies. Sometimes the head needed to be reversed to fit the body they were using—and the mole on his right cheek ended up on his left.

• Although Lincoln's voice is often portrayed in movies as being deep and booming, his actual voice was high-pitched, piercing and shrill. Though unusual, it payed off politically: It carried for hundreds of yards—a distinct advantage in open-air speeches and debates.

## TRY, TRY AGAIN

Lincoln wasn't always a success:

• He lost a race for the state legislature in 1832. He also lost his job.

• His grocery business failed the following year. It took him 15 years to pay off the debt.

• He was elected to the state legislature in 1834, but he lost races for speaker of the house in 1836 and 1838.

• He was elected to Congress in 1846 but was defeated after only two years, and in 1849 lost the race for a land-office seat.

• He lost the U.S. Senate race in 1854 and again in 1858. In between, he lost the Vice Presidential nomination.

• It makes you wonder why he even bothered to run for president in 1860—but he did...and won. He was reelected in 1864.

## HONEST ABE?

• Lincoln's presidential campaigns used dirty tricks to get ahead: During the 1860 Republican National Convention, his campaign managers forged convention passes in order to pack the galleries with Lincoln supporters, shutting out hundreds of his opponent's supporters in the process. Lincoln won the nomination.

• Lincoln wasn't always that honest: After one trip to Springfield, Illinois, he filed for compensation for the 3,252 miles he claimed to have traveled. The actual length of the trip was 1,800 miles.

## ABE FACTS

• Lincoln hated being called "Abe"—friends called him Lincoln.

• He really did carry important documents in his stovepipe hat.

• He was the first President to support womens' suffrage. In 1832, while running for the state legislature, he provided a newspaper with a prepared statement that supported the idea.

• Though the Gettysburg Address is considered the most eloquent oration in American history, the *Chicago Times* hated it. The day after Lincoln delivered it, the *Times* wrote: "The cheek of every American must tingle with shame as he reads the silly, flat and dish-watery utterances of the man who has been pointed out to intelligent foreigners as the President of the United States."

## STRANGE BUT TRUE

Lincoln took his dreams seriously, and believed that strange events foretold the future. According to some accounts, he may even have "predicted" his own assassination.

• On one occasion, he looked into an old mirror and saw two reflections of himself. His interpretation: he would serve a second term as President—but would die in office.

• About a week before his assassination, Lincoln had a dream in which he "awoke" to the sound of sobbing and went to the East Room of the White House—which had been prepared for a funeral. When he asked a guard who had died, he replied: "The President."

• The morning of the assassination, Lincoln told his aides that he had had another dream, one in which he was sailing "in an indescribable vessel and moving rapidly toward an indistinct shore."

**Dr. Seuss designed the first animated color TV commercial in 1949, for Ford.**

# BATTLE OF THE SEXES

*Looking for words of wisdom about love and life? Try TV quotes from the book* Primetime Proverbs, *by Jack Mingo and John Javna.*

## ALL ABOUT MEN

"Men are nothing but lazy lumps of drunken flesh. They crowd you in bed, get you all worked up, and then before you can say 'Is that all there is?' that's all there is."

**—Mrs. Gravas (Latka's mom), *Taxi***

**Cosmetic Clerk:** "You know what the fastest way to a man's heart is?"
**Rosanne:** "Yeah. Through his chest."

***—Roseanne***

## ALL ABOUT WOMEN

"It's not the frivolity of women that makes them so intolerable. It's their ghastly enthusiasm."

**—Horace Rumpole, *Rumpole of the Bailey***

"There she was—dejected, desperate, and stoned. Everything I could hope for in a woman."

**—Louie DePalma, *Taxi***

"It's been proven through history that wimmin's a mystery."

***—Popeye***

## ON MARRIAGE

"In my town, we didn't have datin.' You washed your hair every Saturday night and when you were fourteen, you married your cousin."

**Nurse Laverne, *Empty Nest***

"Well, well, well...So you're going to get married, ha, ha, ha. Welcome to the ranks of the living dead."

**—Kingfish, *Amos & Andy***

"Men are such idiots, and I married their King."

**—Peg Bundy, *Married with Children***

## ABOUT SEX

"With my first husband, it was like a news bulletin: brief, unexpected, and usually a disaster."

**—Mary Campbell, *Soap***

"You can point out any item in the Sears catalog and somebody wants to sleep with it."

**—Det. Stanley Wojohoicz, *Barney Miller***

**More than 44 million Americans say they want to quit smoking. Only 1.3 million will.**

# BREAKFAST SERIALS

*You're not supposed to read this book at breakfast, of course. But you can read it* after *breakfast. Here's the perfect reading fiber.*

## RAISIN' DOUBTS

Everybody knows a raisin is heavier than a cereal flake. So how come all the raisins in Kellogg's Raisin Bran don't end up at the bottom of the box?

The raisins are mixed evenly with the cereal as the boxes are filled. Since the flat flakes pack so densely together, the raisins can't move around much during shipping.

## GETTING FLAKY?

According to one researcher, large doses of cereal may contain enough natural LSD to induce mild euphoria. Dr. David Conning, director of the British Nutritional Foundation, suggests that eating a large bowl of shredded wheat or bran flakes in one sitting may be enough to set you off. This is because LSD is produced by ergot, a common fungal infestation of wheat that may, in some cases, survive food processing. A high-bran diet could result in a daily consumption of 100 micrograms of LSD, four times the minimum dose needed to produce an effect on an inexperienced user of the drug. Eight to ten slices of whole wheat bread, the doctor said, could have the same effect. Turn On, Tune In, Snap, Crackle Pop?

## SO SWEET

Are cereals ashamed of their sugary roots? Three that have been renamed to appeal to the new nutrition-conscious consumer are: Super Sugar Crisp (has become Super Golden Crisp), Sugar Pops (now called simply Corn Pops); and Sugar Smacks (changed to the healthy-sounding but still tooth-aching sweet Honey Smacks). But that doesn't mean they're less sugary—Honey Smacks and Super Golden Crisp are right up there with Froot Loops and Apple Jacks on the list of "high sugar content" cereals, some of which contain more than half their weight in sugar.

**George Washington's false teeth were made of Hippopotomus ivory.**

## SOMETHING USEFUL, FOR A CHANGE

A notorious "Phone Phreak" (a pre-computer hackers of the late 1960s who developed elaborate strategies for getting free phone calls through guerrilla technology), called himself Cap'n Crunch. This was in honor of a "free-inside" premium whistle from the cereal of the same name which, according to legend, was exactly the right frequency for triggering free long distance calls if blown into the phone right after dialing the number.

## STATISTICS:

• Nielsen Marketing Research tells us that last year nearly 2.5 billion boxes of hot and cold cereal were sold in the US.

• The manufacturers of Post cereals use a staggering 75,000,000 pounds of corn, 1,550,000 bushels of wheat and 7,500,000 pounds of rice each year, which they sweeten with 36,000,000 pounds of liquid sugar.

• Kellogg's reports that the average American child consumes 15 pounds of cereal in a year.

• A Cheerios box with a Lone Ranger Frontier Town premium on the box sold for 18¢ in 1948. The price today for this vintage box? $165 to $350 (cereal not included). A full set of the Frontier Town (four maps and 72 models) sells for $7,200 on the collectibles market.

• Potato chips: the new breakfast of champions? A bowlful of Wheaties contains twice as much sodium as a similar size serving of potato chips, according to researchers at *Consumer Reports* Magazine.

## AMERICA'S BEST-SELLING CEREALS

1. Kellogg's Corn Flakes
2. Kellogg's Frosted Flakes
3 General Mills Cheerios
4. Kellogg's Raisin Bran
5. Kellogg's Rice Krispies

**The silkworm can spin a thread more than 1/2 a mile long.**

# CR_ _ SW_ _ D P_ ZZL_ S

*What's an 8-letter word for the smallest library in the house? While you're pondering the answer, here's some crossword puzzle trivia.*

The first crossword puzzle appeared on December 21, 1913, in the pages of the *New York World* newspaper. It was created by a reporter named Arthur Wynn.

Dick Simon, a struggling publisher, was visiting his aunt one afternoon in 1924. She wanted to give her daughter a book of crossword puzzles, but none existed. So Simon and his partner, Lincoln Schuster, published one themselves. It became a bestseller overnight—and made enough money to keep the fledgling Simon and Schuster company afloat.

Crosswords were so popular in the twenties that in 1925 the B & O Railroad put dictionaries on all its mainline trains for its many crossword-solving passengers.

During the Roaring '20s, crossword puzzles even influenced fashions: Clothes made with black and white checked fabric were the rage.

In December, 1925 Theodore Koerner, a 27-year old employee of the New York Telephone Co., shot and wounded his wife after she refused to help him solve a crossword puzzle.

In 1926, a waiter living in Budapest, Hungary commited suicide. He left behind a note—in the form of a crossword puzzle—explaining why he killed himself. His motive: unknown. The police couldn't solve the puzzle.

Today crossword puzzles are the most popular hobby on Earth. The Bible is the most popular Crossword puzzle subject.

What's a 14-1etter word for a crossword maniac? CRUCIVERBALIST.

**More than 28 million Americans buy Christmas presents for their dogs every year.**

# 1ST-CLASS COACH

*It seems as though Vince Lombardi is quoted more often than other football coaches. Here's an example of what he had to say.*

"To play this game, you must have that fire in you, and there is nothing that stokes that fire like hate."

"Pro football...is a violent, dangerous sport. To play it other than violently would be imbecile."

"Winning isn't everything. It's the only thing."

(On his "Winning is everything" quote): "I wish to hell I'd never said the damn thing...I meant the effort...I meant having a goal...I sure as hell don't mean for people to crush human values and morality."

"I think the rights of the individual have been put above everything else...The individual has to have every respect for authority regardless of what authority is."

"The harder you work, the harder it is to surrender."

"Run to daylight."

"A real executive goes around with a worried look on his assistants."

"No one is ever hurt. Hurt is in the mind."

"If you aren't fired with enthusiasm, you'll be fired with enthusiasm."

"If you can't accept losing, you can't win."

"The greatest accomplishment is not in never falling, but in rising again after you fall."

"A school without football is in danger of deteriorating into a medieval study hall."

"There are three important things in life: family, religion, and the Green Bay Packers."

"Football isn't a contact sport. It's a collision sport. Dancing is a contact sport."

"Football is a game of clichés, and I believe in every one of them."

**Sea lions can swim at speeds of up to 25 miles per hour.**

# THE PONY EXPRESS

*Remember those dramatic scenes in TV westerns where everyone's waiting for the Pony Express to arrive with the mail? It turns out that didn't happen very often...or for very long.*

## THE MYTH

The Pony Express was one of the most important links connecting the gold rush towns of the West and large cities in the East. For years, it was the fastest way to send a letter to California; without it the western states might never have developed.

## THE TRUTH

In its short lifetime (18 months—1860-61), the Pony Express *was* the fastest way to send a letter to California. Riders could deliver a letter in 10 days—half the time to send it by sea. But it had its problems:

• Hardly anyone could afford to use it. A single letter initially cost $5.00 to mail, and never dropped below a dollar. The largest customers were newspapers that depended on late-breaking news to keep readers up to date.

• The shipping firm of Russell, Majors & Waddell—founders of the Pony Express—knew their enterprise could never make money with normal business; they counted on winning a contract with the federal government to help cover its enormous costs ($70,000 up front and $4,000 per month). They never got one. The government was more interested in Samuel Morse's telegraph.

• By 1861 the nation's first transcontinental telegraph line was completed—making the Pony Express obsolete overnight. It folded less than two years after its introduction, over $500,000 in debt.

## EXPRESS FACTS

• There wasn't a single pony in the Pony Express. Ponies didn't have the stamina to carry large loads of mail over long distances.

• Few of the riders were adults. Most were teenagers, hired through newspaper advertisements that read: "Wanted: Young skinny wiry fellows, not over 18. Must be expert riders willing to risk death daily. Orphans preferred."

**What state has the highest percentage of literate citizens? Iowa.**

# DON'T CAN IT

*Here are some recycling tips from* The Recycler's Handbook, *by the EarthWorks Group.*

For the recycling novice—in other words, almost all of us—aluminum cans are as close to perfect as you can get: No matter how many of them you have, they're still light enough to carry; you don't need any fancy storage containers—you can even pile them into a paper bag. And you don't have to hunt very far to find someplace to take them—cans are worth so much that there's always someone around who collects them.

The secret is that it's a lot cheaper to recycle aluminum cans than it is to make them out of new metal. So years ago, the aluminum industry set up collection services, and they've been paying top dollar to get cans back ever since.

So if you're wondering where to start recycling, put aluminum cans at the top of your list.

## ALUMINATING FACTS

• Aluminum was worth more than gold when it was discovered. It was first used to make a rattle for Napoleon's son.

• In 1989, Americans used 80 billion aluminum cans. That's the equivalent of about 16 cans for every person on the planet.

• We recycled a record 60% of them that same year.

• Making cans from recycled aluminum cuts related air pollution (for example, sulfur dioxides, which create acid rain) by 95%.

• Recycling aluminum saves 95% of the energy used to make the material from scratch. That means you can make *20* cans out of recycled material with the same energy it takes to make *one* can out of new material.

• Americans throw away enough aluminum every three months to rebuild our entire commercial air fleet.

## WHAT YOU CAN DO

### 1. Find a Place to Take Them

• Virtually all recycling programs accept aluminum cans.

Call recycling centers in your area for more details.

• If you're having trouble finding a recycling center, try the toll-free Reynolds Aluminum hotline: (800) 228-2525. If there's a Reynolds recycling center in your area, they'll tell you where it is.

• Check phone listings under "Scrap Metal." Many scrap dealers aren't interested in small loads, but aluminum is valuable—so they may take it.

• Contact your state recycling office.

**2. Recycle**

***Cans***

• Crushing cans makes storing and transporting them easier. But before recycling, check with your recycler to find out if crushing them is okay. In some states with deposit laws, recyclers prefer to get the cans intact; they need to see the brand and the name of the factory the can came from.

• In most places, it's not necessary to rinse cans...but a large batch of unwashed cans may attract bees and ants.

***Foiled Again***

• Aluminum foil, pie plates, TV dinner trays, etc. are all reusable and recyclable. Lightly rinse them off first if they're dirty (you don't have to waste water—use dishwater).

• Some places request that you keep foil and cans separate. Check with your local recycling center.

***Other Items***

• Containers aren't the only source of aluminum scrap. Other common items include window frames, screen doors and lawn furniture. However, check with your recycling center before including these.

• Is your scrap aluminum? Check it with a magnet; aluminum isn't magnetic. Check small pieces like screws, rivets, etc.

• Remove everything that's not aluminum.

## FOR MORE INFORMATION

**"Aluminum Recycling: America's Environmental Success Story."** The Aluminum Association, 900 19th St., N.W., Washington, D.C. 20006. (202) 862-5100.

# UNCLES & ANT FARMS

*Ever had an ant farm? It's one of those toys people buy you when they're trying to get something "educational" instead of something you can actually play with. Even when you're a kid, you can't help but wonder: Who could have come up with an idea like this?... And where did they get the ants? Here's the answer.*

## THE BEGINNING

It was Independence Day, 1956, when the idea struck. "It just came to me in a flash," "Uncle" Milton Levine says. He was a 32-year-old entrepreneur looking for new products to help expand his line of mail order novelties. "I was at a Fourth of July picnic at my sister's house in the Valley [California's San Fernando Valley]. I saw a bunch of ants around the pool. I saw a bunch of kids, and they were interested in the ants. And it came to me."

• Levine's first ant farms were six inches by nine inches, and sold for $1.98. They consisted of a solid-colored plastic frame that sandwiched a layer of sand between two sheets of transparent plastic. There was a plastic farm scene—barn, silo, farmhouse, and windmill.

• To attract customers, Levine bought a 2-inch ad in the *Los Angles Times*, inviting the curious to "Watch the ants dig tunnels and build bridges" in their own Ant Farm. "I got so many orders, you wouldn't believe it," he says.

•Uncle Milton ran into an unexpected problem, though. The ants in his first farms kept dying—the result of either glue fumes (Levine's former partner's theory) or the booze the assembler used to drink (Levine's theory). Whatever the cause, the problem was eventually solved.

## DOWN ON THE FARM

• The Ant Farm is an enduring product; Over 12 million farms—containing more than 360 million ants—have been sold so far. Most customers are satisfied: the company receives about 12,000 letters each year from happy Ant Farm owners. But not all the letters are positive: one child wrote in complaining that his ants weren't wearing top hats like it showed on the box.

• How do the ants survive weeks on toy store shelves? They don't—the farms are sold empty, with a certificate the owner sends to Uncle Milton Industries for a shipment of free ants.

• Every farm comes with *Uncle Milton's Ant Watchers' Manual*, which tells you how to care for your ants, and gives you information about your new livestock (Do ants talk? Yes. Do ants take baths? Yes).

• One improvement on the Ant Farms of yesteryear: Newer models have connectors for plastic tubes—so you can connect any number of ant farms together and watch the ants crawl back and forth.

## THE ORIGINAL ANT FARMER

• Kenneth Gidney started digging ants in 1959 after answering an ad Uncle Milton had placed in the *Los Angeles Times*. One of his children, Robin Brenner, is still doing it today—she's one of only three diggers that supply the 15 million ants the company sends out each year.

• Not that it's an easy job, according to Brenner. You get bitten a lot. "Sometimes when I'm sitting up late at night, I think 'People don't know how hard this is. They don't know where these ants come from. They don't know how much sleep I'm missing.' "

• Every ant catcher has his or her own technique. Some take straws and blow into antholes, catching the ants as they run out. Brenner's father carefully sliced the tunnels and the kids gathered the ants into coffee cans. Brenner herself digs up the ant tunnels and then sucks up the ants using a car vacuum fixed to a Tupperware container.

• It takes about 10 hours to gather 50,000 ants, for which you can earn about $550. Afterward a half-dozen workers tediously fill little plastic vials with exactly 30 ants each, and these are mailed out to Ant Farm owners.

## ANT FARM FACTS

• All the ants supplied for the Ant Farm are female. In the ant world, there aren't many males, and all they do is mate and die (an anty-climax, if you will). And since the company can't legally ship queen ants, Ant Farm colonies can't reproduce and will eventually dwindle to nothing.

• Out of thousands of varieties of ants, the harvester ant was chosen for the Ant Farm because it's big and is one of the few varieties that will dig in daylight.

• The leading cause of barnyard death is overfeeding. If you exceed the recommended ration of one birdseed or a single corn flake every two days, the food gets moldy, and your ants "buy the farm."

• The next leading dangers are too much sunlight (baked ants). Shaking the farm has been known to cause mass death by shock.

• At a funeral, the live ants always carry the dead ant to the northeastern corner of the farm. If the farm is rotated to a new direction, the pallbearers march into action again, digging up the dead ants and reburying them in the northeast. Why? Nobody knows.

• The technical name for an ant farm (or any ant habitat) is a formicarium.

• Why is Levine called "Uncle Milton"? "Everyone always said, 'You've got the ants, but where's the uncles?' So I became Uncle Milton."

• Ant farms aren't the only culturally significant product Uncle Milton Industries makes. Some others:

—the plastic shrunken heads that hang from rear-view mirrors.

—the Spud Gun, which fires potato pellets

—the once-popular insecticides Fly Cake and Roach Cake

—"100 Toy Soldiers for a Buck"

## ANT FACTS

• In medieval times, it was thought that ants in the house were a sign of good luck and abundance.

• Chinese farmers use ants against pests. A large colony can capture several million insects a year.

# AD NAUSEUM

*Here's a horrible thought: Every day the average American is exposed to 3,000 ads. Today you get to read about them, too.*

In a 1985 Procter & Gamble poll, 93% of the people questioned recognized Mr. Clean, but only 56% of the same group could identify Vice President George Bush.

More American kids age 3-5 recognize Ronald McDonald than Santa Claus or any other entity, real or mythical.

The typical 30-second prime-time TV ad costs about the same to produce as the half-hour program it interrupts.

Advertisers spend about $400 a year on each newspaper subscriber and $300 a year on each television household.

The first advertisement to discuss body odor was a 1919 ad for the deodorant Odo-Ro-No.

The infamous "this is your brain on drugs" ad had an unintentional side effect: Small kids all over the country refused to eat fried eggs, believing they were somehow laced with drugs.

In early cuts of *Die Hard II*, Bruce Willis clearly used a Black & Decker drill in a key scene. When the scene was cut, Black & Decker—which paid for the scene and had planned an expensive promotion campaign around it—sued for damages.

The first recorded singing commercial was for Moxie, the most popular soft drink of the '20s; it was released on disc (on the Moxie label) in 1921.

Michael Jackson's hair-burning Pepsi ads in the mid-1980s boosted Pepsi drinking among 12-20 year olds, the elderly and Japanese. They actually hurt sales among 25-40 year-old blacks, who saw Jackson's plastic surgery and cosmetic touches as a repudiation of his roots.

If you're an average American, you'll spend a year and a half of your life watching TV commercials.

# MORE MYTH CONCEPTIONS

*Here are two more pages of "facts" that everyone knows—but aren't true.*

**Myth:** The song "Chopsticks" was named after the Chinese eating utensils with the same name.
**Truth:** The song was written by Euphemia Allen, a 16-year-old British girl in 1877. She advised pianists to play it with their hands turned sideways, using chopping motions.

**Myth:** Alan Shepard coined the phrase "A-OK" during his first spaceflight in May, 1961. Reason: "OK" by itself could not be heard over the static.
**Truth:** Even *we* thought he said it—we mentioned it in our *Third Bathroom Reader*. But he never did. Colonel "Shorty" Powers—NASA's public relations officer at the time—came up with the phrase himself and attributed it to Shepard, hoping it would catch on. It did—even though most astronauts hated it.

**Myth:** Chinese checkers were invented in China.
**Truth:** The game was invented in England in the 1800s. It was originally called *Halma*.

**Myth:** The Guinea pig originated on the island of Guinea.
**Truth:** It's actually from South America. And it's not a pig—it's a rodent.

**Myth:** Goats can eat anything—even tin cans.
**Truth:** Even if their jaws were strong enough to crunch metal, goats hate the taste of tin cans.

**Myth:** Switching from butter to margarine will help you lose weight.
**Truth:** Margerine may be lower in cholesterol than butter, but it has the same number of calories—so it won't help you lose weight.

**Myth:** The Romans used chariots in battle.

**Truth:** Chariots weren't effective on the battlefield—soldiers couldn't fight while holding onto the reins. The Romans used them only in sports and as transportation.

**Myth:** Dogs sweat through their tongues.

**Truth:** Dogs cool off by breathing rapidly; not by sticking their tongues out. Their tongues don't have sweat glands—and the only large sweat glands they have are in their feet.

**Myth:** Having so many ships in Pearl Harbor when the Japanese attacked in 1941 was one of the worst disasters of World War II.

**Truth:** It may actually have been *lucky:* the ships in port had better air cover, didn't sink as deep, and were much closer to repair facilities than if they had been out at sea.

**Myth:** If too many pores in your skin clog up, you can get sick—even die.

**Truth:** The pores in your skin don't breathe—and you don't need to keep them "open." It is possible to clog all the pores in your body for an extended period of time without suffering any ill effects.

**Myth:** You can tell the age of a rattlesnake by counting the number of rattles it has.

**Truth:** The number of rattles a snake has does increase with age, but not at a uniform rate. Snakes shed their skins more than once a year—and the interval varies with each individual snake.

**Myth:** In high winds, skyscrapers can sway as much as eight feet in any direction.

**Truth:** Even the most limber buildings won't move more than a few inches.

**Myth:** Cold-blooded animals have cold blood.

**Truth:** A "cold-blooded" animal's body temperature changes with the surrounding air temperature. Many cold-blooded animals have body temperatures that are higher than "warm-blooded" animals.

**Given a second chance, 18% of Americans say they would not remarry their spouses.**

# THE GOSPEL ACCORDING TO BOB

*You've heard his songs. Here are a few of his comments.*

"Colleges are like old-age homes; except for the fact that more people die in colleges.

"Just because you like my stuff doesn't mean I owe you anything."

"Art is the perpetual motion of illusion."

"Rock and roll ended with Little Anthony & the Imperials."

"I'd like to see Thomas Jefferson, Benjamin Franklin and a few of those other guys come back. If they did I'd go out and vote. They knew what was happening."

"I'm just as good a singer as Caruso...I hit all those notes and I can hold my breath three times as long if I want to."

"It's always lonely where I am."

"They're just songs. Songs are transparent so you can see every bit through them."

"You can get sex anywhere. If you're looking for someone to *love* you, now that's different. I guess you have to stay in college for that."

"I sometimes dream of running the country and putting all my friends in office. That's the way it works now, anyway."

"I have no message for anyone, my songs are only me talking to myself.."

"On some of my earlier records, I sounded cross because I was poor. Lived on less than 10 cents a day in those times. Now I'm cross because I'm rich."

"Death don't come knocking at the door. It's there in the morning when you wake up. Did you ever clip your fingernails, cut your hair? Then you experience death."

"Money doesn't talk—It swears."

**White House meals were cooked over a fireplace until 1850.**

# THE PIGMENT OF YOUR IMAGINATION

*Do you remember your first box of Crayola Crayons? Here's some info you probably never knew about them:*

## BACKGROUND

In 1885, Joseph W. Binney founded the Peekskill Chemical Company in Peekskill, NY and began producing lampblack, charcoal and red iron oxide barn paint. In 1900 his son and nephew, Edwin Binney and C. Harold Smith, took over, renamed the company "Binney and Smith," and added schoolroom slate pencils to their line of goods.

• In selling to schools, they learned that teachers were dissatisfied with the classroom chalk and crayons available at the time. The chalk was too crumbly and dusty, the European-made crayons too expensive and their colors too anemic.

• Binney and Smith went to work, developing first a "dustless" chalk and then a better-quality crayon. Further research went into finding non-toxic pigments when they discovered that many kids then, as now, thought the colors look good enough to eat.

## WHAT'S YOUR NUMBER?

In 1903 the first boxes of Crayolas rolled off the line, priced at five cents and offering eight colors: red, blue, green, yellow, orange, brown, violet and black. The number of colors available has changed several times since then: By 1949, Crayolas were up to 48 colors; by 1958, 64; and in 1972 eight fluorescent colors were added. The company has stuck with 72 colors ever since. To introduce new ones they have to retire some, most recently in 1990.

## RED SCARE

Crayons, although ageless, are not exempt from the changing world. Consider these examples:

• In 1958, with Cold War xenophobia in full bloom, the company changed the name of "Prussian Blue" to "Midnight Blue."

• In 1962, heightened consciousness brought on by the civil rights movement led Binney and Smith to change the name of "Flesh" to "Peach," recognizing, as the company put it, "that not everyone's flesh is the same shade." On the other hand, the color "Indian Red" still exists.

• In 1990, with much ballyhoo, Binney and Smith discontinued eight of their less-popular colors (Blue Gray, Green Blue, Lemon Yellow, Maize, Orange Red, Orange Yellow, Raw Umber, and Violet Blue) in order to replace them with the brighter colors (Cerulean, Dandelion, Fuchsia, Jungle Green, Royal Purple, Teal Blue, Vivid Tangerine, and Wild Strawberry) that their marketing research indicated that kids wanted.

• The problem: parents. When the colors were introduced, a small knot of protesters picketed the Binney and Smith headquarters, carrying signs with slogans like "We Take Umber-age" and "Save Lemon Yellow." The company refused to back down. But it did make one concession; it promised to ensconce a five foot replica of each color in its "Crayon Hall of Fame," a new feature of its guided tours.

## CRAYON FACTS

• The name *Crayola* comes from combining the French word "craie" meaning a stick of color with "ola" from the word "oleaginous," referring to the oily paraffin wax in the crayons. It was Binney's wife Alice (a schoolteacher, incidentally) who coined the term.

• Surveys have shown that the smell of crayons is one of the most recognized smells in America. Its source: stearic acid, also known as beef fat.

• Four out of five crayons sold in the U.S. are Crayolas. Each year Binney and Smith manufactures more than 2 billion of them. That's enough to produce a giant crayon 35 feet in diameter and 410 feet tall, towering 100 feet taller than the Statue of Liberty.

• 65% of all American children between the ages of 2 and 7 will pick up a crayon at least once today. American kids will spend 6.3 billion hours coloring this year—that's 27 minutes a coloring session, longer if the crayons are brand new.

**James Smithson, founder of the Smithsonian Institution, never visited the U.S.**

# THE PHRASE IS FAMILIAR

*Here are some well-known phrases and the stories behind them.*

**WHEN MY SHIP COMES IN**

***Meaning:*** When financial luck improves.

***Background:*** Before steamships, cargo ships depended on wind, luck and weather. Investors who had a large financial stake in a ship's cargo often waited anxiously, hoping the ship would arrive before they ran out of money.

**PULL OUT ALL THE STOPS**

***Meaning:*** To use every means at your disposal.

***Background:*** Each pipe in an organ contains a "stop" which blocks the flow of air; pulling out specific stops allows sets of pipes to sound. An organist wanting the loudest sound possible "pulls out all the stops."

**THE LION'S SHARE**

***Meaning:*** A greedily large portion.

***Background:*** Taken from an Aesop's fable in which a lion goes hunting with a cow, a goat and a sheep. When the animals catch a deer, the lion divides it into four portions—then takes them all.

**THE BOONDOCKS**

***Meaning:*** A very remote area.

***Background:*** *Bundok* is the Philipino word for mountain. U.S. soldiers brought the term back from the Spanish-American War.

**TO THE HILT**

***Meaning:*** All the way.

***Background:*** A hilt is a handle of a sword or dagger. When you stab as far as you can, it's "to the hilt."

**Researchers say that more than 90% of all Americans bite their fingernails.**

## IN CAHOOTS WITH

***Meaning:*** To conspire with.

***Background:*** Thieves in medieval Germany's Black Forest often shared cabins known as *kajuetes*. They were literally "in kajuetes" with each other.

## NOT WORTH HIS SALT

***Meaning:*** Overpaid.

***Background:*** Before the invention of money, the Romans paid their soldiers in portions of salt, then a very valuable commodity. It was believed to have magical properties. They'd throw it over their shoulder for luck or sprinkle it on food they suspected might be spoiled or poisoned, which explains another salt phrase—"Take it with a grain of salt."

## A DOG EAT DOG WORLD

***Meaning:*** A brutishly hostile world.

***Background:*** An old English saying goes: "dog does not eat dog"—another way of saying "birds of a feather stick together." In a "dog eat dog world" life is so brutal that even natural law is overturned.

## EXAMINE WITH A FINE-TOOTH COMB

***Meaning:*** Look at thoroughly.

***Background:*** The phrase comes from the days before chemical treatment, when the only cure for head and body lice was using a special comb with spaces small enough to trap the tiny bugs. The same device comes up in the old song *Won't You Come Home, Bill Bailey?* in which the singer says she was abandoned with "nothing but a fine-tooth comb"—in other words, a case of the crabs.

## PUT A SOCK IN IT

**Meaning:** Shut up!

**Background:** In early days, handwound Victrolas didn't come with a volume control, and in a small room they could be pretty loud. People discovered that you could lower the sound level by jamming a heavy woolen stocking into the phonograph's horn.

# PIRATE LEGENDS

*Captain Kidd, Blackbeard...their exploits are legendary. But did you know they were real people, too?*

## EUSTACE THE MONK

**Background:** No one knows for sure who inspired the legend of Robin Hood, but Eustace is a strong candidate. He was born in the late 1100s, and really was a priest at one time. He lived in a monastery near Nottingham...until his father was murdered. Then Eustace left religious life forever.

**His Exploits:** At first, he lived as a hermit in Sherwood Forest. But gradually he developed new interests—killing and looting. He built a reputation as a soldier of fortune, and even delved into piracy. His attacks on ships in the English Channel were so effective that King Philip II warned English ships: "if you fall into the hands of Eustace the Monk...do not put the blame on us." Eustace's career as a pirate spanned nearly twenty years. It ended on August 24, 1217, when King Henry III defeated him in the battle of Sandwich and had him beheaded.

**Note:** Eustace stole from the rich, but he probably never gave to the poor. That part of the legend didn't surface until the 1300s.

## CAPTAIN KIDD

**Background:** William Kidd was born in Greenock, Scotland in 1645. He had an unusual background for a pirate; he was a respectable ship owner in New York, and the son of a Presbyterian minister. He never even wanted to be a pirate—he seized only two ships; and only because he had no other choice.

**His Exploits:** The English East India Company hired him in 1695 to work as a *privateer*—a "bounty hunter" who attacks pirate ships in exchange for a share of the recovered loot. But after more than a year at sea, he hadn't caught a single pirate; he had nothing to pay his men with. So in 1697 he let his crew plunder a single ship. But they insisted on raiding another. Kidd refused; he flew into a rage and hit one of his crew members over the head with a bucket. The man died the next day. Fearing mutiny, Kidd backed down and let his crew seize a second ship.

Soon after the second adventure, Kidd and his men finally found a real pirate ship to plunder—the *Resolution*, sailing in the Indian Ocean. Kidd gave the order to attack the ship, but his men refused—and most of them jumped ship to join the pirate crew. Exasperated, Kidd gave up and sailed home.

Though he had committed acts of piracy and murder, Kidd didn't expect to be arrested when he landed in New York. He was friends with the governor, and the East India Company stood to profit enormously from his plunder. Nevertheless, he was seized as soon as he pulled into port, and extradited to England for trial. He was found guilty and was hanged on May 23, 1701.

**Note:** Eleven days before he was scheduled to be executed, Kidd petitioned the House of Commons with a deal: in exchange for a delay in his execution, he would lead a fleet to the spot where he claimed to have buried his treasure. His offer was denied. Searches for Kidd's "lost treasure" have been conducted all over the Northeastern United States and other parts of the world, but nothing has been found. One possibility: it's buried on Oak Island.

## BLACKBEARD

**Background:** Edward Teach was born in Bristol, England in the late 1600s. Like Captain Kidd, he got his start on a privateering ship. But unlike Kidd, he was good at it—so good that in 1713 his captain gave him command of one of the captured ships. That was a mistake—he turned to piracy almost immediately and began plundering English ships.

**His Exploits:** Though his pirate career spanned only five years, Teach came about as close as anyone to living up to pirate lore—even in appearance. According to one historian: "he wore a sling over his shoulders, with three brace of pistols hanging in holsters like bandoleers; he stuck lighted matches under his hat...and his eyes looked fierce and wild...Imagination cannot form an idea of a fury from Hell to look more frightful." He tied his enormous black beard into braids, which he threw back over both ears. He had at least 14 wives—each one in a different port.

Teach operated out of several bases off the coast of South Caroli-

**The TV soap opera "General Hospital" has been on the air for 27 years**

na, which he set up with the help of the state's corrupt governor. But in 1717 his numerous attacks on ships off the New England coast prodded Virginia's *un*corrupt governor into action. Using his own money, he hired Lieutenant Robert Maynard, a privateer, to hunt Teach down.

On November 21, 1718 Maynard found Teach's ship anchored off the coast of the Carolinas. He pulled within shooting distance and opened fire. Teach weighed anchor and tried to flee, but his ship ran aground. He fired back with his cannon, forcing Maynard to send his crew below decks. Seeing so few people on Maynard's ship, Teach assumed that he had killed most of the crew. But when his men tried to board the ship, Maynard's men reemerged from below decks and attacked. Within minutes they had overwhelmed the pirate crew.

While this was going on, Teach and Maynard fought man-to-man—first with pistols, then with cutlasses. Teach came very close to winning. He broke Maynard's blade off at the hilt and knocked him to the ground, but as he was moving in for the kill, one of Maynard's men rushed up and slashed Teach's throat. He kept on fighting, but collapsed and died a few minutes later. Maynard cut off his head and hung it from the ship's bow. The pirates who survived the fight didn't fare any better: all but two were tried for piracy, convicted, and hanged.

## ROBINSON CRUSOE

**Background:** Alexander Selkirk—who inspired the tale of Robinson Crusoe—was born in Largo, Scotland, in 1676.

**His Exploits:** In his early teens he signed up with a privateering expedition, and remained a privateer until 1704. That year he had an argument with his captain—and as punishment, was dumped on an island in the South Seas. He lived there for more than five years, off the wild goats that roamed the island.

Selkirk was rescued in 1709 after a passing ship noticed his signal fire. He returned to Scotland, but never really recovered from his isolation. He remained a recluse, spending much of his time in a cave in his father's garden. He died in 1721. By that time his story had been immortalized in *Robinson Crusoe*, a novel Daniel Defoe had written two years earlier.

# SECTS SCANDALS

*Sex scandals involving famous preachers? Jimmy Swaggert and Jim Bakker were only following a pulpit tradition. As the Bible says, there is nothing new under the sun.*

**THE SINNER: Horatio Alger**. Before becoming one of the most successful American writers of the 19th century, Alger was a preacher. In 1864, at the age of 32, he became pastor of the First Unitarian Parish in Brewster, Massachusetts.

**THE SCANDAL:** More than a few people noticed that he "was always with the boys"—at first this seemed liked commendable interest in their spiritual development, though parishioners began wondering why the eligible bachelor didn't pay attention to any the congregation's single women. An 1866 investigation concluded that he and several of his young charges had committed acts "too revolting to relate."

**JUDGMENT DAY:** Alger didn't deny the charges, but admitted only that he was "imprudent." He resigned and left town. Church officials warned other parishes of his dismissal (without getting specific), and some families threatened legal action. But Alger had promised to abandon his clerical career, and the matter was allowed to die quietly. Resettling in New York, he became a literary success, writing more than 100 books about poverty-stricken boys whose hard work and diligence earned them the attention of rich older men who helped them earn fortune and honor. The shocked parish concealed its findings for more than a century, until the 1970s, when its records were finally made public.

**THE SINNER: Henry Ward Beecher.** The famous Congregational preacher of the 1860s and 1870s (and brother of *Uncle Tom's Cabin* author Harriet Beecher Stowe) was a skilled orator—some called him "the greatest preacher since St. Paul." Pastor of Brooklyn's prestigious Plymouth Congregational Church, where 2,500 people came to hear him weekly, Stowe's eloquent advocacy of abolition, women's rights and Darwinism brought him both fame and an enormous salary of $40,000 a year.

**THE SCANDAL:** In 1874, his close friend and protege, Thomas Tilton, filed suit against Beecher, charging that he had been having an affair with Tilton's wife over several years. Noted feminist writer Victoria Woodhull (with whom Tilton was also suspected of having an affair) dared Beecher to admit his adultery. Beecher would not make a forthright admission of guilt, and the suit went to trial.

The trial itself became a sensation. Ticket scalpers charged $5 for admission passes they had gotten for free; up to 3,000 people were turned away every day; vendors made a killing selling refreshments and binoculars before and after trial sessions. Up against the testimony of 95 witnesses, Beecher declared he was "unable to remember" nearly 900 times.

**JUDGMENT DAY:** The trial ended in a hung jury, and Beecher, free and unabashed, expelled Tilton from Plymouth Church. He continued to enjoy great popularity and influence until his death in 1887.

**THE SINNER: Aimee Semple McPherson.** Pentecostal evangelist, "Queen of Heaven" and founder of the International Church of the Foursquare Gospel, McPherson seemed to have it all: youth, good looks, a large following, and part ownership in the Angelus Temple, the 5,000-seat, $1.5 million Los Angeles church where she preached to the accompaniment of choirs, bell ringers, and an 80-piece xylophone band.

**THE SCANDAL:** On May 18, 1926, the 36-year-old McPherson vanished while swimming in the Pacific Ocean. It was feared she was drowned. Her congregation took to walking into the sea where she was last seen, looking for clues and signs, resulting in the drowning death of one. A few days later, the first of several ransom notes arrived, and police received reports of sightings in Santa Barbara, Denver, El Paso, and Tucson. On June 23, Sister Aimee staggered across the U.S.-Mexican border into Douglas, Arizona with a tale of harrowing escape from kidnapers.

But details of her story failed to check out—for one thing, her ardu-

**Americans spend an average of 76 hours per week in bed; They're asleep for 45 of the hours.**

ous trek across the Mexican desert somehow left her shoes unscuffed. Things got sticky for Sister Aimee. Reporters turned up accounts that McPherson and a married former employee had rented a cottage in Carmel-by-the-Sea, a few hundred miles north of Los Angeles, for ten days in May. Newspapers had a field day, calling it a "honeymoon cottage" and "love nest." A Temple worker told police the kidnaping tale was merely a cover-up for the Carmel tryst. In September, McPherson and others were arrested on charges including "conspiracy to commit acts injurious to public morals."

**JUDGMENT DAY:** During the trial the key prosecution witness—the Temple worker who had blown the cover story—was arrested on a bad-check charge, and it was revealed she had previously been committed to a mental hospital because of a tendency to create elaborate lies. The district attorney dropped the charges against McPherson without explanation. Sister Aimee, who fainted when she heard the news, left the next day for a "Vindication Tour" of the East Coast, but the bad publicity had its effect. She was finished as an influential evangelist. She died at the age of 53 from an accidental overdose of barbiturates.

• • •

## FROM OUR "HEROES OF LITERATURE" DEPARTMENT

A few tales of Mark Twain:

• He got hundreds of photos from people who claimed they were "his exact double." After a while, he got so sick of answering them that he had a form letter printed up: "My dear Sir, I thank you very much for your letter and your photograph. In my opinion, you are more like me than any other of my numerous doubles. I may even say that you resemble me more closely than I do myself. I fact, I intend to use your picture to shave by. Yours thankfully, S. Clemens

• A ruthless businessman he knew announced that "Before I die, I'm going to make a pilgrimage to the Holy Land. I will climb Mount Sinai and read the Ten Commandments aloud at the top."

Twain's reply: "I have a better idea. Stay home in Boston and keep them."

# PRODUCT NAMES

*You probably have some of these products in your house...*
*But do you know how they got their names?*

**AVON PRODUCTS.** Founder D.H. McConnell lived in a small New York town called Suffern on the Ramapo in the 1880s. The name reminded him of Shakespeare's Stratford-upon-Avon.

**TONI HOME PERMANENTS.** Richard Harris began selling "Roll-Wav" home permanent kits through the mail in 1943. For the first time, women could do at home for 25¢ what cost them $10 or more in a beauty salon. But he ran into a problem; the curling chemicals he used were too harsh. "Roll-Wav" flopped. Harris fixed the problem by using a milder curling agent, but something still wasn't right—customers weren't buying. Finally, one of his distributors gave him the advice he needed: "What you need is a *tony* name—one with class." Harris took the advice—literally.

**NOXZEMA.** After more than ten years of mixing up batches of skin cream in his coffeepot, Dr. Avery Bunting, a Maryland pharmacist, hit on a formula he felt was perfect in 1914. But he couldn't find the perfect name—after hundreds of tries he gave up. Then one of his customers walked into the store and said "Doc, you know your sunburn cream has sure knocked out my eczema." Bunding was inspired: The cream that "knocked eczema" became known as *Noxzema.*

**SHELL OIL COMPANY.** Believe it or not, the Shell Oil company got its name because it started out as a *shell shop.* Marcus Samuel owned a London novelty store in the mid-1800s; he began selling shells after getting the idea while on vacation by the sea. Over time his business grew into a large trading company and began selling things other than shells—including *kerosene.*

**MURINE.** Otis Hall, a banker recovering from a serious eye infection in the 1890s, was so impressed with the eye lotion his doctors made for him that he spent years trying to get them to sell it directly to the public. They finally consented—on the condition that its name be derived from its chemical formula: *mur*iate of berber*ine*.

**DIXIE CUPS.** Hugh Moore founded the American Water Supply Company in 1908...but decided that there was more money to be made in supplying paper cups. He changed the company's name to the Individual Drinking Cup Company, then to the Health Kup Co. But his business still wasn't successful. The company next door, The Dixie Doll Company, was doing well at the time. He thought some of their luck might rub off on him if he used their name.

**PRINCE MATCHABELLI.** Georges Matchabelli had it made—or so he thought. A prince with enormous land holdings in southern Russia, Matchabelli was vacationing in Europe when the Bolsheviks seized power in 1919. He lost his entire fortune overnight. But he still had his title—and when he opened an antique shop on New York's Madison Avenue, the well-to-do from all over the world flocked to his store. To maintain their interest, he began making perfumes for individual clients—perfumes he claimed matched their personalities. His customers began ignoring his antiques altogether, asking only about his perfumes. He took the hint.

**PYREX GLASS.** Dr. Jesse Littleton was a scientist who worked for the Corning Glass Works in New York. One morning in 1913, he brought a chocolate cake to work and shared it with the office. After his coworkers finished eating, he told them he had baked the cake in a *glass* pan he'd made out of a battery jar—something they had insisted was impossible. It wasn't. Though heat-resistant glass had been used in industry for more than 20 years, no one had thought of using it to make cooking utensils. Within three years, Corning introduced Pyrex glassware—naming it after the first product they manufactured: a glass *pie* pan.

**RANDOM FACT:** What do electric eels use their electricity for? To detect and kill their prey.

**Renoir's last words: "What a pity I have to go now just when I was beginning to show promise!"**

# UNCLE JOHN'S BATHROOM NEWS

*Bits and pieces of bathroom trivia we've flushed out in the past year.*

## TAKE A STAND

According to a 1991 survey by the Scott Paper Company:

• "You can gauge a person's education by whether they read in the bathroom. More than two-thirds of people with master's degrees and doctorates read in the stall, the survey shows. Only one in two high school grads read while in the bathroom, and 56 percent of those with college degrees do."

• "Fifty-four percent of Americans fold their toilet tissue neatly while 35 percent wad it into a ball before using it."

• "7% steal rolls of toilet paper."

• "More than 60 percent prefer that their toilet paper roll over the top, 29 percent from the bottom. The rest don't care."

## LEFT OUT

• According to *Why Do Clocks Run Clockwise, and Other Imponderables*, here's why toilet flush handles are on the left side:

"Most early flush toilets were operated by a chain above the tank that had to be pulled down by hand. Almost all of the chains were located on the left side of the toilet, for the user had more leverage when pulling with the right hand while seated.

"When the smaller handles near the top of the tank were popularized in the 1940s and 1950s, many were fitted onto existing toilets then equipped with pull-chains. Therefore, it was cheaper and more convenient to place the new handles where they fitted standard plumbing and fixtures."

## STRONGER THAN DIRT

According to a book called *Bigger Secrets*, by William Poundstone, here's a bit of bathroom science you should know about:

• "The combination of Sani-Flush and Comet cleansers can explode. Comet (sodium hypochlorite and grit) is a common all-purpose abrasive, and Sani-Flush (a.k.a. sodium bisulfate) is designed to keep toilet bowls clean. Many think that the combination ought to work all the better.

"The Sani-Flush label warns consumers not to mix it with a chlorine-containing cleanser lest hazardous fumes be released. But few people know which other cleansers contain chlorine, and in any case the label says nothing about explosions. In 1985 Hilton Martin of Satellite Beach, Florida, cleaned the bowl of his toilet with Comet and then hung a Sani-Flush dispenser inside the tank. He noticed the water starting to bubble when the phone rang. While he was in another room on the phone, the toilet detonated. American Home Products has denied that Sani-Flush poses an explosion hazard."

## LIFE-STALLS OF THE RICH AND FAMOUS

If you're *really* famous, you can't even go to the bathroom in peace. Example: In February, 1979, Jacqueline Kennedy was on her way to her nephew's wedding in Gladwyne, Pennsylvania. She pulled into an Arco gas station to answer the call of nature. The owner of the gas station commemorated the event by mounting a plaque in the ladies room: "This room was honored by the presence of Jacqueline Bovier Kennedy Onassis on the occasion of the wedding of Joseph P. Kennedy II and Sheila B. Rauch, February 3, 1989."

## ALL TOGETHER NOW

During a showing of the movie *Airport* on television, the Lafayette, Louisiana Waterworks Department recorded changes in water pressure during the show. Their findings: "At approximately 8:30, a bomb exploded in the airplane, and from then until nine p.m., when the pilot landed safely and the movie ended, almost nobody left his television to do anything—then there was a twenty-six pound drop in water pressure." The department estimates that as many as 20,000 Lafayette residents used the john at the same time. Ratings for other films: *The Good, the Bad, and the Ugly:* a 19 lb. drop in pressure; *Patton:* 22 lbs.

# HERE'S LOOKING AT *YOU*, KID

*Humphrey Bogart is one of the most popular movie stars of all time. Here are some inside facts about two of his most popular films.*

## THE MALTESE FALCON (1941)

The film that made Bogart a star was adapted from a 1929 novel by Dashiell Hammett (who also wrote *The Thin Man*). Warner Brothers bought the screen rights in 1930 and milked the story for all it was worth; they made three different versions of *Falcon* in 10 years.

Bogart's film, the third version, was regarded as a minor picture by Warner Brothers...so they let a screenwriter named John Huston make his directing debut with it.

• George Raft, a popular personality who played slick gangsters, was Warners' first choice for Sam Spade. He turned it down because he didn't like the idea of working for a first-time director. "I feel strongly that *The Maltese Falcon* is not an important picture," he explained.

• It was the fifth time in five years that Bogart (a minor star who specialized in tough gangster roles) was forced to take a part Raft didn't want. Earlier in 1941 Raft even refused to appear in a film if Bogart was cast in a supporting role. He once protested to Jack Warner: "You told me I would never have to play Humphrey Bogart part." After *Falcon*, he never had the chance again.

• Sydney Greenstreet, "the Fatman," had never acted in a movie before *Falcon*. He was an English stage actor who specialized in comedy. He earned an Oscar nomination for his movie debut... and was typecast as a film heavy.

• Mary Astor prepared for her scenes as conniving, unstable Brigid Wonderly, by hyperventilating almost to the point of dizziness. "It gives me the heady feeling of thinking at cross purposes," she said.

• Real life imitates art: In 1975, one of the seven Falcons used in the movie was stolen from its exhibit in a Los Angeles art museum.

## CASABLANCA (1943)

The Oscar winner for Best Film in 1943 started out as an unproduced play called *Everybody Comes to Rick's*. It was written by a New York City school teacher whose inspiration was a visit to a nightclub in southern France in 1938. The club's mix of refugees, Nazis, and French made it, he remarked to his wife, "a marvelous setting for a play."

The rights to the play were purchased by Warner Brothers the day after Pearl Harbor was attacked.

• Legend has it that George Raft was offered the leading role of Rick and, as usual, turned it down. Actually, Raft *wanted* the part...but by this time Bogart was a bigger star and got first choice.

• Ronald Reagan was one of the actors initially considered for Rick.

• *Casablanca*'s famous theme, "As Time Goes By," was included in the original play because the author had been fond of it in college. It first appeared in a 1931 Broadway show called *Everybody's Welcome*.

• Believe it or not, that classic song was nearly cut out of the movie. After *Casablanca* had been shot, the composer who'd scored it decided to write his own tune, because theme songs are worth a lot of money in royalties. But that would have meant reshooting several scenes—and Ingrid Bergman had already cut her hair for her next role (in *For Whom the Bell Tolls*). So reshooting was impossible, the song was left in.

• Dooley Wilson (Sam) didn't really know how to play the piano. He just pretended to finger the keys as he sang, while a studio musician did the playing offstage.

• *Casablanca* won the Oscar for best screenplay, yet the actors never had the luxury of a complete script. In fact, Bogart and Bergman were sometimes handed their lines just before a scene was to be shot. Other times Bogart and the screenwriters would sit around with a bottle of whiskey and argue what should happen next. Ingrid Bergman didn't even know which of the story's main characters she was supposed to love more. She found out when everyone else did—in the final scene.

• Humphrey Bogart's agents took out a $100,000 insurance policy on the actor (a huge amount in those days) during the filming. Bogart's wife was convinced that Bogie was having an affair with Ingrid Bergman and had threatened to kill him if she found them together. The agents decided they'd better not take any chances.

.• Good timing may have been what turned *Casablanca* into a hit. In November 1942, Allied forces launched a successful assault on occupied cities in North Africa, including Casablanca. Less than three weeks later the movie premiered in New York. It opened throughout the rest of the country in January of '43, just as Franklin Roosevelt, Josef Stalin, and Winston Churchill were holding a secret conference—in Casablanca.

• The Germans considered *Casablanca* a propaganda film, and banned it. Even after the war, only a censored version was allowed to be shown; all references to Nazis were cut out.

• After the success of *Casablanca*, Bogart signed a contract that made him the world's highest-paid actor.

**AND NOW...Some Miscellaneous Movie Trivia**

• Actress Jane Wyman broke up with husband Ronald Reagan because, she said, "He talked too much."

• Spencer Tracy and Humphrey Bogart never appeared in a film together because they could never agree on who'd get top billing.

• Actor Peter Lorre specialized in psychotic characters. But in his native Germany he was a student—not a patient—of Sigmund Freud and Alfred Adler.

• Garbo actually said, "I want to be *let* alone."

• Bogart got his distinctive lisp as the result of a childhood accident. A tiny piece of wood lodged in his lip, and the operation to remove it was botched. It left him with a partially paralyzed lip and a permanent speech impediment.

• *Casablanca* was turned into an ABC TV show in 1955. It flopped, and was cancelled after only a few months.

# THE 7 WONDERS OF THE ANCIENT WORLD

*Here's some more useless info you can use to drive your friends and family crazy, contributed by BRI member Phil Catalfo.*

**THE ORIGIN OF THE "7 WONDERS"**

Today we think nothing of 100-story skyscrapers. But in the earliest days of civilization, huge structures were considered superhuman feats. The most impressive of these came to be known as "The Seven Wonders of the World."

• How they got that name is a pretty interesting story in itself. (After all, there were no intercontinental broadcasts to tell people about them.). It turns out that in the timewhen Greece and Rome dominated the course of history in Europe, North Africa and the Middle East, private fleets made money ferrying passengers to "exotic" lands. To tout these destinations, the world's first tourist guidebooks were created.

• Among their most popular attractions were...The Seven Wonders of the World. The earliest list of them on record was compiled by Antipater of Sidonin in the Second Century B.C.

**THE EGYPTIAN PYRAMIDS AT GIZA**

**Built:** Between 2600 and 2500 B.C.

**History:** Three enormous pyramids were erected as burial tombs for Egyptian pharaohs thousands of years before the golden ages of Greece and Rome. The largest, called the Great Pyramid, stands some 450 feet high at its peak; its base takes up 13 acres. The Greeks and Romans were impressed by their size, but, unaware of their religious significance, considered them extravagant.

**Fate:** Still standing. And they still attract millions visitors from around the globe every year.

**THE HANGING GARDENS OF BABYLON**

**Built:** Sometime in the late Seventh or early Sixth Century B.C.

**History:** King Nebuchadnezzar II, who ruled Babylon (near the modern city of Baghdad) between 605 and 562 B.C., built the hanging gardens for his queen, the daughter of the Median king Cyaxares. She was supposedly uncomfortable on the hot Mesopotamian flatlands, and longed for the cool, lofty heights of her mountainous homeland. So Nebuchadnezzar had the enormous garden structure designed and built with elevated terraces containing groves of trees, lush vegetation, fountains and exotic birds. According to contemporary accounts, the gardens were laid out on a brick terrace about 400 feet square and 75 feet above the ground; irrigation was provided by slaves turning screws to lift water from the nearby Euphrates River. The stone used in the construction is not found anywhere on the Mesopotamian plane; historians believe it was ferried down the Tigris River from a far-off mountain quarry.

**Fate:** Destroyed. Archaeologists have been unable to discover and positively identify the remains of the gardens.

## THE TEMPLE OF ARTEMIS (DIANA) AT EPHESUS

**Built:** Circa 550 B.C.

**History:** One of the grandest and most architecturally advanced of ancient temples, the temple of Artemis (whom the Romans called Diana) was located in the Greek city of Ephesus, across the Aegean from modern Greece, on the west coast of what is now Turkey. According to Pliny, it took 120 years to build. It was made entirely of marble, except for its tile-covered wooden roof. It rested on a foundation measuring 377 by 180 feet, and featured 106 columns—each represented by a different king—about 40 feet high.

The Ephesians (the same ones St. Paul preached to) used an especially clever technique for lifting the giant marble stones: They built an inclined plane of sandbags up to the apex of the columns, and dragged the stones up the plane to be laid atop the columns. Then they slit the bags so the sand would empty out, leaving the marble slabs resting in place.

**Fate:** The original temple was destroyed by an arsonist (who said he did it to achieve immortality for his name) in 356 B.C. A replacement of similar design was erected on the same foundation. The replacement was burned by the Goths in 262 A.D. Today only the foundation and parts of the second temple remain. Sculptures from the second temple can be found in the British Museum.

## THE STATUE OF ZEUS, OLYMPIA, GREECE

**Built:** Circa 435 B.C.

**History:** Built by the Greek sculptor Phidias, this depiction of the Greek king of the gods may have been the ancient world's most famous statue. It stood 40 feet high and depicted Zeus—symbol of power, thrower of thunderbolts—on his throne. His robe and ornaments were made of gold, his body of ivory. He wore a wreath on his head and held a figure of his messenger Nike in his right hand, and a scepter in his left.

**Fate:** Destroyed (No one is sure how or when).

## THE MAUSOLEUM AT HALICARNASSUS, IN ASIA MINOR (Southwestern Turkey)

**Built:** About 353 B.C.

**History:** Originally built as a burial tomb for Mausolus, a local ruler in part of the Persian Empire, this huge, white marble edifice stood about 135 feet high, and measured 440 feet around its rectangular base. Above the base was a colonnade formed by 36 columns, and, above them, a stepped pyramid, which, historians believe, held a statue of Mausolus in a chariot.

**Fate:** The top part was destroyed by an earthquake. Only pieces of the building, and its decorations (called friezes) remain; the British Museum holdings include some sculptures from the site. King Mausolus has been immortalized in the word used to name any large tomb.

## THE COLOSSUS OF RHODES

**Built:** Early Third Century B.C.

**History:** According to historians of the time, this huge bronze statue stood astride the harbor at Rhodes, an island in the Aegean. It took the Greek sculptor Chares twelve years to build. Created in honor of the sun god Helios, it stood 120 feet high—roughly the height of the Statue of Liberty—and was made of hollow stone blocks held together by iron bars, a construction technique still used today.

**Fate:** Destroyed by an earthquake in 224 B.C. The iron bars were sold for scrap some 800 years later, in 653 A.D.

## THE PHAROS LIGHTHOUSE AT ALEXANDRIA

**Built:** Sometime during the reign of Ptolemy II (283-246 B.C.)

**History:** Designed by the Greek architect Sostratos, the 400-feet-high lighthouse stood on the island of Pharos in Alexandria's harbor. It achieved such renown that the word *pharos* came to mean "lighthouse." The structure's design was particularly striking: the bottom section, resting on a stone platform, was square; the middle section was eight-sided; and the top section was circular. A fire at the apex provided light.

**Fate:** After helping mariners enter the harbor for *1,500 years*, the lighthouse collapsed in an earthquake.

## SO WHAT ELSE IS NEW?

### Johnny B. Goode, by Chuck Berry

Berry says: "It sounds like it's autobiographical, but it's not. I never lived in Louisiana.... I just improvised the story, typical of what I thought a young, enthusiastic guitar-player from the South would go through. As for the log cabin, I don't think I've actually seen a real log cabin, much less lived in one."

### Etch A Sketch

It was invented in France by Arthur Granjean, who called it "L'Ecran Magique" (The Magic Screen). Representatives of the Ohio Art Company saw it at the Nuremberg Toy Fair in 1959 and decided the toy had possibilities. They purchased the rights to it.

• Ohio Art management decided to introduce their version of it at the New York Toy Fair in February, 1960. They had no idea the toy would become a big success, but they got an inkling on the plane flight to the New York show when company officials started bickering about who would get to play with the prototypes next.

• The toy was officially released to the public on July 12, 1960. More than 60 million of them have been sold to date.

**Einstein's brain is stored in a mason jar in a Wichita, Kansas laboratory.**

# CARNIVAL LINGO

*Next time you wander through a carnival, listen to the hucksters chatting with each other. Here are a few things you might hear them saying, from the marvelous book,* Carnival Secrets, *by Matthew Gryczan.*

**Carny:** Carnival employee.

**Jointee:** A carny who works in one of the booths.

**Ride Monkey:** A carny who operates a ride.

**Kootch:** Strippers.

**Alibi agent:** A game operator who uses undisclosed "rules" (player touched the rail, leaned over the foul line, etc.) to avoid giving out prizes to winners.

**Fixer:** The person who handles complaints about rigged games and payoffs to local police.

**Marks, Tips:** Players

**Chumps:** Naive players.

**Sharpies:** Practiced players who are skilled at winning games.

**Lot lice:** Carnival-goers who don't spend money.

**Patch Money, Ice, Juice:** Money that's used to pay off the police.

**Hey Rube:** A call for help when carnies are in trouble.

**Mitt camp:** Palm readers.

**Circus candy:** Cheap candy in an impressive box.

**Floss:** Cotton Candy.

**Plaster, Slum:** Cheap prizes.

**Donniker:** A toilet.

**Flat stores:** Games set up solely to cheat players as soon as possible.

**Gaff:** Rig a game so that players have absolutely no chance of winning.

**Gig:** Take all of a player's money in one try.

**Two Way Joint:** A game that quickly converts from a dishonest to an honest one in case the police come by.

**Ikey Heyman, G-wheel:** A wheel of fortune with brakes—so the operator can control which number it lands on.

**Burn the lot:** Cheat contestants outrageously because you don't expect to return to the same location again.

**Build up:** Excite a player into spending more money.

**If you floss your teeth, you'll probably use about 5 miles worth of floss in your lifetime.**

# POP CULTURE

*These pages on the history of soda are brought to you by the BRI's Snack Food Division.*

## POPPING OFF

In the early 1800s, the closest thing to soft drinks on the market was "impregnated water," a corked bottle of carbonated water that was sold as a "health tonic." By 1860 makers were adding sugar and flavoring—with mixed success: The corks in the bottles (metal caps hadn't been invented yet) often blew off under the extra pressure created by sugar fermenting in the bottles. This made a popping sound—and the drinks became known as "Soda Pop."

## A CURE FOR WHAT ALES YOU

Selling soda pop to an unitiated public wasn't easy...so most manufacturers tried to boost sales by promoting their concoctions as cures for fever, nausea, dehydration, indigestion, and so on. If the government hadn't passed the Pure Food and Drug Act in 1906, they'd probably be making similar claims today.

Some examples:

**Dr. Pepper:** "Brightens the mind and clears the brain"; an "antidote" to cigarette smoking; and "alone on the bridge defending your children against an army of caffeine doped beverages." (Note: Today's version contains caffeine).

**Hires Root beer:** "Soothing to the nerves, vitalizing to the blood, refreshing to the brain...helps even a cynic see the brighter side of life."

**Moxie "Nerve Food":** "Can recover brain and nervous exhaustion; loss of manhood, imbecility and helplessness. It has recovered paralysis, softening of the brain...and insanity."

**Seven Up:** "Tunes tiny tummies," "For Home and Hospital Use," "Cures Seven Hangovers."

**HIRES ROOT BEER:** Recipes for drinks made from boiled roots date back to the colonial days. But most people didn't want to bother collecting their own roots, so in 1870 Charles F. Hires, a Pennsylvania pharmacist, began selling premixed ingredients through the mail. He originally called his drink "Root Tea," but changed its name to "Root *Beer*" after a friend suggested it would sell better with a stronger name.

Hires' mix sold well, but he realized that bottled soft drinks were the wave of the future. So in 1882 he began bottling his creation—and by 1885 was selling 3 million bottles a year.

**The Sober Truth:** The company ran into trouble in 1895, when the Woman's Christian Temperance Union called for a nationwide boycott of Hires. Reason: the WCTU assumed that, like regular beer, root beer contained enough alcohol to get people drunk. The boycott remained in effect (and devastated sales) until 1898, when an independent laboratory decided to finally *test* Hires' root beer and see how much alcohol it actually contained. Its finding: a bottle of Hires had as much alcohol as half a loaf of bread. The WCTU backed off, and sales returned to normal.

**DR. PEPPER:** In the 1880s, a Virginia pharmacist's assistant named Wade Morrison fell in love with his boss's daughter. The pharmacist "decided the assistant was too old for his daughter" and encouraged Morrison to move on. He did, moving to Waco, Texas, where he bought his own drug store. When one of his employees developed a new soft drink syrup, Morrison named it after the man who got him started in the pharmacy business—his old flame's father, Dr. Kenneth Pepper.

**THE MOXIE GENERATION:** You've probably heard the expression "He has plenty of moxie." But have you heard of the soft drink that inspired it? It was the most popular soda in the U.S. during the '20s—even outselling Coca-Cola.

• What went wrong? The problem wasn't that it started out as a "medicine;" so did Coke. The problem was that it *tasted* like one. It contained gentian root, which has a very bitter aftertaste. Americans wanted a sweeter drink.

## ON JINGLES

• "Things go better with Coke" was the first slogan that appeared on everything Coke did. They worked on it for two and a half years, and spent millions of dollars figuring out how to present it to the public. The first "things go better" jingle was sung by the Kingston Trio. This jingle was also the first in which Coke experimented with rock music. They used the Shirelles for it.

• The "You've got a lot to live . . ." campaign of the mid-1960s was a smashing success for Pepsi.

Pepsi received over ten thousand letters congratulating them. Some people even said they were on the verge of suicide until they heard the ad. The lyrics were written by the songwriter who composed "You Light Up My Life."

## SODA FACTS

• During World War II caffeine was so scarce that Coca-Cola chemists experimented with a substitute made from bat guano. Executives dumped the idea. They thought that if the public identified their drink with bat "droppings," it would doom the company.

• In 1900, Americans were drinking an average of twelve bottles and glasses of soft drink a piece. Today, it's 556 cans each.

• According to the *University of California Wellness Letter*, "If you drink only sugared soft drinks, those 566 cans (at an average of 150 calories each) would add up to about 83,400 empty calories per year."

• Only about five percent of all soft drink caffeine is taken from cola nuts. The other 95% is added during the manufacturing. Where does it come from? Usually the leftovers processed out of decaffeinated coffee.

• Which soda has the most caffeine per serving? Jolt Cola is #1, with 72 milligrams, followed by Mountain Dew (54), Coke (46), Dr. Pepper (40) and Pepsi (38). A cup of coffee contains 50-200 milligrams.

• Research suggests that as many as 950,000 Americans drink Coca-Cola for breakfast.

**Listen closely: On at least one episode, George Burns was the voice of Mr. Ed (the horse).**

# INSTANT HITS

*It usually takes work to write a hit song. But now and then a performer creates one spontaneously. Here are a few of the better-known examples.*

**THE SONG:** "Sweet Dreams" by the Eurythmics (1983)

**THE SITUATION:** Annie Lenox and Dave Stewart, the Eurythmics, had never had a hit. One day they were quarreling so bitterly that it felt like the end of their partnership. Annie was lying on the floor of their studio, curled up in the fetal position. Dave was at the opposite end of the huge room, angrily playing with the recording equipment.

**INSTANT HIT:** As they glared at each other, Stewart fiddled around with his drum machine for a while. He came up with a catchy rhythm...then added a bass line. "It sounded so good," Annie recalls, "that I couldn't resist getting up and playing the synthesizer." Off the top of her head, Lenox began singing: "Sweet dreams are made of this." In thirty minutes the entire song was finished.

They recorded it on their eight-track as a demo tape, but when Stewart took it in to a record company, incredulous record execs told him it was "already perfect." So the "demo" was released; it sold millions of records and established them as major pop celebrities of the early '80s.

**THE SONG:** "What'd I Say," by Ray Charles (1959)

**THE SITUATION:** It was almost 1:00 AM. Ray Charles and his band were playing at a Midwestern night club; they were almost through for the night, but still had about fifteen minutes to go when they played the last song in their repertoire. So Ray just started "noodling."

**INSTANT HIT**: "I couldn't think of nothin' else to play," Ray says. " So I told the guys...'Look, I'm just gonna start this rhythm pattern and just follow me." He also told his back-up singers to repeat whatever he said (which is where the title "What'd I Say" came from). Charles made up the words as he went along. "People went crazy," he recalls, "and so the next night we did the same thing and got the same reaction, in a different town. Somebody came up to me and asked me, 'Listen, where can I buy this record?'

I said, 'Record? What record?' He said, 'But that's a great [song]!' So Charles called up his record producers and said, "Listen, I got a song and I want to record it." He went into the studio on Feb., 18, 1959 and recorded a long version ("because it was for dancing, see?") that was split into Part I and Part II. It became his first record to reach the Top 10 on the pop charts.

**THE SONG:** "Satisfaction," by The Rolling Stones (1965)

**THE SITUATION:** During their tour of North America in 1965, the Rolling Stones spent a night in a Clearwater, Florida, motel.

**INSTANT HIT:** In the middle of the night, Keith Richards woke up with some music running through his head. He got out of bed, recorded it on his tape recorder, and went back to sleep. "In the morning," Richards says, "I still thought it sounded pretty good. I played it to Mick and said the words that go with this are, 'I can't get no satisfaction.' That was just a working title. It could have been, 'Aunt Millie's Caught Her Left Tit in the Mangle,' I thought of it as just a little riff, an album filler. I never thought it was commercial enough to be a single." Jagger wrote lyrics as he sat by the motel swimming pool. But Richards didn't like them; he said the song "sounded too much like a folk song." The song was actually recorded over Keith Richards' objections; he thought it was too corny. It became the band's unofficial anthem, and the #1 song of 1965.

**THE SONG:** "When a Man Loves a Woman," by Percy Sledge (1966)

**THE SITUATION:** Percy Sledge worked as an orderly at Colbert County Hospital in Alabama during the day, and sang with a band called The Esquires Combo at night.

**INSTANT HIT:** One evening the Esquires Combo was playing at a club in Sheffield, Alabama, and Percy just couldn't keep his mind on the songs he was supposed to sing. He was upset about a woman. Overcome by emotion, he turned to bass player Cameron Lewis and organ player Andrew Wright, and begged them to play something he could sing to—anything—it didn't matter what. The musicians looked at each other, shrugged, and just started playing. Percy made up "When a Man Loves a Woman," one of the prettiest soul ballads ever written, on the spot.

**The sperm whale can hold its breath for 82 minutes.**

# W.C. FIELDS FOREVER

*Little-known facts about one of America's classic comedians.*

Fields didn't get his legendary bulbous nose from drinking; he got it as a kid in street fights with neighborhood toughs.

★

His raspy voice, another trademark, was the result of a long series of colds brought on by exposure; a circus hand, he slept outdoors year-round from age 11 till age 15.

★

According to Groucho Marx, Fields had about $50,000 worth of booze stored in his attic. Groucho: "Don't you know that Prohibition is over?" Fields: "Well, it may come back!"

★

Fields' misanthropy was legendary. He liked to hide in the bushes of his San Fernando Valley home and shoot spitballs at passing tourists.

★

He left his mistress, Carlotta Monti, $25,000—to be paid out in 1,000 weekly installments of $25 each.

★

On his deathbed, Fields supposedly said: "I've been thinking about those poor little newsboys out there peddling their papers in cold and rain, working to support their mothers. I want to do something for them." But after a few minutes he sat up in bed and said "On second thought, f--- 'em."

★

Fields had a lifelong fear of returning to the crushing poverty of his youth. He opened hundreds of bank accounts as he traveled, under scores of aliases. Most of the money is still unclaimed.

★

In his 31-year acting career, Fields appeared in 42 films, many of which he wrote and directed as well. Of these, almost a third have vanished or are otherwise not available for viewing.

**The title "Mr." originally applied only to ministers, schoolmasters, and property owners.**

# THE NUMBERS GAME

*You're in the supermarket checkout line and have a few dollars to spare. Should you buy some lottery tickets, or a copy of the* National Enquirer? *Here's some info to help you decide.*

## THE EARLY DAYS

Lotteries in the U.S. may seem like a recent fad, but they date back at least as far as the 1700s. The original 13 colonies were financed with the help of lottery dollars, and the U.S. government used them to help pay for the Revolutionary and Civil Wars. Even the Ivy League universities—Harvard, Yale and Princeton—used them to get started.

State lotteries didn't begin until the 1960s. The first, a $100,000 sweepstakes tied to a horse race, was held in New Hampshire in 1964. Today at least 30 states have lotteries, which generate $17 billion a year in revenues.

## LOTTERY FACTS

- According to *Consumer's Research* magazine, lotteries have the worst odds of any form of legalized gambling. In terms of average payouts, highest percentage is craps (98%), followed by roulette (95%), slots (75-95%), jai alai (85-87%), the race track (83-87%) and, last, the lottery (49%). Only 0.000008% of the 97 million people who play the lottery annually win a million dollars.
- Lotteries with the best odds: Delaware, Maryland, Michigan, Pennsylvania and Washington, DC. The odds of winning their jackpots are 1 in 1000. Worst odds: California and Florida. Their odds are 1 in 14 million.

## WINNERS AND LOSERS

- In 1983, Joseph R. Wyatt, 29, of Union, New Jersey ripped up his lottery ticket—which read "Void if torn or altered" on the back—before realizing it was worth $1,600,000. In tears, he taped his ticket back together and presented it to New Jersey lottery officials, begging them to overlook the rule. They did—he got his money.

• In 1983, Don Temple accidentally threw away a lottery ticket worth $10,000 in a trash can outside a Seattle convenience store. When he realized his mistake, he talked the store into dumping that week's garbage onto the driveway of his father-in-law's home. Temple sifted through the trash for four days, but never found his ticket. The booby prize: he had to pay haulers $200 to take the garbage away.

• In 1985, Donna Lee Sobb won $100 in the California lottery, which qualified her for a $2,000,000 jackpot. But when her photograph appeared in a local paper, a local law officer recognized her—and arrested her on an eight-month-old shoplifting warrant.

• In 1986, California lottery winner Terry Garrett of San Diego was arrested only months after winning $1,000,000—for selling cocaine out of the sports car he had bought with his winnings.

• In 1988, Henry Rich, a computer expert from Harrisburg, Pennsylvania, used a computer at work to forge a winning ticket for a $15,200,000 lottery prize that hadn't been claimed. He had a friend come forward with the fake ticket and explain that he had been using it as a bookmark without realizing that it was the winner. The scheme almost worked: the friend was actually issued a first installment check for $469,989. But lottery officials arrested Rich and his friend when they realized the real ticket had been issued in another part of the state.

• In 1984, Hai Vo, a Vietnamese refugee, spent more than $200 of spare change he had saved up from food stamp purchases to buy California lottery tickets. One ticket won $2,000,000. A week later a couple from Mill Valley, California sued Vo to recover $616.26—the amount they paid in state income taxes that year—claiming Vo had used some of their earnings (in the form of state-subsidized food stamps) to buy the ticket. They lost; Vo kept his winnings.

## THE SAD TRUTH

How much is a $1 million prize *really* worth? The IRS deducts 20% automatically—and state and local taxes are also taken out, leaving about $560,000. The state pays the first $50,000 in cash, but pays out the rest over twenty years, saving another $100,000. Conclusion: the $1 million prize is worth about $468,000.

# DEFINITIONS

*How's your vocabulary? Here's another batch of unusual words you can use to impress your friends and neighbors.*

**Deosculate:** To kiss passionately.

**Pap-hawk:** A child who's breast fed.

**Moirologist:** A person hired to mourn at a funeral.

**Philematophobe:** A woman who hates to be kissed.

**Hippocampine:** Having to do with seahorses.

**Sneckdraw:** A sneaky or mean person.

**Hircine:** Something that smells like a goat.

**Eruciform:** Something that resembles a caterpillar.

**Snoach:** Talk through your nose.

**Fripperer:** A person who sells old clothes.

**Clipster:** A woman barber.

**Girn:** Bare your teeth in anger.

**Snollygoster:** A politician with no interest in issues or principles.

**Butyric:** Having to do with butter.

**Cacogen:** A hostile, unfriendly person.

**Coprology:** The study of pornographic art and writing.

**Napiform:** Shaped like a turnip.

**Natiform:** Shaped like a buttock.

**Hippopotomonstrosesquipedalian:** Having to do with a very long word.

**Phaneromania:** An obsession with picking at your skin.

**Pussock:** An old maid.

**Smell-Feast:** An uninvited guest at a feast.

**Mastodont:** Having teeth that look like a mastadon's.

**Powsowdy:** A broth made from sheep's heads.

**Wallydrag:** A completely useless person.

**Onygophagist:** A person who bites his or her nails.

**Eirmonger:** Someone who sells eggs.

**Fagotist:** A person who plays the bassoon.

# THE MYSTERY OF OAK ISLAND

*The romance of searching for pirates' treasure has been celebrated in dozens of stories since Robert Louis Stevenson's* Treasure Island. *But is there really any buried treasure to be found? Maybe so...on Oak Island.*

## TREASURE ISLAND

In 1795, a teenager named Daniel McGuinnis discovered an unusual, saucer-shaped depression on Oak Island, a tiny island off the coast of Nova Scotia. Next to the hole was an ancient oak tree with sawed-off limbs. And according to legend, a ship's tackle hung from the tree directly over the depression—as if it had been used to lower something very heavy into the hole.

McGuinnis was certain he had found buried pirates' treasure, and with the help of two friends began digging for it. Within minutes they hit rock—which turned out to be a flagstone buried two feet below the surface. They hit another barrier made of oak logs at 10 feet deep; another at 20 feet, and a third at 30 feet. McGuinnis and his friends kept digging—but they never found any treasure and eventually gave up. Still, word of their discovery spread.

## SECOND TRY

In 1803 a wealthy man named Simeon Lynds took up the search. The diggers he hired found another platform at 40 feet, and found several more deeper down. Finally, at 90 feet, the workers found a large stone with strange symbols carved into it. No one could decipher what the stone said, but the workers were convinced they were close to the treasure and kept digging. (The stone was later stolen.) At 98 feet deep, their shovels struck what felt like a wooden chest. But the sun was going down so they stopped for the night.

By the time the workers got back the next morning, the hole had flooded to the top with seawater. And it somehow kept refilling, even as the workers tried to bail it out. They never were able to drain the pit enough to finish digging.

Like McGuinnis, Lynds had hit a dead end.

## AMAZING DISCOVERIES

Lynds wasn't the last person to dig for treasure on Oak Island. In fact, so many excavations have been attempted that the precise location of the original hole—known as the "Money Pit" because so much money has been spent trying to solve its mysteries—has been lost because so many other holes have been dug nearby. Even young Franklin D. Roosevelt supervised a dig in 1909; he followed Oak Island's progress even as president. And the search continues today. Some findings:

• There's at least *some* gold down there. In 1849 treasure hunters sank a drill to the 98 ft. level. Like Lynds, they hit what felt like a wooden chest. They dug through the top into what felt like "22 inches of metal in pieces (possibly gold coins)," through more wood, and into another 22 inches of metal. When they pulled the drill back up to the surface, three links of a gold chain were stuck to it. In nearly 200 years of digging, that's all the treasure that's been found.

• In 1897 another group of drillers dug down to 155 feet. They pulled up a half-inch-square piece of parchment—but that was all. They also hit what they thought was a heavy iron plate at 126 feet, but couldn't pull it up.

• In 1987, an IBM cryptologist finally deciphered an engraving of Lynds' lost stone. The message read: "Forty feet below, two million pounds are buried."

## HIGH SECURITY

• Whoever dug the original pit went to a great deal of trouble to do it. In 1850 explorers resting on a nearby beach noticed that the beach "gulched forth water like a sponge being squeezed." So they dug it up—and discovered it was a *fake*. The beach was actually a manmade network of stone drains that filtered seawater and fed it into the Money Pit. The drains—designed to flood the pit whenever treasure hunters got close to the treasure—had been buried in sand to avoid detection.

• The Money Pit may even be protected by poison gas. On August 17, 1965, treasure hunter Bob Restall blacked out and fell into the pit he had dug. His son and four others tried to rescue him, but they also blacked out and fell in. Restall, his son, and two of the workers were killed. The autopsy finding: death by "marsh-gas poisoning and/or drowning."

**TODAY**

In 1977 the Montreal-based Triton Alliance Ltd., a consortium of 49 investors headed by David Tobias, bought the 128-acre Oak Island for $125,000. They have spent more than $3 million digging for treasure.

• During one drill, Triton's workers found bits of china, glass, wood, charcoal—even cement. But no treasure.

• Perhaps the strangest incident associated with Oak Island occurred in 1971 when Tobias' partner Dan Blankenship lowered an underwater video camera into a water-filled cavity at the bottom of a shaft. On the monitor, Blankenship suddenly saw what looked like a human hand. Horrified, he called over three crew members, who later verified his story. Asked by *Smithsonian* magazine about the legitimacy of his hand-sighting, he answered, "There's no question about it."

**WHAT'S DOWN THERE?**

Oak Island's "treasure," if there is one, could be worth over $100,000,000. Among the many theories of what the Money Pit could be hiding:

**1)** The missing crown jewels of France. The Nova Scotia area was frequented by pirates in the 16th and 17th centuries—when the jewels were stolen. The local Mahone Bay takes its name from the French word *mahonne*, a craft used by Mediterranean pirates.

**2)** Inca gold plundered by Spanish galleons and later pirated by Sir Francis Drake. A carbon analysis of wood samples recovered from the area dated back to 1575, around the time of Drake's explorations. However, there is no record of Drake ever having been to Nova Scotia.

**3)** Captain Kidd's buried treasure. Some believe Kidd buried his treasure there before being extradited and later hanged by the British. Before Kidd was executed in 1701, he offered a deal: "He would lead a fleet to the spot where he had hidden his East Indian

**The *Revenge of the Creature* was Clint Eastwood's first movie.**

treasure, if the authorities would put off his execution. The deal was refused—and Kidd's treasure has never been found." There is, however, no evidence that Kidd was ever near Oak Island.

• Others have their doubts. Some feel that the Money Pit is merely an elaborate decoy, and that the treasure is actually buried in a nearby swamp. Others think it is just a sinkhole. Many doubt whether pirates had the resources and engineering know-how to construct such an elaborate trap.

## POST SCRIPT

Similar Money Pits are rumored to have been found in Haiti and Madagascar, although these discoveries have not been confirmed by archaeologists.

• • •

## ...AND NOW A LITTLE MOOD READING

*Here's a brief quote from* Treasure Island, *by Robert Louis Stevenson. Appropriately, it's the part where they find the spot the treasure should be...and see that it's already been dug up.*

"We were now at the margin of the thicket.

" 'Huzza, mates, altogether?' shouted Merry; and the foremost broke into a run.

"And suddenly, not ten yards further, we beheld them stop. A low cry arose. Long John Silver doubled his pace, digging away with the foot of his crutch like one possessed; and next moment he and I had come also to a dead halt.

"Before us was a great excavation, not very recent, for the sides had fallen in and grass had sprouted on the bottom. In this were the shaft of a pick broken in two and the boards of several packing-cases strewn around. On one of these boards I saw, branded with a hot iron, the name *Walrus*—the name of Flint's ship.

"All was clear to probation. The *cache* had been found and rifled: the seven hundred thousand pounds were gone!"

*If you're into classic books and buried treasure,* Treasure Island *could be a good bathroom reader. The chapters are all about six pages long, and a new copy shouldn't cost more than $3.*

# ZZZ-Z-Z-Z-ZZZ

*According to author Marc McCutcheon, your heart can stop beating for as long as 9 seconds while you're asleep. Here's some more information on sleep from his book,* The Compass in Your Nose.

Sleep deprivation lasting more than 48 hours typically causes hallucinations and psychosis.

The world record for going without sleep is 11 days (264 hours and 12 minutes), a feat considered extremely dangerous by sleep researchers.

30 million Americans suffer from sleep disorders. Most men begin having problems falling asleep in their mid-twenties; women have the same difficulty during their mid-forties.

While normal sleepers change body positions about 30 times per night, insomniacs may toss and turn more than 100 times.

Dream sleep has been observed in all animals studied except the spiny anteater.

Sleep studies show that if your sleeping partner is absent in your sleep, you'll almost always move over to the side of the bed normally occupied by him or her.

An aftenoon nap is healthy. One study indicates that afternoon nappers are 30 percent less likely to suffer coronary artery disease, although the reasons behind this are not yet known.

Humans stay awake far longer than many animals. Bats, cats, porcupines, lions, gorillas, and opossums sleep 18 to 20 hours a day, and some woodchucks snooze for as long as 22 hours.

Pigeons frequently open their eyes during sleep to watch for predators. The dolphin, remarkably, only "half" sleeps: its brain shuts down only one hemisphere at a time.

Horses and rats dream 20 percent or the time during sleep. Cows kept in barns dream 40 minutes per night, while cows sleeping in meadows dream only half as much.

**Idaho grows 120 billion potatoes a year—that's about 500 for every man, woman, and child in the U.S.**

# OFF TO SEE THE WIZARD

*The Wizard of Oz is one of our most enduring modern fairy tales. In the first Bathroom Reader, we explained it as a political allegory. Here are some some other interesting facts about the book and film.*

## THE BIRTH OF THE BOOK

According to some accounts, the land of Oz was created when Lyman Frank Baum, the author, was weaving a tale of fantastical creatures for some neighborhood kids. When one child asked where the imaginary people lived, Baum glanced around. His eyes fell on the labels on his file cabinet; the top was labeled A-N and the bottom, O-Z.

• He didn't write the story down for some time after. But suddenly it took over and demanded to be written: "I was sitting," he wrote later, "in the hall telling the kids a [different] story and suddenly this one moved right in and took possession. I shooed the children away and grabbed a piece of paper and began to write. It really seemed to write itself. Then I couldn't find any regular paper, so I took anything at all, even a bunch of old envelopes." His pencil-written longhand manuscript went right to the typesetter.

• He called his story *The Emerald City*. But his publisher wouldn't release it under that title, citing a long-standing publishers' superstition that any book with a jewel named in its title was doomed to failure.

• So he changed it to *From Kansas to Fairyland*, then *The Fairyland of Oz*, then *The Land of Oz*. They filed for a copyright under this last name, but Baum was still looking for something more colorful and eye-catching. Right before the book was supposed to go to press, illustrator W. W. Denslow pasted a new title over the old one: *The Wonderful Wizard of Oz*.

## FILM FACTS

• Panned by many critics when it was first released in 1939, the

**"We're Off to See the Wizard" was used as a marching song by the Australians in World War II.**

film version of the book was considered a flop. It didn't earn back its initial investment until 1959—twenty years later. Cult status only came as a result of annual TV showings, starting in 1956.

• The cast consisted of 9,200 actors and actresses, including dancing trees, flying monkeys, and 124 midgets as Munchkins. Ray Bolger and Jack Haley were paid $3000 a week; Judy Garland, only $500 a week.

• Dorothy's dog Toto was paid $125 a week, more than twice the wage of each of the 122 midgets hired to play munchkins. Although the little people of Oz were paid $100 a week, their benevolent manager, Leo Singer (Papa), pocketed half. Clearly the Lollipop Guild and Lullaby League were ineffective unions.

• *Oz* was nominated for five Academy Awards. But the competition was fierce and *Gone With the Wind* dominated the event, *Oz* did win for Original Score and Best Song—"Over the Rainbow," written in a car parked outside Schwab's drugstore.

• Ironically, "Rainbow" was the song studio execs wanted to cut out when the finished film was too long. "Why is she singing in a barnyard?" one of the producers had asked. But the director and others complained. Instead, MGM removed a scene (and song) in the Haunted Forest, where Dorothy and crew were attacked by Jitter Bugs (a kind of oversized pink and blue mosquito). The scene, which took five weeks and $80,000 to shoot, has never been found.

## MEET LITTLE DOROTHY

• When the MGM movie was first planned, Shirley Temple was the unanimous choice to play Dorothy. (Likewise, Frank Morgan was the third choice for the Wizard. The lines were written with W.C. Fields in mind. Ed Wynn turned down the part, too.)

• But Shirley Temple wasn't available. While searching for another Dorothy, L.B. Mayer viewed a short called *Every Sunday* and was taken by its star, Deanna Durbin. He told his assistant: "Sign up that singer— the flat one." (He might have been referring to the pitch of Durbin's voice). What the assistant heard was, "Sign up the fat one." He thought Mayer was talking about a different girl in the short, who had a bit of baby fat...so he called Francis Gumm

**The tornado in the "The Wizard of Oz" was a custom-built spinning 35 foot muslin "miniature."**

(quickly renamed "Judy Garland"). But don't cry for Deanna Durbin—she went on to Universal where her movies brought in $100 million in the next 10 years.

• Judy Garland was 16, but she was playing an 11-year-old. So the studio put her on a diet to make her look younger; she was only allowed to eat four days a week. And every morning before filming, her breasts were taped flat so she'd look more like an adolescent.

• MGM's constant attempts at keeping Garland thin with pills and diets may have ultimately cost her life—Garland died in June, 1969 of a drug overdose.

## INSULTS AND INJURIES

• While the Tin Man bemoaned his heartless condition, it was another vital organ that caused him the biggest problems during the filming of *Oz*. Buddy Ebsen, the original tin man, had an extreme allergic reaction when his lungs were coated by the aluminum powder dusted onto his tin makeup. Seriously ill, he spent several weeks in the hospital. He was replaced by Jack Haley.

• The Wicked Witch, Margaret Hamilton, was badly burned on face and hand while filming her dramatic exit from Munchkinland and was off the set for a month. The fire effect went off before she was safely below the trap door. Ironically, a little water thrown her way might have helped.

• She wasn't the only injury: Her double, Betty Danko, was injured when her broom exploded during a stunt shot. Two winged monkeys crashed to the stage floor when their support wires snapped. And Toto too? Yes, Toto too—out of action for a week after being stepped on by one of the witch's huge "O-EE-O"-chanting Winkie guards.

## SHOE FETISH

Although 50 years have passed, at least four pairs of Dorothy's ruby slippers have survived and they bring out-of-sight auction prices (top price so far—$165,000). One pair is on exhibit at the Smithsonian, another at Walt Disney World-MGM Studios. The rest are in private hands…or feet. Over five million people visit the Smithsonian display annually.

# WORLD-CLASS LOSERS

*Have you ever dreamed about having a "sure thing"? It's not always that simple. Here are four stories of people who "couldn't miss"...but did.*

**The Losers:** John Augustus Sutter & James Wilson Marshall
**The Sure Thing:** The largest gold strike in American history.

**Background:** In the 1840s, Sutter was one of Northern California's largest landowners. His headquarters was Sutter's Fort, a trading post near the Sacramento River—an important stopping-point for westward-bound immigrants. Sutter welcomed them all.

One settler, a carpenter named James Marshall, became friends with Sutter. In 1847 they started a sawmill together on the South Fork of the American River at Coloma. Sutter put up the money, Marshall ran the mill, and they split the profits.

**Good Luck:** In January 1848, Marshall had to deepen his mill stream to allow the wheel to turn freely. His digging turned up some bright metal that he realized, after consulting the *American Encyclopedia*, was gold.

It appeared that he and Sutter were rich beyond their wildest dreams.

**Tough Luck:** They kept the secret for a few months. Then word leaked out, and the Gold Rush was on.

First, all of Marshall's workers left to pan for gold. With no laborers, the mill failed.

Then thousands of gold-crazy '49ers flocked to Sutter's land. They slaughtered his livestock for food, trampled his fields and staked claims on his property. He was ruined. The land was legally his, but he couldn't afford the cost of litigation to recover it.

Marshall "became despondent and misanthropic." When he died some 35 years later, he was working as a gardener in Coloma. Sutter died broke in 1880, still petitioning Congress for compensation for his losses.

**On average, Americans spend 40% of their leisure time watching TV.**

**The Loser:** Eli Whitney

**The Sure Thing:** Control of the South's cotton industry.

**Background**: After the Revolutionary War, the outlook for agriculture in the South was pretty grim. The only thing farmers could grow easily was green-seed cotton—an unprofitable crop because it took an entire day for one person to separate a single pound of cotton from the seeds.

In 1793, a young inventor named Eli Whitney overheard several South Carolina planters discussing the possibility of a machine that could clean cotton easily. If someone could invent one, they said, it would "save the South"...and make its inventor a fortune.

**Good Luck:** Whitney was intrigued by the challenge. After only a few days of experimenting, he came up with a working model of a "cotton gin." He received a patent for it in 1794.

**Tough Luck.** Unfortunately, Whitney couldn't cash in on his own creation. The machine was so efficient and amazingly simple that "any country handy man could copy it—and they did." He sued companies that pirated his design, but the courts kept ruling against him. In fact, it took 13 years for Whitney to get even one favorable judgment...and by then the patent had nearly expired.

The cotton gin revolutionized Southern agriculture. In 1792 the U.S. exported about 140,000 lbs. of cotton; by 1800, with the help of Whitney's machine, almost 18 *million* lbs. were being exported annually. However, Whitney never benefitted from it.

**The Loser:** Charles Goodyear

**The Sure Thing:** Control of the "vulcanizing" process that makes rubber useful in manufactured products.

**Background**: Goodyear's hardware store went broke in 1830, and over the next decade he spent a lot of time in debtor's prison. When he wasn't in jail, he was inventing things.

In 1834, he designed a rubber inner tube. He took it to the Roxbury India Rubber company, hoping they'd manufacture it. The company's owners admired his work, but couldn't buy anything; they were broke.

Rubber products, it turned out, were essentially worthless; rubber melted in heat and cracked in cold. "The individual who could unlock the secret to India rubber," the owners assured Goodyear,

**Canine toupees—which attach to the top of dogs' heads with adhesive—are sold in Tokyo.**

"stood to make a fortune."

"To someone forever in debt," recounts *Yankee* magazine, "these words were like throwing a life preserver to a drowning man. The raw material was cheap, and the necessary equipment for cooking rubber could be found in his wife's kitchen: a rolling pin, a marble slab, and a few pots and pans. Vulcanizing rubber became Goodyear's mission in life."

**Good Luck:** After five years of dire poverty, during which he experimented constantly, Goodyear accidentally dropped a batch of rubber and sulphur mixture on a hot stove. When it didn't melt, as he expected it would, he realized he had finally discovered vulcanization.

**Tough Luck:** He had lived off people's charity—and dreams—for so long that none of his family or friends believed in him any more. In fact, it took him three years to find someone who was willing to invest in his discovery.

Finally, in 1854, he perfected the process enough to receive a valuable patent. But he still never made a cent from it. Other companies stole the process and challenged his rights to it. He was forced to spend all the money he could get his hands on defending himself. He died a pauper in 1860, hounded by collection agents.

**The Loser:** Josh J. Evans

**Sure Thing:** A district judgeship in Oklahoma.

**Background:** Frank Ogden had been a popular judge in rural northwest Oklahoma for thirteen years. He normally ran for reelection unopposed, but just before the deadline for filing to run in 1990, it was announced that he had cancer. Doctors speculated that Ogden could last another term. However, Josh Evans decided to run against him. He even tried, unsuccessfully, to get Ogden removed from the ballot.

**Good Luck:** On August ninth, Ogden died. Since write-ins aren't allowed in Okalhoma, Evans looked like a shoo-in.

**Tough Luck:** Evans couldn't even beat a dead man. The local Bar Association endorsed the deceased judge, and the electorate gave him 91% of the vote. The final tally: 9,377 for Ogden; 959 for Evans.

# PRIME-TIME RELIGION

*If God is everywhere, why not on* Gilligan's Island? *TV quotes from the book* Primetime Proverbs, *by Jack Mingo and John Javna.*

### ON RELIGION

"I'm going to take the moment to contemplate most Western religions. I'm looking for something soft on morality, generous with holidays, and with a very short initiation period."

**—David Addison,**
***Moonlighting***

"The pilgrims who drink the water of the Ganges shall trot all the way to the Mosque."

**—Henry Gibson,**
***Laugh-In***

### THE RULES OF HEAVEN

"There's no plea bargaining in heaven."

**—Mark McCormick,**
***Hardcastle & McCormack***

"You don't have to be homely to get into heaven."

**—Hattie Denton,**
***The Rifleman***

**Jean-Paul Sartre** [arriving in heaven]: "It's not what I expected."
**God:** "What did you expect?"
**Sartre:** "Nothing."

*—SCTV*

### ABOUT GOD

"When I was dead I saw God. She looks just like Toody from *The Facts of Life.*"

**—Larry,**
***Newhart***

"God don't make no mistakes—that's how He got to be God."

**—Archie Bunker,**
***All in the Family***

**Gabe Kotter:** "I think God is everywhere."
**Arnold Horschack:** "Even in liver?"

***—Welcome Back, Kotter***

### On FAITH

"All faith must have a little doubt thrown in. Otherwise it just becomes flabby sentimentality."

**—Dr. Loveless,**
***The Wild, Wild West***

"You have to believe in the gods to see them."

**—Hopi the Indian,**
***Gumby***

# THE MONSTER MASH

*This Halloween classic swept across America in 1962—and 1973—like a bat out of...Here's the inside story, from* Behind the Hits, *by Bob Shannon and John Javna.*

## BACKGROUND

In the late '50s, Universal Studios syndicated a package of its greatest monster movies—including *Dracula*, The *Mummy*, and *Frankenstein*, featuring Boris Karloff—to television stations around the country. That's how baby boom kids got their first look at classic horror films. It was love at first sight; by the early '60s, a monster craze was under way. There were monster models, monster trading cards, monster wallets, monster posters...and a monster song: "The Monster Mash," by Bobby "Boris" Pickett.

## KARLOFF DOO-WOP

Bobby was an aspiring actor who made his living singing with a Hollywood rock 'n' roll group called the Cordials at night, while he went on casting calls during the day. He'd always done impressions, and Karloff was one of his best. So one night just for the hell of it, while the Cordials doo-wopped their way thorugh a classic tune called "Little Darlin'," Bobby did a monologue in the middle with a Karloff voice. The crowds loved it. A member of the band suggested that Bobby do more with the Karloff imitation—write an original song, perhaps.

Pickett resisted for a while, but finally he and a friend wrote a monster take-off of Dee Dee Sharp's hit, "Mashed Potato Time." They recorded it at a studio on Hollywood Boulevard, for Gary Paxton's Garpax Records.

## SOUND EFFECTS

Paxton, who'd had his own hit with "Alley Oop" a few years earlier, came up with some clever low-budget techniques to produce the background noises that made the rock 'n' roll's ultimate Halloween party so effective.

For example:

• "The sound of the coffin opening was actually a rusty nail being drawn out of a two-by-four."

• The cauldron bubbling was really water being bubbled through a straw.

• The chains rattling was just the sound of chains being dropped on a tile floor.

"Boris" Pickett thought of "Monster Mash" as a cute novelty tune. But he didn't understand the power of the monster mania that was sweeping America. The song sold a million copies and became a #1 hit in October—just in time for Halloween. One of its fans, who recieved free copies from Pickett, was Boris Karloff.

## RETURN FROM THE DEAD

Pickett followed "Monster Mash" with "Monster's Holiday," and with an album of monster rock 'n' roll. But he had no more monster hits until 1970, when "Monster Mash" was re-released. It was released again in 1973, and it really hit big, reaching the Top 10. Pickett, by then a cabdriver in New York City, attributed its 1973 success, in part, to Nixon's Watergate scandal. "At this point in time, with what's coming down with Watergate, people need some relief from the tension that's building up," he explained.

## ROCKIN' MONSTERS

Before "Monster Mash," the most popular monster tune in rock history was "Purple People Eater," recorded in 1958 by Sheb Wooley. Here's how Wooley came up with it:

• A friend of Wooley's told him a riddle he'd heard from his kid: "What flies, has one horn, has one eye, and eats people?" The answer: "A one-eyed, one-horned flying purple people eater." Wooley thought it was amusing, and wrote a song based on it.

• A short time later,Wooley met with the president of MGM Records to decide on his next single. Wooley played every song he'd written, but still couldn't come up with one the guy liked. "You got anything else?" the president asked. "Well, yeah, one more thing, but it's nothing you'd wanna hear." "Let's hear it."

• It was "Purple People Eater." Wooley recorded it, and three weeks later it was the #1 single in the U.S.

# THE REAL PURITANS

*According to American folklore, the Puritans were stern martinets who wore dark clothes, burned witches and never had sex. That's only partly true.*

**Were the Puritans "puritanical"?**

In many ways, yes. They had little tolerance for differences of opinion. They didn't think much of the concept of democracy, either—John Winthrop, first governor of the Massachusetts Bay Colony, called it "the meanest and worst of all forms of government." The religious freedom they left Europe to find was denied in their own settlements, where religious dissenters were expelled.

**Colonial Christmas.**

They didn't celebrate Christmas—in fact, they made it illegal to do so. A law passed in 1659 levied a 5-shilling fine against anyone "found observing, by abstinence from labor, feasting or any other way, any such days as Christmas day."

On the other hand, the Puritans' reputation for shyness about sex was a fabrication by 19th century historians who were trying to give their Colonial ancestors a moral makeover. In reality, the Puritans considered sex a public concern and regularly discussed it during meetings. They valued sexual intercourse inside marriage to such an extent that, after lengthy public discussion, they expelled a husband from the church community because he had refused to sleep with his wife for over two years. Furthermore, parents and children all slept in close proximity, so youngsters got plenty of sexual education at an early age, with visual aids.

**Animal Husbandry**

Still, deviations from the norm were severely dealt with. In 1647, a 16-year-old from Plymouth, Mass. was "detected of buggery with a mare, a cowe, two goats, five sheep, two calves and a turkey," as Governor Bradford put it. The boy was put to death. "A very sade spectakle it was; for first the mare, and them the cowe, and the rest of the lesser catle, were kild before his face, according to the law, Levitticus 20:15, and then he him selfe was executed."

One of the three original Barbies was a brunette — the rest were blonde.

# OTHER PRESIDENTIAL FIRSTS

*We all know the first president (Washington), the first to resign (Nixon), the first Catholic president (Kennedy), and so on. But who was the first to be interviewed in the nude? Here's the BRI's list of* other *presidential firsts.*

**THE PRESIDENT:** Theodore Roosevelt (1901-1909)
**NOTABLE FIRST:** First president to coin an advertising slogan.
**BACKGROUND:** While he was visiting Andrew Jackson's home in Nashville, Tennessee, Roosevelt was offered a cup of the coffee sold at the nearby Maxwell House hotel. When someone asked if he'd like another cup, Roosevelt replied: "Will I have another cup? Delighted! *It's good to the last drop!*" His words were eventually used by Maxwell House in their ad campaigns.
**Note:** Teddy was also the first president to be blinded while in office. He liked to box, and during one White House bout was hit so hard he became permanently blind in one eye.

**THE PRESIDENT:** James Madison (1809-1817)
**NOTABLE FIRST:** First commander-in-chief to actually command a military unit while in office.
**BACKGROUND:** When the British attacked Washington, D.C., during the War of 1812, President Madison personally took charge of an artillery battery. But that didn't last long; when the Americans started to lose, Madison fled the city.

**THE PRESIDENT:** Benjamin Harrison (1889-1893)
**NOTABLE FIRST:** First president with a fear of electricity.
**BACKGROUND:** President Harrison knew two things about electricity: The White House had just been wired for it; and it could kill people (the electric chair was becoming a common form of execution). That was all he needed to know—he didn't want anything more to do with it. Throughout his entire term, he and his wife refused to turn the lights on and off themselves. They either had the servants do it or left the lights on all night.

**THE PRESIDENT:** Andrew Jackson (1829-1837)
**ACCOMPLISHMENT:** First president to be born in more than one place.
**BACKGROUND:** The following places claim themselves as Andrew Jackson's birthplace: Union County, North Carolina; Berkeley County, West Virginia; Augusta County, West Virginia; York County, Pennsylvania; as well as England, Ireland, and the Atlantic Ocean (he may have been born at sea). His "official" birthplace: Waxhaw, South Carolina.

**THE PRESIDENT:** John Quincy Adams (1825-1829)
**ACCOMPLISHMENT:** First president interviewed in the nude.
**BACKGROUND:** President Adams loved to skinny-dip. In hot weather he'd sneak out for a swim in the Potomac. One morning Anne Royall—a reporter who had been trying to interview him for months—sneaked up while he was swimming, sat on his clothes, and refused to leave until he granted her an interview. He did.

**THE PRESIDENT:** Martin Van Buren (1837-1841)
**ACCOMPLISHMENT:** First president to forget about his wife.
**BACKGROUND:** In his autobiography, Van Buren did not mention his wife Hannah even once.

**THE PRESIDENT:** Warren G. Harding (1921-1923)
**ACCOMPLISHMENT:** First president to pardon a dog.
**BACKGROUND:** One morning Harding read a newspaper article about Pennsylvania dog that had been ordered destroyed because it had been brought into the country illegally. Harding—who loved animals—wrote a letter to the Governor of Pennsylvania. The governor saw to it that the dog's life was spared.

**THE PRESIDENT:** David Rice Atchison (1849-1849)
**ACCOMPLISHMENT:** First president to serve for one day.
**BACKGROUND:** Zachary Taylor was so religious that he refused to take the oath of office on a Sunday. So Atchison, President Pro Tempore of the U.S. Senate, stood in for him until he could be sworn in the next day.

# SMART COOKIES

*Cookies keep the Girl Scouts in the green. That box of Thin Mints or Do-Si-Does you order every season is part of a tradition that's nearly 60 years old.*

**FOUNDING MOTHERS**

After Juliette Low founded the Girl Scouts in 1912, the local troops raised money by selling knitted clothes, baked goods and chickens. Then in 1934, Philadelphia press agent Bella Spewack (who later co-wrote *Kiss Me Kate)* came up with an idea she thought would make fund-raising easier: a vanilla cookie in the shape of the Girl Scout seal. She contracted with a local bakery to make them. One day she heard that reporters were going to interview actresses at a local flower show. Figuring her Girl Scout troop would get free publicity if they showed up selling cookies, she sent a contingent of green-clad cookie-mongers. They got so much publicity and sold so many cookies that within three years, more than a hundred local councils were selling the same professionally-baked cookies. It was the beginning of an American institution.

**NOW IT'S BIG BUSINESS**

• In 1990 the Girl Scouts sold 130 million boxes of cookies, grossing $225 million. That's 13 cookies for every person in the U.S. Average sale per scout? About 100 boxes.

• Some troops now offer "cookie seminars" and toll-free ordering numbers to boost sales. When asked about nutritional value, scouts are coached to respond: "Our cookies contain no preservatives and no artificial colors, and are made of 100% vegetable shortening."

• The *Girl Scout Manual* offers sales tips like this: "Your words and tone of voice must generate the image of someone people trust."

• The greatest cookie seller of all time was Markita Andrews, who sold 60,000 boxes in her twelve years of Girl Scouting. She was so successful that she was hired to make motivational speeches to big companies and appear in a 12-minute sales motivational film, *The Cookie Kid,* produced by Disney.

• Most popular cookies: Thin Mint, followed by Shortbread and Peanut Butter Sandwiches. Least popular: cheese-flavored crackers.

# YOU SEND ME

*Here are the origins of some of the nation's largest people and package movers.*

## GREYHOUND BUSES

In 1914 Carl Eric Wickman opened a Hupmobile car dealership in Minnesota. When business was slow, he used one of the Hupmobiles to drive miners the 4 miles between the towns of Alice and Hibbing, charging 15¢ per trip (25¢ round trip). This enterprise turned out to be very profitable (he made $2.25 the first day), and by 1916 Wickman had expanded it to include long distance routes. He painted the Hupmobiles gray to hide the dust during long journeys...which prompted a hotel owner along one route to comment that they looked like greyhound dogs. Wickman liked the idea. He adopted the slogan "Ride the Greyhounds."

## FEDERAL EXPRESS

When Fred Smith was a student at Yale University, he wrote a term paper outlining his idea for a nationwide overnight delivery service. His Professor gave him a C for the effort....but Smith (who'd inherited a fortune) invested $4 million to start the company anyway. He named it Federal Express because he thought his first major customer would be the Federal Reserve Bank. (Ironically, it wasn't).

## UNITED PARCEL SERVICE

Jim Casey was 19 years old in 1907, when he started the American Messenger company in Seattle. His business consisted of only six messengers, two bicycles, and a telephone...but within a year he added 6 motorcycles and a Model T Ford. By 1918 he was handling the deliveries of 3 of Seattle's major department stores. By the end of World War I, Casey had changed the name of the business to the United Parcel Service, and focused exclusively on delivering for department stores. In 1953 UPS expanded service to 16 metropolitan areas and started expanding its service. Today UPS owns more than 300 aircraft and delivers 600,000 packages every day.

# THE HARDER THEY FALL

*The bigger they are, the harder they fall?*
*Sadly, that was true for these stars.*

**THE STAR:** Veronica Lake, sultry actress known for her "peek-a-boo" hair-style (combed over one eye—in fact, practically covering one whole side of her face).

**ACCOMPLISHMENTS:** A leading box-office attraction of the early 1940s. Made 26 films, including *I Married a Witch* (the inspiration for the TV show, "Bewitched").

**AT HER PEAK**: Her hair-style was so popular that it hampered the war effort. Women working in factories kept getting their "peek-a-boo" hair caught in the machinery. U.S. government officials asked Lake to cut her hair. She did.

**THE FALL:** Without the hair, Lake wasn't special anymore. By the early '50s, her movie career was over. Though she found intermittent work in stage roles, she was reduced at one point to working as a barmaid in Manhattan. She died of acute hepatitis at age 53, on July 7, 1973.

**THE STAR:** D.W. Griffith, the genius regarded as "the father of modern cinema."

**ACCOMPLISHMENTS:** Griffith produced and directed nearly 500 films. The cinematic genres he created—from the epic to the psychological drama—influenced generations of directors. He launched the careers of Hollywood legends Mary Pickford, Douglas Fairbanks, Lionel Barrymore, and many others.

**AT HIS PEAK:** His films had such impact that Woodrow Wilson remarked, when he saw Griffith's *The Birth of a Nation* (the first film shown at the White House), that it was "like writing history with lightning."

**THE FALL:** Griffith's bouts with the bottle inspired him to make *The Struggle*, a 1931 exploration of alchoholism. It bombed. Griffith's own struggle with booze worsened, and his production company folded. Suddenly, he was unable to find work; in the last 17 years of his life, no one in Hollywood would give him a job.

Although his films had earned tens of millions of dollars, he left an estate of only $30,000 when he died in 1948, at the age of 73.

**THE STAR:** "Shoeless Joe" Jackson, one of the greatest players in baseball history. Played for the Philadelphia Athletics (1908-09), Cleveland Indians (1910-15) and Chicago White Sox (1915-20).

**ACCOMPLISHMENTS:** Compiled the third-highest lifetime batting average of all time: .356. Only Ty Cobb, at .367, and Rogers Hornsby, at .358, are higher. In his first full year he hit .408 (but lost the batting title to Cobb, who hit .420).

**AT HIS PEAK:** Between 1910 and 1915, Jackson batted no lower than .331. Cobb called Jackson the greatest natural hitter who ever lived, adding, "He never figured anything out or studied anything with the same scientific approach I gave it. He just swung."

**THE FALL:** After the White Sox lost the 1919 World Series to the Cincinatti Reds, officials learned that eight Chicago players—including Jackson—had agreed to "throw" the Series in exchange for bribes from gangsters. They called it the "Black Sox" scandal.

The revelation outraged the country. A sensational investigation was launched and a grand jury was convened. Jackson, who had hit .375 in the Series (leading all batters), maintained he never accepted any money. He claimed he'd agreed to the plan only because the team's owner, notoriously stingy Charles Comiskey, was paying the players next to nothing. He was found innocent of any criminal wrongdoing, but baseball executives decided to make an example of him (and his teammates). He was banned from baseball for life.

Jackson resettled in his native South Carolina, where he ran a liquor store and played sandlot and textile-league baseball. He died of a heart attack on December 5, 1951, at the age of 63.

**THE STAR:** Joseph McCarthy, U.S. Senator (R-Wisc.) from 1947 to 1957.

**ACCOMPLISHMENTS:** Senator McCarthy did not create the Cold War, but he almost single-handedly fashioned the post-World War II anti-communist hysteria that swept through American society. His 1950 claim that more than 200 Communists had infiltrated the State Department launched a national witch hunt. It ruined hundreds of careers, led to infamous blacklists (especially in the motion picture industry), and, as one magazine put it, "convinced

**Take a deep breath: 47% of smokers have tried to quit four or more times.**

most Americans that their government was riddled with Reds bent on its destruction."

**AT HIS PEAK:** He could make or break careers and reputations. Polls showed that half of all Americans approved of his efforts, while less than one-third disapproved.

**THE FALL:** In April, 1954, a Senate committee began investigating his charge that the U.S. Army was "coddling Communists." Two-thirds of all TV sets in the country were tuned in. TV cameras captured his cruel sneer, his bullying manner, and America saw Army counsel Joseph Welch put McCarthy in his place with the famous words, "Have you no sense of decency, sir?" Welch got a standing ovation and McCarthy's colleagues in the Senate moved to censure him. His political career was effectively over. Always known as a two-fisted drinker, he hit the bottle harder and harder, and on May 2, 1957, he died of liver disease, at the age of 48.

**THE STAR:** Eliot Ness, legendary G-man whose 15-year law enforcement career was highlighted by his campaign against Chicago mob boss Al Capone.

**ACCOMPLISHMENTS:** In 1929, during Prohibition, Ness led the special ten-man Justice Department team known as "The Untouchables," targeting Capone. In 1935, at 32, Ness became Cleveland's youngest director of public safety. He went on to rid the police department of rampant corruption, brought dozens of mobsters to trial, and reduced juvenile crime by two-thirds.

**AT HIS PEAK:** In two years, Ness and his men did more to curtail organized crime in Chicago than federal, state, and local officials combined had in an entire decade. In its first six months alone, the "Untouchables" unit seized nineteen Capone distilleries and six breweries. By 1931 the team had effectively shut down Capone's alcohol-production operations.

**THE FALL:** In the spring of 1942, Ness drove his car, with its unmistakable "EN-1" license plates, into another vehicle—then left the scene. It was reported he'd been driving drunk. Ness denied it, but resigned under pressure two months later. Over the next 15 years, he spiralled downward through a series of failed business ventures, marriages, and an abortive political career. He managed to complete his memoirs, but didn't live to see them in print. When he died of a heart attack, on May 16, 1957, he was $8,000 in debt.

**The bald eagle's nest can weigh as much as a ton.**

# BEAGLE, SHYSTER, & BEAGLE

*This script from the first episode of a long-lost early radio show by the Marx Brothers was recently rediscovered. So close your ears, listen with your eyes, and travel back in time to Nov. 28. 1932, when the first episode of Five-Star Theater aired.*

**SCENE:** *The offices of Beagle, Shyster, & Beagle, Attorneys at Law. Miss Dimple, the receptionist, is polishing her nails. Beagle (Groucho Marx) bursts in.*

**MISS DIMPLE:** Good morning, Mr. Beagle.

**GROUCHO:** Never mind that. Get President Hoover on the phone. There's a picture of me in the police station and it doesn't do me justice. It makes me look like my father. In fact, it *is* my father. Never mind calling the president. Just find out what the reward is.

**MISS DIMPLE:** Mr. Beagle, I've got some letters for you to sign.

**GROUCHO:** Not now, not now! I've had a big day in court.

**MISS DIMPLE:** What was the case?

**GROUCHO:** Disorderly conduct, but I think I'll get off. Why shouldn't I? She hit me first.

**MISS DIMPLE:** Mr. Beagle! You hit a woman?

**GROUCHO:** Well, she was my size. Even smaller. Besides, if it weren't for my own arrests, I'd never get a case. Any calls?

**MISS DIMPLE:** Yes, your creditors have been calling all morning. They said they're tired of phoning and that something will have to be done.

**GROUCHO:** All right. We'll do something. We'll have the phone taken out.

**MISS DIMPLE:** Okay.

**GROUCHO:** There's a good girl. Your salary is raised ten dollars.

**MISS DIMPLE:** Thank you, Mr. Beagle.

**GROUCHO:** It's nothing at all. Say, how about lending me that ten till payday?

**MISS DIMPLE:** But Mr. Beagle, I haven't been paid in weeks. Besides, you overlook the fact—

**GROUCHO:** I've overlooked plenty around here. A fine stenographer you are! What do you do with your time? The floors aren't washed, the windows aren't cleaned. and my pants aren't even pressed.

**MISS DIMPLE:** But Mr. Beagle—

**GROUCHO:** Enough of this small talk. Where's that ten dollars?

*Groucho retires to his office. Soon after, Miss Dimple ushers in a client—a nervous, worried soul named Mr. Jones.*

**JONES:** How do you do, Mr. Beagle. A friend of mine told me you were a good lawyer.

**GROUCHO:** You just *think* he's a friend of yours. Sit down. Have you got a couple of cigars?

**JONES:** Uh...no, I'm sorry.

**GROUCHO:** Well, why don't you send out for some? If you've got a quarter, I'll go myself.

**JONES:** Oh, no, no, Mr. Beagle.

**GROUCHO**: What's the matter? Don't you trust me?

**JONES:** Why—I'd like to talk to you. I'm having trouble with my wife.

**GROUCHO:** You are! Well, I'm having trouble with my wife, too, but I don't go around bragging about it. Hmm. You oughta be ashamed of yourself. Miss Dimple, show this gentleman the door. On second thought, never mind. He saw it when he came in.

**JONES:** But, Mr. Beagle—I came to you for advice. Let me tell you a story. My wife is in love with two men, and—

**GROUCHO:** Ha, ha, ha! Not a bad story. The boys are all repeating it around the club. Now let me tell you one. There were two

**Two out of every three American boys own G.I. Joe dolls.**

traveling men named Pat and Mike—

**JONES:** No, no, Mr. Beagle. I came here with a problem. I'm looking for evidence against my wife.

**GROUCHO:** What you really want is someone to shadow your wife. I've got just the man for you—my new assistant, Emmanuel Ravelli. He looks like an idiot and talks like an idiot. But don't let that fool you. He really is an idiot. You and Ravelli will have a lot in common.

**JONES:** Mr. Beagle, my time is valuable. Let me give you the facts. I married my wife secretly.

**GROUCHO:** You married her secretly? You mean you haven't told her about it? No wonder she runs around with other men.

**JONES:** Mr. Beagle, we must get this divorce—I want your assistant, Mr. Ravelli, to follow my wife.

**GROUCHO:** One thing at a time. Let's get the divorce first and then we can all follow your wife.

**CHICO:** Here I am, boss. You callin' Ravelli?

**GROUCHO:** See here. I don't like your sleeping on the company's time.

**CHICO:** I don't like sleeping on it it, either. Why don't you buy me a bed?

**JONES:** Mr. Ravelli, I've just been telling Mr. Beagle that, much as I regret to say it, my wife is going around with other men.

**CHICO:** She's going around with other men? 'At'sa fine. Hey! You think she like me?

**JONES:** Well, Mr. Ravelli, as long as you're going to trail my wife, I think I ought to describe her to you. She's of medium height and...but never mind, I've got a photograph.

**CHICO:** Hey, 'at'sa fine. Awright. I'll take a dozen.

**JONES:** I'm not selling them

**CHICO:** You mean, I get it for nothing?

**JONES:** Of course.

**CHICO:** Awright. Then I take two dozen.

**JONES:** One picture ought to be enough for the present. There's one man my wife has been paying particular attention to. I'm counting on you to find out who he is. Do you think you can do it?

**CHICO:** Sure, you leave 'im to me. I find out who the man was with your wife. And I find out quick.

**JONES:** Really? How you going to do it?

**CHICO:** Well, first I put on a disguise ...

**JONES:** Yes?

**CHICO:** Then I get a bloodhound ...

**JONES:** Yes??

**CHICO:** Then I go to your house ...

**JONES:** Yes???

**CHICO:** Then I ask your wife.

*(Applause, commercial break)*

*Two weeks later at the offices of Beagle, Shyster, & Beagle.*

**MISS DIMPLE:** Law offices of Beagle, Shyster, and Beagle ...Oh, hello, Mr. Jones. I didn't recognize your voice...Yes, Mr. Ravelli is still trailing your wife ...but it hasn't been long ...just two weeks. We expect Mr. Ravelli in the office this morning. He says he has some news ...Okay, I'll tell Mr. Beagle you'll be in ...Goodbye.

*(Groucho comes in)*.

**MISS DIMPLE:** Good morning, Mr. Beagle—

**GROUCHO:** Miss Dimple, before I forget—call Ravelli and tell him to be sure and oversleep.

**MISS DIMPLE:** But he phoned and said he was coming right in.

**GROUCHO:** In that case, I'm going right back to the poolroom *(he heads for the door)*.

**MISS DIMPLE:** But Mr. Jones is on his way here to talk to you about his divorce.

**GROUCHO:** That's all he ever talks to me about. I'm getting pretty sick of it, too.

**MISS DIMPLE:** But Mr. Beagle, that's your business.

**Each year, Americans consume 19 billion franks—an average of 87 per person.**

**GROUCHO:** Well, I wish he'd keep his nose out of my business. *(Door opens.)*

**MISS DIMPLE:** Shh! Someone's coming in. I think it's Mr. Jones. How do you do, Mr. Jones?

**JONES:** How do you do, Miss Dimple? Morning, Mr. Beagle. About my divorce—

**GROUCHO:** Divorce! You going to start that again? Listen, Jones, can I sell you a ticket to the Firemen's Ball? It's a five-dollar ticket, and it's yours for a buck and a half.

**JONES:** Why, this is last year's ticket.

**GROUCHO:** I know it is, but they had a better show last year.

**JONES:** Mr. Beagle, when will I find out about my divorce case?

**GROUCHO:** See here, Jones, don't change the subject. What about that ticket?

**JONES:** I don't like to appear impatient, Mr. Beagle, but your assistant was supposed to bring in some evidence against my wife. Where is Mr. Ravelli?

**CHICO:** Hey! Who'sa calling Ravelli? Here I am.

**JONES:** Ah, Mr. Ravelli, I'd like to get the results of your investigation. Have you been trailing my wife?

**CHICO:** Sure, I shadow her all day.

**JONES:** What day was that?

**CHICO:** That was Shadowday. I went right to your house—

**JONES**: What did you find out?

**CHICO:** I find your wife out.

**JONES:** Then you wasted the entire two weeks?

**CHICO:** No. Monday, I shadow your wife. Tuesday, I go to the ball game—she don't show up. Wednesday, she go to the ball game—I don't show up. Thursday was a doubleheader. We both no show up. Friday it rain all day—there's a no ball game, so I go fishing.

**JONES:** Well, what's that got to do with my wife?

**CHICO:** Well, I no catcha no fish, but I catch your wife.

**The state with the most outhouses is Alaska.**

**JONES:** You caught my wife—with a man? Who was he?

**CHICO:** I don't wanna say.

**JONES:** I insist that you tell me the man's name.

**CHICO:** I don't wanna tell.

**GROUCHO:** Listen, Jones, my assistant isn't the type of fellow who'd bandy a man's good name in public—

**JONES:** For the last time, gentlemen—who was the man?

**GROUCHO:** Come clean, Ravelli, who was the man with his wife?

**CHICO:** Awright, awright. You maka me tell, I tell you. Mr. Jones, the man with your wife was my boss, Mr. Beagle.

**JONES:** This is an outrage. My attorney going out with my wife!

**GROUCHO:** What do you mean, outrage? Don't you think I'm good enough for her?

**JONES:** I'm going to get a new attorney.

**GROUCHO:** Hmm! I suppose you think we can't get a new client?

**JONES:** Good day! *(He stomps out and slams the door.)*

**GROUCHO:** Ravelli, you did noble work. You can have the rest of the year off. And if you never come back, I'll give you a bonus.

**CHICO:** Well, boss, there's something I wanna tell you.

**GROUCHO:** Go right ahead. I'm not listening.

**CHICO:** You want I should never come back?

**GROUCHO:** In a word, yes.

**CHICO:** Awright, boss, I make you a proposition. If you want I should never come back, I gotta have more money.

**GROUCHO:** Ravelli, it's worth it. (*Applause, theme music*)

**ANNOUNCER:** The crowd in the studio is giving the Marx Brothers a great ovation. We hope you in the radio audience enjoyed them as much as we did. Groucho and Chico will be back again next Monday at this same time.

**The first "streamlined swimsuits" of the early 1900s were made of wool and weighed as much as 20 lbs.**

# PICASSO ORIGINALS

*Pablo Picasso was known for his skill with lines. Here are some you won't see in a museum.*

"We know that art is not truth. Art is a lie that makes us realize truth."

"When I was a child my mother said to me, 'If you become a soldier you'll be a general. If you become a monk you'll become the pope.' Instead I became a painter and wound up as Picasso."

"I am only a public entertainer who has understood his time."

"There are only two kinds of women—goddesses and doormats."

"There are painters who transform the sun into a yellow spot, but there are others who, thanks to their art and intelligence, transform a yellow spot into the sun."

"One starts to get young at the age of sixty and then it is too late."

"There's nothing so similar to one poodle dog as another poodle dog and that goes for women, too."

"You never see anything very great which is not, at the same time, horrible in some respect. The genius of Einstein leads to Hiroshima."

"God is really only another artist. He invented the giraffe, the elephant, and the cat. He has no real style, he just goes on trying other things."

"Ah, good taste! What a dreadful thing! Taste is the enemy of creativeness."

"An artist must know how to convince others of the truth of his lies."

"If only we could pull out our brains and use only our eyes."

"If I like it, I say it's mine. If I don't, I say it's a fake."

"Work is a necessity for man. Man invented the alarm clock."

"You invent something, and then someone comes along and does it pretty."

**Arachibutyrophobia: the fear of peanut butter sticking to the roof of your mouth.**

# LATIN 101

*So you thought Latin was dead?* Latin For All Occasions, *by Henry Beard, brings it back to life. Here are some excerpts:*

**Useful phrase:** "Amicule, deliciæ, num is sum qui mentiar tibi?"
**Meaning:** "Baby, sweetheart, would I lie to you?"

**Useful phrase:** "Perscriptio in manibus tabellariorum est."
**Meaning:** "The check is in the mail."

**Useful phrase:** "Braccæ tuæ aperiuntur."
**Meaning:** "Your fly is open."

**Useful phrase:** "Da mihi sis bubulæ frustum assæ, solana tuberosa in modo Gallico fricta ac quassum lactatum coagulatum crassum."
**Meaning:** "I'll have a hamburger, French fries, and a thick shake."

**Useful phrase:** "Cur non isti mictum ex occasione?"
**Meaning:** "Why didn't you go when you had the chance?"

**Useful phrase:** "In rivo fimi sine rivo sum."
**Meaning:** "I'm up the creek without a paddle."

**Useful phrase:** "Est mihi nulluus nummus superfluus."
**Meaning:** "I do not have any spare change."

**Useful phrase:** "Lex clavatoris designati rescindenda est."
**Meaning:** "The designated-hitter rule has got to go."

**Useful phrase:** "Observa quo vadis, cinaede!"
**Meaning:** "Watch where you're going, you jerk!"

**Useful phrase:** "Tractatorne in Germania Orinetali doctus est?"
**Meaning:** "Was your masseur trained in East Germany?"

**Useful phrase:** "Visne scire quod credam? Credo Elvem ipsum etiam vivere."
**Meaning:** "You know what I think? I think that Elvis is still alive."

**Useful phrase:** "Di! Ecce hora! Uxor mea necabit!"
**Meaning:** "God, look at the time! My wife will kill me!"

**Hitler's favorite movie was *King Kong*.**

# THE TAJ MAHAL

*On the banks of the Jumna River, at Agra, India is a structure considered by many to be the most beautiful edifice ever built—the Taj Mahal.*

## BACKGROUND

In 1628, Shah Jahan became the fifth Mogul emperor of India. Of his four wives, his favorite was one he called *Mumtaz Mahal* (which means "Ornament of the Palace").

• Shah Jahan was known as a benevolent, fatherly ruler. One ritual he—and his subjects—especially enjoyed was "Tula Dan." He would sit on a scale forty feet high, and was weighed against gold coins. When an amount equal to his weight was measured out, the coins were distributed to the poor.

• Mumtaz Mahal, on the other hand, was a bloodthirsty religious zealot and a committed foe of Christianity. She goaded her husband into destroying a Christian colony at Hooghly, on the northeast coast of India. The entire colony was razed. The survivors were marched 1,200 miles from Hooghly to Agra. There, the priests were thrown beneath elephants; the rest were sold as slaves.

## THE MONUMENT

• When Mumtaz Mahal died in 1631, Shah Jahan was so grief-stricken that he disappeared into his quarters for eight days, "refusing food or wine"; all that could be heard coming from his room was a low moan.

• On the ninth day he emerged, determined to build a magnificent tomb as a monument to his beloved. Mumtaz herself, on her deathbed, supposedly whispered into Shah Jahan's ear that he should build " monument of perfect proportions" to symbolize and immortalize their perfect love.

• The project took 22 years. More than 20,000 jewelers, builders, masons and calligraphers worked on it day and night. When they finished, they had created the wondrous white mausoleum which is still regarded—nearly 340 years later—as the most remarkable piece of architecture in the world.

• The main building of the Taj Mahal is on a 186-foot square whose sides have been cut to form an octagon. This rests on a platform 2,000 feet long and 1,000 feet wide. At each of its four corners is a minaret—an Islamic prayer tower—three stories tall.

• Hundreds of tons of imported white marble were used.

• The Taj is adorned with Tibetan turquoise, Chinese jade, Arabian carnelian, and other precious metals.

• According to one account, Shah Jahan showed his appreciation for this masterpiece by ordering the hands of the master builders—and the head of the architect—to be chopped off, so the perfection of the Taj could never be duplicated.

**LATER ON...**

• In first centuries after it was built, the Taj Mahal wasn't a tourist attraction. Until the British Raj (occupation of India), any non-Moslem who entered it was put to death.

• Shah Jahan planned to build a second Taj Mahal, made of black marble, on the opposite bank of the Jumna. (He planned to make it his own tomb.) The two structures were to have been connected by a bridge of solid silver. Construction on this "Black Taj" supposedly was begun in the 1650s, but no traces of its foundation have ever been found. The project was halted when Shah Jahan was deposed by his sons.

• The Mogul spent his last years confined to a suite in Agra's famous Red Fort, where he was imprisoned by his son Aurangzeb, Agra's new ruler. From his window, Jahan could see his monument to Mumtaz—to whom he remained devoted (even though his entire harem was with him). Every day for eight years he sat gazing across the river.

• Jahan finally died at the age of 74, when he took an overdose of aphrodisiacs in an effort to prove his virility.

• Jahan was buried with Mumtaz in the Taj, but their actual remains are not in the main structure. The tombs upstairs are empty; the real ones are in the basement.

**There were 50 soldiers in the U.S. Air Force when World War I.**

## MODERN TIMES

• The domes and minarets of the Taj are so reflective—even in moonlight—that, during the India-Pakistan War, large sections were covered in burlap so that Pakistani aircraft could not use it as a beacon.

• Today, the Taj is threatened by pollution. The river valley where it sits tends to trap corrosive air pollutants, including coal dust and sulfur dioxide, for days at a time. Only about 1% of its surface has been affected, but formerly bright-white marble is now streaked, pitted and yellow. Some of the red sandstone of auxiliary buildings is flaking. Most of the pollution is said to come from two coal-fired power plants, a railroad switching yard and many small coal-burning foundries.

• The Indian government has installed pollution-monitoring gear and promises to relocate the power stations and foundries, but these are long-term propositions. Meanwhile, the race to save the Taj is already being run by frantic workmen who are repairing and replacing slabs of marble as fast as possible.

## THE OTHER TAJ

• Taj Mahal is one of the foremost modern American bluesmen.

• His real name: Henry St. Clair Fredericks.

• Our favorite of his albums: "Natch'l Blues" and "Giant Step." Both are recommended for your bathroom CD player.

• • •

## GOTTA FILL THIS SPACE

*Random quotes about greatness:*

• "A small man can be just as exhausted as a great man." (Arthur Miller)

• "Behind every great man is a woman with nothing to wear." (L. Grant Glickman)

• "Calvin Coolidge—the greatest man ever to come out of Plymouth Corner, Vermont." (Clarence Darrow)

• "The privilege of the great is to see catastrophes from a terrace." (Jean Giraudoux).

# THE PLANE TRUTH

*Occasionally, we get a letter from a reader who confesses he or she has read a Bathroom Reader on an airplane. Well, that's okay with us. To prove it, here's a bit of practical airplane advice from the* Airline Passenger's Guerrilla Handbook, *by George Brown.*

Believe it or not, specialists have actually discovered a medical complaint called "economy class syndrome" (ECS). According to the British medical journal, *The Lancet*, the symptoms can appear several weeks after flights as short as three hours. The syndrome can result in anything from minor body pains and shortness of breath to heart attacks and strokes.

Doctors suspect that cramped legroom in economy class combined with dehydration interrupts the blood flow which causes clots, cutting off the supply of oxygen to various parts of the body. This may account for the results of one study which showed that 18 percent of sudden deaths on airplanes are due to blood clots in the lungs.

The medical specialists reported that the syndrome most often affects smokers, heavy drinkers, those whose feet don't reach the floor (because the seat puts more pressure on the backs of their legs), the elderly and those with a predisposition to coronary heart disease. But it also can affect normally healthy people, in some recorded cases causing them to develop pneumonia-like symptons due to blood clots in the lungs.

The best ways to fight ECS: drink nonalcoholic beverages, don't smoke, take aspirin to thin your blood and exercise on the plane.

**How to Exercise on the Plane**

The best type of exercise on a long flight is to get out of your seat, go to the back of the plane (or, if you're shy, into a toilet cubicle) and engage in traditional calisthenics, such as touching your toes, reaching for the sky and running in place. Avoid doing jumping jacks if you're in the lavatory.

If you can't or don't want to get up, there are certain sets of exercises you can do in your seat. Before you start, be sure to inform your seatmate of what you intend to do. This will prevent him from thinking you're having some sort of seizure, which could lead to his attempting to wrestle a pencil sideways into your mouth to keep you from choking on your tongue—always an embarrassing mistake for both parties.

**The exercises are as follows:**

1. Tighten and release, one group at a time, the muscles in your shoulders, back, buttocks and thighs.

2. By raising your thighs, lift both feet six inches off the floor and rotate them first in one direction and then in the other.

3. Reach up repeatedly toward your overhead light with one arm and then with the other as though trying to block out the light.

4. Bend forward with all your weight, press your crossed forearms onto your knees and, keeping your toes on the floor, repeatedly lift your heels as high as possible.

5. Sitting up, arching your back, repeatedly roll both shoulders forward and then back, first together and then one at a time.

6. Pretending you are on skis, push your knees to the right and your heels and hands to the left. Lift your feet off the floor, and swing your knees to the left and heels and hands to the right. Repeat twenty times.

7. Sitting back, lower your head as far forward as you can. Then, still facing forward, lower it to the left. Then, to the right. Repeat several times.

8. Lay your head back, with your mouth hanging open, and, arching your back, look as far back on the ceiling as you can.

9. With your right hand grab the back of your left armrest and pull your upper body around until you are looking behind you. Hold for ten seconds. Repeat in the other direction.

10. Place your right hand on your left shoulder and your left hand on your right shoulder, and hug yourself. Lean forward as though giving someone a Latin lover kiss. Repeat several times.

11. Sit up slowly, turn towards the aisle and tell the crowd looking at you that you've finished your exercises, so they can all go back to their seats.

# EXPERT OPINIONS

*Being an expert means never having to admit you're wrong. Here are some memorable examples of "expert opinion," quoted in a great book called* The Experts Speak, *by Christopher Cerf & Victor Navasky.*

## ON HEALTH:

"If excessive smoking actually plays a role in the production of lung cancer, it seems to be a minor one."

**—The National Cancer Institute, 1954**

"How do we know? Fallout may be good for us."

**—Edward Teller, 1950**

"A nuclear power plant is infinitely safer than eating, because 300 people choke to death on food every day."

**—Dixie Lee Ray, Washington Governor, 1977**

## ...ON MILITARY STRATEGY:

"I tell you Wellington is a bad general, the English are bad soldiers; we will settle the matter by lunch time."

**—Napoleon Bonaparte at the Battle of Waterloo, 1815**

"I guess we'll get through with them in a day."

**—General George Custer at Little Big Horn, 1876**

## ...ON FILM

"The cinema is little more than a fad. It's canned drama. I'm going to get out of this business. It's too much for me. It'll never catch on."

**—Charlie Chaplin, 1914**

"*Gone With the Wind* is going to be the biggest flop in the history of Hollywood. I'm just glad it'll be Clark Gable who's falling flat on his face and not Gary Cooper."

**—Gary Cooper, 1938**

"You'd better learn secretarial work or else get married."

**—Emmeline Snively (modeling agent) to Marilyn Monroe, 1944**

**Bud Abbott, of Abbott & Costello, was born in a circus tent.**

### ...ON TECHNOLOGY

"Rail travel at high speed is not possible, because passengers, unable to breathe, would die of asphyxiation."

**—Dr. Dionysus Lardener, 1845**

"Heavier-than-air flying machines are impossible."

**—William Thomson, President of the Royal Society, 1890**

"Nuclear powered vacuum cleaners will probably be a reality within 10 years."

**—Alex Lewyt, President, Lewyt Vacuum Cleaner Co., 1955**

"My invention...can be exploited for a certain time as a scientific curiosity, but apart from that it has no commercial value whatsoever."

**—Auguste Lumiere (inventor of the movie camera), 1895.**

### ...ON COMPUTERS

"While a calculator now is equipped with 18,000 vacuum tubes and weighs 30 tons, computers in the future may have only 1,000 vacuum tubes and only weigh 1 1/2 tons."

**—*Popular Mechanics*, 1949**

"I think there is a world market for about five computers."

**—Thomas J. Watson, Chairman of IBM, 1943**

"There is no reason for any individual to have a computer in their home."

**—Ken Olson, President, Digital Equipment Corporation, 1977**

### ...ON POLITICS

"If Richard Nixon is impeached, there will be mass suicides, mass nervous breakdowns, and total demoralization of the country."

**—Helen Buffington, Committee to Re-Elect the President, 1974**

"Dwight D. Eisenhower is a dedicated, conscious agent of the Communist conspiracy."

**—Robert Welch, President, John Birch Society, 1963**

**A typical "lawn" in Austria is planted with cabbages and kohlrabi.**

# LUCKY STRIKES

*Here's proof that the BRI appreciates other kinds of "bowling," too.*

**BIRTH OF BOWLING**

• Bowling originated in German monasteries around 300 A.D. The monks had churchgoers knock down a bottle-shaped object called a *kegel* from a distance to prove their devotion to God. The kegel represented the devil, and upsetting it meant complete absolution from sin.

• Gradually, more kegels (pins) were added and it turned into a secular game. By the 1600s, a version called "nine-pin" had become popular throughout Europe.

• Ninepins was popular in the U.S. in the early 1800s. But because many lanes were located in saloons, the game became associated with drinking. Many states banned it. Bowlers got around the laws by adding a *tenth* pin to the set. Eventually ten-pins became more popular than Ninepins.

## BOWLING LINGO

**Apple:** a bowling ball

**Barmaid:** a pin that's "hiding" behind another pin.

**Bedposts, Snake eyes, Mule ears, Goal posts:** 7-10 split.

**Body English:** using body contortions to change the course of an already thrown ball.

**Cherry:** downing only the front pins when going for a spare.

**Christmas Tree:** 3-7-10 or 2-7-10 splits.

**Cincinnati:** an 8-10 split

**Creeper, powder puff:** a sluggish ball.

**Dead Apple:** a ball with no power when it reaches the pins.

**Golden Gate:** A 4-6-7-10 split.

**Grasshopper:** a ball that sends the pins leaping

**Grandma's Teeth:** a random, gap-filled group of pins left standing.

**Mother-In-Law:** the 7 pin

**Poodle:** a roll right into the gutter.

**Schleifer:** a suspenseful, domino-like strike.

**Woolworth, Dime Store:** 5-10 ("five and dime") split.

# TEA TIME

*Some things you probably never knew about one of the world's most popular beverages.*

According to Chinese legend, tea was discovered in 2737 B.C. by Emperor Shen Nung, when leaves from a nearby plant fell into a pot of boiling water.

◆

Japanese legend differs—it attributes the discovery of tea to Daruma, founder of Zen Buddhism. After nine years of meditating without sleep, it says, Daruma became groggy. This made him mad, so he cut off his eyelids. Blood from his eyes spilled to the ground, and a plant grew from that spot. The drink Daruma made from the plant cured his grogginess.

◆

*All* teas (except herbal teas) come from the same plant—*Camellia Sinensis*. The only things that distinguish one variety of tea from another are blending, added flavors, and the length of time the leaves are allowed to dry, or "ferment."

◆

Tea grows naturally in only one part of the world: the forested region shared by China, India, Burma, and Tibet.

Before the 1700s, the English considered tea a "man's" drink—and sold it only in coffee houses, places considered too rough for women. Thomas Twining changed this in 1706 when he opened London's first tea shop for ladies.

◆

Thomas Lipton, founder of the Lipton Tea Co., owes his success to pigs. Lipton owned a general store in Glasgow, Scotland. To promote it, he dressed up pigs and led them in parades. The pigs, called "Lipton's Orphans," helped Lipton make enough money to buy a tea plantation, and get his start in the tea business.

◆

The tea bag was invented in 1908, by accident. A New York tea importer mailed his customers free samples of his tea, which he packaged in tiny silk bags. When the customers wrote back asking for more of the bags, the importer realized they were using them to steep tea...and began packaging all of his tea that way.

◆

Watch how tea leaves unfold in boiling water. Experts call this "the agony of the leaves."

**The word "Kennedy" actually means "hideous head" in Irish.**

# DEATH OF A CLOWN

*Abbie Hoffman loved to make political points by making Americans laugh. Did somebody take him too seriously? Here's information from a new book,* It's a Conspiracy, *by the American Paranoid Society.*

## BACKGROUND

**Rabble-Rouser**

Abbie Hoffman was best known for co-founding the Yippies, a band of hairy anti-war freaks who assembled outside the Democratic Convention in Chicago to nominate a pig ("Pigasus") for President of the United States in 1968.

• The riots that followed were later blamed on the police, but Hoffman and seven other activists were hauled into court on "conspiracy" charges. They were known as the Chicago 8. After one of the most publicized trials of the '60s, the case was eventually thrown out of court.

**Counterculture King of Satire.**

His social satire (he called it "street theater") always attracted attention:

• When he fluttered three hundred crisp dollar bills down onto the floor of the New York Stock Exchange, there was pandemonium as brokers fought for the money.

• His plan to levitate the Pentagon made the front page.

• He called his second book *Steal This Book!* When no publisher would touch it (because of the title), he published it himself, sold 200,000 copies, and gave most of the money away.

**The Fugitive**

After getting busted for selling cocaine to an undercover policeman, he jumped bail, had plastic surgery and emerged shortly as Barry Freed, an environmental activist in upstate New York.

• Though he was "wanted" by the law, he regularly played softball with the New York State Police, testified to a congressional committee, and was commended by New York's Governor Cuomo for his work.

• As *Newsweek* wrote, "Hoffman may have been the first fugitive

**The state of Pennsylvania is not named after William Penn. It's named after his father.**

surrender with a press agent and a business manager. Before giving up, he summoned ABC's Barbara Walters...for a taping session."

• After a brief sentence, he went back to protest. His next book, *Steal This Urine Test* was an attack on "Reagan's repressive policy." And in 1987 he was back on the streets, getting arrested—along with Amy Carter—in an anti-CIA protest.

## GOING FOR BUSH

• Abbie next took on George Bush, then running for President. In an October, 1988, *Playboy* article he co-authored, Hoffman broke the story of the "October Surprise." He alleged that Reagan supporters had made a deal with Iran to postpone the release of the hostages and keep President Carter from getting re-elected. In his version of the story, Bush had a key role in the conspiracy.

• Presumably, Amy Carter is the person who told Hoffman of her father's suspicions. With his nose for publicity, Hoffman knew it was an explosive story.

• There were rumors Hoffman was assembling a book on the subject. If he was as effective in presenting the story as he was in championing the counterculture during the '60s—and in getting publicity for it—he could have created real headaches for the Republicans...and potentially, the CIA.

## WHAT HAPPENED

On April 12, 1989, when he was unable to contact Hoffman by phone, his landlord entered his house and found him in bed, dead.

## OFFICIAL EXPLANATION

Coroner Thomas J. Rosko reportedly found the residue of about 150 pills and alcohol in Abbie's system. He said, "There is no way to take that amount of phenobarbital without intent. It was intentional and self-inflicted."

## SUSPICIOUS FACTS

• **Hard to swallow:** Hoffman supposedly took 150 pills. One-tenth that number would have been enough to kill anyone.

• **Bad Brakes:** According to conspiracy theorist John Judge in

*Alternative Perspectives on American Democracy*, "When he went to deliver the manuscript to *Playboy* Abbie had an automobile accident....He told his friend and long-time fellow activist David Dellinger, that his brakes had been tampered with."

• **That's Incredible:** The *New York Times* quoted Dellinger as saying: "I don't believe for one moment the suicide thing." The reason: He had spoken with Hoffman recently and reported that Abbie had "numerous plans for the future."

• **No Glory:** His family didn't believe it either. In fact, almost all of Abbie Hoffman's friends were puzzled by the lack of a suicide note—he had a compelling need to express himself. As one of Hoffman's sons said, "Abbie was the kind of guy who, if he was going to do it, would wrap himself in a flag and jump off the top of the ITT building."

## WAS THERE A CONSPIRACY?

### THEORY #1:

**YES.** Somebody was afraid he knew too much and he was sure to create problems for the"Establishment" in the future. A number of journalists think he was able to break the "October Surprise" story with information received from President Jimmy Carter. Moreover, he had made a lot of powerful enemies during the '60s. He was an easy target, given his history of drug use.

### THEORY #2

**NO.** Abbie generated a lot of strong feelings, and the people who loved him had a hard time accepting a suicide verdict. Abbie Hoffman was also a long-time manic-depressive, and was taking medication for it. He was very depressed by the Eighties. One night, he may have hit bottom.

## PARTING SHOTS

"It's hard to believe that Abbie committed suicide—especially so late in the day that he missed The *New York Times*'s deadline."

**—Paul Krassner (Abbie's fellow prankster), in *The Nation***

# SONGWRITER STORIES

*Songwriters often have fascinating stories to tell about their compositions. Unfortunately, we rarely get to hear those tales. Fortunately, there's a great book called* Behind the Hits, *by Bob Shannon and John Javna, full of entertaining stories like these.*

**LOLA, The Kinks**

As songwriter Ray Davies recounts it, he was spending the evening with record producer Robert Wace at a nightclub; Wace was having a bit of luck with a particular young lady. "I'm really onto a good thing here," Wace told Davies, indicating the sultry black woman he was dancing with. But as the night wore on, Davies got a little suspicious. He noticed stubble on the chin of Wace's new girlfriend. Davies decided "she" was a man. Presumably, Wace was so smashed he couldn't tell the difference.

Davies recalls: "I had a few dances with it...him. It became kind of obvious. It's that thrust in the pelvic region when they're on the dance floor. It's never quite the same with a woman."

Davies wrote "Lola" about that incident. But he kept the language deliberately ambiguous ("I'm glad that I'm a man / And so is Lola"), so listeners would never be able to decide whether Lola was a man, a woman...or what.

**HONOLULU LULU, Jan and Dean**

In the early '60s, Roger Christian was one of the top deejays in L.A. He sometimes did live shows at high schools, and his friends, Jan and Dean, often performed with him. One graduation night after a grueling schedule of personal appearances, the exhausted Christian and Jan Berry decided to go to The Copper Penny, an all-night L.A. diner, for something to eat. The two of them co-wrote many of Jan and Dean's hits and this night, as they sat at the table, they started writing another one. They based it on a title that a record company executive had suggested—"Honolulu Lulu."

Christian scribbled the lyrics down on a napkin, and then they paid and left the restaurant. Out front, they said good night. "Give me the napkin," Jan said, "and I'll take it to the studio and write out the arrangements." "I don't have it—you do," Christian replied. "No I don't—you do." "Not me." Suddenly they realized that they'd left it on the table in the restaurant.

They bolted inside to retrieve it, but it was too late. The waitress had already cleared their dishes and everything had been thrown away. Roger and Jan sat down and tried to reconstruct the song, but they just couldn't get the lyrics to work like they had the first time. There was only one thing left to do. They went out to the back of the diner and started sorting through the contents of the dumpster, looking for their napkin in the dark. At about 4:00 A.M., they finally found it. The reward for their treasure hunt? "Honolulu Lulu" hit #11 on the national charts.

**THEY'RE COMING TO TAKE ME AWAY, HA-HAAA!, Napoleon XIV**

In 1966, a 28-year-old New York recording engineer named Jerry Samuels went into the studio to record a song that had no melody and needed almost no instruments. It was recited, not sung, and he used only drums and a tambourine to back himself up. The total cost for studio time was $15.

But if the production of the song was a little unusual, that was nothing compared to the content. Essentially, the "singer" went insane while he was reciting the lyrics. His voice began in a normal tone, and slowly went up until it was as high-pitched as the Chipmunks. What was making him crazy? His dog had run away.

The whole thing was completely bizarre...and very funny.

The first record company Samuels played it for, Warner Brothers, snapped it up. Within a week after releasing the record, more than 500,000 copies had been sold, making it the fastest-selling record in Warner's history.

Although it went on to sell over a million copies, "They're Coming To Take Me Away" was taken off the radio almost immediately. Mental health organizations protested that the record made fun of the mentally ill...and shouldn't receive airplay. That was Napoleon XIV's Waterloo; we never heard from him again.

**Note:** Samuels didn't have any money—or a song—to put on the flip side, so he just reversed the tape. He called it "Aaah-Ah Yawa Em Ekat Ot Gnimoc Er-Yeht."

**Since Massachusetts passed its bottle bill, emergency rooms report 60% fewer glass-related cuts.**

**I PUT A SPELL ON YOU, Screamin' Jay Hawkins**

In the summer of 1954, Screamin' Jay Hawkins, a blues singer with seven records—all bombs—under his belt, was performing at a joint in Atlantic City called Herman's. In the middle of his set, his live-in girlfriend walked in, marched right up to the stage and tossed his house keys at him. Then she disappeared. It looked bad...and it was. Jay went home to find "Good-bye, my love" scrawled in lipstick on the bathroom mirror.

He plopped down on the bed and let out "the most painful" scream of his life. Then he began writing a "sweet ballad" that he hoped would get her back—"I Put a Spell on You."

Hawkins recorded it for the tiny Grand Records in Philadelphia, and it, too, took a dive. He couldn't get his lover back with that record—she never heard it.

It wasn't a total loss, though. In the meantime, Jay incorporated the song into his act and the head of Columbia Records, Arnold Matson, happened to see him perform it in a typically wild manner. Matson loved it. He signed Hawkins to the Okeh label (primarily Columbia's R&B label), and they went into the studio to do a version. But something was wrong. They tried take after take, and Matson still wasn't happy with it. It just wasn't as powerful as when Jay did it live. Why? "Is there something you do when you perform that you're not doing here?" Matson asked."Well," Jay told him, "I usually drink a bit when I'm on stage."

As Hawkins tells it: "So he brought in a case of Italian Swiss Colony muscatel and we all got our heads bent...We all got blind drunk." Hawkins couldn't even remember the session when it was over. "Ten days later the record came out. I listened to it and heard all those drunken groans and screams and yells. I thought, 'Oh, my god!'" It ended in a series of sexual moans, so many radio stations refused to play it. Even after Columbia remastered it to cut out the controversial ending, they couldn't get it on the air. So it never made the charts. But it did become a cult favorite, especially in live performances when Hawkins was carried out in a coffin, wore Dracula capes, and played with snakes. It has also been recorded dozens of times by artists like Creedence Clearwater Revival, and was the theme music for the 1984 cult film, *Stranger Than Paradise*.

**Note:** Jay got his girlfriend back. Not, ironically, because of "Spell," but because she liked the flip side, "Little Demon."

**Humans are the only animals that cry.**

# ROYAL PAINS

*Gossip about some famous kings and a queen.*

## KING WENCESLAS

Was the Christmas carol about "Good King Wenceslas" accurate? Apparently not. The real Wenceslas was King of Bohemia and Holy Roman Emperor in the latter part of the 14th century. According to one source, he was a tyrant who "prowled the street with his cronies at night, breaking into houses, molesting his female subjects, and generally venting his feelings in a riot of cruelty."

He did love his hunting dogs, though; he even slept with them, over the objections of his wife, Johanna. (Even after one of the dogs attacked and killed her while she slept.)

## MACBETH

There really was a Scottish king named Macbeth; he ruled from 1040 to 1057. But according to David Randall in *Royal Misbehavior*, "Although little is known about him, there is no evidence that he was the henpecked social climber portrayed by Shakespeare....[In fact], he was a good and strong enough ruler to survive on the throne for 17 years—which is more than 25 other occupants of that precarious hot spot can claim." Lady Macbeth, granddaughter of King Kenneth III, was known in her time as a "patron of the church"—not as the Shakespearean "royal bitch."

## RICHARD THE LIONHEARTED

Maybe it's because of the legend of Robin Hood that Richard I is remembered as a righteous hero. But according to *Royal Misbehavior*: "He was in reality an absentee monarch who spent no more than ten months of a ten-year reign in England, left the country to the vagaries of his brother John and failed to produce an heir or even, it is said, consummate his marriage. Indeed, his sexual proclivities meant that Robin Hood and his chums were not the only young men...who followed the king with expectations."

## IVAN THE TERRIBLE

Monarchs aren't often as fearsome as their nicknames imply. But Ivan IV, Czar of Russia in the mid-1500s, was worse. "As a child," writes one historian, "he amused himself by throwing cats and dogs from the [200-foot-high] towers of the Kremlin. As Czar, when a group of seventy citizens complained to him of injustices in their town, he ordered hot wine poured over their heads and had them lie naked in the snow. When it was rumored that the city of Novogorod was conspiring to defect to neighboring Lithuania, Ivan exterminated the city, torturing its citizens for five weeks and killing 60,000 people."

He was so terrifying that he could actually scare people to death. In 1569 the girl he'd picked to be his third wife had a heart attack and died when she heard the news.

## CATHERINE THE GREAT

From *They Went That-A-Way*, by Malcolm Forbes: "What you've probably heard about the death of Russian Empress Catherine the Great is wrong. The poor maligned woman, insatiable lover that she was, did not die *in flagrante delicto* with a horse that, according to the famous rumor, crushed her when the truss broke. No, the 67-year-old ruler was alone when she collapsed, having dismissed her lover—a 27-year-old man—earlier that morning."

Apparently Catherine had a stroke in her dressing room and was found on the floor, unconscious. She died the following night without ever coming to.

## KING FAROUK

The last king of Egypt was so corrupt that he once freed a pickpocket from jail just so the prisoner could teach him how to steal. Farouk became as adept at it. "At receptions and parties," says David Randall, "he would move among the company, brushing against dignitaries and their ladies and then slipping off into an ante-room [to] empty his pockets of watches, wallets, lighters, and powder compacts. Eventually an entire warehouse was filled with these items, which even included the ceremonial sword, belt, and medals stolen from the body of the Shah of Persia as the funeral procession passed through Egypt in 1944."

# A FOOD IS BORN

*Those brand names on your supermarket shelf had to come from somewhere, right? Here's the inside scoop on a few famous food products.*

**ANIMAL COOKIES.** Cookies shaped like animals were introduced in England in the 1890s, but in 1902 Nabisco added something new. Recognizing the popularity of P.T. Barnum's "Greatest Show on Earth," they designed a box that looked like a circus cage, labeling it "Barnum's Animals." And to increase sales during the holiday season, they added a string handle that would allow parents to hang the boxes on Christmas trees.

**TABASCO SAUCE.** When Union troops in Louisiana occupied Avery Island and seized Edmund McIhenny's salt mines in 1862, he and his wife fled to Texas. They returned after the war to find that everything they owned had been destroyed—except for a crop of capsicum hot peppers. Desperate, McIhenny decided to try to make a sauce that he could sell to raise money. He aged a concoction of salt, vinegar and peppers in wooden barrels, and poured it into tiny old cologne bottles. He called his creation "tabasco sauce," after Mexico's Tabasco river, because he liked the name.

**WORCESTERSHIRE SAUCE.** When Sir Marcus Sandys, a British nobleman, returned to England from Bengal in the mid-1800s, he brought with him a recipe for a spicy sauce he had tasted in the Orient. He showed it to some chemists he knew in his home county of Worcestershire—John Lea and William Perrins—and asked them to reproduce the sauce exclusively for his use. Lea and Perrins agreed, but over time the sauce became so popular that Sandys gave them permission to sell it to other customers—and eventually sold them the recipe—which the Lea & Perrins Company uses to this day.

**DUNCAN HINES.** Duncan Hines was a traveling restaurant critic in the 1930s. His book *Adventures in Good Eating*—a guide to restaurants along major highways—was so popular that his name became a household word. Hines' notoriety attracted the attention of Roy Park, a New York businessman who was looking for a way to promote his new line of baked goods. He asked Hines to become a partner in the company, and Hines agreed. Together they formed Hines-Park Foods, Inc. in 1948. Their line of cake mixes captured 48% of the American cake mix market in less than *three weeks*.

**YUBAN COFFEE.** John Arbuckle, a turn-of-the-century Brooklyn merchant, sold his own popular blend of coffee. He needed a brand name for it, and decided to make one up using the letters that appeared on the shipments of coffee beans he received:

A B<br>N Y

(Arbuckle Brothers, New York) The combination he liked best was Yban. But it still wasn't quite right—so he added the letter u.

**LOG CABIN SYRUP.** P.J. Towle, a St. Paul, Minnesota grocer, was the first person to blend expensive maple syrup with other, more affordable syrups without losing the maple taste. A big fan of Abraham Lincoln, Towle decided to name the syrup Log Cabin in his honor—and sold it in cabin-shaped tin containers.

**ORVILLE REDENBACHER'S POPCORN.** In the 1950s an agronomist named Orville Redenbacher developed a hybrid strain of popcorn with a higher moisture content than regular corn—resulting in fluffier kernels and fewer "old maids" per batch. But popcorn companies refused to buy it—they insisted the public wanted *cheap* popcorn, not *good* popcorn. Redenbacher disagreed. He began selling to the public directly. Today Orville Redenbacher's is the best selling popcorn in the U.S.

• • •

## WEIGHTING FOR A TRAIN

U.S. President William Taft weighed over 300 pounds. He used it to his advantage: once while stranded at a train station in the country, he was told that the express only stopped for "large parties." He sent a wire to the conductor saying "Stop at Hicksville. Large party waiting to catch train." Once on board, he explained: "You can go ahead. I am the large party."

**blood away from your brain and makes you sleepy.**

# TV OR NOT TV?

*What's a Bathroom Reader without a little TV trivia?*

**THE PARTRIDGE FAMILY**

Love them or hate them, *The Partridge Family* made money. Their show, records, and licensed merchandise reportedly earned $11 million a year. In addition, more than 200,000 people paid $2 each for membership in their fan club—and the *Partridge Family Magazine* sold 400,000 copies a month. They even had 7 hit singles—in spite of the fact that none of them played on the records, and only David Cassidy and Shirley Jones sang on them.

**THE LOVE BOAT.** This show was based on *The Love Boats:* a novel written by a former cruise hostess. She based it on her own experiences.

• The show was always filmed on a real cruise ship, with passengers acting as extras. But before the show's success, it was difficult to get passengers to cooperate; they complained that the film crew was in their way.

**THE BRADY BUNCH.** Executive producer Sherwood Schwartz interviewed 464 girls and boys to find the right Brady kids. He hadn't picked the adult leads yet, but he knew he wanted the kids to have the same color hair as their "parents." His solution: he picked two sets of Brady boys, and two sets of Brady girls (blonde and brunette). When Robert Reed and Florence Henderson were chosen to play the parents, he dumped the kids he didn't need.

**I DREAM OF JEANNIE.** Although network censors had no objection to Barbara Eden's sexy costume or the fact that Jeannie was living with a man for whom she would do anything (anything?), they *did* object to her navel showing. The solution: she had to put a cloth plug in it so it wouldn't show on film.

• Scripts were written by novelist Sidney Sheldon, who was writing scripts for "The Patty Duke Show" at the same time.

The only Hitchcock film to win the Oscar for best film of the year was *Rebecca,* in 1940.

# TWO THUMBS DOWN

*Are book reviews believable? When they're good reviews of* Uncle John's Bathroom Reader *they are, of course. But consider these true-life comments, quoted in* Rotten Reviews *by Bill Henderson*

**Subject:** *Wuthering Heights*, by Emily Brönte
**Reviewer's Comment:** "The only consolation we have in reflecting upon it is that it will never be generally read." —James Lorimer, *North British Review*

**Subject:** *Gulliver's Travels*, by Jonathan Swift
**Reviewer's Comment:** "Evidence of a diseased mind and lacerated heart." —John Dunlop, *The History of Fiction*

**Subject:** *Romeo & Juliet*, by William Shakespeare:
**Reviewer's Comment:** "March 1 [1662]. Saw *Romeo and Juliet*, the first time it was ever acted; but it is a play of itself the worst that ever I heard in my life, and the worst acted that ever I saw these people do." —Samuel Pepys, *Diary*

**Subject:** *Alice in Wonderland*, by Lewis Carroll
**Reviewer's Comment:** "We fancy that any real child might be more puzzled than enchanted by this stiff, overwrought story." —*Children's Books*.

**Subject:** A *Tale of Two Cities*, by Charles Dickens
**Reviewer's Comment:** "It was a sheer dead pull from start to finish. It all seemed so insincere, such a transparent make-believe, a mere piece of acting."—John Burroughs, *Century* magazine

**Subject:** *Anna Karenina*, by Leo Tolstoy
**Reviewer's Comment:** " Sentimental rubbish ...Show me one page that contains an idea." —*The Odessa Courier*

**Subject:** A *Doll's House*, by Henrik Ibsen
**Reviewer's Comment:** "It is as though someone had dramatized the cooking of a sunday dinner."—Clement Scott, *Sporting & Dramatic News*

**Subject:** *Moby Dick*, by Herman Melville
**Reviewer's Comment:** "A huge dose of hyperbolic slang, maudlin sentimentalism and tragic-comic bubble and squeak."—Willima Harrison Ainsworth, *New Monthly Magazine*

**Subject:** *The Great Gatsby*, by F. Scott Fitzgerald
**Reviewer's Comment:** "A little slack, a little soft, more than a little artificial, *The Great Gatsby* falls into the class of negligible novels."—*The Springfield Republican*

**Subject:** *The Sun Also Rises*, by Ernest Hemingway
**Reviewer's Comment:** "His characters are as shallow as the saucers in which they stack their daily emotions, and instead of interpreting his material—or even challenging it—he has been content merely to make a carbon copy of a not particularly significant surface life of Paris."—*The Dial*

**Subject:** *From Here to Eternity*, by James Jones
**Reviewer's Comment:** "Certainly America has something better to offer the world, along with its arms and armies, than such a confession of spiritual vacuum as this."—*Christian Science Monitor*

**Subject:** *Babbitt*, by Sinclair Lewis
**Reviewer's Comment:**"As a humorist, Mr. Lewis makes valiant attempts to be funny; he merely succeeds in being silly. In fact it is as yellow a novel as novel can be."—*Boston Evening Transcript*

## AND THE MOTHER OF ALL "ROTTEN REVIEWS"

**Subject:** *Lady Chatterly's Lover*, by D. H. Lawrence:
**Reviewer's Comments:**"This pictorial account of the day-by-day life of an English gamekeeper is full of considerable interest to outdoor minded readers, as it contains many passages on pheasant-raising, the apprehending of poachers, ways to control vermin, and other chores and duties of the professional gamekeeper. Unfortunately, one is obliged to wade through many pages of extraneous material in order to discover and savor these sidelights on the management of a midland shooting estate, and in this reviewer's opinion the book cannot take the place of J. R. Miller's *Practical Gamekeeping.*" —Ed Zern, *Field & Stream*

**If you live in Kentucky, you're required by law to bathe at least once a year.**

# KENNEDY QUOTES

*Robert Kennedy's legacy is his idealism...and his fatalism. A few of the comments he left for us:*

"One-fifth of the people are against everything all the time."

"I should like to love my country and still love justice."

"Some men see things as they are and ask, 'Why?' I dream of things that could be and ask, 'Why not?' "

"My views on birth control are distorted by the fact that I was seventh of nine children."

"Who knows if any of us will still be alive in 1972? Existence is so fickle, fate is so fickle."

"We give our money and go back to our homes and...our swimming pools and wonder, 'Why don't they keep quiet, why don't they go away?' "

"A revolution is coming—a revolution which will be peaceful if we are wise enough; compassionate if we care enough; successful if we are fortunate enough—but a revolution is coming whether we will it or not. We can affect its character; we cannot alter its inevitability."

"[Freedom] proposes ends, but it does not propose means."

"Every society gets the kind of criminal it deserves."

"What is dangerous about extremists is not that they are extreme, but that they are intolerant. The evil is not what they say about their cause, but what they say about their opponents."

(On learning of his brother's assassination). "I thought they'd get one of us, but Jack, after all he's been through, never worried about it...I thought it would be me."

"Did the CIA kill my brother?"

"With all the violence and killings we've had in the United States, I think you will agree that we must keep firearms from people who have no business with guns." (5 days later, he was assassinated.)

**The emperor penguin can dive to depths of 870 ft. for as long as 18 minutes.**

# REMEMBER THE MAINE!

*In 1898, America declared war against Spain. But was it caused by Spanish atrocities or newspaper profits? Here's information from a new book,* It's a Conspiracy, *by the American Paranoid Society.*

## BACKGROUND

### Itching for a Fight

In the late 1890s, America was bursting at the seams. Having reached the end of its frontier, the nation now looked for new lands to conquer and causes to fight for. As young Teddy Roosevelt, put it, "I should welcome almost any war, for I think this country needs one."

### The Newspaper Wars

• Had Roosevelt worked for a New York City newspaper, he would have found all the fighting he wanted. The city's dailies were locked in a fierce struggle for circulation.

• With seemingly endless millions to spend, young William Randolph Hearst from California bought the *New York Journal* and took on the city's largest daily, the *World*. He started by cutting the paper's price to a penny, though he lost money doing it. Then, to further outrage the *World's* publisher, Joseph Pulitzer, Hearst lured away his most talented people with strapping raises.

• But the real war was on the front pages, and its biggest casualty was the truth. Both papers favored "crime, underwear and indignation." So when Cuban separatists tried to overthrow the rotting empire of Spain, the dailies fought to make each dispatch more lurid than the last.

### Extra! Extra!

• Sample from the *World:* "No man's life, no man's property is safe. American citizens are imprisoned or slain without cause...Blood on the roadsides, blood in the fields, blood on the doorsteps, blood, blood, blood!"

• Sample headline from the *Journal*, responding to a Spanish diplomat's remark—in a private letter—that President McKinley was "a low politician":

"THE WORST INSULT TO THE UNITED STATES IN ITS HISTORY!"

## DATELINE, CUBA

• Offended by press attacks against them, Spanish authorities in Cuba restricted U.S. reporters to Havana. In response, the U.S.S. *Maine* was sent to Havana harbor, "to protect American interests." A quiet three weeks passed. Then, on February 15, 1898, the *Maine* was sunk by a mysterious explosion; 260 men died.

• The *Maine*'s Captain Sigsbee, cabled Washington, "Many killed and wounded...Don't send war vessels...Public opinion should be suspended until further report."

• When Spain's captain-general in charge of Cuba heard the news, he "burst into tears...and sent officers to express regret and organize assistance." The Spanish, joined by a U.S. Navy team, began investigating the cause of the explosion immediately. Their findings were eventually released on March 17.

## JUMPING THE GUN

The papers couldn't wait, though. Hearst's *Journal* led the cry for war with headlines like:

"The Warship Maine Was Split In Two By An Enemy's Secret Infernal Machine" (Feb. 17)

"The Whole Country Thrills With The War Fever" (Feb. 18)

"Havana...insults The Memory Of The Maine Victims" (Feb. 23)

"War! Sure!" (March 1)

• Although the Spanish government finally met the United States' demands about freedom for Cuba—and President McKinley urged restraint—most Americans were howling for war. For example, "Frank James, ex-bandit brother of the legendary Jesse, offered to lead a company of cowboys."

• Ultimately, though, the decision rested on the Navy's findings.

## OFFICIAL EXPLANATION

The Naval Court of Inquiry found that "the *Maine* was destroyed by the explosion of a submarine mine"; however, it was "unable to obtain evidence fixing the responsibility...upon any person or persons." America went to war.

## SUSPICIOUS FACTS

• In addition to Captain Sigsbee's plea to withhold judgment, the *Journal*'s first dispatch from Cuba was also uncertain: "The injured do not know what caused the explosion. There is some doubt as to whether the explosion took place on the *Maine*."

• According to *The Yellow Kids*, "The Navy's new coal-powered warships...like the Maine [had] coal bunkers located near the ship's [gunpowder] magazines. There had been at least a dozen reported incidents on American ships in the previous year, and during one fire…sparks actually ignited wooden ammunition crates before the blaze was brought under control."

• The Navy Secretary "publicly announced his opinion that an explosion in the *Maine*'s magazine had caused the accident," and McKinley himself thought "the catastrophe had resulted from an internal explosion."

• Two days after the explosion, the navy's leading expert on explosives told a reporter that "no torpedo [or mine] as is known to modern warfare can of itself cause an explosion as powerful as that which destroyed the *Maine*."

## WAS THERE A CONSPIRACY?

**Theory #1: YES.** William Randolph Hearst started a war with Spain to boost circulation. His quote to artist Frederick Remington is well-known: "You supply the pictures, I'll supply the war."

• On either side of the *Journal*'s front-page masthead ran the blurb, "How Do You Like The *Journal*'s War?"—until even Hearst saw its tastelessness and removed it.

• If it was a conspiracy, it worked: For the first week after the explosion, the *Journal* averaged 8-1/2 pages on the *Maine*. And the paper's circulation "soared from 416,885 copies on January 9th to 1,036,140 on February 18th."

**Theory #2: YES.** But the navy was also complicit. Unless the Naval Court of Inquiry found that Spain was guilty, it would have had to admit the Navy had been negligent.

• In August, 1897, a bunker fire interrupted a dinner party Captain Sigsbee was hosting on the *Maine*. As he helped his guests down the gangplank he said, "Gentlemen, you have had a narrow escape tonight."

• During the inquiry, Sigsbee likely perjured himself. Although he was vague and "unfamiliar with the ship," he claimed that the day of the explosion he had personally inspected the bunker wall and found it cool. Nobody on the panel believed him.

• Although the navy report was supposed to be delivered to the White House under the strictest confidentiality, its findings were published in the *Journal* before President McKinley even opened the secret document.

**Theory #3: NO.** American industrialists needed a war to distract the public; Hearst was just a bit player, albeit a noisy one.

• A depression had begun in 1893 and showed no signs of ending soon. This was causing widespread strikes, farm revolts and a dramatic growth of the Populist movement.

• As one industrialist put it, "A little war will knock the pus out of Populism." Another noted that "it will take men's minds off domestic concerns."

• With the American frontier used up, untouched lands overseas would give businesses new lands to exploit.

• The American people were undoubtedly whipped up by Hearst and his ilk, but they overwhelmingly supported the war, at least as a fight for Cuban liberty.

**RANDOM QUOTE:**

"The last thing I could imagine is moving in with three other friends, no matter how much I liked them."

**—Betty White, star of "Golden Girls."**

# GOING THROUGH A PHRASE

*Here are some well-known phrases and the stories behind them.*

## TURN A BLIND EYE

***Meaning:*** To ignore something.

***Background:*** Captain Horatio Nelson of the British Navy was blind in one eye. In 1801, he was part of a force attacking French troops in Copenhagen, Denmark. As the tide of battle turned, the command ship signaled for Nelson to withdraw, but Nelson wanted to continue fighting. When he was told that his commander was signalling, Nelson held his telescope up to his sightless eye and declared that he could not see any signal. He continued his attack …and won.

## CHARLEY HORSE

***Meaning:*** A muscle cramp.

***Background:*** In 1640 Charles I of England expanded the London police force. The new recruits were nicknamed "Charleys." There wasn't enough money to provide the new police with horses, so they patrolled on foot. They joked that their sore feet and legs came from riding "Charley's horse."

## BURY THE HATCHET

***Meaning:*** To make peace with an enemy.

***Background:*** Some Native American tribes declared peace by literally burying a tomahawk in the ground.

## SPEAK OF THE DEVIL

***Meaning:*** Someone appears after you mention him or her.

***Background:*** People believed that you could actually summon the devil by saying his name (to be safe, they used nicknames and euphemisms like "the Deuce"). Over time, the expression was used to jokingly imply that your friend was "Old Nick" himself.

**What's the one thing creditors can't seize if you go bankrupt? Your wedding ring.**

## AT THE END OF YOUR ROPE

**Meaning:** Exhausted all possibilities; out of options.

**Background:** Horsemen tied their horses to trees with long lengths of rope so they could graze a large area of land. But when the horse ate all the grass within its reach, it was out of luck, literally "at the end of its rope." An alternate but equally plausible explanation for the phrase has to do with being strung up on the gallows.

## SOW WILD OATS

**Meaning:** Commit youthfully foolish acts.

**Background:** In the 11th century, when England was in the midst of its perpetual war against invaders, many farms were left to go fallow for years, even decades. Many of the grains which had been domesticated over generations reverted to their wild strains. When things settled down on the war front, a lot of the younger men had no experience farming and—eager to get on with it—collected seeds from the wild strains of oats, which grew great leaves and trunks, but few of the "heads" which contain the edible seeds. The plants weren't even worth harvesting.

## WHITE ELEPHANT

**Meaning:** A costly but unwanted object.

**Background:** When the kings of ancient Siam didn't like someone, they sometimes "honored" them with a rare, sacred White Elephant. The beasts cost a fortune to feed and keep in style befitting their high station—but because they were considered sacred, they couldn't be expected to work like normal elephants.

## TO BE AT LOOSE ENDS

**Meaning:** Frazzled and disorganized

**Background:** On old sailing ships, hundreds of ropes went everywhere. If they were allowed to unravel, they quickly became a tangled, disorganized mess. A mark of a good sea captain became the condition of his neatly taped "ends"; you could tell an inefficient and disorganized ship by its number of loose ends.

**Random Quote:** "People don't have much of a sense of humor when they themselves are victimized." —William F. Buckley

# PASS THE KETCHUP

*Can you imagine life without ketchup? One BRI member tells the story of a French visitor who automatically started to pour ketchup on pancakes. When the host stopped him, the surprised visitor asked "Don't Americans put ketchup on* everything?*" Here's a little ketchup history.*

**ORIGIN.** The Chinese invented *ke-tsiap*—a concoction of pickled fish and spices (but no tomatoes)—in the 1690s. By the early 1700s its popularity had spread to Malaysia, where British explorers first encountered it. By 1740 the sauce—renamed *ketchup*—was an English staple, and was becoming popular in the American colonies.

## A BAD APPLE

*Tomato* ketchup wasn't invented until the 1790s, when New England colonists first mixed tomatoes into the sauce. Why did it take so long to add tomatoes? People were afraid to eat them. The tomato is a close relative of the toxic belladonna and nightshade plants; most people assumed the tomato was also poisonous. Thomas Jefferson helped dispel the myth; his highly publicized love of tomatoes helped popularize them.

## KETCHUP FACTS

- Homemade tomato ketchup starts out as a watery gruel that has to be boiled down into a thick sauce—an all-day project that requires hours of stirring. Housewives of the 1870s loved the sauce, but they hated making it. So when Henry J. Heinz began selling bottled ketchup in 1875, he promoted it as a labor-saving device. He used the slogan "blessed relief for Mother and the other women of the household." Today more than half the ketchup sold in the U.S. is made by the H.J. Heinz Co.
- Note: Have you ever poured ketchup on something, wrapped it in aluminum foil, and then noticed later that there were holes in the foil? The ketchup is to blame; it's highly acidic and can actually dissolve small amounts of aluminum if it remains in contact with the metal long enough.

**The average American uses two pine trees' worth of paper products each year.**

# GLASSIFIED INFORMATION

*You don't have to throw glass bottles and containers out with the trash; they're recyclable. Here are more recycling tips from* The Recycler's Handbook, *by the EarthWorks Group*

It's interesting to listen to people talk about why they like glass. The appeal is more than just being able to recycle it easily—they like the way it looks and feels, too.

It's an ancient attraction. Glass bottles and jars have been a part of human culture for more than 3,000 years. We've been recycling them just about that long, too. In fact, it's conceivable that some of the glass you'll use today was once part of a bottle used by Richard the Lion-Hearted or Catherine the Great.

Of course it's not likely, but so what? The point is that recycling glass is a time-honored tradition. It's up to us to keep it going for the next 3,000 years.

## A TOUCH OF GLASS

• Before recycled glass is shipped to manufacturers, it's broken so it'll take up less space. This broken glass is called "cullet."

• When it arrives at the glass factory, the cullet is run through a device which removes metal rings from bottles. A vacuum process removes plastic coatings and paper labels.

• When it's "clean," the cullet is added to raw materials and melted down with them. Most bottles and jars contain at least 25% recycled glass.

• Glass never wears out—it can be recycled forever.

## WHY RECYCLE?

• We save over a ton of resources for every ton of glass recycled. (If you want specifics, it's 1,330 pounds of sand, 433 pounds of soda ash, 433 pounds of limestone, and 151 pounds of feldspar.)

• A ton of glass produced from raw materials creates 384 pounds of mining waste. Using 50% recycled glass cuts it by about 75%.

• We get 27.8 pounds of air pollution for every ton of new glass produced. Recycling glass reduces that pollution by 14-20%.

• Recycling glass saves 25-32% of the energy used to make glass.

• Glass makes up about 8% of America's municipal garbage.

## SIMPLE THINGS YOU CAN DO

### 1. Precycle

• Look for refillable bottles. They're the most energy and material efficient; they can be sterilized and reused up to seven times before recycling.

• Refillables aren't easy to find any more. But if enough consumers speak up at local supermarkets, they'll reappear on shelves. Case in point: Washington's Rainier Brewery, citing its customers' environmental concerns, has recently returned to using refillables for all its single serving bottles.

• An easy way to manage refillables: Get one of the sturdy crates they come in, and store "empties" in it. When the crates are full, take them to the store and exchange the empties for full bottles.

• In some areas of the Midwest and Mountain states, glass is not accepted because there's no market for it. In these areas, consider buying aluminum cans, which are recycled virtually everywhere.

### 2. Store It

• It's safer to pack bottles in boxes or bins than in bags.

• Don't leave the bottles in six-pack carriers; that makes extra processing work for recyclers (they have to remove the bottles).

• If you're selling your glass at a buyback center or dropping it off, you'll probably have to separate it into brown, green and clear glass. The reason: To make recycling profitable, glass factories need to turn brown glass into brown bottles, etc. If colors are mixed, the end product is an unpredictable hue. Glass factories don't like it because their orders are for specific colors.

• If you have any blue or other colored glass containers, recycle them with the brown or green glass—but only in small amounts.

• If the glass is even slightly tinted, sort as colored, not as clear.

• Broken bottles can be recycled, but not everyone accepts them.

• Curbside programs generally accept all colors mixed together; sorting occurs later. Keep glass unbroken if possible—it's easier for the recycling crew to handle.

**3. Recycle**

• Remove lids and caps. You can recycle steel caps with steel cans. (Plastic cap liners are no problem). For aluminum caps, check with the recycling center before including them with aluminum cans.

• It's okay to leave on neck rings, paper and plastic labels—they burn or blow off in the recycling process.

• Dump out food residue and lightly rinse bottles. Old food attracts animals, it's a mess for recyclers, and it stinks. Be sure to empty beer bottles. A drop of beer can turn into a slimy mold.

• Remove rocks and dirt from bottles found in parks, beaches, etc. Even a little stone can ruin a whole load of glass.

**4. Absolutely Don't Include...**

• Windows, drinking glasses, mirrors, Pyrex (baking dishes, coffee pots, etc.), or other glass. Any of these can ruin an entire batch of glass if they slip through at the factory. The reason: They don't melt at the same temperature as bottles.

• Ceramics (coffee mugs, mustard jars, plates, etc.). They don't melt down with the glass, so they contaminate it.

## IF YOUR STATE HAS A "BOTTLE BILL..."

• Not all states accept the same bottles for redemption. Some take only beer and soft drink bottles; others include juice or liquor bottles. Check with stores or recycling centers.

• General Rules: Empty bottles; you may need to sort them by brand to get your deposit back. Broken bottles aren't redeemable.

## SOURCES

**"Glass Recycling: Why? How?"** The Glass Packaging Institute, 1801 K St. N.W., Suite 1105-L, Washington, D.C. 20006.

# ELVIS TRIVIA

*It's become a Bathroom Reader tradition to include a few sections on The King in every book. Here are bits of Elvis gossip.*

Elvis didn't sing well enough to make his high school glee club.

★

Although he has received many co-writing credits, Elvis never wrote a song. His manager (Col. Tom Parker) simply told songwriters that Elvis wouldn't record their songs unless he got credit—and half the royalties.

★

Over the years, Elvis bought more than 100 Cadillacs and gave away around 20 of them. The first one he bought was a pink one for his mom.

★

There are 50 dogs named Elvis registered in Los Angeles county.

★

Elvis's favorite sandwich: grilled peanut butter and banana.

★

Elvis's 1956 two-sided hit, "Hound Dog"/"Don't Be Cruel," is the most popular jukebox selection of all time.

Every day the U.S. Postal Service receives at least one letter on the advisability of issuing an Elvis stamp. Mail is currently running 6 to 1 in favor.

★

According to one author, in 1960 Elvis began secretly dating Frank Sinatra's girlfriend, Juliet Prowse. Sinatra found out and one night showed up at Elvis's dressing room with two "unpleasant companions." Frank and friends "discussed Presley's continued good health." Elvis refused to return Prowse's calls after that.

★

If it wasn't for Colonel Parker torpedoing the offers, Elvis could have starred in *Midnight Cowboy* and opposite Barbra Streisand in *A Star is Born*.

★

Elvis' autopsy revealed that he had at least 10 different drugs in his system at the time of death. Official cause of death: heart failure brought on by "straining at stool." Translation: he died on the pot.

**Rule of thumb: Widowed, divorced, and separated people smoke more than other people.**

# UNCLE JOHN'S BATHROOM CATALOG

*Looking for some "singing" toilet paper? How about "tinkle time targets"? No bathroom reader's bathroom is complete without them. Here are a few key bathroom items you can order by mail.*

**The Little Plastic Cup**

"Everybody's had to do it. The nurse tells you to go into the bathroom at the end of the hall and 'give us a sample.' And how many times have you sat in there until they had to come looking for you and you had to confess, sheepishly, that you 'just couldn't.' Now you can practice at home, and train yourself to avoid the embarrassment (or relive the thrill, if that's your thing)."

**Specimen cup,**
**Item No. 20120**

5 oz. Jerryco Inc.
601 Linden Place
Evanston, IL 60202

**Tinkle Targets**

"Teaching your little boys to aim properly when they're being toilet trained (and after) can be a trying chore. This'll turn boys of any age into sharpshooters. Each pack contains 45 colorful, flushable, non-staining targets. Just float one in the bowl and fire away."

**Tinkle Targets**
**Item # G225**

The Right Start Catalog
Right Start Plaza
5334 Sterling Center Drive
Westlake Village, CA 91361

**Pink Flamingo Toilet Paper**

"Flamingo toilet tissue can help you with any impossible bathroom decorating task. This is an exclusive "The Cat's Pyjamas" design; order their catalog and check out some of their other great flamingo bathroom items like shower curtains, toothbrush holders and towel bars."

**Flamingo Toilet Paper**
**Item # CP756**

The Cat's Pyjamas
20 Church Street
Montclair, NJ 07042

**Gag Black-Hands Soap**

"Looks like regular designer soap, the manufacturers claim. But nobody would guess that when they wash their hands, the black color comes off the soap and stays on them. Easy way to tell which of your friends habitually 'forgets' to wash hands after using the bathroom."

**Black Soap**
**Item # 2419**

Johnson Smith Company
4514 19th Court East
PO Box 25500
Bradenton, FL 34206-5500

**Toity Tunes**

"'A musical novelty! Makes your toilet paper sing!' reads the colorful hang tag. And the battery is INCLUDED! This ingenious, maddening, little electronic device slips inside the toilet paper roll. When the tissue is pulled, what sounds like a mosquito orchestra starts loudly playing one of these old favorites: Christmas Medley, Happy Birthday, My Favorite Things, Home Sweet Home, Wedding March, Love Me Tender, Yesterday, Twinkle Twinkle Little Star, It's a Small World, Over the Rainbow, You Are My Sunshine, When the Saints Go Marching In, and our favorite: The Star Spangled Banner, since true patriots will leap to attention when this starts to play..."

**Toity Tunes**

Funny Side Up.
25 Stump Rd.
N. Wales, PA 19454

• • •

**FROM OUR MUHAMMAD ALI FILES:**

Just before takeoff on a commercial flight, a stewardess asked Ali to make sure his seat belt was fastened. "Superman don't need no seat belt," he protested. She answered: "Superman don't need no airplane, either." He fastened it.

# DRIVE-IN MOVIES

*Although they've all but disappeared from the American landscape, drive-in movies were once the coolest thing around.*

## THE BIRTH OF THE DRIVE-IN

Richard M. Hollingshead Jr. had friends over one summer night in the late 1920s to see his home movies. It was a hot night, and the projector just made it hotter. Seeing his guests' discomfort, the inventor and businessman had an idea—why not show his movies outside?

He put his projector on the hood of the family's model T and projected image onto the white wall of his garage. His guests—and eventually the whole neighborhood—lounged on his car seats and lawn furniture.

Hollingshead knew he had a hit when his guests asked to see more of his home movies. While the picture flickered in front of his eyes, he started thinking about business possibilities.

## COMMERCIAL POTENTIAL

His first idea was that gas stations could keep their patrons amused with short comedies or nature films while filling their tanks. That idea went nowhere. Then one night, he had a vision of an all-car outdoor movie theater where people could watch in the privacy and comfort of their own cars. He started tinkering with the idea, even watching films with his lawn sprinkler going to see if it was possible to watch a movie during a rain storm.

## THE REAL THING

"The World's First Automobile Movie Theater" opened on May 6, 1933 at 2601 Admiral Wilson Boulevard in Camden, New Jersey. It was primitive, yet brilliant—room for 400 cars in seven rows of parking spots tilted at a 5% grade for better reclining and visibility. The site was provided by V. V. Smith, an early investor who happened to have made his fortune in parking lots. On opening night some 600 customers paid 25¢ per car plus 25¢ per person ($1.00 tops) to see *Wife Beware* starring Adolph Menjou.

**George Washington, Thomas Jefferson, and John Adams played marbles even as adults.**

Hollingshead had some trouble with sound. At first he embedded speakers in the ground under each car space, but the floorboards muffled the sounds. Next, he tried huge speakers on either side of the screen. Now everybody in cars could hear every word perfectly—but so could the unhappy neighbors and the freeloaders who watched from just outside the theatre boundary. He abandoned that, too, and next tried individual car speakers hanging on the car windows. Perfect.

Unfortunately, Hollingshead was ahead of his time. Film distributors, seeing the drive-in as a threat to indoor theatres, charged exorbitantly high rental prices and withheld their best first-runs. In 1935, a disgusted Hollingshead sold his theater.

## RISE & FALL

But soon after, drive-in movies caught on. The baby boom of the late 1940s was also an automobile boom. People quickly discovered they could dress casually, bring their own food, smoke, talk, steam up the windows, and bring the kids without paying for a sitter. For teens, roomy back seats provided an arena for love's wrestling matches. The marriage of car and movie seemed perfect.

But not for long. Encroaching suburbia drove up cheap rural land prices, cars got smaller, TV became popular, the opportunities for sexual ecounters expanded, and the quality of the drive-in film fare declined from first run to B-minus. Drive-ins began disappearing from across the landscape, including Hollingshead's original one—its former site is now occupied by a fur store.

## DRIVE-IN FACTS

• Some drive-in theatres even offered drive-in church services on Sunday morning. You didn't have to dress up and you said "Amen!" by honking your horn.

• In the late 1950s and early 1960s, over 4,000 drive-ins operated across the U.S.

• There are only about 1,000 operational drive-ins now. The National Association of Drive-In Operators is defunct.

# NAME THAT TOWN

*The origins of the names of cities and towns are sometimes more interesting than the places themselves.*

**Place:** Anaconda, Montana

**Background:** In Copperopolis, Montana during the Civil War, owners of the local copper mine were strong supporters of the Union cause. Late in the war, word reached them that General Grant's troops were circling Genreral Lee's troops "like an anaconda"—the large snake that wraps itself around its prey and squeezes it to death. To celebrate, they changed the mine's name to Anaconda, and the town eventually followed suit.

**Places:** Bushong and Latham, Kansas

**Background:** In the 1880s, workers for the Missouri Pacific railroad were building a new line through Kansas. To celebrate the success of their hometown baseball team, the St. Louis Browns (who were in the middle of a winning streak) they named 14 stations on the line for their favorite players. Twelve of the stations have been renamed, but Arlie Latham (shortstop) and Doc Bushong (pitcher) are still on the map in Kansas.

**Place:** Pullman, Washington

**Background:** The citizens of this community decided to name their town after George M. Pullman, the rich manufacturer of the Pullman Car...hoping he would shower his namesake with new libraries and other civic gifts. When they invited him to the ceremonies, he sent his regrets, a nice thank you note and a check for $50. That was the last the town heard from him.

**Place:** Eighty Eight, Kentucky

**Background:** Dabney Nunnally was the postmaster of a village 8.8 miles from Glasgow, KY. His handwriting was unreadable, but he could scrawl legible numbers. "Let's call our place 88," he proposed. "I can write that so anybody can read it." Unfortunately for Nunnally, the government insisted that the name be spelled out.

**Place:** Old Glory, Texas

**Background:** Before World War I, this town was called Brandenburg. But anti-German sentiment ran so high during the war that no one wanted to live in a place that sounded German.

**Place:** Naughty Girl Meadow, Arizona

**Background:** The US Board of Geographic Names wouldn't allow them to use the real name—Whorehouse Meadow.

**Place:** Lufkin, Texas

**Background:** Surveyor E. P. Lufkin was laying out a railroad route, and some of his workers were jailed in nearby Homer, Texas for drunkenness. In retaliation, Luflkin rerouted the tracks to miss Homer completely. The newly located station, which he named for himself, flourished; Homer disappeared.

**Place:** Modesto, California

**Background:** Named because the founders were too "modest" to name it after themselves.

**Place:** Truth or Consequences, New Mexico

**Background:** In 1950, the hit radio show *Truth or Consequences* offered free publicity and valuable prizes to any town that would change its name. Hot Springs, NM quickly volunteered and even named the park in the center of town Ralph Edwards Park, after the game show's host

**Place:** Titusville, Florida

**Background:** In 1873, Henry Titus and Charles Rice decided to play a game of dominoes to decide who to name the town after.

**Place:** Tarzana, California

**Background:** Named after Tarzan to honor his creator, Edgar Rice Burroughs, who lived there for many years.

**The only known meteorite fatality was a dog hit in Egypt in 1922.**

# THE PRESS & THE PREZ

*Presidents and the press have a peculiar love-hate relationship. Here are some anecdotes from* If No News, Send Rumors, *a great bathroom reader by Stephen Bates.*

When Paul Hume of the *Washington Post* wrote a harsh critique of Margaret Truman's singing debut, her father Harry wrote back, " I have just read your lousy review buried in the back pages. You sound like a frustrated old man who never made a success, an eight-ulcer man on a four-ulcer job and all four ulcers working. I never met you, but if I do you'll need a new nose and a supporter below."

President Franklin Roosevelt inscribed a photo of himself for the White House press room: "From their victim."

During a trip to India, President Jimmy Carter was shown a pit filled with cow manure, which generated methane gas for energy. ABC's Sam Donaldson said, "If I fell in, you'd pull me out, wouldn't you, Mr. President?" Carter replied, "Certainly—after a suitable interval."

Reporters covering the Kennedys once submitted a detailed questionnaire inquiring about the family's new dog. The First Lady filled it out. When she reached the question, "What do you feed the dog," she wrote: "Reporters."

On his desk President Reagan's press secretary, Larry Speakes, posted a sign: "You don't tell us how to stage the news, and we don't tell you how to cover it."

After the Apollo 11 astronauts returned to earth, President Nixon arranged to send fragments of moon rocks to world leaders. He remarked privately that he hoped to find some "contaminated" pieces to send to reporters.

When he was angry at reporters, Pres. [Franklin] Roosevelt sometimes punished them directly. Once, for example, he ordered Robert Post of the *New York Times* to wear a dunce cap and stand in the corner.

During his 1983 visit to Japan, President Reagan gave a speech praising freedom of the press. At his request, the entire speech was off the record.

After Washington Post reporter Judith Martin described Tricia Nixon as a "24-year-old woman dressed like an ice cream cone who can give neatness and cleanliness a bad name," the White House told Martin she would not be allowed to cover Tricia's wedding.

On Richard Nixon's post-resignation flight to San Clemente, he wandered back through Air Force One. The rear section had previously held reporters; now it held the Secret Service contingent. "Well," Nixon said, "it certainly smells better back here."

When President Johnson was angry with the columnists Evans and Novak, he referred to them as "Errors and Nofacts."

## NIXON ON THE PRESS

• "For sixteen years, ever since the Hiss case, you've had a lot of fun.... [J]ust think of how much you're going to be missing. You won't have Nixon to kick around anymore, because , gentlemen, this is my last press conference."—*News conference, 1962*

• "Don't take it personally, but I'm not going to pay that much attention to you." —*To reporters, 1969*

• "The press is the enemy."—*To aides, 1969*

• If we treat the press with a little more contempt we'll probably get better treatment."—*To aides, 1969*

• "Kicking the press is an art."—*To aides, 1972*

• " I have never heard or seen such outrageous, vicious, distorted reporting in 27 years of public life. I am not blaming anyone for that." —*News conference, 1973*

• "Don't get the impression that you arouse my anger... You see, one can only be angry with those he respects."—*News conference, 1973*

• "I have no enemies in the press whatsoever." —*To the Society of Newspaper Editors, 1984.*

**The moon vibrated for 55 minutes after the Apollo 12 astronauts landed on it.**

# TRY, TRY AGAIN

*Many products we take for granted today were flops when they were first introduced; it took a second—or even a third—effort to find a way to make them successful. Here are a few examples.*

**THE PRODUCT: Timex watches**

**Background:** In 1942, the Waterbury Watch Company stopped making pocket watches and started making fuses for the U.S. military. Sales went up to $70 million, but plummeted to $300,000 after the war. To avoid bankruptcy, the company went back to manufacturing watches. They developed a line of cheap, durable timepieces anyone could afford—"Timex watches."

**First Try:** Salesmen took samples to jewelry stores (where watches were normally sold), expecting quick sales. But at $7.00 each, Timexes turned out to be too cheap and low-class for jewelers. They were used to a fancier product and a bigger profit margin; they refused to stock the watches.

**Second Try:** The company was forced to look for another place to sell its product. They sent salesmen out again, and to everyone's surprise, they found a market in drug stores. Whereas Timex products looked low-class in jewelry stores, they seemed ritzy next to aspirin and cough syrup. Within about a decade, one-third of all watches sold in the U.S. were Timexes.

**THE PRODUCT: Tupperware**

**First Try:** Earl Tupper invented Tupperware in the 1940s. Unlike glass or tin containers, Tupperware's plastic body and innovative airtight seal (based on a paint can design) made it ideal for keeping leftovers fresh. But consumers rejected it—they didn't understand how to use the plastic containers properly, and retailers rarely took the time to demonstrate them. By 1951 Tupper had given up.

**Second Try:** Mrs. Brownie Humphrey Wise, a "house party" saleswoman, came to Tupper's rescue. She was already selling Tupperware alongside other products at house parties, and pointed out to Tupper that the relaxed environment of a house party made it easy

According to recent surveys, 20% of American families don't have a bank account.

to demonstrate its advantages. Tupper agreed—and formed Tupperware Home Parties, Inc., in 1951. The parties worked—Tupperware was a hit. And it still is—today more than 75,000 Tupperware parties are held *every day*.

**THE PRODUCT: Wisk Liquid Detergent**

**First Try:** Unilever introduced Wisk, the first liquid laundry detergent ever, in 1956. It received a lot of publicity, but since it cost more than dry detergents, it wasn't a major success.

**Second Try:** A decade later, Unilever's market research revealed that housewives hated cleaning shirt collars more than any other laundry chore. So the company devised a new strategy for Wisk: They began running commercials that showed "ring around the collar" as the source of lost job promotions, husband-and-wife spats, etc. Their suggested solution: "Wisk around the collar." By 1974 sales of Wisk had tripled, and "ring around the collar" was a household phrase.

**THE PRODUCT: Marlboro Cigarettes**

**First Try:** Philip Morris introduced Marlboro in 1924 with upper-class women in mind—the cigarettes were longer and higher priced than standard brands. They also came with a "beauty tip"—an unfiltered mouthpiece that kept the smoker's lips from touching the cigarette paper. The gimmicks didn't work—Marlboro flopped. As late as 1954, it had less than 1% of the cigarette market.

**Second Try:** When filtered cigarettes were introduced in 1953, Philip Morris decided to dump the "beauty tip" and reintroduce Marlboro with a filter tip. (It was their worst-selling cigarette, and had the least to lose if it bombed). The company also replaced the brand's soft packaging with a new red and white "flip top" box. But women still ignored them, and the brand flopped again.

**Third Try:** In 1954, after 30 years of failures, Phillip Morris decided to forget about women. To attract male smokers, they gave the brand a more "manly" image, running commercials of pilots, hunters, sailors, and cowboys smoking Marlboros. Sales took off immediately; within a year, Marlboro was the fourth most popular smoke in the country. By the 1970s, it had become the most popular cigarette on Earth.

## THE PRODUCT: Vaseline

**Background:** In 1857 a Brooklyn chemist named Robert Chesebrough visited the site of the first oil strike in U.S. history in Titusville, Pennsylvania. The oil workers he chatted with kept mentioning "rod wax" —a substance that collected on oil pumping machinery. They swore it healed their cuts and burns.

Chesebrough took a sample home to study and worked on refining it into a jelly-like product. He deliberately cut and burned himself—and rubbed the Vaseline (a combination of the German word for water—*wasser*—and the Greek word for oil—*elaion)* on his wounds. He found that it did actually speed up healing.

**First Try:** In 1870, Chesebrough set up a Vaseline factory and began mailing free samples to physicians and scientists. He expected to use their endorsements to convince drug stores to carry Vaseline. But they ignored him.

**Second Try:** He had no choice but to go directly to the public. He loaded his wagon with jars of Vaseline and rode around New York state, handing them out to everyone he met along the way. Soon these "customers" began asking local druggists to order refills, and Chesebrough's business took off. By 1912 Vaseline had been written up in medical journals all over the world.

• • •

## AND NOW BACK TO THE SHOW

**Worst sitcom of the '70s:** *Sugar Time!* (From *The Best of TV Sitcoms* by John Javna)

"If this were a horror film, it might be called *The Attack of the Rock-and-Roll Jiggling Bombers*. *Sugar Time!*, starring Barbi Benton (Hugh Hefner's girlfriend), Didi Carr, and Marianne Black, was about a group of braless, spandex-clad rock-and-roll singers who dreamt of stardom, despite their precarious financial condition. The show served a dual purpose. Literally. The late '70s were the era of the jigglers, and producers were looking for any excuse to put both of the jiggling actresses' talents on display. If they could sing (or act), so much the better. Unfortunately in this case, they couldn't. The show was created by James Komack, producer of such classics as *Chico and the Man*, and *The Courtship of Eddie's Father*."

# WHAT'S IN A NAME?

*Interesting facts about names, from* The Best Baby Name Book in the Whole Wild World, *by Bruce Lansky*

## UNUSUAL NAMES

• "Ann Landers wrote about a couple who has six children, all named Eugene Jerome Dupuis, Junior. The children answer to One, Two, Three, Four, Five and Six, respectively."

• "Tonsilitis Jackson has brothers and sisters named Meningitis, Appendicitis and Peritonitis."

• "A couple in Louisiana named their children after colleges: Stanford, Duke, T'Lane, Harvard, Princeton, Auburn and Cornell. The parents' names? Stanford, Sr., and Loyola."

• "In 1979, the Pennsylvania Health Department discovered these two first names among the 159,000 birth certificates issued in the state that year—Pepsi and Cola."

• "Zachary Zzzzra has been listed in the *Guinness Book of World Records* as making 'the most determined attempt to be the last personal name in a local telephone directory' in San Francisco. That happened before his place was challenged by one Vladimir Zzzzzzabakov. Zzzzra reports that he called Zzzzzzabakov and demanded to know his real name (Zzzzra's name is really his own, he says). Zzzzzzabakov told him it was none of his . . . business. At any rate... Zzzzra changed his name to regain his former position. When the new phone book appeared, he was relieved to find himself comfortably in the last place again, as Zachary Zzzzzzzzzzra. Unknown to him, the contender, Zzzzzzabakov, had disappeared."

• "One family which was not terribly successful in limiting its expansion has a series of children called, respectively, Finis, Addenda, Appendix, Supplement and (last but not least) Errata."

## LETTER ALONE

• "Harry S Truman owed his middle name, the initial S with no period, to a compromise his parents worked out. By using only the initial, they were able to please both his grandfathers, whose names were Shippe and Solomon."

**Tokyo dogs have a high baldness rate, because they "apparently lead very stressful lives."**

• "A new recruit in the U.S. Army had only letters for his first and middle names—R B Jones. To avoid problems upon recruitment, he helpfully listed his name as ' R (only) B (only) Jones.' You guessed it—from then on he was, as far as the Army was concerned, 'Ronly Bonly Jones,' and all his records, dogtags, assignment forms and even discharge papers were issued in that name."

## WHAT IN GOD'S NAME?

• "The majority of people in the Western hemisphere have names based on biblical ones. Women outnumber men, yet there are 3,037 male names in the Bible and only 181 female names, with the New Testament a more popular source than the Old."

• "Popes traditionally choose a new name upon their election. The practice began in 844 A.D. when Boca de Porco (Pig's Mouth) was elected. He changed his name to Sergious II."

• "Praise-God Barebones had a brother named If-Christ-Had-Not-Died-For-Thee-Thou-Wouldst-Have-Been-Damned Barebones, who was called 'Damned Barebones' for short."

• "Terril William Clark is listed in the phone book under his new name—God. Now he's looking for someone to publish a book he's written. 'Let's face it,' he reportedly said. 'The last book with my name on it was a blockbuster.'

## LIVING UP TO THE NAME

• "Researchers have found that boys with peculiar first names have a higher incidence of mental problems than boys with common ones; no similar correlation was found for girls."

•"A recent study suggests that about two-thirds of the population of the U.S. is named to honor somebody. Of the people who are namesakes, about 60 percent are named after a relative and 40 percent for someone outside the family."

• "Many people dislike their own names. The most common reasons given for this dislike are that the names "sound too ugly," that they're old-fashioned, too hard to pronounce, too common, too uncommon, too long, sound too foreign, are too easy for people to joke about, and that they sound too effeminate (for men) or too masculine (for women)."

# THE LEGEND OF THE YELLOW RIBBON

*When American troops came home from the Mideast in 1991, people welcomed them with yellow ribbons...as if that was a perfectly natural thing to do. Where did this "tradition" start? With a pop song—which, in turn, came from a* Readers Digest *article. Here's the whole weird story, from* Behind the Hits, *by Bob Shannon and John Javna.*

## INSPIRATION

Songwriter Irwin Levine leaned back and opened the January, 1972 issue of *Reader's Digest*. He skimmed through the magazine and read a few of the articles. Eventually he flipped to the story on page 64. The title said in red letters, "Going Home." And underneath: "Condensed from the New York *Post*." The piece was by newspaper columnist Pete Hamill; it had originally appeared in the New York *Post* on Oct. 14, 1971.

"I first heard this story a few years ago, from a girl I had met in New York's Greenwich Village," Hamill wrote in the introduction. "The girl told me she had been one of the participants. Since then, others...have said that they have read a version of it in some forgotten book, or been told it by an acquaintance who said that it actually happened to a friend. Probably the story is one of those mysterious bits of folklore that emerge from the national subconscious every few years, to be told anew in one form or another."

## THE STORY

The two-page article was about a guy named Vingo, whom six teenagers spotted on a bus headed from New York City to Florida. The kids were going to Fort Lauderdale. Vingo, who'd been in a New York jail for the last four years, was on his way home. But he didn't know if his wife and kids would be there waiting for him. He'd told his wife when he first went in that he'd understand if she couldn't wait. Then he'd told her not to write, and she hadn't.

**During Desert Storm, one ribbon-maker shipped 30 million yards of yellow ribbon in a month.**

"Last week," said Vingo in the story, "when I was sure the parole was coming through, I wrote her again. We used to live in Brunswick, just before Jacksonville, and there's a big oak tree just as you come into town. I told her that if she'd take me back, she should put a yellow handkerchief on the tree, and I'd get off and come home. If she didn't want me, forget it—no handkerchief, and I'd go on through."

This tale was big news in the bus, so as they got to Brunswick everyone watched out the window for the tree. When they saw it, there was a massive celebration—dancing, tears, screaming. The tree was covered with ribbons. Vingo could go home.

## THE SONG

Levine told his partner, Larry Brown, about the article. They both thought it could be a great song, and quickly wrote "Tie a Yellow Ribbon" based on it.

Then they gave it to a record producer, who convinced Tony Orlando to sing it. Orlando, a rhythm and blues fan, thought it was silly. But he couldn't get it out of his head. "I kept singing it around the house...against my will," he recalls.

It affected other people the same way; "Tie a Yellow Ribbon" sold three million copies in two weeks, and became the #1 record of 1973. By now, over a thousand versions have been recorded around the world.

## THE FOLKLORE

**A 1991 wire service report:** "A yellow ribbon made by the wife of former Iranian hostage L. Bruce Laingen was donated yesterday to the Library of Congress, which accepted the bow as a genuine piece of American folklore.

"Shortly after Laingen was captured on Nov. 4, 1979 (when Muslim revolutionaries seized the U.S. Embassy in Tehran), Penne Laingen made the bow from 12 feet of yellow vinyl upholstery material and tied it around an oak tree in the front yard of the Laingen home in Bethesda, MD. When the 52 embassy hostages were freed Jan. 20, 1981, Laingen, the embassy's senior diplomat, returned home and removed the ribbon that had become a national symbol of hope for the hostages' eventual release.

"Laingen's yellow ribbon will be put on permanent display in the reading room of the library's American Folklife Center."

# BOX OFFICE WINNERS

*Who are the real movie superstars? We were surprised by some of the stars on these lists, compliled using the annual info from Quigley Publications.*

## TOP 10 BOX OFFICE STARS

### ...OF THE 1930s

1. Clark Gable
2. Shirley Temple
3. Joan Crawford
4. Will Rogers
5. Wallace Beery
6. Fred Astaire and Ginger Rogers
7. Norma Shearer
8. Marie Dressler
9. Janet Gaynor
10. Sonja Henie

### ...OF THE 1940s

1. Bob Hope
2. Bing Crosby
3. Betty Grable
4. Humphrey Bogart
5. Clark Gable
6. Bud Abbott and Lou Costello
7. Gary Cooper
8. Spencer Tracy
9. Greer Garson
10. James Cagney

### ...OF THE 1950s

1. John Wayne
2. James Stewart
3. Gary Cooper
4. Bing Crosby
5. Dean Martin and Jerry Lewis
6. Bob Hope
7. Frank Sinatra
8. William Holden
9. Randolph Scott
10. Marilyn Monroe

### ...OF THE 1960s

1. John Wayne
2. Elizabeth Taylor
3. Doris Day
4. Paul Newman
5. Jack Lemmon
6. Elvis Presley
7. Rock Hudson
8. Julie Andrews
9. Richard Burton
10. Sandra Dee

### ...OF THE 1970s

1. Clint Eastwood
2. Steve McQueen
3. Paul Newman
4. Barbra Streisand
5. John Wayne
6. Robert Redford
7. Charles Bronson
8. Burt Reynolds
9. Woody Allen
10. Al Pacino

### ...OF THE 1980s

1. Clint Eastwood
2. Eddie Murphy
3. Burt Reynolds
4. Tom Cruise
5. Sylvester Stallone
6. Michael J. Fox
7. Arnold Schwarzenegger
8. Michael Douglas
9. Harrison Ford
10. Dudley Moore

**Origin of the term "bigwig:" King Louis IV of France was a big fan of big wigs.**

# POLITICAL SYMBOLS

*You know what they represent—but do you know where they come from?*

**The Republican Elephant:** First appeared in *Harper's Weekly* in 1874, in a political cartoon drawn by Thomas Nast. Rumors were circulating that President Ulysses S. Grant, a Republican, was going to run for a third term. Fearful of what would happen if Grant were reelected, Nast drew a cartoon of the rumor, incorporating another news story: a false report that wild animals had escaped from the Central Park Zoo and were roaming the streets in search of prey. He drew the Republican Party as a stampeding elephant.

**The Democratic Donkey:** In the 1828 presidential elections, Andrew Jackson's opponents referred to him as a "stubborn jackass." Proud of his reputation for obstinacy, Jackson (a Democrat) began using donkeys in his campaign posters and flyers. Democrats have been doing it ever since.

**The Peace Symbol:** ☮ Created by Gerald Holtom, a British artist, in 1958. A member of the Campaign for Nuclear Disarmament, Holtom was looking for a symbol to promote the antinuclear group that could be easily reproduced on banners. He based it on letters in the semaphore (flag) alphabet that Navy ships use to communicate with each other. The circle stands for the word "total;" the two smaller lines represent the letter N (nuclear), and the long vertical line in the center stands for the letter D (disarmament)—"Total Nuclear Disarmament." It was first displayed at a 1958 peace march in England.

**The Swastika:** Originally a Hindu symbol that represented the sun's daily path across the sky—and that, ironically, was considered a "good luck" symbol before World War II. It has been found on religious artifacts all over the world, from the Middle East to Asia to North and South America. Its image was tarnished forever when Adolf Hitler adopted it as the symbol for the Nazi party.

# UNSUNG HEROES

*Everyone knows about Thomas Edison and Alexander Graham Bell. But the guy who invented the portable vacuum cleaner is anonymous. The folks at the BRI's Division of Practical Science think it's time this injustice is corrected. Here are some heroes we should all recognize.*

**HERO:** Earl Richardson
**WHAT HE DID:** Designed the first practical electric iron.
**THE STORY:** In 1905 Richardson, a California utility worker, decided to improve the electric irons of the day. Existing models weighed as much as 15 lbs, and were warm only while they were sitting in their bases. Richardson's solution: design a lighter iron that stayed hot, even when in use. He succeeded, but still had a problem. Most power companies of the day generated power only in the evenings—their purpose was to provide power for lighting—but women liked to iron during the day. In 1906, Richardson convinced his local utility to generate electricity all day on Tuesdays... and housewives started buying his irons.

**HEROINE:** Josephine Cochrane
**WHAT SHE DID:** Invented the dishwasher.
**THE STORY:** Though she invented the dishwasher, Josephine never washed dishes herself. A wealthy woman of the 1890s, she invented the machine because she was tired of servants breaking her valuable china as they washed it. One afternoon, Cochrane went out into the woodshed alongside her house and began building wire compartments that would hold her dishes. She set these in a large copper boiler, and attached a motor to pump the water and rotate the dishes. Her friends convinced her to patent it; in 1893 one of her machines won top prize at the Chicago World's Fair.

**HERO:** James Murray Spengler
**WHAT HE DID:** Invented the portable vacuum cleaner
**THE STORY:** A failed inventor, Spengler hit rock-bottom in

**Would you like to host the "Tonight Show"? A third of American men say they would.**

1907 and had to take a job as a janitor in an Ohio department store. The mechanical carpet cleaner he used to clean the store's carpets kicked up dust and set off his allergies—so Spengler decided to build a better contraption. He made his first vacuum out of a pillow case, a soap box, an old fan, and some tape; he patented it in 1908. Later he sold the rights to his device to William Hoover, an Ohio businessman, and retired with the money he made.

**HERO: Henry Alden Sherwin**

**WHAT HE DID: Developed ready-mixed paint.**

**THE STORY:** You knew that Sherwin Williams sold ready-mixed paint, but did you know they invented it? The year was 1870, and Sherwin, co-owner of a paint company, wanted to sell pre-mixed colors, so homeowners wouldn't have to mix their own (a risky business). His partners hated the idea, and forced Sherwin out of the company. So he found a new partner, Edward Williams; together they formed Sherwin Williams in 1880.

**HERO: Frederick Walton and Thomas Armstrong**

**WHAT THEY DID: Invented linoleum floors.**

**THE STORY:** Frederick Walton, an Englishman, deserves the credit for inventing linoleum. But Thomas Armstrong, an American, deserves credit for making it what it is today. Walton patented his floor covering, a layer of linseed oil, resin, and cork dust with a woven backing, in 1860. When Thomas Armstrong, a cork maker, heard of Walton's invention, he developed his own cork-based floor covering. Unlike Walton, he experimented with coloring, patterns, and other ideas, giving linoleum the features that made it a fixture in American homes.

**HERO: Edwin Budding**

**WHAT HE DID: Invented the lawn mower.**

**THE STORY:** Edwin Budding was a foreman in an English textile plant in the late 1820s. He was obsessed with a new machine the plant used to shear excess fibers from cotton cloth. He thought a similar machine might help him keep his lawn trimmed, and he set out to make one. Today's mowers are direct descendents of the machine he invented.

**Dentist's lament: An estimated 16% of U.S. women and 13% of U.S. men are toothless.**

# A TOY IS BORN

*We all grew up with them: Raggedy Ann, Legos, Lionel Trains...*

## RAGGEDY ANN

In the early 1900s a little girl named Marcella Gruelle was rummaging through the attic of her parents' Connecticut home when she found a hand-made doll. It was dusty and torn, but Marcella liked it so much that her father repaired it for her. He even gave it a name: Raggedy Ann, (inspired by two poems by James Whitcomb Riley: "The Raggedy Man" and "Little Orphan Annie").

In fact, Marcella spent so much time with the doll that her father (Johnny Gruelle), a cartoonist, started writing and illustrating stories about it. His books—the original *Raggedy Ann* series—made Raggedy Ann one of the most popular dolls of the 20th Century.

## MATCHBOX CARS

In 1952 John Odell and Leslie Smith, owners of a British industrial die-casting factory, started casting toys at night to make extra money. Their first toy: a tiny replica of Princess Elizabeth's Royal Coach. When Elizabeth became Queen in 1953, more than a million of them were sold.

So the partners went into toymaking full time. They created a line of tiny automobiles they called *Matchbox Toys* (because the cars were tiny enough to fit in a matchbox)...then they took it a step further and decided to sell their products in packages that actually *looked* like matchboxes.

## LEGOS

One afternoon in 1954, a shopkeeper complained to Godtfred Kirk-Christiansen, a Danish toymaker, that most modern toys didn't challenge children to think. That night, Christiansen came up with an idea for a new toy: building blocks that locked together, enabling children to use their imagination and build interesting structures that weren't possible with standard blocks. He called his creation *Legos*, from the Danish words *leg godt*, which means "play well." Today they're sold in more than 125 countries.

**Americans spend $10 million a day on potato chips, and $2 million a day on exercise equipment.**

## LIONEL TRAINS

Joshua Lionel Cohen was an inventor in the late 1900s. His earliest creations included fuses for land mines, primitive versions of the electronic doorbell, and something he called a flowerpot light, (a small, battery-operated lamp which was intended to illuminate plants in hotel lobbies). He also invented a tiny electric motor, but couldn't figure out what to do with it. He finally stuffed one into a model train, named it Lionel (after himself), and sold it with 30 feet of track to a novelty store. Within a day or two the store asked for more. Cohen decided to go into train-making full time, and by 1903 his Lionel Train Company had an entire catalog of trains and accessories.

**Note:** Cohen's trains made him rich, but he never earned any money—or credit—for his most famous invention: the battery-operated flowerpot light. It was such a loser that he sold the design to his business partner. The partner started selling the lights *without* the flowerpots—under a new name—*The Eveready Flashlight*.

## CABBAGE PATCH KIDS

Xavier Roberts, a Georgia folk artist, was selling his soft sculpture dolls at a craft fair when a customer walked up and asked him how much the dolls cost. Roberts had a splitting headache. He snapped back: "They're not for sale."—but quickly recovered and said: "They're up for adoption." The idea behind Cabbage Patch Kids was born.

Roberts carried the concept to extremes. He converted an old medical clinic into "Babyland General Hospital," where employees "delivered" his "babies" and gave them "birth certificates" with names like Bessie Sue or Billie Jo. His dolls were ugly, but they still became a national craze in 1983. Customers in one toy store rioted after waiting more than eight hours to buy the dolls. One woman broke her leg—and the store owner had to protect himself with a baseball bat.

**Note:** In 1980 Martha Nelson, a craft artist Roberts had worked with in the past, sued him, claiming he had stolen some of her soft sculpture techniques. The court ruled that Roberts *had* used some of Nelson's ideas, but since she never copyrighted the design, she wasn't entitled to any of the profits.

# CHANDLER SAYS...

*Raymond Chandler was a master of detective fiction. Here's a sample of his style, from his books.*

"When in doubt, have two guys come in through the doors with guns."

"He didn't know the right people. That's all a police record means."

"Guns never settle anything. They're just a fast curtain to a bad second act."

"It was a blonde. A blonde to make a bishop kick a hole in a stained glass window."

"She gave me a smile I could feel in my hip pocket."

"You could tell by his eyes that he was plastered to the hairline, but otherwise he looked like any other nice young guy in a dinner jacket who had been spending too much money in a joint that exists for that purpose and no other."

*On marriage*: "For two people in a hundred it's wonderful. The rest just work at it. After 20 years all the guy has left is a work bench in the garage."

"She had a pair of blue-gray eyes that looked at me as if I had said a dirty word."

"She lowered her lashes until they almost cuddled her cheeks and raised them again, like a theater curtain....That was supposed to make me roll over on my back with all four paws in the air."

"The [dying] General spoke again, slowly, using his strength as carefully as an out-of-work showgirl uses her last good pair of stockings."

"I lit the cigarette and blew a lungful at him and he sniffed at it like a terrier at a rathole."

"Alcohol is like love: the first kiss is magic, the second is intimate, the third is routine. After that you just take the girl's clothes off."

"Los Angeles is a city no worse than others, a city rich and vigorous and full of pride, a city lost and beaten and full of emptiness."

# CN U RD THS?

*The cryptic messages on personalized license plates can be fun...or maddening—as these examples.*

**CAR BRAGGIN'**
FSTRNU
IDSMOKU
2AHSUM
WOWZER
NUN BTR
I XLR8
UDLUUZ
WAY2BAD

**CAR MODESTY**
EYEZOR
HAZRDUS
JUS2LOUD
LOTECH
GASGUZ
H2OLOO
OK4NOW
SHLOMO

**AUTO BIOGRAPHY**
JUSAHIK
NDCENT
I 4GET 2
FMNIST
GAY1
ERLEBRD
IMON2U
IMOKUOK
NVR2OLD
WELLRED
PHAQUE
AIRHED
H82BL8
KUNFUZD
PINHEAD
REDNEK
TRCULNT
XNTRIK
2CRAY Z
BEERFAT
IMNOZEE
CURMUJN
DESPOT
EZ HUMP
FLAKEY
KARMA
I ELVIS

**IT'S A LIVING**
RABBI
TUPRWR
ILSTR8TR
CME4OB
I FIX BAX
MDUC2P
OPNWDE
LITIG8R
ISUEM
SHYSTERR
I ADD4U
I CALQL8
KAR2NST
PNO2R
DCOR8
EDUKTR
GESTALT
MS DONUT
SOUL DR
2THFXR
2BY CME

**JUST FOR FUN**
POLKA
H2O SKE
ROC4EVR
N2HRSES
W8LIFTN
XRCIZE
AV8TR
ICESK8
HAIKU
HDBANGR
ILUV10S
K9SHOW
LV2PUN
PBS YES
SGTPEPR
W8N4SUN
2DA BCHS

**GOOD ADVICE**
BCRE8TV
BCOOL
DOITNOW
B LOGICL
10D 2IT
UBUKLUP

**"If we ever needed a brain, now is the time."—Squiggy, "Laverne and Shirley"**

# I'M GAME

*You can't play board games in the bathroom (not yet, anyway—someone may be developing one right now)...but you can still read about them.*

## START HERE

• The earliest board game on record is the royal game of Ur, which was invented more than 4,000 years ago in Mesopotamia, the site of present-day Iraq. It was a "race" game; the first player to complete the course was the winner. Moves were governed by throwing dice-like objects. Archaeologists believe it is the forerunner of backgammon.

• The Egyptian game of Senet was a best-seller some 4,000 years ago. Even King Tut had one. He liked it so much he was buried with it.

• The first American board game, "The Mansion of Happiness," was produced in 1843. Its theme was Victorian: Players tried to avoid Passion, Idleness, Cruelty, Immodesty and Ingratitude. Drunkeness was punished by a trip to the stocks.

## THE PLAYERS

• *Milton Bradley*: In 1860 he bought a lithographic press and began printing board games. His first game: The Checkered Game of Life. Object: Get to "happy old age" while avoiding "disgrace" and "ruin."

• *The Parker Brothers*: In 1883, about 50 years before Monopoly, George Parker went into the game business. His first product was a card game called Banking. Later, with the help of his brothers Charles and Edward, he revolutionized the toy industry by introducing mass-produced board games.

• *Mark Twain*: The great American author also invented a game. He called it "Mark Twain's Memory Builder: A Game for Acquiring and Retaining All Sorts of Facts and Dates." In the introduction to the rules he wrote: "Many public-school children seem to know only two dates—1492 and 4th of July; but as a rule they don't know what happened on either occasion. It is because they have not had a chance to play this game."

## THE GAME BOARD

If you're going to go to Atlantic City to check out the properties that the Monopoly spaces are named after, be prepared for heartbreak. According to Nathan Cobb, a *Boston Globe* writer who made the pilgrimmage a few years ago:

• You can't take a ride on the Reading Railroad; it's out of business. The only railroad left is Conrail, which doesn't take passengers.

• Advance to St. Charles Place? Forget it. It's gone, replaced by a casino parking lot.

• Kentucky Avenue is a string of burger huts and seedy bars.

• Pacific Avenue is crawling with hookers.

• There's no longer a Community Chest...or the old Water Works.

• You won't find any Free Parking.

• Many of the nineteen other Monopoly streets that still exist are lined with buildings that are boarded up and run down. One wine-guzzling derelict sitting on Oriental Avenue, when told it could be had for $100 on the Monopoly board, declared, "Damn, it ain't worth that much."

## TOKEN FACTS

• Parcheesi, the original male chauvinist game, was created in the 1500s in India by Akbar the Great. It was played in the palace courtyard with young women as game pawns. "Home" was originally the emperor's throne. What Akbar did with the women once he got them all "home" is not documented.

• Backgammon was once known as "Nero's Game."

• There are five legal Scrabble words using 'q' without 'u': faqir, qaid, qoph, qindar and qintar.

• In 1988, the 23rd foreign language version of Monopoly was manufactured—in the USSR. Among the changes: a Russian bear token, real estate names corresponding to Moscow locations (Broadway became the Arbat Mall) and rubles instead of dollars.

# WHAT ALES YOU?

*Here's a bit of information you can use to impress your friends next time you go out for a beer.*

In medieval times, taverns were rough and dangerous places. Glass-bottomed beer tankards were invented so a drinker could take a hefty bottoms-up gulp while still keeping a wary eye on fellow drinkers.

Beer steins were first seen in Europe in the 1500s. Covered containers protected the beer from flies, which were thought to carry the plague.

Eberhard Anheuser, a St. Louis soap maker, bought a failing brewery in 1860 and tried to turn it around. But within 2 years he owed so much money to the local brewer's supply store—owned by Aldophus Busch—that he had to take Busch on as a partner to cancel the debt. Busch married his daughter in 1860, and assumed control of the brewery when he died.

About one out of four beers consumed in the U. S. is a Budweiser. Next most popular domestic beers are Miller Lite, Coors Light, Bud Light, Busch, Miller High Life, Milwaukee's Best, Old Milwaukee, and Coors.

In the late 1860s Adolph Coors stowed away on a ship to America to avoid serving in the German Army. He and a partner founded the Golden brewery in Golden, Colorado in 1873—which he bought outright in 1880.

The reason you spend a lot of time in the john when you drink beer: besides the bulk of liquid that passes through you, the alcohol acts as a diuretic, taking the liquids out of your body and flushing them down the tubes. This dehydration causes a lot of the hangover the next morning. Best prevention? Drink a glass of water or two every time you visit the facilities.

Frederick Miller, royal brewmaster at Germany's Hohenzollern Castle, fled to Milwaukee in 1854 to escape the political strife consuming his country. He founded the Miller Brewing Company in 1855.

Northeasterners and westerners drink more imported beer than elsewhere—more than twice the national average.

**Pigeons are the only birds that can drink water without raising their heads to swallow.**

# NUMBER, PLEASE

*Think of all the numbers you know—your phone number, your address, etc. There's no explanation for most of them. But here are a few we can give you a reason for.*

**NUMBER:** 5280 feet (a mile).
**ORIGIN:** The term *mile* comes from the Latin word *mille*—meaning 1,000. To the Romans it was the distance a soldier could cover in 1,000 paces—about 5,000 feet. But British farmers measured their fields in *furlongs*, which were 660 feet long, and they didn't want to change. So when the mile was introduced in England, it was changed to 5,280 feet—exactly eight furlongs.

**NUMBER:** 60 feet, 6 inches (the distance between the pitcher's mound and home plate in baseball).
**ORIGIN:** The pitching distance was 50 feet until 1893—when some baseball executives changed it to 60 feet. But the surveyor they hired to remap their infield misread their instructions—he thought 60 feet 0 inches was 60 feet 6 inches. The extra 6 inches have been there ever since.

**NUMBER:** Age 65 (when Americans qualify for Social Security).
**ORIGIN:** German Chancellor Otto von Bismarck established the world's first Social Security program in 1881 to undercut the popularity of the socialist movement. He set the retirement age at 65 because he knew he wouldn't have to pay out many benefits—in the 1880s living to age 65 was as likely as living to 105 today. When FDR set up Social Security in the U.S., he copied the German retirement age—not realizing why it had been chosen to begin with.

**NUMBER:** 26 miles, 385 yards (the length of a marathon).
**ORIGIN:** The distance of a marathon was first standardized at 25 miles in 1896. During the 1908 London Olympics, however, Queen Alexandra wanted her grandchildren to see the start of the race. So the starting line was moved back 1 mile and 385 yards—onto the front lawn of Windsor Castle. Marathons are still that length. today.

**Studies show that churchgoers have lower blood pressure than others.**

# BEN FRANKLIN'S ALMANAC

*Here are more bits of wisdom from the man who thought a penny saved is a penny earned.*

"A single man has not nearly the value he'd have in a state of union. He resembles the odd half of a pair of scissors."

"There are more old drunkards than old doctors."

"If a man empties a purse into his head, no man can take it away from him. An investment in knowledge always pays the best interest."

"None preaches better than the ant, and she says nothing."

"He that is good for making excuses is seldom good for anything else."

"In general, mankind, since the improvement of cookery, eats twice as much as nature requires."

"The heart of a fool is in his mouth; but the mouth of a wise man is in his heart."

"He that lives upon hope will die fasting."

"Where there's marriage without love, there will be love without marriage."

"He that falls in love with himself will have no rivals."

"God heals and the doctor takes the fee."

"He that is of the opinion that money will do everything may well be accused of doing everything for money."

"Plough deep while sluggards sleep."

"Three may keep a secret if two of them are dead."

"There was never a good war, or a bad peace."

"Nothing gives an author so much pleasure as to find his works quoted by other learned authors."

"Necessity never made a good bargain."

"At twenty years of age, the will reigns; at thirty, the wit; and at forty, the judgement."

"There are no ugly loves nor handsome prisons."

"Admiration is the daughter of ignorance."

**The Roman Emperor Caligula's last words were: "I'm still alive!"**

# THE COLA WARS

*Some competitors have friendly rivalries, but not Coke and Pepsi. These two have battled for most of this century, taking no prisoners. And the cola wars continue today.*

## BEFORE THE BATTLES

To understand the bitterness between Coke and Pepsi, you have to go back a hundred years to the two pharmacists (both veterans of the Confederate army) who formulated the sticky-sweet brown liquids.

## COKE BEGINNINGS

John Pemberton, a pharmacist in Atlanta, created Coca-Cola as a non-alcoholic "nerve medicine" in 1886.

• He came up with the first Coke syrup by boiling a batch of herbs, coca leaves and kola nuts in his back yard.

• He mixed the syrup with tap water and sold it in his drug store.

• It wasn't until a customer with an upset stomach specifically asked him to mix the syrup with fizzy water that he realized Coke's potential as a soft drink.

• He didn't live to see Coca-Cola become a success. Shortly after he created the drink, Pemberton's health began to fail. He sold the rights to Coke to a group of druggists for about $350; he died in 1888.

## THE NEW REGIME

Only one of Coca-Cola's new owners, Asa Candler, saw the drink's huge potential. By 1891, he had bought complete control of the company for $2,300, and registered *Coca-Cola* as a trademark a few years later. Candler plowed nearly all of the company's early profits back into the business, and kept costs to a minimum (one employee reported earning "$3.00 per week and lots of Coca-Cola").

He had an unmatched flair for promotion, and began the company's tradition of giving away Coca-Cola clocks, fans, calendars, urns, scales, thermometers, and other premiums to storekeepers that ordered Coke syrup.

By 1892 he was selling more than 35,000 gallons of syrup a year, and by the turn of the century, Coca-Cola had become the best known product in America.

## EARLY COMPETITORS

Coca-Cola's meteoric rise had inspired scores of imitators. Coke sued dozens of them for trademark infringement, including the Koke Company, Kola Koke, Coke-Ola, Koko-Cola, Koko-Kola, Ko-Kola, and Coca & Cola. The case against the Koke Company went all the way to the Supreme Court, and Coca-Cola won.

## HITTING THE BOTTLE

According to legend, a mystery man walked into Coca-Cola's offices one day in 1891. He told Candler he knew a way to double the company's sales overnight, and would share his idea for $5,000 (or, some say, $50,000). Candler paid him. The man handed Candler a slip of paper which said, "Bottle it."

Regardless of whether the story is true, Candler resisted bottling Coca-Cola for a long time, fearing that pressurized bottles might explode and expose the company to legal liability. Eventually, a Mississippi candy store owner started bottling the liquid on his own. He had enormous success (and no lawsuits), and five years later, Candler opened his first bottling plant.

At first, Coca-Cola's bottles were indistinguishable from those of other companies, but in 1915 Coke hired an Indiana glass company to design a bottle that customers would recognize "even in the dark." Loosely adapting sketches of a cola nut they found in the *Encyclopedia Britannica*, the glassworkers designed the distinctive bottle that is still in use today.

Candler ran Coca-Cola until 1916, when he turned over control of the company to his sons. His wife's death in 1919 sent him into a deep depression; he tried to shake it off by taking a trip to Europe. While he was away, his sons sold the company to Robert Woodruff, an Atlanta entrepreneur, for $25 million dollars.

**In Boise, Idaho's 1985 mayoral election, Mr. Potatohead received four write-in votes.**

## PEPSI-COLA HITS THE SPOT

Meanwhile, back to 1893: In North Carolina, pharmacist Caleb Bradham decided he wanted to cash in on the success of Coke. At first, he called his imitation "Brad's Drink," but then decided to name it after *pepsin*,a digestive aid, hoping people would buy it as a stomach remedy. Like Pemberton, he didn't see Pepsi's potential as a soft drink until it became popular among people who *weren't* sick.

Bradham paid careful attention to advertising and sales grew to 100,000 gallons of syrup by 1898. Pepsi continued to grow until the end of World War I, when sugar prices shot up from 5 1/2¢ a pound to 22 1/2¢ a pound. To hedge against future shortages, Bradham stocked up on sugar at the higher price. But a few months later, sugar plummeted to 3 1/2¢ a pound, and the company went bankrupt. Bradham returned to his drug store, leaving the soda world.

Roy C. McGargel bought the rights to Pepsi-Cola in 1920 and tried to put the company back on its feet. But he couldn't afford a large advertising budget, and the company faltered. It went bankrupt in 1925, reorganized, and went bankrupt again in 1931.

## SKIRMISH #1: LOFTY GOALS

The day after Pepsi-Cola went bankrupt in 1931, Charles Guth, the president the Loft Candy Store chain, bought it for $10,500. It didn't seem like a wise investment at the time, since Coca-Cola was already the industry giant and was getting bigger every year. But Guth wanted something more than mere money—he bought Pepsi to get *revenge*.

Guth hated the Coca-Cola Company. Even though Loft's 115 candy stores sold 4 million servings of Coke every year, the company had refused to give him a quantity discount. When Guth bought Pepsi for himself, it gave him the chance to dump Coke from Loft stores.

• Coca-Cola was furious: Guth was one of its largest customers, and losing his business hurt. It decided to fight back.

• It secretly sent its employees into Guth's stores to order "a Coke." On 620 occasions, they reported, they were served Pepsi instead. The company sued Guth, claiming he didn't have the right to serve Pepsi to customers asking for "a Coke." Coca-Cola fought the case for more than 10 years. It lost in 1942. The bitterness between the two companies was just beginning.

## SKIRMISH #2: "12 FULL OUNCES, THAT'S A LOT"

Two years after buying Pepsi, Guth had had enough. He couldn't expand sales beyond his own stores, and wanted to sell out. The logical buyer was Coke. Guth offered them the company at a bargain price...and they refused.

Desperate to cut costs, Guth began bottling Pepsi in secondhand beer bottles, which held nearly twice as much soda as normal soft drink bottles. Guth saved money, and hoped the larger serving size would increase sales.

It didn't. Nearly bankrupt, Guth took one last gamble to save his company: He cut Pepsi's price from 10¢ to a nickel, offering twice as much cola as Coke for 1/2 the price. The gamble paid off. By 1938 Pepsi was making $4 million a year and growing fast.

## PALACE COUP

Guth won the battle, but lost it all in an internal power play. By 1935 he had spent so much of his attention and energy building up Pepsi that Loft Candy Stores was on the verge of bankruptcy. Loft's board of directors forced him to resign and hired the Phoenix Security Company to nurse the candy company back to health.

Guth still owned Pepsi-Cola outright; he said he had bought it with his own money. But audits showed that he had bought it using Loft's funds. Upon discovering this, Phoenix Securities hatched a scheme to take control of Pepsi for itself. It bought up much of Loft's nearly worthless stock. Acting on behalf of the candy company, it then sued Guth for control of Pepsi. Phoenix won the suit in 1939. Their scheme had worked—for the bargain basement price of a nearly bankrupt chain of candy stores, Phoenix Securities had taken control of the second most successful soft drink company in the nation.

## SKIRMISH #3: A SMOKING GUN

While Coca-Cola was still the undisputed leader of the cola companies, Pepsi-Cola's booming sales made it nervous. In 1934 it fired the next volley with a trademark infringement suit against Pepsi-

Cola to force it to drop the word "Cola" from its name. Coke had already won similar lawsuits against several companies, and Walter Mack, Pepsi's new president, actually expected to lose.

Everyone else thought Pepsi would lose, too. The widow of the president of Cleo-Cola, which lost a similar lawsuit, visited Mack to commiserate. "My husband thought he was right too," she said, "but they still put him out of business. And I still have a photograph of the check they gave him."

Check? What check? Purely by chance, she given Mack an important piece of evidence proving that Coca-Cola had been bribing soft drink executives to deliberately lose the lawsuits it filed against them, in order to strengthen its trademark position for future cases.

Mack asked the widow for a copy of the check, and introduced it as evidence in court. Caught red-handed, Coca-Cola asked for a two day recess. The next day Robert Woodruff, President of Coca-Cola, met with Mack in a New York hotel. He offered to withdraw the suit, and Mack agreed—but only after forcing Woodruff to sign a statement he had written out on the hotel's stationery: "I, Robert Woodruff, hereby agree that [Coca-Cola] will recognize the Pepsi-Cola trademark and never attack it in the United States."

Coke kept its word. It never again attacked Pepsi's trademark in this country. However, in other countries around the world Coke attacked Pepsi's trademark whenever and however possible.

## SKIRMISH #3: BEG, BORROW & STEELE

By 1949 Pepsi was in trouble again. Coke had recaptured 84% of the U.S. soda market, and Pepsi was again near bankruptcy. The problem: Pepsi's image. Its huge bottles and low price had made it popular during the Great Depression—but they also gave the brand a reputation as a "cheap" drink for people who couldn't afford Coke. Affluent post-war America was returning to Coke.

Luckily for Pepsi, a Coca-Cola vice president named Alfred Steele jumped ship. A former circus showman, Steele's flamboyant antics had been unpopular at Coke, and his career with the company had bottomed out. He quit and become president of Pepsi-Cola, taking 15 other top executives with him. For the second time in its history, Pepsi was being run by a man bent on getting revenge on Coke.

Steele was just what Pepsi needed. He reworked Pepsi's image, updating the company's logo to the familiar circular one used for decades, and switching to fancy swirl bottles. He launched a massive advertising campaign which positioned Pepsi as a superior product, even a status symbol.

In 1955, he married actress Joan Crawford, a former Coca-Cola endorser, and she began appearing in Pepsi ads and publicity events. Her Hollywood glamour helped shake off the brand's "low class" image. Steele succeeded in breathing new life into Pepsi. By the time he died in 1959, he had cut Coke's lead in half.

## SKIRMISH #5: ICE COLD WAR

During the '50s, Pepsi was active in conservative politics. It was a big supporter of Senator Joseph McCarthy and his anti-communist associate, Richard Nixon. In 1959, Vice President Nixon travelled to Moscow to attend an international trade show of American and Soviet products, including Pepsi-Cola. Soviet President Nikita Khrushchev was there, and while touring the Macy's kitchen exhibit the two men got into a heated argument over the merits of communism and capitalism.

Pepsi officials asked Nixon to bring Krushchev to their display to cool off after the debate. Nixon happily obliged, shoving a Pepsi into Krushchev's hand. Photos of the scene were a public relations bonanza for Pepsi: at the height of the cold war, the leader of the Communist world was photographed drinking a Pepsi In one stroke, Pepsi's worldwide image and prestige had finally caught up with Coca-Cola's, and Donald Kendall, Pepsi's overseas operations chief, never forgot Nixon's gesture. A few years late he got a chance to return the favor.

Nixon lost the presidential campaign in 1960, and the California gubernatorial race in 1962. Now unemployed, he was offered the presidency of several universities, considered for the chairmanship of Chrysler, and was even suggested as commissioner of baseball. But he decided to practice law so he could stay active in politics. His wife, Pat, was too embarrassed by his defeat to stay in California, so they moved to New York.

Nixon hadn't practiced law for a long time and wasn't exactly a prestigious figure any more, so he had a hard time finding a firm

**In 1977 there were over 15,000 discos in the United States.**

that would take him. Donald Kendall repaid the Moscow favor by presenting him with the Pepsi account, worth a considerable amount of money. And the job helped keep him in the public eye. He traveled around the world opening Pepsi bottling plants, stopping to meet world leaders. Coincidence: He was in Dallas making a Pepsi-related appearance on Nov. 22, 1963, when JFK was killed.

Even after Nixon was elected President in 1968, his relationship with the company remained close. During his years in office, Pepsi was the only soft drink served at the White House. In 1972, Pepsi won the right to begin selling soft drinks in the USSR after Nixon personally asked the Soviets to "look favorably" on Pepsi's request. Pepsi had pull even when Nixon didn't intervene directly: foreign governments knew that giving Pepsi favorable treatment would score points with the his administration.

## SKIRMISH #6: COKE SHALL RISE AGAIN

In 1962, the same year Nixon became Pepsi's lawyer, a young Georgian named Jimmy Carter lost the Democratic nomination for the state senate. But he suspected election fraud, and hired King & Spalding, Atlanta's most prominent law firm, to challenge the results. They succeeded: Carter was declared the Democratic nominee, and went on to win the election.

The law firm got Carter together with officials from another of its clients: the Coca-Cola Company. Company officials saw immediately that he had potential as a national candidate. They introduced him to the inner circle of Georgia's corporate and industrial leaders, whose money and support would later prove crucial in Carter's campaigns for governor and president.

Carter remained close to Coca-Cola for the rest of his career. As governor he often used the company's jets on official trips, and when his 1976 presidential campaign started losing steam, he turned to Coke's image makers to film his campaign commercials.

As early as 1974 he admitted the company's role in developing his knowledge of foreign affairs: "We have our own built-in State Department in the Coca-Cola company. The provide me ahead of time with...penetrating analyses of what the country is, what its problems are, who its leaders are, and when I arrive there, provide me with an introduction to the leaders of that country."

Like Nixon, Carter returned the favor after being elected president. One of the first acts of his administration: removing the White House Pepsi-Cola machines and replacing them with Coke.

After Carter was elected, Portugal allowed Coke to be bottled and sold in the country—lifting a ban that was more than 50 years old. Not long afterward, U.S. government approved a $300 million emergency loan to the country. And when China opened its markets to American companies during Carter's term, Coke was the one that got the nod.

## SKIRMISH #7: PEPSICO STRIKES BACK

In the mid-1960s, the Pepsi-Cola Company (renamed *Pepsico*) began diversifying into the snack-food and restaurant business eventually buying Kentucky Fried Chicken, Pizza Hut and other popular chains, in part so they could switch their soda fountains over to Pepsi-Cola. Pepsico's diversification strategy worked: by 1979 the company succeeded at the unthinkable—the company had grown larger than Coca-Cola. While undiversified Coke still sold more soft drinks and had higher profits, Pepsi was gaining even there. And now Coke's own surveys were showing that younger drinkers preferred the taste of Pepsi. Coke decided to act.

## A SHOT TO THE FOOT: NEW COKE

In 1985, the Coke company announced it was replacing the old Coke formula with one a new one. Extensive marketing tests indicated that people preferred New Coke over both the old product *and* Pepsi.

But the marketing tests didn't anticipate the huge negative reaction to tinkering with a beloved old product. It was a major embarrassment for Coca-Cola. Pepsi declared victory, consumers revolted, and within two months old Coke was back—in the form of "Classic Coke." Today it outsells New Coke by a ratio of 4 to 1.

Today, the makers of the sweet liquids continue their bitter battle.

**In the Civil War, the Union army used kites to drop leaflets behind Confederate lines.**

# NOW AND ZEN

*If all of the world can be seen in a grain of sand, as some Zen masters say, why not on TV? Cosmic quotes from the book* Primetime Proverbs, *by Jack Mingo and John Javna.*

## SELF KNOWLEDGE

"I am what I am and that's all that I am."

**—Popeye, *The Popeye Show***

"The blossom below the water knows not sunlight. And men, not knowing, will find me hard to understand."

**—Caine, *Kung Fu***

## COSMIC THOUGHTS

"There's a time to be Daniel Boone, and there's a time to be a plumber."

**—MacGyver, *MacGyver***

"The butcher with the sharpest knife has the warmest heart."

**—Village saying, *The Prisoner***

"A day without grapes is like a day without apples."

**—Kelly Robinson, *I Spy***

"There's a big difference between making instant coffee and bringing a Rastafarian back from the dead."

**—Ricardo Tubbs, *Miami Vice***

## EVERYTHING IS EVERYTHING

"I know they're blue berries, but they might not be blueberries. And while all blueberries are blue berries, not all blue berries are blueberries."

**—Alex Reiger,*Taxi*"**

## RULES FOR LIVING

"No good deed goes unpunished."

**—B.J. Hunnicut, M*A*S*H**

"Most people's lives are governed by telephone numbers."

**—Narrator, *Hitchhiker's Guide to theGalaxy***

"No river is shallow to a man who cannot swim."

**—Paladin, *Have Gun Will Travel***

# FIRST HITS

*Here are the inside stories of the first hit records for three of the most successful music acts in history—the Beatles, Elvis, and Simon & Garfunkel—from* Behind the Hits, *by Bob Shannon and John Javna.*

## THE BEATLES

**First Hit:** "Love Me Do," 1962

**BACKGROUND:** The tune was written by Paul McCartney, who called it "our greatest philosophical song." He skipped school and wrote it when he was sixteen years old.

By the time the Beatles went to London in 1962 to try to get a recording contract, it was one of their best numbers.

They played it at their audition...but the record executive assigned to work with them, George Martin, wasn't particularly impressed. Still, he agreed to give them a contract—and even make "Love Me Do" their first single—provided they got a new drummer.

**THE SESSION:** The recording session took place on September 11, 1962, at Abbey Road Studios. The Beatles arrived with a new drummer, Ringo Starr...But Martin didn't trust him and brought his own session drummer, Andy White, to make the record. Ringo was despondent, so Martin took pity on him; he recorded several versions with Ringo, and several with White. (In fact, Ringo played on the English hit, and White was the drummer on the single released in America.) It took seventeen takes to get the song right. By the time they were done, John Lennon's lips were numb from playing the harmonica so much.

**IT'S A HIT.** On October 4, 1962, "Love Me Do" was released in England on Parlophone Records. It surged into the Top 20 and established the Beatles as a viable commercial group. But behind the scenes was manager Brian Epstein, making sure that the Beatles succeeded. He bought 10,000 copies himself, knowing that was the minimum amount their record company had to sell to make a disc a best-seller. Epstein's gimmick worked. The record company was impressed and got behind the Beatles' next single, "Please Please Me," which reached #1 in Britain and started a chain of events that revolutionized popular music.

In America, in 1962, no one wanted any part of the silly "Love Me Do." Capitol Records, which owned the rights to the song, practically gave it to Vee Jay Records, which later issued it on an album called "Introducing the Beatles."

On May 2, 1964, about a year and a half after it was first released, "Love Me Do" became the Beatles' fourth American #1 record.

## ELVIS PRESLEY

**First Hit:** "Heartbreak Hotel," 1956

**BACKGROUND:** The headline on the front page of the *Miami Herald* read, "Do You Know This Man?" Below it was a photograph of a suicide victim. Who was he? The story explained that he'd left no clue about his identity behind—only a pathetic hand-written message that read, "I walk a lonely street." It asked the family—or anyone who recognized the photo—to get in touch with the police.

**THE SONG:** In Gainesville, Florida, a songwriter named Tommy Durden read the paper and was struck by the suicide note. Now *that* was a great line for a blues tune, he mused. The more he thought about it, the more he liked it...so he hopped in his car and drove over to Mae Axton's house to work on it. Mae was Tommy's collaborator in songwriting; she was also a local TV and radio personality. When Elvis Presley had come to town earlier in the year, she'd befriended the young singer and reportedly assured him that she'd be the one to write his first million-seller.

Mae agreed that the suicide line might make a good song, but couldn't stop thinking about how the guy's family would suffer when they found out about him. He might have walked a lonely street, but at the end of it there was surely going to be heartbreak for the people who loved him. So Mae decided there should be a "heartbreak hotel" at the end of "lonely street." From there it took fifteen minutes to write the whole song.

**IT'S A HIT:** A friend of Mae's named Glen Reeves dropped by her house and agreed to tape a version of the song in a pseudo-Elvis style—so Elvis would be able to imagine how he'd sound on the tune. Then Mae, demo in hand, drove up to Tennessee to play it for Elvis. "Hot dog, Mae!" Presley is said to have exclaimed, "Play it again!" Legend has it that when he recorded the song, Elvis copied Reeves's version note-for-note.

In exchange for agreeing to make it his first RCA record, Elvis got an equal share of the writer's credit. "Heartbreak Hotel" went to the top of the charts, establishing Elvis as the most popular new singer in America.

## SIMON & GARFUNKEL

**First Hit:** "Hey Schoolgirl," 1957

**BACKGROUND:** Paul Simon got to know Artie Garfunkel in P.S. 164 in Queens when they both appeared in their sixth-grade graduation play, *Alice In Wonderland.* Paul was the White Rabbit, Artie was the Cheshire Cat. Because of their mutual interest in music, they became close friends, and when they were fourteen, they began writing songs together.

**THE SINGERS:** According to Paul Simon: "We were fifteen years old when we signed a contract with Big Records as Tom and Jerry. 'Hey Schoolgirl' was the first song we recorded. To go along with the Tom and Jerry thing, I took on the stage name of Tom Landis and Artie took Jerry Graph. I picked Landis because I was going out with a girl named Sue Landis at the time and Artie picked Graph because he used to [keep track] of all the current hit records on big sheets of graph paper.'Hey Schoolgirl' was sold in both 45 and 78 RPM; on the 45 it says by Landis-Graph, but on the 78 it's got P. Simon and A. Garfunkel."

**IT'S A HIT:** The song was released in 1957 and sold 120,000 copies, peaking at #54 after being on *Billboard's* "Top 100" for nine weeks. "You can't imagine," says Simon, "what it was like having a hit record behind you at the age of sixteen. One month Artie and I were watching 'American Bandstand' on television and the next month we were on the show." They had to follow Jerry Lee Lewis playing "Great Balls of Fire." It's one of the few "Bandstand" shows not preserved on tape.

"Hey Schoolgirl" was "Tom and Jerry's" only hit. Simon says he bought a red Impala convertible with the royalties.

## IF THE SHOE FITS...

In ancient Inca weddings, the bride and groom weren't considered "officially" married until they had taken off their sandals and traded them with one another.

# OH, MARILYN

*Some little known facts about the life of the ultimate Hollywood icon.*

Marilyn Monroe was born Norma Jean Mortenson, an illegitimate child, on June 1, 1926 in Los Angeles. Her mother, Gladys Pearl Baker, was a negative cutter in a Hollywood film studio. Her father, Edward Mortenson, was a baker.

★

Norma Jean's mother entered a sanitarium when she was three, and sent Norma Jean to live with her aunt. Her aunt later dumped her in a Los Angeles orphanage, where she was neglected and sexually abused.

★

Norma Jean spent much of her childhood in foster homes. She married an aircraft worker at age 16—to avoid getting sent to yet another foster home.

★

She was was discovered by an Army photographer whose boss had told him "to take some morale-building shots of pretty girls for *Yank* and *Stars and Stripes*." The photographer's boss: a soldier named Ronald Reagan.

She stuttered as a child: "It comes back sometimes," she said. "Once I had a small part with a scene in which I had to climb a staircase and I couldn't bring out my line. The director rushed over and shouted: 'You don't actually stutter?' 'Y-y-you th-think not?' I said to him."

★

Early in her career, Monroe was desperate for money. So she agreed to pose nude for a calendar, and was paid the standard modeling fee. To date more than 1 million copies of the photos have been sold, generating more than $750,000 in profits. Marilyn's share: $50.

★

Marilyn never understood why men were so attracted to her: "Why I was a siren, I hadn't the faintest idea. There were no thoughts of sex in my head...I had no thoughts of being seduced by a duke or a movie star. The truth was that with all my lipstick and mascara and precocious curves, I was as unsensual as a fossil. But I seemed to affect people otherwise."

# TEARS IN THE SNOW

*All's fair in love, war...and politics. But did somebody go just a little too far to win in '72? Here's information from a new book called* It's a Conspiracy, *by the American Paranoid Society.*

## BACKGROUND

As election year 1972 got underway, all eyes turned to New Hampshire, the nation's first primary. The Republican candidate would be President Richard Nixon, of course. But his re-election was not the foregone conclusion it seems in retrospect. Among other issues, his handling of the Vietnam war made him vulnerable.

• The Democrats' early favorite, Ted Kennedy, had been knocked out by Chappaquiddick. Of the eleven Democrats running, Senator Ed Muskie—Hubert Humphrey's 1968 running mate—looked like the strongest candidate. In the polls, a Muskie-Nixon race was dead even.

• Because Muskie was from Maine, he was expected to win the New Hampshire primary easily. But experts said a really impressive victory might clinch the nomination for him early.

## WHAT HAPPENED

• William Loeb, owner and editor of New Hampshire's largest newspaper (the *Union Leader*)—and an arch-conservative—had been sniping at his liberal neighbor for years, nicknaming him "Moscow Muskie."

• Loeb also constantly repeated claims that Muskie had called French-Canadian descendants "Canucks," an unforgivable ethnic slur. This offended nearly half the state's voters.

• A little more than a week before the primary, Loeb ran a story about Mrs. Muskie headlined, "Big Daddy's Jane," slurring the candidate's wife as a heavy boozer with an itch for dirty stories.

**A government study of U.S. eating habits turned up a man who drank 64 cups of coffee a day.**

• It was a serious accusation in conservative New Hampshire. Muskie, terribly stung by the cheap shot at his wife, took the attack personally. He took the fight to Loeb the next day.

• Standing on a flatbed truck in a driving snowstorm outside *Union Leader* offices, the senator called Loeb ,"a gutless coward." Then Muskie, slump-shouldered and weary from campaigning, stood in the blizzard and wept.

• It was touching, but it killed him in the polls. Broadcast endlessly on the news, Muskie's emotional moment made him look like a basket case. As *Time* put it: "The moment of weakness left many voters wondering about Muskie's ability to stand up under stress."

• Muskie still won the primary, but with such a small margin that his campaign lost its momentum and soon collapsed.

## THE OFFICIAL EXPLANATION

Since there were no allegations of a conspiracy at the time of the incident, there were no official explanations denying one.

## SUSPICIOUS FACTS

• Loeb's source for the "Canuck" story was a letter from Paul Morrison in Deerfield Beach, Florida. However, when veteran reporter David Broder looked for Morrison, he could not be found.

• In fact, the Muskie camp was *plagued* with bizarre incidents. In March, 200 letters on *Citizens for Muskie* stationery were sent to supporters of Henry Jackson, a Muskie rival. The letters—which created tension between the Democratic camps—contended that Jackson had fathered an illegitimate child, and was later arrested on "homosexual charges."

• Some voters in largely white New Hampshire got calls at 2 or 3AM from representatives of the "Harlem for Muskie Committee" who promised "full justice for black people."

• Sometimes, the skulduggery was really intricate. "At a Muskie fund-raiser for 1300 people in Washington, D.C., several arrivals weren't planned: 200 pizzas nobody ordered, two magicians, and 16 ambassadors from African and Middle Eastern countries who, though entirely out of place, had to be treated courteously and fed."

**It took 1,700 years to complete the Great Wall of China.**

## WAS THERE A CONSPIRACY?

**Theory #1: YES.** Ed Muskie was systematically harrassed and embarrassed to destroy his candidacy.

• The reporters who later broke the Watergate story said the "Canuck" letter and all the other tricks were part of a "massive campaign of political spying and sabotage conducted on behalf of the re-election effort by the White House and Nixon campaign officials."

• The "Canuck" letter was said to have been written by White House PR man Ken Clawson, but he denied it. According to Nixon's master of dirty tricks, Donald Segretti, Muskie's Washington fund raiser almost had one more guest: "We also made inquiries about renting an elephant, but were unable to make the arrangements."

• In time, all of Nixon's '72 adversaries were destroyed in one way or another. The Democrats' eventual nominee, George McGovern, was scuttled by leaks that his running mate had been in a mental hospital; George Wallace, whose strong appeal to conservatives might have drawn votes from Nixon, was shot in the stomach; and Ted Kennedy never ran because of Chappaquiddick. Coincidences?

**Theory #2: NO.** Loeb acted on his own.

• In light of the facts that came to light after Watergate, that's pretty hard to believe. The real question is, how far did the Nixon tricksters go in undermining the democratic process?

## PARTING SHOTS

Muskie later said that though he was upset, he had not actually cried: it was melting snow running down his face. Whatever—it cost him the election. "It was," as he put it, "a bitch of a day."

# SOLUTIONS

## POP QUIZ, PAGE 687

1. Her eyes
2. Discovered by accident
3. Stearic acid from beef fat
4. At a picnic
5. Missionaries, because they were embarassed by all that bare skin
6. A crocodile
7. From his father's cowlick
8. Shirley Temple, W. C. Fields
9. Trick question—it *was* Bogart
10. Moe, Shemp, and Curley
11. Actually Vance was one year *younger*
12. Stabbed during a fight over a hunting dog
13. *Scrambled Eggs*
14. One
15. Two. Exactly the same. (There's one long groove on each side.)
16. Plastic
17. TV show
18. Money

## HOW LONG, PAGE 727

1. B; 2. B; 3. A; 4. C; 5. C; 6. C; 7. B; 8. A; 9. B;
10. A; 11. B; 12. B; 13. A; 14. B; 15. B; 16. A; 17. A; 18. B.

## PUNS:

1. "People who live in grass houses shouldn't stow thrones."
2. "Repaint, and thin no more."
3. "Let your pages do the walking through the yellow fingers."
4. "It takes two Wongs to make a white."
5. "I wouldn't send a knight out on a dog like this"
6. "A Benny shaved is a benny urned."
7. "The Czech is in the male."
8. "A weigh a day keeps the doctor an apple."

# THE LAST PAGE

**FELLOW BATHROOM READERS:**

The fight for good bathroom reading should never be taken loosely—we must sit firmly for what we believe in, even while the rest of the world is taking pot shots at us.

Once we prove we're not simply a flush-in-the-pan, writers and publishers will find their resistance unrolling.

So we invite you to take the plunge: "Sit Down and Be Counted!" by joining The Bathroom Readers' Institute. Send a self-addressed, stamped envelope to: B.R.I., 1400 Shattuck Avenue, #25, Berkeley, CA 94709. You'll receive your attractive free membership card, a copy of the B.R.I. newsletter (if we ever get around to publishing one), and earn a permanent spot on the B.R.I. honor roll.